*Children's
Writers'
& Artists'*
**YEARBOOK
2026**

Praise for the *Yearbook*

'Take the great advice that's in this *Yearbook*.'
David Almond

'[An] impressive raft of advice and notes on every aspect of the business.'
Quentin Blake

'Riffle these pages and turn your dream into an ambition.'
Frank Cottrell-Boyce

'To find your way as a children's author, *CWAYB* should be your first port of call.'
Sarah Crossan

'Between the covers of this book is everything you need to know to get published.'
Julia Donaldson

'Contains a wealth of essays, articles and advice.'
Frances Hardinge

'Stuffed full of useful facts to help you get writing (and drawing).'
Liz Pichon

'Whenever people ask me about how to get their work for children published ... the first words to come out of my mouth are always: *Children's Writers' & Artists' Yearbook*.'
Michael Rosen

'A goldmine of invaluable information.'
Francesca Simon

'Filled with practical and creative advice.'
William Sutcliffe

'I wish you all the luck in the world. Don't be a ninny like me, practically giving up at the first rejection. Consult the excellent *Children's Writers' & Artists' Yearbook*.'
Jacqueline Wilson

Children's Writers' & Artists' YEARBOOK 2026

TWENTY-SECOND EDITION

The essential guide for children's writers and artists
on how to get published and who to contact

BLOOMSBURY YEARBOOKS
LONDON · OXFORD · NEW YORK · NEW DELHI · SYDNEY

BLOOMSBURY YEARBOOKS
Bloomsbury Publishing Plc
50 Bedford Square, London, WC1B 3DP, UK
Bloomsbury Publishing Ireland Limited,
29 Earlsfort Terrace, Dublin 2, D02 AY28, Ireland

BLOOMSBURY, BLOOMSBURY YEARBOOKS, WRITERS' & ARTISTS' and the Diana logo are trademarks of Bloomsbury Publishing Plc

This edition published 2025

Copyright © Bloomsbury Publishing Plc, 2025

All rights reserved. No part of this publication may be: i) reproduced or transmitted in any form, electronic or mechanical, including photocopying, recording or by means of any information storage or retrieval system without prior permission in writing from the publishers; or ii) used or reproduced in any way for the training, development or operation of artificial intelligence (AI) technologies, including generative AI technologies. The rights holders expressly reserve this publication from the text and data mining exception as per Article 4(3) of the Digital Single Market Directive (EU) 2019/790

Bloomsbury Publishing Plc does not have any control over, or responsibility for, any third-party websites referred to or in this book. All internet addresses given in this book were correct at the time of going to press. The author and publisher regret any inconvenience caused if addresses have changed or sites have ceased to exist, but can accept no responsibility for any such changes

A catalogue record for this book is available from the British Library

ISBN: PB: 978-1-3994-2127-0; eBook: 978-1-3994-2126-3

2 4 6 8 10 9 7 5 3 1

Typeset by DLxml, a division of RefineCatch Limited, Bungay, Suffolk
Printed and bound in Great Britain by CPI Group (UK) Ltd, Croydon, CR0 4YY

To find out more about our authors and books visit www.bloomsbury.com and sign up for our newsletters.

For product safety related questions, contact productsafety@bloomsbury.com

Writers' & Artists' team
Editor Alysoun Owen
Assistant editor Eden Phillips Harrington
Articles copy-editor Lisa Carden
Listings editors Lisa Carden, Rebecca Collins, Lauren MacGowan
Editorial assistant Alice Glasspool
Editorial assistance Sophia Blackwell (poetry), Kathryn Alley, Zara Relphman
Production controller Rachel Murphy

A note from the Editor

The Editor welcomes readers to this edition of the *Children's Writers' & Artists' Yearbook*.

Every year I sit down to draft this note to introduce readers to the delights in these pages, in particular the brand-new articles. This year, we have a large crop of new pieces – which means fresh advice, lots more encouragement and a wealth of inspiration. Andy Darcy Theo's article on page 29, *Debut dilemma: your publishing options*, describes how he first considered self-publishing, only to be picked up by one of the Big Five publishing houses. He, like many of our contributors, puts his success down to a mix of 'hard work' and 'luck'. This book exists to show you how hard work can pay off and that luck does exist (even if at times it might feel it is in short supply).

Jamie Smart's *Creating successful comic books* (page 251) adds a further key ingredient to the recipe for success: finding joy in what you create; obsession can help too! In *The next chapter ... being a successful self-published author* (page 25), Griselda Heppel updates us on her writing career and endorses the DIY route.

If you are a budding poet, Laura Mucha (*Writing poems for children*, page 173) shares how you might get your work into print and into the hands and ears of readers. But how do you know who your readers are? Finn Longman unpacks that question and helps you decide in *Writing for YA or adults: how do you know?* on page 165. Some of the broader challenges of writing for children are explored by Tom Tivnan in *The children's publishing year: the highs, the lows, the trends* on page 3.

If you are starting to look for an agent to represent your work, turn to the articles by Lydia Silver, *The author-agent contract* on page 189 and *The many hats of a literary agent* by Christabel McKinley on page 196. If you are intrigued by the role of writers in the shadows, read *What does a ghostwriter do?* by Sam Binnie on page 135. And for the perfect pairing of practical and inspirational advice that demonstrates the delights and benefits of creative collaboration, I recommend the articles by Siân Roberts (*Picture books: the illustrator's story*, page 236) and Sital Gorasia Chapman (*Picture books: the writer's story*, page 240) respectively.

Good luck, work hard, enjoy the ride – and have this book as your trusted guide. As Ross Montgomery says in his *Foreword* to this edition (page ix), once you finished your book ... or poem ... or comic ... or play, that's when 'you suddenly [realise] that you had absolutely no idea what to do next'. The information between these covers will help you decide what those next steps are for you.

Alysoun Owen
Editor

vi A note from the Editor

All articles, listings and other material in this yearbook are reviewed and updated every year in consultation with the bodies, organisations, companies and individuals that we select for inclusion. To the best of our knowledge the websites, emails and other contact details are correct at the time of going to press.

Our **Listings subscription** service gives you access to the entire database of contacts in the latest edition of this *Yearbook* and the *Writers' & Artists' Yearbook*, plus hundreds of additional online-only listings entries. www.writersandartists.co.uk/resources/listings

Writers' & Artists' Yearbook Short Story Competition

The annual *Writers' & Artists' Yearbook* Short Story Competition offers published and aspiring writers the chance to win a place on an Arvon Residential Writing Week (worth £985). In addition, the winner's story will be published on the Writers & Artists website.

To enter the competition, submit a short story (for adults) of no more than 2,000 words, on the theme of 'play' by 13 February 2026 to waybcompetitions@bloomsbury.com. For full details, terms and conditions, and to find out more about how to submit your entry, visit www.writersandartists.co.uk/competitions.

For advice on short stories, see *Writing short stories for children* by Julia Green on page 145.

ARVON is the UK's home of creative writing, offering a wide range of in-person and online courses led by acclaimed writers. From poetry and fiction to screenwriting and memoir, their courses cater to writers of all levels, providing expert guidance, inspiration, and a supportive community. Alongside an extensive online programme of Writing Days, Weeks, Months, and Masterclasses, Arvon hosts immersive Residential Writing Courses in three historic countryside houses. Here, writers can step away from daily life to focus on their craft and make real progress on their projects.

Contents

A note from the Editor ... v
Foreword – Ross Montgomery ... ix

Books

The publishing process

The children's publishing year: the highs, the lows, the trends – Tom Tivnan ... 3
Authentic inclusion in children's books – Beth Cox ... 8
What are children's publishers looking for? – Rebecca Hill ... 12
Winning opportunities: the role of a small independent publisher – Bella Pearson ... 14
Getting published: the author's story – Nicola Garrard ... 18
Getting published: the agent's story – Abi Fellows ... 20
Getting published: the publisher's story – Rosemarie Hudson ... 23
The next chapter … being a successful self-published author – Griselda Heppel ... 25
Debut dilemma: your publishing options – Andy Darcy Theo ... 29
Give and take: finding partners to help build your writing career – Tom Palmer ... 33

Listings

Children's book publishers UK and Ireland ... 37
Children's book publishers overseas ... 57
Children's audio publishers ... 78
Children's book packagers ... 79
Children's bookshops ... 81
Books, sites and blogs about children's books ... 88

Inspiring writers

Making a writer – Sarah Crossan ... 93
From dream to reality – Frank Cottrell-Boyce ... 95
A solitary dream – Alice Oseman ... 97
Words are my happy place – Smriti Halls ... 99
If at first you don't succeed … – Frances Hardinge ... 101
My way into a different world – Sally Green ... 103
How do you do it? – William Sutcliffe ... 105
Journey to publication: the summit is worth the climb – M.G. Leonard ... 107
Following your heart: my journey to publication – Hannah Gold ... 109
The long and winding road to publication – Paul Stewart ... 113

The writing craft

Connecting with your readers – Clare Povey ... 119
Plotting and pace in your middle-grade adventure – Christopher Edge ... 123
Writing real characters into fiction – Elle McNicoll ... 126
Creating your cast of characters – Aisling Fowler ... 129
World-building in your fantasy fiction – L.D. Lapinski ... 132
What does a ghostwriter do? – Sam Binnie ... 135

Writing for different genres

Writing adventures in the real world: children's non-fiction – Isabel Thomas ... 141
Writing short stories for children – Julia Green ... 145
Writing magic into fiction – Kiran Millwood Hargrave ... 148
Reinventing old stories for new readers – Deirdre Sullivan ... 151
Writing mystery and adventure stories – H.L. Dennis ... 154
Write using your empathy superpower – Camilla Chester ... 158
Writing hopeful climate fiction – Lauren James ... 161
Writing for YA or adults: how do you know? – Finn Longman ... 165
Writing about love and loss for children – Natasha Farrant ... 169

Poetry

Writing poems for children – Laura Mucha ... 173
From gigging to getting published – Joseph Coelho ... 177

Listings

Poetry organisations ... 179

Literary agents

Submission to a literary agent (the when, what and how…) – Hannah Sheppard ... 185
The author–agent contract – Lydia Silver ... 189
Finding an agent for your picture book – Jodie Hodges ... 192
The many hats of a literary agent – Christabel McKinley ... 196
Submitting your sci-fi/fantasy novel to an agent – Molly Jamieson ... 200
Why teachers make great children's writers – Kate Scarborough ... 203
The life and works of a literary scout – Sophie Clarke ... 207

viii Contents

Listings
Children's literary agents UK and Ireland — 210
Children's literary agents overseas — 224

Illustration
Pitching your work to an illustration agent – Anna Zieger — 233
Picture books: the illustrator's story – Siân Roberts — 236
Picture books: the writer's story – Sital Gorasia Chapman — 240
How to become a book illustrator: Q&A with Dapo Adeola — 244
Do judge a book by its cover – Thomas Taylor — 248
Creating successful comic books – Jamie Smart — 251
How to create a graphic novel – Isabel Greenberg — 254

Listings
Illustration agents — 258

Magazines and newspapers
Writing for teens – Chloe Rhodes — 263

Listings
Magazines and newspapers for children — 266
Magazines about children's literature and education — 269

Stage, screen and audio
Adapting children's books for stage and screen – Emma Reeves — 271
Children's literature on radio, podcast and audio – Neville Teller — 275
Writing for visual broadcast media – Jayne Kirkham — 280

Listings
Children's television and radio — 284
Theatre for children — 288

Societies, prizes and festivals
Society of Authors — 297
Writers' Guild of Great Britain (WGGB) — 300
Alliance of Independent Authors — 304
Society of Children's Book Writers & Illustrators — 305
Seven Stories – The National Centre for Children's Books — 309
Federation of Children's Book Groups — 311
National Literacy Trust — 313

Listings
Societies, associations and organisations — 315
Children's book and illustration prizes and awards — 333
Prize winners — 349
Opportunities for under-represented writers — 350
Children's literature festivals and trade fairs — 352

Resources for writers
How BookTok can help you engage with your readers – Beth Reekles — 361
ISBNs: what you need to know — 365
Who's who in publishing — 368
Glossary of publishing terms — 370
Self-publishing children's books – Jeremy and Alex Thompson — 375
Paid-for publishing services: *Is it a steal?* — 378
Public Lending Right — 381

Listings
Libraries — 386
Software for writers — 392
Publishing services for independent authors — 395
Children's writing courses and conferences — 398

Copyright and contracts
Copyright 101: top tips – Sarah Burton — 403
Author–Publisher contracts — 407
Copyright Licensing Agency — 411
Authors' Licensing and Collecting Society — 413
DACS (Design and Artists Copyright Society) — 415

Money, tax and benefits
Managing your finances: a guide for writers – Jonathan and Louise Ford — 417
National Insurance contributions – Sarah Bradford — 428

Index — 437

Foreword

Ross Montgomery

So you decided to write a children's book. You cherished an idea for months, years, decades maybe, until you finally took a bold leap into the unknown and started writing it. You worked at it in dribs and drabs, questioning yourself every step of the way, until – at long last – you finished it. You wrote a book! Which is when you suddenly realised that you had absolutely no idea what to do next.

If this is you – hi! You've come to the right place. Whenever someone asks me for advice about publishing their kid's book, I always say, 'there's nothing I can tell you that isn't covered better in the *Children's Writers' & Artists' Yearbook*'. So well done for taking a second bold leap and buying this book. If you haven't bought it yet, and you're just standing in a bookshop reading this: stop it, this isn't a library. And trust me, just buy it – it's worth it.

Let me explain my own journey. After I left uni, I got a job as a teaching assistant at a primary school. That meant that I still had school holidays, which was great, until I realised that all my friends were in full-time employment and I had six weeks with absolutely nothing to do. I had an idea for a kids' book, so I spent my holidays writing it, and the holidays after that, too: after a year, I suddenly found myself with a finished book. Which is when I realised that I was totally clueless, and found myself where you are now.

I've got no idea how I heard of the *Writers' & Artists' Yearbook*: I probably googled WHAT THE HELL DO I DO and clicked on the first link. At the time, I didn't even realise there was an edition specifically for children's books: had I known it existed, I would have absolutely bought that one instead. But the 2012 general edition still gave me everything I needed: I can say, with absolute confidence, that I wouldn't have been published if I hadn't bought it and read the essays inside.

That's your next step – read the essays. Read them all. Guzzle their collected wisdom. Note, however, that your primary reaction will be one of confusion. 'Hang on a tick!' you'll say to yourself, probably out loud. 'These essays all contradict each other! Some tell me to submit boldly to get an agent's attention – others tell me to be demure – some tell me to resubmit to show enthusiasm – others tell me to not pester! So what's the right answer?'

The thing is, they're all right. Back then, I thought that there was one single path to 'cracking' publishing: if I followed the rules and got it right, then I'd get in. But if I made a single mistake – a weak opening paragraph! A punctuation error in my covering letter! – then my manuscript would be flung into the brazier that all agencies having burning in their central foyer, stoked by underpaid interns, and my name would be added to a giant chalkboard titled DO NOT PUBLISH.

The reason why different approaches are correct, I've learned, is that this is an industry made up of people, and different people like different things. There's no hard and fast rule for how to get published – anyone who tells you otherwise is lying – but if I could offer one concrete piece of advice, it would be not to go into this process aiming to get published by anyone, at any cost. You want to find the agent and/or publisher that is the right fit for you: you won't be every agent's cup of tea, and they won't be yours, no matter how brilliant your book is.

So read the essays – understand that this is an industry with expectations around submissions, but that these expectations vary from agency to agency and from agent to agent.

Think about why a particular agent would be a good fit for you – perhaps they represent an author who was a huge inspiration to your own book. Maybe the best agent for you is a famous and established name, with an illustrious list and thousands of followers on social media: or maybe it's an unknown who's just starting out, and who can devote time, hunger, drive and energy to getting your book published, even if it takes them years.

For the record, here's what I did: I read the essays, and made a shortlist of 50 (50!!! too many) agents. I got lots of lovely rejections, complete with kind explanations about why my book wasn't for them (you should take these seriously, by the way; they mean what they say), a few more abrupt impersonal ones, a manuscript returned without a covering letter so I didn't even know who had rejected me, and loads of silence. But by then, thanks to going through the process, I felt more confident – so much so that I started submitting by email as well, looking online and thinking on my feet.

That was how I ended up submitting my manuscript to Pat White at Rogers, Coleridge and White. She didn't reply to me, but her assistant did: she was building her own list at the time, read my email, liked the chapters and asked for more. We had a meeting, she asked me to make changes to the manuscript – again, this is common – and having seen that I responded well to edits, she made an offer to represent me. We went out on submission, entered into an auction, accepted an offer, and I was published.

That assistant was Claire Wilson, who's now a director at RCW, and who has been my agent ever since. She has a list of authors that would make your eyes water: I don't think I'd be writing still if I hadn't had her in my corner these last fifteen years, fighting for me at every turn and devoting tireless time and effort to making sure my books are the best they can be. I know that I got extremely lucky: picked up on my first round of submissions (even if that round was pretty large), indirectly finding the perfect agent for me, getting a publisher on the first round.

That may not be your journey. You may not find success on your first round of agent submissions, or even your second or third; you might get an agent, only to not find a publisher for your first book; you might get published, only to discover that it's just the start of a long and challenging journey, filled with ups and downs. I don't know a single author, myself included, whose career has been a smooth upwards trajectory of success: but it doesn't matter. This is an industry made up of people who started out by taking a bold leap into the unknown, not because they knew they would succeed, because they believed they had something to share.

If that sounds like you – hi! You're in the right place. And don't worry if you feel nervous. I wouldn't be where I am now if I hadn't picked up this book 15 years ago, baffled and scared but full of hope, and started reading. Take courage: everything you need is right here, right now, in your hands.

Good luck!

Ross Montgomery is an award-winning children's author of over 30 books. His first book *Alex, The Dog and the Unopenable Door* (Faber & Faber 2013), published while he was working as a primary school teacher, was nominated for the Costa Children's Book of the Year and the Branford Boase Award, and selected as one of *The Sunday Times* Top 100 Modern Children's Classics. His other books include *The Midnight Guardians* (Walker 2020) – selected as a Waterstones Children's Book of the Month and chosen as a *Guardian's* Children's Book of the Year – and *Ten Delicious Teachers* (Walker 2021), a picturebook co-written with Sarah Warburton. His most recent book, *I Am Rebel* (Walker 2024) was named the Waterstones Children's Book of the Year. Find out more at www.rossmontgomery.co.uk and follow him on Instagram, Facebook and X @mossmontmomery.

Forewords from previous editions

FIRST EDITION

Any book I write, any book you write, may be a catalyst for a child, may turn him into a reader, may turn her into a writer. That's supreme (a recently acquired favourite word of mine), just supreme.
Michael Morpurgo (author of *War Horse* and Children's Laureate 2003–05)

SECOND EDITION

When you have a story turned down you still have the story. It is perhaps a cliché, but no idea is ever wasted.
Julia Donaldson (author of *The Gruffalo* and Children's Laureate 2011–13)

THIRD EDITION

On the road to becoming a published author, every writer has to take a first step. Make the *Children's Writers' & Artists' Yearbook* yours. I'm glad I made it mine.
Meg Cabot (author of *The Princess Diaries*)

FOURTH EDITION

I believe the *real* secret of my success is the fact that I started doing many school and library visits early on, talking about my books. In fact I don't think there's a single county in the UK where I haven't given a talk.
Jacqueline Wilson (author of *Tracy Beaker* and Children's Laureate 2005–07)

FIFTH EDITION

I think I gathered that poetry was something that you could listen to, play with and rummage around in. There were also some kinds of poems that you could think were possible examples of the sort of thing you could write.
Michael Rosen (author of *We're Going on a Bear Hunt* and Children's Laureate 2007–09)

SIXTH EDITION

I will always remember the moment when my agent rang to tell me that my first book was going to be published. For me, that's the day I became a writer.
Francesca Simon (author of *Horrid Henry*)

SEVENTH EDITION

The great advantage of such a personal approach is that the advice you find there is not merely prescriptive. In fact, though there is useful advice to be had, nothing is certain.
Quentin Blake (knighted for 'services to illustration' and Children's Laureate 1999–2001)

EIGHTH EDITION

You must write something. You must do some work. And only then will this book become something that could CHANGE YOUR LIFE FOR EVER.
Andy Stanton (author of the *Mr Gum* series)

NINTH EDITION

As soon as I started to write it, I knew that it was the best thing I'd ever written, that it was somehow the culmination of everything I'd done before, and to my astonishment I knew that it was a book for the young. I had a sense of liberation, of new possibilities opening up.
David Almond (author of *Skellig*)

TENTH EDITION

I suppose, though, that everything that had happened until [I was an author] was good training and I'd learned the skills needed for the job. So when young aspiring writers ask me for advice on writing I always say, not 'Get a job', but 'Get a life'.
Charlie Higson (author of the *Young Bond* series)

ELEVENTH EDITION

> Here's my advice to anyone who wants to write or illustrate children's books: Be persistent. I know lots of people who have had their first efforts turned down or ideas rejected. But if the comments from publishers are positive, keep going and don't give up.

Liz Pichon (author and illustrator of the *Tom Gates* series)

TWELFTH EDITION

> Before we walked on the Moon we had to spend hundreds of years imagining it. Before I became a writer I spent a lot of time pretending to be a writer... all the pragmatic guidance [*Writers & Artists*] offered helped crystallise my thoughts and turn the dream into an ambition. When you think about it, that is magic.

Frank Cottrell-Boyce (author of *Millions*)

THIRTEENTH EDITION

> Even now, when I look at the *Writers' & Artists' Yearbook*, I still recall everything it symbolised for me. It looks too heavy for the shelf, packed to the binding with hunger, trepidation, determination and hope. It's still a little intimidating. Opportunities often are.

Frances Hardinge (author of *The Lie Tree*)

FOURTEENTH EDITION

> I never really believed I'd be a published writer – it seemed less likely than winning the lottery – but I believed in my story.

Sally Green (author of *Half Bad*)

FIFTEENTH EDITION

> If I wanted to achieve my dream of writing for a living, I had to believe in myself, otherwise no one else would. I found a way out of my shame and into a pattern of work that I loved.

Sarah Crossan (author of *One*)

SIXTEENTH EDITION

> There is a right and a wrong way to make a submission to an agent; there isn't a right and a wrong way to write a novel. Everyone finds their own method.

William Sutcliffe (author of the *Circus of Thieves* series)

SEVENTEENTH EDITION

> Most important for me, I found my voice. At that time there were no working-class, multi-ethnic British families in children's books – and only a few in adult books.

Patrice Lawrence (author of *Orangeboy*)

EIGHTEENTH EDITION

> My journey to publication would have been easier and quicker if I'd read the *Children's Writers' & Artists' Yearbook* before I began my epic climb, but I got here in the end. So, dear climber, put this book in your backpack and don't just smell it, read it from cover to cover.

M.G. Leonard (author of *Bettle Boy*)

NINETEENTH EDITION

> Whenever I bemoan the lack of space to escape to, I remember that I wrote a Number One bestseller standing up in my living room with a child on one hip and another toddling on the floor – which helps lend a bit of perspective.

Smriti Halls (author of *I Love You Night and Day*)

TWENTIETH EDITION

> It will be difficult, there will be rejection, and at times you'll wonder: 'Why am I doing this?'. But deep down you know why – it's because you can't not do it, because something is calling you on this adventure.

Joseph Coelho (poet and Waterstones Children's Laureate 2022–24)

You can find the full versions of the Forewords to the 11th, 13th, 14th, 15th, 16th, 17th, 18th, 19th, and 20th editions in this Yearbook.

Books

The publishing process

The children's publishing year: the highs, the lows, the trends

Given the pressures on young people these days, it may come as no surprise that many are reading less. It is certainly a significant cause for concern, though, and in this article Tom Tivnan explores that and other key challenges for children's publishing over the past year.

Many issues have been on the minds of those in Britain's children's book sector over the past 12 months, but none more so than the decline in reading for pleasure among kids. In fact, the problem is so acute the terminology around it has changed with industry professionals now referring to it as 'the reading crisis'; an acknowledgment we are at DEFCON 1 and the trade needs a punchier way to emphasise that, similar to environmental activists' adoption of 'climate emergency' over 'climate change'.

The reasons for worry are manifold, but let's start with the bleak statistics. The National Literacy Trust's (NLT) autumn 2024 report revealed that 34.6% of eight to 18 year-olds said they enjoy reading in their spare time, the lowest level since the charity began its annual survey two decades ago. Reading frequency is at an all-time nadir, with just 29% of primary school age children (five to 10 year-olds) reporting they read in their free time; that drops to fewer than 20% in early secondary (11 to 14s).

Another good reason to shift the terminology is that the 'for pleasure' part might have had some folk missing the seriousness and perhaps wondering: 'So what if kids aren't reading Dav Pilkey's *Dog Man* (Scholastic) series in their spare time? As long as they are doing their school work, they should be OK.' Well, no. There are mountains of nigh-incontrovertible research demonstrating that the more children read for pleasure, the better their performance at school, combined with positive outcomes like improved mental health, enhanced future job prospects and eventual higher median income. There are even several intriguing studies suggesting that in literacy tests, elementary students who only self-select books to read for pleasure surpass those who only read assigned school work. So bin your homework, kids, and just hunker down with Jeff Kinney's *Diary of a Wimpy Kid: Hot Mess* (Puffin 2024). You'll do better in the end.

The invisible privilege

The reading crisis, of course, is part of broader socio-economic currents and policy issues – a growing disparity between rich and poor, a shaky global economy, swingeing cuts to school and library budgets, to name a few. Plus, wider behavioural trends – first and foremost is the far greater amount of time children now spend looking at screens. I know this is anecdotal but I am writing this shortly after convincing my visiting 13-year-old nephew to read a novel – and a fun book, Bill Wood's *Let's Split Up* (Scholastic 2024) – rather than play Fortnite. Goodness me, the drama.

Anyway, the Waterstones Children's Laureate Frank Cottrell-Boyce hit the nail on the head when the NLT survey came out in describing the benefits of reading for pleasure as an 'invisible privilege'. It is that invisibility that is the problem – a reversal of the slide requires investment from governments from which the positive outcomes may not be visible for a generation. It is a rare politician who has the courage to look beyond the next election cycle – or even the next 24-hour news cycle.

But the book trade is taking steps both because politicians are not, and, quite frankly, since it has skin in the game: if we lose the kids, they won't grow up to be adult readers and book-buyers. But it should be underscored that most in the children's sector wholeheartedly and uncynically believe in the ability of books to change lives. There are practical initiatives afoot like the NLT and Penguin Random House-backed Libraries for Primaries project in which the publisher and charity provide books and resources for schools that do not have a library or dedicated reading for pleasure space. The scheme hit its 1,000th opening in June 2024, but there is still some way to go, with nearly 1,900 more schools in Britain still without a library. Doing the maths, that means 2,900 schools in Britain have no state-funded library, a statistic which should enrage any sensible-thinking person.

A number of big houses have recently launched or are kickstarting their own schemes, like the Hachette Raising Readers initiative and HarperCollins' A Year of Reading for Pleasure programme. But many in the trade are urging bigger, broader swings such as a generic publicity campaign, a sort of 'Got Milk?' for reading. The UK Publishers Association is seriously mulling this option, though who among its members will pony up the dough remains the sticky question. But with the government's shameful relative inaction, the trade has come to the conclusion that it cannot afford to do nothing.

Trendwatch: short, sweet and full of pics

The reading crisis is having a direct effect on what children's editors are on the hunt for. I am writing this having just returned from the 2025 Bologna Children's Book Fair, the annual hootenanny where the international kids' publishing and agenting community congregates to sell and acquire books (and eat gelato and sip Aperols in the sunshine, which I am sure has nothing to do with the fair's ongoing popularity). At BCBF 2025, there was a trend for shorter books (across all age ranges) and illustrated titles for younger readers to help address the reading crisis.

Broadly, the feeling on the former is that as reading for pleasure has decreased, so have literacy levels and attention spans: as a result, commissioners want titles with lower word counts. Claire Wilson, children's specialist superagent at RCW (rep for megastars Katherine Rundell, Alice Oseman, Catherine Doyle, Anna James etc.) and president of the UK's Association of Authors' Agents, called this trend 'meeting readers where they are … If attention spans are shorter and reading confidence has dropped, it is our job to create books that will appeal in that context, so we don't lock a generation of readers out of the chance to discover the life-changing power of reading'.

And highly illustrated books in the early years and younger readers space – roughly 2 to 8 years-old – were sizzling hot at BCBF 2025, largely because they hit the age range when children (hopefully) begin forming that lifelong habit. Big announcements at Bologna included Magic Cat Publishing inking celeb chef Jamie Oliver for a series of interactive board books with art by Adrian Johnson, and Hachette Children's Group signing up *Kid Potato*, a 'younger middle-grade' (7 to 8 year-olds) series by debut author/illustrator Neil Coslett. Simon & Schuster Children's Books even launched an entire new imprint, Little Simon, to cater to the early years space.

Keeping it real

Closely aligned to the 'meeting readers where they are' movement is a hunger by publishers for 'real YA'. Young Adult fiction has had a huge resurgence over the past few years –

particularly in its fantasy and romance subgenres – as it has been surfing the BookTok wave (for the uninitiated – users enthusing about books on the TikTok app). YA is ostensibly geared at 13 to 18 year-olds but for a long time its core readership has been actual adults: women in their twenties. Indeed, many of YA's biggest stars write with this crossover audience in mind, such as Lauren Roberts, the formerly self-published American author whose *Powerless* (Simon & Schuster) series was the huge YA breakout of 2024, earning £2.7m through bookshops, according to the industry sales monitor Nielsen BookScan. While editors will not be foregoing the titles that appeal to adults anytime soon, in late 2024 and into 2025 there has been a flurry of YA acquisitions aimed squarely at teens – and their current reading levels.

Another hot trend which in part addresses the reading crisis is graphic novels. Kids' comics are booming in the UK (as they are on the adult side), part of a wider recognition of the literary merit of the form after decades of snootiness. But also that comics are useful in attracting reluctant readers, particularly boys whose reading falls off far more precipitously than girls as they advance through the school years. BookScan's Children's Comic Strip Fiction category had its biggest year in 2024, up 18% to £19.3m – and it has continued to boom thus far in 2025, rising nearly 20%. The genre is, however, currently dominated by just three author/illustrators. Pilkey, *Bunny vs Monkey* (David Fickling Books) creator Jamie Smart and *Heartstopper*'s (Hodder Children's) Oseman were responsible for the top 29 kids' comics in 2024 and 68% of the entire category's sales. But publishers are betting on further growth and are hungry for new graphic novel stars with a raft of huge deals of late, such as the *Tiny Hercules* series by Jon Lock and Nich Angell being snapped up by Macmillan Children's and Scholastic inking fantasy duology *Wilomina* from Glasgow-based Metaphrog (AKA partners John Chalmers and Sandra Marrs). Additionally, there have been launches of new comics-specific imprints like Scholastic's Graphix and David Fickling Books' The Phoenix Comic Books, and a surge of graphic novel adaptations of recent and classic titles, such as artist Fred Fordham taking on Phil Earle's bestselling, award-winning *When the Sky Falls* (Andersen Press).

Sales strong but a middle-grade muddle

With the above gloominess about reading for pleasure, you could be forgiven for thinking there has been a crisis at the tills, too. Nope. Not even close. Sure, there was a slight dip year-on-year in children's sales through BookScan across 2024, down less than 1% to £433.3m. That still represented the third-best annual return for kids' books sales since accurate records began, and all three of those years have come since 2022. At this writing, 2025 has started off 3% up on the same period in 2024 and there is an outside chance that it could end up as the best sales year in history. The biggest author in Britain in 2024 was from the children's sector – the mighty Julia Donaldson, who with illustrators such as Axel Scheffler and Lydia Monks, was worth £17.1m to British booksellers – as were five of the top ten.

Amid the successes there are interesting changes afoot in the kids' market, one of which is the decline in middle-grade fiction. (Middle grade is roughly aimed at 8 to 12 year-olds, but like all the age-range categories, this is elastic and hugely subjective for each reader.) For many years middle grade was the driver of the British children's sector, the space for all-conquering goliaths like Kinney, David Walliams and J.K. Rowling. But in 2024, middle-grade sales continued its half-decade slump, slipping to £99.2m, 5% down on 2023 and the first time in 11 years (barring the pandemic period) in which the category failed to generate more than £100m.

At first glance, you could put middle grade's 2024 drop on the shoulders of Walliams and Rowling as the category's circa-£5m decline at the shops was almost exactly their combined sales contraction. Weep no tears, as in these 'down' years – a mere £9m for Rowling, a paltry £4.8m for Walliams – are totals that 99.9% of writers will fail to generate in their lifetimes. But as 2024 had some notable success – Kinney had a banger, as did Katie Kirby, author/illustrator of the *Lottie Brooks* (Puffin) series – there is something more going on. And that can be seen at the very top, as there were few hits: in 2024, just one middle-grade, Kinney's *Hot Mess*, exceeded the £1m threshold through BookScan, the fewest seven-figure titles for 11 years; in 2023, the category had seven £1m-plus earners.

What is happening is almost assuredly ruction at the retailers with the supermarkets and WHSmith's High Street stuttering. I equivocate because BookScan is forbidden from revealing individual booksellers' market shares, so we cannot say with forensic certainty where the trouble lies, but most publishers admit that these two channels – which have long been the wheelhouse for bestselling middle grade – have faltered. The supermarkets are down mainly because since the pandemic, most of them have stocked fewer books. This is why a lot of supermarket-friendly adult authors – celeb chefs, big-brand crime authors – have also had across-the-board sales declines over the past few years.

The troubles of WHS High Street have been a long spiral of a shrinking footprint and contracting sales – and a stark contrast to its booming sister division, WHS Travel, the retailer's outposts in train stations and airports. There seemed to be a policy of managed decline by WHS's head honchos over the past decade and a half, with little High Street investment resulting in shabby, unloved shops and unimaginative book ranges. Given all that, WHS High Street was still vital as it remained important in certain categories (including middle grade) and often had stores in towns where it was the sole bookseller. In early 2025, WHS sold its 480 High Street shops to investment firm Modella Capital for a relatively cut-price £76m. The WHS name – which will continue in the 1,200 Travel shops – was not part of the deal, so the shops will be rebranded TGJones. There is some melancholy here, as this means WHS will disappear from Britain's high street after 233 years. But Modella says it has a 'clear-cut strategy' for the chain's future and maybe this was the reprieve that was desperately needed.

Freshen it up

I know this is veering into mentionitis territory, but let's return to the current reading crisis and the seemingly counterintuitive ongoing robust children's books sales. How can these two things co-exist? A big reason is one of the most important things to remember about the kids' market: in the main, the purchasing is not done by the reader. It is by harried parents, doting grandparents and worried uncles (like me) who careen around bookshops in a panic, wondering what would be appropriate to buy. The result is we tend to go back to the tried and true. As I write this, the three bestselling picture books in the UK in 2025 were all first published over 25 years ago, all authored by the dearly departed: Eric Carle's *The Very Hungry Caterpillar* (Puffin 1969), Judith Kerr's *The Tiger Who Came to Tea* (HarperCollins Children's 1968) and *Guess How Much I Love You?* (Walker 1994) by Sam McBratney (I should note McBratney's illustrator, Anita Jeram, is still very much among the living).

The children's publishing year: the highs, the lows, the trends

These brilliant classics endure because of their quality. But they also continue to sell because retailers still give them plenty of shelf and table space. There is a concern among many agents that this 'legacy' end of the children's market is squeezing fresher voices out and there is an urgent call for booksellers, Waterstones in particular, to be bolder in seeking newer authors to promote and direct customers to. The level of nostalgia purchasing that one sees in kids' books simply does not happen in the adult market, and it is almost certainly because the end user is choosing what they want to read. And getting more kids reading has to be the ultimate end game.

Tom Tivnan is Managing Editor of *The Bookseller*. Tom was a freelance writer and his work has appeared in the *Glasgow Herald*, the *Independent*, the *Daily Telegraph* and the *Times Literary Supplement*. Before joining *The Bookseller* in 2007, he worked as a bookseller for Blackwell's in the UK and for Barnes & Noble in the USA. He wrote the text for *Tattoed by the Family Business* (Pavilion 2010) and his debut novel is *The Esquimaux* (Silvertail 2017). Follow him on Twitter @tomtivnan.

See also ...
- *From dream to reality*, page 95
- *A solitary dream*, page 97
- *Creating successful comic books*, page 251

Authentic inclusion in children's books

Beth Cox, inclusion and equality consultant, shares advice on how to make books authentically inclusive, based on over 20 years' experience in publishing, and explores why inclusion is vital for the wellbeing of all children.

Whilst inclusion and diversity may, disappointingly, not be the 'hot topic' across publishing that it once was, it's not a fad that can or should be forgotten. Inclusion is something that needs to be embedded and permanent if we want publishing to be a truly creative industry. But what do we mean by inclusion and diversity and are the terms interchangeable? There are two core approaches in this area when it comes to the content of books: books that focus on or teach about 'diversity' or a particular facet of it, and books that just happen to include a diverse range of characters. The former certainly have a place – they help us understand things that we don't have lived experience of, they open up conversations, and they show the challenges that many marginalised people face. However – and it's a big however – if books 'about' diversity are all that children are exposed to, they are still 'othering'; they still say, 'This is different', 'This is unusual', 'People with this experience only have challenges and face suffering, never joy'. I refer to these types of books as 'diverse books'.

What we need more of are 'inclusive books'. These are great stories (or high-quality content if non-fiction) that include a diverse range of characters incidentally. In such books, the reason that characters are traditionally marginalised is incidental or a natural part of the plot, the characters are fully rounded and more than the aspect(s) that make them 'different'. Because all humans are different. All humans are diverse. Talking about 'diverse books' suggests there is a 'norm' – a white, heterosexual, male, cisgender, nuclear family norm. But there is no such thing. Normal is subjective.

At this point I want to emphasise that, when I talk about inclusion and diversity, I'm referring to all facets of diversity and the many ways in which all humans are 'different'. A lot of the time the focus is solely on ethnic diversity, but no one facet exists in isolation, and they often intersect, which impacts experiences of marginalisation.

Why is inclusion so important?

The most common answer to this question is the 'windows and mirrors' explanation, first introduced by Emily Style in 1988 and expanded on by Rudine Sims Bishop in 1990 to include 'sliding doors'. The approach explains that books should be windows onto that which is outside a reader's experience and mirrors for them to see themselves. The sliding door is a metaphor for how books allow a reader to step into and experience a world created by an author. Now, there is absolutely nothing wrong with this analogy, but it's only part of the reason inclusive books are important. They do so much more than this.

The limitation with the windows and mirrors analogy is that, even if such a book exists, a reader might not come across a book that reflects their personal experience. Books that present a stereotypical 'norm' again and again and again suggest there is just one way of being. However, if books represent a multitude of ways of being, if books show that there are a multitude of ways to be happy, readers will see, regardless of whether their own precise experience is reflected, that it's okay and safe for everyone to be exactly who they are. That whoever they are – that's okay. They are of value. They are enough. They belong. Inclusion in books isn't just important as a way of challenging marginalisation and discrimination, it is important for the mental wellbeing of every child (and adult).

I've been working in publishing for over 20 years and since 2005, when I joined the steering group for Scope's 'In The Picture' project, I've been committed more than ever to making books inclusive. Thankfully, the way inclusion is thought about and approached in the industry has changed a lot in that time. When Alexandra Strick and I founded Inclusive Minds in 2013, our focus was very much on convincing publishers of the need for incidentally inclusive books and exploring the barriers they faced in creating these, as well as seeking solutions. More recently, Inclusive Minds has been able to focus on supporting authors and publishers to ensure authenticity, mainly through its network of Authenticity Advocates – young people with lived experience of marginalisation who are willing to be connected with publishers, authors and illustrators to help them build authentic characters and plots.

It's important to be clear that Authenticity Advocates are NOT sensitivity readers. Sensitivity readers are too often brought in at a very late stage in the publishing process to 'check' that there is nothing in a book that could 'cause offence', but this isn't an effective approach. Not only is it too late in the publishing process to make large changes, should core problems be identified, but it can lead to authors feeling as though they are being censored because they had already pretty much finalised their text. If an author doesn't have the relevant lived experience themselves, working with people who do should happen as early as possible, ideally as part of the research and development process. They should be having conversations when they are building characters and working out plots to enable them to sense-check the authenticity of their ideas and build in nuance that only someone with lived experience would know about. This will result in a much more authentic representation than doing a sensitivity check at the end of the book.

So, where do you start?

The first piece of advice I always give is to **focus on similarities first**, not differences. Often when a traditionally marginalised character appears in a book there is an emphasis on what makes them different. But this approach can 'other' them further. The way readers initially engage with characters is by identifying things they have in common. This is what builds empathy – a reader's sense that 'Oh, *I* do/feel/think that' (or that someone they know does). Once a connection with a character has been made, it's easier to explore or understand what might make that character different, if that's even necessary, without danger of them being othered. After all, this is how we make friends. We initially connect with people because of something we have in common, and then, as a friendship develops, we find out how we are different; we have conversations that might challenge our thinking; we understand how their 'normal' is different from ours.

Very closely linked to this is **ensuring that your characters are fully rounded** – that they are more than the aspect for which they are marginalised. Humans are multifaceted and should be treated as such. Everyone has a multitude of hopes, interests, passions, concerns, fears. Know who your character is, inside and out. Even if that isn't all explored in the text, it will ensure that they come across as a real person rather than a caricature.

Be aware of your world-view and any privilege you may hold. Regardless of how much research you do and how many people you speak to, you will still write or approach a project from your own personal perspective and experience. It's important therefore to try to look at your work dispassionately if you can, and consider how your writing might come across to someone with a different lived experience from yours. This isn't an easy thing to do, but the more you understand about inclusion and the various facets of diversity, and the more you try, the easier it becomes. Overthinking is a positive skill here. You need to consider all the possible ways that something could be perceived, and whether one of these interpretations will perpetuate a stereotype. Of course, there will be a point where you have to accept that one book can't do everything, and times when you might decide that, although a character could perpetuate one stereotype, they challenge many others. And that's fine. The important thing is for that to be a conscious decision.

Consider what you have done to ensure authenticity. Basing a character on what you've been exposed to in other media isn't enough, as the media is often based on stereotypes. What research has gone into the plot and character to ensure that these will ring true?

Finally, remember that **this is a constant learning journey.** After so many years I'm still learning all the time. I also look back at some of the things I've done in the past with the awareness that I would do them differently now. You might still get something wrong; in that case the most important thing is to apologise and ask, or see, how you can learn from it.

Where can you get support?

The good news is that you don't have to go on this journey alone. I realised, after working on numerous books over the years, that if authors, illustrators, editors, designers and publishers understood the basic principles of inclusion, the children's book landscape could be transformed much more quickly. So I designed a programme based on everything I've learned, not just about inclusion, diversity and equality, but also about creating books and, most importantly, about combining the two.

Foundations for Inclusion offers a unique combination of training, implementation tasks, mindset work and live group sessions with me to help anyone who is self-employed in the children's book world, including authors and illustrators, understand and explore those basic principles. I also deliver a version of this programme, the **Inclusion Incubator**, to publishers, along with tailored training and consultancy.

And if you want to explore the best inclusive books, I'd highly recommend becoming a member of and purchasing books from **Letterbox Library**, who curate the most authentic inclusive books and sell them individually or in collections. But please do support by buying from them, as their sales fund their valuable curation work.

Beth Cox is an inclusion and equality consultant and editor, and founder of Beth Cox Inclusion Consultancy Ltd. She has worked in the publishing industry since 2003 and was at Child's Play International Ltd for almost eight years before becoming self-employed. From 2005–08 she was on the steering group for the lottery-funded Scope 'In the Picture' project. She is the co-founder of Inclusive Minds alongside Alexandra Strick and speaks on inclusion at conferences across the UK and overseas. She's currently involved in facilitating the Reflecting Disability project. Beth is the author of four books in the *Level Headers* series and *All Bodies are Wonderful* (shortlisted for the Royal Society's Young People's Book Prize in 2024), all published by B small publishing. For more information visit www.bethcox.co.uk and connect on LinkedIn at www.linkedin.com/in/bethinclusion.

Authentic inclusion in children's books

Further resources

- **Inclusive Minds**

Organisation with a large network of Authenticity Advocates (young people with lived experience of marginalisation, who can be connected to book creators).
   www.inclusiveminds.com

- **Beth Cox Inclusion Consultancy Ltd.**

Inclusion and equality training and consultancy. Including the Inclusion Incubator (for publishing organisations) and Foundations for Inclusion (for freelancers, authors and illustrators) which combines training, implementation tasks and consultancy.
   www.bethcox.co.uk

- **Reflecting Realities**

The 2019 report has a useful section on exemplifications of good practice and reiterates in detail the various 'degrees of erasure' by which ethnically marginalized characters are kept in the background. The section on ensuring children's literature reflects realities provides useful questions to ask when producing or working on inclusive books.
   https://clpe.org.uk/research/reflecting-realities

- **Reflecting Disability**

The Arts Council has funded a project to build on Reflecting Realities which will look at the representation of disabled people in UK children's books. A framework for assessing quality and quantity of representation was developed in 2024, and in 2025 a team of reviewer used this to review books published in 2024. If further funding is granted, this data will then be analysed to create a report. Keep up to date on Instagram @ReflectingDisability or sign up for updates:
   www.reflectingdisability.co.uk

- **What is intersectionality?**

A simple explanation from Kimberlé Crenshaw who coined the word.
   www.youtube.com/watch?v=sWP92i7JLlQ

- **The Danger of a Single Story**

Chimamanda Ngozi Adichie's TED Talk
   www.ted.com/talks/chimamanda_ngozi_adichie_the_danger_of_a_single_story

- **Inclusive and accessible to all? An evaluation of children's picture books and their representation of physical disability**

Dissertation by Caroline Linnea Oestergaard.
   https://whatcarolineread.co.uk/inclusive-and-accessible-to-all.html

What are children's publishers looking for?

Editorial director Rebecca Hill highlights the key ingredients of a children's book that will inspire the passion of an editor, publishing team and readers. She urges writers to focus on their craft, knowing that a great book relies on a great story, one with its own fully developed world that captures the reader from start to finish.

Stories! Each year publishers send thousands of books out into the world, into the hands of eager children, so how can you make sure your story gets to the top of a publisher's pile? Every editor is a fan of reading, but the truth is we get sent more material than we can hope to acquire. What we are all looking for when we open up a new manuscript is a story that allows us to do what we love best ... *read*.

It really is that simple. What I'm looking for when I start a story is to be that writer's biggest fan. The books we publish at Usborne have all given me that feeling of wanting to shout about them from the rooftops: 'Listen to this sentence, everybody! Turn the page and gasp, dear reader ... Hide under the covers and tremble, if you dare dive into this one.' Stepping into a world that is thoroughly developed, and has characters that live and breathe, is a feeling unlike any other. So, if a book can hook me in and make me laugh, make me cry, affect me more than anything else I've read that week, I know that's the one to be passionate about. And passion is what every editor needs – first at an editorial meeting, then at an acquisition meeting and at every available opportunity after that, until that book ends up on a bookseller's table.

As an editorial director, when I'm building Usborne's list I'm always aware of providing a book for every reader. After all, there are lots of tastes that need catering for. But it is essential to see a company's passion for each and every book – from the very first editorial meeting when a submission is discussed. That is exactly what is needed to make a book a success because, beyond the editor's door, a whole team of people will need to love and champion a book: the cover designer, the sales teams, the publicist, the rights team and the marketing department. Without company-wide passion a book could disappear, but with it a book will fly, because we come together to become its superfans.

But before editors even start reading a story and becoming superfans, we make judgements based on your **title**. The title is the crucial 'first sell' of your book to the reader; I can't emphasise enough that a title needs to work hard, and you need to work hard on making it right. As publishers, we are not looking for a set of clumsily arranged buzz words – *The Secrets of the Forbidden Girl in the Magical Dragon Kingdom with Unicorns* – but we are looking for a title that tells us what kind of book you are writing. Strong titles should shine a light on something about your novel, be that the character, the tone or the central interest. Great titles should make us want to know what your book is about. Great titles should make us want to read on.

After the title, the **start** of your story is essential. I so often find myself getting distracted from the story in front of me by a plot that doesn't quite know where it is heading, or a character that doesn't leap out from the pages to ensure I don't return to the demands of office life. Make sure your opening is as strong and grabby as you can make it, without throwing the whole of the kitchen sink in there. Openings are the reason we carry on but, more importantly, they are the reason *children* carry on reading, and that is who we, as editors, are always thinking of when we read. Child readers are harsher than any editor, so make sure you work on making your opening as perfect as you can get it. That prologue – do you actually need it? Where should the first chapter start? Often the story gets going just before your inciting incident, so make *that* the kicking off point!

And carry that **guiding light**; ask yourself, what was it that made you want to write this book? What idea? What theme? What was it you wanted to say? What is it you want children to feel? Make sure you keep those things with you when writing and editing, and keep coming back to them, because what editors want to see, when looking for books to acquire, is authors who are in control of their material; authors who understand how their world is built and understand who their characters are; authors who will tell me at some stage of the editing process: *No, no! My character would never do that, but they would do this instead.*

Always, always think about your **audience**. The children's book market is split into age groups, and you need to be aware of what works for those categories – what content is appropriate, what subjects appeal and what word counts are expected.

Then there's the **ending**: this is another area that I often work hard on with authors. Plan where you want your story to go, and what message and emotion you want to leave the reader with. Make sure that when we finish your book we want to thrust it straight into someone else's hands to read!

But how do publishers *really* decide what to publish?

There are many important things for a publisher to consider when acquiring a book. Will children love it? Will international publishing partners want to buy the rights? Does the author have many more stories to tell? If it is a series, how quickly can the author write the next book? Does this book fit the type of publishing house that we are? Is this something that is missing on our list, or is it something that the competition is doing well with? I always hope the answer to all of these questions is 'Yes', but the truth is, my mind is set when I'm about a third of the way through a book – because by then I have fallen in love with the story.

After that comes the editing, the positioning, the building up of the campaign, the writing of sales material, the development of a cover … These things all combine to help make a great story into a great book. Great stories will always find readers, because stories make us who we are, and help us to become what we want to be.

So, how *do* you make sure your book gets to the top of the editor's pile? Focus on your craft! When the market is ever-changing, do publishers really know what trend is coming next? Can we look into a crystal ball and see what will become a bestseller? I'll let you into a secret here: the answer is no and … erm … no. But I do know a good story, as soon as it arrives on my desk. I open it up, settle down, and then I read, and read and read – doing what every editor loves best. All I want is a story that won't let me stop reading.

Rebecca Hill is fiction editorial director at Usborne Books. She was named Editor of the Year at the British Book Awards 2019, the first children's editor ever to win this coveted prize. Rebecca has acquired and published bestselling authors Holly Bourne, Peter Bunzl, Sophie Anderson and P.G. Bell alongside award-winning titles such as *After the Fire* by Will Hill, winner of the 2018 YA Book Prize, and *Kick* by Mitch Johnson, winner of the Branford Boase Award 2018.

See also…
- *Who's who in publishing*, see page 368
- *Glossary of publishing terms*, see page 370

Winning opportunities: the role of a small independent publisher

Bella Pearson tells of the goals and values that drive her work as a children's publisher, and the excitement and reward of bringing the work of talented creators to fruition, as well as the hard work and resilience required by authors, illustrators and publishers. She advises aspiring writers and artists to focus on developing creative confidence and an authentic voice, to be open to all possibilities and ready for ups and downs on the journey to publication and success.

I have worked in children's publishing for nearly 25 years (can that really be true?!) and the landscape now is so very different to when I started. After working in an independent children's bookshop and completing an MA in Children's Literature, my first job was as editorial assistant to publishing director Philippa Dickinson at Transworld Children's Books in 1999. This was followed by an almost 17-year stint working with David Fickling at David Fickling Books in Oxford, firstly when it was an imprint of Random House Children's Books and then as an independent company. And then, lo, in 2018 I was presented with the opportunity to set up my very own publishing company. Setting up Guppy Books single-handedly was the hardest thing I've ever done, but also the most exciting and rewarding (not counting giving birth to my children, by the way!). From the age of 12, I had wanted to be a publisher (as a child I thought that meant I could read all the time – and oh how I wish that was the case …) and the concept of curating my *very own* list of children's books was a dream. So I took the plunge, deciding that – based on my track record – if I could continue acquiring the same kind of books I had previously, I would be able to create a sustainable, communicative, transparent and innovative publishing company that would provide a good home for authors and illustrators from around the world.

Guppy Books is small and independent, producing between eight and ten books of fiction each year for children aged 5–18 – entertaining, thought-provoking, eclectic, original and inclusive books for young readers of all ages, ability, background. We produce a selection of books that will comfort, stimulate, illuminate, or provide escape for young readers (as well as their carers), individual books that stand out from the crowd and create readers of the future. If (… another dream here) in ten years' time, any child was to wander into a Guppy Bookshop, they would find something that they loved to read. That's the aim. Reading brings SO much value to lives, in so many ways, and children's books are simply the best. Our books range from highly illustrated texts for five-to-eight year-olds (such as the *Ghost Scouts* series (2021–) by Taylor Dolan) to comical intertextual series for emerging readers (e.g. *Knight Sir Louis* by the Brothers McLeod, 2020–); high-octane adventures for the more confident reader (e.g. *Ghostlight* (2022) by Kenneth Oppel) to the stunning *Maggie Blue* fantasy trilogy (2021–) by Anna Goodall for children aged 10+, to thought-provoking novels for young teens, such as *Song Beneath the Tides* (2020) by Beverley Birch. We also look at different ways of telling stories: *Tsunami Girl* (2021), written by Julian Sedgwick and illustrated by Chie Kutsuwada, is a part-prose part-manga novel for readers aged 12+; the *Bronte Mettlestone* series (2017–) by Jaclyn Moriarty is an intricately-woven magical series for readers wanting to be transported into an accessible fantasy world; and Louisa Reid's verse YA novels are quick and immersive reads for young adults, highly impactful and beautifully crafted.

At the time of writing, Guppy has published 32 titles in just under four years. We have been shortlisted for almost all the key children's book awards (the Costa Children's Book Award, the Yoto Carnegie Medal, the Branford Boase Award), as well as recently winning the Waterstones Overall Book Prize in 2023 (… more about that exciting moment below). See *Children's book and illustration prizes and awards* section starting on page 333. We've had five *Sunday Times* Book of the Week slots, as well as our other titles receiving reviews in all the broadsheets; our authors are out there doing school events and attending book festivals (Edinburgh, Hay, Cheltenham, Young Adult Literature Convention (YALC) to name a few); we've sold translation rights and optioned film rights; and in 2023 Guppy was shortlisted for the Newcomer of the Year in the Independent Publishers Guild Awards.

Okay, that's enough boasting! Because it's not all prizes and glory. Publishing is a very strange business. And it can be a very difficult one for all involved, especially for you, the creators – the authors and illustrators. It can be lonely, it can feel as if the industry is closed, opaque and, on top of that, everyone else seems to be doing it better. It's easy to watch other creatives having success and to feel left behind – though I can guarantee that they, too, will have had their insecure moments. An aspiring writer or artist's journey goes up and down; there is no simple upward trajectory, unfortunately, even for the most successful. And then, getting a deal is far from the end of the road. Even when you are published – at that stage, perhaps, by foreign publishers or film companies – it can feel like a long process of rejection: book sales aren't as strong as you hoped; there's an award shortlisting you aren't included on. As a small independent publisher, we try to help our authors through this process as much as we can. We aim to be as communicative and transparent as possible. We're small – we keep in regular touch with our authors and illustrators; we try to provide as much clarity as possible, especially to debut authors when they first set out. It is so important to us that all our authors have a positive experience of being published by Guppy. Although we can't control everything that happens when the book goes out in the world, we can be there every step of the way on the journey – to do our very best for each title individually and to be supportive when things don't work out quite as planned.

We also want to be small enough to remain concentrated on our backlist – we don't intend simply to move on each month. Indeed, it's a backlist that provides the bedrock of a small publishing company – and to ignore this would be foolish. Although I would never say to any author/artist that we want to publish everything they write or illustrate, we are there for the long term rather than for a single book. When Guppy takes on a book, we take on the author and hope to sustain a relationship with them (though, equally, we would completely understand the need to move on when the time is right).

The other thing I was intent on, when setting up Guppy, was to be as open as possible to the multitude of writers out there who neither have an agent or have been previously published. But as a small publisher (or to be honest, even as a larger publisher), it is impossible to be open to submissions all year round. The number received would be so high that, in order to respond to everyone, we simply wouldn't have time to do the actual work of producing any books. But there is another way … In the spring of 2020, when suddenly the world had shut down and the summer was stretching out ahead of us in a very different way, it felt like the perfect time to hold the first Guppy Open Submission competition. Over the course of a week, we invited unpublished and unagented writers to submit the first 2,000 words or so of their young adult novels (one year we ask for YA, and the following year for middle grade). In that first pandemic year we had nearly 400 submissions. We whittled this down to a longlist of around 35, and subsequently a shortlist of ten which was read by a selection of expert judges. I also offered an editorial session for all shortlisted authors. We then went on to choose a winner who was offered a contract with Guppy Books. It was an overwhelming but incredibly exciting experience – to receive so many submissions in one week, and of such high quality too.

In 2020, 23-year-old law student, Nadia Mikail, won the prize with her extraordinary YA post-apocalyptic novel, *The Cats We Meet Along the Way*, which Guppy published in February 2022. And just over a year later, in 2023, this very novel went on to win the hugely prestigious Waterstones Children's Book Prize (see page 347). Florentyna Martin, head of children's buying at Waterstones, said: 'Booksellers were overwhelmed by the tenderness woven through each chapter; the moments of silence between the characters are as truthful and evocative as their conversations. Mikail has ultimately crafted a novel of hope, set against an eventful road trip, that encourages us to share stories and dreams'. We have sold rights all over the world, and the book comes out in America this autumn. What an extraordinary achievement for Nadia! And for Guppy too – all as a result of remaining open to the huge wealth of talent which does not come via the traditional, agented route. The following year the competition was open to middle-grade writers, and James Dixon's evocative and tender book, *The Billow Maiden* (2022), was crowned the winner, while runner-up Carrie Sellon's *Pizza Pete and the Perilous Potions* (illustrated by Sarah Horne) will be published later in 2023. And in 2024 we'll be publishing Olivia Collard's fabulously funny LGBTQ+ YA novel, *Apocalypse Cow*. I have no doubt that all these talented writers will be names of the future, and all through this open and inclusive process. I can't wait for the next one!

So what advice do I have for writers and artists trying to get a break? Well, most of all, have confidence in your own voice/style. I can't remember how many times I've been asked what 'voice' is, and what makes one voice work when another doesn't; frankly, I wish I had an easy answer. It's different for everyone. But confidence and authenticity have a big part to play – don't try to be someone or something you're not. Write from the heart, and tell the story YOU want to tell. And it is important to remember that your voice/style might not be right for one editor, but it could be right for another. I also suggest you watch what is out there for reference, context, and enjoyment! But don't restrict yourself as a result. We didn't choose to publish *The Cats We Meet Along the Way* because it was *like* something else or was '*the next* … [insert your favourite title]'. No, it was an outstanding book in its own right and showed an originality of storytelling, a strong and compulsive spine and authenticity of voice.

It's important to recognise that everyone's journey is different. Author A might have a six-figure deal one year and five years later find themselves looking for a new publisher; Author B might submit over years and finally land a small deal, before winning a huge award; Author C might never publish traditionally and decide to self-publish with great success. There's a whole myriad of possibilities, and everyone's journey is different. But they have one thing in common: they keep going, keep writing, keep illustrating – and hopefully will go on doing so for a very long time.

Winning opportunities: the role of a small independent publisher 17

Bella Pearson has worked in children's publishing for over 25 years. After working in an independent children's bookshop, she completed an MA in children's literature and then moved into publishing at Transworld Children's Books. In 2001 she began work as an editor with David Fickling, helping set up his eponymous list under the umbrella of Random House, leaving as publishing director in 2018 to set up her own publishing company Guppy Books. Bella won the Branford Boase Award for Siobhan Dowd's *A Swift Pure Cry* (Penguin Random House 2006) in 2007 and has been shortlisted a further seven times. For three years she was a mentor at The Golden Egg Academy, and has also edited for many children's publishers including Puffin, Chicken House and Oxford University Press. See https://guppybooks.co.uk for more information and follow on X @guppybooks.

See also...
- *Children's book and illustration prizes and awards*, page 333
- *What are children's publishers looking for?*, page 12

Getting published: the author's story

In this, the first of three articles tracking the course of her debut novel, *29 Locks*, from concept through to publication and beyond, author Nicola Garrard describes what motivated her to write it: the steps, decisions and people involved in each stage of the process, and the highs and lows encountered along the way.

My journey to publication was unplanned. I'd been a secondary English teacher since 1998, but I never thought to write a novel until 2017, when one of my loveliest students was stabbed to death in London. I started writing with a clear intention: to show how poverty, knife crime and child criminal exploitation rot childhoods but also how young people resist and succeed. Having taught boys groomed by gangs for many years, I was able to illustrate the pressures to which they are exposed and celebrate their many special qualities which are often unappreciated by wider society.

These early attempts at writing developed into the story of an inner-city teenager, Donny, who was raised in poverty and exploited by gangs, but who gets the opportunity to leave London, learn about boats and make friends with rural teenagers. He then returns, via the eponymous 29 canal lock gates, to take his revenge on the drugs importers who have hurt his family, friends and community. I wrote the first draft rapidly when my young children were asleep and hit 'send' to literary agents as soon as it seemed 'finished'. I wouldn't advise you to do this but, perhaps because of its emotive subject and the passion with which I wrote, a number of agents quickly replied with variations of 'This is important but needs work … Try this …' and I was thrilled to be telephoned by a top agent. Encouraged by 'revise and resubmit' requests, I returned to the manuscript and worked with Islington teenagers and former students who had been groomed by gangs to make sure my representations of their lived experience and London dialect were respectful and accurate.

A few months later, I submitted a draft to the Lucy Cavendish Fiction Prize and the Mslexia Children's Novel Award; both competitions shortlisted *29 Locks*. At this point I was made four offers of representation. I met the agents and chose The Good Literary Agency, which was founded by Nikesh Shukla and Julia Kingsford to promote under-represented voices, such as BAME, working class, disabled and LGBTQ+ writers. I was star-struck when Nikesh Shukla appeared with the TGLA team for coffee and signed my copies of his YA novels. I had never met a novelist before! The other agencies were equally impressive, but I wanted my writing to generate income that would one day be reinvested into under-represented writers. As a teacher committed to social justice, I needed my writing career to align with those values.

After signing with TGLA I completed a new draft, taking on board the editorial suggestions of the agency team which works collegiately on their titles. Next, my agent Abi Fellows pitched in person to publishers. There was immediate interest. Abi took me to meetings with a publishing director, head of PR and commissioning editor at 'Big 5' publishing house in central London. Sadly, *29 Locks* did not clear the acquisitions stage. This is an aspect of publishing that is seldom acknowledged: that a writer can find literary representation yet still not find a publisher. Having sailed through all the milestones –

prize shortlistings, signing with an agent, submission to publishers – my Young Adult novel stumbled at the last post.

But my agent didn't give up. I was delighted when, many months after I had accepted the idea that *29 Locks* might never be published, Abi phoned with an offer from Rosemarie Hudson at HopeRoad. It was a perfect fit. When I looked up HopeRoad, I discovered that their remit is to further Asian, Caribbean and African diaspora stories, and to fight negative cultural representations. As a Black publisher, with decades of experience, Rosemarie was uniquely placed to champion *29 Locks* and its multicultural cast of characters. She was also keen to build opportunities in publishing, such as commissioning a young illustrator whose degree portfolio was inspired by the Bristol Black Lives Matter movement. HopeRoad's editor, Joan Deitch, brought decades of publishing experience to bear on the final stages of structural revision, copy-editing and preparation of the manuscript for publication. My overwhelming sense was that the entire team of this small, award-winning independent publisher wanted to make my novel the best it could be and to bring Donny's story to readers.

Since publication, throughout the publicity and promotion phase, Rosemarie and her friendly team give ongoing support. Rosemarie sends encouraging texts before I do an event or interview, and recently called to give me a much-needed pep talk about writing my next novel. I'm told that this level of attention would be unlikely with a large publisher, and I am very grateful for her kind and supportive introduction to the industry. As a result, my experience of publishing has been enormously fulfilling and *29 Locks* was soon recognised in literary prizes, such as the Branford Boase Award (see page 335), and reviews, making the *Financial Times* 'Best Books of 2021' list.

Abi, an enthusiastic but pragmatic agent who manages my expectations, is always available to answer questions about publishing, contracts and marketing, and to guide my next steps following a successful debut. We were both very excited to be consulted in the choice of actor for the upcoming audiobook of *29 Locks* and, as a rule, I follow her advice whenever opportunities arise. I would advise aspiring authors to be open to independent publishers, and to manage their expectations because – even with an outstanding manuscript – there remains a huge element of luck. Say yes to all promotional opportunities sent your way, be energetic in generating your own, and remember that the right agent and publisher for you are the ones who care deeply about your story's intentions and the readers for whom it was written.

As a small indie, HopeRoad doesn't have the budget of large publishers to place their titles in trade publication listings, supermarkets and on bookseller's shop tables, but their high-quality production values, personal touch and passionate belief in *29 Locks* has already inspired support from award-winning authors, reading organisations, librarians, teachers, reviewers, grass-roots youth organisations and the readers who matter: teenagers seeking to make sense of the world, develop empathy with others, and most importantly, find hope. I am deeply grateful to Abi and Rosemarie who have brought my story to their hands.

Nicola Garrard is the author of *29 Locks* (HopeRoad 2021), *21 Miles* (HopeRoad 2023) and *On the Edge* (Old Barn Books 2025). Nicola has appeared at the Hay Festival of Literature and Arts, Chichester Festival and Petworth Festival Literary Week, Farnham Literary Festival and BilliLit, and is a regular guest on BBC Radio London. Her words and poetry have been published in *The Frogmore Papers*, *Mslexia*, the *Guardian*, the *W&A Guide to Getting Published* (Bloomsbury 2019) and by IRON Press. For more information see www.nicola-garrard.co.uk or follow her on X @nmgarrard and Instagram @nicolagarrard7.

Getting published: the agent's story

In this second of three articles tracking the course of Nicola Garrard's debut novel *29 Locks* from concept to publication, Abi Fellows recounts how she came to sign Nicola as one of her first authors at The Good Literary Agency (TGLA) and supported her along that journey. She describes the qualities she looks for in books to add to her list, and in their authors, and what her multifaceted role as literary agent entails.

Often, when I do workshops and panels, writers ask that golden question: what are agents looking for? For me personally, as an agent, what is most important is the potential for impact. Because I work across fiction and non-fiction, for adults and for children, this potential can manifest in a number of ways. My list is very diverse, but what unites my authors is their commitment to, and passion for, creating narratives that spark conversation, raise awareness, advocate for positive change and engender hope – narratives for readers who haven't seen themselves, their histories and their stories in books before, or enough.

The importance of representation is at the forefront of my mind when I'm considering children's publishing specifically. When I first read the manuscript of *29 Locks*, I had been volunteering as a school governor in southeast London schools for several years and was acutely aware of the issues that Nicola's writing shone a spotlight on: grooming, gang violence and knife crime. I also knew that teachers were always looking for ways to open up conversations with their students about the realities of young people's lives, realities which are – sadly – often challenging and bleak, in a way that British-originated YA fiction doesn't always acknowledge. The thing that struck me most on my first reading of *29 Locks* was the impact it could have in terms of raising awareness about issues which have been neglected by politicians but which impact a huge number of teenagers, and younger children too. To jump forward for a moment, this was hammered home to me when Nicola told me about the number of safeguarding referrals made at one of the schools she visited, after *29 Locks* was published, for a session with the students. It is devastating that the novel's themes and plot resonate with so many young people, but also heartening to know that, because of seeing themselves in the novel, some youngsters felt better equipped to ask for help.

Authors often wonder whether agents are more moved by polish than by potential. Potential is the thing that excites me, personally, coupled with talking to the writer and believing they have the tenacity and persistence writers need to progress from manuscript to published book. Most agents these days will do some editorial work (some more than others), and, to be sure that your vision is aligned with theirs, I would always advise writers to ask any prospective agents about this. I'm lucky enough to be able to invest both my own time and energy and the support of colleagues when giving editorial feedback, and I was able to use this collegiate approach when working with Nicola ahead of submission.

Working on an edit – or more often several edits – before submitting a book to publishers is one of my favourite parts of the job. While my client is hard at work redrafting, based on the feedback that I have given them, I am busy perfecting my pitch and drumming up some buzz with editors. Cultivating relationships with editors is a vital part of an agent's job, as we need to keep up to date with what editors are looking for and how their lists are evolving. Alas, this is not all 'Call my Agent'-style long lunches and parties (although we're grateful to see some of these events returning); it also involves phone calls, Zooms, office meetings, reading published books to keep an eye on the market, and a little bit of stalking editors on X (Twitter). But even with the most enthusiastic pitch and a superb manuscript, submissions don't always go quite as we agents hope. In Nicola's case, wider conversations about the market at that time were a tricky road bump that we had to navigate. The least fun part of an agent's job is having to make the call to say that an anticipated offer has not come through after all – but it's where we go together, as agent and author, from that point that is important.

Rejection is a part of an agent's life, just as it is an author's, and we don't talk about this enough as an industry. In fact, I think we are overly keen to give the impression that all debuts sell overnight in massive pre-empts. Would it were so! There are many routes to publication, not all of them quick or direct, and resilience is a huge necessity of life for most authors. It's important to be aware that the journey to publication can have unexpected hiccups along the way. But we agents are a tenacious species, and the key thing is to find an ally and champion of your work who will hold tight during these challenging times. As agents we are here to give moral support to our authors whilst they are waiting for news of an offer. This can be a time in a writer's career when working on something else is a great distraction. In Nicola's case, she was buzzing with new ideas so it made sense to start exploring those, talking together about her wider goals and what the strategy for her career should look like moving forward.

Choosing an agent is generally a decision that is made in a moment of excitement, and it marks a great stage of achievement in a writer's life. It's important to consider what kind of advisor that person is going to be in the tougher moments and how you will communicate when things are tricky. It's worth remembering that it is not always an author's first book to go on submission that lands a deal. This can be down to shifting trends and tastes more than the quality of the work itself. I'm a great believer in never giving up on a project and will always keep my ear to the ground for unexplored opportunities, new imprints and editors. And that is how I ended up having a very fortuitous conversation with Rosemarie at HopeRoad about *29 Locks*. Key for both Nicola and I was to hold on to our belief in what made *29 Locks* special and the impact it could have, a belief which – happily – Rosemarie and her team at HopeRoad shared. We knew we needed a publisher who would put this book out into the world sensitively and in a way that would enable both the book and Nicola to have the impact that had motivated her to write it.

Agents are often thought of as the 15-percenters who do the deal, keep their commission, and move on. But our work encompasses so much, both before and after the deal is done. Once the contract is signed, the agent's role shifts into one of overseeing, occasional troubleshooting, and a lot of cheerleading. In the case of *29 Locks*, (HopeRoad 2021) the publishers made my job very easy. One of the things that I love about working with independent publishers is the personal touch and the shared vision that runs through the team, along with the vast amount of energy that goes into every single launch. Particularly important was that the team fully supported Nicola's wish to use the book to create opportunities for up-and-coming creatives, such as the artist who designed the cover and the young actor who voiced the audio edition.

I am thrilled that, in HopeRoad, we found powerful advocates and collaborators who shared our vision of the impact *29 Locks* could have. Its publication is a wonderful example of how author, agent and editor can work together as a team.

Abi Fellows is a literary agent who has worked at DHH Literary Agency since 2023. She has previously worked as a literary agent at The Good Literary Agency, Georgina Capel Associates, as a literary scout at Rosalind Ramsay Ltd, and also as a bookseller at Blackwell's and on the sales team at Faber & Faber. Abi has a BA in English Literature from Bristol University and an MA in English Literature from UCL. See www.dhhliteraryagency.com/abi-fellows for more information and follow her on X @AbiRFellows.

Getting published: the publisher's story

Following on from the author's story and that of the agent, Rosemarie Hudson, publisher at HopeRoad, describes her role and experience as commissioning editor of *29 Locks* by Nicola Garrard (published in 2021), and gives advice for other new authors on how to tackle the publishing process.

On my first reading of the manuscript for *29 Locks*, I was immediately struck by the relevance of the content and also deeply moved by the loving relationship between the main protagonist, Donny, and his addicted mother. The story was written with so much passion – passion, and sometimes anger, at the suffering of the young hero and his contemporaries in their real-life settings of inner-city deprivation.

By publishing *29 Locks* (HopeRoad 2021), I hoped the story would inspire young readers *not* to take up the knife or a life of drugs. I vowed to do my very best for this book, because it was a story that was worth telling and sharing. There was no need to give the manuscript out to any of our readers, nor to spend much time deliberating about my decision – I fell in love with Nicola's story immediately and by the end of Chapter One I knew it was perfect for our Young Adult list. The story reminded me so much of the late, award-winning author Alex Wheatle's debut novel *Brixton Rock* (which I published in 1999 and has been republished by others since) in its rawness and in its depiction of Brenton Brown's struggles in that book. Alex, in fact, later read the proofs of *29 Locks* and gave us a lovely quote for the front cover of the book, saying that the text 'crackles off the page'.

From the very start, I could see that *29 Locks* had a distinct selling point: I knew I could promote it well to the public and get it into schools, libraries and bookshops. Teachers and librarians, as well as booksellers, are real experts when it comes to knowing what readers want and what sells well, so asking them for their views and tapping into their knowledge is an important part of being a publisher.

Publishers also have an eye on book prizes, as being longlisted, shortlisted or winning a prize can propel a title up the sales charts. I sensed that *29 Locks* would shine in the YA fiction category of some of our most prestigious prizes. Suzi Feay, writing for the *Financial Times*, loved it and it became one of her Best Books for YA readers for 2021. At the time of writing this piece, *29 Locks* was on the longlist for the Branford Boase Award 2022 (see page 335) and the Berkshire Book Award. At HopeRoad we feel that *29 Locks* is a classic book that will continue to sell.

It is worth noting that we did not use many professional reviewers pre-publication; these can be especially valuable for quotations and endorsements to use in marketing. Instead, we sent the proofs out to real 'beta' teenage readers, and to reading groups in young offenders' institutions, from whom we received original and enthusiastic feedback. The book resonated with these readers in a way that is truly authentic; many could see their own lives, and choices they had made, reflected in the text. As publishers, we are really grateful for their input as it helped confirm my own views about Nicola's manuscript and to hint at a receptive market for her story.

To sign Nicola up as one of our authors, I swiftly contacted her literary agent Abi Fellows who, at the time, was at the Good Literary Agency. We negotiated and arrived at an agreement that worked well for all of us. The cover design for the book was hugely important – it is what readers see first, so needs to have impact and compel them to pick it up. We needed a cover that properly reflected the content and was fresh as well as enticing. Our brilliant designer, James Nunn, working alongside his gifted mentee Olivia Anthony, came up with our fabulous design, which sums up exactly the mood of the novel.

Nicola is a dream debut author to work with; a little anxious at first, she dapted speedily to the publishing process. An extremely hard worker, Nicola's own ideas came thick and fast, and she's a great communicator. It's important for publisher and author to work well together, and especially key in finding the right copy-editor to work with an author – someone who is on their wavelength. When Nicola learned that Joan Deitch had worked on *Brixton Rock* back in the day, she was reassured; they loved working together. One of the high points of the whole process for me was the launch event, which took place on 'Word on the Water', the London Bookbarge on the Regent's Canal towpath. I also enjoyed reading the reviews that confirmed our own high regard for the book. It was a joy to watch Nicola talking about her book during interviews. With her talent at communication, she takes great pleasure in visiting schools and discussing the book and its themes.

Were there any downsides to the whole process? Yes! Thanks to Covid, the book had to be put back from a summer publication to an autumn one. Getting everything done on time, when staff illness (which had an impact throughout the industry) was delaying deadlines and causing breaks in the chain of production, caused quite a bit of panic. Schedules were turned upside down. And, of course, during Covid we couldn't take advantage of public events, as they were cancelled (and Zoom will never replace face-to-face!).

Here is my top advice for all new authors:

- **Know the market.** Know who you are writing for – who is your book aimed at? Who is your reader? Make sure you have a good story to tell, one that is believable, and write it well. Persevere. Rejection and dejection are part of the learning curve; they are not the end of the world. And success does not always come with the first book.
- **Research and read.** Know where to look for information about publishers who produce books like your own. This book, *Children's Writers' & Artists' Yearbook*, is a key resource. Also, do plenty of research in the bookshops and online. Find out who is publishing what. Read a lot.
- **Get your work edited.** You need to have it edited by a professional before you send it out to an agent or publisher. A good copy-editor will help with presentation and polish. Always check the Acknowledgement pages at the end of books in the same genre as your own, as they can give valuable clues about the copy-editors and agents that the author worked with.
- **Work hard.** Be prepared to work hard both at the editing stage and at publication. Once your book has been acquired, the work does not stop there. Social media helps to sell books, so be on top of your game. Post publication, be prepared to do interviews, to be in the public eye and to travel to events to promote your book. Don't be shy. Your publisher and their team will support you at all times. And finally ...
- **Keep writing.**

Rosemarie Hudson is a publisher and commissioning editor, and the founder and managing director of HopeRoad (www.hoperoadpublishing.com).

The next chapter ... being a successful self-published author

Self-publishing offers authors a way to get into print on their own terms and without having to contend with the traditional gatekeepers of the publishing industry. But what comes after that first flush of pride at printed copies? Griselda Heppel explains all here.

In 2015, I wrote a piece for the *Children's Writers' & Artists' Yearbook* entitled 'An indie's journey to award-winning success'. I had just brought out my children's novel, *Ante's Inferno*, and was on a high. Not only had my first-ever published book taken a Gold Wishing Shelf Award but it had won the People's Book Prize, both of which are judged exclusively by readers. It had also been runner-up in *Writing Magazine's* self-publishing prize, in which high production and design values were important judging criteria, alongside quality of writing; a powerful endorsement of how far self-publishing had distanced itself from its negative 'vanity press' image. Sales were buoyant, with a reprint needed within six months of publication. I felt vindicated, both for daring to believe I'd written a book children would like, and for the publishing method I'd chosen.

Self-publishing hadn't been my original plan. Like all aspiring authors, I sent off my manuscript to publishers and agents, many of whom liked it but were concerned children would be confused by the combined themes of classical mythology and the First World War in the story of 12-year-old Ante's journey through Hell. Having tried the book out on 40 or so readers aged nine to 16, I knew they were wrong. Children love getting their teeth into a story that offers more than one level of complexity, provided it's gripping enough, and the fact that they are so often underestimated in this respect never ceases to amaze me.

High-quality professional self-publishing

I began to research other ways of getting into print. The thought of going it alone, arranging the design, typesetting, production, printing and distribution myself, overwhelmed me, and instead I looked for a professional company that would take charge. I found Matador, which, as an imprint of trade publishing company Troubador, had expertise in all these areas, producing books of a quality to vie with the best traditionally published. Once they accepted my manuscript (not a given – Matador will turn away work they judge not to meet their standard), they took on the production process, leaving me free to take care of the jacket. I commissioned Hilary Paynter, a leading wood engraver, to create – with graphic designer Pete Lawrence – a dark and scary image of Ante's path down through Hell. The Matador design team liaised with me on page design and typeface, and I was thrilled with the final printed book.

Over the next few years, I followed *Ante's Inferno* with two more titles. My first book having been inspired by Dante's *Inferno*, the theme for my second seemed a no-brainer. No one – as far as I knew – had yet centred a children's story on one of the greatest (and oldest) of world legends: Dr Faustus, the man who makes a pact with a demon. How about a tale of a 13-year-old boy, beset by problems, stumbling on the means to call a magic spirit to his aid? What could possibly go wrong?

Thus *The Tragickall History of Henry Fowst* (2015) was born. After this came *The Fall of a Sparrow* (2021), a ghostly thriller, in which 11-year-old Eleanor, sent away to school a long way from home, finds herself confronting the supernatural in the shape of a strange little boy who, to her horror, knows all about her. For both books I followed the same path as *Ante's Inferno*, in getting the manuscript publication-ready as much as the publishing itself.

Have your manuscript critiqued by writing experts

Readers will have no idea how many rewrites a novel has gone through before it reaches them. With *Ante's Inferno*, I learnt from scratch, responding to input from agents, editors and mentors before sending what I thought was a finished draft to a literary consultancy for an editorial report. How wrong I was! Their critique identified a major structural problem. Resolving this, and tightening up the writing overall, meant that the book eventually submitted to Matador was much stronger and better paced than before.

While tough criticism can be difficult to take on board at first, I'd always recommend that a writer, whatever publishing route they're on, has their work looked at by someone who can give genuinely helpful feedback. I submitted all my books for professional critiques and was glad I did. Fresh eyes will spot inconsistencies and problems you're too close to see, and they will be better able to judge the fundamental issues of writing and story quality. Writing courses will also deepen your understanding of the craft, whatever stage you're at. A workshop run by Cornerstones Literary Consultancy helped with story structure and character creation, and I took away from it techniques I've used ever since. As a result, I made sure all three novels were as good as they could possibly be before handing them over to Matador. Each has a jacket engraved and designed by Hilary Paynter and Pete Lawrence, making them as beautiful to look at and handle as they are (I hope) exciting to read.

My rags to riches experience ... or not

So where have I got to with my publishing career? Ha, I know what you're thinking. Half a dozen bestsellers under my belt, bookshop windows full of my titles, queues stretching down the street and round the block for every book signing, global sales soaring…

Erm, not exactly. It hasn't quite worked out like that.

There's something very seductive about the rags to riches myth in self-publishing. Nor, since the advent of the internet, is it always a myth. E.L. James famously sold around 250,000 digital and POD copies of *Fifty Shades of Grey* before signing a traditional publishing contract, and other examples abound of highly successful digitally self-published authors in genres such as romance, thriller, fantasy and science fiction.

The trouble is, children don't, as a rule, read e-books. For them, the feeling of the book in their hands, the lure of illustrations, even the smell of ink and paper, still hold a kind of magic (they do for me, too), and parents are far more likely to browse book shops and libraries with their offspring than buy them an e-reader. This is where marketing comes in, something needed by all books, however they are published. You may have written the best, the most exciting story in the world, but if keen readers – or in this case, their parents – don't know about it, they can't buy it. Around 10,000 new children's titles are published every year in the UK. That's an awful lot of competition vying for space on bookshop shelves stacked with the output of previous years, let alone the great classics that never go out of print. Yes, you can always browse internet bookshop sites, but that can be even more challenging when there are hundreds of thousands of titles to go through.

It's all about the marketing

Marketing budgets are key here. Large publishing houses can afford expensive advertising campaigns as well as deals with major book chains to place their wares prominently in shop windows and on display tables. Smaller presses, whether offering traditional or partnership publishing, simply can't compete on this level, making it harder for their titles to get noticed. Instead they must rely on free publicity, sending out copies to journalists and book bloggers judged likely to review them, with authors expected to contribute by promoting themselves on social media, posting articles online and engaging with their readers. The days when a writer delivered their final manuscript to a publisher before skipping lightly away are well and truly gone.

Awards can help. The prizes *Ante's Inferno* won undoubtedly raised its profile, leading to increased sales. A dozen years on it's still my bestseller, recently undergoing its fifth print run. In terms of independent publishing, this counts as a great success, when you bear in mind that the average self-published book sells 250 copies, with 90 per cent of self-published books selling fewer than 100 (see Nicholas Rizzo, https://wordsrated.com/self-published-book-sales-statistics, 30 January 2023). In this light my books have done very well indeed, with *The Tragickall History of Henry Fowst* and *The Fall of a Sparrow* due for reprinting, and *Ante's Inferno* way out in front.

The marketing strategy that works for me

I never expected sales beyond my wildest dreams. What I wanted was to write and produce the kind of books that gripped me as a child, using my love of classical myths and legends to create exciting adventure stories from some of the greatest pieces of world literature. I banked on the hope that what appealed to me would appeal to present day children, and was delighted to find, from pre-publication feedback from numerous young readers, that it did. All I had to do was come up with a marketing strategy to get my books known that wouldn't bankrupt me.

Reader, I found it. It seems the best way to connect with child readers is to go and talk to them. And I do. I offer a variety of school workshops for Years 5–8, each one centring on one of my books. Along with discussing plot structure, world building and creating believable characters, the students learn about the themes inspiring my stories: classical mythology, the mediaeval idea of Hell and World War I (*Ante's Inferno*); Elizabethan magic and the Faustian pact (*The Tragickall History of Henry Fowst*); ghost stories and gothic horror (*The Fall of a Sparrow*). I've visited all kinds of schools: single-sex, mixed, day schools, boarding schools, independent and state schools, on World Book Day and at other times in the year. Every time, I am bowled over by my audience's enthusiasm and their hunger for stories that are exciting, yes, but also emotionally complex and mentally stimulating. Queues formed for signed copies afterwards, doing wonders for my sales statistics. There's also nothing more inspiring for a writer than to spend time with the audience she's writing for and to see her books through their eyes.

A rewarding experience... but not necessarily financially

While I've found self-publishing hugely rewarding, to interpret that as hugely financially rewarding would be somewhat wide of the mark. If anything, learning about the costs of book production has raised my respect for all publishers. Clouds have been gathering in recent years. Matador's production charges for *The Fall of a Sparrow* in 2021 were significantly higher than for *Ante's Inferno* in 2012, as were their fees for trade marketing and distribution. Rises are to be expected, as that's a space of nine years and it reflects the price increases felt right across the industry for paper and distribution of physical books, in part due to Brexit and the war in Ukraine. In theory, then, the price of the finished book should also rise, but book prices have barely increased in the last couple of decades, and children's titles in particular are expected to be affordable. Large publishing companies can get round this through long print runs, reducing the cost of individual copies, and (hopefully) achieving enough bestsellers to make up for the slower ones.

But smaller companies have less elbow room and, according to Sam Jordison of the Galley Beggar Press, things are getting worse. Between 2015 and 2023, he estimates the production costs on a print run of 3,000 copies to have more than doubled ('Canaries in the Coal Mine', *The Author*, Spring 2025), meaning that once retailer discounts, returns refunds and author royalties are accounted for, sales that nine years ago would have shown a small profit are now making a loss. And that's without any mention of marketing.

Would I take the plunge into self-publishing now, in these tougher conditions? Absolutely. My books may not have made my fortune, but they're out there. They've all been adopted as class readers in primary schools, and I was intrigued to discover that a professor at Melbourne University recommends *The Fall of a Sparrow* to teenagers planning to read English at university.

As an English graduate and lover of literature, I can think of no greater compliment.

Griselda Heppel is the author of three self-published novels: *Ante's Inferno* (2012), winner of the People's Book Prize Children's Award, *The Tragickall History of Henry Fowst* (2015) and *The Fall of a Sparrow* (2021). To find out more, go to www.griseldaheppel.com and www.griseldaheppel.wordpress.com.

See also ...
- *Self-publishing children's books,* page 375

Debut dilemma: your publishing options

Preparing yourself for a self-publishing journey only to be spotted by one of the Big Five publishers is a dream for many children's authors: for Andy Darcy Theo, it's a dream that came true. In this article, he explains the twists, turns and lessons he's experienced along the way.

If you had told me a few years ago that *The Light That Blinds Us* would end up traditionally published by one of the Big Five and become an instant bestseller, I honestly don't know if I would have believed you. I dreamt big over the decade I spent writing my *Descent into Darkness* series, but the path to publishing is rarely straight, and my journey was particularly unusual. It was a mix of determination, strategic decision-making, a lot of hard work and – honestly – luck.

Why fantasy?

Fantasy is the genre I grew up loving. Books, films, TV – I couldn't get enough of it, especially viral YA fantasy books from the mid-2010s. I adored how it served as a vehicle to deal with real-world issues like identity and belonging, through the lens of magic, myth and powers. I was always drawn to themes like found family, revenge and mythology.

When I first began on BookTok, initially as just a reader looking for book recommendations, I never anticipated others to love this genre as much as I did. BookTokers were shouting about their favourite tropes like enemies-to-lovers and morally grey heroes, and they were posting aesthetic videos and dramatic quotes which seemed to go viral all the time. Perhaps it was the escapism we were all seeking that made us love fantasy, especially in the wake of the pandemic. When I first started posting about the book I had written, *The Light That Blinds Us*, it seemed to connect with readers who wanted to see the magic in the mundane and follow a found family of bickering teenagers as they sought to save their world from corruption.

Building on BookTok

I didn't start my TikTok account with a grand marketing plan. Well, I was advised by Harper Collins' Author Academy to join a social media platform to build a following in order to reassure potential publishers that I was willing to promote my books, but truly never thought that I would get a publishing deal from it. I shared snippets about my writing process, character aesthetics, world-building behind the scenes and small emotional teases without giving away too much of the plot in the hopes that it would find potential readers. Primarily, though, I grew my account through reading and reviewing other viral books and doing silly bookish skits, with my most viral signature series being the 'How to become the perfect book boyfriend' videos. This gained me tens of thousands of followers who I would later try to convince to care about me personally and about the book series I had been writing for half of my life.

I tried querying for years, but to no avail. Through TikTok, I garnered interest from an agent and an editor who saw my posts, although it didn't go much further than that. It felt like the higher powers were gatekeeping, or maybe my book just wasn't what was needed in the market as a YA fantasy, despite there being such an evident love for it online.

That was when I realised that I didn't need permission to publish my books, as I could see first-hand on BookTok how much self-published authors were thriving.

At that time, around 2022–3, self-publishing seemed like the clear path forward for me. I'd have complete autonomy: full creative control over the cover design, the marketing, the timeline. I was ready to invest in professional editing and cover design because I wanted *The Light That Blinds Us* to be the best version of itself; I had been writing it since the age of 13 and just wanted to share it with the world. I thought it was now or never: given that I was also working full-time as a teacher, I was worried my dream would soon get sidelined for this more practical, realistic career. Self-publishing also had the advantage of speed and meant I could offer my story to my followers while the excitement was still fresh. The journey was not the one I had initially envisioned, to be honest. I had imagined getting an agent first, going through a formal submission process, then getting published traditionally. This route didn't seem to be on the cards for me, though.

I researched extensively, and I really mean that. The other incredible thing about BookTok was that it served as a platform for me to learn about how to self-publish. I spent countless hours preparing to go down that route and even paid for an editor and ran a competition where I asked my followers to vote on their favourite cover from a selection for *The Light That Blinds Us*. It was a few weeks before I was about to self-publish that a DM in my inbox caught my attention.

The DM that changed everything

I got a message through on TikTok from the editorial director of a Big Five publisher – the same editor who was involved in the acquisition of Lauren Roberts, author of the bestselling *Powerless* series. I thought it was a fluke, but I sent my book anyway and emailed back and forth for a couple of weeks before we arranged a Zoom call. That was then she said that she loved my book and wanted to publish it.

I cried. I'm not ashamed to admit that – I've probably posted a video of me crying on TikTok too, as I wanted to document my entire publishing journey. The moment of external validation from a professional in the field who was able to get it into bookstores around the country, and hopefully around the world too, was a moment I will never forget. I felt all the more empowered as I had done this without an agent, although in retrospect, I wish I had got one at this point onward before I signed any deals.

Pros and cons: Self-publishing vs traditional

Having researched self-publishing and now being a traditionally published author of both *The Light That Blinds Us* and its sequel, *The Dark That Hides Us*, I can say with honesty that both paths have advantages and disadvantages.

Self-publishing pros, traditional publishing cons

- **Creative control**: You make all the decisions about the book when self-published – from your cover to your release date to the story itself. In trad publishing, however, your voice can sometimes be lost, especially if unagented (like I was).
- **Higher royalties**: Generally, self-published authors earn a larger percentage per book sold, although sales may be lower given the challenges of getting copies into physical bookstores.
- **Speed**: As soon as your book is written and edited, you can publish it. You don't need permission from a dozen people or to wait for a year (or more), which is often the case

with trad publishing. Writers who can pump out many books in one year might prefer this snappier route where they aren't tied down to any legal contracts or options etc.

Self-publishing cons, traditional publishing pros
- **Financial investment**: Upfront costs for editing, design, formatting and marketing can add up for self-publishing, whereas this doesn't apply for trad publishing. Here, you get an advance payment made in instalments and then (a much smaller percentage of) royalties if you earn out your advance from your book sales. I can't stress enough the importance on getting an agent to negotiate and advocate for you, otherwise you run the risk of being exploited or taken advantage of by less-scrupulous larger corporations.
- **Limited reach**: I knew it would be so difficult to get into bookstores as a self-published author, or to sell any translation rights, or to produce an audiobook version, which is how I mostly consume books nowadays. By being traditionally published, we have sold translation rights in numerous territories and have managed to have special editions with huge booksellers such as Waterstones and The Works, which I don't think would have been possible otherwise.
- **Workload**: I found it so difficult juggling all the complex roles when contemplating self-publishing. I wasn't just the author, but also the editor, designer, marketing manager, publicist etc. It was exhausting just thinking about it. While authors still do a lot of heavy lifting with promotion and marketing with trad publishing – this was especially the case for me, as I had a social media presence and my publishers really utilised this – I have learned to trust my publishing team to do what they do best in their respective fields.

What I'm up to now
Right now, I'm deep in the whirlwind of author life: bookstore signings, author panels and festivals, excitement about fan art and theories, the surreal joy of seeing my book in readers' hands. It's exhilarating, exhausting, and more rewarding than I ever imagined. *The Light That Blinds Us* became an instant bestseller and the highly anticipated sequel, *The Dark That Hides Us*, have benefited from the special editions I mention above, which have had a profound impact on sales too. I adore seeing more and more readers discover this series and fall in love with the complex, diverse cast of characters and the magical world I have built. They make all the stress of publishing worth every second and every new wrinkle on my forehead (I've just turned twenty-six, bear in mind).

I'm currently writing the third book in the *Descent into Darkness* series and I am loving it, especially now that I'm now teaching part-time due to my books' successes. I can't wait to continue to do what I've always felt I was meant for, to chase my dreams and kindle my spark. I am extremely ambitious, but I would rather live a life naively hopeful than one filled with regret.

Writing advice
No matter what genre you write or which path you choose, here's what I've learned about writing and publishing.
- **Connect**: First, start building your audience early by utilising platforms like TikTok, Instagram, YouTube, X etc. It's incredible for inspiration, but also to share your writing journey and snippets of your book so that you build excitement and connect with potential readers. But don't cold-sell to them! Immerse yourself in the community, make friends, be kind and enjoy being a reader again.

- **Network**: Surround yourself with a network of friends who altruistically care for you and shout about your achievements so loudly that you don't think to pay attention to those who aren't looking. Writing is a solitary activity, but publishing isn't. I can't thank my author friends enough for helping to educate me, uplift me, reassure me and cheer me on.
- **Reflect**: Lastly, and I have only recently learned this the hard way, but please make sure you stop to smell the roses. In the chaos of publishing, it's easy to lose sight of why you write. I found myself constantly comparing myself to other authors, typically more successful and more viral authors who had been doing it a lot longer than I have. This drained me of my hope and forced me to become hyper-critical of myself and my dream. Imposter syndrome doesn't help either, whether you're traditionally published and a bestseller or if you are self-published with hundreds of readers and fans. My advice is to appreciate that writing is what we love; that is the dream, and publishing is just the way we share our joy with readers who may also love our stories.

Andy Darcy Theo is a bestselling author and teacher, with a background in clinical psychology. The first two books in his *Descent into Darkness* series are *The Light That Blinds Us* (Simon & Schuster 2024) and *The Dark That Hides Us* (Simon & Schuster 2025). Follow Andy on both Instagram and TikTok @andydarcytheo.

See also ...
- *Self-publishing children's books*, page 375

Give and take: finding partners to help build your writing career

Getting a publishing deal is (quite understandably) the main goal for all authors. Once your book is in print, though, you need to think about getting it to the widest possible audience. In this article, Tom Palmer explains the many benefits of working with a partner to do just that.

Questions

Even before I start planning a book – when it is just an idea knocking round my head – I ask myself two things.
1. How am I going make my book as authentic as possible?
2. How am I going to promote my book when it comes out?

These might seem like very separate issues for you to think about. One is about research and planning before a word of your text has been written. The other is about after all the words have been written, rewritten, edited, proofread and printed. Connecting the two, though, can make a huge difference to whether a book gets published and whether it sells. Think about the book you are writing and ask yourself these questions:
- What is it about?
- Where is it set?
- When is it set?
- Who are the characters?

Once you have answered those, ask yourself two more.
1. Who can you partner with to make this book accurate and authentic?
2. Which partner – when the book is published – can help you spread the word about it?

And, then, when you have the answer to those two questions, ask yourself the most important question of all. *How can you help them?*

Partnerships

Below are some of the range of organisations I have worked in partnership with:
1. A museum that used to be a warship.
2. A chocolate manufacturer.
3. A Holocaust education charity.
4. A village school in the Lake District.
5. A charity that supports military families.

How to attract a partner organisation
- What is your book about?
- What organisations does it link with?
- What do those organisations need? What are their aims?
- How can you help them achieve those aims?
- What can they do for you, from research to promoting your book?

Arctic Star

I wanted to write a book about the Royal Navy during the Second World War. There are lots of children's books about soldiers, plenty about airmen too, but very few about sailors. I saw a gap in the market: the book would be called *Arctic Star*.

This idea was inspired by my wife who used to work on board HMS Belfast, once a warship, now a museum on the Thames in London. As usual, I asked myself the what (WW2 naval warfare), who (young sailors), when (1943) and where (on a warship).

My first research was to visit the outstanding Imperial War Museum (IWM) website and trawl through their online audio and photograph files. Awesome material. But there was still so much I didn't understand. So I contacted HMS Belfast, also part of the IWM. I told them I was planning a book about the ship's role in the Arctic convoys – to be called *Arctic Star* – and could they help me, please?

Some museums and organisations don't reply to these approaches. But if you do your research, discover the name of an individual involved and have already done some groundwork, they often do. HMS Belfast did reply. I asked them for all the help they could give me to tell the story of their ship. Then I offered to help them do the work they are funded to do. If I could help them tell their story and if I could help drive visitors to their museum, then they had a good reason to invest time and goodwill in me and *Arctic Star*.

They introduced me to a veteran of the Arctic convoys and I interviewed him. They gave me a private tour of the ship. They answered countless questions I had about what might happen to the characters in the book. And then – when I had written the first draft – they checked it and advised me on how to make my book more accurate.

No money changed hands. But we both benefit wonderfully from our partnership. My book is accurate. Many of its 30,000 readers have gone on to visit HMS Belfast with their families, but all of them now know the story that the Imperial War Museum and HMS Belfast are trying to tell.

Off Side

For the third book in my Football Detective series – *Off Side* – I fixed on the trafficking of young footballers from Ghana and Nigeria to Europe as a crime for my child sleuths to solve. This illegal or forced movement of young people is a major violation of human rights and usually ends in catastrophe for them and their families.

Again, I asked myself the what (African football), who (young footballers), when (today) and where (Ghana).

How was I going to find out about all of that? This was as far out of my experience and knowledge as you could get. (Other than the football.)

I talked to some people and read around about organisations that were already tackling football trafficking. I narrowed it down to Right to Dream, a football academy that guides young Ghanaian footballers away from corrupt and bogus football agents. I contacted them and asked, if I came to Ghana for my research, if I could meet them and see their work? They said yes.

I paid for the travel and accommodation myself, using a quarter of the money I had been advanced for the book. I had an extraordinary week meeting young footballers, seeing them train and play games, but also hearing about how their lives can go horribly wrong.

Knowing I was going to Ghana, and aware of the work Divine chocolate do as part of their fairtrade campaign for local farmers to be paid properly for their cocoa beans, my wife suggested I contacted the company. She phoned them. I was travelling to Ghana, she explained. I'd like to visit one of your farms and meet the families you support so I could write accurately about their lives. They said yes, too.

Both Divine and Right to Dream helped me because they saw I wanted to help tell their story, boost their campaigns and that the books (and the publicity the books might attract) would enhance their profile and help the people they support.

Since the book was published, I have done events alongside both charities, supporting their work. This has given my book a higher profile that it might have had otherwise. Many schools in the UK work with the Fairtrade Foundation on Fairtrade Fortnight and my book is one of those most used to help tell the story and make it engaging to children.

After the War

When my wife heard a radio programme about a group of Holocaust survivors who came to the English Lakes direct from the liberated concentration camps, she insisted I listen to it. And that I do a book about or even with them. I was unsure. Did I have the confidence?

The story of these Windermere Children has been told by the Lake District Holocaust Project (LDHP) who use a website, a museum and their speakers and work in schools and across the UK to help tell this story. A film has been made about them (*The Windermere Children*).

I needed careful guidance into how to write a story based on the story of Holocaust survivors. The LDHP project leader – Trevor Avery – introduced me to his research and to some of the survivors. I was able to get primary source material to write my book with that help. He did this generously, once he trusted I was approaching the project in good faith.

As a result my book, *After the War*, is accurate and respectful, based entirely on testimony. LDHP's help was invaluable: I'd never have been able to write the book without it. But our working together has had benefits for them, too. My book has led to 10,000 children learning about the Holocaust. Many of those children have visited the museum and used the LDHP website, all of which has raised the profile of the organisation's work and its ultimate purpose of educating people about the Holocaust.

Angel of Grasmere

While I was writing *After the War*, I read and heard stories about other events in the Lake District during the Second World War – stories I wanted to follow up on.

So I knew the where my next book would be set. Cumbria. And the when: during the Second World War. These two questions were answered. But I wasn't so sure on the who and the what.

But when I was writing *After the War*, I needed to try it out on a group of readers. *After the War* is set in Ambleside. Grasmere School was just up the road. It seemed a good fit. The school's Year 6 students read the book and – with their teachers – gave me feedback that made me change it significantly. It was a great help for me. The school got something out of it, as well. They met an author, worked with an author, and felt empowered that an author had changed his book after they had shared their responses with him.

And so I decided the next book – *Angel of Grasmere* – would be set in their village, because I wanted to work with them again. We worked on ideas together, researching settings together. They read the first draft and we launched the book together. Their input made my book authentic.

The result was the school got to help write a book from an idea to publication, empowering the children and enhancing their education. The teachers were pleased. And so was I.

Rugby Academy

Having worked with the RAF Museum and a school with many RAF children as pupils in another partnership, I was keen to tell a story featuring Forces kids. This was around the time I wanted to fill another gap in the children's book market. Rugby books. Sometimes two ideas blend to become something bigger than the two ideas on their own. Rugby and Forces families did that for me.

I asked my usual questions. What and who is the story going to be about? Children in the forces and who play rugby. Where will it be set? A school with lots of children whose parents are in the forces. When? Now.

So how would I reach military children and their families?

Reading Force are a UK charity who use the power of reading together to help support Forces families, particularly those where a parent has been deployed. At the core of their offer is enabling and encouraging military parents and their child to read the same book and talk about it by letter, telephone or Zoom. They also put on events to encourage forces families to sign up, usually hosted in the children's schools.

I had been really lucky to collaborate with Reading Force before, when I had delivered reading workshops to children and parents in schools as part of their work. While working with them, I met Forces families and talked to parents and children about the unique situations they face and what it is like to be a young person with Forces parents. I found out how children have to live for months each year missing one parent, sometimes both, aware that they are in harm's way. I also learned how many Forces families are required to move from one base of deployment to another every two years. Making friends can be challenging. It's a world a lot of people cannot imagine. And – until I heard their stories – I had no idea myself.

Thanks to working with Reading Force, I was able to represent military children authentically. I created a series of three books for Reading Force about rugby where the child characters are all coping with having parents deployed in military conflict.

The above case studies are examples of partnerships that have played out well. Plenty of approaches don't bear any fruit but – if you persist and make it clear you have a lot to contribute as well as to ask for, and make your case clearly – partnerships are a great way of operating as an author. And while both parties benefit in predictable ways, gains can also come in exciting and unpredictable ways too.

There is another partnership that helped start and maintain my writing career. My wife's influence will have become clear in the case studies above. Of all the partnerships I've been part of, this is the one that has had the greatest impact.

Tom Palmer is a children's author from Yorkshire. He writes historical and sports fiction for ages 7–13 years. Tom has been published since 2008 and in 2024 he passed 1,000,000 book sales. He has won 30 book awards, including four UK national awards. Before he was an author, he worked as a bookseller, in library reader development and at book festivals. For more information, visit: www.tompalmer.co.uk.

Children's book publishers UK and Ireland

There are changes to listings in this section every year. We aim to provide a comprehensive list of publishing imprints, the name or brand under which a specific set of titles are sold by a publisher. Any one publisher might have several imprints, which are included either under a publisher's main entry or in some cases as entries themselves. Information is provided in a way that is of most use to a reader. The listings that follow are updated by the Writers' & Artists' editors based on information supplied by those listed.

The country code for phoning UK offices from overseas is +44.
*Member of the Publishers Association or Publishing Scotland
†Member of Publishing Ireland, the Irish Book Publishers' Association
‡Member of the Independent Publishers Guild
sae = self-addressed envelope
MS = manuscript (MSS = manuscripts)

Some of the smaller companies listed are also members of the Indie Press Network, formed in 2023 to represent publishers with five or fewer employees.

Acair*
An Tosgan, 54 Seaforth Road, Stornoway, Isle of Lewis HS1 2SD
email info@acairbooks.com
website https://acairbooks.com/
Facebook www.facebook.com/acairbooks
X @acairbooks

Scottish Gaelic children's books and a wide range of titles in Scottish Gaelic and English. Founded 1977.

Alanna Max
38 Oakfield Road, London N4 4NL
email info@alannamax.com
website www.alannamax.com
Co-publisher Fay Erek, Editor-At-Large Anna McQuinn

Children's picture books. See website for submissions guidelines. Founded 2012.

Amgueddfa Cymru – Museum Wales‡
Cathays Park, Cardiff CF10 3NP
tel 029-2057 3235
email post@museumwales.ac.uk
website www.museumwales.ac.uk
X @AmgueddfaBooks
Head of Publishing Mari Gordon

Trade and special interest books based on the Welsh national collections and research of Amgueddfa Cymru, Wales's national museums. For adults, schools and children, in both Welsh and English. Founded 1907.

Andersen Press*
6 Coptic Street, London WC1A 1NH
tel 020-7840 8701
email anderseneditorial@penguinrandomhouse.co.uk
website www.andersenpress.co.uk
Facebook www.facebook.com/andersenpress
X @andersonpress
Instagram @andersonpress
Managing Director Mark Hendle, Publisher Klaus Flugge

Picture books, fiction for 5–8 and 9–12 years and YA fiction. Publisher of the *Elmer* series by David McKee, the *Little Princess* series by Tony Ross, *The Proudest Blue* by Ibtihaj Muhammad, S.K. Ali and Hatem Aly, *The Bolds* series by Julian Clary and David Roberts, as well as award-winning fiction by Phil Earle and Kwame Alexander. Founded 1976.

Arcturus Publishing‡
26–27 Bickels Yard, 151–153 Bermondsey Street, London SE1 3HA
tel 020-7407 9400
email info@arcturuspublishing.com
website www.arcturuspublishing.com
Facebook www.facebook.com/arcturusbooks
X @arcturusbooks
Instagram @arcturusbooks
Editorial Manager Joe Harris (children's)

Children's non-fiction, including activity books, reference, education, practical art, geography, history and science. No unsolicited MSS. Founded 1993.

Aurora Metro‡
80 Hill Rise, Richmond TW10 6UB
tel 020-8948 1427
email submissions@aurorametro.com
website www.aurorametro.com
Facebook www.facebook.com/AuroraMetroBooks
X @aurorametro
Managing Director Cheryl Robson

YA fiction and plays for young people. Submissions: send synopsis and three chapters. Runs a biennial competition for women novelists (odd years): Virginia Prize for Fiction. Entry fee for submission of either an adult or YA novel. Imprints: Amber Lane Press, Aurora Metro Books, River Light Press and Supernova Books. Founded 1990.

Award Publications
The Old Riding School, The Welbeck Estate, Worksop, Notts. S80 3LR
tel (01909) 478170
email info@awardpublications.co.uk
Facebook www.facebook.com/awardpublications
Instagram @award.books

Picture story books, fiction, early learning, information and activity books for 0–12 years. No unsolicited material. Refer to social media sites for details of submission windows. Founded 1972.

b small publishing*‡
website www.bsmall.co.uk
Managing Director Catherine Bruzzone, *Publisher* Sam Hutchinson

Activity books and foreign language learning books for 2–12 years. Written in-house. No unsolicited MSS. Founded 1990.

Badger Learning*
Oldmedow Road, King's Lynn, Norfolk PE30 4JJ
tel (01553) 816083
email info@badgerlearning.co.uk
website www.badgerlearning.co.uk
Publisher Sarah Rudd

High interest/low reading age fiction and non-fiction for 7–16 years. The range also includes educational and teacher resources. Series include: *WOW! Fiction, WOW! Facts, Teen Reads, Full Flight* and *Graphic Novels*. Email for submission guidelines. Founded 2001.

Barrington Stoke*
18 Walker Street, Edinburgh EH3 7LP
tel 0131 392 9400
email barringtonstoke@harpercollins.co.uk
website www.barringtonstoke.co.uk

Short fiction and non-fiction for children, specially adapted and presented for reluctant, struggling and dyslexic readers. Includes books for ages 5 to YA, with reading ages of 6–9. No unsolicited submissions. All work is commissioned from well-known authors and adapted for reluctant readers. Imprint of HarperCollins Publishers. Founded 1998.

Big Picture Press
Victoria House, Bloomsbury Square, London WC1B 4DA
tel 020-3770 8888
email hello@bonnierbooks.co.uk
website www.bonnierbooks.co.uk
X @BigPicturePress

Boutique range of illustrated gift books. Collaborates with artists such as Chris Wormell (*Planetarium*) and Ximo Abadía (*The Speed of Starlight*). An imprint of Bonnier Books UK. Founded 2013.

Bloomsbury Publishing*‡
50 Bedford Square, London WC1B 3DP
tel 020-7631 5600
website www.bloomsbury.com
Facebook www.facebook.com/BloomsburyPublishing
X @BloomsburyBooks
Bluesky @BloomsburyPublishing.bsky.social
Instagram @bloomsburypublishing
Founder & Chief Executive Nigel Newton

Independent publisher with authors who have won the Nobel, Pulitzer and Booker prizes. Offices in London, New York (page 67), New Delhi, Oxford and Sydney (page 57). MSS must normally be channelled through literary agents, with the exception of academic and professional titles. Founded 1986.

BLOOMSBURY CONSUMER DIVISION
Managing Director Ian Hudson
Imprints: Absolute Press, Bloomsbury Children's Books, Bloomsbury Circus, Bloomsbury Press, Bloomsbury Tonic (wellbeing), Harry Potter, Head of Zeus - Zephyr and Raven Books.

Bloomsbury Children's Books
Publishing Director & International Editor-in-Chief Rebecca McNally

Children's fiction and non-fiction, graphic novels. No unsolicited MSS.

Bloomsbury Education
Head of Education Helen Diamond, *Editorial Director* Hannah Rolls (educational fiction & poetry), *Commissioning Editor* Joanna Ramsay (early years & CPD), *Commissioning Editor* Emily Evans (primary & CPD)

Educational fiction and non-fiction, children's poetry, teacher resource books and CPD titles. Imprints: Andrew Brodie and Featherstone Education. Submissions by email: education-submissions@bloomsbury.com. Look at recently published titles and catalogues to gauge current publishing interests. Much of the list is educationally focused and publishes in series. Allow 8–10 weeks for a response.

Children's book publishers UK and Ireland

Bog Eyed Books
39 Coptefield Drive, Belvedere DA17 5RL
email info@bog-eyed-books.com
website https://bog-eyed-books.com/
Facebook www.facebook.com/bogeyedbooks
X @bogeyedbooks
Instagram @bogeyedbooks
Directors Gary Northfield, Nicky Evans

Children's comic books of all genres, mystery, historical and bizarre. Hosts events in comic bookshops. Founded 2016.

Bonnier Books UK*‡
Victoria House, Bloomsbury Square,
London WC1B 4DA
tel 020-3770 8888
email hello@bonnierbooks.co.uk
website www.bonnierbooks.co.uk
Facebook www.facebook.com/bonnierbooksuk
X @bonnierbooks_UK
Ceos Sarah Benton, Jonathan Perdoni, *Managing Director of Black & White Publishing Group* Tim Whiting, *Managing Director of Zaffre Publishing Group* Sarah Benton, *Managing Director of Children's Trade* Helen Wicks, *Editor-at-Large* Carole Tonkinson

Publishes across a wide variety of genres for different ages and has a number of adult and children's imprints. Children's trade: Autumn Publishing, Big Picture Press (page 38), Hatch Press, Hot Key Books (page 45), Igloo Books (page 46), Piccadilly Press (page 51), Studio Press (page 54) and Templar Books (page 54). Founded 2015.

The Book Guild
Unit E2 Airfield Business Park, Harrison Road, Market Harborough, Leics. LE16 7UL
tel 0116 279 2299
email info@bookguild.co.uk
website www.bookguild.co.uk
Facebook www.facebook.com/thebookguild
X @BookGuild
Instagram @thebookguildpublishing
Managing Director Alex Thompson, *Operations Director* Chloe May

Children's fiction and non-fiction; see website for submission details. The Book Guild is part of Troubador Publishing. Founded 1996.

Books on the Hill Press
20 Hill Road, Clevedon, Somerset BS21 7NZ
email info@booksonthehill.co.uk
website www.booksonthehill.co.uk
Facebook www.facebook.com/booksonthehill
X @booksonthehill
Instagram @booksonthehill
Publisher Alistair Sims

Dyslexia-friendly books for adults and children. Also a bookshop. Founded 2019.

Bright Red Publishing*
Mitchelston Drive Business Centre,
Mitchelston Drive, Kirkcaldy KY1 3NB
tel 0131 220 5804
email info@brightredpublishing.co.uk
website www.brightredpublishing.co.uk
Facebook www.facebook.com/BrightRedBooks
X @_BrightRed
Instagram @bright_red_publishing
Directors John MacPherson, Alan Grierson

Educational publishing for Scotland's students and teachers. Founded 2008.

The British Museum Press
Great Russell Street, London WC1B 3DG
tel 020-7323 8000
email publicity@britishmuseum.org
website www.britishmuseum.org/publishing
Head of Publishing Claudia Bloch

Books for children, young readers and families, in collaboration with award-winning publisher Nosy Crow (page 49). Titles range across picture books, activity books and illustrated non-fiction. Founded 1973.

Buster Books
16 Lion Yard, Tremadoc Road, London SW4 7NQ
tel 020-7720 8643
email enquiries@mombooks.com
website www.mombooks.com/buster
Facebook www.facebook.com/BusterBooks
X @BusterBooks
Instagram @buster_books

Picture books for 0–5 years, reference, activity and fiction for 5–12 years. Publishes approx. 60 titles a year. Publications include puzzle books, such as the bestselling *Clever Kids* series, and a wide selection of children's illustrated non-fiction, colouring, drawing, sticker, activity, fiction and picture books. Titles range from enlightening books, such as the *A Day in the Life* comic series and *Am I Made of Stardust?* by Dr Maggie Aderin-Pocock, to quirky picture books, such as *Does a Bear Poo in the Woods?* and *The Dinosaur Department Store*, and the *Sherlock Bones* series of fiction puzzle adventures. No unsolicited MSS. Founded 1985.

Cambridge University Press & Assessment*‡
University Printing House, Shaftesbury Road,
Cambridge CB2 8BS
tel (01223) 358331
email directcs@cambridge.org
website www.cambridge.org
Facebook www.facebook.com/CambridgeUniversityPress
X @CambridgeUP
Chief Executive Peter Phillips, *Managing Directors* Mandy Hill (academic), Jill Duffy (UK education), Rod Smith (international education)

For children: curriculum-based education books and software for schools and colleges (primary, secondary and international). For all learners: ELT. Founded 1534.

Campbell – see Pan Macmillan

Candy Jar Books
Mackintosh House, 136 Newport Road, Cardiff CF24 1DJ
tel 029-2115 7202
email submissions@candyjarbooks.co.uk
website www.candy-jar.co.uk/books
Facebook www.facebook.com/CandyJarLimited
X @Candy_Jar
Head of Publishing Shaun Russell

Non-fiction and fiction for children 7+ years. Will consider unsolicited MSS. Check website for submission details. Founded 2010.

Cassava Republic Press
Studio C11, Mainyard Studios, 94 Wallis Road, London E9 5LN
email info@cassavarepublic.biz
website https://cassavarepublic.biz/
Facebook www.facebook.com/CassavaRepublic
X @cassavarepublic
Instagram @cassavarepublicpress
Publishing Director Bibi Bakare-Yusuf

Contemporary Black and African writing. Aims to bring high-quality fiction and non-fiction for children to a global audience. Has offices in Abuja and London. Founded 2006.

Catnip Publishing
320 City Road, London EC1V 2NZ
tel 020-7138 3650
email editorial@catnippublishing.co.uk
website www.bouncemarketing.co.uk/publisher/catnip-publishing
X @catnipbooks
Managing Director Robert Snuggs

New and previously published titles from picture books to teen fiction. Acquires new titles from overseas publishers, reissues out-of-print titles by top authors and commissions original fiction for 7–9 years, 9–12 years and YA readers. Publishes 15–20 books a year. Recently published books by Pippa Goodhart, Jason Beresford, Berlie Doherty, Sarah Baker, Sophie Plowden, Joan Lingard, Keris Stainton and Anne Booth. Will only consider agented submissions. Founded 2005.

CGP
Coordination Group Publications, Broughton House, Broughton-in-Furness, Cumbria LA20 6HH
tel (01229) 715766
email ewt@cgpbooks.co.uk
website www.cgpbooks.co.uk
Facebook www.facebook.com/cgpbooks
Instagram @cgpbooks.uk

Educational books centred around the National Curriculum, including revision guides and study books for Reception, KS1, KS2, KS3, GCSE, iGCSE and A level. Subjects include maths, English, science, history, geography, computing, ICT, computer science, psychology, business studies, economics, religious studies, design and technology, PE, music, French, German, Spanish, sociology, 11+, 13+ and functional skills. On the lookout for top teachers at all levels, in all subjects. Potential authors and proofreaders should fill in the application form found on the website, ready for when a project comes up in their subject area. Founded 1996.

Chicken House
2 Palmer Street, Frome, Somerset BA11 1DS
tel (01373) 454488
email hello@chickenhousebooks.com
website www.chickenhousebooks.com
X @chickenhsebooks
Instagram @chickenhousebooks
Managing Director & Publisher Barry Cunningham, *Deputy Managing Director* Rachel Hickman

Fiction for 7+ years and YA. No unsolicited MSS. See website for details of *The Times*/Chicken House Children's Fiction Competition for unpublished writers. Part of Scholastic. Founded 2000.

Child's Play (International)
Ashworth Road, Bridgemead, Swindon, Wilts. SN5 7YD
tel (01793) 616286
email office@childs-play.com
website www.childs-play.com
Facebook www.facebook.com/ChildsPlayBooks
Bluesky @childsplaybooks.bsky.social
Instagram @childsplaybooks
Chair Adriana Twinn, *Publisher* Neil Burden

Children's educational books: board, picture, activity and play books; fiction and non-fiction. Founded 1972.

Christian Education
Suite 5–6, Pure Offices Ltd, 1 Devon Way, Longbridge Technology Park, Birmingham B31 2TS
tel 0121 472 4242
email sales@christianeducation.org.uk
website https://shop.christianeducation.org.uk/, www.retoday.org.uk
Facebook www.facebook.com/RETodayServices
X @IBRAbibleread

Incorporating RE Today Services and International Bible Reading Association. Publications and services for teachers and other professionals in religious education including *REtoday* magazine, curriculum booklets and classroom resources. Also publishes bible reading materials. Founded 2001.

Cicada Books*

Studio 31A, Archway Studios, Bickerton House,
25–27 Bickerton Road, London N19 5J
email info@cicadabooks.co.uk
website www.cicadabooks.co.uk
X @cicadabooks
Instagram @cicadabooks

Independent publisher of award-winning, highly illustrated children's books, specialising in non-fiction, picture books and graphic novels. Publishes 10–12 titles per year. Founded 2009.

Colourpoint Creative†

Colourpoint House, Jubilee Business Park,
21 Jubilee Road, Newtownards, Co. Down BT23 4YH
tel 028-9182 0505 (within UK), +353 (0)48 9182 0505 (Republic of Ireland)
email sales@colourpoint.co.uk
website www.colourpointeducational.com
X @colourpointedu
Commissioning Editor Wesley Johnston

Textbooks for Northern Ireland CCEA board. Educational textbooks for KS3 (11–14 years), KS3 Special Educational Needs (10–14 years), GCSE (14–16 years) and A Level/undergraduates (17+ years). Not primary. Subjects include, but not limited to, biology, business studies, chemistry, design and technology, English, French, geography, history, HE, ICT, Irish, life and health sciences, LLW, MVRUS, PE, physics, politics, RE and science. Full submission by email only including details of proposal, sample chapter/section to show ability to connect with target age group, qualification/experience in the subject, full contact details. Textbooks, workbooks and electronic resources all considered. Founded 1993.

Cranthorpe Millner Publishers‡

9 Hills Road, Cambridge CB2 1GE
tel 020-3441 9212
email enquiries@cranthorpemillner.com
website www.cranthorpemillner.com
Facebook www.facebook.com/CranthorpeMillner
X @CranthorpeMillner
Instagram @cranthorpemillner
Managing Director Kirsty Jackson

Fiction and non-fiction: picture books, chapter books, middle-grade, teen and YA. Founded 2018.

Crown House Publishing*‡

Crown Buildings, Bancyfelin, Carmarthen SA33 5ND
tel (01267) 211345
email books@crownhouse.co.uk
website www.crownhouse.co.uk
Facebook www.facebook.com/CrownHousePub
X @CrownHousePub
Bluesky @crownhousepub.bsky.social
Instagram @crownhousepub
Directors David Bowman, Karen Bowman

Award-winning independent publisher specialising in the areas of education, coaching, business training and development, leadership, NLP, hypnotherapy, psychotherapy, self-help, personal growth and children's books. Founded 1998.

Independent Thinking Press

email books@independentthinkingpress.com
website www.independentthinkingpress.com

CPD books and resources for teachers and school leaders, including business, training and development, coaching, health and wellbeing, NLP, hypnosis, counselling and psychotherapy. Publishes a range of children's books.

Dinosaur Books

88 Turney Road, London SE21 7JH
tel 020-7737 6737
email info@dinosaurbooks.co.uk
website www.dinosaurbooks.co.uk
X @dinosaurbooksco
Bluesky @DinosaurBooksCo.bsky.social
Instagram @dinosaurbooksco
Director Sonya McGilchrist

Chapter books for children 5–14 years. Submissions by email only: submissions@dinosaurbooks.co.uk. Founded 2014.

DK*

(formerly Dorling Kindersley)
20 Vauxhall Bridge Road, London SW1V 2SA
tel 020-7139 2000
website www.dk.com
Facebook www.facebook.com/dkbooks
X @dkbooks
Bluesky @dkbooks.bsky.social
Instagram @dkbooks
Ceo Paul Kelly

Illustrated and narrative books for children. Fiction and non-fiction. Non-fiction: reference and education. Part of Penguin Random House UK. Founded 1974.

DK Flip

Chapter books, early middle grade, middle grade, teen, graphic and YA.

Dref Wen

28 Church Road, Whitchurch, Cardiff CF14 2EA
tel 029-2061 7860
website www.drefwen.com
Facebook www.facebook.com/drefwen
X @dref_wen
Instagram @drefwen
Directors Roger Boore, Anne Boore, Gwilym Boore, Alun Boore, Rhys Boore

Welsh-language publisher. Original, adaptations and translations of foreign and English-language full-colour picture story books for children. Also activity books, novelty books, Welsh-language fiction for children 7–14 years, teenage fiction, reference, religion, audiobooks and poetry. Educational material for primary and secondary school children in Wales and England, including dictionaries, revision guides and Welsh as a Second Language. Publishes approx. 50 titles a year and has 450 in print. No unsolicited MSS. Founded 1970.

The Educational Company of Ireland
12 Ballymount Road, Walkinstown,
Dublin D12 R25C, Republic of Ireland
tel +353 (0)1 450 0611
email info@edco.ie
website www.edco.ie
Facebook www.facebook.com/edcoireland
X @edco_ie

Educational (primary and post-primary) books in the Irish language. Publishes approx. 60–70 titles each year and has 600–700 in print. Ancillary materials include digital resources, concrete resources and CDs. Submissions to: amolumby@edco.ie. Please include: a brief description of the project's scope and content, table of contents, sample chapter and biographical details. Allow three months for response. A member of the Smurfit Kappa Group Plc. Founded 1910.

Elsewhen Press
Alnpete Limited, PO Box 757, Dartford,
Kent DA2 7TQ
tel 07956 237041
email info@elsewhen.co.uk
website https://elsewhen.press
Facebook www.facebook.com/ElsewhenPress
Bluesky @elsewhen.press.bsky.social
Instagram @elsewhenpress
Managing Director Alison Buck, *Editorial Director* Peter Buck

Small independent publisher of speculative fiction (including sci-fi, fantasy, paranormal, horror and alternative history), for ages YA upwards. Digital-first publisher. For submission guidelines see website. Founded 2011.

Everything with Words
5th Floor, 30–31 Furnival Street, London EC4A 1JQ
tel 020-8771 2974
email info@everythingwithwords.com
website www.everythingwithwords.com
Editor Mikka Haugaard

Literary fiction for children and YA. Accepts unsolicited MSS. Send synopsis, brief bio and first 50 pages. Founded 2016.

Express Publishing
Greenham Business Park, Newbury,
Berks. RG19 6HW
tel (01635) 959759
email inquiries@expresspublishing.co.uk
website www.expresspublishing.co.uk
Facebook www.facebook.com/expresspublishing
X @expressELT
Instagram @expresspublishing
President Jenny Dooley

ELT materials and digital resources. Founded 1988.

Faber & Faber*‡
The Bindery, 51 Hatton Garden, London EC1N 8HN
tel 020-7927 3800
website www.faber.co.uk
X @FaberChildrens
Publisher Leah Thaxton (children's)

Independent publisher of fiction, non-fiction, poetry, drama, film, graphic novels and children's books. The children's and YA list publishes books to support teachers, libraries and book clubs with relevant, inclusive and necessary stories, from picture books to YA fiction, non-fiction and poetry. The FAB Prize (page 337), which champions unpublished authors and illustrators of colour, is now in its tenth year. Founded 1929.

CJ Fallon
Ground Floor, Block B, Liffey Valley Office Campus,
Dublin D22 X0Y3, Republic of Ireland
tel +353 (0)1 616 6400
email editorial@cjfallon.ie
website www.cjfallon.ie
Executive Director Brian Gilsenan

Educational textbooks. Founded 1927.

Farshore Books – see HarperCollins Publishers

David Fickling Books‡
31 Beaumont Street, Oxford OX1 2NP
tel (01865) 339000
website www.davidficklingbooks.com
Facebook www.facebook.com/davidficklingbooks
X @DFB_storyhouse
Bluesky @dfbstoryhouse.bsky.social
Instagram @dfb_storyhouse
Publisher David Fickling, *Publishing Director* Liz Cross

Independent publisher of picture books, novels and non-fiction for all ages, as well as graphic novels. Currently not accepting unsolicited MSS. Founded 1999.

Fincham Press
University of Roehampton, School of Humanities,
Fincham Building, Roehampton Lane,
London SW15 5PH
email finchampress@roehampton.ac.uk
website https://estore.roehampton.ac.uk/product-catalogue/fincham-press
Facebook www.facebook.com/finchampress
X @finchampress

Titles are commissioned, edited and published by a team based in English and creative writing, part of the School of Humanities and Social Sciences.

Children's book publishers UK and Ireland

Creative writing anthologies, a journalism anthology. Founded 2014.

Firefly Press*
Britannia House, Caerphilly Business Park,
Van Road, Caerphilly CF83 3GG
email hello@fireflypress.co.uk
website www.fireflypress.co.uk
Facebook www.facebook.com/FireflyPress
X @fireflypress
Bluesky @fireflypress.bsky.social
Publisher Penny Thomas

Fiction for 5–19 years. Founded 2013.

Five Quills*
71–75 Sheldon Street, Covent Garden,
London WC2H 9JQ
email info@fivequills.co.uk
website www.fivequills.co.uk
Facebook www.facebook.com/www..fivequills.co.uk
X @5Quills_kids
Instagram @fivequillsforkids
Publisher Daniela Schneider, *Editorial Director* Natascha Biebow

An independent children's book publisher of picture books and chapter books for readers 3–9 years. Currently not accepting submissions. Founded 2017.

Floris Books*
Canal Court, 40 Craiglockhart Avenue,
Edinburgh EH14 1LT
email floris@florisbooks.co.uk
website www.florisbooks.co.uk
Facebook www.facebook.com/FlorisBooks
X @DiscoverKelpies
Bluesky @florisbooks.bsky.social
Commissioning Editors Sally Polson, Eleanor Collins

Children's board books, picture books and story anthologies. Approx. 50 titles each year. Founded 1976.

Kelpies
website www.discoverkelpies.co.uk
Facebook www.facebook.com/DiscoverKelpies
X @DiscoverKelpies

Contemporary Scottish children's books: picture books (3–6 years), young readers series (6–8 years) and novels (8–15 years). Annual Kelpies Prize (page 339).

Flying Eye Books
27 Westgate Street, London E8 3RL
tel 020-7033 4430
email subs@flyingeyebooks.com
email gnsubs@flyingeyebooks.com
website www.flyingeyebooks.com
Facebook www.facebook.com/flyingeyebooks
X @flyingeyebooks
Bluesky @flyingeyebooks.bsky.social
Instagram @flyingeyebooks

Children's board books, picture books, illustrated non-fiction, graphic readers, comics and graphic novels. Founded 2013.

Fox Eye Publishing‡
85 Highway Road, Leicester LE5 5RF
email info@foxeyepublishing.com
website https://foxeyepublishing.com/
Director Salma Thadha

Children's and classic books. Home of *Classic Editions*. Founded 2004.

From You To Me
Studio 100, The Old Leather Factory,
Glove Factory Studios, Holt, Wilts. BA14 6RJ
tel (01225) 866225
email hello@fromyoutome.com
website www.fromyoutome.com
Facebook www.facebook.com/fromyoutome
Instagram @fromyoutome_ltd
Founder Neil Caxon, *Publisher* Helen Stephens

Bespoke and illustrated gift books. Authors and illustrators see Work With Me page on the website for details of current opportunities. Founded 2009.

Galore Park Publishing*
Carmelite House, 50 Victoria Embankment,
London EC4Y 0DZ
tel 020-7873 6412
website www.galorepark.co.uk

Educational textbooks and revision guides for students studying at independent schools. *So You Really Want To Learn* range of textbooks for children 11+ years and *Junior* range for children 8–10 years. Courses include Latin, French, English, Spanish, maths and science. Part of Hachette Learning. Founded 1999.

Gemini Books Group
Marine House, Tide Mill Way, Woodbridge,
Suffolk IP12 1AP
email customerservice@geminibooks.com
website www.geminibooks.com
Instagram @geminibooksgroup
Founder & Managing Director Marcus E. Leaver,
Publishers Dan Graham, Lisa Dyer

Illustrated non-fiction books for children. Founded 2023.

Graffeg‡
24 Stradey Park Business Centre, Mwrwg Road,
Llangennech, Llanelli SA14 8YP
tel (01554) 824000
email croeso@graffeg.com
website https://graffeg.com/
Facebook www.facebook.com/graffegbooks
X @graffeg_books
Instagram @graffegbooks
Founder Peter Gill

Non-fiction illustrated books and illustrated fiction for children. Open to submissions – see website for guidelines. Founded 2003.

Cadno
Middle-grade and YA fiction in English and Welsh.

Graffeg Bach
Welsh language children's fiction.

W.F. Graham
2 Pondwood Close, Moulton Park, Northampton NN3 6RT
tel (01604) 645537
email books1@wfgraham.co.uk
website www.wfgraham.co.uk

Activity books including colouring, dot-to-dot, magic painting, puzzle, word search and sticker books. Founded 1956.

Guppy Publishing*
Bracken Hill, Cotswold Road, Oxford OX2 9JG
tel 07884 068983
email bella@guppybooks.co.uk
website www.guppybooks.co.uk
Facebook www.facebook.com/guppybooks
X @guppybooks
Bluesky @guppybooks.bsky.social
Instagram @guppypublishing
Director Bella Pearson

Children's and YA fiction for 5–18 years. Illustrated books for newly emerging readers, fiction for middle-grade readers and novels for YA. Poetry, prose and graphic novels. No unsolicited submissions outside the Guppy Open Submission Competition (run annually in May). Founded 2019.

Hachette Children's Trade*
Carmelite House, 50 Victoria Embankment, London EC4Y 0DZ
tel 020-3122 6000
email editorial@hachettechildrens.co.uk
website www.hachettechildrens.co.uk
Facebook www.facebook.com/hachettechildrens
X @HachetteKids
Instagram @hachettechildrens
Ceo Hilary Murray Hill

Baby and preschool books, picture books, illustrated gift, fiction, non-fiction, series fiction, books for the school and library market and licensed publishing. Imprints include: Hodder Children's Books, Laurence King Children's Books, Little, Brown Books for Young Readers, Orchard Books, Orion Children's Books, Quercus Children's Books, Pat-a-Cake, Franklin Watts, Wayland Books, Welbeck Children's Books and Wren & Rook. Owner of Enid Blyton Entertainment. Generally only accepts submissions sent via an agent. Occasionally holds periods of open submissions for a limited time or a specific genre. See social media channels for details. Founded 1986.

Hachette Learning*
Carmelite House, 50 Victoria Embankment, London EC4Y 0DZ
tel (01235) 827720
website www.hoddereducation.co.uk, www.galorepark.co.uk, www.risingstars-uk.com
Ceo Seshni Jacobs

School and college publishing. Imprints: Galore Park, Hodder Education, Rising Stars and RS Assessment. Part of Hachette UK. Founded 1960.

Hachette UK*
Carmelite House, 50 Victoria Embankment, London EC4Y 0DZ
tel 020-3122 6000
website www.hachette.co.uk
Facebook www.facebook.com/pages/Hachette-UK
X @hachetteUK
Ceo David Shelley, Deputy Ceo Richard Kitson, Ceo Adult Trade Katie Espiner, Ceo Education Seshni Jacobs, Managing Director, Children's Trade Ruth Alltimes

Hachette UK comprises three publishing divisions: Adult Trade, Children's Trade and Education. Hachette group companies: Bookouture, Hachette Australia (page 58), Hachette Book Publishing India; Hachette Children's Trade (above), Hachette Ireland, Hachette Learning (above), Hachette New Zealand, Headline Publishing Group, Hodder & Stoughton, Little, Brown Book Group (page 47), John Murray Group, Octopus Publishing Group and Orion Publishing Group. Founded 1986.

Happy Yak
2nd Floor, 1 Triptych Place, London SE1 9SH
tel 020-7000 8084
website www.quartoknows.com/happy-yak
Instagram @happyyakbooks
Associate Publisher Rhiannon Findlay

Preschool, picture books and illustrated non-fiction for children from birth upwards, with a focus on fun, accessible content and contemporary illustration. A children's imprint of Quarto Group Publishing UK. Founded 2021.

HarperCollins Publishers*
The News Building, 1 London Bridge Street, London SE1 9GF
tel 020-8741 7070
Alternative address 1 Robroyston Gate, Robroyston, Glasgow G33 1JN
tel 0141 772 3200
website www.harpercollins.co.uk
Facebook www.facebook.com/HarperCollinsPublishersUK
X @HarperCollinsUK
Ceo Charlie Redmayne

Children's fiction and non-fiction across various imprints. All fiction and trade non-fiction must be submitted through an agent. Owned by News Corporation. Founded 1817.

Children's book publishers UK and Ireland

Magpie
Publisher Natasha Bardon
YA fantasy and sci-fi.

Collins
website www.collins.co.uk
Managing Director Alex Beecroft

Children's fiction and non-fiction. Education publisher for UK and international school curriculums, revision and home learning support. Reference publishing, including dictionaries and atlases. Imprints include: A–Z, the National Trust and Times Books. Children's imprints include: Barrington Stoke and Rocket Bird Books.

Farshore Books
website www.farshore.com
Managing Director & Publisher Cally Poplak

Children's fiction, YA, graphic novels, picture books, non-fiction, film/TV, toy and gaming. Imprints include: Electric Monkey, Expanse and Red Shed.

HarperCollins Audio
Group Technology & Digital Director Joanna Surman, *Audio Publishing Director* Fionnuala Barrett

Trade fiction and non-fiction audiobooks for children, as well as standalone audio projects. Publishes in excess of 75,000 audiobooks each year.

HarperCollins Children's Books
Managing Director & Publisher Cally Poplak

Children's fiction, YA fiction, graphic novels, picture books and non-fiction. Also film/TV tie-in brands. Imprints: Harper Fire and Kumusha.
All submissions to come via agents.

Hawthorn Press‡
Hawthorn House, 1 Lansdown Lane, Stroud, Glos. GL5 1BJ
tel (01453) 757040
email info@hawthornpress.com
website www.hawthornpress.com
Facebook www.facebook.com/HawthornPress
X @HawthornPressUK
Bluesky @hawthornp.bsky.social
Instagram @hawthornpress
Director Martin Large

A small, ethically aware press. Series include *Early Years*, *Steiner/Waldorf Education*, *Crafts*, *Storytelling* and *Parenting*. Founded 1981.

Head of Zeus - Zephyr – see Bloomsbury Publishing

Henningham Family Press
130 Sandringham Road, London E8 2HJ
tel 07976 843290
website https://henninghamfamilypress.com/
Facebook www.facebook.com/HenninghamPress
Instagram @henninghampress
Publishers David Henningham, Ping Henningham

Makes artists' books by hand that are collected by libraries and museums. Since 2018 the studio has sold fiction paperbacks in bookshops. Novels have been shortlisted for The Goldsmith's Prize, Republic of Consciousness Prize, British Book Awards and longlisted for The Walter Scott Prize. Founded 2006.

Hogs Back Books‡
34 Long Street, Devizes, Wilts. SN10 1NT
tel (01483) 506030
email enquiries@hogsbackbooks.com
website www.hogsbackbooks.com

Children's picture books and teenage fiction. Welcomes texts and submissions from illustrators but cannot return material without prior arrangement. Founded 2009.

Holler
2nd Floor, 1 Triptych Place, London SE1 9SH
tel 020-770-9000
website hwww.quarto.com/Holler
Publisher Debbie Foy

Part of Quarto Group Publishing UK, non-fiction imprint of 12+/YA. Genres include: biography, social issues, self-help and wellbeing and graphic non-fiction. Founded 2024.

Hopscotch
St Jude's Church, Dulwich Road, London SE24 0PB
tel 020-7501 6736
email orders@hopscotchbooks.com
website www.hopscotchbooks.com
Associate Publisher Angela Morano Shaw

Teaching resources for primary school teachers. A division of McGraw-Hill Education. Founded 1997.

Practical Pre-School Books
website www.practicalpreschoolbooks.com
Early years teaching resources.

Hot Key Books
Victoria House, Bloomsbury Square, London WC1B 4DA
tel 020-3770 8888
email hello@bonnierbooks.co.uk
website www.bonnierbooks.co.uk/imprints/hot-key-books
X @HotKeyBooksYA
Executive Publisher Emma Matthewson

Literary teen and YA fiction, some books also suitable for an adult audience. An imprint of Bonnier Books UK. Founded 2012.

Hungry Tomato‡
F15, Old Bakery Studios, Blewetts Wharf, Malpas Road, Truro TR1 1QH
tel (01872) 242246
email claudia@hungrytomato.com
website www.hungrytomato.com
Facebook www.facebook.com/hungrytomatoltd

Instagram @hungrytomato
Director John Twiggs

Educational content for children aged 3–12 years. Offering a diverse range of titles across three imprints: Beetle Books, The Big Questions and Hungry Tomato. Founded 2011.

I Am a Bookworm*
35 Manor Close, Templecomb, Somerset BA8 0LA
email hello@iamabookworm.co.uk
website www.iamabookworm.co.uk
Facebook www.facebook.com/iamabookwormuk
Instagram @i_amabookworm

An independent publisher of children's novelty books, board books, activity books and light books for children aged 0–5 years. Founded 2011.

Igloo Books
Cottage Farm, Mears Ashby Road, Sywell, Northants. NN6 0BJ
tel (01604) 741116
email customerservices@igloobooks.com
website www.igloobooks.com
X @igloo_books

Children's: fiction, licensed books, novelty, board, picture, activity books and education. Not currently accepting submissions. Founded 2005.

Illuminate Publishing
Carmelite House, 50 Victoria Embankment, London EC4Y 0DZ
tel (01235) 827720
email sales@illuminatepublishing.com
website www.illuminatepublishing.com

Teaching and learning resources. Publishes across a wide range of secondary subjects: academic and vocational. Part of Hachette UK. Founded 2010.

Ivy Kids
2nd Floor, 1 Triptych Place, London SE1 9SH
tel 020-770-9000
website www.quarto.com/Ivy-Kids
Publisher Georgia Buckthorn

Part of Quarto Group Publishing UK. Sustainably printed books in fiction and non-fiction for children about the environment and the living world. For submission guidelines see website. Founded 2015.

IWM (Imperial War Museums) Publishing‡
Lambeth Road, London SE1 6HZ
tel 020-7416 5000
email contact@iwm.org.uk
website www.iwm.org.uk
Facebook www.facebook.com/iwm.london
X @I_W_M

Titles published draw on the expertise and archives of the museum, produced both in-house and in partnership with other publishers. Founded 1917.

Jolly Learning*‡
77 Hornbeam Road, Buckhurst Hill, Essex IG9 6JX
tel 020-8501 0405
email info@jollylearning.co.uk
website www.jollylearning.co.uk
Director Gilbert Jolly

Educational: primary and English as a Bilingual Language. Publishes approx. 25 titles each year and has 300 in print, including *Jolly Phonics Extra*, *My Jolly Phonics* and *Jolly Dictionary*. Imprint: Jolly Phonics. Unsolicited MSS are only considered for add-ons to existing products. Founded 1987.

Miles Kelly Publishing
Harding's Barn, Bardfield End Green, Thaxted, Essex CM6 3PX
tel (01371) 832440
email hello@mileskelly.net
website www.mileskelly.net
Facebook www.facebook.com/MilesKellyPublishing
Instagram @mileskellypub
Director Gerard Kelly

Illustrated non-fiction and fiction titles for children and family: activity books, board books, story books, picture books, poetry, reference, posters and wallcharts. Age groups: preschool, 5–10, 10–15 and 15+ years. Owned by HarperCollins Publishers. Founded 1996.

Kelpies – see Floris Books

Knights Of*
97 Granville Avenue, Brixton Village, London SW9 8PS
website https://knightsof.media
Facebook www.facebook.com/KnightsOf
X @_KnightsOf
Instagram @_knightsof
Managing Director Aimée Felone

Children's commercial fiction publisher, championing authors and illustrators from diverse backgrounds. Founded 2016.

Kube Publishing‡
Markfield Conference Centre, Ratby Lane, Markfield, Leics. LE67 9SY
email info@kubepublishing.com
website www.kubepublishing.com
Facebook www.facebook.com/KubePublishing
X @kube_publishing
Instagram @kubepublishing
Managing Director Haris Ahmad

Children's books of a Muslim interest. Founded 2006.

Ladybird Books
One Embassy Gardens, 8 Viaduct Gardens, London SW11 7BW
tel 020-7139 3000

Children's book publishers UK and Ireland

email ladybird@penguinrandomhouse.co.uk
website www.ladybird.co.uk
Facebook www.facebook.com/ladybirdbooks
X @ladybirdbooks
Instagram @ladybirdbooks

Publishes books across a wide range of formats for children 0–7 years. They include tactile books for babies, nursery rhymes, classic fairy tales and reading schemes, alongside licensed character publishing. Part of Penguin Random House UK. Founded 1867.

Lantana Publishing
Clavier House, 21 Fifth Road, Newbury RG14 6DN
email info@lantanapublishing.com
website https://lantanapublishing.com/
Facebook www.facebook.com/lantanapublishing
X @lantanapub
Instagram @lantana_publishing
Ceo Alice Curry, *Commissioning Editor* Katrina Gutierrez

Children's book publisher and social enterprise, publishing inclusive books by authors from under-represented groups from around the world. Looking for inclusive picture books for babies and toddlers, and fiction and non-fiction for 5–8 years and 9–12 years. Authors should send full MS, illustrators their portfolio and link to their website and author-illustrators a complete book dummy. See submissions page on website. Founded 2014.

Leckie*
1 Robroyston Gate, Glasgow G33 1JN
email leckiescotland@harpercollins.co.uk
website www.leckiescotland.co.uk

Education textbooks and revision guides specifically for the Scottish Curriculum for Excellence. Published under Collins Education, part of HarperCollins Publishers. Founded 1989.

Frances Lincoln Children's Books
1 Triptych Place, Second Floor, London SE1 9SH
tel 020-7700 9000
email peter.marley@quarto.com
website www.quartoknows.com/Frances-Lincoln-Children's-Books
Facebook www.facebook.com/Quartokids
X @QuartoKids
Publisher Peter Marley

Illustrated children's books: picture books, visual storytelling, non-fiction, gift books and cultural diversity. Welcome submissions from writers who have a book idea in one of the imprint's focus areas. Check website for current catalogue. Follow the instructions in the submission guidelines to submit a proposal. Imprint of Quarto Group Publishing. Founded 1983.

Little, Brown and Company Books for Young Readers
30 Victoria Embankment, London EC4Y 0DZ
tel 020-3122 7000
website www.littlebrown.co.uk/genre/childrens-teenage-educational/childrens
Facebook www.facebook.com/LittleBrownYoungReaders
X @littlebrownyr
Instagram @littlebrownyoungreaders
Ceo Charlie King

Picture books, chapter books, middle grade and YA fiction and non-fiction. Submissions via agent only. Founded 1926.

Little Door Books*
email submissions@littledoorbooks.co.uk
website www.littledoorbooks.co.uk
Instagram @littledoorbooks
Publisher Alan Windram

Award-winning family-run independent publisher of children's books, publishing between two and five books a year. Works collaboratively with emerging and established authors and illustrators. Not currently accepting unsolicited MSS. Accepting new illustrator submissions. Check website regularly for change in submission status. Founded 2016.

Little Island Books
7 Kenilworth Park, Dublin D6W XV34, Republic of Ireland
tel +353 (0)85 228 3060
email info@littleisland.ie
website www.littleisland.ie
Facebook www.facebook.com/LittleIslandBooks
X @LittleIslandBks
Founder Siobhán Parkinson

Children and YA. Non-fiction: science and nature, and myths and mythology. Fiction: fantasy, humour, historical and mystery. Founded 2010.

Little Tiger Press
1 Coda Studios, 189 Munster Road, London SW6 6AW
tel 020-7385 6333
email contact@littletiger.co.uk
website www.littletiger.co.uk
Publishing Director Thomas Truong, *Publisher* Jude Evans, *Editorial Director (Picture Book Studio)* Steph Stansbie, *Editorial Director (Caterpillar Studio)* Patricia Hegarty, *Editorial Director (Bespoke Studio)* Sam Sweeney, *Associate Editorial Director (Liontree Studio)* Becky Davies, *Editorial Director (Fiction Studio)* Lauren Ace

Children's books: board books, novelty board books, picture books, activity books, children's fiction, YA fiction and non-fiction. Founded 1987.

LOM ART
16 Lion Yard, Tremadoc Road, London SW4 7NQ
tel 020-7720 8643
email enquiries@mombooks.com
website www.mombooks.com/lom
Facebook www.facebook.com/MichaelOMaraBooks
X @OMaraBooks
Managing Director Lesley O'Mara

Illustrated non-fiction for children. Publishes approx. ten titles a year. Titles include *Fantomorphia*, *Maybe the Moon*, *The Van Gogh Activity Book* and *Life Lessons I learned From My Cat*, plus a range of artist-led drawing, colouring and picture book titles. Submissions including sae will be returned by post. Imprint of Michael O'Mara Books. Founded 2015.

Mabecron Books
3 Briston Orchard, St Mellion, Saltash, Cornwall PL12 6RQ
tel (01579) 350885
email ronjohns@mabecronbooks.co.uk
website www.mabecronbooks.co.uk
X @mabecronbooks

Children's picture books and books with a Cornish or West Country subject. Linked to bookshops in Falmouth, St Ives and Padstow. Founded 1998.

McGraw-Hill Education*
email emea_schools_intl@mheducation.com
website www.mheducation.co.uk
Facebook www.facebook.com/mheducationemea
X @mhe_emea

Educational publisher and digital solution provider for primary and secondary education in English language arts, maths, science and other subject areas, including intervention and learning support. Founded 1988.

Magic Cat Publishing*‡
Unit 2, Empress Works, 24 Grove Passage, London E2 9FQ
email s.griffiths@magiccatpublishing.co.uk
website www.magiccatpublishing.co.uk
Instagram @magiccatpublishing
Directors Jenny Broom, Rachel Williams

A small, award-winning, independent children's publisher of family-focused non-fiction and gift books. Founded 2019.

Mama Makes Books‡
49 Newlands Road, Tunbridge Wells, Kent TN4 9AS
email info@mamamakesbooks.com
website www.mamamakesbooks.com
Facebook www.facebook.com/mamamakesbooks.com
X @mamamakesbooks
Instagram @mamamakesbooks
Director Penny Worms

A small, independent children's publisher of illustrated books for children 0–8 years: baby books, novelty, early learning and non-fiction. Founded 2020.

Mantra Lingua
Global House, 303 Ballards Lane, London N12 8NP
tel 020-8445 5123
email info@mantralingua.com
website https://uk.mantralingua.com/
Facebook www.facebook.com/Mantralingua
X @mantralingua
Managing Director Robene Dutta

Bilingual picture books and educational resources for UK, US, Swedish and German audiences. Looking for illustrators with ability to draw racially diverse faces and authors and storytellers with ability to interpret or imagine modern city lives. Commission and royalty-based relationships with print runs covering between ten and 15 language editions. Founded 2002.

Maverick Arts Publishing
Suite 1, Hillreed House, 54 Queen Street, Horsham RH13 5AD
tel (01403) 256941
email submissions@maverickbooks.co.uk
website www.maverickbooks.co.uk
Facebook www.facebook.com/Maverick-Childrens-Books
X @maverickbooks
Managing Director Steve Bicknell, *Managing Editor* Kimara Nye

Picture books, early readers, graphic reluctant readers, junior fiction and middle grade. For submissions, please see submission guidelines page on website. Submissions by email only. Founded 2009.

Kevin Mayhew
Fengate Farm, Rattlesden, Suffolk IP30 0SZ
tel (01284) 374495
email info@kevinmayhew.com
website www.kevinmayhew.com
Facebook www.facebook.com/KevinMayhewPublishers
X @kevinmayhew
Director Barbara Mayhew

Christianity: prayer and spirituality, pastoral care, preaching, liturgy worship, children's, youth work, drama, instant art and education. Music: hymns, organ and choral, contemporary worship, tutors, piano and instrumental. Submissions guidelines on website. Founded 1976.

The Mercier Press†
82 Ballyhooley Road, St Lukes, Cork T23 Y3V2, Republic of Ireland
email info@mercierpress.ie
website www.mercierpress.ie
Facebook www.facebook.com/MercierPress

X @MercierBooks
General Manager Mary Feehan

Children's fiction and non-fiction on subjects related to Irish literature, folklore and history. Founded 1944.

Moonlight Publishing*
2 Michaels Court, Hanney Road Hanney Road, Southmoor, Abingdon, Oxfordshire OX13 5HR
email info@moonlightpublishing.co.uk
website https://moonlightpublishing.co.uk/
Facebook www.facebook.com/moonlightpublishinguk
X @moonlightpubl
Instagram @moonlightpublishingltd
Managing Director John Clement

An independent, family-run publisher of illustrated information books for children 4–10 years. Founded 1980.

My Kind of Book
12 Clearburn Crescent, Edinburgh EH16 5ER
tel 07813 705840
email ailie@mykindofbook.org.uk
website https://mykindofbook.org.uk/
Facebook www.facebook.com/100043995404469
Instagram @mykindofbook
Director Ailie Finlay

A not-for-profit publisher that researches, creates, adapts and gifts books for children with additional needs, particularly those with complex and profound needs. All profits are re-invested into the company for further research and book creation. Founded 2020.

Neem Tree Press
95A Ridgmount Gardens, London WC1E 7AZ
tel 020-7993 5581
website www.neemtreepress.com
Facebook www.facebook.com/neemtreepress
X @neemtreepress
Instagram @neemtreepress
Ceo & Publisher Archna Sharma, *Coo* Alison Savage, *Senior Editor* Cecilia Bennett

Fiction, non-fiction and children's and YA books including translation and short stories. See website for submission guidelines. Imprint of Boundless. Founded 2013.

North Parade Publishing
3–6 Henrietta Mews, Bath BA2 6LR
email info@nppbooks.co.uk
website www.nppbooks.co.uk
Facebook www.facebook.com/NPPBooks
Instagram @northparadepublishing
Director Peter Hicks

Independent publisher of a range of nursery titles that embrace a variety of formats that include textured board books, sound books and lift-the-flap books. Also publishes books for older children in the *Wonders of Learning* series that explore everything from botany to robotics. For illustrator submissions, see website. Founded 2001.

Nosy Crow*‡
Wheat Wharf, 27A Shad Thames, London SE1 2XZ
tel 020-7089 7575
email hello@nosycrow.com
website www.nosycrow.com
Facebook www.facebook.com/NosyCrow
X @nosycrow
Instagram @nosycrow
Group Ceo Kate Wilson, *Publishing Directors* Kirsty Stanfield (fiction), Louise Bolongaro (picture books), Rachel Kellehar (non-fiction, preschool & activity)

Independent publisher of child-focused, parent-friendly children's books. Publishes in partnership with The National Trust and The British Museum. Founded 2010.

The O'Brien Press†
12 Terenure Road East, Rathgar, Dublin D06 HD27, Republic of Ireland
tel +353 (0)1 492 3333
email books@obrien.ie
website https://obrien.ie
Facebook www.facebook.com/TheOBrienPress
Bluesky @theobrienpress.bsky.social
Instagram @theobrienpress
Directors Ivan O'Brien, Kunak McGann

Children: picture books, fiction for all ages, illustrated fiction (for ages 3+, 5+, 6+ and 8+ years); novels (10+ and YA): contemporary, historical and fantasy. Non-fiction. No poetry or academic. Unsolicited MSS (sample chapters only), synopses and ideas for books welcome. Submissions will not be returned. Further information available on website. Founded 1974.

Old Barn Books*‡
Warren Barn, Bedham Lane, Fittleworth, West Sussex RH20 1JW
email ruth@oldbarnbooks.com
website www.oldbarnbooks.com
Facebook www.facebook.com/oldbarnbooks
X @oldbarnbooks
Instagram @oldbarnbooks

Independent publisher of picture books, gift books and teen and YA fiction. Interested in the natural world and promoting empathy. No unsolicited submissions. Founded 2015.

Michael O'Mara Books*‡
16 Lion Yard, Tremadoc Road, London SW4 7NQ
tel 020-7720 8643
email enquiries@mombooks.com
email publicity@mombooks.com
website www.mombooks.com
Facebook www.facebook.com/MichaelOMaraBooks
X @OMaraBooks

Instagram @omarabooks
Chairman Michael O'Mara, *Managing Director* Lesley O'Mara

Children's illustrated fiction and non-fiction. See website for submission guidelines. Imprints: Buster Books (page 39), LOM ART (page 48), O'Mara Books. Founded 1985.

Otter-Barry Books‡
Little Orchard, Burley Gate, Herts. HR1 3QS
tel (01432) 683288
email info@otterbarrybooks.com
website www.otterbarrybooks.com
X @otterbarrybooks
Publisher Janetta Otter-Barry

Illustrated books for children 0–11+ years. Authors and illustrators include Jackie Morris, Joseph Coelho, Chitra Soundar, Petr Horáček and Ken Wilson-Max. Founded 2015.

Owlet Press
tel 07920 446328
email sam@owletpress.com
website www.owletpress.com
Facebook www.facebook.com/owletpress
X @owletpress

Independent publisher working with established and new, under-represented authors and illustrators. Founded 2017.

Oxford University Press*
Great Clarendon Street, Oxford OX2 6DP
tel (01865) 556767
email enquiry@oup.com
website https://corp.oup.com/
Facebook www.facebook.com/OUPAcademic
X @OxUniPress
Instagram @oxunipress
Ceo Nigel Portwood

Children's books (fiction, non-fiction and picture books) and educational texts and resources (foundation, primary, secondary, technical and university). Also encyclopaedias, ELT and foreign language learning. Founded 1478.

Children's and Educational Division
Picture books, fiction, poetry, educational resources and dictionaries.

Palazzo Editions
15 Church Road, London SW13 9HE
email info@palazzoeditions.com
website www.palazzoeditions.com
Facebook www.facebook.com/palazzoeditions
X @palazzoeditions
Instagram @palazzoeditions
Publishers Rob Nichols, Jon Rippon

Illustrated non-fiction for children. Founded 1998.

Pan Macmillan*
6 Briset Street, Farringdon, London EC1M 5NR
tel 020-7038 5000
email publicity@macmillan.com
website www.panmacmillan.com
Facebook ww.facebook.com/panmacmillanbooks
X @panmacmillan
Ceo Joanna Prior

For children: fiction and non-fiction including popular reference. Founded 1843.

Campbell
Early learning, pop-up, novelty and board books for the preschool market.

Kingfisher
Children's illustrated non-fiction.

Macmillan Children's Books
Children's books.

Tor
website https://torpublishinggroup.com/imprints/tor-books/
Facebook www.facebook.com/torbooks
X @torbooks
Instagram @torbooks

Sci-fi and fantasy.

Two Hoots
Illustrated children's books.

Pearson UK*
80 Strand, London WC2R 0RL
email schools@longman.co.uk
website www.pearsoned.co.uk
Facebook www.facebook.com/pearsonplc.uk
X @Pearson_UK
Instagram @pearsonhighereducation
Ceo Andy Bird

Consists of five divisions: Virtual Learning, Higher Education, English Language Learning, Workforce Skills and Assessment and Qualifications. Founded 1998.

Penguin Random House Children's UK*
One Embassy Gardens, 8 Viaduct Gardens, London SW11 7BW
tel 020-7139 3000
website www.penguin.co.uk/company/publishers/penguin-random-house-children-s
X @PenguinKids
Instagram @randomhousekids
Managing Director Francesca Dow

Books for toddlers to YA. Formats: board books, activity books, picture books, graphic novels, novels and non-fiction. Imprints: Alfred A. Knopf Books for Young Readers, Bright Matter Books, Crown Books for Young Readers, Delacorte Press, Delacorte Romance, Doubleday Books for Young Readers,

Children's book publishers UK and Ireland

Dragonfly, Ember, Joy Revolution, Labyrinth Road, Little Golden Books, Make Me A World, Princeton Review, Random House Books for Young Readers, Random House Graphic, Random House Studio, Rodale Kids, and Yearling Books. Part of Penguin Random House UK. Founded 1925.

Penguin Random House UK*
One Embassy Gardens, 8 Viaduct Gardens, London SW11 7BW
tel 020-7139 3000
website www.penguin.co.uk
Facebook www.facebook.com/PenguinRandomHouse
X @PenguinUKBooks
Ceo Tom Weldon

Penguin Random House UK group companies which publish books for children: Penguin Random House Children's UK. Founded 2013.

PG Online
The Old Coach House, 35 Main Street, Tolpuddle, Dorset DT2 7EW
email sales@pgonline.co.uk
website www.pgonline.co.uk
Facebook www.facebook.com/pgonlinepub
X @pgonlinepub

Educational resources and textbooks. Provides lesson resources for science, design and technology, maths, computer science and business. Works with all major examination boards including AQA, Cambridge, OCR, Pearson Edexcel and BTEC qualifications. Founded 2013.

Phaidon Press
2 Cooperage Yard, London E15 2GR
tel 020-7843 1000
email enquiries@phaidon.com
website www.phaidon.com
Facebook www.facebook.com/phaidoncom
X @phaidonpress
Instagram @phaidonpress
Ceo Bob Miller, *Vice-President & Publisher* Deborah Aaronson, *Associate Publisher, Children's Books* Maya Gartner

Visual arts and illustrated books for children. Founded 1923.

Piccadilly Press*
Victoria House, Bloomsbury Square, London WC1B 4DA
tel 020-3770 8888
email hello@bonnierbooks.co.uk
website www.bonnierbooks.co.uk/imprints/piccadilly-press
Facebook www.facebook.com/piccadillypressbooks
X @PiccadillyPress
Instagram @piccadillypress
Editorial Director Ruth Bennett

Publishes books primarily for readers 5–12 years. Titles can be standalone stories or part of a series. Imprint of Bonnier Books UK. Founded 1983.

Pikku Publishing‡
7 High Street, Barkway, Royston, Herts. SG8 8EA
tel 07763 877656
email info@pikkupublishing.com
website https://pikkupublishing.com/
Instagram @pikkubooks

Original, illustrated books for 3–9 years. Strong focus on nature themes. Founded 2016.

Poolbeg Press
Grange Hill, Baldoyle, County Dublin D13 N539, Republic of Ireland
tel +353 (0)1 806 3825
email info@poolbeg.com
website www.poolbeg.com
Directors Kieran Devlin, Barbara Devlin

Children's and teenage fiction. Imprints: In a Nut Shell and Poolbeg. Founded 1976.

Post Wave Publishing
Runway East Bloomsbury, 24–28 Bloomsbury Way, London WC1A 2SN
email hello@postwavepublishing.com
website https://postwavepublishing.com/
Facebook www.facebook.com/people/Post-Wave-Publishing
Bluesky @postwavebooks.bsky.social
Instagram @postwave_books
Managing Director Emma Hopkin, *Publisher* Emma Blackburn, *Editorial Director* Joanna McInerney

Publisher of original and translated books for young children. Publishes preschool, picture books, activity and non-fiction. No middle grade or YA. Please see submission guidelines on website. Founded 2006.

Priddy Books
The Smithson, 6 Briset Street, London EC1M 5NR
website www.priddybooks.com
Instagram @priddybooks
Publisher Sam Priddy

Baby/toddler and preschool books: activity books, board books, novelty books and picture books. Founded 2000.

Prim-Ed Publishing
Unit 2A, Block E, Waterford Road Business Park, New Ross, Co. Wexford Y34 NC82, Republic of Ireland
tel +353 (0)5 144 0075
email marketing@prim-ed.com
website www.prim-ed.com
Managing Director Seamus McGuinness

Educational publisher specialising in copymasters (photocopiable teaching resources) for primary school and special educational needs. Books written by practising classroom teachers. Founded 1993.

Pure Indigo
Publishing Department, 17 The Herons, Cottenham, Cambridge CB24 8XX
tel 07981 395258
email ashley.martin@pureindigo.co.uk
website www.pureindigo.co.uk/publishing
Commissioning Editor Ashley Martin

Children's books: develops innovative junior series fiction in-house. Also develops software products that complement the product range. Sometimes authors and illustrators are commissioned to complete project-based work. Currently closed to submissions. Founded 2005.

Pushkin Press‡
New Wing, Somerset House, Strand, London WC2R 1LA
email books@pushkinpress.com
website www.pushkinpress.com
Facebook www.facebook.com/PushkinPress
X @pushkinpress
Publisher Adam Freudenheim, *Publishing Director* Laura Macaulay, *Senior Commissioning Editor* Daniel Seton

Contemporary children's fiction and non-fiction, including graphic novels. Imprints: Pushkin Children's Books, Pushkin ONE, Pushkin Press, Pushkin Press Classics and Pushkin Vertigo. Founded 1997.

Quarto Group Publishing UK‡
1 Triptych Place, 2nd Floor, 185 Park Street, London SE1 9BL
tel 020-7700 9000
website www.quarto.com
Ceo Alison Goff, *Managing Director* Karine Marko

Children's picture books and general children's non-fiction. The UK division of The Quarto Group includes six children's imprints: Frances Lincoln Children's Books (page 47), Happy Yak (page 44), Holler, Ivy Kids (page 46), Quarto Children's Books and Wide Eyed Editions (page 56) and words & pictures. Founded 1976.

Ransom Publishing*‡
Unit 7, Brocklands Farm, West Meon GU32 1JN
tel (01730) 829091
email orders@ransom.co.uk
website www.ransom.co.uk
Managing Director Jenny Ertle, *Creative Director* Steve Rickard

Children's fiction and non-fiction, phonics and school reading programmes, and books for children and adults who are reluctant or struggling readers. Also publishes books in a dyslexia-friendly format. Range covers high interest age/low reading age titles, quick reads and reading schemes. Currently not accepting unsolicited submissions. Founded 1995.

Raven Books
Publishes fiction and non-fiction for children 8–14 years.

Really Decent Books‡
156 Newbridge Road, Bath BA1 3LE
tel (01225) 334747
email info@reallydecentbooks.co.uk
website www.reallydecentbooks.co.uk
Facebook www.facebook.com/reallydecentbooks
X @ReallyDecent
Instagram @reallydecentbooks
Publisher Phil Dauncey

Independent publisher of books for babies, toddlers and children. Founded 2012.

Rily Publications‡
PO Box 25, Caerphilly CF83 9FL
email shop@rily.co.uk
website www.rily.co.uk
Facebook www.facebook.com/RilyPublications
X @GwagsRilyeBooks
Instagram @gwasgrilypublications
Publishing Director Lynda Tunnicliffe, *Head of Publishing* Rachel Lloyd

Family-run, award-winning, publisher of Welsh language versions of popular books. Publishes original content. English-language imprint: Dragon Press. Founded 2001.

Rockpool Children's Books
6 Kitchener Terrace, Ferryhill, Co. Durham DL17 8AX
tel 07711 351691
email stuarttrotter3@gmail.com
website www.rockpoolchildrensbooks.co.uk
Facebook www.facebook.com/RockpoolChildrensBooks
X @rockpooltweets
Instagram @rockpool_childrens_books
Publisher & Creative Director Stuart Trotter

Independent publisher of quality children's picture books plus picture book design, story writing, illustration, and 'All About Picture Books' workshop. Print on Demand: www.rockpool.alburybooks.com. Founded 2006.

Ruby Tuesday Books‡
6 Newlands Road, Tunbridge Wells, Kent TN4 9AT
tel (01892) 557767
email shan@rubytuesdaybooks.com
website www.rubytuesdaybooks.com
X @RubyTuesdaybks
Bluesky @rubytuesdaybooks.bsky.social
Instagram @rubytuesdaybks
Publishers Ruth Owen, Shan White

Children's books for ages 0–16 years, with over 150 in print. See website for submission guidelines. Founded 2008.

SAGE Publishing*‡
1 Oliver's Yard, 55 City Road, London EC1Y 1SP
tel 020-7324 8500
email info@sagepub.co.uk
website www.sagepublishing.com
Facebook www.facebook.com/SAGEPublishing
X @SAGE_Publishing
Instagram @sage_publishing

Journals, books and library products for the educational, scholarly and professional markets. Founded 1965.

Scallywag Press*
10 Sutherland Row, London SW1V 4JT
tel 07910 278462
email publisher@scallywagpress.com
website www.scallywagpress.com
X @scallywagpress
Instagram @scallywagpress
Contact Sarah Pakenham

Works with new and established authors and illustrators. Currently not accepting unsolicited MSS. Founded 2018.

Schofield & Sims*
7 Mariner Cour, Wakefield, West Yorkshire WF4 3FL
tel (01484) 607080
email editorial@schofieldandsims.co.uk
website www.schofieldandsims.co.uk

Educational: nursery, infants and primary, also posters. Founded 1901.

Scholastic*
Euston House, 1 London Bridge, London SE1 9BG
tel 020-7756 7756
website www.scholastic.co.uk
Facebook www.facebook.com/Scholastic
X @scholasticuk
President & Ceo Peter Warwick

Children's fiction, non-fiction: picture books and education resources for primary schools. Owned by Scholastic Inc. Founded 1964.

Scholastic Children's Books
tel 020-7756 7761
email submissions@scholastic.co.uk
website www.scholastic.co.uk
X @scholasticuk
Fiction Publisher Lauren Fortune, Non-Fiction Publisher & Licensing Elizabeth Scoggins, Editorial Director, Illustrated Books Sophie Cashell

Activity books, novelty books, picture books, fiction for 5–12 years, teenage fiction, series fiction and film/TV tie-ins. Imprints: Alison Green Books, Klutz and Scholastic. No unsolicited MSS. Unsolicited illustrations are accepted, but do not send any original artwork as it will not be returned.

Scholastic Educational Resources
Thorney Leys Business Park, Unit 18F, Witney, Oxfordshire OX28 4GE
tel (01993) 893456
Publishing Director Rachel Morgan

Professional books, classroom materials, home learning books and online resources for primary teachers. GCSE support material.

Scripture Union
Trinity House, Opal Court, Fox Milne, Milton Keynes MK15 0DF
tel (01908) 856000
email hello@scriptureunion.org.uk
website www.scriptureunion.org.uk
Facebook www.facebook.com/scriptureunionews
X @SUEnglandWales
National Director Dave Newton

Christian books and bible reading materials for children. Educational and worship resources for churches. Also children's fiction. Age groups: under 5, 5–8, 8–10 and YA. Publishes approx. 40 titles each year for children and YA and has 200–250 in print. Will not consider unsolicited MSS. Founded 1867.

Shepheard-Walwyn (Publishers)
Suite 108. 4. Little Portland Street London W1W 7JB
tel 020-8241 5927
email books@shepheardwalwyn.com
website www.shepheardwalwyn.com, www.ethicaleconomics.org.uk
Facebook www.facebook.com/ShepheardWalwynPublishers
X @SWPublishing
Instagram @swpublishers
Director K. Toth

Books for children with a focus on the environment. Publishing partner of The School of Philosophy and Economic Science, London. Founded 1971.

Simon & Schuster UK*
222 Gray's Inn Road, London WC1X 8HB
tel 020-7316 1900
email enquiries@simonandschuster.co.uk
website www.simonandschuster.co.uk
Facebook www.facebook.com/simonschusterUK
X @simonschusteruk
Ceo tbc, Managing Director Rachel Denwood (children's), Publishing Director Ali Dougal (children's)

Children's and YA fiction, picture books, novelty, pop-up and licensed character. Founded 1986.

Children's Books
Books for all ages, across all genres, including picture books, chapter books, novels for 8–12 years, YA and non-fiction.

Little Simon UK
Contact Jane Buckley

Board and novelty books for 0–5-year-olds from a mix of new and established authors. Also oversees in-house IP projects.

Simon & Schuster Audio
website www.simonandschuster.co.uk/audio
Publisher Alice Twomey

Fiction, children's, YA and non-fiction audiobooks.

SRL Publishing
email admin@srlpublishing.co.uk
website www.srlpublishing.co.uk
Facebook www.facebook.com/srlpublishing
X @srlpublishing
Instagram @srlpublishing
Publisher Stuart Debar

The world's first climate positive publisher, small independent press of YA fiction. Founded 2014.

Studio Press*
Victoria House, Bloomsbury Square,
London WC1B 4DA
tel 020-3770 8888
email hello@bonnierbooks.co.uk
website www.bonnierbooks.co.uk/imprints/studio-press
X @StudioPress
Managing Director Helen Wicks, *Head of Studio Press* Stephanie Milton

Pop culture trends and health, wellbeing and environmental issues. Publishing partner to major brands including Disney, Marvel and Harry Potter. Creators of the bestselling *Ultimate Football Heroes* series for children. An imprint of Bonnier Books UK. Founded 2015.

Sweet Cherry Publishing*‡
Unit 4u18, The Book Brothers Business Park,
Tolwell Road, Leicester LE4 1BR
tel 0116 253 6796
email info@sweetcherrypublishing.com
website www.sweetcherrypublishing.com
Facebook www.facebook.com/sweetcherrypublishing
X @sweetcherrypub
Instagram @sweetcherrypublishing
Director A. Thadha

Children's fiction series. Children's picture books, novelty books, gift books, board books, educational books and fiction series for all ages. Also welcomes YA novels and series. See website for submission guidelines. Founded 2011.

Clock Tower Publishing
Marginalised and diverse voices trade fiction, including standalone and series titles.

Every Cherry
Accessible books for the SEND community.

Ta-Ha Publishers‡
tel 020-8670 1888
email editor@tahapublishers.com
website www.tahapublishers.com
Facebook www.facebook.com/tahapublishers
Instagram @tahapublishers
Managing Director Abia Afsar-Siddiqui

Family-run small independent Islamic publisher of children's books with Islamic cultural elements, often with illustrations. Founded 1980.

Tarquin Publications
Suite 74, 17 Holywell Hill, St Albans AL1 1DT
tel (01727) 833866
email info@tarquinbooks.com
website www.tarquinbooks.com

Mathematical models, puzzles, codes and logic and paper engineering books for children. Publishes 7–8 titles each year and has over 100 in print. Do not send unsolicited MSS. Send a one-page proposal of idea. Founded 1970.

Taylor & Francis Group*
4 Park Square, Milton Park, Abingdon,
Oxon OX14 4RN
tel 020-7017 6000
email enquiries@taylorandfrancis.com
website https://taylorandfrancis.com/
Ceo Penny Ladkin-Brand, *Managing Director, Books* Jeremy North

Academic and reference, including education. Imprints include: CRC Press, Routledge, and Taylor & Francis. Founded 1798.

Templar Books
Victoria House, Bloomsbury Square,
London WC1B 4DA
tel 020-3770 8888
email hello@bonnierbooks.co.uk
website www.bonnierbooks.co.uk/imprints/templar-books
X @templarbooks
Publisher Sophie Hallam

Children's imprint. Series include the *Ology* series, *Jonny Duddle's Gigantosaurus* titles and the *Amazing Baby* range of board and novelty books. Imprint of Bonnier Books UK. Founded 1978.

ThunderPoint Publishing*
Bryn Heulog, Talley, Llandeilo SA19 7YH
email info@thunderpoint.co.uk
website www.thunderpoint.scot
X @thunderpointltd

Fiction and non-fiction. Books that reflect the wide range of communities in Scotland, especially under-represented voices. YA (age 15+). Submission guidelines on website. Founded 2012.

Tiny Owl Publishing
366 Woodstock Road, Oxford OX2 8AE
email info@tinyowl.co.uk
website www.tinyowl.co.uk
Facebook www.facebook.com/tinyowlpublishing
X @TinyOwl_Books
Instagram @tiny_owl_publishing
Publisher Delaram Ghanimifard

An independent publisher of global children's literature. Picture books for ages 3–11. Aims to promote diversity and human rights values. Founded 2015.

Tippermuir Books*
3 Graham's Place, King Street, Perth PH2 8HZ
email wavmail@tippermuirbooks.co.uk
website http://tippermuirbooks.co.uk
Facebook www.facebook.com/people/Tippermuir-Books
X @tippermuirbooks
Instagram @tippermuirbooks
Directors Paul Philippou, Matthew Mackie, Rob Hands

Children's fiction and non-fiction including poetry with a cultural and social importance. Submissions welcome. Founded 2009.

Troika*
Troika Books Well House, Green Lane, Ardleigh, Colchester, Essex CO7 7PD
email info@troikabooks.com
website www.troikabooks.com
Publisher Martin West, Publicity, Marketing & Editorial Roy Johnson

Picture books, poetry and fiction with a focus on diversity for all ages. Founded 2012.

Trotman Indigo Publishing‡
18e Charles Street, Bath BA1 1HX
email info@trotman.co.uk
website https://trotman.co.uk/
Managing Director Sarah Cambell

Professional and educational publisher of books by contemporary careers education influencers. Founded 1969.

Two Windmills
Marine House, Tide Mill Way, Woodbridge, Suffolk IP12 1AP
tel (01394) 386651
email customerservice@twowindmills.com
website www.twowindmills.com
Instagram @twowindmills
Founder & Managing Director Marcus E. Leaver,
Publishers Dan Graham, Steve Munnings

Children's activity, novelty, picture, reference, character, gift and early learning books. Founded 1999.

UCLan Publishing‡
The Media Factory, University of Central Lancashire, Preston PR1 2HE
email uclanpublishing@uclan.ac.uk
website https://uclanpublishing.com/
Facebook www.facebook.com/uclanpublishing
X @publishinguclan
Bluesky @uclanpublishing.bsky.social
Instagram @uclan_publishing
Publisher Hazel Holmes

A commercial business based at the University of Central Lancashire, publishers of early years, middle-grade, teen and YA fiction. Currently closed to submissions. Founded 2010.

Usborne Publishing‡
83–85 Saffron Hill, London EC1N 8RT
tel 020-7430 2800
email help@usborne.co.uk
website www.usborne.com
Facebook www.facebook.com/UsbornePublishing
X @usborne
Directors Nicola Usborne, Publishing Director Jenny Tyler (editorial)

An independent, family publisher of books for children of all ages, including baby, preschool, novelty, activity, non-fiction and fiction. Looking for imaginative children's fiction. No unsolicited MSS. Founded 1973.

Wacky Bee Books*
17A Electric Lane, Brixton, London SW9 8LA
tel 07938 819510
email louise@wackybeebooks.com
website www.wackybeebooks.com
Facebook www.facebook.com/wackybeebooks
X @wackybeebooks
Instagram @wackybeebooks
Threads @wackybeebooks
Director Louise Jordan

Publishing books with a buzz for children 3–12 years. Picture books for 3+ years, early readers for 5–7 years and general fiction for 8–12 years. Submission enquiries by email to submissions@wackybeebooks.com. Founded 2014.

Walker Books*‡
87 Vauxhall Walk, London SE11 5HJ
tel 020-7793 0909
website www.walker.co.uk
Facebook www.facebook.com/walkerbooks
X @walkerbooksuk
Instagram @walkerbooksuk
Publishing Director Shannon Cullen

Publishes activity books, novelty books, picture books, fiction for ages 5–8 and 9–12, YA fiction, series fiction, film/TV tie-ins, plays, poetry, digital and audio. Publishes approx. 300 titles each year and has 2,000 in print. Imprints include: MITeen Press,

MIT Kids Press, Walker Books, Walker Entertainment and Walker Studio. Write to the editor, enclosing sae, and allow six months for response. Founded 1980.

The Wee Book Company
website www.theweebookcompany.com
Facebook www.facebook.com/theweebookcompany
X @theweebookco
Director Susan Cohen

Children's fiction. Founded 2018.

What On Earth!*‡
The Black Barn, Wickhurst Farm, Leigh, Tonbridge, Kent TN11 8PS
tel (01732) 464621
email info@whatonearthbooks.com
website www.whatonearthbooks.com
X @whatonearthbook
Bluesky @whatonearth.bsky.social
Instagram @whatonearth_books
Founder & Ceo Christopher Lloyd *Publisher* Natalie Bellos

Publishes children's non-fiction books. Founded 2010.

Wide Eyed Editions
2nd Floor, 1 Triptych Place, London SE1 9SH
tel 020-7700 9000
website www.quartoknows.com/Wide-Eyed-Editions
Publisher Georgia Buckthorn

Children's non-fiction. Imprint of Quarto Group Publishing UK. Founded 2014.

Wildthought Books
Box Wildthought, 245 Gladstone Street, Nottingham NG7 6HX
email submissions@wildthoughtbooks.co.uk
website https://wildthoughtbooks.co.uk/
Facebook www.facebook.com/61574004987163
Instagram @wildthought_books
Co-founder Ronny Worsey

Independent publisher of children's fiction and non-fiction. See submissions page on website for guidelines and genres. Founded 2024.

ZigZag Education
Unit 3, Greenway Business Centre, Doncaster Road, Bristol BS10 5PY
tel 0117 950 3199
email submissions@publishmenow.co.uk
website www.zigzageducation.co.uk, www.publishmenow.co.uk
Development Director John-Lloyd Hagger, *Strategy Director* Mike Stephens

Secondary school teaching resources: English, maths, ICT, geography, history, science, business, politics, PE and media studies. Founded 1998.

ZunTold‡
email elainebous@gmail.com
website https://zuntold.com/
Facebook www.facebook.com/zuntoldbooks
X @zuntold
Instagram @zuntold_books
Director Elaine Bousfield

New fiction for children and young people to support mental health. Also supports young people in their own writing. Interested in middle-grade fiction (9–12 years), teens, YA and crossover fiction. Agent submissions send a copy of synopsis and the first three chapters. Submissions opened for authors without an agent in June (YA, new adult and crossover fiction) and in December (for middle-grade fiction). No picture books. Founded 2016.

Children's book publishers overseas

Listings are given for children's book publishers in Australia (below), Canada (page 59), France (page 62), Germany (page 62), Italy (page 63), the Netherlands (page 63), New Zealand (page 64), South Africa (page 65), Spain (page 66) and the USA (page 66).

sae = self-addressed envelope
MS = manuscript (MSS = manuscripts)

AUSTRALIA

*Member of the Australian Publishers Association

ACER Press
19 Prospect Hill Road, Private Bag 55, Camberwell, VIC 3124
tel +61 (0)3 9277 5555
email proposals@acer.org
website www.acer.org/au
Facebook www.facebook.com/acer.edu.au
X @acereduau
Ceo Lisa Rodgers

Publisher of the Australian Council for Educational Research. Produces a range of books and assessments including professional resources for teachers, psychologists and special educational needs professionals. Founded 1930.

Affirm Press
28 Thistlethwaite Street, South Melbourne, VIC 3205
tel +61 (0)3 8695 9623
email info@affirmpress.com.au
website https://affirmpress.com.au/
Facebook www.facebook.com/affirmpress
X @affirmpress
Ceo & Publishing Director Martin Hughes

Non-fiction, fiction and young fiction. Owned by Simon & Schuster. Founded 2010.

Allen & Unwin*
83 Alexander Street, Crows Nest, NSW 2065
Postal address PO Box 8500, St Leonards, NSW 1590
tel +61 (0)2 8425 0100
website www.allenandunwin.com
Chairman Patrick Gallagher, Ceo Robert Gorman, Publishing Directors Jane Morrow (Murdock Books), Eva Mills (children & YA), Cate Paterson (Allen & Unwin and Atlantic Books)

Fiction for children 5–9 and 10–13 years, teenage fiction, series fiction and narrative non-fiction. Imprints include: Albert Street Books, Allen & Unwin, Atlantic Books, Crows Nest, Inspired Living, Joan, Murdock Books, Pier 9. Submission guidelines: will consider unsolicited MSS (but not picture book texts). Will only accept MSS through the electronic Friday Pitch system. Founded 1990.

Bloomsbury Publishing*
Level 6, 387 George Street, Sydney, NSW 2000
tel +61 (0)2 8820 4900
email au@bloomsbury.com
website www.bloomsbury.com/au
Facebook www.facebook.com/bloomsburypublishingaustralia
X @BloomsburySyd
Managing Director Cristina Cappelluto

Supports the worldwide education and children's publishing activities of Bloomsbury Publishing: caters for the Australia and New Zealand territories. Bloomsbury Publishing (page 38) founded 1986.

Brolly Books*
Suite 330, 45 Glenferrie Road, Malvern, VIC 3181
tel + 61 (0)3 9533 8863
email emma@brollybooks.com
website https://brollybooks.com/

An independent Australian publishing house specialising in Australian children's books, boxed picture jigsaws and general non-fiction. Founded 1997.

Cambridge University Press & Assessment Education Australia*
477 Williamstown Road, Private Bag 31, Port Melbourne, VIC 3207
tel +61 (0)3 8671 1400
email enquiries@cambridge.edu.au
website www.cambridge.org
Chief Executive Peter Phillips

Academic, educational, reference and ESL. Founded 1534.

Cengage Learning Australia*
Level 7, 80 Dorcas Street, South Melbourne, VIC 3205
tel +61 (0)3 9685 4111
website www.cengage.com.au

Educational books. Founded 2007.

EK Books
Unit 11, 201 Main Street, Gosford, NSW 2250
website www.ekbooks.org
Facebook www.facebook.com/ekbooksforkids
X @ekbooksforkids

Instagram @ek_books
Ceo Gareth St John Thomas

An imprint of Exisle Publishing. Independent children's publisher on a mission to publish books with heart on issues that matter. Publishes fiction and non-fiction for 0 years to YA, on themes including mental health, environmentalism and creative learning. Founded 2013.

ELK Publishing
PO Box 2828, Toowoomba, QLD 4350
tel +61 (0)4 0030 1675, +61 (0)4 7592 3670
email contactus@elk-publishing.com
website www.elk-publishing.com
Facebook www.facebook.com/elkpublishing
X @elkpublish
Instagram @elkpublishing
Founder & Ceo Selina Kucks

Independent publisher of children's and educational literature. Provides opportunities for unknown artists and illustrators to collaborate with in-house authors and offers internships to university students. Founded 2009.

Hachette Australia*
Level 17, 207 Kent Street, Sydney, NSW 2000
tel +61 (0)2 8248 0800
email reception@hachette.com.au
website www.hachette.com.au
Facebook www.facebook.com/HachetteAustralia
X @HachetteAus
Instagram @hachetteaus
Ceo Louise Stark

General, children's: picture books, fiction for children 5–8 and 9–12 years, teenage fiction and series fiction. Accepts MSS via website. Founded 1971.

Hardie Grant Children's Publishing*
Ground Floor, Building 1, 658 Church Street, Richmond, VIC 3121
tel +61 (0)3 8520 6444
email info@hardiegrantchildrenspublishing.com.au
website www.hardiegrant.com/au/hardie-grant-childrens-publishing

The young readers' division of one of Australia's largest independent publishers. Publishes a diverse list of fiction, non-fiction, graphic novels and picture books, including two imprints of illustrated titles: Bright Light and Little Hare. Check website for details of when submissions are accepted. Founded 2002.

HarperCollins Publishers (Australia)*
PO Box A565, Sydney South, NSW 1235
tel +61 (0)2 9952 5000
website www.harpercollins.com.au
Facebook www.facebook.com/HarperCollinsAustralia
X @HarperCollinsAU

Children's and reference. Founded 1989.

Little Book Press*
PO Box 76, Hilton Plaza, SA 5033
email admin@littlebookpress.com.au
website https://littlebookpress.com.au/
Facebook www.facebook.com/lbpress
Instagram @littlebookpress
Publishing Director Alyson O'Brien

Award-winning publishing house of Raising Literacy Australia (RLA) – a not-for-profit organisation. Publishes baby books and picture books for pre-school children. Founded 2017.

McGraw-Hill Australia*
Level 33, 680 George Street, Sydney, NSW 2000
website www.mcgraw-hill.com.au
Facebook www.facebook.com/MHEducationANZ
X @MHeducationAU

Educational publisher: higher education, primary education and professional (including medical, general and reference). Division of the McGraw-Hill Companies. Founded 1964.

New Frontier Publishing*
Suite 83/20–40 Meagher Street, Chippendale, NSW 2008
tel +61 (0)2 9660 4614
email info@newfrontier.com.au
website www.newfrontier.com.au
Facebook www.facebook.com/newfrontierpublishing
X @nfpublishing
Instagram @newfrontierpublishing

Activity books, board books, picture books, middle-grade fiction, dictionaries, textbooks for children 2–12 years. Unsolicited MSS accepted. Understanding of existing list crucial. Downloadable submissions pack available via website. Founded 2002.

Pan Macmillan Australia*
Level 25, 1 Market Street, Sydney, NSW 2000
tel +61 (0)2 9285 9100
email pan.reception@macmillan.com.au
website www.panmacmillan.com.au
Facebook www.facebook.com/PanMacmillanAustralia
X @macmillanaus
Publishing Director Ingrid Ohlsson

Commercial and literary fiction, children's and YA fiction, non-fiction and character products, general non-fiction, sport, cookery and lifestyle. Founded 1843.

Penguin Random House Australia*
Sydney office Level 3, 100 Pacific Highway, North Sydney, NSW 2060
tel +61 (0)2 9954 9966
email information@penguinrandomhouse.com.au
Melbourne office Level 28, 2 Southbank Blvd, Southbank, VIC 3006
website www.penguinrandomhouse.com.au
X @PenguinBooksAus

Children's book publishers overseas

Ceo Julie Burland, *Publishing Directors* Holly Toohey, Jess Malpass (Head of Launch)

General fiction, non-fiction, children's and illustrated. MS submissions for non-fiction accepted, unbound in hard copy addressed to Submissions Editor. Fiction submissions are only accepted from previously published authors, or authors represented by an agent or accompanied by a report from an accredited assessment service. Imprints: Arrow, Bantam, Ebury, Hamish Hamilton, William Heinemann, Michael Joseph, Knopf, Penguin, Viking and Vintage. Subsidiary of Bertelsmann AG. Founded 2013.

University of Queensland Press*
PO Box 6042, St Lucia, QLD 4067
tel +61 (0)7 3365 7244
email reception@uqp.com.au
website www.uqp.com.au
Facebook www.facebook.com/uqpofficial
X @UQPBooks
Instagram @uqpbooks

Children's and YA, also fiction, non-fiction and poetry for all ages. Founded 1948.

Rhiza Edge
PO Box 302, Chinchilla, QLD 4413
tel +61 (0)7 3245 1938
email editor@rhizaedge.com.au
website www.rhizaedge.com.au
Facebook www.facebook.com/rhizaedge

Issue-based stories for YA readers. Imprint of Wombat Books. Founded 2018.

R.I.C. Publications
5 Bendsten Place, Balcatta, WA 6021
tel +61 (0)8 9240 9888
email mail@ricpublications.com.au
website www.ricpublications.com.au

Teaching resources in all formats, including boldline masters, workbooks and digital content. Founded 1986.

Scholastic Australia*
76–80 Railway Crescent, Lisarow, Gosford, NSW 2250
tel +61 (0)2 4328 3555
website www.scholastic.com.au
Facebook www.facebook.com/ScholasticAustralia
X @scholasticAUS
Instagram @scolastic_au
Managing Director David Peagram

Children's fiction and non-fiction. Founded 1968.

Tale Publishing*
email talepublishing@gmail.com
website https://talepublishing.com/

Children's fiction and non-fiction. See website for submission windows. Member of the Small Press Network. Founded 2015.

Wombat Books*
PO Box 302, Chinchilla, QLD 4413
tel +61 (0)7 3245 1938
email website@wombatrhiza.com.au
website www.wombatrhiza.com.au
Facebook www.facebook.com/wombatbooks
Publisher Rochelle Manners

An independent publisher of children's picture books and books for early readers. YA and adult imprint: Rhiza Edge. Founded 2009.

CANADA

*Member of the Canadian Publishers' Council
†Member of the Association of Canadian Publishers

Annick Press†
665 Gerrard Street East, Toronto, ON M4M 1Y2
tel +1 416-221-4802
email annickpress@annickpress.com
website www.annickpress.com
Contact David Caron

Preschool to YA fiction and non-fiction. Approx. 25% of books are by first-time authors. Founded 1975.

Breakwater Books†
PO Box 2188, St John's, NL A1C 6E6
tel +1 709-722-6680
email orders@breakwaterbooks.com
website https://breakwaterbooks.com/
Facebook www.facebook.com/breakwaterbooksltd
X @breakwaterbooks
President & Publisher Rebecca Rose

Fiction, non-fiction for children and YA. Also educational resources. Founded 1973.

Common Deer Press†
1745 Rockland Avenue, Victoria, BC V8S 1W6
website www.commondeerpress.com
Facebook www.facebook.com/commondeerpress
X @commondeerpress
Instagram @commondeer-press
Publisher & Acquiring Editor Kirsten Marion

Publishes books for children and teens. Founded 2017.

Dundurn Press†
1382 Queen Street E, Toronto, ON M4L 1C9
tel +1 416-214-5544
email submissions@dundurn.com
website www.dundurn.com
Facebook www.facebook.com/dundurnpress
X @dundurnpress

Instagram @dundurnpress
Managing Editor Elena Radic

YA fiction. Founded 1972.

Fitzhenry & Whiteside
209 Wicksteed Avenue, Unit 51, East York, ON M4G 0B1
tel +1 905-477-9700
email hdoll@fitzhenry.ca
website www.fitzhenry.ca
Facebook www.facebook.com/FitzWhits
X @FitzWhits

Trade, educational and children's books. Fiction and non-fiction. Publishes first-time authors. Emphasis is on Canadian authors and illustrators, subject or perspective. Will review MS/illustration packages from artists. Submit outline and copy of sample illustration. For illustrations only, send samples and promotional sheet. Founded 1966.

Guernica Editions†
1241 Marble Rock Road, Gananoque, ON K7G 2V4
website https://guernicaeditions.com/
Facebook www.facebook.com/guernicaed
X @guernica_ed
Instagram @guernicaeditions
Founder/Co-publisher Michael Mirolla, *Co-publisher* Connie Guzzo-McParland

YA fiction and non-fiction that address social issues. Imprints: Guernica World Editions, MiroLand and 1366Books. Submission guidelines: please check website. Founded 1978.

HarperCollins Publishers (Canada)*
22 Adelaide Street West, 41st Floor, Toronto, ON M5H 4E3
tel +1 416-975-9334
email hcOrder@harpercollins.com
website www.harpercollins.ca
Facebook www.facebook.com/HarperCollinsCanada
X @HarperCollinsCa

Literary fiction and non-fiction, history, politics, biography, spiritual and children's books. Founded 1989.

House of Anansi Press and Groundwood Books†
128 Sterling Road, Lower Level, Toronto, ON M6R 2B7
tel +1 416-363-4343
email publicity@houseofanansi.com
website https://houseofanansi.com/
Facebook www.facebook.com/groundwoodbooks
X @GroundwoodBooksPr
President Semareh Al-Hillal, *Publisher* Karen Brochu, *Editorial Director* Douglas Richmond

Groundwood Books publishes books for all ages, including fiction, picture books, graphic novels and non-fiction. House of Anansi Press is a publisher of literary fiction. Founded 1978.

Kids Can Press†
25 Dockside Drive, Toronto, ON M5A 0B5
tel +1 416-479-7000
email customerservice@kidscan.com
website www.kidscanpress.com
Facebook www.facebook.com/kidscanbooks
X @kidscanpress
Editorial Director Yasemin Uçar

Middle-grade/YA fiction and non-fiction. Publishes picture books, young readers, middle readers and YA titles. Approx. 10–15% of books are by first-time authors. Submit outline/synopsis and between two to three sample chapters. See website for submission guidelines. Founded 1973.

McGraw-Hill Canada*
300 Water Street, Whitby, Ontario, ON L1N 9B6
website www.mheducation.ca
Facebook www.facebook.com/mcgrawhillcanada
X @mcgraw_canada

Education and trade. Founded 1972.

Nelson Education*
2005 Sheppard Ave E, Suite 700, Toronto, ON M2J 5B4
tel +1 416-752-9448
website www.nelson.com
Facebook www.facebook.com/NelsonClassroom
X @NelsonClassroom
Instagram @nelsonclassroom
President & Ceo Steve Brown

Education: K–12. Creator of digital platform, Edwin. Founded 1914.

Nimbus Publishing
3660 Strawberry Hill, Halifax, NS B3K 5A9
tel +1 800-646-2879
website https://nimbus.ca/
Facebook www.facebook.com/nimbuspub
X @nimbuspub
Instagram @nimbuspub

Children's picture books and fiction, literary non-fiction, social and cultural history, nature photography, current events, biography, sports and cultural issues. Founded 1978.

Oberon Press
203–145 Spruce Street, Ottawa, ON K1R 6P1
tel +1 613-238-3275
email oberon@sympatico.ca
website www.oberonpress.ca

Children's fiction and non-fiction by Canadian writers. Currently not accepting submissions. Founded 1985.

Orca Book Publishers†
1016 Balmoral Road, Victoria, BC V8T 1A8
tel +1 800-210-5277
email orca@orcabook.com
website www.orcabook.com
Facebook www.facebook.com/orcabook
X @orcabook
Publisher Andrew Wooldridge

Books for children and YA. Will consider MSS from Canadian writers only. No submissions by fax or email. See website for submission guidelines. No poetry. Founded 1984.

Pajama Press†
11 Davies Avenue, Suite 103, Toronto, ON M4M 2A9
website https://pajamapress.ca/
Facebook www.facebook.com/pajamapress
X @pajamapress1
Instagram @pajamapressbooks
Publisher Gail Elizabeth Winskill

Children's: picture books, new board books for the very young, early chapter books for new readers, and middle-grade and YA novels for pre-high school audiences. Also literary non-fiction. Publishes 18–20 titles a year. Not currently open to unsolicited submissions. Founded 2011.

Pearson Canada*
26 Prince Andrew Place, North York, ON M3C 2T8
tel +1 800-361-6128
website www.pearson.com/ca/en.html
Facebook www.facebook.com/pearsonhighereducationCA
X @pearson
Instagram @pearsonhighereducation

Academic, technical, educational, children's and adult trade. Founded 1998.

Penguin Random House Canada*
320 Front Street West, Suite 1400, Toronto, ON M5V 3B6
tel +1 416-364-4449
website www.penguinrandomhouse.ca
Facebook www.facebook.com/penguinrandomca
X @penguinrandomca
Instagram @penguinrandomca
Ceo Kristin Cochrane

Children and YA. No unsolicited MSS; submissions via an agent only. Imprints: Appetite (Appetite by Random House), Doubelday Canada (Anchor Canada, Bond Street Books and Doubleday Canada), Knopf Canada (Alchemy by Knopf Canada, Knopf Canada and Vintage Canada), McCelland & Stewart (Emblam Editions, McCelland & Stewart, Signal and Strange Light), Penguin Canada (Allen Lane, Hamish Hamilton, Penguin Canada and Viking), Random House Canada (Random House Canada and Vintage Canada). Subsidiary of Penguin Random House. Founded 2013.

Red Deer Press
209 Wicksteed Avenue, Unit 51 Toronto, ON M4G 0B1
tel +1 800-387-9776
email rdp@reddeerpress.com
website www.reddeerpress.com
Facebook www.facebook.com/reddeerpress
X @reddeerpress
Publisher Holly Doll, *Children's Editor* Beverly Brenna

Literary fiction, sci-fi, non-fiction, children's illustrated books YA fiction and teen fiction. Publishes books that are written or illustrated by Canadians and that are about or of interest to Canadians. Publishes 14–18 new books a year. Children's picture books MSS from established authors with a demonstrable record of publishing success are preferred. Currently accepting new MSS. Imprint: RJS (Robert J. Sawyer) Books (sci-fi). Founded 1975.

Ronsdale Press†
125A–1030 Denman Street, Vancouver, BC V6G 2M6
tel +1 604-738-4688
email info@ronsdalepress.com
website www.ronsdalepress.com
Facebook www.facebook.com/ronsdalepress
X @ronsdalepress
Publisher Wendy Atkinson

Publishes literary fiction, non-fiction, young reader chapter books and poetry. Not currently accepting picture books. Founded 1988.

Scholastic Canada*
175 Hillmount Road, Markham, ON L6C 1Z7
tel +1 800-268-3860
email custserv@scholastic.ca
website www.scholastic.ca
Facebook www.facebook.com/ScholasticCanada
X @scholasticCDA
Instagram @scholasticcda
Art Director Andrea Casault

Publishes books for children, parents and teachers through a variety of businesses including Scholastic Book Clubs and Book Fairs, Scholastic Education, Classroom Magazines, Trade and Éditions Scholastic. Publishes recreational reading and educational materials for children and young people, ages 0–14 in both English and French. Its publishing focus is on books by Canadians. No unsolicited, unagented submissions are being accepted at this time. Canadian artists may submit electronic samples of their work along with their website/contact information to the art director. Founded 1957.

Second Story Press†
20 Maud Street, Suite 401, Toronto, ON M5V 2M5
tel +1 416-537-7850
email info@secondstorypress.ca
website https://secondstorypress.ca/
Facebook www.facebook.com/secondstorypress

X @secondstory
Instagram @_secondstory

Feminist-inspired fiction and non-fiction for adults, children and YA. Founded 2015.

University of Toronto Press
800 Bay Street, Mezzanine, Toronto, ON M5S 3A9
tel +1 416-978-2239
email publishing@utpress.utoronto.ca
website www.utorontopress.com
Facebook www.facebook.com/utpress
X @utpress
Vice President Antonia Pop

Non-fiction, monographs, textbooks and academic books, ESL/EFL, teacher reference, adult basic education and school texts. Imprints: Aevo, Irwin, New Jewish Press, Rotman and University of Toronto Press. Founded 1901.

Tundra Books
320 Front Street West, Suite 1400, Toronto, ON M5V 3B6
tel +1 416-364-4449
email submissions@tundrabooks.com
email art@tundrabooks.com
website www.penguinrandomhouse.ca/imprints/TU/tundra-books
Facebook www.facebook.com/tundrabooks
X @TundraBooks
Bluesky @tundrabooks.bsky.social

Children's and YA picture books and novels. A division of Penguin Random House Canada. Founded 1967.

FRANCE

l'école des loisirs
11 rue de Sevres, 75006 Paris
tel +33 (0)1 4222 9410
email edl@ecoledesloisirs.com
website www.ecoledesloisirs.fr
Facebook www.facebook.com/ecoledesloisirs
X @ecoledesloisirs

Specialises in children's literature from picture books to YA fiction. Founded 1965.

Flammarion
87 Quai Panhard Et Levassor Cedex 13, Paris, Île-de-France 75647
tel +33 (0)1 4051 3100
website https://editions.flammarion.com/
Facebook www.facebook.com/Editions_Flammarion
X @Ed_Flammarion

Children's imprints include: Aubier, Arthaud, Autrement, Champs, Climats, Etonnants Classiques, Flammarion, GF, Jeunesse, Père Castor and Tribal. Founded 1875.

Père Castor
Children's picture books, junior fiction, activity books, board books, how-to books, comics, gift books, fairy tales, dictionaries and records and tapes. Covers 0–16 years.

Gallimard Jeunesse
5 rue Gaston Gallimard, 75328 Paris
tel +33 (0)1 4954 4200
website www.gallimard-jeunesse.fr
Facebook www.facebook.com/GallimardJeunesse
Instagram @gallimard_jeunesse
Children's Publisher Hedwige Pasquet

Publisher of children's fiction and non-fiction including board books, novelty books, picture books and pop-up books. Founded 1911.

Hachette Livre/Gautier-Languereau
Building Louis Hachette, 58 rue Jean, Bleuzen, CS 70007 – 92178 Vanves
tel +33 (0)1 4392 3030
website www.gautier-languereau.fr
Ceo Pierre Leroy

Picture books for children. Imaginative stories for children 2–10 years. Publishes approx. 55 titles each year. Will consider unsolicited MSS. Allow four months for response. Contacts on website. Founded 1885.

Editions Sarbacane
35 rue d'Hauteville, 75010 Paris
tel +33 (0)1 4246 6207
email administration@sarbacane.net
website www.editions-sarbacane.com
Facebook www.facebook.com/fanpage.editions.sarbacane
X @esarbacane
Instagram @editionssarbacane

Activity books, board books, picture books and YA fiction, fiction for children from preschool age to adult. Founded 2001.

Le Sorbier
25 boulevard Romain Rolland, 75014 Paris
tel +33 (0)1 4148 8000
website www.editionsdelamartiniere.fr
Facebook www.facebook.com/editionsdelamartiniere_off
X @ed_LaMartiniere
Instagram @editions_de_la_martiniere

Picture books for children up to 10 years and illustrated reference books for 9–12 years. Imprint: De La Martinière Jeunesse. Founded 1992.

GERMANY

Carlsen Verlag
Postfach 50 03 80, 22703 Hamburg
tel +49 (0)40 398040

email info@carlsen.de
website www.carlsen.de
Facebook www.facebook.com/kanaeleWE
X @carlsen_verlag
Directors Renate Herre, Joachim Kaufmann

Children's picture books, board books and novelty books. Illustrated fiction and non-fiction. Teenage fiction and non-fiction. Publishes both German and international authors including Stephenie Meyer, J.K. Rowling and Philip Pullman. Publisher of the *Harry Potter* series. Imprint: Chicken House Deutschland. Age groups: preschool, 5–10 years, 10–15 years and 15+ years. Unsolicited MSS welcome but must include a sae for return. Do not follow up by phone or post. For illustrations, submit no more than three colour photocopies and unlimited b&w copies. Founded 1953.

dtv Verlagsgesellschaft mbH & Co. KG
Tumblingerstraße 21, 80337 Munich
tel +49 (0)89 38167282
email verlag@dtv.de
email junior@dtv.de
website www.dtvjunior.de
Facebook www.facebook.com/dtvVerlag
Instagram @dtv_verlag
Editor-in-Chief Susanne Stark

Fiction and non-fiction for children, teenagers, YA and young general fiction. Founded 1971.

Carl Hanser Verlag
Vilshofener Straße 10, 81679 Munich
tel +49 (0)89 998300
email info@hanser.de
website www.hanser-literaturverlage.de
Facebook www.facebook.com/HanserLiteraturverlage
X @hanserliteratur
Instagram @hanserliteratur, @hanser.hey
Children's Publisher Saskia Heintz

Hardback books for all ages from preschool to YA. Board books, picture books, fiction and non-fiction. Age groups: 3–10, 10–15 and 15+. Founded 1993.

ITALY

De Agostini Editore
Via Giovanni da Verrazano 15, 28100 Novara
tel +39 02-380861
website www.deagostini.it
Facebook www.facebook.com/eAgostiniPublishingUK
Instagram @deagostini_official

Illustrated children's books. Founded 1901.

Edizioni Arka srl
Via Milano 73/175, 20010 Cornaredo Milan
tel +39 02-4818230
email daisy.zonato@edizioniel.it
website www.arkaedizioni.it

Picture books and general fiction from preschool to 10+ years.

Edizioni El/Einaudi Ragazzi/Emme Edizioni
Via J. Ressel 5, 34018 San Dorligo della Valle TS
tel +39 040-3880311
email edizioniel@edizioniel.it
website www.edizioniel.com

Activity books, board books, picture books, pop-up books, non-fiction, novels, poetry, fairy tales, fiction. Age groups: preschool, 5–10, 10–15 and 15+ years. Founded 1974.

Giunti Editore
Via Bolognese 165, 50139 Florence
tel +39 055-50621
email info@giunti.it
website www.giunti.it
Facebook www.facebook.com/GiuntiEditore
X @GiuntiEditore
Managing Director Martino Montanarini

Activity books, board books, novelty books, picture books, colouring books, pop-up books and some educational textbooks. Founded 1841.

Arnoldo Mondadori Editore (Mondadori)
Via Mondadori 1, 20090 Segrate, Milan
tel +39 02-75421
email stampalibri@mondadori.it
website www.mondadori.it
Facebook www.facebook.com/MondadoriLibri
X @Mondadori
Instagram @librimondadori

Activity books, board books, novelty books, picture books, painting and colouring books, pop-up books, how-to books, hobbies, leisure, pets, sport, comics, poetry, fairy tales, education, fiction and non-fiction. Age groups: preschool, 5–10, 10–15 and 15+ years. Founded 1907.

Adriano Salani Editore
Via Gherardini 10, 20145 Milan
tel +39 02-34597624
email info@salani.it
website www.salani.it
Facebook www.facebook.com/AdrianoSalaniEditore
X @salanieditore
Instagram @salani_editore
Ceo Gianluca Mazzitelli

Picture books, how-to books, comics, gift books, fiction, novels, poetry and fairy tales. Age groups: preschool, 5–10, 10–15 and 15+. Founded 1862.

THE NETHERLANDS

Lemniscaat BV
Vijverlaan 48, 3062 HL Rotterdam
tel +31 10-2062929

email info@lemniscaat.nl
website www.lemniscaat.nl
Publisher Jesse Goossens

Independent children's book publisher of picture books, juvenile novels and YA literature. Founded 1963.

Rubinstein Publishing

Prinseneiland 43, 1013 LL Amsterdam
tel +31 20-4200772
email info@rubinstein.nl
website www.rubinstein.nl
Facebook www.facebook.com/uitgeverijrubinstein
X @uitgeverijrubinstein
Instagram @uitgeverijrubinstein
Publisher Juliette van Wersch

Independent publisher of audiobooks for children. Also produces novelty books. Founded 1985.

Van Goor/Van Holkema & Warendorf

PO Box 23202, 1100 DS Amsterdam
tel +31 20-2364200
email info@de-leukste-kinderboeken.com
website www.de-leukste-kinderboeken.nl, www.bestofyabooks.nl

Picture books, learn-to-read books, middle-grade (literary) fiction, non-fiction and YA. Founded 2009.

NEW ZEALAND

*Member of the New Zealand Book Publishers' Association

The Cuba Press

Level 6, 138 Wakefield Street, Te Aro, Wellington 6011
email hello@thecubapress.nz
website www.thecubapress.nz
Facebook www.facebook.com/TheCubaPress
Instagram @thecubapress
Director Mary McCallum, *Publisher* Paul Stewart

Children's fiction with Aotearoa New Zealand setting. Children's imprint: Ahoy! Founded 2018.

Edify*

PO Box 444, Whitianga 3542
tel +64 (0)9 972 9428
email orders@edify.co.nz
website www.edify.co.nz
Facebook www.facebook.com/edifynz
X @edifynz

Publishes in the New Zealand educational market. Exclusive representatives of Pearson and the educational publisher Sunshine Books. Founded 2013.

HarperCollins Publishers (New Zealand)*

Unit H, 63 Apollo Drive, Rosedale, Auckland 0632
tel +64 (0)9 443 9400
email publicity@harpercollins.co.nz
Postal address PO Box 1, Shortland Street, Auckland 1140
website www.harpercollins.co.nz
Facebook www.facebook.com/Harpercollinsnz
X @HarperNZ

Children's non-fiction titles by New Zealand authors. Submissions to: nz.submissions@harpercollins.co.nz. Founded 1989.

Huia Publishing*

PO Box 12–28, Thorndon, Wellington 6144
email info@huia.co.nz
website https://huia.co.nz/
Facebook www.facebook.com/huiapublishers
X @huiapublishers
Directors Eboni Waitere, Pania Tahau-Hodges

A Māori owned, independent publisher producing innovative and inspiring books and resources. Founded 1991.

Massey University Press*

Private Bag 102904, North Shore Mail Centre, Auckland 0745
email editorial@masseypress.ac.nz
website www.masseypress.ac.nz
Facebook www.facebook.com/masseyuniversitypress
X @masseyunipress
Instagram @masseyuniversitypress
Publisher Nicola Legat

Children's. Founded 2016.

New Zealand Council for Educational Research

Box 3237, Education House, 178–182 Willis Street, Wellington 6140
tel +64 (0)4 384 7939
email info@nzcer.org.nz
website www.nzcer.org.nz
Facebook www.facebook.com/nzcer
X @nzcer

Education, including educational policy and practice, early childhood education, educational achievement tests, Māori education, schooling for the future, curriculum and assessment. Founded 1934.

Penguin Random House New Zealand*

Private Bag 102 902, North Shore, Auckland 0745
tel +64 (0)9 442 7400
email submissions@penguinrandomhouse.co.nz
website www.penguin.co.nz
Facebook www.facebook.com/PenguinBooksNewZealand
X @PenguinBooks_NZ
Instagram @penguinbooksnz
Publishing Grace Thomas

Children's fiction and non-fiction. Imprints: Black Swan, Godwit, Penguin, Puffin Books and Vintage. Part of Penguin Random House. Founded 2013.

SOUTH AFRICA

*Member of the Publishers' Association of South Africa

Cambridge University Press & Assessment, Africa*
Unit OW3A Old Warehouse Building,
Black River Park, 2 Fir Street, Observatory,
Cape Town 7925
tel +27 (0)21 412 7800
email cambridge-sa@cambridge.org
website www.cambridge.org
Publishing Director Johan Traut

Textbooks and literature for sub-Saharan African countries, as well as primary reading materials in 28 African languages. Founded 1534.

Human & Rousseau – see NB Publishers

Macmillan Education South Africa
4th Floor, Building G, Hertford Office Park,
90 Bekker Road, Vorna Valley, Midrand 1685
tel +27 (0)11 731 3300
Postal address Private Bag X19, Northlands 2116
website www.macmillan.co.za
Managing Director Mandla Balisa

Educational titles. Founded 1843.

Maskew Miller Learning*
10 Freedom Way, Milnerton, Cape Town 7441
Postal address PO Box 396, Cape Town 8000
tel +27 (0)21 532 6000
email info@mml.co.za
website https://mml.co.za/

Provides learning materials, technologies and services for use in schools, TVET colleges, higher education institutions and in home and professional environments. Founded 2010.

NB Publishers*
12th Floor, Media24 Centre, 40 Heerengracht,
Cape Town 8001
tel +27 (0)21 406 3033
email nb@nb.co.za
website www.nb.co.za

General: Afrikaans fiction, politics, children's and youth literature in all the country's languages, non-fiction. Imprints: Best Books, Human & Rousseau, Kwela, Lux Verbi, Pharos, Queillerie and Tafelberg. Founded 1950.

New Africa Books
Unit 13, Athlone Industrial Park,
10 Mymoena Crescent, Cape Town 7764
tel +27 (0)21 467 5860
email info@newafricabooks.co.za
website https://newafricabooks.com/
X @DavidPhilipPub
Instagram @newafricabooks
Contacts Dušanka Stojaković, Nerina van Wyngaarden Lindhout, Cheraldine Smit, Felicity Solomons

Award-winning independent publisher of picture books publishing approx. 60 titles per year. Fiction, non-fiction and comics with South African content in all South African languages. Imprints: David Philip and New Africa Books. Founded 1971.

Oxford University Press Southern Africa*
Vasco Boulevard, N1 City, Goodwood,
Cape Town 7460
tel +27 (0)21 596 2300
email oxford.za@oup.com
website www.oxford.co.za
Facebook www.facebook.com/OxfordSASchools
Instagram @oxford_university_press_sa
Managing Director Africa Karen Simpson

Pre-primary education, primary education, secondary education, higher education, TVET, dictionaries, atlases, literature, children's books, home learning, reading schemes, ELT, online and offline learning solutions, professional development services. Produces educational material and support for Grade R to 12, TVET, higher education, and home learning in all official written South African languages. Founded 1586.

Shuter and Shooter Publishers*
45 Willowton Rd, Willowton, Pietermaritzburg 3201
tel +27 (0)33 846 8700
email sales@shuters.com
website www.shuters.co.za
Facebook www.facebook.com/shuterandshooter
X @shuters

Core curriculum-based textbooks for use at foundation, intermediate, senior and FET phases. Supplementary readers in various languages, dictionaries, reading development kits and charts. Literature titles in English, isiXhosa, Sesotho, Sepedi, Setswana, Tshivenda, Xitsonga, Ndebele, isiZulu and Siswati. Founded 1925.

Via Afrika
11th Floor, Media24 Centre, 40 Heerengracht,
Cape Town 8001
Postal address PO Box 5197, Cape Town 8001
tel +27 (0)21 406 3528
email info@viaafrika.com
website www.viaafrika.com
Facebook www.facebook.com/ViaAfrikaZA
X @ViaAfrikaZA
Instagram @viaafrikaza
Ceo Christina Watson

Publishes educational content and learning experiences in all appropriate formats by learners, TVET students and teachers. Creates material for Via Afrika Digital Education Academy where courses are offered online in both asynchronous and synchronous options to provide teachers with South African Certificate of Education endorsed training with Professional Development Points. Founded in 1949.

SPAIN

Grupo Anaya
website www.grupoanaya.es
X @hachettelivre

Non-fiction: education textbooks for preschool up to 15+ years. Part of Hachette Livre. Founded 1984.

Editorial Cruilla
C/Roger de Llúria 44, 4th, 08009 Barcelona
tel +34 902 123 336
email editorial@cruilla.cat
website www.cruilla.cat
Facebook www.facebook.com/SMEspana
X @SM_Espana

Activity books, novelty books, fiction for children 5–8 and 9–12 years, teenage fiction and poetry. Publishes approx. 120–130 titles each year. Subsidiary of Ediciones SM. Founded 1984.

Destino Infantil & Juvenil
Carrer de Llull 51, 60–4A, 08005 Barcelona
email destinojoven@edestino.es
website www.planetadelibros.com/editorial/destino-infantil-juvenil/23
Facebook www.facebook.com/kidsplanetlibros
X @TeenPlanetLibro
Instagram @kidsplanetlibros

Fiction for children 6–16 years. Picture books, pop-up books, fiction and some unusual illustrated books. Founded 2002.

Libros del Zorro Rojo
Carrer de Pallars 5–3, 08018 Barcelona
email rights@librosdelzorrorojo.com
website www.librosdelzorrorojo.com
General Director Fernando Diego García, Editorial Director Diana Hernández Aldana

Independent publisher of illustrated titles for readers of all ages. Founded 2004.

Editorial Libsa
C/ Puerto de Navacerrada, 88, Pol. Ind. Las Nieves, 28935 Móstoles (Madrid)
tel +34 916 572 580
email libsa@libsa.es
website www.libsa.es
Facebook www.facebook.com/LibsaEditorial
X @edicioneslibsa

Publisher of highly illustrated mass market books: activity books, board books, picture books, colouring books, how-to books and fairy tales. Founded 1980.

Penguin Random House Grupo Editorial
Luchana 23, 1A, 28010 Madrid
tel +34 915 358 190
website www.penguinrandomhousegrupoeditorial.com
Facebook www.facebook.com/penguinlibros
X @penguinlibros
Instagram @penguinlibros

Preschool activity, novelty and picture books through to YA fiction. Also a packager and printer. Part of Penguin Random House. Founded 2013.

Vicens Vives SA
Avenida Sarriá 130–132, 08017 Barcelona
tel +34 932 523 700
email rrhh@vicensvives.es
website www.vicensvives.com
Facebook www.facebook.com/vicensvives
X @vicensvives
Instagram @vicensvives

Activity and novelty books, fiction, art, encyclopaedias, dictionaries, education, geography, history, music, science, textbooks, posters. Age groups: preschool, 5–10, 10–15 and 15+ years. Founded 1960.

USA

*Member of the Association of American Publishers Inc.

Abingdon Press
810 12th Ave South, Nashville, TN 37203
tel +1 800-251-3320
website www.abingdonpress.com
Facebook www.facebook.com/AbingdonPress
X @AbingdonPress

General interest, professional, academic and reference, non-fiction and fiction, youth and children's non-fiction and Vacation Bible School, primarily directed to the religious market. Imprint of United Methodist Publishing House. United Methodist Publishing House founded 1789.

Harry N. Abrams
195 Broadway, 9th Floor, New York, NY 10007
tel +1 212-206-7715
email abrams@abramsbooks.com
website www.abramsbooks.com

Children's books. Imprints: Abrams, Abrams Appleseed, Abrams Books for Young Readers, Abrams ComicArts (imprints: Kana, Megascape and Surely Books), Abrams Fanfare, Abrams Image, Abrams Press, Amulet Books, Magic Cat, The Overlook Press and Taunton Press. Founded 1949.

Children's book publishers overseas

Aladdin Paperbacks – see Simon & Schuster Children's Publishing Division

All About Kids Publishing
7680 Monterey St. #307, Gilroy, CA 95020
tel +1 408-337-1152
email lguevara@aakp.com
website www.allaboutkidspub.com
X @LindaGu55410941
Instagram @allaboutkidspub
Publisher Mike G. Guevara, Editor Linda L. Guevara

Fiction and non-fiction picture books and chapter books. See website for submission guidelines. Does not accept submissions by email unless there is a call for submissions, postal and with a sae only. Founded 2001.

Astra Publishing House
19 West 21st Street, #1201, New York, NY 10010
email info@bmkbooks.com
website https://astrapublishinghouse.com/imprints/astra-young-readers/
Facebook www.facebook.com/astrakidsbooks
X @astrakidsbooks
Instagram @astrakidsbooks
Publisher Betsy Wollheim

Activity books, picture books, fiction, non-fiction and poetry for 18 years and under. Publishes 80 titles each year. Check website for submission guidelines. Imprints: Astra House (adults), Astra Young Readers, Calkins Creek, Daw Books (adults), Hippo Park, Kane Press, minerva, mineditionUS, Toon Books and WordSong. Founded 1991.

Atheneum Books for Young Readers – see Simon & Schuster Children's Publishing Division

Barefoot Books
23 Bradford Street, Concord, MA 01742
tel +1 617-576-0660
email publicity@barefootbooks.com
website www.barefootbooks.com
Facebook www.facebook.com/barefootbooks
X @BarefootBooks
Editorial Director Emma Parkin

Independent publisher of children's fiction and non-fiction. Currently not accepting MS submissions or queries. Accepts illustrator samples via mail only. Please mail samples (no original artwork) for the attention of the editor. Length: 500–1,000 words (picture books) and 2,000–3,000 words (young readers). US branch founded 1998.

Bloomsbury Publishing USA*
1385 Broadway, New York, NY 10018
tel +1 212-419-5300
email Contact-USA@bloomsbury.com
website www.bloomsbury.com/us

Supports the worldwide educational and children's publishing activities of Bloomsbury Publishing: caters for the US market. For submission guidelines see website. Established in 1998 as an American subsidiary of Bloomsbury Publishing. Founded 1986.

Calkins Creek Books – see Astra Publishing House

Candlewick Press*
99 Dover Street, Somerville, MA 02144
tel +1 617-661-3330
email bigbear@candlewick.com
website www.candlewick.com
Facebook www.facebook.com/candlewickpressbooks
X @candlewick
Bluesky @candlewickpress.bsky.social

Books for babies through teens: board books, picture books, early readers, first chapter books, novels, non-fiction, novelty books, poetry, graphic novels. Publishes 70 picture books, 40 middle readers and 30 YA titles each year. Founded 1991.

Candlewick Entertainment
Media-related children's books, including film/TV tie-ins.

Charlesbridge Publishing
9 Galen Street, Watertown, MA 02472
tel +1 617-926-0329
email development@charlesbridge.com
website www.charlesbridge.com

Fiction and non-fiction board books, picture books and middle-grade books for preschool up to 14 years. YA novels for readers 14+ years. Non-fiction list specialises in nature, concept, history and science. Publishes roughly 60% non-fiction and 40% fiction. Send full MSS for board books and picture books. Send first three chapters, a chapter outline, and plot summary for MSS longer than 30 pages. No queries. Electronic submissions only: childrens.submissions@charlesbridge.com. Responds to MSS of interest. For illustrations, send art postcards or electronic query with samples, pdf or jpg portfolio, and website: design.submissions@charlesbridge.com. Founded 1980.

Chicago Review Press
814 North Franklin Street, Chicago, IL 60610
tel +1 312-337-0747
email frontdesk@jpg.com
website www.chicagoreviewpress.com

Non-fiction activity books for children. Imprint Zephyr publishes professional development titles for teachers. Interested in hands-on educational books. See website for submission guidelines. Imprints: Academy Chicago Publishers, Amberjack Publishing, Chicago Press Children's, Council Oak Books, Duet

Books, Interlude Press, Lawrence Hill Books and Parenting Press. Founded 1973.

Chronicle Books
680 Second Street, San Francisco, CA 94107
tel +1 415-537-2000
email hello@chroniclebooks.com
website www.chroniclebooks.com,
www.chroniclebooks.com/titles/kids-teens
Facebook www.facebook.com/chroniclekidsbooks
X @ChronicleKids
Instagram @chroniclekidsbooks
Chairman & Ceo Nion McEvoy

Traditional and innovative children's books. Looking for projects that have a unique edge – in subject matter, writing style or illustrative technique – that will add a distinctive flair. Interested in fiction and non-fiction for children of all ages as well as board books, decks, activity kits and other unusual or 'novelty' formats. Publishes 60–100 books each year. For older readers, submit outline/synopsis and three sample chapters. No submitted materials will be returned. Response approx. three months. Part of the McEvoy Group along with Princeton Architectural Press and and Galison/Mudpuppy. Founded 1967.

Dawn Publications
PO Box 4410, Naperville, IL 60567-4410
tel +1 800-432-7444
website www.sourcebooks.com/dawn-publications.html

Publishes books and educational materials with the Earth and climate as themes. An imprint of Sourcebooks eXplore, the children's non-fiction division of Sourcebooks. Founded 1979.

Dial Books – see Penguin Young Readers

Doubleday – see Penguin Random House

Dover Publications
1325 Franklin Ave, Ste 250, Garden City NY 11530
website https://store.doverpublications.com/
Facebook www.facebook.com/doverpublications
X @doverpubs
Instagram @doverpublications

Activity books, novelty books, picture books, fiction for children 5–8 and 9–12 years, teenage fiction, series fiction, reference, plays, religion, poetry, audio and CD-Roms. Also adult non-fiction. Will consider unsolicited MSS but write for guidelines. Founded 1941.

EDCON Publishing Group
9316 East Raintree Drive, Suite 120, Scottsdale, AZ 85260
tel +1 800-826-4740
email info@edconpublishing.com
website www.edconpublishing.com

Supplemental instructional materials for use by education professionals to improve reading and maths skills. Includes early reading, *Classics* series, *Easy Shakespeare*, fiction and non-fiction, reading diagnosis and vocabulary books. Founded 1970.

Eerdmans Publishing Company
4035 Park East Court SE, Grand Rapids, MI 49546
tel +1 616-459-4591
website www.eerdmans.com
Facebook www.facebook.com/eerdmans
X @eerdmansbooks
Instagram @eerdmans
President & Publisher Anita Eerdmans

Independent publisher of a wide range of religious books, from academic works in theology, biblical studies, religious history and reference to popular titles in spirituality, social and cultural criticism and literature. Founded 1911.

Eerdmans Books for Young Readers
website www.eerdmans.com/youngreader

Picture books, biographies and middle-reader fiction and non-fiction. Publishes 18–22 books a year. Stories that celebrate diversity, stories of historical significance and stories that relate to current issues are of special interest. Accepts unsolicited submissions. Send to Acquisitions Editor; responds in four months only to submissions of interest. For illustrations, send photocopies or printed media and include a list of previous illustrated publications. Send to Art Director. Samples will be kept on file and not returned.

Enchanted Lion Press
248 Creamer Street, Studio 4, Brooklyn, New York, NY 11231
website https://enchantedlion.com/
Facebook www.facebook.com/enchantedlion
X @EnchantedLion
Bluesky @EnchantedLion.bsky.social
Publisher Claudia Zoe Bedrick

An independent children's book publisher of illustrated books from around the world. Founded 2003.

Encyclopaedia Britannica
325 North La Salle Street, Suite 200, Chicago, IL 60654-2682
tel +1 312-347-7159
email contact@eb.com
website www.britannica.com
Facebook www.facebook.com/BRITANNICA
X @Britannica
Instagram @Britannica

Encyclopaedias, reference books, almanacs, videos and CD-Roms for adults and children 5–15+ years. Founded 1999.

Enslow Publishers
40 Industrial Road, Box 398, Berkeley Heights, NJ 07922
tel +1 800-398-2504
email customerservice@enslow.com
website www.enslow.com
Ceo Roger Rosen

Provides fiction and non-fiction content across the K-12 space. Aims to inspire readers to become lifelong learners. Imprint West 44 Books. Owned by Rosen Publishing. Founded 1976.

Evan-Moor Educational Publishers
10 Harris Court, Suite C-3, Monterey, CA 93940
tel +1 800-714-0971
email marketing@evan-moor.com
website www.evan-moor.com
Ceo Judy L. Harris

Educational materials for parents and teachers of children (3–12 years): activity books, textbooks, how-to books and CD-Roms. Subjects include maths, geography, history, science, reading, writing, social studies, art and craft. Publishes approx. 50 titles each year and has over 500 in print. Fewer than 10% of books are by first-time authors. Query or submit outline, table of contents and sample pages. Responds to queries in two months and MSS in four months. See website for submission guidelines. For illustrations, send résumé, samples and tearsheets to the Art Director. Primarily uses b&w material. Founded 1979.

Farrar, Straus Giroux Books for Young Readers
175 Fifth Avenue, New York, NY 10010
website https://us.macmillan.com/fsg/

Books for toddlers through to YA: picture books, fiction and non-fiction for all ages, and poetry (occasionally). Publishes 70 hardcover originals plus 10 paperback reprints each year and has approx. 500 titles in print. Approx. 10% of books are by first-time authors. No unsolicited MSS. An imprint of Macmillan Children's Publishing Group. Founded 1946.

The Feminist Press
365 Fifth Avenue, Suite 5406, New York, NY 10016
website www.feministpress.org
Facebook www.facebook.com/feministpress
X @feministpress
Publisher Margot Atwell

Cutting-edge fiction, activist non-fiction, literature in translation, hybrid memoirs and children's books. Publishes 12 to 15 books a year. Founded 1970.

Flux
2297 Waters Drive, Mendota Heights, MN 55120
tel +1 888-417-0195
email submissions@northstareditions.com
website www.fluxnow.com
Facebook www.facebook.com/FluxBooks
Instagram @fluxbooks
Managing Editor Meg Gaertner

YA in all genres. Particularly interested in out-of-the-box narratives in a unique voice. See website above for submission guidelines. Accepts electronic submissions only. Open to submissions during the following reading periods: February–March, June–July and October–November. Submissions sent outside of these periods will be deleted unread. Flux is an imprint of North Star Editions. Founded 2006.

Free Spirit Publishing
6325 Sandburg Road, Suite 100, Golden Valley, MN 55427
tel +1 612-338-2068
email acquisitions@freespirit.com
website www.freespirit.com
Facebook www.facebook.com/freespiritpublishing
X @freespiritbooks

Non-fiction materials for children and teens, parents, educators and counsellors. Specialises in self-help materials for kids and teens which empower young people and promote positive self-esteem through improved social and emotional health. Topics include: self-esteem and self-awareness, stress management, school success, creativity, friends and family, peacemaking, social action and special educational needs (i.e., gifted and talented, children with learning differences). Authors are expert educators and mental health professionals who have been honoured nationally for their contributions on behalf of children. Founded 1983.

Fulcrum Publishing
7333 W Jefferson Ave, Ste. 225, Lakewood, CO 80235
email orders@fulcrumbooks.com
website www.fulcrumbooks.com
Facebook www.facebook.com/Fulcrumbooks
X @fulcrumpublishing

Independent publisher for children exploring conservation, American culture, civics and the American West. Founded 1965.

Gale, part of Cengage Group*
27555 Executive Drive, Suite 270, Farmington Hills, MI 48331
tel +1 800-877-4253
website www.gale.com
Facebook www.facebook.com/GaleCengage
X @galecengage

Education publishing for libraries, schools and businesses. Serves the K–12 market with the Gale imprint. Founded 1954.

Gecko Press
241 First Avenue North, Minneapolis, MN 55401
tel +1 612-332-3344
email geckopress@lernerbooks.com
website www.geckopress.com

Facebook www.facebook.com/geckopress
X @geckopress
Instagram @geckopress
Publisher-at-Large Rachel Lawson

Children's books: picture books, junior fiction and non-fiction. Translates and publishes award-winning children's books from around the world and a small number of own titles. Selects books strong in story, character, illustration and design. An imprint of Lerner Publishing Group. See website for submission guidelines. Founded 2005.

Gibbs Smith

570 N Sportsplex Drive, Kaysville, UT 84037
tel +1 800-835-4993
email info@gibbs-smith.com
website www.gibbs-smith.com
Facebook www.facebook.com/gibbssmithbooks
X @gibbssmithbooks
Instagram @gibbssmithbooks

An employee-owned, independent publisher of home reference, cookery, non-fiction and children's books. The Gibbs Smith Education division is the nation's leading publisher of state history programmes. All unsolicited queries, submissions and correspondence should be via email. Responds only to projects of interest. Founded 1969.

Gryphon House

PO Box 10, 6848 Leon's Way, Lewisville, NC 27023
tel +1 800-636-0928
email info@gryhonhouse.com
website www.gryphonhouse.com
Facebook www.facebook.com/gryphonhouseinc
X @GryphonHouse
Instagram @ghbooks
President Rebecca Berlin

Early childhood (0–8 years) resource books for teachers and parents. Looking for books that are developmentally appropriate for the intended age group, are well researched and based on current trends in the field, and include creative, participatory learning experiences with a common conceptual theme. Send query and/or a proposal. Founded 1971.

Hachai Publishing

527 Empire Boulevard, Brooklyn, New York, NY 11225
tel +1 718-633-0100
email info@hachai.com
website www.hachai.com
Facebook www.facebook.comhachai-publishing
X @haichaipub

Jewish books for children 0–8+ years. Welcomes unsolicited MSS. Specialises in books for children 2–4 years and 3–6 years. Looking for stories that convey the traditional Jewish experience in modern times or long ago, traditional Jewish observance and positive character traits. Founded 1988.

Hachette Book Group*

1290 Avenue of the Americas, New York, NY 10104
tel +1 212-364-1100
website www.hachettebookgroup.com
Facebook www.facebook.com/HachetteUS
X @HachetteUS
Instagram @hachetteus
Chairman Michael Pietsch, *Ceo* David Shelley

Publishing groups: Grand Central Publishing; Hachette Audio; Hachette Nashville; Little, Brown and Company; Little, Brown Books for Young Readers; Orbit; Perseus Books and Workman. Imprints: Grand Central: Balance, Forever, Forever Yours, Legacy Lit, Twelve and Vision. Hachette Nashville: Center Street, Ellie Claire, FaithWords, Worthy Books and WorthyKids. Little, Brown and Company: Back Bay Books; Little, Brown Audio; Little, Brown Spark; Mulholland Books; and Voracious. Little, Brown Books for Young Readers: LB Kids, LB Ink, Christy Ottaviano Books and JIMMY Patterson. Orbit: Redhook. Perseus Books: Avalon Travel, Basic Books, Black Dog & Leventhal, Bold Type Books, Hachette Books, Hachette Go, Moon Travel, PublicAffairs, Rick Steves, RP Studio, Running Press, Running Press Kids and Seal Press. Founded 1996.

Handprint Books

413 Sixth Avenue, Brooklyn, New York, NY 11215–3310
tel +1 718-768-3696
email cmf@handprintbooks.com
website www.handprintbooks.com
Publisher Christopher Franceschelli

A range of children's books: picture and story books through to YA fiction. Welcomes submissions of MSS for works ranging from board books to YA novels. For novels, first query interest on the subject and submit a 7,500-word max. sample. Accepts MSS on an e-submission basis only. Artwork should be sent as small jpg files. Artists' website addresses may also be submitted. No series fiction, licensed character (or characters whose primary avatar is meant to be as licences), 'I-Can-Read'-type books or titles intended primarily for mass merchandise outlets. Imprints: Blue Apple, Handprint Books and Ragged Bears Founded 2000.

HarperCollins Publishers*

195 Broadway, New York, NY 10007
tel +1 212-207-700 0
website https://corporate.harpercollins.com/us/
X @HarperCollins
President & Ceo Brian Murray

For children, publishes fiction (literary and juvenile poetry) and non-fiction (education and history). No unsolicited material; all submissions must come through a literary agent. HarperCollins Children's Books imprints: Allida, Amistad, Clarion Books,

Greenwillow Books, Harper, Harper Alley, Heartdrum, Quill Tree Books, Storytide, Versify and Walden Pond Press. Founded 1817.

History Compass
25 Leslie Road, Auburndale, MA 02466
tel +1 617-332-2202
email info@historycompass.com
website www.historycompass.com

Publishes historical fiction for younger readers. Publishes *Get a Clue!* (grades 2–8) and *Adventures in History* series (grades 4–8). Other series include *Perspectives on History* (grades 5–12+) and *Researching American History* (8–15 year-olds and ESL students). Founded 1990.

Histria Books
7181 N Hualapai Way Suite 130-86, Las Vegas, NV 89166
email info@histriabooks.com
website https://histriabooks.com/
Facebook www.facebook.com/HistriaBooks
X @histriabooks
Instagram @histriabooks
Director Kurt Brackob

Children's non-fiction. Imprints: Addison & Highsmith, Center for Romanian Studies, Guadium, Histria Academic, Histria Kids, Prende Publishing and Vita Histria. Founded 1996.

Holiday House*
50 Broad Street, Ste 301, New York, NY 1000
tel +1 212-688-0085
email info@holidayhouse.com
website www.holidayhouse.com
Facebook www.facebook.com/HolidayHouseBks
X @holidayhousebks
Instagram @holidayhousebks

General fiction for children. Publishes about 60 picture books, 10 young reader, 10 middle reader and 30 YA titles each year. Approx. 20% of books are by first-time authors. Send entire MSS. Only responds to projects of interest. Will review MS/illustration packages from artists: send MS with dummy and colour photocopies. Imprints: Margaret Ferguson Books and Neal Porter Books. Founded 1935.

Houghton Mifflin Harcourt
3 Park Avenue, Floor 19, New York, NY 10016
tel +1 212-598-5730
website www.hmhco.com
Facebook www.facebook.com/houghtonmifflinharcourt
X @hmhco
Instagram @houhtonmifflinharcourt
Ceo Jack Lynch

Reference, fiction and non-fiction for adults and young readers. Also educational content and solutions for K–12 teachers and students. Divisions include Center for Model Schools (formerly ICLE), Heinemann and NWEA. Founded 1832.

Center for Model Schools
Dedicated to ensuring that every child attends a model school.

Heinemann
Provides professional resources and a provider of educational services for teachers, kindergarten through college.

NWEA
Provides assessment and learning solutions for educators.

Impact Publishers
5674 Shattuck Avenue, Oakland, CA 94609
tel +1 805-466-5917
email customerservice@newharbinger.com
website www.newharbinger.com/about-us/impact-publishers
Facebook www.facebook.com/newharbinger
X @newharbinger
Instagram @new-harbinger-publications

Psychology and self-improvement books and audio tapes for children, families, organisations and communities. Only publishes non-fiction books that serve human development and are written by highly respected psychologists and other human service professionals. Rarely publishes authors outside of the USA. See website for guidelines. Imprint of New Harbinger Publications. Founded 1970.

Jolly Fish Press
2297 Waters Drive, Mendota Heights, MN 55120
tel +1 888-417-0195
email publicity@northstareditions.com
website https://northstareditions.com/jolly-fish-press/

Publishes new voices in middle-grade fiction. Imprint of North Star Editions. Founded 2011.

Just Us Books, Inc.
395 Pleasant Valley Way, Suite B, West Orange, NJ 07052
tel +1 973-672-7701
email info@justusbooks.com
website https://justusbooks.com/
Publishers Cheryl Hudson, Wade Hudson

Publishers of Black-interest books for young people, including preschool materials, picture books, biographies, chapter books and YA fiction. Focuses on Black history, Black culture and Black experiences. Currently accepting queries for YA titles, targeted to readers 13–16 years. Work should contain realistic, contemporary characters, compelling plot lines that introduce conflict and resolution, and cultural authenticity. Also considers MSS for picture books and middle-reader chapter books. Send a query letter, one-to-two page synopsis and a brief author biography that includes any previously published work, plus an sae. Imprint: Sankofa Books. Founded 1988.

Kaeden Books
PO Box 16190, Rocky River, OH 44116
tel +1 800-890-7323
email info@kaeden.com
website www.kaeden.com
Facebook www.facebook.com/kaedenpublishing
X @kaedenbooks
Instagram @kaeden-publishing

Educational publisher specialising in early literacy books and beginning chapter books. See website for when open to submissions and guidelines for submissions. Founded 1986.

Kane Press – see Astra Publishing House

Alfred A. Knopf – see Penguin Random House

Lee & Low Books
381 Park Avenue South, Room 1401, New York, NY 10016
tel +1 212-779-4400
email general@leeandlow.com
website www.leeandlow.com
President Tom Low

Children's book publisher specialising in multicultural literature that is relevant to young readers. Focuses on fiction, non-fiction and poetry for children 5–12 years, for middle graders and YA 13–18 years. Of special interest are realistic fiction, historical fiction and non-fiction with a non-white protagonist, a distinct voice or unique approach. Does not consider folktales or animal stories. Offers two writing contests per year for debut picture book writers and novelists. Writers of colour and/or of Native nations are especially encouraged to submit. Imprints: Bebop Books, Children's Book Press, Cinco Puntos Books, Dive Into Reading, Lee & Low, Lee & Low Games, Shen's Books and Tu Books. Please visit website to see current guidelines and needs. Potential authors will be contacted by email or phone within six months if interested. Founded 1911.

Lerner Publishing Group
241 First Avenue North, Minneapolis, MN 55401
tel +1 800-328-4929
email info@lernerbooks.com
website www.lernerbooks.com
Publisher Adam Lerner

Independent publisher of children's books for K–12 schools and libraries: picture books, fiction for children 5–8 and 9–12 years, teenage fiction, series fiction and non-fiction. Subjects include biography, social studies, science, sports and curriculum. Publishes approx. 300 titles each year and has about 1,500 in print. Publishing Group includes: Carolrhoda Books, Carolrhoda LAB, Darby Creek, ediciones Lerner, First Avenue Editions, Gecko Press (page 69), Graphic Universe, Kar-Ben Publishing, Lerner Publications, Lerner Classroom, Lerner Digital, Millbrook Press, Twenty-First Century Books and Zest Books. Lerner Publisher Services partners include: Anderson Press, Big & Small, Cheriton Children's Books, Creston Books, Full Tilt Press, Hungry Tomato, Intergalactic Afikoman, JR Comics, Knowledge Books, Lantana Publishing, Live Oak Media, Lorimer Children's & Teens, Maverick Arts Publishing, New Frontier Publishing, Page Education Foundation, Planting People Growing Justice Press, Quarto Library, Red Chair Press, Ruby Tuesday Books, Souring Kite Books and We Do Listen. No unsolicited submissions for any imprint. Founded 1959.

Lightbox Learning Books
276 5th Avenue, Suite 704 #917, New York, NY 10001
tel +1 866-649-3445
website https://openlightbox.com/
Facebook www.facebook.com/learnwithlightbox
X @lightboxedu
Instagram @learnwithlightbox

Educational publisher: children's non-fiction titles. Founded 1979.

Little, Brown and Company Books for Young Readers
1290 Avenue of the Americas, New York, NY 10104
tel +1 212-364-1100
website https://www.hachettebookgroup.com/imprint/little-brown-books-for-young-readers
President Sally Kim, Editorial Director Denise Roy

Picture books, chapter books, and middle grade and young adult fiction and non-fiction. Founded 1926.

LB Kids
website www.hachettebookgroup.com/imprint/little-brown-books-for-young-readers/lb-kids
Novelty and board books.

LB Ink
website www.hachettebookgroup.com/imprint/little-brown-books-for-young-readers/little-brown-ink
Graphic novels and graphic non-fiction.

Christy Ottaviano Books
website www.hachettebookgroup.com/imprint/little-brown-books-for-young-readers/christy-ottaviano-books
Publisher Christy Ottaviano

Imprint of author-illustrators encompassing literary and commercial fiction and non-fiction from pre-shool to YA.

JIMMY Patterson Books
website www.hachettebookgroup.com/imprint/little-brown-books-for-young-readers/jimmy-patterson

Founded by James Patterson, publishes Patterson's children's books and others that fit the style and genre.

Margaret K. McElderry Books – see Simon & Schuster Children's Publishing Division

McGraw-Hill Professional*
1325 Avenue of the Americas, 7th Floor, New York, NY 10019
website www.mhprofessional.com
Facebook www.facebook.com/mcgrawhilleducation
X @MHEducation
Ceo Simon Allen

Divisions and imprints: Business, Education and Test Prep, International Marine and Ragged Mountain Press, Medical and Open University Press. To find individual editorial contacts check website. Founded 1966.

Macmillan Publishers*
120 Broadway, New York, NY 10271
tel +1 646-307-5151
email press.inquiries@macmillanusa.com
website https://us.macmillan.com/
Facebook www.facebook.com/MacmillanUS
X @MacmillanUSA

Imprints for children: Macmillan Children's Publishing Group, FSG Books for Young Readers, Feiwel & Friends, First Second, Holt Books for Young Readers, Kingfisher, Neon Squid, Odd Dot, Priddy Books, Roaring Brook, Starscape/Tor Teen, Square Fish, Swoon Reads and Young Listeners. Founded 1843.

Mitchell Lane Publishers
2001 S.W. 31st Avenue, Hallandale, FL 33009
tel +1 800-223-3251
email customerservice@mitchelllane.com
website https://mitchelllanepub.com/
President Phil Comer

Non-fiction and fiction titles for young readers, middle readers and YA. Imprints: EZ Readers, Little Mitchie, en Español, mlp pbk and MLP Fiction. Founded 1962.

Thomas Nelson Publisher*
PO Box 141000, Nashville, TN 37214
tel +1 800-251-4000
email publicity@thomasnelson.com
website www.thomasnelson.com

Bibles, religious, non-fiction and fiction general trade books for adults and children. Owned by HarperCollins Publishers. Founded 1798.

North Star Editions
2297 Waters Drive, Mendota Heights, MN 55120
website www.northstareditions.com
Facebook www.facebook.com/northstareditions
X @nseditions
Instagram @northstareditions

Publishes Flux (page 69), a YA fiction imprint, and Jolly Fish Press (page 71), a middle-grade fiction imprint. Other imprints include: Apex, Focus Readers, Little Blue House, North Star Classroom, North Star Kids and Press Box Books. Founded 1939.

NorthSouth Books
600 Third Avenue, 2nd Floor, New York, NY 10016
tel +1 917-699-2079
website www.northsouth.com
Facebook www.facebook.com/NorthSouthBooks
X @NorthSouthBooks
Instagram @northsouthbooks
Publisher Herwig Bitsche, *Managing Director* Andie Krawcyzk, *Editorial Director* Alisha Berger, *Senior Editor* Alex Robertson

Publishes 25–30 titles a year including Spanish/bilingual titles under their imprint Ediciones NorteSur. Publishes fresh, original, picture books with universal themes that could appeal to children 3–8 years. Accepting agented picture book submissions from authors and illustrators. Guidelines on submissions: accepts picture book MSS (1,000 words or less). Typically, does not acquire rhyming texts (although have been exceptions for simple/original text). Authors do not need to include illustrations. Illustrators can send work for consideration via postcards/pdfs emailed to: submissions@northsouth.com. Founded 1961.

The Overlook Press – see Abrams Books for Young Readers

Richard C. Owen Publishers
PO Box 585, Katonah, NY 10536
tel +1 914-232-3903
website www.rcowen.com
X @RichardOwen43
Publisher Richard C. Owen

Books for grades K–6. Books for young learners: seeks high-interest stories that children 5–7 years can read by themselves. Interested in original, realistic, contemporary stories, as well as folktales, legends and myths of all cultures. Non-fiction content must be supported with accurate facts. Length: 45–1,000 words. Also beginning chapter books up to 3,000 words. Founded 1982.

Pearson Education*
One Lake Street, Upper Saddle River, NJ 07458
tel +1 201-236-7000
email communications@pearsoned.com
website www.pearson.com/en-us.html
Facebook www.facebook.com/PearsonNorthAmerica
X @PearsonNorthAm
Instagram @pearsonofficial

Educational secondary publisher of scientifically researched and standards-based instruction materials for today's grade 6–12 classrooms. Subjects include: arts, mathematics, modern and classical languages, science, social studies, careers and technology. Part of the Curriculum Division of Pearson Education, Inc. Founded 1966.

Pelican Publishing
990 N. Corporate Drive, Suite 100, New Orleans, LA 70123
tel +1 504-684-8976
email editorial@pelicanpub.com
website www.arcadiapublishing.com/pages/pelican-publishing
Publisher & President Scott Campbell

Gulf South children's books. Email a query letter, outline if chapter book and résumé. No unsolicited MSS for chapter books. Most young children's books are 32 illustrated pages when published so their MSS will be 1,100 words maximum. Proposed books for middle-grade readers (8+ years) should be at least 90 pages. Brief books for readers under 9 years may be submitted in their entirety. Founded 1926.

Penguin Random House*
1745 Broadway, New York, NY 10019
tel +1 212-782-9000
website www.penguinrandomhouse.com
X @PenguinUSA
Ceo Nihar Malaviya

Consists of 300 independent imprints and brands, more than 15,000 new print titles and close to 800 million print, audio and ebooks. Committed to publishing children's fiction and non-fiction print editions, and is a pioneer in digital publishing. Book brands include storied imprints such as Doubleday, Viking and Alfred A. Knopf (USA); Ebury, Hamish Hamilton and Jonathan Cape (UK); Plaza & Janés and Alfaguara (Spain); and Sudamericana (Argentina); as well as the international imprint DK. Founded 2013.

Penguin Young Readers*
1745 Broadway, New York, NY 10019
tel +1 212-366-2000
website www.penguin.com/children
Facebook www.facebook.com/penguinkidsbooks
X @penguinkids
President Jen Loja

Publishes under a wide range of imprints and trademarks including: Kathy Dawson Books, Dial Books, Dutton, Grosset & Dunlap, Kokila, Nancy Paulsen Books, Penguin Workshop, Philomel, Puffin, G.P. Putnam's Sons, Razorbill, Speak, Viking and Frederick Warne. Penguin Young Readers is a division of Penguin Group, a Penguin Random House company. Founded 1935.

Puffin – see Penguin Young Readers

Quarto Publishing Group – Walter Foster Publishing
100 Cummings Center, Suite 265D Beverly, MA 01915
tel +1 978-282-9590
email walterfoster@quarto.com
website www.walterfoster.com
Group Publisher Anne Landa, *Senior Managing Editor* Karen Julian

Instructional art books for children and adults. Also art and activity kits for children. A division of Quarto Publishing Group US. Imprint of The Quarto Group. Founded 1976.

Random House Children's Books*
1745 Broadway, New York, NY 10019
tel +1 212-782-9000
website www.rhcbooks.com, www.randomhouse.com/teachers
President & Publisher Barbara Marcus

An English-language children's trade book publisher. Creates books for preschool children through YA readers, in all formats from board books to activity books to picture books, graphic novels, novels and non-fiction. Imprints: Alfred A. Knopf, Anne Schwartz Books, Beginner Books, Bright Matter Books, Crown, Delacourt Press, Doubleday, Dr Seuss, Dragonfly Books, Ember, Golden Books, Joy Revolution, Labyrinth, Little Tiger, Make Me A World, Random House Books for Young Readers, Random House Graphic, Random House Studio, Rodale Kids, Step into Reading, The Princeton Review, Underlined, Wendy Lamb Books and Yearling Books. Part of Penguin Random House. Founded 1925.

Razorbill – see Penguin Young Readers

Roaring Brook Press
120 Broadway, New York, NY 10271
tel +1 646-600-7861
website https://us.macmillan.com/publishers/roaring-brook-press/
Publisher Jennifer Besser

Picture books, chapter books, novels and graphic novels in fiction and non-fiction for young readers, 0–18 years. Publishes about 70 titles a year. Does not accept unsolicited MSS or submissions in print or digital. Division of Holtzbrink Publishers. Part of Macmillan Children's Publishing Group. Founded 2002.

Running Press Group
123 South Broad Street, Fl 27, Philadelphia, PA 19107
email perseus.promos@perseusbooks.com
website www.runningpress.com
Facebook www.facebook.com/runningpressbooks
X @running_press
Publisher Shannon Connors Fabricant

General non-fiction, science, history, children's fiction and non-fiction, cookbooks, pop culture, lifestyle and illustrated gift books. Imprint of Hachette Book Group. Founded 1972.

Running Press Kids
Picture books, activity books, YA fiction. Publisher of the *Doodles* series.

Sasquatch Books
1904 Third Avenue, Suite 710, Seattle, WA 98101
tel +1 206-467-4300
email custserv@sasquatchbooks.com
website www.sasquatchbooks.com
Facebook www.facebook.com/SasquatchBooksSeattle
X @sasquatchbooks
Instagram @sasquatchbooks

Non-fiction children's. Will consider queries and proposals from authors and agents for new projects that fit into the company's West Coast regional publishing programme. Imprints: Little Bigfoot (children's), Sasquatch Adult and Spruce Books. Founded 1986.

Scholastic*
557 Broadway, New York, NY 10012
tel +1 212-343-6100
email news@scholastic.com
website www.scholastic.com
Facebook www.facebook.com/scholastic
X @scholastic

Children's, education and technology. Divisions: Scholastic Book Clubs, Scholastic Book Fairs, Scholastic Education, Scholastic Magazines and Scholastic Trade. Imprints include: Acorn, AFK (Away From Keyboard), Branches, Cartwheel Books, Chicken House, Graphix, Klutz, Little Shepherd Books, Orchard Books, Point, PUSH, Scholastic Early Learners, Scholastic en español, Scholastic Nonfiction, Scholastic Focus, Scholastic Paperbacks and Scholastic Press. Founded 1920.

Simon & Schuster Children's Publishing Division*
1230 Avenue of the Americas, New York, NY 10020
tel +1 212-698-7200
website www.simonandschuster.com/kids
President & Publisher Jon Anderson

Preschool to YA, fiction and non-fiction, trade, library and mass market. Division of Simon & Schuster. Founded 1924.

Aladdin Books
Vice-President & Publisher Valerie Garfield
Publishes commercial middle-grade fiction with an emphasis on adventure, fantasy and humour. Accepts query letters with proposals for middle-grade series and single-title fiction, middle-grade and commercial non-fiction. Send MS for the attention of the Submissions Editor.

Atheneum Books for Young Readers
Vice-President & Publisher Justin Chanda
Picture books, chapter books, mysteries, biography, sci-fi, fantasy, graphic novels, middle-grade and YA fiction and non-fiction. Covers preschool–YA. Approx. 10% of books are by first-time authors. No unsolicited MSS. Send query letter only. Responds in one month.

Beach Lane Books
website www.simonandschusterpublishing.com/beach-lane
Publisher Allyn Johnston
Picture books.

Boynton Books
Board books by author and illustrator, Sandra Boynton.

Little Simon
website https://simonandschusterpublishing.com/little-simon/
Facebook www.facebook.com/simonkids
X @simonskids
Instagram @simonkids
Publisher Valerie Garfield
Books for young children.

Margaret K. McElderry Books
Vice-President & Publisher Justin Chanda
Picture books, easy-to-read books, fiction (8–12 years and YA), poetry and fantasy. Covers preschool to YA. Approx. 10% of books are by first-time authors. No unsolicited MSS. Responds in three months. Samples returned with sae.

Denene Millner Books
website https://simonandschusterpublishing.com/denenemillnerbooks/
Publisher Denene Millner
YA and children's books by Denene Milner.

Salaam Reads
email salaamreads@simonandschuster.com
website https://simonandschusterpublishing.com/salaam-reads/
Senior Editor Deeba Zargarpur
YA, middle-grade and young children's books that explore Muslim life. For submission guidelines, see website.

Simon & Schuster Books for Young Readers
Vice President & Publisher Justin Chandu
Publishes a wide range of contemporary, commercial, award-winning fiction and non-fiction that spans every age of children's publishing. Seeking challenging and psychologically-complex YA novels; also imaginative and humorous middle-grade fiction. No unsolicited MSS. Send query letter only. Responds in two months.

Simon Spotlight
website https://simonandschusterpublishing.com/simon-spotlight/
Editorial Director Siobhan Ciminera
Imprint for developing licensed properties and brands.

Books

Sourcebooks
PO Box 4410, Naperville, IL 60567-4410
website www.sourcebooks.com
Publisher & Ceo Dominique Raccah

Independent publisher in a wide variety of genres including fiction, romance, children's, YA, gift/calendars and college-bound. Imprints include: Bloom Books, Cumberland House, Dawn Publications (Dawn Publications), Duo Press, Hometown World, Little Pickle Press, Poisoned Pen Press, Put Me In The Story, Simple Truths, Sourcebooks, Sourcebooks Casablanca, Sourcebooks eXplore, Sourcebooks Fire, Sourcebooks Jabberwocky, Sourcebooks Kids, Sourcebooks Landmark, Sourcebooks Young Readers and Sourcebooks Wonderland. Founded 1987.

Tachyon Publications
1459 18th Street, #139, San Francisco, CA 94107
tel +1 415-285-5615
email Tachyon@tachyonpublications.com
website https://tachyonpublications.com/
Facebook www.facebook.com/Tachyon-Publications
X @TachyonPub
Publisher Jacob Weisman

Smart sci-fi, fantasy and horror, as well as occasional mysteries, memoirs, YA and literary fiction. Founded 1995.

Teacher Created Resources
12621 Western Avenue, Garden Grove, CA 92841
tel +1 800-662-4321
email custserv@teachercreated.com
website www.teachercreated.com

Educational materials. See website for guidelines. Founded 1977.

Tor Publishing Group
120 Broadway, 22nd Floor, New York, NY 10271
tel +1 212-388-0100
email enquiries@tor.com
website https://torpublishinggroup.com/
Facebook www.facebook.com/torbooks
X @torbooks
Instagram @torbooks

YA and middle-grade. Genres: sci-fi, fantasy, mystery, thriller, horror, romance, magical realism, speculative fiction, humour and contemporary fiction. Founded 1980.

Bramble
website https://torpublishinggroup.com/imprints/bramble/
Facebook www.facebook.com/BrambleRomance
X @brambleromance
Instagram @brambleromance

Fantasy romance.

Forge
website https://torpublishinggroup.com/imprints/forge-books/
Facebook www.facebook.com/forgereads
X @forgereads
Instagram @forgereads

General fiction, both contemporary and historical, thrillers, mysteries and suspense, Westerns and Americana, military fiction and non-fiction.

Nightfire
website https://torpublishinggroup.com/imprints/tor-nightfire/
Facebook www.facebook.com/tornightfire
X @tornightfire
Instagram @tornightfire

Fantasy horror.

Tor
website https://torpublishinggroup.com/imprints/tor-books/
Facebook www.facebook.com/torbooks
X @torbooks
Instagram @torbooks

Sci-fi and fantasy.

Tor Teen/Starscape
website https://torpublishinggroup.com/imprints/tor-teen/
Facebook www.facebook.com/torteen
X @torteen
Instagram @torteen

Sci-fi and fantasy for YA.

Tordotcom Publishing
website https://torpublishinggroup.com/imprints/tordotcom/
Facebook www.facebook.com/tordotcompub
X @tordotcompub
Instagram @tordotcompub

Fantasy sci-fi.

Union Square & Co.
33 East 17th Street, New York, NY 10003
tel +1 800-367-9692
email editorial@sterlingpublishing.com
website www.unionsquareandco.com
Facebook www.facebook.com/UnionSqandCo
X @unionsqandco
Instagram @unionsqandco

Children's board books, picture books and non-fiction. Imprints: Boxer Books, EM & Friends, Flashkids, Hearst Books, Knock Knock, Puzzlewrright Press, Sparknotes, Sterling Ethos, Union Square & Co. and Union Square Kids. Part of the Hachette Book Group. Founded 1949.

Viking – see Penguin Young Readers

Albert Whitman & Company
250 South Northwest Highway, Suite 320, Park Ridge, Illinois, IL 60068

Children's book publishers overseas

tel +1 847-232-2800
email mail@albertwhitman.com
website www.albertwhitman.com

Books that respond to cultural diversity and the special educational needs and concerns of children and their families (e.g., divorce, bullying). Also novels for middle-grade readers, picture books and non-fiction for children 2–12 years. For submissions guidelines see website. Founded 1919.

WordSong – see Astra Publishing House

Workman Publishing Company*

1290 Avenue of the Americas, New York, NY 10104
email info@workman.com
website www.workman.com
Facebook www.facebook.com/workmanpublishing
X @workmanpub
Instagram @workmanpub
Publisher Lia Ronnen

General non-fiction for adults and children. Imprints Algonquin, Algonquin Young Readers, Artisan, Page-a-Day, Storey Publishing, Timber Press, Workman, Workman Calendar and Workman Kids. Owned by Hachette Book Group. Founded 1968.

World Book

180 North LaSalle Street, Suite 900, Chicago, Illinois 60601
tel +1 800-729-5800
email international@worldbook.com
website www.worldbook.com
Facebook www.facebook.com/WorldBook
X @worldbookinc
Instagram @worldbookinc

Publisher of authoritative, age-appropriate and reliable print and digital educational and reference materials for children and adults. Trade companies include children's book publisher Bright Connections Media and Incentive Publications which specialises in supplemental resources for children and teachers. Founded 1917.

WorthyKids

6100 Tower Circle, Suite 210, Franklin, TN 37067
email IdealsInfo@hbgusa.com
website www.worthykids.com
Facebook www.facebook.com/worthykidsbooks
X @worthykidsbooks
Instagram @worthykidsbooks

Picture books, board books and middle-grade novels for children (1–12 years). Email to request submission guidelines. Digital submissions not accepted. Due to the large volume of submissions, the company only responds to those of interest to the publishing programme. Potential authors should become familiar with current books before submitting. Agents welcome. Imprint of the Hachette Book Group. Founded 1944.

Yen Press

150 W 30th Street, 19th floor, New York, NY 10001
email yenpress@hbgusa.com
website www.yenpress.com
Facebook www.facebook.com/yenpress
X @yenpress

Graphic novels and manga in all formats for all ages. Founded 2006.

Children's audio publishers

Many of the audio publishers listed below are also publishers of print and electronic books.

Audible
email partners-uk@audible.co.uk
website www.audible.co.uk
X @audibleuk
Instagram @audible_uk

Producer and seller of digital audio entertainment, including fiction and non-fiction audiobooks for adults and children. Publishers interested in exploring business opportunities with Audible may email the address above, or find out more about turning print books into audiobooks at www.acx.com. Founded 1995; acquired by Amazon 2008.

Audiobooks.com
email acquisitions@audiobooks.com
website www.audiobooks.co.uk/
Facebook www.facebook.com/audiobookscom
X @audiobooks_com
Instagram @audiobooks_com

Subscription audiobook service offering a wide range of fiction and non-fiction genres, as well as some children's titles. Publishers interested in having their titles included in the company's library may get in touch via the email address above.

Barrington Stoke – see page 38

BookBeat
email info@bookbeat.com
website www.bookbeat.com/uk
X @BookBeatUK
Instagram @bookbeat

Digital streaming service for adult and children's audiobooks across a variety of fiction and non-fiction genres. Monthly subscription model (from £6.99). Owned by Bonnier. Founded 2017.

The Educational Company of Ireland
Ballymount Road, Walkinstown, Dublin D12 R25C, Republic of Ireland
tel +353 (0)1 450 0611
email info@edco.ie
website www.edco.ie
Facebook www.facebook.com/EdcoIreland

Irish language CDs. Trading unit of Smurfit Kappa Group – Ireland. Founded 1910.

W. F. Howes Ltd
Unit 5, St George's House, Rearsby Business Park, Gaddesby Lane, Rearsby, Leicester LE7 4YH
tel (01664) 423000
email info@wfhowes.co.uk
website www.wfhowes.co.uk
X @wfhowes
Instagram @wfhowes

Audiobook publisher, distributing its content through all leading consumer and library vendors. Authors include bestselling writers such as Jilly Cooper, Val McDermid, Mark Dawson and David Nicholls. UK subsidiary of RBmedia. Founded 1999.

Kobo
website www.kobo.com/gb/en
X @kobo

Audiobook streaming service, for a monthly fee. Offers fiction, non-fiction, adult, children's and YA titles.

Naxos AudioBooks
5 Wyllyotts Place, Potters Bar, Herts. EN6 2JD
tel (01707) 653326
email info@naxosaudiobooks.com
website www.naxosaudiobooks.com
X @NaxosAudioBooks
Managing Director Anthony Anderson

Recordings of classic literature, modern fiction, non-fiction, drama and poetry. Founded 1994.

Penguin Random House UK Audio (Children's)
Penguin Studios, One Embassy Gardens, Nine Elms Lane, London SW8 5BL
website www.penguin.co.uk/company/publishers/audio

Contemporary and classic literature for younger listeners. Authors include Malorie Blackman, Charlie Higson, Roald Dahl and Eoin Colfer.

Children's book packagers

Many illustrated books are created by book packagers, whose particular skills are in the areas of book design and graphic content. In-house editors match up the expertise of specialist writers, artists and photographers who usually work on a freelance basis.

Global Blended Learning
Singleton Court, Wonastow Road, Monmouth NP25 5JA
tel 0845 5480261
email hello@globalblendedlearning.com
website www.globalblendedlearning.com

Primary, secondary academic education (geography, science and modern languages) and co-editions (travel guides, gardening and cookery). Multimedia (CD-Rom programming and animations). Opportunities for freelancers. Founded 1985.

Hawcock Books
242 Bloomfield Road, Bath BA2 2AX
tel 07976 708720
website www.hawcockbooks.co.uk
Instagram @davidhawcock

Designs and produces highly creative and original pop-up art and 3D paper-engineered concepts. Most experience is in developing, providing editorial assistance, printing and manufacturing pop-up books and novelty items for the publishing industry. Also undertakes demanding commissions from the advertising world for model-making, point-of-sale and all printed 3D aspects of major campaigns.

I Am a Bookworm*
35 Manor Close, Templecomb, Somerset BA8 0LA
email hello@iamabookworm.co.uk
website www.iamabookworm.co.uk
Facebook www.facebook.com/iamabookwormuk
Instagram @i_amabookworm

An independent publisher of children's novelty books, board books, activity books and light books for children aged 0–5 years. Founded 2011.

Little People Books
The Home of BookBod, Knighton, Radnorshire LD7 1UP
tel (01547) 520925
email littlepeoplebooks@thehobb.tv
website www.littlepeoplebooks.co.uk
Director Grant Jessé

Packager of audio, children's educational textbooks and digital publications. Parent company: Grant Jessé UK. Founded 2018.

Orpheus Books
2 Hewlett Place, Cheltenham, Glos. GL52 6DQ
tel (01993) 774949
email info@orpheusbooks.com
website www.orpheusbooks.com, www.Q-files.com
Executive Directors Nicholas Harris, Sarah Hartley

Produces children's books and ebooks for the international co-editions market: non-fiction and reference. The creators of Q-files.com, the online educational resource for schools and libraries. Founded 1993.

The Puzzle House
Ivy Cottage, Battlesea Green, Stradbroke, Suffolk IP21 5NE
tel (01379) 384656
email puzzlehouse@btinternet.com
website www.thepuzzlehouse.co.uk
Partners Roy Preston, Sue Preston

Editorial service creating crossword, quiz, puzzle and activity material for all ages. Founded 1988.

Red Bird Publishing*
Kiln Farm, East End Green, Brightlingsea, Colchester, Essex CO7 0SX
tel (01206) 303525
email info@red-bird.co.uk
website www.red-bird.co.uk

Innovative children's activity packs and books produced with a mix of techniques and materials. Activity books, novelty books, picture books, painting and colouring books, teaching books, posters, hobbies, nature and the environment, science. Age groups: preschool, 5–10 and 10–15. Authors are specialists in their fields. No unsolicited MSS. Founded 1998.

Storymix
The Wenta Business Centre Colne Way, Watford, Hertfordshire WD24 7ND
email jasmine@storymix.co.uk
website www.storymix.co.uk
Facebook www.facebook.com/storymixstudio
X @storymixstudio
Director Jasmine Richards

Multi-award-winning inclusive children's fiction studio. Works with publishers to create fiction for children and teens, and offers paid collaboration opportunities to writers and illustrators of colour. Actively looking to add emerging and established talent to our database of creatives. To apply: www.storymix.co.uk/write-for-us. Founded 2019.

Toucan Books
128 Aldersgate Street, Suite 106, London EC1A 4AE
tel 020-7250 3388
website www.toucanbooks.co.uk
Contact Ellen Dupont

International co-editions: editorial, design and production services. Non-fiction only. Founded 1985.

David West Children's Books
11 Gebe Road, Barnes, London SW13 0DR
tel 020-8876 1405
email lynn@davidwestbooks.com
website www.davidwestchildrensbooks.com
Proprietor David West, *Partner* Lynn Lockett

Packagers of highly illustrated children's non-fiction books. Specialises in science, art, geography, history, sport and flight. Produces 20 titles each year. Opportunities for freelancers. Founded 1986.

Working Partners
9 Kingsway, 4th Floor, London WC2B 6XF
tel 020-7841 3939
email enquiries@workingpartnersltd.co.uk
website www.coolabi.com/books
Managing Director Chris Snowdon

Creators of children's and YA fiction: animal fiction, fantasy, horror, historical fiction, detective, magical and adventure. Unable to accept any submissions. Pays advance and royalty. Retains copyright on all works. Selects writers from samples based on specific brief provided. Part of the Coolabi Group. Founded 1995.

Children's bookshops

The bookshops in the first part of this list specialise in selling new children's books and are good places for writers and illustrators to check out the marketplace. Most of them are members of the Booksellers Association and are well known to publishers. A list of secondhand and antiquarian children's bookshops follows. Independent Booksellers Week usually takes place each year in June or July, but check online for further information: https://booksellers.org.uk/campaigns/independentbookshopweek.

The Alligator's Mouth
2A Church Court, Richmond, Surrey TW9 1JL
tel 020-8948 6775
email info@thealligatorsmouth.co.uk
website www.thealligatorsmouth.co.uk
Facebook www.facebook.com/alligatorsmouth
Bluesky @alligatorsmouth.bksy.social
Instagram @alligatorsmouth
YouTube @thealligatorsmouth519

Independent children's bookshop stocking works for all ages from babies to teenagers. Runs regular story-time sessions, book clubs and author events.

Bags-of-Books
1 South Street, Lewes BN7 2BT
tel (01273) 479320
email bagsofbooks@bags-of-books.co.uk
website https://bags-of-books.co.uk
Facebook www.facebook.com/leweschildrensbookshop
X @BagsofBooks
Instagram @bagsofbookslewes
Proprietor Rachel Givertz

Independent children's bookshop situated within a 16th-century building. Extensive selection of fiction and non-fiction from babies up to 18 years. Hosts author visits and runs a books-for-schools programme.

Bert's Books
54 Goodwin Court, Swindon SN1 4BB
email bert@bertsbooks.co.uk
website https://bertsbooks.co.uk/
Facebook www.facebook.com/BertsBooks/
Instagram @bertsbooks
Founder Alex Call

Online bookshop with a focus on diversity. Offers books in monthly bundles, including YA titles. A bricks-and-mortar shop opened in May 2022. Founded 2019.

Blackwell's Bookshop, Children's Dept
Blackwell's Bookshop, 48-51 Broad Street, Oxford OX1 3BQ
tel (01865) 333611
email oxford@blackwell.co.uk
website https://bookshop.blackwells.co.uk/bookshop/home
Facebook www.facebook.com/blackwellbooks
Instagram @blackwelloxford

Based on the first floor of Blackwell's flagship bookshop, the children's department stocks over 10,000 titles for younger readers.

The Blue House Bookshop
10 Bootham, York YO30 7BL
tel (01904) 927838
email karen@thebluehousebookshop.co.uk
website www.thebluehousebookshop.co.uk
Facebook www.facebook.com/bluehousebookshop
Instagram @thebluehousebookshop
Proprietor Karen Walker

Independent specialist children's bookshop offering a range of fiction and non-fiction to young readers. Supplies books for schools and can advise on book choices and runs creative writing courses for children. Founded 2019.

The Book Burrow @ Aardvark Books & Café
The Bookery, Manor Farm, Brampton Bryan, Bucknell SY7 0DH
email aardvaark@btconnect.com
website www.aardvark-books.com
Facebook www.facebook.com/AardvarkBooks
Instagram @aardvarkbookscafe
Proprietors Sheridan and Sarah Swinson

Bookshop and play space with a castle, enchanted forest, pirate cabin and princess seat. Extensive range of books, mostly new but some secondhand and rare. Children's events throughout the year. BA member.

Book Corner
24 Milton Street, Saltburn-by-the-Sea TS12 1DG
tel (01287) 348010
email jenna@bookcornershop.co.uk
website www.bookcornershop.co.uk
Facebook www.facebook.com/p/Book-Corner-Saltburn
Instagram @bookcornersaltburn
Proprietor Jenna Warren

Independent bookshop with dedicated children's section, stocking books for all ages from babies to young adults. Also stocks fiction and non-fiction for adults, and hosts author visits.

The Book House
93 High Street, Thame, Oxon OX9 3HJ
tel (01844) 213032
email office@thebookhousethame.co.uk
website www.thebookhousethame.co.uk
Instagram @the_book_house
Proprietor Brian Pattinson

Specialises in children's books alongside a wide range of titles for all ages.

The Book Nook
First Avenue, Hove BN3 2FJ
tel (01273) 911988
email info@booknookuk.com
website www.booknookuk.com
X @booknookhove
Proprietors Vanessa Lewis, Julie Ward

Specialist children's bookshop set in a child-friendly environment with author events, regular story-time, book clubs, cafe and pirate ship. Previous winner of Children's Bookseller of the Year category at *The Bookseller* Industry Awards.

Booka Bookshop and Café
26–28 Church Street, Oswestry, Shrops. SY11 2SP
tel (01691) 662244
email hello@bookabookshop.co.uk
website www.bookabookshop.co.uk
Facebook www.facebook.com/bookabookshop
Instagram @bookabookshop
Proprietors Carrie and Tim Morris

Independent bookshop and cafe offering a wide range of books, cards and gifts. Hosts a regular programme of author talks and signings, organises themed events, runs bookclubs and works with schools and local libraries. Previous winner of Independent Bookshop of the Year category at *The Bookseller* Industry Awards. A second branch was opened in Bridgnorth in 2023.

Bookbugs and Dragon Tales
41 Timberhill, Norwich NR1 3LA
tel (01603) 964022
email leanne@bookbugsanddragontales.com
website https://bookbugsanddragontales.com
Facebook www.facebook.com/people/Bookbugs-and-Dragon-Tales/100039029726821/
X @Bookbugsdragon1
Instagram @bookbugsdragontales
Proprietors Dan and Leanne Fridd

Independent bookshop offering a wide range of books and events for children and their families. An events space that hosts bookclubs, classes and other interactive opportunities is also available. Founded 2019.

The Broadway Bookshop
6 Broadway Market, London E8 4QJ
tel 020-7241 1256
email books@broadwaybookshophackney.com
website www.broadwaybookshophackney.com
Proprietor Jane Howe

General independent bookshop specialising in literary fiction with a strong selection of children's books for all ages.

Browns Books For Students
5 Redcliff Road, Melton, East Yorkshire HU14 3RS
tel (01482) 384660
email customer.services@brownsbfs.co.uk
website www.brownsbfs.co.uk
Facebook www.facebook.com/BrownsBFS
X @BrownsBFS
Instagram @BrownsBFS

Supplier of books and educational resources across the UK and internationally. Offers next-day delivery, an extensive ebook catalogue, in-house stock-selection team and shelf-ready book servicing.

Chicken & Frog
30 Crown Street, Brentwood, Essex, CM14 4BA
tel (01277) 230068
email info@chickenandfrog.co.uk
website https://chickenandfrog.com
Instagram @thechickenandfrog
Proprietors Jim and Natasha Radford

Independent bookshop and tuition centre. Weekly sensory rhyme time, creative writing and handwriting sessions. Regular events for children and families, book clubs (in person and online), school supply and consultation.

Children's Bookshop (Huddersfield)
80 Lidget Street, Lindley, Huddersfield HD3 3JR
tel (01484) 658013
email hello@childrensbookshuddersfield.co.uk
website www.childrensbookshuddersfield.co.uk
Facebook www.facebook.com/ChildrensBookshopHuddersfield
X @Lindley_Books
Instagram @Lindley_Books
Contact Nicola Lee

Independent bookshop stocking a wide selection of titles for children, from picture books to YA. Also offers services to schools.

Children's Bookshop (Muswell Hill)
29 Fortis Green Road, London N10 3HP
tel 020-8444 5500
email admin@childrensbookshoplondon.co.uk
website www.childrensbookshoplondon.com
Instagram @childrensbookshoplondon
Proprietor Sanchita Basu De Sarkar

Oldest-running children's bookshop in the UK. Stocks approximately 12,000 titles and 25,000 books for children from newborn to young adult. Offers services for schools, charities, and individual companies, as well as an events programme. Named

Children's Bookseller of the Year and Book Retailer of the Year at the 2024 British Book Awards. Founded 1974.

DRAKE The Bookshop
26–27 Silver Street, Stockton-on-Tees TS18 1SX
tel (01642) 909970
email books@drakethebookshop.co.uk
website www.drakethebookshop.co.uk
Instagram @drakethebookshop
Proprietors Richard Drake, Melanie Greenwood

Independent bookshop with strong children's offering, as well as events and initiatives aimed at young readers and schools. The shop runs three children's book groups (Teen Readers, High-Rise Readers and Young Bookworms) and offers a selection of dyslexia-friendly titles. Founded 2015.

ebb & flo bookshop
12 Gillibrand Street, Chorley, Lancs. PR7 2EJ
tel (01257) 262773
email diane@ebbandflobookshop.co.uk
website www.ebbandflobookshop.co.uk
Facebook www.facebook.com/ebbandflobookshop
X @ebbandflobooks
Instagram @ebbandflobookshop
Proprietor Diane Gunning

Small independent bookshop stocking books for children and adults, plus toys, cards and gifts. Supplies books to local schools, including library restocks and topic boxes. Hosts a regular story-time for preschool children (call ahead to book) as well as author events and holiday workshops.

The Edinburgh Bookshop
219 Bruntsfield Place, Edinburgh EH10 4DH
tel 0131 447 1917
email mail@edinburghbookshop.com
website www.edinburghbookshop.com
Bluesky @edinburghbookshop.bsky.social
Instagram @theedinburghbookshop
Proprietor Marie Moser

Four-time Scottish Independent of the Year winner. Events programme includes author visits, book signings, book clubs and a story-time for the under fives. Founded 2007.

Far from the Madding Crowd
20 High Street, Linlithgow EH49 7AE
tel (01506) 845509
email info@maddingcrowdlinlithgow.com
website www.maddingcrowdlinlithgow.com
Facebook www.facebook.com/FarFromTheMaddingCrowdLinlithgow
Instagram @maddingcrowdbooks

Independent bookshop with eclectic range of titles, including a dedicated children's and preschool section. Strong influence from Scottish publishers. Free storytelling on Fridays at 2pm: tickets must be booked in advance.

Foggie Toddle Books
18 North Main Street, Wigtown DG8 9HL
tel (01988) 402896
email hello@foggietoddlebooks.co.uk
website https://foggietoddlebooks.co.uk
Facebook www.facebook.com/FoggieToddleBooks
X @FoggieToddler
Instagram @foggietoddlebooks
Proprietor Jayne Baldwin

Independent children's bookshop and publisher named after the Scots word for bumblebee. Stocks new, second-hand and vintage books for age groups from babies to YA. Also produces and sells a range of Bookshelf and Booktown products designed by local artists. Member of the Booksellers Association.

Ginger and Pickles Children's Bookshop
51 St Stephen Street, Edinburgh EH3 5AH
tel 0131 285 8069
email hello@gingerandpicklesbookshop.com
website www.gingerandpicklesbookshop.com
Facebook www.facebook.com/gingerandpickleschildrensbookshop
Instagram @gingerandpicklesbookshop

Independent children's bookshop catering for young readers from birth to teenage years. Founded 2020.

Golden Hare Books
68 St Stephen Street, Edinburgh EH3 5AQ
tel 0131 225 7755
email mail@goldenharebooks.com
website www.goldenharebooks.com
X @GoldenHareBooks
Instagram @goldenharebooks
Owner Mark Jones

Stocks books for readers of all ages. Holds regular book groups and author events. Runs a book subscription and offers bookshop membership. Previous winner of Independent Bookshop of the Year at the British Book Awards.

Harbour Bookshop
2 Mill Street, Kingsbridge, Devon TQ7 1ED
tel (01548) 857233
email hello@harbourbookshop.co.uk
website www.harbourbookshop.co.uk
X @HarbourBookshop
Instagram @harbourbookshop_devon
Proprietor Jane Fincham

Well-established independent bookshop with an extensive range of children's books for all ages. Next-day delivery available. Also works with primary and secondary schools and holds children's book events and celebrations.

Heath Educational Books
Willow House, Willow Walk, Whittaker Road, Sutton, Surrey SM3 9QQ
tel 020-8644 7788

email orders@heathbooks.co.uk
website www.heathbooks.co.uk
Proprietor Richard Heath

Supplies books to schools and teachers throughout Europe. Large showroom.

Jacqson Diego Story Emporium
444 London Road, Westcliff on Sea, Essex SS0 9LN
tel (01702) 344262
email stories@jacqsondiego.com
website www.jacqsondiego.com
Facebook www.facebook.com/jacqsondiego
Instagram @jacqsondiego

Independent bookshop specialising in fiction and non-fiction for children and young people. Regular events include bookclubs and writing groups. Also runs bespoke book-related services for schools and nurseries, including author visits, library audits, consultancy and workshops. BA member. Founded 2011.

Letterbox Library
Unit 13 Mainyard Studios, 679 High Road, Leyton E10 6RA
tel 020-8534 7502
email info@letterboxlibrary.com
website www.letterboxlibrary.com

Online booksellers, specialising in children's books that celebrate inclusion, equality and diversity. Curated Book Packs for schools. Founded 1983.

Madeleine Lindley
Book Centre, Broadgate, Broadway Business Park, Chadderton, Oldham OL9 9XA
tel 0161 683 4400
email books@madeleinelindley.com
website www.madeleinelindley.com
Facebook www.facebook.com/madeleinelindleyltd
Instagram @teacher_books

Supplies books to schools and nurseries, provides information services and runs open days and training courses for teachers. Hosts author/publisher events for teachers and children.

The Little Bookshop
47 Harrogate Road, Chapel Allerton, Leeds LS7 3PD
tel 0113 212 3465
email hello@thelittlebookshopleeds.co.uk
email skipton@thelittlebookshops.co.uk
website www.thelittlebookshopleeds.co.uk
Facebook www.facebook.com/thelittlebookshopleedskids
Instagram @thelittlebookshops
Proprietor Cheryl Duffield

Independent bookshop specialising in books for children; also stocks adult titles. Carries a wide range of diverse and inclusive books and also provides subscription service for readers of all ages. Holds regular author events for children and adult. Also has regular storytimes outside of school holidays, and daily craft sessions weekdays during school holidays (see website for dates). Offers services for schools, including creating and ordering book lists, as well as arranging author events and book fairs. Founded 2017; a second location opened in Skipton in November 2023.

The Mainstreet Trading Company
Main Street, St Boswells, Scottish Borders TD6 0AT
tel (01835) 824087
email books@mainstreetbooks.co.uk
website www.mainstreetbooks.co.uk
Facebook www.facebook.com/Mainstreet.Trading.Company
X @mainstreethare
Instagram @mainstreethare
Proprietors Rosamund and Bill de la Hey

General bookshop with a particular focus on children's books. Previous winner of Independent Bookseller of the Year category at the *The Bookseller* Industry Awards.

Moon Lane Ink CIC
300 Stanstead Road, London SE23 1DE
tel 020-3489 7030
email info@moonlaneink.co.uk
website www.moonlaneink.co.uk
Facebook www.facebook.com/moonlaneink
Instagram @moonlaneink

Community-interest company dedicated to raising equality in children's books; equality of access, representation and roles in the publishing industry. In addition to a bookshop, runs enterprise workshops for children as well as a range of events. Founded 2018.

Nickel Books
9 Merlin Close, Sittingbourne ME10 4TY
tel 07731 152089
email enquiries@nickelbooks.co.uk
website www.nickelbooks.co.uk
Instagram @nickelbooks
Proprietor Andrea Don

Mail-order, school books supply, visits, fairs, fetes and events. Specialises in children's books, from birth to teenage; also books for parents.

Norfolk Children's Book Centre
Church Lane, Alby, Norwich NR11 7HB
tel (01263) 761402
email marilyn@ncbc.co.uk
website https://ncbc.co.uk, https://uk.bookshop.org/shop/norfolkcbc
Facebook www.facebook.com/norfolkchildrensbooks
Instagram @norfolkchildrensbooks

Independent bookshop established for over 35 years, specialising in books for children and teachers. Offers storytelling and school booksales within East Anglia,

Children's bookshops

as well as nationwide conference book displays and mail order. Other services include school library assessment and rejuvenation, and topic-based approval collections.

Octavia's Bookshop
24 Black Jack Street, Cirencester, Glos. GL7 2AA
tel (01285) 650677
email info@octaviasbookshop.co.uk
website www.octaviasbookshop.co.uk
X @octaviabookshop
Proprietor Octavia Emanuel

Independent bookshop in which more than half the stock is dedicated to children's titles, from buggy books to teen fiction and classics. Previous winner of the Children's Independent Bookseller of the Year category at The Bookseller Industry Awards.

The Oundle Bookshop
13 Market Place, Oundle, Peterborough PE8 4BA
tel (01832) 273523
email oundlebookshop@colemangroup.co.uk

General bookshop with extensive children's selection.

Owl and Pyramid
8 Fore Street, Seaton EX12 2LA
tel (01297) 598030
email owl.pyramid@yahoo.com
website https://uk.bookshop.org/shop/OwlandPyramid
Facebook www.facebook.com/owlpyramid
Instagram @owlandpyramidbookshop

Independent bookshop with a strong children's section. Founded 2014.

Peters
120 Bromsgrove Street, Birmingham B5 6RJ
tel 0121 666 6646
website www.peters.co.uk
Facebook www.facebook.com/Petersbooksbirmingham
Instagram @petersbooks

Specialist supplier of children's books and library furniture to schools, nurseries, academies and public libraries, with a book and furniture showroom, online ordering facilities and ten specialist children's librarians. Also provides a library design and installation service and hosts regular professional development events for teachers and librarians, featuring speakers, authors and illustrators.

Pickled Pepper Books
10 Middle Lane, Crouch End, London N8 8PL
tel 020-3632 0823
email info@pickledpepperbooks.co.uk
website www.pickledpepperbooks.co.uk
Instagram @pickledpepperbooks
Proprietors Urmi Merchant, Steven Pryse

Family-run specialist children's bookshop with a weekly programme of events for preschoolers including baby sensory sessions, music and drama sessions, Italian and French classes, and storytimes. After-school events include both middle-grade and teen book clubs, and illustration classes. Also hosts regular interactive author events, as well as theatre and puppet shows in the upstairs performance space. Works closely with nurseries, primary schools and secondary schools to deliver bespoke author talks and books to support reading.

The Rabbit Hole
21 Market Place, Brigg DN20 8LD
tel (01652) 408534
email therabbithole.brigg@outlook.com
website www.therabbitholebrigg.com
Facebook www.facebook.com/therabbitsbrigg
X @Therabbits21
Instagram @therabbithole.brigg
Proprietors Mel and Nick Webb

Community-focused bookshop with a strong emphasis on children's books. Also runs events and workshops and offers a range of services to schools. Named Midlands Bookshop of the Year at the 2023 British Book Awards. Founded 2017.

The Rocketship Bookshop
5 Bridge Street, Salisbury SP1 2ND
tel (01722) 237172
email info@rocketshipbookshop.co.uk
website https://rocketshipbookshop.co.uk
Facebook www.facebook.com/rocketshipbookshop

Independent bookshop catering predominantly for children and young people, although a specially curated selection of adult titles is also available. Hosts author events and supports Salisbury Literary Festival.

Round Table Books
97 Granville Avenue, Brixton Village, London SW9 8PS
email bookshop@roundtablebooks.co.uk
website www.roundtablebooks.co.uk
Instagram @roundtablebooks
Co-Directors Aimée Felone, Meera Ghanshamdas, Jasmina Bidé

Inclusive children's bookshop, launched by the Knights Of, an independent children's publisher that champions authors and illustrators from diverse backgrounds. Founded 2019.

The Secret Bookshelf
38 Scotch Quarter, Carrickfergus BT38 7DP
tel 07936 000078
website https://uk.bookshop.org/shop/Thesecretbookshelf
Facebook www.facebook.com/TheSecretBooks1
X @Thesecretbooks1
Instagram @secretbookshelfcarrickfergus

Independent bookstore of the year (Ireland), stocking a range of adult general fiction and with a dedicated children's room stocking fiction and non-fiction from age 0–12. YA books also stocked, with an emphasis on Irish authors and their work. Children's events, including storytelling and crafting, held during holiday periods. Adult events held throughout the year, including book groups, writing space and classes, and special events.

Seven Stories – see page 309

Seven Stories Bookshop
30 Lime Street, Ouseburn Valley, Newcastle upon Tyne NE1 2PQ
tel 0300 330 1095
email bookshop@sevenstories.org.uk
website www.sevenstories.org.uk/shop
X @7Stories

Independent specialist children's bookshop. Offers a hand-picked range of books to browse, from board and picture books to middle-grade, non-fiction books and YA titles, as well as a handful of poetry and plays. Hosts frequent author and illustrator events, alongside a monthly Book Club.

Simply Books
228 Moss Lane, Bramhall, Cheshire SK7 1BD
tel 0161 439 1436
email enquiries@simplybooks.info
website www.simplybooks.info
Facebook www.facebook.com/p/Simply-Books
Instagram @simplybookshq
Editor Co-owner and Managing Director Ben Johns, *Co-owner and Director* Karen Johns

Independent bookshop with strong children's selection, as well as regular events and reading groups for adults and children readers.

Storytellers, Inc.
7 The Crescent, St Anne's on Sea, Lytham St Anne's, Lancs. FY8 1SN
tel (01253) 781690
email info@storytellersinc.co.uk
X @storytellersinc
Proprietors Carolyn Clapham, Katie Clapham

Independent bookshop with dedicated children's section. Supplies books to local schools. Also runs a monthly book group for adults. Previous winner (North) in the Independent Bookshop of the Year category at *The Bookseller* Industry Awards. Founded 2010.

Tales On Moon Lane
21 Canterbury Rd, Whitstable CT5 4HJ
email info@talesonmoonlane.co.uk
website www.talesonmoonlane.co.uk
Instagram @talesonmoonlane
Proprietor Tamara Macfarlane

Specialist children's bookshop dedicated to improving equality in children's literature.

West End Lane Books
277 West End Lane, London NW6 1QS
tel 020-7431 3770
email info@welbooks.co.uk
website www.welbooks.co.uk
X @WELBooks
Instagram @westendlanebooks

Independent family-owned bookshop carrying fiction and non-fiction books and stationery. Specialises in signed and special edition books, and hosts occasional book launches and author talks. Also runs school events. Founded 1994.

Winstone's Hunting Raven Books
10 Cheap Street, Frome, Somerset BA11 1BN
tel (01373) 473111
email winstonebooks3@gmail.com
Facebook www.facebook.com/HuntingRavenBooks
X @HuntingRavenBks
Instagram @huntingravenbooks
Proprietor Wayne Winstone, *Manager* Tina Gaisford-Waller

Award-winning independent bookshop with extensive range of books and gifts for all ages and a strong children's section. Holds events and signings throughout the year. South-West Independent bookshop of the year 2020. Other Winstone's bookshops can be found in Sidmouth and Sherborne.

Wonderland Bookshop
64 Carolgate, Retford DN22 6EF
tel (01777) 948580
email hello@wonderlandbookshop.co.uk
website https://wonderlandbookshop.co.uk
Facebook www.facebook.com/WonderlandBookshop
X @Wonder_Bookshop
Instagram @wonderlandbookshop
Proprietor Helen Tamblyn-Saville

Specialist children's bookshop stocking titles for readers from birth to teens (also orders in titles for adults on request). Includes dyslexia-friendly and LGBTQ+ shelves. Also offers services for schools, including library advice, author visits (in person or online) and school wishlists. Named independent Bookshop of the Year (Midlands region) 2022 and Highly Commended Children's Bookshop of the Year 2022 at the British Book Awards. Founded 2019.

BOOKSELLERS FOR COLLECTORS

Blackwell's Rare Books
48–51 Broad Street, Oxford OX1 3BQ
tel (01865) 333555
email rarebooks@blackwells.co.uk
website https://blackwells.co.uk/rarebooks/
Instagram @blackwellrare

Deals in early and modern first editions of children's books, among other subjects.

Bookmark Children's and Illustrated Books

Orchard Close House, Wye Lane, Marlborough, Wiltshire SN8 1PJ
tel (01672) 512415 / 07788 841305
email leonora.f.smith@gmail.com
Contact Leonora Smith

Mail-order bookseller, specialising in books for collectors, ranging from antiquarian to modern. A wide range of first editions, novelty and illustrated books, chap-books, ABCs, annuals, etc. Also a selection of vintage toys, games, greetings cards and illustrated postcards, dolls and nursery china. Member of PBFA, selection of stock on PBFA website, occasionally exhibiting at PBFA book fairs in London, Bristol, York, Devizes, Brighton and Oxford. Established 1973 by Anne Excell.

The Children's Bookshop – Hay-on-Wye

Toll Cottage, Pontvaen, Hay-on-Wye, Herefordshire HR3 5EW
tel (01497) 821083
email sales@childrensbookshop.com
website https://childrensbookshop.com/
Facebook www.facebook.com/ChildrensBookshopHayOnWye

Second-hand and antiquarian children's books.

Henry Sotheran

4 Cecil Court, London WC2N 4HE
tel 020-7439 6151
email rh@sotherans.co.uk
website www.sotherans.co.uk
Facebook www.facebook.com/sotherans
Instagram @sotheranslondon

Large showroom with hundreds of important children's books spanning two centuries, specialising in first editions and illustrated works by pivotal artists. Opening hours: Mon–Fri 9:30am–6:00 pm. Two specialist catalogues issued annually, available free on request.

Stella & Rose's Books

Monmouth Road, Tintern, Monmouthshire NP16 6SE
tel (01291) 689755
email enquiry@stellabooks.com
website www.stellabooks.com
X @stellarosebooks

Specialists in rare, out-of-print children's and illustrated books, also carrying a large and varied general stock (over 25,000 books in stock). Stock available for sale via website. Specialist lists issued regularly. Open Tuesday to Sunday; see website for opening hours. Single items or collections purchased. Founded 1991.

Books, sites and blogs about children's books

These listings include some of the best print and online resources about children's books for readers, writers and illustrators.

BOOKS

The Oxford Companion to Children's Literature
by Daniel Hahn
Published by Oxford University Press (2015, 2nd edition)

An indispensable reference book for anyone interested in children's books. Over 900 biographical entries deal with authors, illustrators, printers, publishers, educationalists and others who have influenced the development of children's literature. Genres covered include myths and legends, fairy tales, adventure stories, school stories, fantasy, science fiction, crime and romance. This book is of particular interest to librarians, teachers, students, parents and collectors.

The Reading Bug – and how you can help your child to catch it
by Paul Jennings
Published by Penguin Books (2004)

Paul Jennings is a well-known children's author who explains, in his unique humorous style, how readers can open up the world through a love of books. He cuts through jargon to reveal simple truths about reading, which should enable adults to infect children with the reading bug.

Sticks and Stones: The Troublesome Success of Children's Literature from Slovenly Peter to Harry Potter
by Jack Zipes
Published by Routledge (2001)

Jack Zipes – translator of the Grimm tales, teacher, storyteller and scholar – questions whether children ever really had a literature of their own. He sees children's literature in many ways as being the 'grown-ups' version', a story about childhood that adults tell kids. He discusses children's literature from the 19th century moralism of Slovenly Peter (whose fingers get cut off) to the wildly successful *Harry Potter* books. Children's literature is a booming market but its success, this author says, is disguising its limitations. *Sticks and Stones* is a forthright and engaging book by someone who clearly cares deeply about what and how children read.

1001 Children's Books You Must Read Before You Grow Up
by Julia Eccleshare
Published by Cassell Illustrated (2009)

An introduction to the best of children's literature, ranging from international classics to contemporary writers. Reviews of each book are accompanied by line drawings and artwork from books themselves. A number of authors including Michael Morpurgo and Jacqueline Wilson also write about their favourite books. The reviews are ordered according to the book's publication date, from past to present, and age range of the reader.

The Ultimate Book Guide
Edited by Leonie Flynn, Daniel Hahn and Susan Reuben
Published by A&C Black (2009)

Over 700 entries covering the best books for children aged 8–12 years, from classics to more recently published titles. Funny, friendly and frank recommendations written for children by their favourite and best-known authors including Anthony Horowitz, Jacqueline Wilson, Celia Rees, Darren Shan, David Almond and Dick King-Smith. Plus features on the most popular genres.

The Ultimate First Book Guide
Edited by Leonie Flynn, Daniel Hahn and Susan Reuben
Published by A&C Black (2008)

Comprehensive reference to help children aged 0–7 years with their first steps into the world of books. Covers board books and novelty books, through to classic and contemporary picture books, chapter books and more challenging reads. It includes recommendations and features from top authors and experts in the field of children's books, including former Children's Laureate Michael Rosen, Tony Bradman, Malachy Doyle and Wendy Cooling. There are also special features on a variety of topics and themed lists, and a selection of cross-references to other titles children may enjoy.

Books, sites and blogs about children's books

The Ultimate Teen Book Guide
Edited by Daniel Hahn and Leonie Flynn
Published by A&C Black (2010, 2nd edn)

Listings of over 750 books that might interest teenage readers, recommended and reviewed by authors such as Melvin Burgess, Anthony Horowitz, Meg Cabot, Eoin Colfer and Philip Pullman. Reviews cover the classics to cult fiction, and graphic novels to bestsellers, and each is cross-referenced to other titles as suggestions of what to read next. The book also contains essays on areas of teenage writing including *Race in Young Adult Fiction* by Bali Rai and *Off the Rails* by Kevin Brooks. There are also the results of a national teen readers' poll, plus reviews from teen readers.

ONLINE

Armadillo
website www.armadillomagazine.co.uk

An online magazine about children's books, including reviews, interviews, features and profiles. New issues are posted at the end of March, June, September and December. It was founded in 1999 by author Mary Hoffman as a review publication for children's books.

BBC Bitesize
website www.bbc.co.uk/bitesize

Information about UK schools' curriculum. Useful for those wishing to write for educational publishers but also for keeping abreast of curricular topics.

The Bookbag
website www.thebookbag.co.uk

A UK-based website focused on great reviews about children's books, there are also booklists and information about book awards, as well as articles and author interviews.

Books for Keeps
website http://booksforkeeps.co.uk

Featuring a quarterly online magazine for children's books including book reviews and features.

The Bookseller
website www.thebookseller.com

A magazine for the publishing industry, sharing news on author deals, book launches and industry features to subscribers. Some content is available for free, including the fortnightly *Chapter and Verse: The Art of Selling Children's Books* podcast.

BookTrust
website www.booktrust.org.uk

Dedicated children's reading charity, this is a useful site for professionals working with young readers. Information on events, prizes, books, authors, etc.

BookTrust Great Books Guide
website www.booktrust.org.uk/book-recommendations/great-books-guide-2024-25

BookTrust's independent annual 'pick of the best' in children's paperback fiction published in the previous calendar year. It is designed to help parents and those interested in children's reading to select books for children, from babies to teenagers.

Branford Boase Award
website www.branfordboaseaward.org.uk

The website for the annual children's book award dedicated to debut children's writers and their editor. Includes a writing competition for young people.

The Carnegies
website https://carnegies.co.uk

This website follows the only UK children's book award where the winners are selected by specialist children's librarians. The website includes a 'shadowing' area for schools to leave their comments about the books, plus interviews with shortlisted authors. See page 336.

CBBC
website www.bbc.co.uk/cbbc

Website of the CBBC channel with games, activities and news for children.

The Children's Book Council
website www.cbcbooks.org

The Children's Book Council in the USA is dedicated to encouraging literacy and the enjoyment of children's books. The website includes reviews of children's books published in the USA, forthcoming publications and author profiles. A good site for checking out the US marketplace.

Children's Laureate
website www.booktrust.org.uk/what-we-do/childrens-laureate

Official website of the Children's Laureate with resources and activities for children.

Children's Literature
website http://childrenslit.com/

US website of the Children's Literature Comprehensive Database (CLCD), a subscription database with over 120,000 reviews of children's books. Plus links to US author and illustrator websites.

The Federation of Children's Book Groups

website http://fcbg.org.uk/

The FCBG runs an annual children's book award, judged by children, and a network of local groups for those interested in finding out more about children's books and authors. See page 311.

Goodreads for Children

website www.goodreads.com/genres/childrens

The Amazon-owned website supports consumer reviews about books for children that can be researched by categories including middle grade and picture books, etc.

The Horn Book

website www.hbook.com

US website hosting *The Horn Book Guide Online*, a comprehensive, fully searchable database of over 70,000 book titles and reviews for children and young adults (YA). Also includes a regular newsletter sharing an interview with an author or illustrator, *Authors & Illustrators talk with Roger*, and and a monthly e-newsletter for parents, *Notes from the Horn Book*.

National Literacy Trust

website www.literacytrust.org.uk

The organisation is focused on developing literacy among adults and children and its website documents its activities. See page 313.

Picture Book Den

website http://picturebookden.blogspot.com

An independent website created by professional children's authors based in the UK and Ireland where they share their passion for picture books, with blogs on getting published and creating picture books.

Quentin Blake Centre for Illustration

website https://qbcentre.org.uk

The brainchild of author and illustrator Quentin Blake, it celebrates all forms of illustration, runs regular talks and events and supports schools-based activities. See page 318.

ReadingZone

website https://readingzone.com

A magazine-style website, created with Arts Council support, dedicated to children's books including monthly book reviews by teachers and librarians as well as children, chapters to download, author interviews, news, activities and a regular newsletter. There are distinct areas for teachers, librarians, families, children and teenagers.

Scottish Book Trust

website www.scottishbooktrust.com

Information on books for children of all ages in Scotland plus a national programme of events with children's writers: author tours, festivals, writing competitions and exciting activities.

Seven Stories

website www.sevenstories.org.uk

The Seven Stories National Centre for Children's Books, based in Newcastle, provides regular events and exhibitions dedicated to children's literature which are highlighted on its website. See page 309.

The Story Museum

website www.storymuseum.org.uk

Stories from around the world to watch, hear, read and tell.

Toppsta

website https://toppsta.com

A children's book review website that invites children and adults to review books for children and teenagers.

Words & Pictures

website www.wordsandpics.org

The online magazine of SCBWI British Isles, an organisation of writers and illustrators of children's books, with advice on writing, illustrating, news, blogs and activities. See page 305.

World Book Day

website www.worldbookday.com

Providing a range of resources for children and teenagers, from writing and illustration masterclasses to quizzes, activities and reading ideas.

Inspiring writers

Making a writer

Sarah Crossan describes what led her to take her writing seriously, put her secret dream of being a writer into practice and – with time and resolve – achieve her goal.

I never thought a person like me could be a writer. I was an incredibly ordinary child, have become an even more ordinary adult and believed many untruths about writing and writers. Firstly, I didn't come from a family connected to the literati, which I perceived as a major problem, though at the time I probably hadn't even come across the word 'literati'. Secondly, I wasn't privately educated and didn't have anything close to a BBC newsreader's accent – grand drawback. Finally, and perhaps most importantly, I didn't own a serious-looking scarf. You know the ones. All proper artists own them.

When I went to university, to study Philosophy and Literature, my fears about what went into making a writer were compounded as I carefully stalked the creative writing students: they all seemed aloof, important and occasionally sad, hanging out in the humanities building, wearing oversized jumpers and, yes, their scholarly scarves.

After my undergraduate degree, convinced writing wasn't for me (and secretly hating all those creative writing students who'd spent three years smugly impersonating Margaret Atwood), I went off to study teaching. It was a way to make books a part of my daily life. And I was actually really good at it. The students fell in love with words and sentences, with poems and novels. I even convinced a class of hardened Shakespeare haters (one of whom offered to steal my car for £50 so I could pick up the insurance money!) to perform scenes from *Romeo and Juliet*, as well as partake in some Renaissance dancing. I loved teaching – my job was about books and kids, words and relationships.

Then came an afternoon that changed everything – a lesson that had an outcome missing from my planning notes. I was teaching poetry, encouraging students to write about their dreams, their hopes, how they saw their lives developing. I believed in those kids. I knew they could be anything they wanted to be if they just puffed out their chests and did some hard work. They wrote wonderful poems. They wrote moving poems. And then, at the end of the lesson, one child put up his hand and asked a question: 'Have you always wanted to be an English teacher, Miss?'. Now, a more sensitive person might have read some subtext into this, namely *'Why are you a teacher, Miss? You're terrible at your job.'* But I don't think that's what he meant. He genuinely wanted to know whether or not I'd lived my dreams, so shyly I explained that, as well as being a teacher, I wanted to be a writer, a poet and a novelist, but that I didn't think I quite had what it took. The boy frowned, as did a few other students, and angrily replied, 'Well you have a bit of cheek then, don't you, telling us to live our dreams when you haven't even done it yourself. Have you even tried?'

Despite being young, I was a strict teacher; I never tolerated rudeness, but in that moment I was dumbstruck – because he was right. Who was I to lecture them on bravery and risk when I had never taken myself nor my own desires seriously? Instead of asking him to leave the room, where I could speak to him about his tone of voice, I quietly said, 'You're right. I've been too afraid to try.'

On the basis of that very bald conversation, I applied to go back to university and study creative writing – which I did the very next year, annoying the head teacher who had to find a replacement for the next academic year at short notice.

And so I began to write. And I began to take my writing seriously. Rather than going to the cinema when friends asked, I started to say, 'Sorry, I can't. I'm writing.' When they seemed irritated by my resolve, I didn't care. If I wanted to achieve my dream of writing for a living, I had to believe in myself, otherwise no one else would. I found a way out of my shame and into a pattern of work that I loved.

That doesn't mean a contract came quickly; it didn't. It was another ten years of graft and fine-tuning my skills before I found an agent, listed in the *Writers' & Artists' Yearbook* in the children's section, who seemed to fit the bill. I sent her my book and astonishingly she took me on within days. We are still together, for better or for worse, and when I start to flounder and find myself wondering if I should pack it all in, she reminds me that I don't need anything to succeed except a dash of self-belief and a bit of hard work. Oh, and my serious writerly scarf, of course. Everyone needs one of those!

Sarah Crossan is the award-winning author of the young adult novel *One* (Bloomsbury 2015) which won the CILIP Carnegie Medal, the YA Book Prize, the CBI Book of the Year Award and the CLiPPA Poetry Award in 2016. Also published by Bloomsbury, her books *The Weight of Water* (2011) and *Apple and Rain* (2014) were both shortlisted for the CILIP Carnegie Medal. Her latest books are *Where The Heart Should Be* (Bloomsbury 2024), and her second novel for adults *Hey, Zoey* (Bloomsbury Circus 2024). Sarah was Laureate na nÓg, the Irish Children's Laureate, from 2018–20. Her books have been translated into more than 25 languages.

From dream to reality

Frank Cottrell-Boyce provides his own winning formula for writing success.

Infallible spell for transforming yourself into a successful children's writer ... (it worked for me)

1. Acquire copy of current *Children's Writers' & Artists' Yearbook*.
2. Riffle pages. Inhale deeply of the fragrance of future fulfilment.
3. Place volume prominently on kitchen table or other work surface. You will remark an immediate alteration in the atmosphere. This alteration is caused by certain properties inhering in the vivid hues of its cover.
4. If working in a public space, insert Post-it notes and other bookmarks in profusion. Recall that the more attention the book attracts the more power it generates.
5. At certain intervals you may refresh the spirit by opening the book. Do not select the page. Allow the book to offer certain pages to your attention.
6. If the book offers you those pages on which are written the names of agents, consider all their descriptions to assay which ones reverberate most mellifluously in your heart. Seek out their addresses on Google Street View that you may see their doorways. Remember that each of these doorways is a portal to another, richer world. While you know not yet which doorway you will take, picture yourself walking through the doorway with your manuscript in hand (see note 1 below).
7. If the book offers you the pages describing festivals, then consider those festivals – the green rooms wherein great steaming buckets of latte stand next to towers of cupcakes, where the conversation is polished so that the very air doth seem to shine. See, in your imagination, yourself bedecked with lanyard and shepherded by volunteers to the tent where eager children wait to hear you speak (see note 2).
8. If the book offers you the pages describing literary awards then inscribe in your imagination the name of your book beneath those of past winners (see note 3).
9. Before closing the volume always riffle and inhale. The air thus imbibed is of a special type and potency. It is called Inspiration.
10. Maintain these habits and observe these practices until your ends are obtained.

Notes:
1. So you do have to write the book first.
2. Or you won't have anything to read out from.
3. And when you've written it, give it a title.

Before we walked on the Moon we had to spend hundreds of years imagining it. Before I became a writer I spent a lot of time pretending to be a writer. The ostentatious use of the *Writers' & Artists' Yearbook* (WAYB) in public places was a big part of that pretence. But it also helped me turn that pretence into a reality. I had never met a writer or indeed anyone who wanted to be one. The book showed me that it wasn't a 'dream' that somehow 'came true' but a job that involved work and meetings and word counts and layouts and invoices.

All the pragmatic guidance it offered helped crystallise my thoughts and turn the dream into an ambition. When you think about it, that is magic.

Frank Cottrell-Boyce is an award-winning author and scriptwriter and the current Waterstones Children's Laureate. His children's books include *Millions* (*New York Times* bestseller and winner of the CILIP Carnegie Medal 2004), *Framed* (2005), *Cosmic* (2008), *Chitty Chitty Bang Bang Flies Again* (2011), two further *Chitty Chitty Bang Bang* titles, *The Astounding Broccoli Boy* (2015), *Runaway Robot* (2019), *Noah's Gold* (2021), *The Wonder Brothers* (2023) and *The Blockbusters!* (2025). All published by Macmillan Children's Books. In 2012 he won the Guardian Children's Fiction Prize for *The Unforgotten Coat* (Walker Books 2012). *Millions* was made into a movie by Oscar-winning director Danny Boyle. Frank has written scripts for *Doctor Who* and for a number of feature films, and also the script for the opening ceremony of the 2012 London Olympics.

A solitary dream

Bestselling YA author, Alice Oseman, details how she managed to secure an unexpected publishing deal in her late teens with help from the *Writers' & Artists' Yearbook*.

The story of my path to publication has always had an air of novelty: a 17-year-old schoolgirl writes a novel about a depressed 16-year-old, gets an agent at eighteen, and is published by nineteen. Around the time of publication, my adolescence was what most people wanted to talk about. Most interviews I gave were focused on the inspiring story of a 'teenage author', even landing me a spot on BBC Breakfast and in national newspapers. I don't deny it was an incredible sequence of events, and one for which I will be grateful for the rest of my life. Of course, at the time, I was mostly frustrated that people didn't want to talk with me about the actual content of the book.

Ten years on from the publication of *Solitaire*, I find myself looking back with more empathy towards those journalists and media professionals who were so awe-struck by my journey. Getting published so young, and so quickly, is rare. It's the ultimate dream of many a young writer. So how, exactly, had I managed to achieve this? There were no classes on how to become an author at school. I'd never even met an author before. But somehow, armed with just a manuscript, a dream and an internet connection, I had launched my career.

Throughout my youth, my writing was a secret. I didn't tell anybody I wrote stories, especially in secondary school, where it felt like a cringeworthy hobby that would send me plummeting down the social hierarchy. I didn't tell my parents, because then they would ask me questions about what I was writing, and I didn't want to talk with anyone about it. My writing was mine, not to be judged by anyone else, and it could be whatever I wanted it to be.

The urge to share my writing felt like it came out of nowhere, but it most likely grew from the academic and career pressures that British teens face at the age of sixteen. We had to begin considering A-level options, which would lead to degree choices, which would lead to a career, which would lead to – well, the rest of our lives. And suddenly I realised that the thing I would be most happy doing for the rest of my life was writing stories.

I began writing *Solitaire* for fun. It took me around five months to complete the first draft, and by the end of those five months, I fervently believed that this book was good. It was worthy of publication. I had a confidence in my writing that I – an anxious, shy teenager – had never felt about anything else in my life. I wanted to share my work. I wanted *Solitaire* to be published. I wanted to become an author. I wanted to try.

So, as a child of the digital age, I went online. I searched 'how to become an author' and read all the blog posts I could find. I made notes. I learned about 'literary agents' and 'slush piles' and 'querying'. I purchased the *Writers' & Artists' Yearbook 2013*, read through its articles many times over, and highlighted the agents I wanted to reach out to.

Soon I could see a path towards achieving my dream, but I also knew that if this didn't work out, life would roll on. I hoped for the best but had nothing to lose.

I'm sure you can guess the end of this story: I was very fortunate and had a positive response from one of the nine agents I contacted, who then helped me improve the book and eventually land a publication deal. That part of the story feels less important to discuss, because that's where 'luck' really comes in. Talent and skill is required, of course, but finding an agent who is looking for a book like yours requires a luck component. Things could easily have not worked out because I'd contacted the wrong people at the wrong time, which is why so many writers – published or not – stress the importance of persistence and determination in the querying process. I certainly like to imagine that if things hadn't worked out, I would still be writing, still be dreaming, and still be trying.

Because that's what I see when I look back at that time. A young writer who, all on her own, decided to try.

Finding the confidence to try is not easy, especially now. We are living in an age of information but also of convenience; a time where it is so much easier to look outwards and find distraction rather than look within at our own hopes and dreams. Acting upon those hopes and dreams requires grit, tenacity, perseverance and usually some boring admin, but it is ultimately an act of self-love. Going for your dreams and trying your best is powerful, no matter the outcome.

If there's one thing that I'd love for you to take away from my tale of teenage authordom, it's this: when it comes to dreaming of creative success, the only person who can make that happen is you. You must take the first step, and then the steps that follow. You must fight for your work, advocate for your talent, educate yourself and never give up. Do not bow down to self-doubt, to comparison, to distraction or to 'what ifs'.

You can make it happen. But only if you try.

Alice Oseman is an award-winning author, illustrator and screenwriter. Creator of the million-copy bestselling *Heartstopper* books (HarperCollins Children's Books 2018–) and their enormously popular Netflix adaptation, Alice has also written several standalone YA novels, including *Solitaire* (HarperCollins Children's Books 2014), *Radio Silence* (HarperCollins Children's Books 2016) and *Loveless* (HarperCollins Children's Books 2020).

Words are my happy place

Award-winning children's novelist Smriti Halls discusses how her love for words grew into a lifelong desire to write.

Words are my happy place. Playing with them, nudging them, giving them a little squeeze. From as far back as I can remember they've been my companions, filling me to the brim with joy. It wasn't much of a surprise, then, that they became the tools of my trade – as teacher, copywriter, staff writer and editor. Any excuse to keep tinkering. The surprising bit was that those same words started prodding at ME – playing with me, nudging me, giving *me* a little squeeze ... Soon they were filling me to the brim with stories of my own that I felt compelled to write – books that reflected my own passions, preoccupations and perspectives; stories I wanted the world to hear, written in my own voice.

Pursuing this path seemed neither sensible nor sane and, at first, I tried to ignore it, knowing full well that I didn't have the luxury of an office or even a desk at home – much less the idyllic writer's shed, den or hut to retreat to. But those mischievous words wouldn't let me go. I quickly realised that writing in my spare time, around a full-time job, daily commute and three gorgeous children, was not sustainable. And so, gathering all my courage, I plunged into the life of a full-time, freelance writer.

How I longed for a room of my own (frankly I'd have made do with a small cupboard) – just somewhere to shut the door and concentrate for five minutes together – but that simply wasn't an option. Instead, I focused on grabbing the moments I could, in the space that was available. I negotiated with my husband for some clear working days and accepted every offer of help. I paid for a childminder (and tried not to be put off by the sound of pound coins clinking into an invisible jar, for every word not written). And little by little, one by one, with comedic haphazardness, my books began to be written – at the library, in my sister's spare bedroom, on the train, in waiting rooms and coffee shops. I wrote at the kitchen table, kneeling up to the sofa, with babies asleep in the back of the car, whilst on holiday, and once (only once) I got out of bed and wrote the first draft of a picture book at three in the morning. On one memorable camping trip, I charged across several fields in the rain, was pursued by a bull and lost a shoe in a ditch – all in pursuit of a pub where I could use the WiFi to send off a manuscript. Naturally, the minute I got there, out of puff, dishevelled and smelling fragrantly of manure, the laptop ran out of charge.

It's now over ten years since my first picture book was published and, in that time, that has grown from one to over 50 titles – brought to life by a host of incredible illustrators. Some have seen success, others none at all, but I'm proud of every single one. Each is fingerprinted with love and is a snapshot of my life at a single moment. Together, they are a photo album of the joys, the tears – and the tantrums, too! The books I write are created right in the centre of my topsy-turvy, everyday life. That obviously brings significant challenges (*No, you may not build a den out of my proofs!*), but whenever I bemoan the lack of space to escape to, I remember that I wrote a Number One bestseller standing up in my living room with a child on one hip and another toddling on the floor – which helps lend a bit of perspective.

I'm humbled to know that some of the words I've written have walked alongside people in their deepest, most profound moments. They've been used in beauty and brokenness, used as marriage vows and as last rites; I sometimes wonder whether their creation, amidst the idiosyncrasies and imperfections of my own life, imbues them with something that speaks into the real-life moments of other people's lives. I don't know. What I *do* know is that not a word would have been written if I'd waited for what I foolishly believed were the ideal circumstances.

So, my advice? a) Don't waste time trying to get everything in order – embrace the chaos and roll with it. b) Enjoy your work and the pleasure it brings you. c) Even if the path might not look as you expected, it might be leading somewhere spectacular ... You won't find out unless you get started, so get going and enjoy the journey!

And if you need just one trusty friend for the road, you won't find better than the *Children's Writers' & Artists' Yearbook*. It was placed into my hands when I first started out and I recommend it to everyone who asks me for advice. It's a one-stop welcome to the world of publishing – an invaluable guide to who's who and what's what. For anyone new to the business, it's worth its weight in gold.

As for me, I'll still daydream about my writing room (and you have an open invitation to come and visit me there one day), but for now I'll be content living in and out of words. *They're* my happy place.

Smriti Halls is a multi-award-winning, bestselling children's author whose books have been published in more than 40 languages worldwide. Her titles include picture book *Rain Before Rainbows* (Walker Books 2020) and the *I'm Sticking With You* series (Simon & Schuster 2021–23) as well as *Publishers Weekly* #1 bestselling *I Love You Night and Day* (Bloomsbury 2014). Smriti has been a judge for several awards and prizes, including the Costa Book Award, The Week Jr Awards and the BookTrust Lifetime Achievement Award and is a Patron of the School Library Association (SLA) as well as a former BookTrust Writer-in-Residence. Find out more at www.smriti.co.uk or on Instagram @smriti_halls_author.

If at first you don't succeed ...

Frances Hardinge describes the steps she took, as a hopeful young writer, to brave rejection, persevere and grow in confidence, and the friends and resources that helped her find where her writing belonged and gain that first momentous book contract.

I was in my teens when I bought my first copy of the *Writers' & Artists' Yearbook*. Back then, the *Children's Writers' & Artists' Yearbook* didn't exist. But in those days I wasn't an adult writing children's fiction, I was a teenager trying my hand at adult fiction.

Buying the book felt significant – a little intimidating, in fact. I sensed that I was making a promise to myself. I wouldn't keep my stories safely hidden away. I would send them off to be judged, and expose my fragile, iridescent bubble-dreams to the jagged edges of the real world. In effect, I had *bought* some of my cowardly excuses into non-existence: '*I can't send my work off, I don't know where to start!*'; '*I don't know what to send, or where!*'. Well, now I did.

And whenever I let schoolwork or other commitments eat up all my time, I'd spot the *Yearbook* on my shelf, fire-engine red. A silent, insistent reminder of my promise to myself. A gentle but much-needed boot in the rear.

I meticulously typed out my stories on the roaring, ill-tempered electric typewriter I'd bought from my sister for five pounds. Every time I made an error and had to perform Tipp-Ex surgery, I agonised over it and considered typing the whole page again.

And all the while I was gripped by a crippling fear that my first submission might be my only chance, and that if I messed it up badly all would be lost. The submissions editor would look coldly at my clunkiest metaphor, or scowl at my Tipp-Ex, and then stride away to the dark chamber where the editor collective kept the Terrible Tome of Authors We Must Never Publish. They would add my name to the list, and from that moment all my other submissions would be doomed. Prospective editors would consult the book, see my name in blood-red letters, shake their heads and throw my manuscript in the bin.

Only after a few trembling submissions did I start to suspect that the Terrible Tome didn't actually exist. Rejection slips arrived in the post, but didn't bring the apocalypse with them. Occasionally there was an actual rejection letter. (My favourite of these effectively said: 'We rather liked your story, and we wish we knew what it was about.') Eventually I realised that I had nothing to lose but the cost of two stamps and a spoonful of pride. If I was turned down it didn't matter. All that mattered was that I kept trying.

By my twenties, I was subscribing to *Writers' News* and *Writing Magazine* to supplement the *Yearbook*. I now typed my stories on a little Franken-puter that my boyfriend had cobbled together from parts of discarded, elderly computers. My friends and I set up a small writers' group, which gave me a regular deadline to keep me writing. With their feedback I became more confident, and less precious about editing my work.

And one day, after sending a short story to a little independent magazine, I received an answer that wasn't a 'no'. This was the first in a series of 'not-no' responses. However, when I received my first book contract a few years later, it was thanks to my good friend Rhiannon Lassiter. She realised something I hadn't – that my peculiar dark fairy tales were actually children's fiction. Rhiannon persuaded me to try writing a children's novel, then wrested my first five chapters from my unwilling hands and marched off with them to her editor.

The *Children's Writers' & Artists' Yearbook* would have been invaluable to me as a young, aspiring children's writer, if I'd had the sense to realise that that was what I was. The latest editions of the *Yearbook* are even richer and more useful than those I bought in my teens and twenties, with more information on agents, prizes, courses, conferences, digital publishing and self-publishing, and a wealth of essays, articles and advice.

Even now, when I look at the *Writers' & Artists' Yearbook*, I still recall everything it symbolised for me. It looks too heavy for the shelf, packed to the binding with hunger, trepidation, determination and hope. It's still a little intimidating. Opportunities often are.

Frances Hardinge is the award-winning author of *Fly by Night* (Macmillan Children's Books 2005), winner of the 2006 Branford Boase Award, *Twilight Robbery* (Macmillan Children's Books 2011), shortlisted for the Guardian Children's Fiction Prize, and *Cuckoo Song* (Pan Macmillan 2014), which won the Robert Holdstock Award for Best Novel at the British Fantasy Awards 2015. *The Lie Tree* (Macmillan Children's Books 2015) won the Costa Book of the Year 2015 award, the 2016 UKLA Book Award (12–16 category), the 2016 *Boston Globe* Horn Book Fiction Award and the 2016 *Los Angeles Times* Young Adult Literature Prize and was also shortlisted for the Independent Booksellers Week Award 2015, the *Guardian* Children's Fiction Prize 2015 and the 2016 Carnegie Medal. The sequel, *A Skinful of Shadows* (Pan Macmillan 2017), won the Dracula Society's Children of the Night award. Her other books include *Gullstruck Island* (Macmillan Children's Books 2009) and *A Face Like Glass* (Pan Macmillan Children's 2012). Her latest book is *The Forest of a Thousand Eyes* (Two Hoots 2024), a collaboration with award-winning illustrator Emily Gravett. She has been nominated for the Astrid Lindgren Memorial Award twice in 2021 and 2024. Find out more at www.franceshardinge.com.

My way into a different world

Sally Green describes how, later in life, she found herself hooked on the creative process of writing and, by applying hard work and good advice, made her way into the world of the professional writer.

I remember the beginning of my writing career quite clearly. It was a sunny afternoon in June 2010, I was 48 years old and doing housework and I had an idea for a story. I'd never written anything before (no diary, no dabbling in short stories, no childhood dreams of being an author), but what did I have to lose other than a few hours of my time? Anything had to be more interesting than hoovering, and no one would ever read the story but me, so I sat down and wrote.

At school I'd learnt the basics of grammar and punctuation, but I always felt inhibited about my writing and that I lacked imagination. Now I realize that everyone has imagination, but being brave and comfortable enough to risk expressing it is the hard thing. By June 2010 schoolgirl inhibitions were a distant memory, although learning wasn't, as the previous year I'd begun to study Social Sciences with the Open University. Because of the OU course I had developed the habit of writing – I had to produce regular assignments and I enjoyed closing the door on the outside world and immersing myself in a new topic. I loved the process of putting ideas and words together and creating something, even if it was only a rather poor essay on politics.

So that June afternoon, with no more essays to write, I repeated the procedure but instead of an essay I began a short story about a girl who didn't know that she was a witch. I didn't have much of a plan – I just wrote, and I continued the next day and the next. After two weeks of this I had to admit to myself that the story wasn't that short; in fact I was probably writing a novel, and it was now taking up all my time. I was hooked. Possibly I was in love too – with my characters. I was obsessed with them, thinking about what they'd do and how, and why. I carried on writing and by September 2010 my story was complete and definitely not short (136,000 words). It wasn't atrocious but there were things wrong with it, though I wasn't even sure what those things were (the narrative point of view was jumping all over the place). I was desperate to improve and so I switched my OU course to Creative Writing, studying hard and all the while working on my manuscript.

I never really believed I'd be a published writer – it seemed less likely than winning the lottery – but I believed in my story. I wanted to try to get it published, but I had a problem: I didn't know a thing about the publishing world. However, I had heard about the *Writers' & Artists' Yearbook* and I found a rather battered copy at my local library. As soon as I started leafing through it I knew I'd found a book I could trust. I devoured its advice. It became my Bible, a source of knowledge and comfort. It was my way into a different world – the world of the professional writer.

I decided to try the traditional route of getting an agent who would then help me find a publisher, and so I listed the agents who accepted manuscripts for YA books, googled them and chose a few I thought might be interested in my story. I submitted to eight agents and within a few months received five brief replies saying 'No' (though the non-replies were fairly clear No's too). However, one reply was different: it was still a 'No', but the agent said she liked my writing style though the story 'didn't have the necessary edge for today's market'. I was delighted. OK – it was a rejection, but an agent from a prestigious London literary agency liked my writing style! I was over the moon. Better yet, I was fired up – I knew I could do edgy better than most people, and I knew that I could improve on the manuscript that I'd sent out. My mindset, once I decided I'd try to get published, was that I would write at least three novels before I'd give up, so starting again didn't daunt me. I gave myself a year to rewrite the story and immediately set to work. Best of all, I'd been released from the cage that I hadn't realised I was still in; I'd been told to be edgy, and to do that I had to let go of my writing inhibitions and make the story mine.

A year later I was back in the library with the *Writers' & Artists' Yearbook*, following its advice about covering letters and synopses (much better advice than the, often American, tips I'd seen online) for what turned out to be my first published novel.

I would have been lost without *Writers' & Artists' Yearbook* to guide me, and I'm delighted there is now this *Children's Writers' & Artists' Yearbook*. It's a wonderful resource – it's *the* resource for writers.

Sally Green is the author of two internationally acclaimed, award-winning trilogies of young adult fantasy novels, *Half Bad* (*Half Bad*, *Half Wild* and *Half Lost*) and *The Smoke Thieves* (*The Smoke Thieves*, *The Demon World* and *The Burning Kingdoms*) published by Penguin Random House in the UK. *Half Bad* (2014), which was Sally's debut novel, was named Waterstones Best Book for Teenagers 2015 and was shortlisted for the YA Book Prize and the Branford Boase Award in 2015. *Half Bad* was adapted into a Netflix series released in 2023. Sally is on Instagram @SallyGreenWriter, X @Sa11eGreen, and her website is www.sallygreenwriter.com

See also...
- *Writing for teens*, page 263

How do you do it?

After more than two decades as a published author William Sutcliffe has only one answer to the often-asked question 'How do you do it?'. He shares the most important piece of advice he has to offer and reminds writers to enjoy every step of the long journey they are embarking upon.

In the 25+ years that I have been writing and publishing books I have been to scores of literary events, both as a speaker and an audience member. If I had to agglomerate all the questions I've heard put to authors into one overarching meta-question, it would be this: 'How do you do it?'. Sadly, my agglomerated meta-answer to that question would have to be 'I don't know.' Every published writer frequently gets asked for advice, and most of them have only one truly essential tip to offer: buy the *Writers' & Artists' Yearbook*. The key turning point in every professional writer's life is when writing shifts from being a hobby or a dream into a source of income. For making that transition, this book is the Bible.

To get published, you don't have to know someone; you don't have to know someone who knows someone; you don't have to live in Hampstead; and you don't need a degree in English literature. You do, however, need to understand that publishing is a business and that, like every other business, it operates in a way that seems obvious and transparent to insiders, but is opaque and confusing to outsiders. This is what makes the *Writers' & Artists' Yearbook* an essential reference book for everyone who hopes to make a living as a writer. Trying to get published without it is like setting off on a hike without a map.

When put to a writer, the question 'How do you do it?' can mean two things. If it means 'How do you get published?', you are holding the answer in your hands right now. Not everyone who hopes to find a publisher will achieve that, not by a long shot, but if you want to give your work in progress the best possible chance of finding an agent and ultimately a publisher, all the answers you need are right here. Of course, the other thing that question often means is 'How do you write a good book?'; and for that one, there are no clear-cut answers. Moreover, when it comes to key questions such as getting started, editing, plotting, characterisation and getting unstuck when you are stuck, for every writer there is a different solution. There is a right and a wrong way to make a submission to an agent; there isn't a right and a wrong way to write a novel. Everyone finds their own method.

The fascinating essays in this volume contain a wealth of experience from many of Britain's finest children's authors. None of these essays will tell you how to write like those authors, but they will open your thoughts onto how you should write – how to get your personality onto the page; how to tell a unique story in an original way; how to navigate your own path through the craft of writing. These essays are the second-best resource there is for hearing the secrets of good children's writing. The best resource, of course, is the novels themselves.

Read them. Read them once as a reader, then again as a writer – which is to say with the eyes of a hyena. Pull the books to pieces. Think about the word choices, the structure, the characterisation, the pacing, the world-building. Read the books you love ruthlessly and critically. Read the books you don't love in the same way, and hone your sense of where your literary taste sits. There is no objective scale of good and bad. You need to make your own. This gimlet-eyed reading is essential, because only when you have done it to others will you be able to do it to your own prose. To write for children you have to tap into a playfulness in your imagination, but when it comes to editing and rewriting you have to be brutal. Any word or sentence that isn't doing a useful job has to go.

This book is filled with practical and creative advice for writers at every stage of a writing career, but I would like to leave you with the simplest and most important advice there is: enjoy it. When you write, pour yourself into the work. Think of the blank page not as a scary place but as a path to freedom. Writing can take you anywhere. If you really apply yourself to the task, whether you get published or not, that journey will be worthwhile.

William Sutcliffe writes for adults, young adults and children and is the author of 12 novels, including three titles in his *Circus of Thieves* series, published by Simon & Schuster Children's: *Circus of Thieves and the Raffle of Doom* (2014), *Circus of Thieves on the Rampage* (2015) and *Circus of Thieves and the Comeback Caper* (2016). His YA books are *The Wall* (2014) which was shortlisted for the CILIP Carnegie Medal, *Concentr8* (2016), shortlisted for the YA Book Prize, *We See Everything* (2017), *The Gifted, The Talented and Me* (2019) and *The Summer We Turned Green* (2021), all published by Bloomsbury. William's novels for adults include the international bestseller *Are You Experienced?* (Hamish Hamilton 1997), *New Boy* (Penguin 1996), *Bad Influence* (Hamish Hamilton 2004) and *Whatever Makes You Happy* (Bloomsbury 2008), which was adapted into a Netflix film with the new title, *Otherhood*, in 2019. He is also a screenwriter. His work has been translated into 28 languages. Follow him on X @Will_Sutcliffe8.

Journey to publication: the summit is worth the climb

M.G. Leonard shares the obstacles she faced on her journey to publication, how she overcame them and what she learnt about the requirements for middle-grade novels along the way.

To me, the feat of becoming a published author was as daunting as climbing Mount Everest … people say they want to do it but the odds of getting to the top are slim and the probability of getting hurt is high. Few people try and even fewer succeed.

Stage One of my ascent was to have the idea for my book – and it crawled into my brain on six legs with an exoskeleton and two pairs of wings. My story was going to be about beetles, an ecological entomological adventure, and so I enthusiastically began researching the bugs – which I thought would take a couple of weeks but actually took six years, because there are over 400,000 known species of beetle and I hadn't known that.

Stage Two was to write the book. During this time, I bought the *Writers' & Artists' Yearbook* and put it on a shelf beside my desk. I would flick through the pages inhaling the smell of an industry I longed to be a part of. Foolishly, I didn't read it. Including false starts and real-life obstacles to creativity, like getting divorced and being a single working mum, it took me four years to complete a draft of my manuscript.

Finally, I was moving to Stage Three of the climb – getting an agent! I'd fantasised about finding my literary best friend, the Clyde to my Bonnie, who would belay for me on the toughest part of the ascent – submitting to publishers. But then I got the fear. What if I sent my book to every single agent in the *Writers' & Artists' Yearbook* and they all hated it? I would crash to earth, a failure (cue sad music). I chose procrastination as my avoidance technique: I took the *Yearbook* and went through every agent, putting the ones I thought looked good (all of them) into a spreadsheet; I typed out all their details into columns (there was absolutely no need to do this), including their submission preferences. Then one day I'd completed my long list of possible agents … there was nothing else I could do other than submit.

At this point, I must confess that I presumed my book about a 13-year-old boy and a sentient giant rhinoceros beetle was for adult readers. I have no defence for this other than I thought: I am an adult, the story came out of my brain, so it must be for adults. As you might guess from this assumption, I hadn't got a clue about how the publishing industry worked. Despite spending a large percentage of my life in libraries and bookshops, I hadn't considered the categories books are sorted into or where my story might fit amongst them. I hadn't thought about what happened after you got an agent. I figured my agent would tell me that. This was an error.

I submitted to four agents on my list. Three rejected me with no feedback. I added a column to my spreadsheet in which to put insults about agents who rejected me. The fourth agent asked for the full manuscript and I sent all 120,000 words of it to them, only to receive a swift reply telling me my book was middle grade (I didn't know what this meant) and that they only represented adult fiction and YA (I didn't know what this meant either). They informed me a middle-grade debut shouldn't exceed 60,000 words and politely suggested I do some market research and edit my book accordingly.

I fell to the ground with a sickening thud. But I'm not a quitter, and a year later, on maternity leave, I began submitting again. This time I'd bought a copy of the *Children's Writers' & Artists' Yearbook* and focused my attention on understanding the rock face I was climbing. I read the whole book, cover to cover, learning about the business and drawing courage from author essays about their journey to publication. It's rare to find a book that's as useful as it is inspiring, but this book is essential reading for aspiring children's authors. Equipped with new knowledge, I began my second ascent, able to see the hand- and footholds that others had used before me.

Once again, I submitted to four agents; once again, three of them rejected me. One said a book on beetles wouldn't sell. Another was rude about my protagonist. I was rude about both of them in my spreadsheet. However, I took on board the agent's concerns about my protagonist and revised my opening chapters. The fourth agent requested my full manuscript. I submitted my 60,000-word book, with a more likeable protagonist, and held my breath … Eventually, I was rewarded with a real-life phone call! Unfortunately, I had a six-month-old baby, so it went to voicemail.

I can still remember repeatedly listening to that voicemail. It was surreal, like getting a message from the other side. The agent said they liked my beetle book and that I could write, but that the manuscript needed work; it had a flabby fourth act and a problematic ending. They told me to call the Golden Egg Academy. This was not the news I'd been hoping for, but it was a crevice into which I could insert my fingers and heave myself a little further up the mountainside. At the Golden Egg Academy, I discovered I'd written a middle-grade book with a YA ending and got a lesson in story structure. I edited my book again. Finally, I had a manuscript fit for submission, and the Golden Egg Academy helped me find both my agent and my first publishing deal.

My journey to publication would have been easier and quicker if I'd read the *Children's Writers' & Artists' Yearbook* before I began my epic climb, but I got here in the end. So, dear climber, put this book in your backpack and don't just smell it, read it from cover to cover. Heed the advice you're given, only be rude in spreadsheets, and don't give up. See you at the top.

M.G. Leonard is the bestselling, award-winning writer of children's books *Beetle Boy*, *Beetle Queen* and *Battle of the Beetles* (Chicken House 2016–18), the *Adventures on Trains* series with Sam Sedgman (Macmillan Children's 2019–22) and *The Twitchers* quartet (Walker Books 2021–24). Her books have been translated into over 40 languages. *The Highland Falcon Thief* (Adventures on Trains) has been optioned for cinema and *Beetle Boy* is being developed as a live-action series for TV. *Beetle Boy* won the Branford Boase Award (2017), and was shortlisted for the Waterstones Children's Book Award and longlisted for the Carnegie Medal. *The Highland Falcon Thief*, won the Books Are My Bag Readers Award 2020 for Children's Fiction and the Children's Fiction Book of the Year 2021 in the British Book Awards. The series has won international awards and been nominated for two Edgar awards in America. *Twitch* (*The Twitchers* quartet), won the Sainsbury's Fiction Children's Book Award in 2021, Best Crime Fiction Novel for Children Crimefest Award 2022 and was nominated for the Carnegie Medal. *Spark* was shortlisted for the Wainwright Prize for Nature Writing 2023. M.G. also wrote the acclaimed story *The Ice Children*, produced with full cast and orchestration by Audible (Macmillan 2023). Her latest book is *Hunt for the Golden Scarab* (Macmillan 2025). Find out more at www.mgleonard.com and follow M.G. on X @MGLnrd.

Following your heart: my journey to publication

Rejection is always painful. In this article, Hannah Gold explains how pain – along with a polar bear – spurred her forward to achieve her dream of becoming a published children's author.

I always wanted to be a children's author. It was the Big Dream. But I was in my mid-forties by the time this dream came true. That's the thing with dreams – sometimes they have to take a few detours along the way. But in my twenties, I didn't understand that. After leaving university, I was impatient for overnight success and to fulfil my destiny as a rockstar multi-millionaire author. And when it didn't happen immediately, it was a huge blow. But sometimes life has other designs for you – far better than the ones your younger self could have envisioned. Every author has a different publishing journey. And I share mine to show you my ups, my downs and the key turning point that made all the difference.

Naïve beginnings

I had always dabbled in writing – magazine articles, short stories – and had even trained as a copywriter. But it wasn't until my late twenties that I wrote my first book. Somehow, I'd managed to snag this writer-in-residence gig at a swanky boutique hotel in Sydney, Australia. And honestly, I had the best time. In the two months of my residency, I managed to scribble together a book. And I was very proud of that book. It felt mystical and profound and most importantly, mine. Upon my return to the UK, I picked up my trusty copy of the *Writers' & Artists' Yearbook* (back then, there was no children's version) and duly sent the manuscript of my book off to the sum total of one agent.

I genuinely thought that's all it would take.

Suffice to say, this agent let me know that what I *thought* was a book actually was just a collection of pages thrown together. Was my ego crushed? Yes. But it was also a pivotal moment. I realised that perhaps this dream job wouldn't just fall into my lap. Even though I considered myself a decent writer, I would have to *learn* how to write a book. This learning process took six whole years – studying the craft, reading lots, taking part in various critique groups and so on. By this point, the collection of whimsical pages had morphed into a moody young adult (YA) paranormal romance. It was the *Twilight* era and I believed that this was the type of book which would sell. Back then, I thought you had to write to the market in order to succeed.

I picked up a newer edition of the *Yearbook* (still in the era of the red cover) and sent this book off to approximately ten agents. I quickly received ten rejections. A bit of a blow. But there was one shining light. There was one agent who did like my writing and who – despite turning down this manuscript – asked to see any future work of mine. And that tiny crumb was enough to sustain me.

I was determined to stick to YA. Not because I loved the genre, but because I was still convinced this would be my best shot. I then spent another six years writing a new paranormal romance. When it was finished in 2017, I submitted the first three chapters to about twenty agents and lo and behold, this time I got four full manuscript requests.

This is it! I thought. My moment has arrived.

My lowest point

Unfortunately, all four agents subsequently rejected me.

Despite all the success that has happened since, I still remember how much these four rejections stung. How deeply I felt the disappointment as one by one, the agents said 'no'. I have a vivid and sharp memory of sobbing on my husband's shoulder and saying 'it's never going happen for me'. Being rejected is horrible. It *hurts*.

Once I had mopped up my tears, I tried to be philosophical. Okay, all four had turned me down, but I was getting closer. Surely that was evidence I was heading in the right direction? This was good. But there was a comment from one of the agents that I just couldn't shake out of my head. They had said my writing was too 'sentimental' and while that wasn't intended as an insult, I saw it as a personal affront.

I resented myself for being too emotional, too sentimental, too wrong. If only I were someone else (insert 'edgier', 'more dynamic', 'funnier', 'better'), I would land an agent.

After this, I kind of gave up for a while, until – at the end of 2018 – a friend suggested that I 'go back to my writing' as I was feeling pretty lost. It was the best advice anyone could have given me. It was life-changing, in fact. This time I decided not to write YA. I had realised by this point that trying to follow the market wasn't working for me. Instead, I would write a children's book. This was the dream, right? And now in my mid-forties, there really was nothing else to lose. Except perhaps a bit of pride if my dream didn't work out.

The Last Bear

I can't pinpoint when the idea of writing about a polar bear came to me. But one day, there he was in my head – fully formed and gazing at me with his dark chocolate eyes. There was a story he wanted to tell and I, for some reason, was the person he had chosen to tell it to.

Unlike my previous attempts at writing YA, this time the story arrived quickly – almost as if it existed already and was merely waiting for me to commit it to paper. I wrote a first draft in about three months and I poured every last bit of myself in it. If you've read *The Last Bear*, then you'll know it's a very emotional story. It came from a raw, authentic place. It came from *me*.

The sentimentality that I had once perceived as an insult, suddenly became my secret weapon. It became my *strength*. Because there's no getting away from it: I am sentimental! I am emotional. I adore big, sweeping gestures, powerful feelings, raw intensity – anything that gets the heartbeat thudding. And rather than shy away from who I am deep down, I chose to embrace this side of me. Because I knew intuitively that in being honest with myself, I would also find honesty with my readers.

Agent journey

I knew *The Last Bear* was special. I don't want this to sound arrogant – I just *knew*, deep down, it was The One. It was a gut feeling. Now it was just a matter of finding an agent who agreed with me.

And hurrah! By now a shiny green children's version of the *Writers' & Artists' Yearbook* had appeared on the market. Oh! The immense joy of knowing there was this literal catalogue of possibility without having to filter out all the grown-up stuff first. I pored over it, gobbling up the author stories. Feeling inspired and buoyed up with fresh possibility, I subsequently drew up a list of about fifteen agents.

A couple of days later, I was sitting at my desk, undoubtedly daydreaming of my big break, when something compelled me to pick up the *Yearbook* again. And this is when the magic happens. (We are children's authors – we can believe in magic!) The book seemed to miraculously fall open at a random page and on that page was a listing of agencies in the UK. One of these agencies was RCW.

Working at RCW was the agent Claire Wilson. For some unfathomable reason, I had missed her off my original list. But not only did she represent the author of one of my all-time favourite books, *Rooftoppers* (by Katherine Rundell, Faber & Faber 2013), but after some quick research on what was then called Twitter, she also seemed to represent the ecological values I wanted in an agent. She seemed terribly out of my reach but nevertheless I felt a small and very insistent voice urging me to submit to her.

That was in mid-September 2019. By the end of November, she had offered representation.

Dream publishing journey

After we did some light edits over the festive period and in early January, Claire submitted the manuscript to publishers. I honestly had no idea what to expect. But I don't think, even in all my wildest dreams, I expected events to move quite so fast.

Within twenty-four hours of submission, we had our first offer via email. Ironically, I was sat on the very same sofa where only three years before I had sobbed on my husband's shoulder over my latest rejection. But this time I was crying for a different reason. I was crying because I could not believe it was finally happening to me.

Later on in that same week, I met up with the interested publishers – one of whom was HarperCollins Children's Books. My prospective publisher told me how wonderful he thought the book was – but the clincher for him? The fact it made him cry. That's when he knew they had to publish my book.

My sentimentality had finally paid off.

Publication and beyond

The Last Bear was released in the middle of lockdown in early 2021, but despite a tough start, somehow the book took on a life of its own and thrived.

Shortlistings, major prizes, trophies, fancy publishing lunches, big festivals and overseas travel all followed. It was the best of everything. It was and still is the dream author life. And then the sales! So many sales that keep on coming.

And all of that has been amazing. It really has. If there is one advantage to being published in your forties, it's that sense of knowing what you want. And I knew I always wanted the book to be big.

But you know the best thing?

It's the love. Booksellers, teachers and readers young and old in many countries have taken the book to their hearts. I still receive messages almost daily from readers all over the world telling me how much they love my books. How much the story means to them. How much it has touched their hearts.

And I couldn't ask for any greater gift than that.

There is only one you

The message here is not to be like me. Yes, you might be the kind of writer who writes emotionally powerful books. You might even aspire to write the kind of books I do. But you might not.

The message here is to be true to you. Whoever *you* are. Don't shy away from your innate character, your strengths, your true self. Be *you*, unashamedly, on the page, because in being you, you will reach the people who were always destined to be your readers. You will find your tribe.

And you never know, one day you could pick up the latest edition of the *Children's Writers' & Artists' Yearbook* and spot your name in it.

I hope so.

Hannah Gold is a children's author passionate about writing stories that share her love of the planet. *The Last Bear*, her middle-grade debut, became an instant classic and international bestseller upon release in 2021. A *Sunday Times* Book of the Week, it went on to win both the Waterstones Children's Book Prize and The Blue Peter Book Award and has been translated into 27 languages. She is also the author of *The Lost Wha*le, which won the Edward Stanford Children's Travel Book of the Year in 2023. Her latest books include *Turtle Moon* (2024) and *Finding Bear* (2025), the bestselling sequel to *The Last Bear*. All books are illustrated by award-winning illustrator Levi Pinfold and published by HarperCollins Children's Books. Hannah is an ambassador for the Whale and Dolphin Conservation Charity. Find out more at: www.hannahgold.world and follow her on X @HGold_author and Instagram @hannahgold_author.

The long and winding road to publication

Paul Stewart tells how he achieved his childhood dream of becoming a writer, championing illustrated books for children, and shares his experience of the submission process, rejection and success, and finding the ideal collaboration.

When I was at school, other boys in my class wanted to be footballers or train drivers. One wanted to be an astronomer. Me, I didn't have a clue. Possibly a singer in a band. Then, when I was eight, I was given a prize by a music teacher. Her husband worked for Collins and the prize was a book: *The Phantom Tollbooth* by Norton Juster, with illustrations by Jules Feiffer (Collins 1962). She apologised that it was an uncorrected proof, but thought I would love it. She was right. The novel took me to somewhere wonderful and, from that moment on, I knew I wanted to be a writer.

I started work on my own children's novel – as well as drawing the pictures to accompany it. I soon discovered two things: writing was more difficult than I'd thought, while illustrating was beyond me. I abandoned the project, but I never lost that new-found enthusiasm for my future career.

At university I studied English, choosing Lancaster because they offered a unit in Creative Writing. Then I applied for a (then almost unknown) writing MA at UEA, run by Malcolm Bradbury and Angela Carter. By the end of the course I had a folder of 20 short stories and an idea for a novel. One of those stories – a reimagining of Andersen's *The Snow Queen*, called *Ice* – was published in a literary magazine, *Bananas*. I still remember the thrill of reading their letter of acceptance: '… we'd like to use it in the next issue due out at the end of this month.' It was my first short story in print. I'd arrived.

I hadn't, of course. The other 19 stories – separately and as a collection – were not published, and the novel remained an idea. I decided that if it was indeed true that you should write about what you know, then I needed to know more. It was time to go travelling.

This was back before computers. Up until then I had been writing on an olive-green Olympia SM3 – allegedly a portable typewriter, but Charles Atlas would probably have had problems lugging it about. So I bought a lightweight Olivetti Lettera 32 and, following Malcolm's parting comment – 'I don't have the address but it is, like all the other addresses, in the *Writers' & Artists' Yearbook*' – got hold of a copy. Then I set off.

I lived in Greece, Germany and Sri Lanka; I travelled through Europe, India, parts of the Far East, Australia, the US, Kenya. I had numerous jobs – factory packer, security guard, fork-lift truck driver, bank operative, translator, EFL teacher, you name it – and I wrote something every day. The typewriter went everywhere I went, and each time I completed a piece of writing, I would search through the *Yearbook* for an appropriate publication. A growing number of magazines and publishers in the UK received examples of my work.

Most, to their credit, were kind in their rejections. Many offered advice. I always tried to match the manuscript to the publication, though not always successfully. A leading women's magazine responded to one story with the comment: 'The idea was ingenious but … we do try to keep death out of our stories.'

I also discovered that I was receiving letters from people I'd actually heard of: Robert McCrum, Bill Buford, Paul Samwell-Smith (ah, yes … still nurturing dreams of singing in a band, I'd also submitted a cassette of songs for appraisal). The thrill of communicating with famous people was tempered by the fact that they were sending me rejection letters – one after the other they arrived, enough to paper my walls, and I was feeling increasingly disheartened, though unable to stop writing.

It was this optimistic response from Tom Maschler of Jonathan Cape that set me back on track: 'The above said [i.e. the inevitable rejection], I don't like to lose sight of you because frankly I am convinced that you will make it as a serious writer, and think it likely that we would want to publish you in the future if we had the opportunity.'

I was in Sri Lanka in the '80s when civil war broke out. The school I'd been teaching in was closed, and I returned to England to find that the adult novel I'd almost completed over there suddenly seemed flippant and superficial. So I went back to the children's book I'd been musing over for more than two decades and, three months later, *The Thought Domain* was finished. Published by Viking in 1988, it was my first children's novel in print. For a second time, I'd arrived.

Largely on the strength of that published book, I was taken on by a literary agent. This took a lot of the hard work – and inevitable heartache – out of the process of trying to find a home for my scribblings. I now had someone to do it for me. Three years later, a deal was secured for a book I'd been researching. Based on a true story I'd stumbled upon in Kenya, it was accepted by – yes – Jonathan Cape. In 1991, my first adult book, *Trek*, was duly published. I'd *arrived* …

Apart from that one book (and even *Trek* itself reads like a *Boy's Own* tale of gung-ho misadventure), it was children's literature that I pursued. I liked the discipline of writing for a younger audience, as well as the rigour, clarity and sincerity it demands. My early books were our-world-but-with-a-twist fantasies, often starting with a simple What if…? premise. What if there was a dimension where our thoughts were stored? What if a child was born able to communicate with animals? What if a video machine could record our nightmares?

After the publication of *The Thought Domain*, I submitted fresh proposals in the form of the first three chapters of the new work, a rough outline of the entire novel and a working title, in order to gauge whether my primary editor thought it had legs. If he didn't, my agent would send it to other publishers. I had, by this time, given up teaching EFL to devote myself to writing full time. I did not intend to return to the classroom. Not only did I generate my own stories, but I also started taking on commissions – writing to order, following briefs. I wrote football stories, puzzle adventures books, graded readers, horror and fantasy novels; I had short stories published in themed anthologies.

All these pieces of work, even the ones for older children, were illustrated. I considered this a good thing; I still do. There is, I believe, something perverse about using pictures to lure children into the world of books and then, when they've cracked reading, to remove them. It feels almost like a punishment. If I'd been able to I would have illustrated my own texts but, since I wasn't good enough, the next best thing was to find an illustrator I could work closely with.

This proved far from easy. Publishers often keep authors and illustrators apart. An American editor once explained that this was company policy, as authors 'tend to bully illustrators'. A likely story! Had there been closer cooperation between me and my various illustrators, however, maybe a scene I'd written about a boy on a bike being attacked by a slavering dog wouldn't have been depicted by an old bicycle leaning up against a wall. I mentioned my disappointment to my editor and was given a new illustrator – based in Tasmania ...

It was at a publisher's party in London that I first got talking to Chris Riddell. Beforehand, we had seen each other at the nursery our two sons went to, but we'd never spoken. On our train journey home that evening we talked about working together and, after a couple of false starts, produced a picture book about a rabbit and a hedgehog: *A Little Bit of Winter* (Andersen Press). It was my first picture book and my first collaboration.

The year was 1998, and that wasn't the only work we had published ... Working together on *Rabbit and Hedgehog*, we'd both realized how much we enjoyed the collaborative process. Chris drew me a fantasy map entitled *The Edge*: 'Here's the world,' he said. 'What happens in it?'. It was at this stage that we tested our ability to work together to the max. This wasn't a 12-page spread picture book; it would be a long novel for 11-year-olds, illustrated throughout. There were times when we both wondered whether it would ever be completed, but finally, 15 months later, *Beyond the Deepwoods* (Doubleday 1998) – the first of what would become a 13-part fantasy series, *The Edge Chronicles* – was on the shelves. I'd arrived. Again!

Oddly, the series nearly didn't happen. I'd spoken to my editor at the time about the idea. She thought pictures would make the fantasy look too young. 'Not Chris's pictures', I assured her and, though unconvinced, she suggested I send in the proposal. In the usual way, I printed up the three chapters we'd completed, plus a rough synopsis of the book and outline of the world, and included a wad of Chris's pictures. The envelope came back return of post. Being a writer with a string of rejections under his belt, I naturally assumed they'd dismissed it out of hand as a rubbish idea. It was two days later when a tentative phone enquiry revealed that a youngster on a Youth Opportunities scheme had decided to tidy up the office and sent back all the manuscripts that were lying around – ours included. I've often fantasized about other novels that might have been rejected in the same batch ...

Chris and I have written and illustrated more than 40 books together to date. One of us will come up with a very general idea, then we talk, talk, talk. If that initial idea starts to fly, we set about building a self-contained world – with maps, characters, names, back histories – for the two of us to immerse ourselves in; a place where we discover the stories that will turn into books. A flying box containing an ominous warning became the first *Far-Flung Adventure* – *Fergus Crane* (Doubleday 2004); a Victorian delivery lad with an insight into the supernatural became the *Barnaby Grimes* novels; a trio of aliens on a spurious mission to Earth became *The Blobheads*; humans versus killer robots – *Scavenger*; cowboys and dragons – *Wyrmeweald*.

Since Chris and I come to a piece of work from different perspectives, the text itself goes through many revisions. Although it is immensely enjoyable working with someone else – the writing, the events, the festivals, plus the fact that 'writer's block' is impossible if two of you are working together on a piece – collaboration is never easy. If we had tried working together when we'd first left college, it might not have worked. By the time we did start, I think we were both old enough to realize that the finished item was of far more importance than our individual egos. And certainly, none of the books we produced together could have been done by either of us alone.

Looking back on my writing career, it seems to have been so arbitrary. I kept thinking I'd arrived, only to discover that it was not my final destination – that there was always somewhere else to go to. All I know is that, ever since first realizing that 'I wanted to be a writer', everything has been geared towards making that a possibility. Publishing is currently changing. I wonder where I will arrive at next …

Paul Stewart is a bestselling author of children's and adult books. He is co-creator (with Chris Riddell) of the *Edge Chronicles* series, the *Far-Flung Adventures* series including *Fergus Crane* (Gold Smarties Prize winner), *Corby Flood* and *Hugo Pepper* (both Silver Nestlé Prize winners), as well as the *Barnaby Grimes* series (published by Penguin Random House), and the *Free Lance*, *Wyrmeweald* and *Scavenger* trilogies. His other books include two *Muddle Earth* adventures and the *Blobheads* series (for younger readers), published by Macmillan Children's, and the *Rabbit and Hedgehog* picture books (Andersen Press). *Brian the Brave* (Otter-Barry Books 2019), the second picture book he has worked on with illustrator Jane Porter, won the 2020 Derby Children's Book Award, while *A Little Bit of Hush* was published in 2022. Barrington Stoke has re-issued both the *Free Lance* trilogy and his *Football Mad* series. Paul has written six titles for OUP's *Hero Academy* series and a biography of footballer Alex Oxlade-Chamberlain (Scholastic 2021). His latest book is *Mabel and the Big Wide World* (Otter-Barry Books 2024). For more information see www.EDGECHRONICLES.co.uk.

The writing craft

Connecting with your readers

Clare Povey explores how a writer can reach out and grow valuable connections with a wider readership. She shares her tips on how best to establish and maintain a strong author–reader relationship, through web content, social media, teachers, schools, libraries and bookshops.

Every writer wants to be read. I believe that every writer writes the book that they want to read themselves. Why else would we spend hours of our lives typing or scribbling away, with no guarantee that anyone other than ourselves (and a few lucky family members or friends) will get to see it? Connecting with your readers has to start with yourself. It's essential that you, the writer, find the story that you are most passionate and excited about because, without this, you will struggle to engage with your readers. Believe me, children can sniff out insincerity.

The first proper story I wrote was one I absolutely wanted to read. For full disclosure, it was my own take on *Holes* (Bloomsbury Children's 2015) by Louis Sachar. In my version, a girl character named Clara (we'll ignore how this is one letter off my own name) is sent to Camp Green Lake and shakes things up. It was my very own fan fiction; I reread it until the pages started to wear thin and tear. Since then, I have carried that same energy into all the stories I've written. So, although my first piece of advice seems simple, I can assure you that being genuine is a starting point for any meaningful author–reader relationship.

How do you successfully reach beyond your one-person audience and find wider readers for your work? Every writer – whether agented or unagented, whether they have published with a larger publisher or an independent, or have self-published – can feel this an overwhelming task, but the advice in this article should be relevant.

My debut middle-grade book *The Unexpected Tale of Bastien Bonlivre* (Usborne) was published in September 2021. While bookshops were open then (thankfully), there were still certain restrictions in place. I wasn't able to get into schools immediately, and I also work full-time, so it was a challenge to organise school events to promote the book. This meant that, for the first six months of my book being out in the world, I had to find and use different ways of connecting with potential readers.

Promotional disclaimer

I must acknowledge, at this point, that I was lucky enough to receive the September 2021 slot for Waterstones Children's Book of the Month. This promotional opportunity definitely helped my book reach a really wide audience in its early days – the size of audience that any author, especially a debut author, would dream of. It meant that my book sat in the window of every Waterstones bookshop across the UK (all 283 of them at the time), as well as being clearly placed on tables and displayed next to the till for a whole month. It was an opportunity that I will be forever grateful for, but I appreciate that it is also something that a writer has no control over; your publisher pitches your book to Waterstones and the head team of retail experts decides which story gets the coveted slot.

But, as a writer, establishing connections and maintaining them is something you need to grow for a lifetime, not just a single month. So much of the publishing world is out of your control, so it is important to focus on the things that you can do and take accountability for yourself. How, then, can you connect with your readers? Beyond summoning the bookish child inside you and demanding an answer, here are my five top tips on how you can connect and communicate best with your readers. All of these tips are interconnected, but I've broken them down into five separate points for clarity.

1. Create and organise your own content

A writer does not necessarily need a website (it's something you will have to pay for, as well as maintain and update), but you do need to build up a bank of content. By content, I mean blogs, articles, Q&A features, short videos or audio clips ... anything that can be used for promotional purposes. Having a variety of content available to offer to teachers, librarians and parents is a great way to expand the scope of your book. I have a Resources area on my website that allows me to put worksheets, links to articles and blogs, reading lists, historical facts and much more all in one place. Teachers can directly download resources for their classrooms, as well as access the first chapter of my book.

You don't need to be an expert video editor or design whizz to create content. I use the free versions of Canva (www.canva.com) and Clipchamp (https://clipchamp.com/en/) and am learning as I go. But I do keep my publishers in the loop about what I'm up to. I created a 'villain' worksheet for my school events (see section on School visits below) and the Usborne marketing and design team redesigned it into something much more professional looking. Communication is key – because, even though I love learning new skills, I'm not an expert designer or video editor. If you need help, don't be afraid to ask for it.

2. Find your corner of X (Twitter)

Social media isn't for everyone. If you're reading this and thinking 'Nope, not going anywhere near that cesspool,' that's your choice. But, be aware that the online children's fiction writing and book community contains some of the most supportive people you could ever hope to meet. I have met so many writers, book bloggers, booksellers, librarians and teachers through social media. I'll go into more detail about each one of these communities below, but I cannot overstate how useful and rewarding it has been to connect with others digitally. I have found my own tiny corner of the internet that is generous, kind and supportive.

While you might not be reaching your main readership through social media, especially if you are writing for children up to the age of 12, you will still connect with the people who buy books for your younger readers. Other children's fiction writers are not your competition, but your co-workers. They will support your book and recommend you to their own readers, and in turn you can shout about their writing and make friends for life.

3. Reaching out to teachers and librarians

There are so many brilliant primary school teachers and librarians who are incredibly engaged with the children's publishing world. They truly care about making sure that every single child feels seen. I've met a number of teachers who are passionate about literacy and want authors to get involved. Here are some ways that have allowed me to connect:

• Ask if any schools would like to enter an author pen-pal correspondence with you. You could contact a local school or even get in touch with your old primary school.

• Go to your local library to discover what reading resources are especially useful for children. Accelerated Reader (www.renaissance.com/products/accelerated-reader), for example, is a programme that is used in many schools to encourage reading for pleasure.

• Get involved in online chat and keep an eye out for hashtags such as: #teachertwitter, #edutwitter, #primaryschoolbookclub.

4. The brilliance of bookshops and booksellers

It's well worth calling up or going into your local bookshop(s) and introducing yourself. It's hypocritical of me to tell you not to be shy because, even after visiting dozens upon dozens of bookshops, I still quietly mutter, 'My name's Clare and I wrote that book over there…' (*points ambiguously to a shelf in the distance*). Bookshops can't stock every single book that has been published (unless they're a Tardis in disguise). I guarantee they will want to hear from you and, if they don't have copies of your book in store, be assured that they will be ordering after your visit.

Once you connect with a bookseller, you can ask whether they might be interested in running an event with you or organising a signing. For all of the big glossy promotions and huge marketing and publicity campaigns, bookseller recommendations are still one of the most useful selling tools. How many times have you walked into a bookshop, only planning to buy just one book on your list, and then left with a dozen new recommendations from a friendly bookseller? Booksellers help your books to live a long and happy life, and to be read by new readers time and time again.

5. School visits

A school visit is one of the most direct ways to connect with your readers. In the *Writers' & Artists' Guide to Writing for Children and YA* (Bloomsbury 2019), author Linda Strachan has written a comprehensive guide for writers on how to navigate school visits. I do implore you to get that book and read it, so you can make the most out of any school visits you organise.

Think about what strands of your story would work best for a school event and how this will relate to your readers. For example, I lead assemblies and workshops creating mystery, adventure stories and how to create authentic villains in a responsible way. Villains are a big part of my books and I always give a reading of my main villains and then immediately follow it up with a 'Guess the Villains' quiz, where I include villains from other books, films and TV shows.

Not every writer is able to visit schools in-person, but there are still other ways of connecting with schoolchildren. Virtual workshops and Q&As are more popular than ever, and this is a great way to reach your readers from your home office desk or kitchen table. Alternatively, if you don't have time in your working day to offer virtual school visits, creating pre-recorded videos – whether it's a five-minute creative writing exercise challenge or a much longer workshop session – is another great way to maintain a connection with schools. You can also reuse any recordings as content for other schools or organisations, or upload it to your website.

A note to remember:

You can do as much or as little of this as you want. You might agree to write a blog for free; you might offer a visit to a school in a low-income area that would love to have an author visit but just doesn't have the financial means. As an author, you are in control of what you say 'Yes' and 'No' to. You never have to do anything you feel uncomfortable with. I always remind myself that connecting and growing readers is a marathon, not a sprint. Focus on what you can control and enjoy it – because, when you're having fun, your readers will too.

Clare Povey is an author, avid language learner and the proud owner of four Blue Peter badges. Her middle-grade novels include *The Unexpected Tale of Bastien Bonlivre* (Usborne 2021), which was a Waterstones Children's Book of the Month, *The Unexpected Tale of the Bad Brothers* (Usborne 2022) and *The Wanderdays: Journey to Fantome Island* (Usborne 2024). Her next book, *The Midnight Sweet Factory*, will be published in September 2025. She also wrote the mystery play, *The Book of Eternity*, for the Northern Opera Group. Clare is the Content and Partnership Manager of the Writers & Artists website. Born and raised in Barking & Dagenham, Clare was motivated to create the W&A Working-Class Writers' Prize in 2018. For more information see www.clarepovey.com. Follow her on X @ClareFPovey or Instagram @clarefpovey.

See also...
- *Why teachers make great children's writers*, page 203

Plotting and pace in your middle-grade adventure

Christopher Edge understands the highs and lows, twists and turns that are needed to hold the attention of middle-grade fiction readers with a thirst for adventure. Here he shares valuable advice on how to structure a plot and drive forward an emotionally engaging storyline that has all the essential elements.

'Adventure is just bad planning.' So said the great Norwegian explorer, Roald Amundsen, who was the first man to reach both the North and South poles but who, as far as I know, never wrote a single word of children's fiction – so I really wouldn't go listening to him when it comes to planning your middle-grade adventure.

But what is a 'middle-grade adventure'? Well, the first part is easy to define, as middle-grade is the term the publishing industry uses to describe novels for children aged 9–12. Now, I'm a subscriber to C.S. Lewis's dictum that the best children's books which can be enjoyed at the age of ten are equally worth reading at the age of 50 and beyond, so when we talk about middle-grade we're definitely not talking about fiction that is any way middle-of-the-road or second-rate. These are the stories that can shape young readers' lives, opening doors into new realities, allowing them to escape into other lives, and inspiring them to step boldly forward to mark their own place in the world. And as for adventure, I'd argue it's not so much a genre but more an attitude that's woven into the fabric of children's fiction. Whether it's fantasy, mystery, historical, contemporary, science fiction or even comedy, from Lewis Carroll's *Alice's Adventures in Wonderland* (Macmillan 1865) to *Rowley Jefferson's Awesome Friendly Adventure* by Jeff Kinney (Penguin Random House 2020), the drumbeat of adventure can always be heard as we turn the pages of the novels we find on the bookshelves labelled 'Fiction 9–12'.

This is certainly true of my own fiction. I find it difficult to pin the stories I write down to a single genre, but adventure is an 'ever-present'; from *The Many Worlds of Albie Bright* (Nosy Crow 2016) where Albie climbs inside a cardboard box to travel to parallel universes in search of his mum, to *The Infinite Lives of Maisie Day* (Nosy Crow 2018) where Maisie's adventures are contained within the four walls of her home after the universe outside her front door disappears. In children's fiction there are no hard-and-fast rules about where adventure can be found and, in stories such as *The Longest Night of Charlie Noon* (Nosy Crow 2019) which begins, 'Once upon a time, three kids got lost in the woods', I've enjoyed twisting familiar tropes into unexpected new shapes. But why do readers of middle-grade fiction have such a thirst for adventure? In surveys about children's reading habits, such as Scholastic's biennial *Kids & Family Reading Report*, children aged 9–12 respond that they want books that have characters that look like them; this reaffirms the need for all readers to find themselves represented in the fiction they read, but also that they want characters they wish they could be like because they're smart or strong or brave. So this thirst for adventure could be viewed as a form of wish fulfilment, as young readers seek out stories in which they can see idealised reflections of themselves, placed in exciting and dangerous situations. For these readers, reading can be role-play, their identification with the heroes and heroines of middle-grade fiction offering them a vicarious agency they might not be able to find in their everyday lives.

I think another reason why such a rich thread of adventure runs through middle-grade fiction can be found in the world-view of its readers. Still shaping their understanding of the world around them, these are curious readers who read with fearless eyes. Their tastes aren't fixed in the same way that an adult readers often are. This isn't a jaded audience, but it is an audience with high expectations who will only keep turning the pages of a story if it delivers on its promise of adventure. So how can you craft a middle-grade adventure that will keep these readers turning the pages? The first thing to consider is plot. Now plot is just another name for story – it's the sequence of events that take place in a narrative. And the plotting stage is where you decide exactly what these events will be and the best way to structure them. This is a stage of writing that I love. For me, stories rarely land in my brain fully formed. The initial spark of inspiration might arrive in the form of a character, a situation, or a setting. For *The Infinite Lives of Maisie Day*, I had an image of a girl opening her front door to find an infinite darkness outside. Like any spark of inspiration, this image initially existed in what Russell T. Davies dubs 'the quantum state of Maybe' – with seemingly infinite possibilities it could spawn in terms of the story sparking in and out of existence inside my mind. Through a process of asking questions, researching ideas, and making connections, I started to shape these possibilities into a definitive storyline.

But how could I be sure that the plot I was building was taking the right shape? Lots of theories about story structure come from the world of film. From the three-act structure of set-up, confrontation and resolution, with key scenes that tip the story from one act to the next, to mythic structures such as the 'Hero's Journey' where a protagonist heeds a call to adventure, faces tests, trials and challenges before seizing their reward, screenwriting formulas seemingly offer a short cut to crafting the perfect plot. However, I must admit I don't consciously hold any theories like these in the front of my mind when plotting my adventures. For me, the plot always grows from character or, more accurately, plot and character grow together.

Stories are about change and change is driven by character. Examining your protagonist's motives can help you to build your plot, as you consider the actions they might pursue as they try to attain their goal. In *The Many Worlds of Albie Bright*, the motive that spurs Albie to set out on his adventure is his desire to see his mum again, with this goal fuelling his creation of the Quantum Banana Theory – the invention that enables him to travel into parallel worlds. Handily, this universe-hopping device also gave me a skeleton structure for the story, as Albie journeys through these alternate universes in search of the one where his mum is still alive. Now if your protagonist achieves their primary goal straight away, there's not much of a story – so you need to think about what's going to stand in their way. This could be an antagonist whose own motives and goals place them in conflict with your protagonist. In every adventure there needs to be obstacles, complications and confrontations which your protagonist has to navigate to get closer to their goal. Some scenes might shine brightest in your mind at this point, but thinking about the cause-and-effect of these key moments can trigger ideas for other scenes and help you start to sequence these into a coherent plot. I sometimes draw a flow chart to plot the action of the story – this helps me to visualise the links between different events and keep track of how characters develop.

Every scene should have a purpose that drives the plot forward; deciding what this is can help you to focus on the details that matter when you start writing. Begin each scene as far into the action as possible and as soon as the purpose is achieved that should be your signal to end the scene. Each scene should contain the seeds of the next and, as the story moves forward, you want to keep raising the stakes – but you also need to vary the rhythm of the story so that it doesn't become predictable for the reader. Think about the rhythm you want to create, perhaps balancing action-packed scenes with quieter moments of description and dialogue that slow the narrative pace and give the reader a chance to catch their breath.

Now every adventure must come to an end. Some authors only discover the ending of a story through the act of writing it, but I usually find mine before I even write the very first line. At the outset I have a clear picture in my mind of the opening scene and also the climax of the story, with these two moments tracing the emotional arc of my protagonist's adventure. In *The Many Worlds of Albie Bright*, Albie's journeys through different parallel worlds show him the alternative lives he could have lived, and these experiences change Albie and help him to come to an understanding of what he's really searching for as the story reaches its climax. An adventure isn't just an action-packed sequence of events but an emotional journey too, as characters make discoveries, find out things about themselves, and are changed by their experiences.

Writing itself can be an adventure, so don't be afraid to follow your own path. There will be trials and challenges along the way, and you may even feel lost at times as you hack through the thickets of a first draft – but always try to take pleasure in the journey. And when you make it to the end, the reward you find can be greater than any treasure hoard: it's the sight of a young reader turning the pages of your story, their eyes shining with excitement as they escape into a world of adventure.

Christopher Edge is an award-winning author whose novels for children include *Twelve Minutes to Midnight* (2012), *The Many Worlds of Albie Bright* (2016), *The Jamie Drake Equation* (2017), *The Infinite Lives of Maisie Day* (2018), *The Longest Night of Charlie Noon* (2019), *Escape Room* (2022) and *Black Hole Cinema Club* (2024), all published by Nosy Crow, and *Space Oddity* (Chicken House 2021). His latest novel is *Escape Room: Game Zero* (Nosy Crow 2025). He is also the author of guides to creative writing for children and teenagers, *How to Write Your Best Story Ever!* (OUP 2015) and *How to be a Young #Writer* (OUP 2017), and works as a freelance publishing and education consultant. For more information see his website www.christopheredge.co.uk and follow him on Instagram @christopheredge.

See also...
- *Writing mystery and adventure stories*, page 154

Writing real characters into fiction

Elle McNicoll explores what is meant by describing fictional characters as 'real', a quality that is achieved through 'the exposure of the human condition within an imagined story' in a truthful and relatable way. She relates her experience as a neurodivergent author and how her authentic, lived experience is portrayed in her fiction, and asks other writers to examine their own truth as authors.

As an author, I'm not entirely settled upon what 'real' means anymore. In children's publishing, writing 'real characters' may refer to an author choosing to write contemporary fiction, with characters whose fictional world – or rather the one that the author feels they inhabit – greatly resembles our own and there are no fantastical elements involved. That's not on my résumé.

So why have I been asked to write about creating 'real characters'? Sometimes this refers to an author who chooses to use historic events and people as a stimulus for their story. Perhaps their children's novel is set aboard the Titanic, or maybe it uses WWII as a background. Patience Agbabi brilliantly incorporated Samuel Johnson into her fabulous trilogy for children, *The Leap Cycle* (Canongate Books 2020–23). That is not on my résumé, either. I have not written gritty, realistic novels, nor have I used historical figures as members of my ensemble cast. Both are noble pursuits, but they have not been mine. So again, why have I been asked to write about 'real characters'? It's because I'm neurodivergent and my fiction is unapologetically so. Every author is different, and every author has their own point of view. It's why we read. Books are windows into other people's minds, a way to view how fellow travellers see the world. No literary window looks out onto the exact same landscape as another, so every author brings individuality.

With that disclaimer out of the way, let me say that some viewpoints are promoted more than others. Some writers are considered the default, while the rest of us are treated as charming novelties. A writer with a neurodevelopmental disability, for example, will be asked to talk about their personal life, and even their trauma, far more than their work. Your book may win every literary prize, won on literary merit and awarded by your peers and readers, but the press will only ever want to hear about which parts are 'true' and which are 'made up'. I'm a bestselling, award-winning children's author, with a CBBC adaptation of my debut novel (*A Kind of Spark*; Knights Of 2020) which was described as 'groundbreaking', but I'm mostly asked about my darkest moments. I'm asked about my diagnosis, something that every neurodivergent person should be allowed to hold close to them. I'm asked about how my brain works in comparison to my neurotypical peers, who make up the majority (but not all) of the publishing industry. My neurotypical colleagues on panels answer questions about character development and plot structure. I'm asked to explain why children who are like me deserve to be in stories. I'm asked about what is 'real'.

If you are reading this, we are peers or perhaps even colleagues. I won't presume to tell you how to write, how to publish, how to illustrate. But I am here to tell you that there is no such thing as 'real' in what I do. I use my authentic, lived experience to portray neurodiversity in my books, that is true. Perhaps that is as real as anything *can* be in a children's story. I hope so. I'm heartened and moved by the many letters I receive from readers saying, 'Addie is just like me!' or 'Cora is like me at school'. Good writing, like great acting, needs the truth. A great story is an imagined circumstance, narrated authentically. I don't necessarily believe in the maxim 'Write what you know' – unless we're discussing marginalised people.

So many neurotypical writers have had a go at writing about my brain. I woke up one day and decided it was time *I* actually tried it. And it felt very exposing. Telling all my secrets about dancing hands, heightened senses, masking and processing difficulties. Bad handwriting, social exclusion and the sky falling over things others don't even see. It was vulnerable. It was frightening. But it was truthful. It was, I suppose, real.

It was one candid nettle in a garden of fictional flowers.

But why does the industry insist on treating majority writers like authors and marginalised writers like biographers? We are imaginers, too – perhaps more than anyone; I'll return to that later. It is the truthful and relatable aspects of any fictional character that makes them 'real', not the life of the author. Othello is real to us because his jealousy is something that has spiralled out of control, but it comes from a place that many of us own in our hidden hearts. We love Anne Shirley of L.M. Montgomery's *Anne of Green Gables* (L.C. Page & Co. 1908) because we have all, at some point, wished our hair were a different colour or our face another face. Jo March is not real. In the literal sense. But, to millions, she is real in the soul. Her ambition, her bluster, her clumsy manners. Her yearning for something more.

It is the exposure of the human condition within an imagined story that makes characters 'real' – the vulnerable and brave choice of the author to say, 'I see the world like this. Perhaps people like this exist? Perhaps a world like this is real to you, as it is to me. Or maybe we could make it.'

Every story, no matter the trimmings, asks: 'What am I? Who am I when the light goes out?'. A checklist or a cheat sheet cannot accomplish this kind of portrayal, and it will not connect with the reader. An expert on birds will never truly know what it feels like to fly. So, what is your truth as an author? Not your past, not your biography, but your *truth*? The truth is not synonymous with fact when it comes to storytelling.

So I'll ask again: What is your truth? What do you know to be true? Or believe to be true? What is your point of view? I could have written a novel containing the facts of my life. I could have written a memoir disguised as a children's story. Instead, I plucked a hidden, painful handful of truth dust from my ribs and scattered it onto the page, alongside plenty of imagination. Readers are archaeologists. They can always find and connect with the truth and the 'real' parts … if they're really looking. I wrote about a young witch who could see through the supernatural veil of an ancient city, but what made her real to people was her struggle in school. Her stubbornness. Her pride. Her learning difficulty and her refusal to let people shame her for it. The truth, as I know it.

You can write about the most magical, the most impossible. In children's fiction, there is no impossible. But if you want people to connect with your fiction, add a little of your truth. And again – remember that the truth, in stories, is not objective. I write books where children who have been historically oppressed and miscounted are the heroines: I know that can be true.

I write about characters who learn about their own prejudice and prove in their actions that people can change and grow and make the world a more encouraging place: I know that will be true.

I write about worlds that can be changed by these incredible children and the courage they inspire in others. I write about things that may not have happened but that, in telling them, I can reach through the pages and show young readers they are not alone, they can chart the course. They can decide the path. I can give them permission to be brave: I know that is true.

None of it is real. As a storyteller, I'm not interested in real. I'm tired of remembering things that were real. I'm interested in the truth. And you should be, too. Only in telling the truth in our stories can we create something real for the reader. Our humanity, our fingerprint, our unique view on the human condition and our fellow passengers to the end of the story – that is the only thing that can make your writing 'real'.

Elle McNicoll is a bestselling and award-winning Scottish children's author, currently living in North London. Her debut novel, *A Kind of Spark* (Knights Of 2020) won the Blue Peter Book Award and the Waterstones Children's Book Prize. Her second novel, *Show Us Who You Are* (Knights Of 2021) was one of *The Bookseller*'s Best Books of 2021. Her third book, *Like a Charm*, was published in 2022 and its sequel, *Like a Curse*, in February 2023. Elle is also co-writer for the *A Kind of Spark* CBBC series. Her latest books include *Keedie* (Knights Of 2024), *Some Like it Cold* (First Ink 2024) and *Wish You Were Her* (First Ink 2025). Neurodivergent herself, Elle is an advocate for better representation of neurodiversity and disability in publishing and the media; she founded the Adrien Prize, to recognise children's fiction that explores the disability experience. For more information see https://ellemcnicoll.com.

Creating your cast of characters

Aisling Fowler considers the power of fictional characters to engage young readers, and gives advice on how to know and develop your characters fully, in a way that draws readers with them on an emotional journey.

The breadth of children's literature is enormous, but no matter what type of book a child loves to read, one thing remains constant: it's the characters that take our young readers by the hand to lead them through the story. Authors hope that their fictional characters will engage a reader emotionally, compelling them to devour chapter after chapter. But how, as writers, can we create characters who feel *real* enough to do this? I think there are two parts to this: 1) not to think of your characters purely as made-up creations, but as people just as real as anyone you might know – with all the depth, complexity and contradictions that go along with that; 2) getting to know those characters inside out, so their authenticity sings off the page when you write them.

In my case, it was the main character of the *Fireborn* series (HarperCollins 2021–24), Twelve, who was the first spark of the story for me. She sprang into my imagination with her axes in hand and full of a fiery anger that took me by surprise. She immediately felt strong – but getting to know her thoroughly took a while. I started by asking her questions such as: Why are you so angry? Where is your family? What are those axes for? Through this, Twelve's personality, back story, and many features of the fantastical world of Ember pulled into focus.

When I started writing my first draft, I thought I knew Twelve well. But by the end she was vastly different – not purely because of the journey she'd been on, but also because I'd got to know her better through the act of writing her story. She was no longer abstract; I'd seen her in a variety of situations and discovered her responses to different characters. She felt more complete, more authentic, more three-dimensional. I was delighted – until I realised this meant rewriting how she was portrayed earlier in the book.

For some of us, perhaps those who lean more towards being 'pantsers' (seat-of-the-pants types) than plotters, this is how we ultimately get to know our main characters: we write them and discover them on the page. For those more organised individuals who want to have a clearer idea before they begin, though, there are a multitude of possible methods. You could interview your character, or write test scenes – which is particularly useful, in my opinion, for working out group dynamics. How about reading your character's horoscope, writing diary entries for them, or even giving them the Myers–Briggs personality test? Your imagination is the limit here … anything goes. This will all help you discover your character's strengths and weaknesses, their personality and backstory. But to identify what truly drives them, their goals and motivations for behaving the way they do, you will have to go even deeper, and ask trickier questions: What do they want most? Or even, what do they *think* they want but what do they *actually* want? What do they need (whether acknowledged by them or otherwise)?

Once you've achieved this deep knowledge of your main character, it's time to start thinking about their story arc through your book. How will their experiences change them? How will they grow? This might be immediately obvious or take some careful thought, but your character's emotional journey is every bit as important as their physical one. It's worth thinking about it in conjunction with your plot to make sure these two crucial aspects of the story are working together to draw your reader ever onwards. In *Fireborn*, Twelve is haunted by her past, tormented by the guilt of what happened to her family and obsessed with thoughts of revenge. I knew almost immediately that her arc needed to be a journey towards acceptance and self-forgiveness, one that would allow her to open up enough to allow friendships to blossom. In a way, her entire quest to rescue a kidnapped girl is a vehicle which lets that emotional shift take place in her. Many of the decisions I made about the plot were informed by how Twelve would react and whether that reaction moved her closer to or further from the goals of greater inner peace and friendship.

I can't think of many children's books (or any?) where there is a single, solitary character. At some point, you'll need to consider the wider cast, those sidekicks who'll be beside your main character on their journey. It's definitely worth getting to know these secondary characters just as well as you know your protagonist. Ideally, each of them needs to feel entirely distinct, with their own desires and story arcs through the book – these might end up being important sub-plots. As you did for your main character, identify their personalities and back story as well as their goals and motivations. Ask yourself how they differ from the main character and from each other. What sets each character apart?

In any group, real or imagined, there are usually complex dynamics at play. The chances are that this is true in your story too. Does everyone get on equally well, or are some closer than others? Does anyone feel left out? Do your characters bring out the best in each other, or the worst? Does one of them compensate for a lack of a particular trait in another? These are things worth thinking about carefully and I'll illustrate this with a couple of examples from *Fireborn*. Twelve has almost-impenetrable defensive walls around herself and is very prickly towards the other characters. I wanted the story to end with her having made friends, but it was very clear to me that Twelve herself would not be building any bridges. That meant I needed at least one of the other characters to be both kind and persistent enough to do that for her. These ended up being key traits in a secondary human character called Six. Another example involves Twelve's pet squirrel, Widge. I was worried that, because of those walls I mentioned, a reader would find Twelve unlikeable. I wanted to show there was more to her than raw anger. The solution came through Widge, who at the start of the story is her only friend. Early on, it's only through him that we see a different, softer side to Twelve. As he was a non-human character, I didn't feel I was compromising the coherency of Twelve's determination to remain alone – he's a squirrel: different rules apply than to the human characters.

In both examples, the sidekicks are compensating for flaws in my main character, working under cover to make her more relatable, while also (hopefully) staking their own claim on the reader's affections. It's important to remember that, with each new character, there's another chance to engage your young reader – another opportunity for them to find something they relate to, something that speaks to them and makes them care about your characters on a deeper, emotional level. It's this that can make a story utterly compelling. We can probably all think of a book that kept us up way past our bedtime, one that we couldn't stop reading because we had to know what happened to the characters we cared about so much. But, as writers, how do we invite this degree of connection? My take on it is this: we can like a character for their strengths and admire them for their triumphs, but to *love* them, to root for them with every fibre of your being, to cry for them, you need to see their vulnerabilities, their fears, their moments of weakness and the way they face adversity. Almost inevitably, this means putting them in difficult situations. Although this article is about creating characters, don't forget that it's your plot which showcases them. The two things can (and perhaps should) develop in tangent. Don't be afraid to think something like: 'My character is brave – how can I use the story to show this?'.

Let's take a step back. You now have your cast of characters and you know each of them well. It's time to consider how they can be portrayed clearly on the page. Remember that, particularly in the early chapters, their every word and action should be reinforcing who they are, drawing a clear, defined picture in your reader's mind. Consider what you know about each character: how will those things affect the way they speak, the language they choose to use? What about the way they dress, or their attitude towards others? Perhaps even the names you choose for them can help show who they are. This doesn't mean your characters can't have hidden depths, or behave surprisingly, but you need coherence in terms of who you know they are and the journey they're on, both individually and together. From the very first page, you want every character – but especially your main character – to feel as three-dimensional as possible.

In early drafts of *Fireborn*, I found differentiating subsidiary characters difficult. This was because I didn't know them well enough and needed to spend more time with them one-on-one. Later, to make each one feel more unique, I gave them habits or quirks unique to them. For example, one of my characters has a stutter, another constantly uses 'obviously' in his sentences, Twelve bites her lip when she's nervous, and Widge nibbles her hair. These are small things, but if you choose the traits carefully in a way that is authentic to the character, they can act as a shorthand which builds a clearer picture for your reader.

Creating believable characters is at the very heart of what we do as writers for children. Through your characters, young readers will experience ways of thinking and living that are different to their own – and perhaps, through that lens, they'll make more sense of their own lives and beliefs. Maybe your characters will even encourage young readers to question the world around them, show them that they can make a difference, empower them to be the people they want to be. The characters *you* create can do this. So, create them with love, don't be afraid of making them deep or complex and, above all, enjoy the process.

Aisling Fowler is the author of middle-grade fantasy novels *Fireborn: Twelve and the Frozen Forest* (2021), *Fireborn: Phoenix and the Frost Palace* (2023) and *Fireborn: Starling and the Cavern of Light* (2024), all published by HarperCollins. Aisling worked as a support worker and then as a nurse, before rediscovering her childhood love of writing. Follow her on X @fowler_aisling and Instagram @aislingfowler.

World-building in your fantasy fiction

L.D. Lapinski explores the creative art of world-building, with its imaginative potential and hidden depths, and has advice on how writers can bring their fantasy worlds, and the characters that navigate through them, to life in a way that engages and absorbs young readers.

World-building is such a strange and magical thing: using just your mind, you are bringing entire populations, places and universes almost to life. Creating a new reality that can feel as precious and vulnerable and enticing as the one we live and breathe in is a fantastic exercise, and one that seems increasingly tempting. The world you build for your characters to explore is not an empty set; it can have as much character as your hero, or as much menace as your villain. The world you create takes your reader on a journey, which can be close to home or as far flung as you desire.

I have always created imaginary places and worlds. Reading and writing have been my creative escape for as long as I can remember (and possibly even further back than that), and I have very fond memories of spending a rainy holiday in a caravan hunched over, drawing a detailed map and plotting a vast history for 'The World of Bunny Rabbits'. The real world wasn't appealing right then, so I made my own. And I'm still doing it. My first novel for children 9+, *The Strangeworlds Travel Agency* (Orion Children's 2020), arrived in bookshops at the start of the Covid-19 pandemic and, though it was a very unexpectedly fiery baptism, I hope it offered an escape to young readers looking for ways to get away from our world and into others.

However, simply hurling a new world at a reader does not a story make. Novels are, at their very heart, entertainment. The story needs to seize us by the wrist and drag us along a journey, not simply abandon us, mapless, in a new place with no sense of direction. Any world you create is there to work with and for your characters – it is a backdrop that you can change; to fit and make the most impact in your story. And, although your characters may navigate it with ease, the world they explore and tell the reader about still needs to be strong and 'real' enough to support their narrative journey. And this support is quite a literal concept when it comes to fantasy worlds!

Picture a penguin. Add the David Attenborough-style narration, if you like, as the camera pans back to reveal that the tiny penguin has hitched a ride on the top of an iceberg, and the iceberg drops deep into the depths below, far more of it below the waterline than above it. This iceberg, and the penguin, is your world-building. As you might expect, there is always so much more going on below the surface when writing fantasy books, but in this analogy what's really important for you to focus on isn't the iceberg at all. It's the penguin. As the writer, that tiny wee penguin is the amount of world-building you're actually going to have the space and words to include in your children's book. The iceberg above the surface is the amount and detail that you, your editor, and your agent will know. And, sadly, that huge mass below the surface is everything that not one other person will ever, ever, see. You might not even write it down.

Then surely we can get rid of it? Well, you could do. Take the iceberg away and the penguin would be able to swim for a bit. But it wouldn't be able to keep it up forever, and eventually it would get eaten by a sea leopard. The iceberg, even the unseen and unwritten part, protects and supports the penguin on its journey. In the same way, your characters and their journey could not carry on for very long without the supporting detail and facts of your world-building.

Tell me again how a world should feel

In *The Strangeworlds Travel Agency* series, Flick and Jonathan have travel to over 20 different worlds in the space of five stories. Hardly a great feat for them, given that there are 743 magical suitcase-portals in the travel agency, but certainly a challenge for me to keep a handle on when writing. Such a plethora of worlds could rapidly have felt overwhelming and difficult to keep track of, but – rather than begin an encyclopaedic collection of notes – I consciously crafted the worlds so that each one would appear distinct, without having to deep-dive into the history of each one, particularly since some of the characters' visits are rather fleeting.

I designed each individual world to evoke a specific emotional reaction from both the characters and the reader, and in such a way that each reaction would not be deliberately repeated. I created one world written to be deliberately frightening, another to be innocently joyful, one to be calm and soothing, and so on. In doing so, I was able both to show off the vast potential of *The Strangeworlds Travel Agency*'s magical suitcases, and to ensure that each of the worlds visited by the reader would be memorable. Even if the name of the place was forgotten, a younger reader might remember that one world was 'the scary one' and another 'the funny one', because they will relate to the world in the same way that Flick and Jonathan do. The characters' emotional reaction would be tied to the setting and what happened there, and will be mirrored by the reader, who wants to find out more and find out what will happen next.

Fantasy rules! Okay ...?

Who runs the world? Well, you do! The great thing about fantasy world rules is you get to make them up. And they can be as 'normal' or as outlandish as you like. They don't even have to serve a purpose beyond being entertaining! If everyone has to stand on their chair and shout 'WAHOOEY!' after eating, you can make that a rule. Perhaps this is never explained – and that's completely fine too. But how many of those rules you want to include is dependent on several factors: firstly and most importantly, your readers (and probably your characters) are children. Whether they are visiting this world for a brief visit like in *Strangeworlds*, or they live there full time, they are only going to focus on the aspects of their world that are the most pressing and interesting to them – the parts of their world that are driving their story, and their journey, forward. And if this element is shouting WAHOOEY, your characters might not bother mentioning the complex political systems of their world. Thinking again of the penguin atop the iceberg of world-building and how aware it may be about what's going on below it, remember that, however much you might know your fantasy world inside and out, your reader wants your characters to navigate the world you have built, not to read a travel guide about it.

Secondly, the amount of description you have space to include will always be restricted by the word count. There's nothing wrong with having enough world-building potential to fill a 500,000-word book, but editors and agents generally prefer shorter books (and it helps to keep printing costs down!). Tell readers what they need to know straight away, and use the rest of your imagined rules as iceberg-style unseen support for the story. It's still important, it's just out of sight.

Think fast!

Anyone familiar with video games will know that at the start of a game there is often a video, less than three minutes long, in which the world of gameplay is introduced – a few minutes of speedy world-building for games that can take dozens of hours to complete. I checked a few of these out, and on average an introductory video accounts for about 0.1% of total gameplay time. That's like doing all your introductory world-building in the space of a paragraph that takes up about one third of a page. That sounds pretty extreme, doesn't it?

Actually, no. A decent chunky paragraph at the start of a book can work extremely hard, just as the intro to a video game might. That initial chunk of world-building description introduces what sort of world this is, whether there's anything readers can recognise and relate to, whether there's magic or not, and it sets the scene for other, smaller bits of world-building which can be 'confettied' through the rest of the story. A first world-building paragraph has to be enticing; it may be the deciding factor as to whether someone carries on reading your book or not, having picked it up in a shop to browse through. The first impressions the reader of your fantasy world receives need to be rich, engaging … and brief. Readers should want, nay *need*, to know how your characters are going to navigate this wonderful or terrifying new place. They may even have an initial idea about the sort of problems they may encounter or the fun they might have. That early paragraph of world-building is advertising the journey your characters are about to go on; show off the best bits, and leave the details for later. And if, as in *The Strangeworlds Travel Agency*, the concept of your world is what you want to showcase rather than a description of a place, remember to hint at the richness of its potential but leave the reader hungry for more. Your character's journey is to get from A to B (whether this is physically or emotionally), but your reader's journey is to find out the details and to get thoroughly lost in your new world of fantasy and magic.

To be able to build a world for young readers to explore is a wonderful thing. Whether or not we can ever throw open the doors to our fantasy worlds completely, by writing them down at all we are inviting readers to wander within, to make up their own minds about the potential dangers or excitements – and inspiring them to create escapes of their own.

L.D. Lapinski is the author of the *Artezans* trilogy: *JAMIE*, *Stepfather Christmas* and *The Biggest Christmas Secret Ever*; and *The Strangeworlds Travel Agency* series. They have also written for BBC IP *Doctor Who* with *Doctor Who Icons: Charles Darwin & the Silurian Survival*. Their first speculative fiction book for adults, *Some Body Like Me* was published by Gollancz, and their debut graphic novel *KickFlip*, created with Logan Hanning, was published in 2025. Lapinski's books are published around the world in 16 languages. They have an MA in Creative Writing from Nottingham Trent University, and have been honoured with the University's Outstanding Alumnus award. Lapinski's work has been nominated for the Yoto Carnegie Medal, Polari Prize, Branford Boase and more. For more information see www.ldlapinski.com. Follow them on social media @ldlapinski.

See also...
- *Writing magic into fiction*, page 148

What does a ghostwriter do?

Writing can be a solitary business – but it doesn't have to be. Some authors benefit enormously from collaborating with experienced, skilled ghostwriters like Sam Binnie. Read on to find out her thoughts on the process.

Everyone has a book in them, runs the old adage. But at the heart of any great book is an idea and sometimes turning an idea into a polished manuscript is too big a task for a new writer to do alone.

Writing a book with or for you whilst remaining 'invisible' is what a ghostwriter does; capturing another person's unique voice, and then combining it with clever plotting and good-quality writing, such that readers are carried along until the final page. And those ghostwriters, although hidden in the shadows, are in fact within arm's reach: once accessible only through big publishers or a well-connected agent, the internet has changed all of that. Search online for 'ghostwriter services' and you'll find a wide selection of professionals offering these sought-after services. With a deep understanding of story and of human nature, these passionate and accomplished writers are in high demand, helping turn aspiring authors' ideas into complete books.

Of course, there have always been the lone hermits who toiled away, producing masterpieces with little to no intervention. But if that doesn't appeal to you, or your strengths lean toward collaboration, then an invisible co-author might be just what you're looking for. There's no need to abandon your dreams of writing your book because you're short on time or skills: finding a professional, experienced and creative ghostwriter could mean the difference between your idea remaining in your imagination and it seeing the full light of day, whether the project is a sweeping piece of historical children's fiction or a charming ten-page picture book with 100 words and your own beautiful illustrations.

Professional ghostwriting is about crafting compelling, original, authentic narratives instead of using technical copywriting skills or asking ChatGPT to produce the chapters until you've hit your word count. Ghostwriters have spent their days developing their skills, from editing to mentoring and teaching, to producing their own award-winning work. So, who better to help that book finally take shape than an experienced ghost?

I am one of them, and have found myself at home at The London Ghostwriting Company (LGC). We work closely with our authors at every stage in their journey, from the moment a prospective client contacts us and shares details about the book they need help with, sometimes even bringing us a first draft that needs an appraisal or edit.

More often, our clients will state they're not writers and need our help because they have an idea that they're desperate to see become something and be shared with the world. And like many of us, they want that meaningful connection through creative collaboration.

We then consider which of our writers to be the best fit for the project. The client and ghostwriter meet for video calls or in person, and these don't have to be dry, literary occasions: I've spent some opening sessions swapping recipes or reminiscing about shared memories of the 1990s. Creative writing is meant to bring enjoyment to both parties; it's about ensuring a creative flow through which author and ghostwriter can build a book together.

The working sessions themselves can be somewhat therapeutic for our authors. The creative process is frequently cathartic and transformational, and it goes without saying that all memoir types offer a confessional space in their creation. Interview sessions can involve a ghostwriter walking an author through their more challenging thoughts and memories to capture the themes or emotions the author wants to see on the page; the best books often come from the most open clients, those who can be honest about where they've been in life, their bad decisions and their good luck. When I worked on a glossy celeb tell-all, the author could completely open up about some truly punishing moments in their life because they knew they had total control over what would appear in the book under their name. Until then, they hadn't had the opportunity to talk about those events to someone free of judgement and direct emotional connection, who could approach their story from an outsider's perspective. Every author is amazed at how much a good ghostwriter can draw out of them, with a combination of active listening and leading suggestions, and clear steps towards the final goal of their book coming to life.

If you are working with a ghostwriter, make sure you have some say in how the sessions are shaped: if distance allows, do you want to meet at the same time every week in your favourite cafe, comparing cakes while plotting each twist and turn? Or would you prefer a video meeting and correspondence over email and document notes? The author should feel comfortable sharing their ideas and giving feedback. Ultimately, the author has complete control of a project, so while ghostwriters can advise clients on style, structure and publishing trends, their mission is always to create the book the client wants. As we say at LGC, it's 'your story, your book'.

Each ghostwriter will have their own way of doing things. At LGC we have a wider team that means there is always more support at hand and no ghostwriter is left entirely to their own devices: projects are fully supervised by our in-house staff to keep everyone on the agreed-upon track; work is further developed by one of our editors for another perspective; and, when the time is right, we assist with final submissions to agents and publishing houses.

How long does it take? It all goes back to the project. Books of 60,000+ words can be written in four months on the fastest-possible turnround, but occasionally large amounts of research can see a book take several years. Usually, the whole project – from point of contact to publisher submissions – will average between 12 and 18 months.

At the beginning of the writing process, we produce an outline of the project, a detailed chapter breakdown, and a pitch. These components are the scaffolding, and while aspects can and do change during the writing, it means both writer and author are on the same page (pun intended) throughout the whole process.

Beyond this, it's then the job of the ghost to write and edit all iterations until the number of changes requested hits zero and everyone feels the book is complete. At this point, we begin the technical work of proofreading and submissions. From exciting but foggy thoughts to solid lines of tightened, edited and polished prose, it's deeply satisfying for both ghostwriter and aspiring author to see the book weigh anchor and sail into the real world.

But this world of agents and publishers is when the work really starts. We'll refine the proposal and cover letter, highlighting exactly which features of the project an agent will want to see and advising our authors where to send their book. When a book sells to a publisher, it becomes the publishing house's task to print, publicise and market it to potential purchasers, and we can sit back and enjoy the client's success. If the client wants to self-publish, we can advise who to consider there too. There are some fantastic hybrid options available for writers today, so all in all there is going to be a home for every creation.

Writing a book requires a lot of time, patience and practice that, for many, is just too demanding to do by themselves. But when there is too much to process, working collaboratively with an expert can work wonders. Showing your writing to people you know can also feel exposing. Will the reader get your jokes? Will they understand your subplots? Your theme? A good ghostwriter will offer an objective approach with non-judgemental support, and allow you to take all the credit for both your ideas and the wonderful book you've worked towards all this time.

There are some key things to consider when starting work with a ghostwriter:

- What is the genre of your book? What is the age range? What books might compare with it? You may not be able to answer these initially, but as you talk through your book with your new co-writer, they can guide you on these topics.
- What stage is your story idea at? A good writer can't give you your initial idea, but they can help you talk through your premise and unpack a story's theme to uncover all of the underdeveloped areas, and then polish your full project into a sellable title.
- Are you ready to collaborate? Ghostwriting is most productive when clients are committed to communicating and sharing ideas: co-writers need to know when you like or dislike what they're doing.
- How do I find a ghostwriter? Literary agents and publishers might be able to assign writers on their books to projects, but going direct to a ghostwriter 'for hire' will guarantee a quick and focused response. Try online searches or word-of-mouth recommendations; some collectives, agencies and companies work exclusively as ghostwriters without the desire to share credit on the cover, although this can be a way to negotiate lower rates. Don't be shy about asking for links and samples to get a feel for a ghost's writing too.
- Do I really need a ghostwriter, editor or mentor? Consider where your project is, as well as your own goals. If you want to get the words down on paper (as it were) yourself, outsourcing to a ghostwriter would not appeal, in which case a book mentor or good freelance editor will coach you through what you've already produced. Most writers tend to wear many hats and operate as anonymous scribes or active editors, mentoring and consulting as is necessary.
- Is it cheating? Not at all! Some of the most popular books of the last 2,000 years have been ghostwritten, from religious texts to *The Three Musketeers*, old *Hardy Boy* novels and the *Nancy Drew Mystery Stories*, to almost every celebrity and political memoir. Everyone is good at something: maybe your talent is storytelling, and you can leave the writing of that story to your ghost. Every book starts somewhere, and hiring a ghostwriter could be the start of yours.

Sam Binnie is a professional writer of fiction and non-fiction. She has ghostwritten a *Sunday Times* bestselling celebrity memoir, created a guidebook to the multi-award-winning *Wolf Hall* books and written four of her own novels. She has interviewed Pulitzer Prize-winning authors, copy-edited art books, cookery books and major industry handbooks, and runs corporate copywriting workshops and creative writing sessions in schools. Her writing has appeared in *VICE* magazine, the *Guardian* and *Harper's Bazaar,* and she won the Orange Short Story Prize in 2005. She works as an editor and ghostwriter at The London Ghostwriting Company on fiction and non-fiction titles.

Writing for different genres

Writing adventures in the real world: children's non-fiction

Isabel Thomas explores the exciting world of children's non-fiction, and shares her tips for writing the perfect pitch.

Why write non-fiction?

Children's non-fiction is so much more than 'books with facts'. It's a different way for writers to reach young readers, to take them on a journey that makes them laugh, or cry, or bubble over with enthusiasm. It inspires children to explore their world – and to change it.

The last decade has seen an exciting renaissance in the genre. Dozens of new children's non-fiction imprints have launched, and publishers are investing in lavish illustrations and large formats. Bookshops and libraries have reconfigured their shelves to make space for titles big enough to dive into. Children's non-fiction titles appear in bestseller charts, award shortlists and festival programmes. Readers – and their families – are demonstrating a huge appetite for bold and beautiful adventures in the real world.

It's an exciting time to write and illustrate children's non-fiction, and the scope for creativity is huge. I've written picture books, comic strips and biographies where text and illustrations play together on the page. I've created coffee table tomes, activity books packed with paper engineering, and hands-on crafts and experiments.

All these books have something in common: a good children's non-fiction book is nothing like a textbook. It's an opportunity to tell a complete story that helps children connect bite-sized facts with the bigger picture.

Where do I begin?

Find something that excites YOU, and then work out the best way to pass that excitement on to young readers. For me, it's science and nature.

Next, get specific. My first book was about blue and purple foods, an extension of an existing series. As debuts go it was low key. But it gave me the confidence to offer my services as a science writer to other publishers. Finding your niche is useful for winning that first commission, but it's not enough to know your subject area in depth. To make a topic irresistible to children, you need to know your readers too.

Spend time with children and immerse yourself in their world. Not just literature, but TV, films, apps and playground trends. Children's non-fiction competes with all of these things. I volunteer as a school governor and STEM Ambassador, roles that keep me in touch with curriculum change, and the influences that shape children's lives. I also read at libraries and run school events. Over 200 books into my career, I've become an expert in thinking like an eight-year-old.

Finding your angle

The value of a non-fiction book lies not just in the information delivered – which must of course be accurate and up-to-date – but in the way it's presented. How will you hook your reader, so that your book educates *and* entertains? Play with ideas, make connections and take your readers on a journey. It might be through humour, adventure or quirky details. Or it might be by making a complex topic simple enough to give a child that 'wow' moment.

An original angle is essential if your book is to stand out on a crowded shelf. Instead of listing facts about space, weave them into an alien's guide to the solar system, or a book of rocket science for beginners. If you're writing about life cycles, how about a zookeeper's handbook, or a hypothetical battle of lion versus tiger?

Developing your idea

At this point, a fiction author would write the first draft, ready to polish to perfection. The advice for non-fiction is rather different: don't write the book!

Children's non-fiction is usually a team effort, combining the author's ideas with those of talented editors, illustrators and designers to create something extraordinary. Unless you are pitching a picture book, there is usually no need to write the entire manuscript up front. Instead, develop a proposal and a few sample spreads, and make these as polished as possible. Once your idea has been commissioned, the editor will work with you to refine the approach, perfect the pacing of content and finalise the text features.

Don't forget to visit bookshops and libraries as you develop your idea. Holding the latest children's non-fiction books in your hands is much more revealing than looking at covers online. Get a feel for the typical extent and word count for each age group. How will you build knowledge and understanding over 48, 64 or 96 pages? Will you write a picture book with 20 words per page, or a reference book with 200? Read as many examples as you can to absorb the language level. Make a note of the page features that non-fiction writers use to break up the text into manageable chunks.

Writing a proposal – dos and don'ts

Children's non-fiction authors work with publishers in several different ways. The first will be familiar if you already write fiction. Pitch an original idea and negotiate an advance and royalty. Some non-fiction authors work with literary agents; others pitch directly to publishers. When I worked as a non-fiction commissioning editor, I was equally happy to hear from both. I worked without an agent for the first decade of my writing career, and used the excellent Society of Authors (see page 297) for advice on contracts.

Even if your initial idea is not the right one at that time, pitching is a good way to introduce yourself. Editors often come to non-fiction writers with a subject in mind and ask for a text treatment – a fresh new approach that will work for their market. In this case, the remuneration may be a one-off fee, higher than the advance for a similar title. Either way, your first task for each new title is to write a concise and engaging proposal to make the case for your idea.

Begin with an **overview** that showcases your style and tone. It should be good enough to become the back-cover blurb (and it often does). Follow this attention-grabbing introduction with a longer **description**. Explain why the book is timely, perfect for the target age group and why you are the best person to write it. There's no need to send the whole manuscript (unless you are writing a short picture book). Instead provide a **breakdown of the structure**, showing how you build engagement and understanding. Finally, include two or three pages of **sample text** to bring the idea to life.

DO:
- **Explain why you are pitching to this publisher.** Visit bookshops and scour catalogues, including the rights catalogues that publishers produce for book fairs. Find out what makes their books special. Then show why your idea and their list are a perfect match.
- **Come up with an attention-grabbing title** that hints at both subject matter and approach. Humorous and irreverent or lyrical and atmospheric? Hands-on activities or narrative adventure?
- **Point out anything that might drive sales**, such as anniversaries, curriculum links or exhibitions. Remember to work at least 18–24 months ahead – illustrated non-fiction takes around a year to journey from manuscript to shelf.
- **Showcase your voice.** Ten years ago, children's non-fiction often had a formal tone, edited to match house style. Today, a unique voice will help you stand out.

DON'T:
- **Claim that there is no competition.** More often than not, this points to a lack of research. Competition can prove that a topic is in demand. Publishers will always offer books on dinosaurs, space and animals, and are hungry for creative new approaches to these popular themes. Compare your idea to existing titles – ideally successful ones! Explain why your approach will be different (and better).
- **Include illustrations.** Unless you're an author-illustrator, it's the publisher's role to find an illustrator that the audience will love (often, but not always, with your approval). Instead, note down ideas about the type of illustrations you think would work well, as part of your overall vision for the book.
- **Mention how much your family and friends like the idea.** Publishers get many proposals saying 'tested on my kids'. It's better to showcase the skills and experience that make you an expert in your subject area or target audience – or both!

Writing the book – three golden rules

1. Research is key
One of the best things about writing for a living is the chance to dive into a subject. You might be writing for ten-year-olds, but you'll need to understand your topic in much greater depth. To avoid introducing errors, track down original sources. If you read an interesting article, find the original research too. Better still, interview the author. Insist on – and carefully record – at least two sources for every fact (and never make one of those sources Wikipedia). And be warned – when you're interviewing stuntwomen, scientists or astronauts, job envy is an occupational hazard!

2. Be playful
Hooking the audience doesn't end with a creative angle. Every page, paragraph and sentence must work hard to weave in the information you'd like to cover, while keeping readers engaged.

Make good use of text features, such as infographics, charts, text boxes and quotes. They can help you to bring interesting facts to the fore, enticing a reader to explore the rest of the page. They also help to pace the flow of information, making complex topics or arguments easier to follow.

Resist the temptation to include everything. First drafts are often double the length of the final text, and the real work comes in deciding what to leave out.

3. Think visually

Illustrations are a key ingredient in children's non-fiction. Sourcing these illustrations (whether buying photographs or commissioning illustrators) is the job of the publisher. But briefing them is the job of the author.

Think like an art director – how will information be broken up into chunks and displayed on the page? What diagrams will help you to explain a difficult concept? Will you include cartoons and visual jokes? An information book might need simple photo briefs, while a graphic text demands detailed descriptions of every panel. Create a wish list, to be realized by a talented illustrator and designer.

Building a writing career

Children's non-fiction authors develop valuable skills: the ability to carry out in-depth research, to build bridges between prior knowledge and new information, and to craft a story that educates and entertains. These skills are in demand outside book publishing – by companies, charities and organisations that want to create outreach resources, by children's magazines, museums and science centres, and by producers of educational websites, blogs and vlogs. Writing other types of non-fiction content helps you keep your voice and ideas fresh. It can also be another way to reach your audience if you have an idea that's close to your heart, but find that there is no commercial demand for it in book form.

Promoting your books is another area where creative ideas and an appetite for pitching will help you to shine. As a non-fiction author, you are well placed to **design and run** events linked to your writing. For example, write and introduce yourself to to organisations and museums linked to the subject(s) you write about; suggest topics for radio or podcast discussions; pitch magazine and newspaper articles; offer to run hands-on sessions in bookshops and public libraries; help children unleash their own non-fiction writing power in an educational workshop. Events are a direct way to keep in touch with your readers, and you'll come away with dozens of ideas for new books.

Nothing beats the feeling of discovering something wonderful for the first time. Whether I'm writing a biography, an activity book or a picture book, I aim to give readers the same feeling. If I can encourage children to pick up a book, think 'wow', and keep reading, I know I've done a good job. But if they read something that encourages them to close the book, head outside and explore the world ... well, then I know I've done a *great* job.

Where will your next non-fiction adventure take you?

Isabel Thomas has written more than 280 non-fiction titles for young audiences, published by Bloomsbury, What on Earth? Books, Oxford University Press, Puffin, Laurence King, Ladybird, Collins, Pearson, Phaidon, DK, Rising Stars, Raintree, Schofield & Sims, QED, Welbeck, Weldon Owen, Wide Eyed and Wren & Rook in the UK, and translated into more than 30 languages around the world. Her narrative non-fiction picture books *Moth: An Evolution Story* and *Fox: A Circle of Life Story* (both published by Bloomsbury) were winners of the AAAS Subaru Prize for Excellence in Science Books. Isabel's most recent publications include *Frog: A Story of Life on Earth* (Bloomsbury 2025), *The Bedtime Book of EVEN MORE Impossible Questions* (Bloomsbury 2024) and *Exploring the Universe: A Complete Guide to the Cosmos* (Phaidon 2025). Isabel's short online course in developing and pitching non-fiction for young audiences is available via Domestika. Find out more at www.isabelthomas.co.uk and follow her on Bluesky @isabelthomas.co.uk and Instagram @isabelthomasbooks.

Writing short stories for children

Julia Green describes the power and the pleasure of a well-written children's short story, and its essential attributes. She encourages aspiring short story writers to read, study, practice, experiment and aim high.

Primary School. I'm maybe eight or nine. We're reading a short story in class, from an ancient hardback collection of stories and poems illustrated with line drawings, with a faded blue and green cover. I can't remember the title of the anthology, but I do remember one story, about a lonely man making sand sculptures on the beach – Weymouth, in my memory. And the atmosphere – slightly melancholy, a sense of loss, the way that I often felt as a child when it was time to leave the beach – the tide coming in, late afternoon, the beach emptying out. The man walks away, the sea washes in and erases the sculptures... Later on, aged 13 or 14, in an English lesson we read Ted Hughes' short story *The Rain Horse*, which is all atmosphere – a field, the rain, the threatening horse, a young man's sense of terror.

Why have these particular short stories stayed in my mind over so many years, out of all the others we read as children? Perhaps it's the strong sense of place, the use of vivid detail to create a landscape and a moment in time through the appeal to all the senses. And a strong *feeling*: sadness, sense of loss, fear. It's partly in what is *not said*; an effective short story doesn't waste words. It leaves a space for the reader to imagine, to fill in the gaps. We enter into the story world, stay a short time, and leave again – but as a reader, we're left with the sense that something has changed forever. We've glimpsed something, felt something, of lasting significance. The short story as 'an arrow in flight', as the Irish writer Mary Lavin described it.

We are talking here about **the short story as a form in itself**; not a short book for children, like a picture book, or an illustrated story for young children which is short in length but is in essence a short novel – though much of what I am saying here would apply to these forms of story, too. And we are thinking of the **audience** as children aged from about four, when a child might be listening to the story being read aloud rather than reading for themselves, to about 12. Publishers and booksellers classify readers older than that as 'teen' or 'young adult' rather than children. It is helpful for a new writer to be aware of this. Writing for a four- or five-year-old is obviously very different from writing for someone of 9-12 years. Think about how appropriate the theme or experiences and emotions in your story would be for the age group you want to write for. Alternatively, first write the story you want to write, and *then* think about that question of audience. The problem for many new or unpublished writers is a mismatch between the style/language/content of the story and the age and interest of the 'audience': the child reader. Of course there are many notable exceptions to this, but as a *beginner writer* it's helpful to think about making the age of your main character just a little older than the age of your readers. You will need to be aware of the language and style, too, to make it appropriate for the intended audience.

If you want to write short stories for children, the important thing, of course, is to *read* many! Immerse yourself in the form. You might reread stories you enjoyed as a child, to re-experience them with your adult 'writer' mind, namely reading as-a-writer, alert to the way the story has been written. Examine closely: 1) the language, the way words and sentences work, how much or little description there is, how dialogue is used, how much or how little 'action' or 'plot'; 2) the pace (how quickly do things move along?); 3) what the story is actually 'about'; 4) the form of the short story, studying this is the best way of learning how to do it yourself (not so that you write in exactly the same way – we can only ever write authentically as ourselves – but to help you think about the different options open to you, and the tools of your trade). Make notes for yourself in a notebook.

Read contemporary short stories for children, too, to see what is being published now. Fashions change. Haunt bookshops and libraries. Look at anthologies of short stories published for children, such as *Moonlight Magic* (Stripes 2016) or *My Kind of School* (A&C Black 2008), edited by Tony Bradman; collections for different age groups, such as *The Puffin Book of Stories for Five-Year-Olds* (Penguin 1996) edited by Wendy Cooling, or *Funny Stories for 5-Year-Olds* (Pan Macmillan 2016), edited by Helen Paiba. These contain stories by different writers, new and old.

Read collections of short stories by individual authors, too. These are usually by established authors (it is very rare for a brand-new writer to have a collection of stories accepted for publication):

- Nicola Davies' *Up on the Hill* (Walker 2008) consists of three separate short stories about children who live in the country.
- Michael Morpurgo wrote a memorable collection, published as *The White Horse of Zennor and other stories* (Mammoth 1982).
- Leila Berg's wonderful *Little Pete Stories* (Methuen) for very young children written in the 1950s were groundbreaking in their time for the way she showed 'real' children, feeling strong emotions including anger.
- Emma Carroll's *When We Were Warriors* (Faber 2019) contains three short stories linked to her popular historical novels for children.
- David Almond's collection *Counting Stars* (Hodder Children's 2000) illustrates the richness of the short story form in the hands of a master storyteller. These layered, rich, strange and beautiful stories are based on his childhood in Felling in the North-East of England and transcend the usual publishing boundaries of 'age groups'. Almond wrote them before he wrote the prize-winning *Skellig* (Hodder Children's 1998), but they weren't published until after he was established as a successful novelist for young people.

Read these stories and then, as a 'writing exercise' in your writing notebook (of course you have one of these!), take real incidents or experiences from your own childhood as the material for a short story, so as to get in touch with the real, raw emotions of childhood and to help you find an authentic voice in your writing. (Note: this might end up as a short story '*about*' childhood as distinct from a story '*for*' children, two subtly different things.)

One of the great satisfactions of writing a short story is that sense of having the complete story in your hand, so you can 'see' it all at once, with its beautiful, honed shape. You can polish and perfect it, and learn much that will help you with all your writing, particularly about precision and brevity, voice and tone, and about the significance of endings. Aim high. Only the very best writing is good enough for children.

As children's writers, we have other things to consider as well as mastery of the short form. A contemporary short story for children is likely to be commissioned by an editor, via an agent, on a particular theme, to be published alongside other stories by other writers on that same theme. For example, I have been asked to write stories about children and animals suitable for several 'winter' anthologies, about the experience of primary school and on the theme of friendship for children of primary school age (up to age 11). The challenge is to write a story that will be original and different enough from the others in the collection, that will appeal to the age group, be accessible, reflect the diversity of the world we live in and be enjoyable and engaging. The story needs to feel complete, to give the reader that satisfaction of a happy (or happy/hopeful *enough*) ending. It needs to take the reader into its world and introduce the main character (in my case always a child) swiftly and immersively, and to do this within a word limit (in these examples, 1500 words).

So, like a novel but in very condensed form, the story has to establish a character, a setting and a situation. It must take the reader on some kind of 'journey' with ups and downs, as the character does things (takes certain actions) to try to resolve the 'situation' (problem/issue). And then it must swiftly reach an ending – in such a way that the situation you established at the beginning is either resolved or changed in some way. You might ask yourself these questions: What does my character want? What do they DO, to try to get it? How does it all work out? (Do they get what they wanted ... or something else, unexpected?)

In a story for children, it is usually a good idea to put the child at the centre of the action, to make them ACTIVE (rather than passive, having things done TO them). **Write from the child's perspective**. Find a voice that feels fresh and authentic and contemporary. Experiment with first person or close-up third person as a way of bringing your child reader close to the action. Children want to immerse themselves in the story.

I write realistic stories, but a short story might be in any genre: fantasy, science fiction, supernatural, funny, historical. It can be a good way to **try out something new**, in terms of style or genre, before committing to a longer project. And some ideas just come as 'short'; you know that's the form they need to take. After I'd written a commissioned short story about a girl and a seal pup, I went on to write a novel, *Seal Island* (OUP 2014). The short story had led me into a longer story in a similar setting with a similar central character, but with more incidents, more characters, more developed themes and the longer time-frame that a novel allows.

When we are learning, nothing we write is ever wasted, whether it gets published or not. We write first and foremost for ourselves. **Practising the short story form will improve all your writing.** There are short story competitions which can give you the benefit of a deadline, and sometimes a subject or theme, too. Having the constraints of a word count can be strangely liberating. Set yourself a deadline, a word count, and a subject, and see what magic happens. The mind plays games. A character will arrive, and a place – all stories have to happen somewhere – and before you know it, the story will start to emerge. Keep asking questions: *What if…? Supposing she….* Write it, one word, one sentence at a time. Write the first draft, fast. Then – cut, cut, cut! Polish. Make it beautiful. Make it the best story it can be. Write the story only *you* can write.

Julia Green is the author of more than 20 novels and short stories for young people. She is Emeritus Professor in Writing for Young People at Bath Spa University and founded the MA Writing for Young People, which has launched the careers of more than 70 writers for children and young adults. Her most recent novels for children are *The House of Light* (2019) and *The Children of Swallow Fell* (2020), both published by OUP Children's, a picture book *The Boy Who Sailed the World* (2022) and her latest novel, *Ettie and the Midnight Pool* (2024) published by David Fickling Books. She is currently writing a collection of short stories and a new novel for young people. For more information see www.julia-green.co.uk or follow her on X @JGreenAuthor.

Writing magic into fiction

Kiran Millwood Hargrave recommends the techniques she uses to feed and inspire her magical stories, and guides us through each stage of the process that allows a writer's fantastical ideas to come to fruition.

All fiction is a kind of magic: a conjuring. From your imagination, you are building whole people, whole worlds, making them so vivid and tangible your reader will be able to touch them, see them, wish they lived in your stories – but how do you layer magic upon magic and introduce a fantastical strand to your story? Perhaps you call it fabulism, perhaps magical realism, perhaps fantasy. They are all branches of the same enchanted tree, and here are my experiences of reading – and rooting my own stories in – magic.

Roots

My earliest love was the *His Dark Materials* trilogy by Philip Pullman. Read first when I was ten, much of it admittedly flew over my head, but I didn't mind because *how* it flew! Like witches on yew twigs, like swan daemons swirling, like angels stirring the clouds. I believe we all have 'books of power', as I term them, often discovered when we are young, that are keystones for the sort of stories we wish to write.

When I look at my own 'books of power', they largely fall into what I used to call magical realism. This was incorrect, as I came to learn magical realism refers to those writing in the South American tradition, addressing issues of colonialism. The better term is fabulism. Alongside Pullman's epic trilogy are: *Skellig* by David Almond, the *Chrestomanci* books by Diana Wynne Jones, *The Wolves of Willoughby Chase* by Joan Aiken, *Journey to the River Sea* by Eva Ibbotson and the ubiquitous *Harry Potter* series by J.K. Rowling. All hold very different, varying systems and approaches to 'magic', and often my first task when writing a novel is to decide where I want my book to sit within that spectrum. My debut, *The Girl of Ink & Stars* (Chicken House 2016), plunges into fully-fledged fantasy; my second novel, *The Island at the End of Everything* (2017) finds magic in nature, and my third, *The Way Past Winter* (2018), is folkloric in its telling and so sits on the border of fabulism.

Ask: what are your 'books of power'? Do they tell you about the sort of books you love, and give you an insight, as I believe, into the sort of books you should probably be writing? Some of you will be fantasy fans, while others may prefer that world to be recognisable but knocked slightly ajar to let some magic in. I like to keep my 'books of power' on my desk throughout my current writing project (the books change from project to project). It's an excellent procrastination exercise, but also an inspiring one.

Shoots

Your books of power are on your desk; perhaps you're listening to a film soundtrack (Enya is my writing jam); maybe you have a scented candle wafting snatches of 'Mystical Forest' towards you – and now you're ready to write. It's all possibility ... like new shoots of green life emerging in spring. Some of you will plunge straight in, others will plan your narrative to within an inch of its life, but as a self-confessed 'pantser' (as in by-the-seat-of-your-pants vs 'planner') I wholly condone the former. There is nothing more exciting to me than plunging into the adventure alongside your characters and, as they take on more life, letting them make the decisions.

That said, I started my writing life as a poet; a bit of structure has always helped me and I give this to myself in the form of a map. This piece of advice is probably most useful to those of you writing a quest narrative – something where the characters travel through landscape – but I've also worked on maps of houses, or schools or streets. As soon as the perimeters of the places your characters will inhabit are solid, your imagination can run wild. Often these places also help to define the sort of magic you'll encounter in your world: if it's rife with mountains and dragons, you're probably reaching for an alternate universe, the rules of which you get to decide; if it's a secret door in an otherwise ordinary garden, you've got a beautiful set-up for fabulism. But my main advice at this stage is not to worry about labelling *what* sort of magic you're choosing. Let your story tell you what will work.

When I say 'draw a map', it does not need to be a work of art. My map for *The Girl of Ink & Stars* was a clumsily drawn circle with childish landmarks, with the routes of my characters plotted through the landscape in different colours for each. The plan for *The Way Past Winter* was even more basic: a house, some trees, some mountains, the sea and an arrow pointing 'North'. Think of it as storyboarding, as they do for films. You have your whole story on one piece of paper – and you can always rip it up and start again.

Rings

I can only speak to describe my own experience of writing – and everyone is different – but I like to charge through my first draft, full pelt towards the conclusion. This results in very short, fast-paced first drafts, but it means that the fear of the blank page is conquered. Something is easier to improve than nothing, so I would encourage you to write your first draft quickly, too. Then, the real work begins.

A tree grows rings as it ages, and so too will your story. These next drafts are for firming up its core, and finding the confidence to set down more firmly what you perhaps only gestured at in first drafts. I would argue this is not the time for brutal editing. Rather, luxuriate in bringing your story more fully into being. If you've written a fantasy, full of mermaids and talking animals, give them their back stories. If you've written in magical objects that transport your character into parallel worlds, think about how they feel, smell, look, where they came from. Put in all those details you would want as a reader: colour your world in. Check that your characters' names suit them and the world they inhabit. Research any asides that observant readers will appreciate and think how clever you are. Enjoy playing around, giving credence to ideas that may not quite be working, but that you think *could* – with just one more draft (or three).

This stage takes the longest for me, but it is also the most fun. It's when I experiment and learn the most about myself as a writer, and about what I want this story to do, and what I want a reader to take from it.

Branches

This next stage may appear to be misleadingly titled, as it implies growth when actually it's very likely that your manuscript will shrink – but editing really *is* like growing branches; it's also a little bit about hacking off the weaker ones.

As a reformed poet, editing holds a special place in my heart. I love it, because finally I know what my story is, and editing will help me get it there. But I know not everyone shares my enthusiasm for hacking at sentences or scenes that took weeks/months/years to write. So my advice to you is this: look at it as *giving* your story something, not taking something away. Only by editing can you find the sub-plots worth growing, and those that need pruning. Only by editing can you find the heart of your story, and make it sing.

Buds

Now you're ready to submit (I hugely dislike this word: when I was on 'submission' to agents I made a spreadsheet to keep track of where/when/who and my husband changed all the headings to things like 'date soul delivered' to denote when I sent out the manuscript, and 'poop or not poop?' to indicate whether I got a full request or a meeting/rejection … humour helps!). Speaking from experience, the waiting is possibly the worst bit of all. Even when you're waiting to hear from, and often being rejected by, publishers, at least you and your agent are in it together. So hang in there, and give yourself the best possible chance of success by taking special care when choosing which agents you send to.

I made a list from the *Children's Writers' & Artists' Yearbook* and thoroughly researched this shortlist, breaking it into a top-tier I wanted to send to first, and then a second to help me get straight back on the horse if those initial queries bore no fruit. Look at those who represent the writers of your 'books of power', and pop them on the list too. Aim high. I did, and I ended up with my first choice of agent. But there was something I did not do right, and that I would urge you to do – that is to classify what exactly I had written.

I've mentioned that one of my 'books of power' was *His Dark Materials* by Philip Pullman, but another was *One Hundred Years of Solitude* by Gabriel Garcia Marquez and a third was *The Border Trilogy* by Cormac McCarthy. If that sounds like a confused list, it was, and it made for a confused manuscript. Fraught with long descriptions of landscape, and far too much pathetic fallacy, I wasn't sure what I had written. This showed in my query letter, which announced *The Girl of Ink & Stars* (then *The Cartographer's Daughter*) as a 'magical-realist YA/crossover adventure story'… Yes, I really did write all that down, and press 'send'. Luckily, my wonderful agent saw past it, but you can help yourself enormously by really pinning down what sort of book you've written. This is the only point at which this really matters, I would argue. Until you send your book to agents, just follow your instincts and write in whatever way your story needs you to write it. Once you have an agent, they can help you nail down what exactly you've written. We sent *The Girl of Ink & Stars* out as an adventure story and let the fantasy element come as a surprise.

That's why I've called this section 'buds' – it's about making your story look as appealing as possible, making it impossible for them *not* to want to represent you, and showing that you really know what you're talking about and are taking this seriously. So, finesse what you call your book. Perhaps it's a 'YA coming-of-age story with magic', like Harry Potter, or a 'fast-paced action adventure story' like Percy Jackson. Comparisons to other successful books on the market are always a good idea, but you should highlight how your book differentiates itself too.

Know that you are not alone in your fear and trepidation … or your big dreams. I look forward to reading your no-doubt magical stories.

Kiran Millwood Hargrave is the *Sunday Times* bestselling author of 12 novels for children and adults, including *The Girl of Ink & Stars*, *Julia and the Shark*, *The Mercies* and the *Geomancer* Trilogy. Her work has won major international prizes such as the British Book Awards Children's Book of the Year and the Waterstones Children's Book Prize 2017, the Janis Baltvilks Award, the Prix Rive Gauche à Paris, a Betty Trask Award and the Wainwright Prize. Her work has been translated into more than 30 languages and optioned for stage and screen. For more information see www.kiranmillwoodhargrave.com. Follow her on Instagram @kiran_mh.

Reinventing old stories for new readers

Deirdre Sullivan shares her fascination for retellings of fairy tales and the possibilities that arise from looking with fresh eyes at these stories, reworking their age-old power to inspire, influence and connect with young adult readers.

I think we all remember the first stories that spoke to us – however we encountered them, from the mouths of teachers or caregivers or by ourselves, transported by a book. Different voices speak to different readers, and Hans Christian Andersen's *The Little Mermaid* and Oscar Wilde's *The Nightingale and the Rose* spoke to me. I had learned to expect a 'happily ever after', in the way we all do, so these melancholy stories defied my expectations and lodged themselves in my heart, like a shard of the Devil's mirror.

In college I was introduced to the work of Jack Zipes and his anthology, *Don't Bet On The Prince* (Gower 1987) by a friend (to whom the book is dedicated), and I became acquainted with a greater breadth of fairy-tale retellings, in female voices. I had encountered feminist fairy tales before (a small Irish publisher, Attic Press, had published a children's series of these that I used to hunt for in libraries and secondhand bookshops), but revisiting them at the tail end of my adolescence was as potent as a poisoned comb to the skull. Fairy tales have always had what Marina Warner calls a 'suspect whiff of femininity', but I had been raised on stories told by men. Soon I was discovering Madame Leprince de Beaumont and Dortchen Wild. Female tellers had been there all along, it seemed, if you only took the care to look more closely. From then on, fairy-tale motifs wound themselves through my writing, both subtly and explicitly. I became hungry for more fairy-tale retellings, and devoured stories by the likes of Emma Donoghue, Robin McKinley, Neil Gaiman, Aimee Bender, Francesca Lia Block, Isabel Allende and Margaret Atwood.

In the summer of 2015 my publisher, Little Island, approached me about publishing a collection of my fairy-tale retellings. I was instantly excited about it. It felt right. I dusted off some old stories and began work on some new ones. As the collection progressed, though, I ended up writing 12 brand-new retellings, to ensure the themes and voice felt uniform. It wasn't a hardship. When I write, I feel like I am in conversation with myself and with the stories I have been told about the world around me. I run my hands over their edges, and I try to notice new details I am drawn to. I write what I know, but also what I fear and what I love.

Tangleweed and Brine (Little Island 2017) is a book that centres the female experience of the world within the fairy-tale realm. I wanted to write about bodies, and how terrifying and messy they can be. I wanted to talk about being a woman in a society built by and for men. I wanted to talk about fear, but also anger. I wanted to write about the lessons that the world teaches girls, drip by drip or all at once. I was 12 when the last Magdalene laundry closed, and until 2018, I had lived my whole life in the shadow of the eighth amendment. My country was structured in a way that let me know, that let us all know – over and over again – how little women's lives mattered. That casts a shadow, and when I began to piece together the stories for the collection it was largely women in the shadows I was drawn to

– women with bodies that didn't fit societal expectations, women used as pawns for political gain, women who try to find the right thing in a wrong world. It is a sad book, and an angry book, but there are moments of freedom there as well.

... Because there is a witchcraft to being female. From the whisper networks to tampons slipped underneath a cubicle by some kind hand, we find support in each other. There's a shared struggle that binds us. And no one knows that more than a teenage girl. Adolescence can be a very dangerous and lonely place, but there is a power in it, too, an alchemy: changing bodies, fluctuating emotions, the dawning realisations; it's a heady time, and an intense one. It's that mixture of dependence and independence, of forging your own path and being guided along the one envisioned for you. It is a time in my life I remember sharply, and a time that will continue to inspire me. I facilitate creative writing workshops for teenagers, and they are incisive and passionate readers who can enjoy books while recognising their faults. Before *I Want to Know That I Will Be Okay* was published, I would often be asked when I would write a book 'for adults'; this was generally framed as a compliment. I brush it off quietly, saying things like 'Oh, you never know', and continuing to write the things I want. I most often write for young adults for the same reason that I tell the stories I do – because they inspire me.

I'm aware that *Tangleweed and Brine* came out at an opportune moment. There was something of a fairy-tale zeitgeist in the air, as well as increased discussion of feminism with the #MeToo movement started by Tarana Burke gaining traction in 2017, when the book had just been published. People, and young people in particular, were becoming increasingly comfortable confronting and unpacking previously unspoken things, looking at the way the world worked and articulating why that wasn't good enough. Whispers were becoming shouts. And my book was not alone – around that time Melissa Albert, Sarah Henning, Louise O'Neill and Daniel Lavery also had books out that reworked or built on old stories and turned them into something of their own. There was something in the air that made writers look at the tales they had been told and hold them up to the light with fresh eyes. And each of us saw something different and built something that was our own from that. There may be a lot of talk about trends in YA but we are all living in the same world; we experience a lot of similar things, consume a lot of the same media, hear the same news headlines. The same inspiration can take two people on very different journeys ... I love that.

My advice for someone who wants to rewrite fairy tales would be to be aware of what is out there – to read and reread to give you a sense of what can be done and has been done. Then to listen to yourself. In tarot readings, there are the prescribed meanings of the cards, but sometimes a reader will find themselves drawn to a detail or a symbol; they may not know why, but something about it calls to them. That sense of moving away from what a story is supposed to be towards what it could become for you in this moment – that little, precious space is inspiration. And it's worth worrying at those details like a dog, until you've chewed it into something that's yours alone. With old stories, the more familiar people are with them, the more of a shorthand you can use; a shoe, a wolf, an apple becomes symbolic. Whatever world you put it into, the old story will be humming underneath like a familiar tune. The reader will sense it pulling at them, making them remember when it first spoke to them and all the ways it has spoken to them since. When you retell a fairy tale, you are invoking something very old and very powerful; there's a responsibility to get it right, but a satisfaction when something clicks.

I had two big 'clicks' of this kind when writing *Tangleweed and Brine*. One of them came from years of trying and the other came to me in a dream. The second way was far easier, but I think the first was more satisfying. I had put a lot of 'Little Mermaids' into the collection at first, as it's a story I'm drawn to time and time again. As someone who feels like they spend a lot of time on the outside wondering how people work, I found the mermaid character spoke to me. I grew up beside the ocean, and the tang of salt air was never far away when I was small. The story of *The Little Mermaid* brought me my first sad ending and my first Disney princess, and both of those left small dents on my heart. I had to cull a fair few mermaids as I drafted *Tangleweed and Brine*, but I remember sitting in a café thinking that I could just have my mermaid kill the prince and return to the ocean, and feeling so happy for her. I'm not normally in favour of murder, but I wanted that little tongueless girl – who'd walked on glass for love – to choose herself. And so, in my story, I asked her to do that – and she did. The child I was when I first encountered that story wouldn't have been fond of it ending in a stabbing, but it made sense for me to follow the path not taken in the Andersen story … and to send my mermaid home. The second magic click came with *Bluebeard*. I didn't know what to do; I'd written what was turning into a tender little love story, but the fairy tale demanded a roomful of murdered wives and I just didn't think the *Bluebeard* I had written would do that (#notallbluebeards). I worried and wondered about it for ages, tweaking other stories while I did (one of my favourite things to do when I get blocked on a project is to start something else, even a ridiculous thing; it provides the distance you need to stand back and see what must be done to set things right). It took a dream to point me in the right direction. I woke up with an image seared into my brain: a room full of dead men. And that gave me the key I needed to unlock my version of the story, where the secret is not the things that Bluebeard has done, but who he is and what he has survived.

I care a lot about these old stories. I have tried to inhabit them respectfully, but my experience is only one experience, and that's not enough for such an intricate world. The stories we tell matter. They can and should change. Your voices matter. I look forward to the next retelling and the next one – the same old story, through a different lens, a different heart.

Deirdre Sullivan is an award-winning writer and teacher from Galway. She has written eight acclaimed books for young adults, including *Savage Her Reply* (Little Island 2020), *Perfectly Preventable Deaths* (Hot Key Books 2019) and *Tangleweed and Brine* (Little Island 2017), as well as a collection of short fiction for adult readers, *I Want to Know That I Will Be Okay* (Banshee 2021). Her latest book, *Wise Creatures* (Hot Key 2023), is a young adult horror, exploring the different ways we can be haunted.

Writing mystery and adventure stories

H.L. Dennis shares her own imaginative method of creating and refining a story, and bringing adventures and emotions fully to the page, using the structure and inspiration of a film-maker's craft.

I'm going to tell you a secret. I'm not a writer at all ... actually, I'm the Chief Executive of my very own Imagination Headquarters. It's a game I play, and it makes writing such an adventure that I'm going to let you in on the mystery of how it works. Not everyone will like this method, but you just might ... so I hope you'll enjoy it too.

I've never been to film school – but being the Ceo of Imagination HQ is like being an entire studio working on a film. After all, a good book plays like a film inside our heads. We watch as characters experience triumph and despair, happiness and pain. And, if the story is a good one, we feel those emotions too. That's my aim: to generate emotion in the reader, to make them laugh, gasp or cry. I want readers to feel, to believe, to remember. I hope they'll adventure with me, racing through the pages of my story as the mystery unfolds.

So now let me show you how it works – in Imagination HQ – as I try to achieve this.

Time for popcorn ...

It begins with the 'popcorn stage'. This is a time that fuels my spirit – when I'm reminded of the power of good stories. I watch film and TV avidly, re-watching sections, trying to understand the storyteller's craft. I analyse moments when I'm on the edge of my seat, and I break down scenes where I'm sobbing or screaming at the screen. I try to establish exactly how the lighting, music and camera angles make me feel. Then I use exactly the same close analysis on my favourite books; I reread extracts over and over, in precisely the same analytical way. I immerse myself in adventures and mysteries well told. Only then am I ready to start work myself.

Stage One: Development

1. Find the theme – First of all, your story needs to get the 'green light'. You must know why this story needs telling and why it's you who needs to tell it. The theme is the light that guides all the decisions later. It's why the story is emotionally significant. Your job isn't to preach, but to explore a theme that matters to you

My series *Secret Breakers* (Hodder Children's 2012–) was about children's hidden potential. Working as a teacher at the time, I was concerned about how education rated some skills more highly than others. You, too, need to find an area that fascinates, angers, worries or intrigues you. Find something that makes you *feel*; this will become the 'why' that lights your way.

2. Choose your story world – In *Secret Breakers* I wanted to celebrate the abilities of children to do more than adults thought possible. The world of code-cracking was a perfect fit. You might choose to explore the theme of fairness, for example, through the world of sport or science, theatre or space travel. So find a world where you can explore your theme. Ground your adventure in this particular, chosen world.

3. Prepare the trailer – Film trailers pare back films to their basic elements. Trailers give us a sense of the story's 'palette'. They prepare us for high octane, thrilling action or quiet, sinister mystery. We know what to expect because trailers sell us emotions the film promises to deliver. Your adventure could be created in a range of different tones, so establish the emotional impact you want by analysing film trailers. Then attempt to write a basic summary of a story, noting what you want the reader to feel as they read.

Stage Two: Pre-production

1. Select your locations – If you can set your story anywhere – real or imagined – be purposeful and selective about every single location you use. In my *River of Ink* series (Hodder Children's 2017–) I explored the theme of what makes a life worth living. I chose the world of alchemy to do this and, as the elixir of life was central to this theme, I focused on river locations for my adventure. You need to make every location work to support the story. Choose contrasting locations, intriguing locations, locations that will provoke emotion! Work as a 'location scout', visiting places you can't visit in reality – via guidebooks or the internet.

2. Cast the characters – We care about stories because we care about characters. Make sure you rigorously audition every member of your cast, to be certain they're worthy of screen time. The hero of an adventure becomes such after she is tested and because of the difficult choices she makes. We must feel for the characters – even the villains. Make us cheer on an underdog, empathise with the lost soul, root for the character who is scared just like us.

You need characters who give elements of contrast to your theme. In *River of Ink*, a girl with a life ruled by schedules would learn the value of spontaneity. Characters must change as a result of their adventures, so think about how you'd like your character to be in the final stage of your story, then work backwards to create your character at the beginning. Audition a cast of contrasting characters and show us what they're truly like, through their actions and interactions, decision-making and discoveries.

*I like to set up Pinterest boards at this stage – with pictures of locations, sketches of characters and quotes that support my theme. This helps create a sense of tone and sets me up for the more technical stages ahead.

Stage Three: Production

1. Prepare the shooting schedule – You can now begin to sketch out the major arc of an adventure. Think about: an inciting incident; times of crisis when all hope seems lost; then the ultimate life-changing climax. Why is the mystery your characters are trying to solve so important? What obstacles are in the way? What is there to gain or lose? Just as you didn't settle for mediocre locations or cast, make sure the stakes are as big as possible, as meaningful as they can be and the most likely to provoke emotion. We need our characters to be scared about losing everything in order for the adventure to mean everything to us.

2. Compose the storyboard – By this I don't mean a drawn storyboard (although this might be just your thing); take the schedule and break it into scenes. It's important, particularly in mysteries, to work out what needs to be revealed when and in what order. You might also have an idea about some key set pieces, and indeed the finale which you're working towards. I envisioned one particular scene, at the end of *Secret Breakers* Book Six, before I ever wrote the words 'Book One: Chapter One'. I was always striving towards this culmination of the adventure – a point when the characters were at their most desperate, and the risk of making the wrong decision the most intense. I could see the weather in the scene, and even hear the musical soundtrack in my head. Here my characters' emotions were at their most raw (and hopefully the reader's would be too!).

The big reveal of the mystery must be worth the pay-off, so give the finale a massive amount of your time, energy and thought. Your ending must deliver all the emotional punch you planned from the trailer stage. Be sure to build anticipation as your storyboard develops; keep the adventure moving, the characters changing, and the stakes increasing.

3. Rehearse the scenes – Now I've worked out the gist of what will happen in each scene and, finally, I get to rehearse. A film director might shoot the same scene many times – you can too.

Don't offer your reader your first thoughts about how to show that scene. Try lots of different ways of 'staging' it. For this, I find the 'record card' system really satisfying: on record cards, jot down how variations of each scene could look. Experiment by changing camera angles and focusing on one character more than others or elevating one emotion over another. Try different ways of revealing character through dialogue and actions. The aim of these rehearsals is to choose a version of the scene that will best generate the suspense, worry, fear or elation in the reader you hoped for. Don't settle. Be the director who demands the ultimate take.

4. Make a rough cut – By this stage I've worked through all the angst of how best to show something; I've built up tension by heightening anticipation; I've put characters through the very worst situations they (or I) could imagine. So now I cut together the ultimate version of each scene and begin to type them out in a document labelled 'My Book'. This is my Director's Cut – and now it's ready for editing.

Stage Four: Post-production

1. Add effects – Every single scene must be worthy of the reader's time. So I cut, I tighten, I search for the most powerful phrase, the truest character reaction, the most poignant beat to build emotion. You can speed up shots or change the lighting to get closer to the characters and show their emotions more clearly. It's fun to scrutinise every page, every paragraph and every sentence, to make sure it's the best it can be.

2. Check continuity – Now I ask whether the whole thing hangs together as one seamless piece. Does the internal logic of the whole adventure make sense? Does the mystery unfold without stuttering or confusing? It's time to ask if you've done everything you promised the reader you would. The record cards are packed away and it's time to focus on the whole story you've created, splicing together the joins so no-one can see the technicalities of your craft!

Stage Five: Distribution

Release – This is it. You've created a story. You've written an adventure full of emotion, twists, turns and cliffhangers, which all build to the solution of your mystery and the emotional punch you guaranteed! Now, at last, it's time to grab your copy of the *Children's Writers' & Artists Yearbook* and – if you have any of those record cards left – use them to jot down a list of agents to approach. It's time to send your story out into the world to find its audience.

Writing mystery and adventure stories

Time for popcorn again
And now you wait …

Remember though – some people might dislike my suggestions about how to create a story; some fear that such a technical approach might clutter the magic of creation. There's also a chance your story might not resonate with all who read it, but that is part of the adventure – the mystery of the power of words. I personally believe magic *can* come from design, emotion from knowing direction and a powerful story through purposeful attention to detail.

So, if at every stage of the operation of Imagination HQ you've worked hard and refused to settle for mediocre, then you need to relax now and trust in your process. You *will* find an audience. The right reader is waiting. Just enjoy another bowl of popcorn, while your story makes its way out into the world to find them.

H.L. Dennis is the award-winning author of the *Secret Breakers* six-book series and the *River of Ink* quartet, both published by Hodder Children's Books. *Secret Breakers: The Knights of Neustria* (2013) was nominated for the Carnegie Medal and the series was optioned for a live action TV series in 2024. *River of Ink: Genesis* was selected as a BookBuzz book by BookTrust 2016 and included in their Deaf Awareness Week Recommendation List 2019. Helen worked for 20 years as a junior school teacher before becoming a full-time writer. She has an MA in Creative Writing Education and the Arts from Sussex University. For more information see www.helendennisbooks.com and www.hldennis.com. Follow her on X @HLDennisauthor and Instagram @helendennisauthor.

Write using your empathy superpower

Empathy is an important skill for children and adults alike to learn and practise. In this article, Camilla Chester explains how writing with empathy can yield tremendous results for authors and readers.

When I visit schools, there are two main writing tips that I pass on. The first is a quote that an Open University writing tutor shared with me. It's been adapted over the years, so I've never known exactly who first came up with it, nor exactly what they said, but I find it incredibly useful: *read like a writer and write like a reader.*

Children are sometimes initially confused by this idea, until we put on our 'writers' hats' and listen to a piece of prose and pick out techniques of the craft. When the time comes for the children to write for themselves, I encourage 'free flow', letting the mind wander and the natural storytelling, that is within us all, to come to the fore. However, it's my second tip, write using your empathy superpower, that this article will delve into a little deeper.

I'd like to explain how the process of writing *Call Me Lion* – a story about a boy with Selective Mutism (SM) – led to me actively using this as a key writing tool and I hope to pass on its benefits to you as fellow writers for children, whether you are published or not. Before I wrote *Call Me Lion*, I was a self-published author. I believe what helped me to finally create a book that attracted interest from the traditional publishing industry, was using my empathy superpower. Perhaps my personal experience might inspire you to think differently about how you'll approach your current or next work in progress.

The voice of Lion (Leo) came to me whilst out walking my dog, Stanley, and it was only when I sat down to write the book that I realised Lion was unable to speak to anyone outside of his immediate family. I should say that neither I nor my children have a diagnosis of SM and, before writing the book, I had never had any direct experience of it. When Leo came to me as a fully formed boy, though, convincing me to tell his story, I knew I had a social responsibility to portray his SM with accuracy and sensitivity. But how?

As I'm sure you're aware, the usual ways to carry out research for a book are to trawl the internet, watch YouTube clips, seek out documentaries, read widely (fiction and non-fiction), and generally load yourself up with information. I did all this, but it didn't feel enough. I wanted to find people that lived with SM every day. I needed to feel that I had permission to write Leo's story from children who recognised themselves in him.

It wasn't particularly hard to find the Selective Mutism Information and Research Association (SMiRA) and I sent an email, via their website, explaining that I was a children's author looking for readers to check my handling of SM within my current story. I was still, at this stage, naively approaching this from a 'sensitivity read' angle. Very kindly, SMiRA agreed to help, and I wrote a request that they shared with their Facebook Support Group. I had a flurry of email responses which I responded to by sending a PDF of the draft, along with some guidance questions. A few never replied, but I did get a core group of families who stuck by me throughout the process. One relationship that came from the SMiRA connection, in particular, is the reason the book is dedicated to the memory of James Redrup. That, however, is a whole other story.

The feedback I received from families, particularly the children themselves, was moving and heartfelt. Based on that, I knew that what I had written to date wasn't a true portrayal of SM. It was startlingly clear that I had 'tagged' the condition onto the character rather than making it central to his life. This is a common risk of writing. Initially it threw me and for a while I was stuck, still focusing too much on plot. Following additional advice from my critique group around story structure, however, I rewrote the book entirely. I had Leo's voice and emboldened by the support I had received, and would continue to receive from the members of SMiRA, the new story emerged quickly. Whilst I was writing, I truly experienced the emotions of Lion and once I'd finished, I knew I'd produced the best work of my career so far. It went on to attract a lot of interest among various commissioning editors and was finally published in June 2022 by Firefly Press.

Contacting SMiRA was the best decision I ever made as a writer, and it has completely changed the way I now approach research. It meant that I linked directly with children, families and healthcare professionals with real-life stories to tell about SM. With their words, I was able to truly understand and feel Leo's experiences of living with the condition. What I didn't realise then, but do now, was that this experience had activated my empathy superpower. Forming relationships with individuals who *were* Leo gave me confidence and assurance that I was being accurate and sensitive in how I wrote his story. This is what the organisation Inclusive Minds also strives to do; if you're embarking on telling a story which is outside your personal experience, I would strongly encourage you to contact them for help and support. There is also a wonderful article written by Beth Cox, founder of Inclusive Minds, called *Authentic Inclusion in Children's Books*, that you can read in this edition of the *Yearbook*.

We can only ever truly perceive the world through our own, personal lens, but authors, like actors, have the chance to walk for a while in someone else's shoes. If we do this well, then our readers will make the same journey, and this can only be a good thing. The more we can empathise and understand one another, the greater our compassion. Understanding a condition like SM has had a profound effect on me and I see every day, by how Lion's reach continues to ripple out, that it is touching others too.

The children and families who were involved in helping me shape *Call Me Lion* have, crucially, also gained personal reward from the experience. Through my email correspondence with parents, I frequently heard how empowered and valued the children felt by working on the project. These are children who, quite literally, are never heard. One mum told me her daughter had taken the part of Scar in her school production of *The Lion King*. This was incredible to hear and, because Leo's aspires to perform in that very musical in the West End, it was so relevant to the book that I was stunned. Many of these families came to the launch of *Call Me Lion*, and even though the children were unable to talk to me, I could see the powerful impact that being part of the book's creation had on them.

Working on the project showed the children that their experiences were not only valid, but vital to my understanding of their world and ability to write the book. Indeed, there's a section in *Call Me Lion* where Leo writes a letter to his friend Richa to explain to her how his SM works; these words came directly from one of the children I worked with. There are examples of this throughout the book and although every child with SM will have a different experience, I know that *Call Me Lion* is helping all readers to understand the condition more. On a more practical note, I made sure to include a section at the back of the book taken from SMiRA's leaflet about SM for primary schools which offers helpful information and methods to help quiet children and/or those diagnosed with SM. I know, from visiting schools and from the feedback I've received, that the book is working to raise understanding and compassion, not just about SM but for quiet children in general, who often feel anxious or unsure, particularly in school or in social situations.

However, I do want to say here that – like Leo and the children I worked with – the book is about far more than SM. It's uplifting and fun, full of dance and laughter. It's about family and friendships and a hilarious dog called Patch. Leo lives with SM, but it doesn't define him; he's capable and brave and incredibly loveable. It's vital that children feel seen and fairly represented within children's fiction, and I'm a strong believer that stories centred around disabilities should be empowering, honest and inspiring.

I'm thrilled that *Call Me Lion* has gone on to become such a successful book. One of its most significant achievements was being selected as part of the *Read for Empathy* list which is produced every year by a charity called EmpathyLab. Through EmpathyLab training, I learned from Professor Robin Banerjee, Professor of Developmental Psychology and Pro-Vice-Chancellor for Global and Civic Engagement at the University of Sussex, that empathy has three parts to it. First is resonating with someone else's emotions. Second is thinking, using reasoning and imagination to try and understand why they are feeling the way they are. And the third element is acting, feeling inspired or motivated to help.

Empathy, I have seen, is something that can be taught and practised. EmpathyLab works with teachers, librarians and schools to encourage children to develop their empathy superpowers through fun activities such as creating paper glasses that magically allow the wearer to really see others, or having a child 'become' a character in a story who other children can question. All of this is hugely beneficial to the school environment. When children can empathise, their ability to connect and interact is vastly improved. They have much stronger social relationships, which help their mental health. When children feel connected, they feel secure and ready to learn. They are kinder to one another, so there is less negative behaviour. Empathy leads to more developed, pro-social attitudes and the ability to make positive change.

Empathy isn't just a superpower for children, however. Adults, particularly those of us writing for children, need to flex their empathy superpower too. We know that reading for pleasure is immensely powerful, activating an area of our brain that enables us to really feel and experience the emotions of the character(s). But this works both ways. We, as writers for children, can use our own ability to empathise with others to create characters that are wholly different from ourselves and write outside of our own personal experience. To do that, we have to actively listen and connect on a deeper level to the characters and the lives that we are trying to portray. In short, we need to empathise. It is crucial that we understand ourselves and our personal lens of the world to write, but we must also make sure that what we are writing comes authentically and genuinely from the point of view of the character(s) we portray, and not only our own, limited view.

Camilla Chester is a dog walker who writes. She is the author of three self-published children's novels as well as *Call Me Lion* (Firefly Press 2022). Find out more at: www.camillachester.com/.

Writing hopeful climate fiction

Bestselling author and self-confessed literary activist Lauren James has advice for writers on how to promote climate awareness and avoid potential pitfalls when dealing with climate change and the planet in children's fiction.

From the beginning of my writing career, I've wanted to write about climate change. But my writing is focused on character and story. It's funny and romantic. For a long time, writing a book about a topic that is discomforting at best and soul-crushing at worst felt impossible.

The turning point came when I realised that I could focus on characters who are actively working to slow climate change. I'm not interested in dark dystopias about a climate-ravaged planet. We know the dangers already – and I feel strongly that in children's and YA literature we should not be telling a generation that their future is broken. I want to read – and write – inspiring, optimistic stories. After all, the books that reach the widest audiences, that have the best chance of spreading awareness, are enjoyable ones.

After seven years of writing, my sixth novel, *Green Rising* (Walker Books 2021), was the result. It centres on teenagers who can grow plants from their skin. These 'Greenfingers', as they are called, use their powers to rewild the planet, and stand up to profit-hungry corporations. The novel shows how positive environmental changes – involving kelp forests, peatlands, reforestation – can help store carbon in huge quantities. I expected the writing process to be depressing. But, in fact, immersing myself in the climate debate helped me to stop feeling helpless. Instead of trying desperately to ignore the monster looming in the corner of my vision, I was facing it head-on. I was doing something.

Writing the novel, and another climate novella, *The Deep-Sea Duke* (Barrington Stoke 2021), led me to setting up the Climate Fiction Writers League. I was inspired in part by the Women Writers Suffrage League, a UK-based awareness-raising organisation, founded in 1908 and disbanded in 1918 after the UK granted (some) women the right to vote. The League's prospectus asserted that 'A body of writers working for a common cause cannot fail to influence public opinion'. This has become our own League's guiding principle. Fiction is one of the best ways to inspire passion, empathy and action. We also partner with many other climate activism groups at events and panels, and by publishing essays and interviews.

Researching the climate crisis

I'm not great at reading scientific publications – it feels too much like homework. But I am good at wasting time on social media. So I tricked myself into researching climate change through online resources although, often, the science has been obscured by politics or disinformation campaigns. Take geoengineering – slowing the global temperature increase by, for instance, using a solar mirror in space, or spraying chemicals into the atmosphere to reflect light away from the planet. These ideas are supported by the fossil fuel industry, which wants to be able to continue selling its products while ostensibly supporting climate action. However, we have no firm idea what knock-on effects geoengineering might have on the planet.

I wanted to explore *Juliana v. US* and other similar legal cases in which young plaintiffs have argued that the US government has violated their constitutional rights by failing to act on climate change. In 2023, the landmark case *Held v. State of Montana* resulted in a historic first, when it was ruled that 'the plaintiffs have proven that as children and youth, they are disproportionately harmed by fossil fuel pollution and climate impacts'. Over the next few years we are going to see the consequences of these legal precedents ripple around the world.

I'm interested in the way youth activist groups like Extinction Rebellion are treated by the press – as extremist terrorists and moral heroes standing up for the planet, often simultaneously. I also wanted to investigate how billionaires are investing money in accessible space tourism, rather than fixing Earth, and how the new, trendy NFT (non-fungible token) art and bitcoin use huge amounts of power to create cryptocurrency. I wanted to highlight the issues related to carbon emissions, like metal poisoning from coal ash, microplastics and the garbage patches in the ocean. And I wanted to do it all in a positive way, in a book for teenagers. It was a lot to tackle.

Representing all views

I tried to look at both sides of the debate, because the way that climate deniers talk about the topic can often be really helpful for creating narratives. (Why not let them do the hard work of being creative with arguments?) The Ceo of an oil company, a billionaire trying to launch a space mission or a politician with investments in fossil fuels don't see themselves as the 'bad guys'. To them, they're community-builders, providing jobs and energy to keep the world running. I tried to put myself in their shoes so I could write characters who felt the way they might. For example, space-race billionaire Elon Musk tweeted that he didn't want to pay tax on his companies' profits because: 'My plan is to use the money to get humanity to Mars and preserve the light of consciousness'. In my novel *Green Rising*, space-race billionaire Edgar Warren uses a similar justification in an argument with the novel's teenage protagonist Theo.

I also subscribed to a very niche geoengineering forum. Eavesdropping on scientists' highly technical bickering gave me a lot of insight into the people working at the forefront of this issue, on both sides of the equation.

Making science engaging

In the writing, I tried not to get bogged down in the science. Story always has to come first. I looked for ways to tie science into other fields, like archaeology or linguistics. In *Green Rising*, for instance, my characters plan to use their 'Greenfingers' powers of growing plants to launch an illegal protest against fossil fuel companies, power plants and vehicle manufacturers. I wrote extracts from their online discussions in an activists' forum, dramatising their doubts concerning the science of such topics as solar seeding.

I keep an eye out for interesting, well-known science stories that might provide a way to talk about something more complicated, and for debunked or disproven theories from the past that tell us a lot about people's knowledge level – and motivations – at the time. I also try to think about big concepts in terms of historical events. How can we look at archaeology to get a new perspective on climate change? How might the present day look from a far-future or far-past point of view? Has something like this ever happened before on Earth? What might a climate disaster look like in a far-future world set on another planet? In my novella *The Deep-Sea Duke*, butterfly-like aliens are forced to flee their planet after burning fossil fuels has raised the temperature too high for their caterpillar offspring to survive. Problems arise when the planet they migrate to has the wrong type of environment (fully oceanic) and the butterflies introduce an invasive species to their new home (a rambunctious ferret pet). The book is aimed at ages 8+, and uses this humorous lens to comment on real-world issues.

Should fiction be political?
Ultimately, climate change is a political topic. It's unavoidable. The end of the world is profitable. From trading stock market futures on water scarcities, to increased crop yields in extreme weather, business will thrive as the planet collapses. My characters are angry they're being told to reduce their climate footprint, that they're being made to feel guilty about their personal pollution when industry is responsible for the vast majority of emissions.

From a legal perspective, there were things I couldn't do – I wasn't allowed to mention real life companies or people by name, and had to create fictional versions of certain things. But in *Green Rising*, I tried to capture the feeling of being part of the ongoing green revolution, to show what it feels like to grow up in a time of unprecedented existential fear. I wanted to write about young people who are turning that fear into hope and action, pushing against the enormous weight of the existing establishment. I have since edited an anthology of uplifting climate stories aimed at ages 9+, *Future Hopes* (Walker Books 2024). Throughout the process, I was able to advise contributors including M.G. Leonard, Tolá Okogwu, Neal Shusterman and Louie Stowell on how to create positive future worlds for their stories.

Writing advice
My top tips for writers who want to include climate change in their work:
- Read climate fiction in a variety of genres, not just science fiction and fantasy.
- Consider the activism going on outside the very vocal UK/US groups. Activists from the countries most affected by climate change are often ignored in the media.
- Inspire activism – but be aware that readers don't want to be made to feel guilty.
- Convey the seriousness of the situation without making action seem futile.
- Show how climate change is no longer a long-term issue but something happening right now.
- Use your frustration in your writing – but be aware that most people don't want to read an angry book.
- Remember that hope and optimism will inspire more action than anything else. Fiction can inspire a huge amount of empathy, which is a force that can be used collectively to inspire change on a global level.

Hopeful climate fiction reading list
A Cloud Called Bhura: Climate Champions to the Rescue by Bijal Vachharajani (Speaking Tiger 2019)
Onyeka and the Academy of the Sun by Tolá Okogwu (Simon & Schuster 2022)
Beauty and the Bin by Joanne O'Connell (Pan Macmillan 2021)
How to Save the World with a Chicken and an Egg by Emma Shevah (Chicken House 2021)
The Summer We Turned Green by William Sutcliffe (Bloomsbury 2021)
The Tale of a Toothbrush by M.G. Leonard (Walker Books 2020)

Lauren James is the pen name of Wren James, the bestselling author of many YA novels, including *Last Seen Online* (2024), *Green Rising* (2021), *The Reckless Afterlife of Harriet Stoker* (2020), *The Quiet at the End of the World* (2019) and *The Loneliest Girl in the Universe* (2017), all published by Walker Books. They are a Royal Literary Fund Royal Fellow, freelance editor and screenwriter, and founder of the Climate Fiction Writers League. For more information see https://wrenjames.co.uk and you can follow them on Instagram @wrenjameswriter.

A version of this piece first appeared in *The Author*, the journal of the Society of Authors (Spring 2022 Vol. 133.1).

Writing for YA or adults: how do you know?

The rise in popularity of YA books over the past two decades or so has changed the publishing landscape dramatically, but what really distinguishes YA from adult fiction? And if you're an aspiring author, which category is the best fit for you? Read on for Finn Longman's advice.

Looking at my career to date, one might make several assumptions: that I've written roughly the same number of YA books and adult books; that I've moved on from YA to adult; that my choice of age category is decided by the books' genre. After all, I sold three YA thrillers first, and then three adult fantasy novels. In fact, none of these assumptions would be accurate. My first published novel, *The Butterfly Assassin*, was the fifteenth book I wrote, and I've drafted a total of 24 novels, around 16 of which are YA and six are adult (the remaining couple sit uneasily between categories). I've written plenty of YA fantasy, too, though I've yet to write any adult thrillers, and I've certainly not left the category behind, even if I'm focusing on adult fiction at present.

Writing on both sides of this divide means I've spent quite a lot of time pondering exactly what makes a book YA rather than adult, especially when writing YA books that hover around the upper age limits of the category and contain a great deal of murder and trauma. It can be tempting to wonder how much it matters, and to assume the line is an arbitrary marketing category that agents or publishers will decide for you, rather than something you need to worry about as a writer. After all, more and more adults are reading YA, and many voracious teenage readers enjoy adult books, too, so the categories must have some overlap. And YA can be just as complex, challenging, well written and original as adult fiction: surely all you'd have to do is change the age of your protagonist, and you could slot neatly into either box?

Well … not quite.

Age matters

First, on a practical level, as an author you need to know whether you're writing adult or YA fiction, because agents and publishing imprints tend to focus on one or the other. Genre is subjective and loosely defined – a lyrically written novel set in the past with some magical elements may find itself being labelled 'literary', 'historical', or 'fantasy' depending on where it's likely to sell best that year, which may not be the same place it would have found itself ten years earlier – but age categories are less so. An agent may represent all genres of adult fiction, but not touch children's books, or be an absolute whizz at placing even the most genre-bending children's literature with a publisher, but never go near adult books. There are, as always, exceptions, and even agents who focus on one area may be willing to branch out for an existing client with guidance from colleagues, but it's never wise to assume you'll be the outlier, and agent specialisms aren't listed for show or to inconvenience you. (If you know you plan to write both, though, this is something to consider when querying, and ask an agent about on your first call with them.)

But it also matters on a story level. I firmly believe that there are very few themes you can write about in adult fiction that you can't also tackle in YA (with the exceptions being things like 'the joys of retirement and grandchildren', and you could probably even make that work if spinning it from the right angle). YA readers are bright, curious and living in the real world: they can handle moral complexity and difficult issues, and many young readers take a bloodthirsty delight in character suffering. And they don't need to be patronised. I have never intentionally simplified my language for a teenage audience: they're analysing Shakespeare and endless poetry in GCSE English, so I know they can keep up.

But YA is not adult fiction, and while I might write about some of the same themes in both – trauma, bodily autonomy, pain, justice vs punishment, destructive cycles of violence, and so on – I wouldn't approach them in the same way, because YA readers need something different from authors than adult readers do. Adults have, on the whole, more life experience, as well as more years of engaging with stories and processing narratives, and they can use that experience to draw connections and figure things out for themselves. They'll be coming to fewer concepts for the first time, and they'll have more personal reference points to help them interpret challenging stories. Everything is new to somebody, of course, and not every teenager is living a safe, sheltered life – more's the pity – but as a general rule, there's a greater responsibility in YA to guide your reader through the narrative, not merely in terms of comprehension but also in terms of emotional processing and working through moral questions.

There are other 'rules' about what makes YA what it is, all of which have their exceptions. It usually has teenage protagonists, for example, though not all books with teenage protagonists are YA, as adult books can sometimes have younger characters. This is especially true in genre fiction, where age in years might not correspond to role and experience in the world. YA is often about new experiences and 'firsts' (first love, first grief, first steps into independence), allowing an audience who are also experiencing those things for the first time – or may be doing so in the next few years – to process them alongside characters.

In reality, it can be hard to pin down on paper why one narrative is YA and one is adult, but the difference is meaningful, however intangible. There is a certain contract between reader and author, a relationship that has been created, and I feel the responsibilities of that relationship strongly when I write YA. It isn't that I'm careless when writing for adults – but I will take less responsibility for my readers' emotions, and leave more of the thematic questions unanswered, in the expectation that they'll grapple with them for themselves. I know the relationship I have with the readers of *The Butterfly Assassin trilogy*, and it's not the same relationship I have with readers of my forthcoming book *The Animals We Became*, which I'm editing as I write this – I'm approaching their overlapping themes from entirely different angles, and asking something different of my readers in the process.

Why I write YA

I started to write YA by accident. I was a teenager, and those were the stories I was marinating in, and I naturally began writing things I wanted to read. Though you don't have to be a teenager yourself, I believe the reading YA stage is essential. Yes, it's the best way to learn the expected pacing, genre conventions and stylistic demands of the category – but more than that, if you don't read this category, don't enjoy it or think it has anything interesting to say, why would you want to write it? Why would you want to join a conversation you haven't been listening to? All stories are in dialogue with other stories; I began writing YA because those were the conversations I was participating in as a reader, and I found I had something to say.

I think anybody who was a keen reader growing up can point to a children's or YA book that changed their life, and that's one of the things that's so rewarding about the category: YA readers are at a formative stage, and you have the potential to shape them forever. That power is thrilling, but also terrifying. The same might be said of the readers themselves. Passionate YA readers are a delight – but have you ever met an obsessed teenager? I mean, a truly, truly obsessed one? I have. I was one. Nothing quite compares to a 15 year-old who has just made a book their entire personality. Meeting those readers is a phenomenal experience: their opinions are genuine and unfiltered, and for the most part, they will tell you them, though some will be shy and simply slip you a note telling you what your book meant to them, which you can reread for the next three years and cry over every time you're feeling discouraged. Teenagers are so thoughtful and emotional and creative: who wouldn't want to write for them?

And then there are the books themselves. YA books have an immediacy and crisp pace that makes them both challenging and rewarding to write. Teenagers have busy lives, crammed with school, homework, after-school clubs, part-time jobs and social drama – so there's no time to hang around. Everything on the page has to be there for a reason. I'll be the first to grumble about a strict word limit, but it has made me a better writer, as has the careful balancing act of providing context and explaining details without ever making it seem like I don't trust my readers to keep up.

Plus, over the past ten to 15 years, YA has become a space of great diversity of characters, with a big emphasis on telling previously unheard stories and giving more teenagers the chance to see themselves in books. It's an opportunity for me to write the stories I couldn't find as a teenager – such as bloody, murderous, friendship-focused stories for older teenagers, without any of the romance I found so off-putting at that age.

Finally, I think being a teenager is a fundamentally strange, dystopian experience. It's a space of bodily change, perpetual emotional crisis, and a profound lack of autonomy or control over your life – and that combination creates a pressure-cooker that is narratively and psychologically fascinating. It's a great space for stories because it's a crucible of human experiences, and because all of us, at some point, went through it, even if the details varied.

Why I write Adult

More recently, I've drifted into writing adult books, and most of the new premises and concepts I come up with fall naturally into this space. This is partly that I'm reading a lot more adult fiction these days, and so these are the stories I'm responding to, the narrative shapes I'm working within and the conversations I'm trying to enter.

Writing adult books is neither easier nor harder overall than YA – just different. I enjoy it because I feel it gives me greater freedom to lean into niche, specialist, or esoteric ideas, with the expectation that my readers will keep up. It's not that I think all adults have a good general grounding in medieval studies (sadly, they don't, or explaining my academic research would be much easier) – but I do expect them to have a greater ability to parse, process and engage with the unfamiliar, using reference points they do have to keep up, and that lets me dive deeper into ideas.

I also like that, as noted above, I feel less responsibility for managing my readers' feelings and guiding their conclusions about the moral questions I'm posing. That gives me a lot more leeway to pose moral questions without answering them – including those to which I don't have the answers, but which I'm using narrative as a way to work through. And when it comes to traversing those darker corners of human nature, I don't have to worry so much about whether something's 'too much'.

Then there's the release from plot constraints. The characters are usually adults, so I don't have to kill off all their parents to give them the freedom to experience plot, and they don't have to balance their double life with their homework. More seriously, I can write characters with life experience, with particular specialisms, with in-depth knowledge – characters can be more different from each other, because they've had more years to grow into their own personalities.

Adult fiction, too, feels like a space that enables and rewards genre specialism, and allows you to work in conversation with the specific conventions and history of the genres you write. YA books are very rarely segregated by genre in bookshops and libraries, and YA readers often read across genre boundaries, still working out what they like. YA as a category, too, is young and fast-moving, with generations of readers moving on and new ideas and genre mixes rising to the fore. In adult fiction, genre divisions have greater weight, and while genre-fluid readers still abound, other readers will have been immersed in particular genres for years. That provides the opportunity to build on those shared reference points, entering into more specific traditions that have developed over years and decades, and digging deeply into the genre conventions you're following or subverting, knowing that your readers bring that context and their own mental libraries to the conversation.

Which should you write?

Nobody can tell you whether you would enjoy writing YA or adult books more – and for all that many people on the internet will probably claim otherwise, nobody can tell you which is likely to be more successful, or to make you more money. (I will say, however, that if you want to be published in hardback in the UK, YA is probably not going to be the category for you – these practicalities are worth bearing in mind.) But here are a few questions that might help you figure it out for yourself:

1. What do you read?
2. What do you love about it?
3. What stories haven't you found yet that you've been looking for?
4. What are you trying to say, and who are you trying to say it to?
5. What life experience does it speak to?

Whether you seek the relative freedom of adult fiction or the more constrained but equally passionate and original creativity and care of YA, there will be a space where your stories fit. The best way to find that space is to read widely and enthusiastically until you find the literary conversation you'd like to join, and then read even more to understand the language of that dialogue. Then join it – with your own voice, your own words, and your own stories. You have something to say, so let it be heard.

Finn Longman is a Cambridge-based writer and medievalist. Their novels include *The Butterfly Assassin* (Simon & Schuster 2022) and its sequels, all YA thrillers; their first adult book, *The Wolf and His King* will be published by Gollancz in late 2025. Find out more about Finn at https://finnlongman.com.

Writing about love and loss for children

Natasha Farrant considers the responsibility shouldered by authors who write about love and loss for children and teenagers; how such novels can be a valuable opportunity for young readers to explore challenging emotions and life experiences.

Years ago, when I started out working in children's publishing and before I was published myself, I went to a lecture given by Anne Fine. A member of the audience asked her what the difference was between writing for children and writing for adults. She replied that you could write about all the same subjects, whatever the age of your readers, but that you would tell the story differently. It was all a question, she said, of the angle at which you shone the light. I want to explore that question here in relation to writing about loss and love, because these are subjects I have returned to again and again in my own books.

Even as I write this, I read in *The Bookseller* that authors John Boyne, Malorie Blackman and Sam Copeland, presenting their titles at the Penguin Random House Children's Showcase, 'spoke of transgender issues, experiences of psychosis and how to cope with anxiety as a small child'. And this focus on difficult themes is by no means new to children's literature. From *The Railway Children* to *The Secret Garden*, *Matilda* to *Journey to the River Sea* and *Harry Potter*, authors have dealt with parental imprisonment, poverty, bereavement, loneliness, persecution, child neglect – all huge issues; all, one way or another, connected with loss.

'Struggle and hardship are the essential ingredients of narrative', writes Trisha Lee, theatre director and founder of MakeBelieve Arts, in *Princesses, Dragons and Helicopter Stories* (Routledge 2015). She goes on to quote Kieran Egan in *Teaching as Storytelling* (University of Chicago Press 1989) who believes that it is our desire to explore global concerns with binary opposites – good and evil, fair and unfair, cruel and kind – that engages us with fiction. This is true whatever age the reader. It's up to us, the reader, to make that exploration as engaging, accessible and, dare I say it, as age-appropriate as possible.

My first book for young people, *The Things We Did For Love* (Faber 2012), is a Second World War love story based on the massacre which took place at Oradour-sur-Glane, near Limoges in South West France, in 1944. Years later, a friend still hasn't got over my writing this: 'A children's book! About a massacre!' Well, it wasn't a children's book, as was made clear by the cover. I have no desire to give it to a child – frankly, there are gentler ways for them to learn about man's brutality to man. But teenagers are a different matter. The novel deals with subjects most teens I know are familiar with: sex and desire, jealousy, shame, the awareness that although they long to do the right thing they often feel coerced by social pressure to do the opposite. Most teenagers, by dint of the online world we live in, do know about war. My book offers them a chance to reflect further on what it means.

What, though, makes it a book for teens, and not for adults? It's a tricky question. A book for young people doesn't mean adults can't enjoy it too. It doesn't mean it can't have adult characters. It doesn't mean, for example, that the characters can't have sex. Sex! How often have I heard book pitches along the lines of 'It's a love story, but don't worry, it's for teens so it doesn't have sex in it' – as if teenagers didn't have sex! In *The Things We Did For Love* my teenage protagonists Arianne and Luc have sex. In fact, Arianne uses sex, rather naively thinking that if she sleeps with Luc, he won't join the Resistance and leave her. I don't show them having sex. I show rose petals leading up to a door (corny, but I couldn't resist), and I show that door closing. But we know perfectly well what is happening, and it's the sort of device that's used in plenty of grown-up fiction.

So again, if I can show torture and I can (sort of) show sex, what makes this a book for teens rather than adults? How have I shone the light? Well, there's the characters, I guess – three of the main protagonists are teenagers; one is a child (and one is a fully-grown man, but we'll put that to one side). They have teen and childhood preoccupations, like falling in love and doing homework. Arianne is trying to fill the gap left by her dead mother and her imprisoned father. She believes she may have found her answer in Luc. She believes she can use her love for him to keep him from harm. And the unnamed teenage narrator, after the massacre, writes that the lovers will be together forever. As adults, we suspect that this is unlikely. As teenagers, it's important (I think) to believe that it is true. Maybe that is the key – that belief in the redemptive power of love.

One of my golden rules, when writing for young people, is this: do not leave the reader without hope. Do not destroy that belief that the world can do better. It's difficult, if you're writing about certain subjects. Climate change is a classic example. But I would suggest that if you see no future for humanity yourself, then perhaps writing for young people is not for you. There are various forms of redemption to be found in *The Things We Did For Love*. They were hard to find, in the bleakness of that event, but the focus of the book (and indeed its inspiration) is the small acts of heroism I discovered in the course of my research and which give the book its title. Because writing for children comes with a certain responsibility.

Scientific research has shown that 'when we connect with a story, parts of our brain related to a particular emotion or action light up, and our neurons start firing as if we were engaged in the activity ourselves' (Kieran Egan; *Princesses, Dragons and Helicopter Stories*). And what is true for us as adults is even more true for a child, during the plastic years of brain formation. Philip Pullman writes about his experiences of playing at Davy Crockett in the suburbs of Adelaide when he was growing up: 'When we children play at being characters we admire, doing things we value, we discover areas and depths of feeling it would be hard to reach otherwise. Exhilaration, heroism, despair, resolution, triumph, noble renunciation, sacrifice: in acting these out we experience them in miniature or, as it were, in safety' (*Daemon Voices: Essays on Storytelling*, David Fickling Books 2017). He goes on to write that, through play, he was 'building patterns of behaviour and expectation into my moral understanding'.

As children play, so they read. They *live* the books they love, and these books offer tremendous opportunity to learn about love and loss and everything in between. They will shape their young readers and make them who they are. And yet, remember this. When you are writing for children, know that you are writing for some of the toughest, most critical readers there are, who will not suffer unnecessary babble. Know that that babble includes you pontificating on love and loss, on how sad your heroine is, or how hard she is crying, or how slowly time is passing. Never forget that other golden rule: 'Show don't tell.' *Show* the loss. *Show* the emotion. *Show* the redemptive love. Use every writing trick at your disposal – metaphor, imagery, leitmotiv – to make them come to life. They're never going to live your book if they're bored.

My middle-grade book *The Children of Castle Rock* (Faber 2018) traces the grief of the main protagonist, Alice, as she mourns the death of her mother. The book opens as she prepares to leave her family home forever. Rather than linger on Alice's emotions, I choose to focus on her refusal to leave without taking her mother's commemorative rosebush, which is dug up and squished into the car. The rosebush then reappears periodically – on a balcony, as a watercolour and eventually in a new garden – in a way which shows the reader without spelling it out that Alice, without forgetting, is nevertheless learning to move on.

As I wrote the story, I asked myself these questions: What has Alice lost? What does she want? What does she need? These are the questions which drive the plot. Alice has lost her mum, her dad is completely unreliable and her home is sold. She needs to rebuild a sense of family, she wants her dad to do this for her but she needs to understand that he never will. These are the questions which give the novel emotional depth and a sense of purpose. They are not what make it an exciting read, though. The excitement comes from the fact that, in her pursuit of these needs, Alice runs away from boarding school, camps on a Scottish beach, almost drowns, breaks into a house and gets chased onto a stack of rocks by a bunch of Italian gangsters, where she gets cut off by the tide … and in the end conquers both her fear of losing her dad and her fear of heights by abseiling down a cliff.

Even as I write this, I'm aware how complex this question of responsibility is. It is absolutely not about watering down difficult subjects, but it's about rendering them in such a way that a child can explore them – as Pullman writes in the quote I cited earlier – in safety. Children, like all readers, will take what they can and what they need from a story. A child who has experienced severe loss will be alive to Alice's grief. A child with less experience of loss may simply enjoy the adventure. The story may lead to greater understanding; it may simply entertain. All forms of reading are valid.

In *The Children of Castle Rock*, as in all my other books, I have tried to acknowledge that bad things do happen, that the people you love are not always reliable, but that there are others who love you if you can open your eyes and heart to them. I have also tried to fulfil my other responsibility as a writer, which is to make my story as cohesive, exciting and as good as I possibly can. But there my task as a writer is finished. Alice's story is in the world, to be completed in as many ways as there are readers. Which is just as it should be.

Natasha Farrant is a writer and literary scout. Her books include *The Rescue of Ravenwood* (Faber 2023), the Costa winning *Voyage of the Sparrowhawk* (Faber 2020), *The Girl who Talked to Trees* (Zephyr 2021), *Eight Princesses and a Magic Mirror* (Zephyr 2019), *The Children of Castle Rock* (Faber 2018), as well as *The Things We Did for Love* (Faber 2012) and four titles in her popular, Faber published children's series *The Diaries of Bluebell Gadsby*: *After Iris* (2013), *Flora in Love* (2014), *All About Pumpkin* (2015) and *Time for Jas* (2016). Her latest book is *The Secret of Golden Island* (Faber 2024). For more information visit www.natashafarrant.com, and follow her on X @NatashaFarrant1.

Poetry
Writing poems for children

Poetry can be a huge source of support, solace and strength, particularly for children. In this article, Laura Mucha explains what it means to her as both a reader and poet, and how to go about writing it.

I started writing poetry when I was bedbound following a car accident. I couldn't socialise. I couldn't exercise. I couldn't go to work. But I could read and write poetry.

The smallness of it felt manageable, safe – unlike having my health ripped away from me age 29. It provided a code and a container for me to explore what I was feeling when I couldn't articulate it to myself, let alone anyone else.

I didn't mean to write for poems for children; they just came out that way. As well as writing poems, I devoured them. I read myriad collections and anthologies for children and adults. I also read the same stanza every day for years – a small package of words that helped me believe I could get through this monstrously difficult period.

> NEW EVERY MORNING (an excerpt)
> Every day is a fresh beginning;
> Listen, my soul, to the glad refrain,
> And, spite of old sorrow and older sinning,
> And puzzles forecasted and possible pain,
> Take heart with the day, and begin again.
> Susan Coolidge, from *A Few More Verses* (1889)

I eventually left my career as a lawyer and am now a full-time poet and author. I write poetry, fiction and non-fiction for children and young people, and non-fiction for adults. And I'm evangelical about the benefits of writing (and reading) poetry.

Why write poetry for children?

One defining feature of poetry is the use of white space. It can say a huge amount without adding any extra words. It can make the reader speed up or slow down. It can create a breath, improve comic timing, or create surprise by splitting a line at a certain point – so the reader thinks, 'What?! That is not what I thought the next line was going to say…'

White space is one of the key ingredients that makes poetry a brilliant way into reading and writing for young people. It makes the page less intimidating. Yes, there are words on it, but the white space holds those words, balances them, helps them breathe, gives them space, makes them feel more manageable. A child learning to read may not feel comfortable reading a page crammed to the margins with words, but they might read a poem.

Perhaps this is why recent National Literacy Trust research found that poetry is incredibly popular, with over half of children surveyed actively engaging with poetry in some way. And because poetry often explores difficult, emotional things, it can help young people who wouldn't normally embrace literacy to express what's really going on for them. Teachers regularly tell me that it's often the students who they think are the least confident in writing that write the most powerful poems.

Poems can change the way we think. They can give us a moment to delight in the musicality of language. To pause. Observe. Reflect. They can hold difficult things that might otherwise feel overwhelming. They can make us stop and pay attention amid the busyness of life. They can let us laugh. Relax. Rest.

Poems are often small, but the work that has gone into them is usually vast. I'll give you an example: I was recently commissioned to write a poem for the Somerset House Soil exhibition. I read hundreds of children's poems (written as part of the project), watched two documentaries, read nine books and every published poem I could find on the subject. I then wrote 60 drafts of a poem, 40 drafts of a different poem (also about soil), then returned to the original. The final poem was just 82 words.

Poems may not include many words, but those that are included work incredibly hard to deserve their place.

Ok, you've persuaded me. How do I start?

A blank piece of paper can be intimidating, but there are many ways in:
• Read and listen to lots of poems (the Children's Poetry Archive is a brilliant, free place to start), watch films, listen to music. When you see or hear a line you like, try writing a poem from that.
• Pay attention to something that's upsetting you, making you laugh or going round and round in your head. What is it? Why is it making you feel or think something? How could you translate this into something that children the age you are writing for will understand and relate to?
• Look at artwork and write down as many things that pop into your mind as possible.
• Sit down and write a list of everything you've done in the last week. Is there anything that surprised you?

At this point, you *must* pause any inner critic / editor thoughts. You *have* to make a mess, you *have* to allow yourself to come up with *all* the ideas you can, and that means *allowing* yourself to come up with ideas that might be *terrible*. That's part of the process.

Editing comes *later*.

I hate what I've written

At some point, you will find you have a collection of words. You may like them, you may feel there is potential there, you may not.

Don't worry if you don't. I write things I don't like all the time. I was commissioned to write a poem that empowered young people, and wrote five poems that didn't work. Thankfully by this point, I'd been writing long enough that I had faith that I would write something good in the end. And I did. One night, at 1am when I couldn't sleep, an idea popped into my head and I wrote a first draft of the poem that was eventually published.

When you write something you don't like, it's important NOT to think 'Argh, this is useless. I can't write poetry!' Instead think, 'This is part of the process' and 'I will get there'. Because you will (with lots of determination and study).

Then what?

Once you have something you're vaguely happy with, now comes the part that is the hardest to teach but the most fundamental.

Editing.

I studied poetry for years before I fully realised what editing was. The penny dropped when, during one of her workshops, Katy Evans-Bush showed me the 17 drafts that Elizabeth Bishop wrote of her poem, 'One Art'. Seeing each and every draft, with all Bishop's manuscript scribbles and changes, helped my head get around what can be an incredibly nebulous process.

My editing process can involve adding words, removing them, shuffling, changing the order of stanzas, cutting them (sometimes only to decide I want them back in), pausing the writing process to research something and check what I'm saying is accurate, reading aloud, getting feedback from a trusted person, taking a break so that I can come back to the poem with fresh eyes, deciding I can't figure out how to make a poem work, working on another poem, then coming back to the original and realising I can.

I love editing because I'm working from a set of words. They may not be perfect, but I'm no longer dealing with a blank page or an idea floating round in my head. I'm working with *something*. All I have to do is make it the best it can be.

But editing can also be a *total* pain.

The 60 drafts of the Somerset House poem are a great example of this. Writing and editing children's poetry is not an efficient process. You *have* to go down dead ends and write things you choose not to include. Or at least that's my experience.

Don't give up

Sometimes you might feel like a poem should go in the bin.

Don't put it in there.

Put it in a folder of 'I can't use right now' poems, because you may be able to use it in the future. I wrote a poem called 'Dear Ugly Sisters' while sitting in the bath. It consisted of a long list of chores scribbled on the back of a soggy envelope, and that's where it lived for eight years, until a brilliant poet gave me an idea of how to change it into something else. The poem won *The Caterpillar* Poetry Prize, has been featured in the press, displayed on public transport and printed in bestselling anthologies. And for eight years it was *horrendous*.

If you stick at studying, writing and reading children's poetry, you will get better and better. And as you do, you might figure out how to rework earlier poems that were previously bin-worthy. But there may also be some that you will never be happy with, and that's okay.

What do I do with what I've written?

Agents often don't represent poets unless they write more than just poetry. Poetry sales are usually small, so they can't afford to spend the time on it. But there are some agents that will.

I began by writing (a lot), I spent *years* attending poetry courses and reading widely around poetic technique, as well as multiple editions of the *Children's Writers' & Artists' Yearbook*. I eventually submitted to children's poetry magazines, won a couple of competitions, and was published in anthologies before finally publishing a collection. It was a long process – about ten years from writing my first poem to having my first collection. And the vast majority of poems I wrote in that time did not make the cut.

That was my journey. But there are many other routes in, for example sharing poems on social media and building a following that way. While the journey to publication can vary, what I don't think changes is the importance of committing to and studying the craft. It can take a huge amount of time. But it's worth it!

Conclusion

Children's poetry is unlikely to make you big bucks. Bookshops don't give poetry much shelf space. Poetry doesn't usually get translated much, so you (and publishers) miss out on additional income or cheaper printing costs from larger print runs.

But that's not why I write it.

Writing and studying poetry improves everything else I write. Whether that's a picture book for three- to six-year-olds or non-fiction for adults, every single one of my books include poetic technique – and is all the better for it.

I use poetry to teach creative writing to young people. I can't write a chapter with students in an hour's session, but we can write a draft poem – and in doing so, we can explore not only poetry, but the creative writing (and editing) process more generally.

When I finish a poem, it gives me a full-bellied ahhh-everything-has-slotted-into-place-as-if-it-always-belonged-there feeling that other forms of writing don't give me in the same way.

And my hope is that some of my poems will provide the laughter, insight, wisdom, or delight that poems have given me, both as a child and as an adult. Or the comfort, connection and hope that Susan Coolidge gave me when I was bedbound – even though she died long before I arrived on this planet.

So no, writing children's poetry won't earn me big bucks. But it might be the most valuable thing that I do.

Laura Mucha is a poet and Author-in-Residence in the Department of Public Health & Primary Care, University of Cambridge. Her books have been described as 'stunningly original' by BookTrust, 'fantastic' by the *Daily Mail*, 'brilliant' by the *Daily Telegraph*, 'a must for every school library and classroom' by *The School Librarian* and 'a marvellous feat' by Richard Curtis. In 2024, she won Children's Book of the Year 2024 (Non-Fiction) in *The Week Junior* Awards with *Welcome to Our Table* (Nosy Crow 2023). She also broke the Guinness World Records title for Largest Poetry Lesson (Multi Venue) together with 43,516 young people around the world. Follow her @lauramucha and see more of her work at lauramucha.com.

From gigging to getting published

Former Waterstones Children's Laureate, Joseph Coelho, chronicles his journey to becoming a published author, poet and playwright, highlighting the importance of seizing opportunities as they arise.

You should put this book back where you got it! Honestly – put it back, back up on the shelf and step away. That way everything can stay exactly the same and you'll be safe ... You're still here! Okay – so you're prepared for the consequences of flicking through these pages, of delving into this book's knowledgeable depths? You have been warned ... your life is about to be changed.

When I first started putting pen to paper in the early noughties, it was as a performance poet. I took to the stage at Battersea Arts Centre, the Poetry Society or some other gig in a cafe or bar, rushing from my day job selling advertising in my ill-fitting suit and shakily putting my name down on the open mic list. And the reward for my careering around central London? A chance to read my poems to a live audience and sometimes, *sometimes* I might get paid for my efforts. Getting paid was rare, but it didn't matter – I had the writing bug and a little thing like 'rarely getting paid' wasn't going to stop me. I gigged for years, mainly around central London, and spent my days running from one horrible job to the next – working as a transport planner, gym instructor and (during a low period) a tequila boy. Slowly but surely, I started to get known on the circuit and would be invited to perform at paid gigs. Through the brilliant performance poetry organisation Apples and Snakes, I found a whole host of paid opportunities, from doing R&D (research and development) as a writer for theatre shows to leading creative writing sessions in schools to engage young people with poetry. Life was good but, in order to make ends meet, I found I was saying yes to every opportunity going. Most of these gigs were educational – wonderful, rewarding educational gigs – but not necessarily taking my career in the direction I needed it to go.

It was at this juncture I started to actively look for ways of being published as a writer and playwright. I started googling, attending workshops and taking advantage of mentoring schemes run by organisations like Spread the Word and Arvon. I spoke to other writers who had managed to get a play put on or get a book deal, and I found that they all kept mentioning one book – this book, the book you now hold in your hands.

Flicking through the pages of *Children's Writers' & Artists' Yearbook* (*CWAYB*) felt conspiratorial, like I was glimpsing top secret files. There were articles from authors I respected, lists and lists of organisations offering opportunities, and a compendium of agents. I started to research playwrights and authors whose work was similar to the sort of things I was writing. I made lists of top agents to approach, and I started to send out my pitches. Whereas before I had been sending approaches to agents out in the dark, now I was focused – I knew who represented who and, when I started to get replies and meetings, I knew how to impress. I was wise to the industry I wanted to be a part of, and that was in no small part because of the information gifted to me by the *CWAYB*.

Since those early days thumbing through *Children's Writers' & Artists' Yearbook* over 15 years ago, much has changed: I'm now a fully-fledged author and playwright with over 30 books under my belt, and many plays besides; and I was the Waterstones Children's Laureate from 2022 to 2024– an honour that the nervous young writer who first picked up a volume of this book could never have imagined. It's been a long and a bumpy road carving out space for myself as a writer, but I have loved (and continue to love) every minute of it. It's not easy and it's not for everyone – but not everyone makes the effort to get to know the industry. You, dear reader, are not like everyone; you have this book in your hands, which already tells me a lot about you. You are actively researching, you are finding out about an industry which wants and needs your voice, your stories, your illustrations, your poems, plays, TV series and films. So … write, illustrate, put ink to paper, finger to keyboard and use the knowledge contained in these pages to set you on your course. It will be difficult, there will be rejection, and at times you'll wonder: 'Why am I doing this?' But deep down you know why – it's because you can't *not* do it, because something is calling you on this adventure. And there is no treasure without trial, so rise to the challenge, dearest of readers, and know that you have already taken that first essential step.

Joseph Coelho, Waterstones Children's Laureate 2022–24, is an award-winning performance poet, playwright and children's author. His first poetry collection *Werewolf Club Rules* was published by Frances Lincoln in 2014 and won the CLPE CLiPPA Poetry Award 2015. His other books include the critically acclaimed *Luna Loves...* series (Andersen Press 2017–), *If All the World Were* (Lincoln Children's Books 2018), the CLiPPA-shortlisted collection of poems, *Overheard in a Tower Block* (Otter-Barry Books 2017), *The Girl Who Became a Tree* (Otter-Barry Books 2019), which was shortlisted for the 2021 CILIP Carnegie Medal, the middle-grade series *Fairytales Gone Bad* (Walker 2020) and YA novel *The Boy Lost in the Maze* (Otter-Barry Books 2022). Joseph has also published non-fiction titles including *How to Write Poems* (Bloomsbury 2017). For more information, see www.thepoetryofjosephcoelho.com.

Poetry organisations

Below are some organisations which provide budding poets with opportunities to develop their skills, and to perform and engage with audiences and other poets.

WHERE TO GET INVOLVED

A range of organisations – from local groups to larger professional bodies – exist for emerging and established poets to access support or to learn more about others' work. A concise selection appears below.

Literature Wales
Tŷ Newydd Writing Centre, Llanystumdwy, Cricieth, Gwynedd LL52 0LW
tel (01766) 522811
email post@literaturewales.org
website www.literaturewales.org
Instagram @llencymru_litwales
Executive Director Claire Furlong, Artistic Director Leusa Llewelyn

National company for the development of literature in Wales. Working to inspire communities, develop writers and celebrate Wales' literary culture. Activities include the Wales Book of the Year Award, the National Poet of Wales, Children's Laureate Wales and Bardd Plant Cymru schemes, creative writing courses at Tŷ Newydd Writing Centre, and various writer-development initiatives. The organisation is a member of the Arts Council of Wales' Arts Portfolio Wales.

The Poetry Book Society
Milburn House, Dean Street, Newcastle Upon Tyne NE1 1LF
tel 0191 230 8100
email enquiries@poetrybooksociety.co.uk
website www.poetrybooks.co.uk
Facebook www.facebook.com/poetrybooksoc
Instagram @poetrybooksociety

Book club for readers of poetry founded in 1953 by T.S. Eliot. Every quarter, expert poet selectors choose one outstanding publication (the PBS Choice), and recommend four other titles; these are sent to members, who are also offered discounts on other poetry books. The PBS produces the quarterly membership magazine, the *Bulletin* (available to all members), which contains the poet selectors' reviews of the Choice and Recommendations, interviews with international poets, reviews and listings. Also offers a range of educational memberships for secondary school libraries with expert teaching tips and posters to inspire students with a love of poetry.

The Poetry Business
Campo House, 54 Campo Lane, Sheffield S1 2EG
tel 0114 438 4074
email office@poetrybusiness.co.uk
website www.poetrybusiness.co.uk

Publishes pamphlets by young poets between the ages of 17 and 24 under The New Poets List imprint; runs the literary magazine, *The North*. Also organises a national pamphlet competition for young poets, writing days and residential courses. Publishes illustrated poetry anthologies for children under the Small|Donkey imprint. Founded 1986.

Poetry Ireland
(Temporary office) 3 Great Denmark Street, Dublin 1, D01 NV63, Republic of Ireland
tel +353 (0)1 678 9815
email info@poetryireland.ie
website www.poetryireland.ie
Director Liz Kelly, Publications Manager Paul Lenehan

Committed to achieving excellence in the reading, writing and performance of poetry throughout the island of Ireland. Receives support from The Arts Council (An Chomhairle Ealaíon) and The Arts Council of Northern Ireland and enjoys partnerships with arts centres, festivals, schools, colleges and bookshops at home and abroad. Creates performance and publication opportunities for poets at all stages of their careers. Publishes *Poetry Ireland Review* three times a year, *Trumpet* once a year and an online journal of work by early career poets who participate in the Introductions/Ceadlínte programme.

The Poetry Society
22 Betterton Street, London WC2H 9BX
tel 020-7420 9880
email info@poetrysociety.org.uk
website www.poetrysociety.org.uk
Instagram @thepoetrysociety

A leading voice for poets and poetry in Britain. Founded in 1909 to promote a more general recognition and appreciation of poetry, the Society has nearly 4,000 members. Its education, commissioning and publishing programmes, as well as a packed calendar of performances, readings and competitions, help it to champion poetry in its many forms.

The Society also publishes education resources for teachers and educators; organises high-profile events including an Annual Lecture and National Poetry Day celebrations; runs Poetry Prescription, a critical appraisal service; and provides an education advisory service, INSET packages for schools and networks of schools, a poets in schools service, school membership, youth membership and a website.

Competitions run by the Society include the annual National Poetry Competition, with a first prize of £5,000, and the Foyle Young Poets of the Year Award.

Tower Poetry

Christ Church, Oxford OX1 1DP
tel 07849 625906
email tower.poetry@chch.ox.ac.uk
website www.chch.ox.ac.uk/towerpoetry
Facebook www.facebook.com/towerpoetry
X @towerpoetry
Instagram @towerpoetry

Exists to encourage and challenge everyone who reads or writes poetry. Funded by a generous bequest to Christ Church, Oxford, by the late Christopher Tower, the aims of Tower Poetry are to stimulate an enjoyment and critical appreciation of poetry, particularly among young people in education, and to challenge people to write their own poetry.

WHERE TO GET INFORMATION

Your local library is a good first port of call and should have information about the poetry scene in the area. Many libraries are actively involved in spreading the word about poetry as well as having modern poetry available for loan.

Alliance of Literary Societies (ALS)

email allianceoflitsocs@gmail.com
website www.allianceofliterarysocieties.org.uk
Chair Marty Ross, Secretary Anita Fernandez-Young

Umbrella organisation for over 100 literary societies and groups in the UK. It provides support and advice on a variety of literary subjects, as well as promoting cooperation between member societies. It publishes a twice-yearly members' newsletter, *Not Only But...* ALS holds an AGM weekend which is hosted by a different member society each year, moving around the UK, or online. Founded 1973.

Arts Council England

tel 0161 934 4317
email enquiries@artscouncil.org.uk
website www.artscouncil.org.uk
Instagram @aceagrams

National development agency for the arts in England, providing funding for a range of arts and cultural activities. It supports creative writing including poetry, fiction, storytelling, spoken word, digital work, writing for children and literary translation. Also funds a range of publishers and magazines as well as providing grants to individual writers. Contact the enquiries team for more information on funding support and advice.

Arts Council of Wales

Bute Place, Cardiff CF10 5AL
tel 0845 873 4900
email information@arts.wales
website https://arts.wales
Facebook www.facebook.com/celfyddydau
Instagram @celfcymruarts

Independent charity with three regional offices; its principal sponsor is the Welsh Government. It is the country's funding and development agency for the arts, supporting and developing high-quality arts activities. Its funding schemes offer opportunities for arts organisations and individuals in Wales to apply, through a competitive process, for funding towards a clearly defined arts-related project. Founded by Royal Charter 1994.

Manchester Poetry Library

Manchester Metropolitan University, Grosvenor Building, Cavendish Street, Manchester M15 6BG
email poetrylibrary@mmu.ac.uk
website www.mmu.ac.uk/poetry-library
Instagram @mcrpoetrylibrary
Director Becky Swain

Public poetry library: free and open to all. Aims to expand access to poetry and to encourage the writing of it at all levels, from primary school to professional publication. Core collection includes 19th- to 21st-century poetry in English from around the world, as well as poetry in translation. Audio and print versions available. Runs events that celebrate the role of local communities and languages.

National Association of Writers' Groups

Old Vicarage, Scammonden, Huddersfield HD3 3FT
email info@nawg.co.uk
website www.nawg.co.uk

Aims to bring cohesion and fellowship to isolated writers' groups and individuals, promoting the study and art of writing in all its aspects. There are many affiliated groups and associate (individual) members across the UK.

National Poetry Library (Children's Collection)

Level 5, Royal Festival Hall, Southbank Centre, London SE1 8XX
tel 020-7921 0943
email info@poetrylibrary.org.uk
website www.nationalpoetrylibrary.org.uk
Facebook www.facebook.com/NationalPoetryLibrary
Instagram @nationalpoetrylibrary

Comprises thousands of items for young poets of all ages, including poetry on audio and film. The library has an education service for teachers and writing groups, with a separate collection of books and materials for teachers and poets who work with children in schools. Group visits can be organised, allowing children to interact with the collection in various ways, such as engaging with war poetry via the Letters Home booklet, or becoming a Poetry Library Poetry Explorer. Children of all ages can join for free and borrow books and other materials. A special membership scheme is available for teachers to borrow books for the classroom. Contact the library details on membership and opening times.

Northern Poetry Library

Morpeth Library,
Morpeth Sports and Leisure Centre,
Gas House Lane,
Morpeth Northumberland NE61 1SR
tel 01670 620391
email mylibrary@northumberland.gov.uk
website http://northernpoetrylibrary.org.uk

Largest collection of contemporary poetry outside London, housing over 15,000 titles and magazines covering poetry published since 1945. Founded 1968.

Scottish Poetry Library

5 Crichton's Close, Canongate, Edinburgh EH8 8DT
tel 0131 557 2876
website www.scottishpoetrylibrary.org.uk
Facebook www.facebook.com/scottishpoetrylibrary
Instagram @splscotland
Director Asif Khan

Houses over 45,000 poetry-related items: books, magazines, pamphlets, recordings and the Edwin Morgan Archive (featuring rare works by Morgan and others). The core of the collection is contemporary and classic poetry written in Scotland – Scots, Gaelic and English – but classic Scottish poetry as well as contemporary works from almost every part of the world are also available. All resources, advice and information are readily accessible, free of charge. The SPL has its own shop and holds regular exhibitions and poetry events, including reading and writing groups and outreach projects throughout the nation; see website for details. Closed Friday to Sunday. Founded 1984.

ONLINE RESOURCES

There is a wealth of information available for poets at the click of a mouse; the suggestions below are a good starting point.

The Children's Poetry Archive

website https://childrenspoetryarchive.org

World's premier online collection of recordings of children's poets reading their work. Visitors to the website may listen, free of charge, to the voices of contemporary English-language poets and of poets from the past. Featured poets include Allan Ahlberg, Michael Rosen and Valerie Bloom, but the Archive is added to regularly. The website has a range of search options, so that users can search by theme, poet name, lyric, and so on. Supported by the T.S. Eliot Foundation.

LoveReading4Kids.co.uk

website www.lovereading4kids.co.uk
Instagram @lovereadingkids

Independent literature recommendation site designed to inspire and inform parents about the best new reads in children's publishing from toddlers to YA, including poetry. Now features an online bookstore with social purpose where 25% of money spent can be donated to a school of the buyer's choice, to spend on books. Features include: filter by age range and interest; downloadable opening extracts; exclusive reviews from children's book experts; and authentic reader reviews from children.

Now part of LoveReading4Kids, the LoveReading4Schools portal supports schools across the UK wanting to embed a reading for pleasure culture. On their school dashboard, they can create their own recommended reading lists and share these with their pupils' parents, so that they can make better informed purchasing decisions for their children both at home and at school. Eligible schools can also apply for between £1,000–£5,000 credit to spend on books through the LoveReading4Kids Funding For Schools Scheme. Founded 2005.

The Poetry Kit

email info@poetrykit.org
website www.poetrykit.org
X @thepoetrykit

Collates a wide variety of poetry-related information, including events, competitions, courses and more for an international readership.

Poetry Space

email susan@poetryspace.co.uk
website www.poetryspace.co.uk

Specialist publisher of poetry and short stories, as well as news and features, edited by Susan Jane Sims. Operates as a social enterprise with all profits being used to publish online and in print, and to hold events to widen participation in poetry. Submissions of poems, stories, novel extracts, photographs and artwork accepted all year for Young Writers' and Artists' Space (18s and under; work by under-16s particularly welcomed).

Seven Stories – The National Centre for Children's Books

email info@sevenstories.org.uk
website www.sevenstories.org.uk
Facebook www.facebook.com/7Stories
Instagram @7stories
Ceo Wendy Elliott

Dedicated to the art of children's books. Its website features a blog and online catalogue that may be of use to researchers and authors.

Teachit: English Teaching Resources
6th floor, Capital Tower, 91 Waterloo Road,
London SE1 8RT
website www.teachit.co.uk/english
Facebook www.facebook.com/teachit.uk
X @TeachitEnglish

Resource website for teachers, with over 20,000 pages of classroom worksheets, PowerPoint presentations and activities that have been written and edited by experienced English teachers. The website provides free PDFs, and subscribers can access teaching packs, templates and downloadable posters designed for Key Stages 3, 4 and 5.

WHERE TO CELEBRATE POETRY

Festival information should be available from Arts Council England offices (see page 315). See also *Children's literature festivals and trade fairs* on page 352.

The British Council
British Council Customer Service UK,
Bridgewater House, 58 Whitworth Street,
Manchester M1 6BB
tel 0161 957 7755
email uk-literature@britishcouncil.org
website https://literature.britishcouncil.org
Instagram @britishcouncil

Information on events, authors and projects.

Imagine: Writers and Writing for Children
Southbank Centre, London SE1 8XX
tel 020-7960 4200
website www.southbankcentre.co.uk/events/imagine/imagine-festival/
X @southbankcentre
Takes place February

An annual festival celebrating writing for children. Features a selection of poets, storytellers and illustrators.

Ledbury Poetry Festival
The Barrett Browning Institute, Homend,
Ledbury HR8 2AA
tel (01531) 634156
email director@poetry-festival.co.uk
website www.poetry-festival.co.uk
Artistic Director Chloe Garner
Takes place June, July and throughout the year

The UK's biggest celebration of poetry and spoken word, attended by poets from all over the world. Established and upcoming talents take part in a wide variety of events, from masterclasses, walks, talks and films through to breakfasts, music, exhibitions and bike rides. International Poetry Competition launches every February.

WHERE TO WRITE POETRY

Arvon
Lumb Bank – The Ted Hughes Arvon Centre,
Heptonstall, Hebden Bridge,
West Yorkshire HX7 6DF
tel (01422) 843714
email lumbbank@arvon.org
Totleigh Barton, Sheepwash, Beaworthy, Devon EX21 5NS
tel (01409) 231338
email totleighbarton@arvon.org
The Hurst – The John Osborne Arvon Centre,
Clunton, Craven Arms, Shrops. SY7 0JA
tel (01588) 640658
email thehurst@arvon.org
website www.arvon.org

Hosts residential creative writing courses and retreats in three rural writing houses. With the opportunity to live and work with professional writers, participants transform their writing through workshops, one-to-one tutorials, time and space to write. Five-day courses and shorter courses are available in a wide range of genres, including writing for children and young adults, fiction, poetry, theatre and creative non-fiction. An online programme of writing courses, masterclasses and live readings also runs year-round. Grants and concessions are available to help with course fees. Founded 1968.

City Lit
1–10 Keeley Street, London WC2B 4BA
tel 020-7831 7831
email writing@citylit.ac.uk
website www.citylit.ac.uk
Facebook www.facebook.com/CityLit

Offers classes and courses (online and in-person) on poetry appreciation and writing for children, as well as a wide range of other topics.

The Poetry School
Ground Floor, 1 City Square, Park Row,
Leeds LS1 2ES
website www.poetryschool.com
Instagram @thepoetryschool

Teaches the art and craft of writing poetry, with courses in Leeds, London and around the UK, ranging from evening classes, small seminars and individual tutorials, to one-day workshops, year-long courses and an accredited MA. Activities for beginners to advanced writers, with classes happening face-to-face and online. Three termly programmes a year, plus professional skills development projects and CAMPUS, a social network for poets.

Tŷ Newydd Writing Centre
Llanystumdwy, Cricieth, Gwynedd LL52 0LW
tel (01766) 522811

email tynewydd@literaturewales.org
website www.tynewydd.wales
Instagram @canolfantynewydd

Tŷ Newydd, the former home of Prime Minister David Lloyd George, has hosted residential creative writing courses for writers of all abilities for over 30 years. Open to everyone over the age of 16. Courses cover everything from poetry and popular fiction to writing for the theatre, developing a novel for young adults. No qualifications are necessary. Staff can advise on the suitability of courses, and further details about each individual course can be obtained by visiting the website, or contacting the team by phone or email. Tŷ Newydd also offers courses for schools, corporate courses and away days for companies, and is home to Nant, the writers' retreat cottage located on site. Tŷ Newydd Writing Centre is run by Literature Wales, the national company for the development of literature in Wales.

HELP FOR YOUNG POETS AND TEACHERS

National Association of Writers in Education (NAWE)
Tower House, Mill Lane, off Askham Fields Lane, Askham Bryan, York YO23 3FS
tel 0330 333 5909
email admin@nawe.co.uk
website www.nawe.co.uk

Advocates for creative writing: enhancing knowledge and understanding of the subject, supporting writers and good practice in teaching and facilitation in all settings. NAWE promotes creative writing as both a distinct discipline and an essential element in education generally. Its membership is national and international and includes those working in Higher Education, freelance writers working in schools and community contexts, and the teachers and other professionals who work with them. It runs a national directory of professional members offering workshops, talks and other services, produces a fortnightly opportunities bulletin and holds an annual national conference. Professional Membership includes public liability insurance cover.

Professional Graduate Membership is available for university creative writing students who have recently graduated and aims to support the move from student to working as a professional writer in education and the community, offering the benefits of Professional Membership at a discounted rate.

Poetry Society Education
The Poetry Society, 22 Betterton Street, London WC2H 9BX
tel 020-7420 9880
email educationadmin@poetrysociety.org.uk
website www.poetrysociety.org.uk
X @poetryeducation
Instagram @thepoetrysociety

An arm of The Poetry Society, one of the UK's leading poetry organisations, aiming to facilitate exciting and innovative education work. For over 30 years it has been introducing poets into classrooms, providing free downloadable learning resources and producing accessible publications for pupils. It develops projects and schemes to keep poetry flourishing in schools, libraries and workplaces, giving work to hundreds of poets and allowing thousands of children and adults to experience poetry for themselves.

Through projects such as the Foyle Young Poets of the Year Award and Young Poets Network, The Poetry Society gives offers talent-development opportunities and exposure to young writers and performers. A network for poets and teachers, Cloud Chamber, is free to join and provides opportunities to share knowledge and best practice. Schools membership and Youth membership offer a range of benefits, including quarterly Poetry Society publications, books and posters.

Young Poets Network
email educationadmin@poetrysociety.org.uk
website https://ypn.poetrysociety.org.uk
Facebook www.facebook.com/YoungPoetsNetwork
X @youngpoetsnet

Free online platform from The Poetry Society comprising features about reading, writing and performing poetry, plus new work by young poets and regular writing challenges. Open to anyone under the age of 25.

YOUNG POETRY COMPETITIONS

Children's competitions are included in the competition list provided by the Poetry Library: this is free online at www.southbankcentre.co.uk/venues/national-poetry-library/write-publish/competitions.

Foyle Young Poets of the Year Award
The Poetry Society, 22 Betterton Street, London WC2H 9BX
tel 020-7420 9880
email fyp@poetrysociety.org.uk
website https://foyleyoungpoets.org
Facebook www.facebook.com/thepoetrysociety
X @PoetrySociety
Bluesky @poetrysociety.bsky.social
Instagram @thepoetrysociety

Annual competition for writers aged 11–17. Prizes include books, mentoring and talent development opportunities, such as publication and performance. Deadline 31 July. Free to enter. Founded 2001.

Christopher Tower Poetry Competition

Christ Church, Oxford OX1 1DP
tel 07849 625906
email tower.poetry@chch.ox.ac.uk
website www.chch.ox.ac.uk/towerpoetry
X @TowerPoetry

Annual poetry competition (open from October to February) from Christ Church, Oxford, aimed at students aged between 16 and 18 in UK schools and colleges. The poems should be no longer than 48 lines, on a different chosen theme each year. Free to enter. Prizes: £5,000 (1st), £3,000 (2nd), £1,500 (3rd). There will also be ten commended awards of £500 each.

Further reading

Addonizio, Kim, *Ordinary Genius: A Guide for the Poet Within* (W.W. Norton 2012)
Bell, Jo and Jane Commane, *How to Be a Poet: A 21st-Century Guide to Writing Well* (Nine Arches Press 2017)
Bell, Jo and guests: *52: Write a Poem a Week – Start Now, Keep Going* (Nine Arches Press 2015)
Blackwell, Sophia, *Writers' & Artists' Poetry Writers' Handbook* (Bloomsbury, 2022)
Chisholm, Alison, *A Practical Guide to Poetry Forms* (Compass Books 2014)
Fairfax, John and John Moat, *The Way to Write* (Penguin Books, 2nd edn revised 1998)
Greene, Roland et al., *Princeton Encyclopedia of Poetry and Poetics* (Princeton University Press, 4th edn 2012)
Hamilton, Ian and Jeremy Noel-Tod, *The Oxford Companion to Modern Poetry in English* (Oxford University Press, 2nd edn 2014)
Kowit, Steve, *In the Palm of Your Hand: A Poet's Portable Workshop* (Tilbury House, 2nd edn 2019)
Maxwell, Glyn, *On Poetry* (Oberon Books 2017)
Oliver, Mary, *Rules for the Dance: Handbook for Writing and Reading Metrical Verse* (Houghton Mifflin 1998)
Padel, Ruth, *52 Ways of Looking at a Poem: A Poem for Every Week of the Year* (Vintage 2004)
Padel, Ruth, *The Poem and the Journey: 60 Poems for the Journey of Life* (Vintage 2008)
Roberts, Philip Davies, *How Poetry Works* (Penguin Books, 2nd edn 2000)
Sampson, Fiona, *Poetry Writing: The Expert Guide* (Robert Hale 2009)
Sansom, Peter, *Writing Poems* (Bloodaxe 1993, repr. 1997)
Whitworth, John, *Writing Poetry* (A&C Black, 2nd edn 2006)

Literary agents
Submission to a literary agent (the when, what and how...)

Hannah Sheppard offers practical advice on the process of submitting your finished work to a literary agent and provides top tips and inside knowledge on how to find the representation that might be right for you.

Congratulations! You've finished your novel. This is a huge achievement – not everyone manages to see the task through to completion (I know this from experience ... twice). But, what should you do next? At the risk of being a complete bore – unless you've already done this, now you need to *get back to work and start editing.*

Honing your final manuscript
The first rule of submitting to literary agents is: ***don't* submit your first draft**. It's time to read your work objectively. Where does the pace drop? Where do the characters do things that don't fit with their motivations? Remember that section you really love but know, if you're honest, isn't moving the plot forward? Cut it.

Find a critique partner (social media and local writers' groups can be a good place to start); read and give feedback on their novel in return for feedback on your own. You'll learn as much from exercising your inner editor on someone else's work as you will from the feedback they give you.

Go back and re-write. Do it again. Do it until, hand on heart, you cannot see another thing that might need changing. Then print your freshly edited story in a font you haven't seen it in before (alternatively stick the manuscript on your e-reader or phone, or read it aloud to yourself); this will help you see the words with fresh eyes and make it easier to spot any lingering typos, word repetitions or slightly awkward sentences, so you can fix those. Only now are you ready to start thinking about submitting to a literary agent, and first, you'll need to decide who to submit to.

Making your agent list
The second rule of submitting to literary agents is: ***don't* send your work to everyone**. Agents have different tastes and specialisms and there's enough information out there to help you narrow down a list of those who might be suitable for your manuscript. The amount of time authors spend waiting for a response to submissions would be a lot shorter if everyone stuck to this rule!

Luckily, you currently have in your hand the fount of all knowledge when it comes to literary agents – well done. Make your way through the *Children's Writers' & Artists' Yearbook* (but not yet, finish reading this first) looking for agents who represent your genre, and make yourself a longlist. Then look these agents up online – nearly all will have a website, many will also have social media accounts, and if you keep hunting you might find articles they've written and also their manuscript wish lists. All of this will give you some clues as to whether each agent might be right for you and your work.

It's also worth thinking about what's important to you when it comes to this relationship. Do you want someone who is a cut-throat dealmaker who is all about the business side of publishing, or someone a little more approachable? (If I'm honest, they're all pretty lovely – I haven't met many of the first kind.) Do you want someone who will be hands-on editorially or do you feel like you've got that covered? My top piece of advice is to find someone you can ask basic questions to without feeling stupid ... because there are going to be a lot of those. Quite honestly, there's no reason you *should* know all about how this industry works. Publishing can be flummoxing at times – even for someone who's been working in it for over 20 years.

After researching everyone on your longlist, put them into some sort of order – from those who feel like the closest fit in terms of their list and who you think you might gel with personally, down to those who could be a bit of wild card but are not completely beyond the realms of possibility. But if an agent says they don't represent your genre, it's unlikely they're going to start doing so just because of *your* book; this is about their publishing contacts as much as anything – and you want an agent who knows the right editors to sell your work.

Putting together a submission package

After selecting the agents to approach, you'll need to prepare your submission package, and the third rule of submitting to literary agents is: ***always* follow their guidelines**. As well as your *manuscript* (usually the first three chapters or 10,000 words, and always from the beginning of your manuscript), the submission package should generally include a *synopsis* and a *cover letter*. But it's important to check exactly what each agent wants and how they want it sent. These may be different for every agent on your list. Yes, that may be tiresome, but the guidelines are there to enable your chosen agent to get through their inbox as fast as possible (they've worked out a system that works for them) and get an answer to you. And if an author appears to think they're above following the guidelines, I ask myself – why would I want to work with someone who doesn't respect me? Could I feel confident promoting them to editors I have good working relationships with? The harsh truth is, I don't even need to read the material in these cases.

There's a lot of great advice online about writing a synopsis (see for example, www.writersandartists.co.uk/advice/synopsis) but, in short, this should be one page of A4, size 12 font (typically Times New Roman or something similarly readable), single-spaced. Don't play with the margins or shrink the font; think about the person who has to read it – if it's tiny, densely packed text, you've probably lost them. White space on the page is always good.

A synopsis should be a very functional overview of your protagonist's emotional journey. This isn't about trying to wow an agent with your style (but be sure to proofread – try using the different font trick mentioned above). You don't need to include every plot point or introduce every character, but agents do need to know the cause-and-effect structure of your plot – all of it. We *want* the spoilers here please. An agent needs to know that the mechanics of your story work; from this they can see where there might be structural issues to address.

For your cover letter, it's good to strike a professional yet personable tone. This isn't a casual approach, but an agent does want to see some of your personality, to judge whether you're someone they might work well with. Opposite is the kind of letter I like to see – the focus is very much on the character and story, rather than themes or why the author wrote it.

Submission to a literary agent (the when, what and how...)

(1) Dear Hannah/Ms Sheppard

(2) I'm writing to submit *Romeo and Juliet*, a tragic love story for YA readers, complete at 75,000 words.

(3) When Romeo Montague and Juliet Capulet fall in love, it enrages their feuding families. Can they find a way to be together before Juliet is married off to someone else?

(4) Juliet can't even remember what started the argument between her family and the Montagues, it's been going on so long, and as a result she hasn't seen her childhood friend Romeo for years. But when fate brings them together at a school dance which Romeo and his friends have gate-crashed, the connection is immediate. They are meant to be together. Surely their families will see that? But they don't. And in an effort to keep Romeo and Juliet apart, Juliet's family arrange a marriage between Juliet and a friend of her father. Horrified, Romeo and Juliet hatch a plan to escape together, but a series of mixed messages and missed connections lead to disaster.

(5) *Romeo and Juliet* will appeal to readers of *Othello* and *Antony and Cleopatra* and fans of Christopher Marlowe.

(6) I am a debut writer who has ...

(7) I am submitting to you because ...

(8) Yours sincerely/Regards ...

---

(1) I'm happy with either style. Some agents prefer more formality ... but, above all, spell it correctly.

(2) Clearly state your title, target market and word count.

(3) This is your short elevator pitch – it's great to have something like this prepared for chance encounters with an agent, but also for post-publication when you're at promotional events in front of an audience and you're asked to introduce your book. A useful structure is: When A (inciting incident) happens, B (protagonist) must do C (action) otherwise/ before D (stakes) happen.

(4) This gives you a chance to expand a little on the story. You want to focus on the main story line and the emotional journey of your protagonist, making sure that the stakes are clear – knowing what the character stands to lose is important for emotionally engaging your reader. Think of this paragraph a little like the blurb on the back of a book; you want to make me care about the character and intrigue me. The synopsis is where you give the full story.

(5) This is your chance to position your work within the market and demonstrate that you understand the area you're writing into. Try not to include only the mega-sellers, as that suggests you don't read widely in the market – and it's important that you do.

(6) We don't need a huge amount of information about you at this point, but try to include anything pertinent, e.g. have you joined SCBWI; are you part of a writers' group; have you completed a writing course or won a writing competition? None of this is essential, but anything you have done will show how seriously you're taking your writing. My top tip here is **keep it positive**. So, for example, if you haven't won any writing competitions, just don't mention them.

(7) Show that you've done your research and understand a little about the particular agency and agent you're submitting to. Have you read an article in which I talked about my love for the type of story you've written? Does it fit with something my agency has mentioned on its manuscript wish list? Are you a huge fan of one of our existing clients and feel your mutual fandom of that body of work suggests we might like yours too?

(8) Polite sign off ... Use your actual name, not just initials or a pseudonym, even if that's what you want to write under. The agent is going to have a working relationship with you.

A few final top tips:
- Use your own, professional email address – almost all submissions are via email now. My agency does not accept hard copy submissions, and many agencies have the same policy. Don't use an email address you share with your partner or one that was funny when you were a student. Email accounts are easy and free to set up, so have a separate one for your work.
- Make attachment file names as useful as possible … 'synopsis for Hannah' is not very helpful (I receive hundreds with a similar description). Instead include your name and the title of your book.
- Try testing the water by contacting four or five agents initially, to see what response you get. That will give you the chance to tweak your submission. Maybe start midway down the list you drew up of those to contact. If you start getting positive reactions, you can always quickly send the submission to the agents at the top of the list too.
- Brace yourself for a long wait. Agents don't do this to torture you; we're very busy and we use our office time working for our existing clients. This means reading submissions happens in the evenings and at weekends. When my submissions were open generally I would typically receive ten a day. Now that we're only open for one week a month, I get between 200 and 300 within that window.
- Start writing your next book, so that you're not focused solely on the fate of the first one you send out. This should ideally be something new rather than a sequel, just in case your first submission doesn't work out.
- Usually a gentle nudge is fine if you haven't heard back within the time stated on the agent's website, but always stay polite. Definitely update an agent if you've been offered representation, and withdraw the submission if you accept that representation.
- If you get feedback, take it seriously. I'm so busy that I rarely give personalised feedback and only when I think there's something easy to fix which would make a significant difference to an author's chances.
- Remember that rejections are part of the process. They don't always mean your book or your writing is bad; they can simply mean that yours wasn't the right book for that agent at that time. There's a lot of luck and serendipity involved here too.
- If all you are getting are standard rejections, take some time out to think about whether you need to do more work. Perhaps you should get a professional assessment on your manuscript? Or maybe it's time to begin a different project (luckily you followed my earlier tip and have already started one, right?).
- Keep an open mind, the right agent for you might not be the person you initially put at the top of your wish list. How you get on at a personal level when you chat with an agent will be important.

So that's it … you're ready to start submitting. Good luck, hold your nerve and keep trying.

Literary agent **Hannah Sheppard** worked as an in-house editor with Macmillan Children's Books and Headline Publishing Group before joining the DHH Literary Agency in 2013. In 2023, she launched the eponymous Hannah Sheppard Literary Agency. She represents authors across children's fiction and commercial adult fiction. For more information, visit www.hs-la.com and follow Hannah on Instagram @hannah_litagent and Bluesky @hannahlitagent.bsky.social.

The author–agent contract

Finding an agent to fight your corner is the dream for many children's authors. But how does the relationship work? In this article, Lydia Silver explains the vital roles each party needs to play.

When I first joined my agency, I was handed two double-sided A4 pages, and told they were the most important pieces of paper I'd ever handle. Were they woven by angels, or imbued with a dark curse that needed to be locked away in a secret library? No – they were the brand new draft of our author–agency contract.

Since that first day, I've signed over 50 of those contracts, but I never stop feeling the responsibility and weight of them. Each of those contracts represents an author who has chosen to work with me, the relationship we hope we have with each other, and potentially years of working together; joining our creative minds and our business acumen to develop a life-long career for both of us. It represents their hopes and dreams, the love and time they've poured into their writing, and the anticipation of the deals I will make for them in the future. I don't foresee there ever being a time when signing them becomes everyday, because ultimately they're the foundation of everything I do.

As you can tell from this, the idea of a contract is something that elicits some strong reactions. In the legal sense, a contract makes things official, and having one is a mark of success – you've written something so great that someone wants to make legal promises to you about it. But it isn't just a piece of paper. A contract is a set of obligations, going both ways between an author and an agent, and it outlines the basis of what your relationship should be. Yes, there's legal jargon there, but at its core, the contract basically says this is who we are, and this is what we will do for each other.

This might sound a little intimidating and scary! But don't worry. The *really* scary contracts, the ones with clauses about delivery and royalties and copyright, are the ones that an agent can guide you through. For this article, we're looking at the contract before that, the one between you and the agent. This will be the first contract you sign in publishing and ultimately, it's the most important one too. Once you and your agent are a team, they're on your side to help you through every other contract and situation you might encounter. The contract is a set of promises between you, and they're promises agents take seriously. Every other promise is made off the back of these.

One final thing before we go into more detail – I love working with authors. I want them to feel empowered to ask questions about the industry, to dive in and learn more. Any good agent will feel the same so this article is just a jumping-off point, and you should always ask your agent about any questions you have. If we don't know the answer (and we normally do), we can go and find it. It's your career; you have the right to be informed about it!

What promises do agents make?

This question is pretty much the same as 'what does an agent do?'. Put simply, we promise to represent you and your interests to publishers, to sell your work as best we can, and to be in your corner throughout your career. On a more complex level, our promises can be broken down into before, during and after selling your work.

Before we can sell your work, we have to get it ready. For some authors and illustrators, this means working in a hands-on way with us to edit, reshape and package your concept.

Coming from an editorial background, this is a part that I really love. It's so exciting when you discover something that has that spark of specialness, and you know that with a little bit of shaping, some tweaking of the plot and a nice tight line edit or a shift in order of your portfolio, you're going to have something that takes people's breath away. My clients would probably say my edits are hugely harsh, but the market is tough and you need to blow editors' socks off. So one of my promises is to make the book the best I can, before I go any further.

Once we've done that, my next promise is to do my utmost to sell it. That starts well before I actually send the book to editors. Publishing runs on meetings over coffee or in the office or occasionally (for our very favourite editors) over wine, and at every meeting, editors will ask 'so, what do you have coming up?'. There are also twice-yearly book fairs where for a week, we'll have meetings every half hour to pitch new titles. Well before I'm actually sending a book out, I'll be speaking to editors, putting together a list of the people I want to send it to, and making sure everyone is ready to load up their Kindles and get reading the moment this manuscript lands in their inbox.

When the manuscript is ready to go out … it's time for the fun part! My promise here is to get the best deal possible for my authors. That doesn't just mean big money, but great royalties, a motivated marketing team, a good editorial connection … there are so many components to a strong deal and one of the things an agent does is weigh all of them up and guide their clients to what might be the best fit for them. A good agent will get you money – a *great* agent will get you a career.

Finally, once the deal is done and the real work starts, we promise to be on hand for anything and everything that might come up. Whether that's a cover you're not sure about, a deadline you suddenly can't make, or a new shiny idea you just have to discuss with someone, we are here for it. Over the years, some of my clients have become great friends and people whose careers I care deeply about, and all of that starts with my initial promise, made when we first sign that contract, to do the best I can for them as a creator.

What do you promise to us?

As I said at the top, contracts go both ways. So if an agent is making all these promises to you, do you have to promise them things back? Well, yes – and there's no hiding from it, a big part of what you're promising is money.

As agents, we don't get paid until you get paid. This is a core, fundamental part of how agents and agencies operate, so if you ever find an agent who is asking for money upfront, it's a scam. It breaks my heart a little that there are so many unscrupulous people out there who know how much authors and illustrators want to be published and will use that to take advantage of them, but they exist, and it's important to be aware of that.

The standard commission for authors is 15% in the UK and 20% internationally. Sometimes there are variations on this, and often the rates for illustrators are a little different, but an agent should be able to talk you through why that is if it's the case. And trust me, your agent will work for that commission! In exchange for this portion of the money you make through publishing, your agent becomes your editor, career coach, business manager and even therapist (although ideally you wouldn't need that feature of us too often). And before you have a book deal, we will still do all this work for you: we're just doing it for free.

But as well as the tangible, financial side of the contract, there are other promises that an author makes to an agent. You promise to share your work with us. You promise to keep us informed of things that might affect it. You promise to fulfil any obligations that come with your contract with a publisher, and most importantly of all, you promise to trust us. It's that trust that makes the contract, and the entire author–agent relationship, work.

How do you find an agent?

If all of these promises ultimately come down to trust, how do you find the right agent that you can trust and that trusts you? Over the years, I've been surprised by how many people are concerned that an agent might not have their best interests at heart, but I do understand how hard it is to place your trust and your work with someone you don't know yet. These contracts are big commitments! So you need to be confident that the agent you're working with is the right fit.

There are multiple ways to research and find agents, and I suspect every querying author has a different approach. But these are some of my favourites:
- The *Children's Writers' & Artists' Yearbook*, which you already hold in your hands. Well done, that's the first major step towards a successful agent relationship.
- Conferences and talks can be a good way to get a feel for an agent's working style and how they talk about their job. Everyone has a different approach (my signature is worryingly enthusiastic) and you'll be able to sense if theirs is a good fit for you.
- Looking online will show you exactly what an agent claims to be looking for at that moment. We all write wishlists where we call for our dream projects, and talk about others that we've enjoyed to give a sense of our tastes. If you look at our social media, we're often talking about the latest releases and successes for our clients, so you can see exactly what we're working on.
- The acknowledgements page at the back of a book is your secret weapon in an agent search. Find a book you love, and see if they thank the agent at the back. Now you know you and the agent have a similar taste, and that they're loved by their current clients too.
- Speaking to other authors can be a fantastic step, if you know people or have the right networks. If I've offered someone representation, I'm always happy for them to reach out to my clients and have an honest conversation about what exactly working with me is like.

And finally, I'd hope that you can always ask the agent themselves. We understand just how hard it is to find an agent and just what your work means to you. Every time I read a manuscript or open a submission, I'm honoured that this creator has trusted me with what might be their life's work. Being in a position to make these promises to an author is a huge privilege, and one that brings me an enormous amount of joy. And at the core of it, isn't that what writing is all about?

Lydia Silver joined the Darley Anderson Children's Agency in 2018, having started her publishing career in Egmont's editorial team. Her clients range from YA to picture books, and include *Sunday Times* and *New York Times* bestsellers, Carnegie-shortlisted illustrators, and multiple prize-winners. Follow her on Instagram @lydiarsilver and on TikTok @da_childrens.

Finding an agent for your picture book

Jodie Hodges explains the opportunities and options for aspiring picture book authors and illustrators, sharing her experience and essential advice on how to find representation and build a successful career in this creative sector.

I've been a literary agent for nearly 15 years; apart from a post-university six months as a bookseller, it is the only adult job I've ever known. Every day I count myself lucky that I was second choice for a position as assistant to Rosemary Canter at Peters, Fraser & Dunlop, one of the only children's literary agents at the time, and that her first choice turned down the job! Working with Rosemary, the agent of children's book luminaries like Giles Andreae, William Nicholson and Benjamin Zephaniah, was a privilege that gave me an incomparable grounding in the job of literary representation. We moved to United Agents in 2007 and, when Rosemary died in 2011, I inherited her list, combining it with my own fledging group of authors and illustrators of children's books. Working equally with new and established talent affords me a perspective on building careers – allowing me to see how things have changed and what remains the same, and I'm lucky enough to represent a fantastically varied list of creators across all age groups in children's publishing.

I love working with picture book creators; I enjoy the variety, the creativity, the collaboration. Picture book authors and illustrators in the children's market are in a particularly fortunate position, having the opportunity to publish multiple books (strategically managed by a good agent, of course!) and therefore to give themselves several chances of having a hit. I choose to represent both authors and illustrators of picture books, which gives me a full picture of this area of the market and the chance to work on lots and lots of different books (… I so enjoy doing this job, so why wouldn't I want to work on as many books as I can?).

So what is a picture book?

When I say 'picture books', I'm mainly talking about colour illustrated books of around 12 double-page spreads with a text of about 500 words, aimed at a shared reading experience for an adult alongside a child under seven. Traditionally these would be fictional stories but, increasingly, narrative non-fiction is also published in this format. There are longer picture books, of course, and baby books, but the vast majority of picture books fall within that definition.

Picture books can be created by one person, an author-illustrator, such as Rob Biddulph. They can also be collaborations between an author and an illustrator, such as *The Littlest Yak* (Simon & Schuster Children's UK 2020) written by Lu Fraser and illustrated by Kate Hindley. When a picture book is a collaboration, it's usually the case that the publisher has acquired the text first and then searches for a suitable illustrator, commissioning them to bring the text to life visually. More rarely, a book might start from an illustrator's image or character which a publisher then commissions a writer to create a text for – as with *Dogs in Disguise* (HarperCollins Children's 2021) written by Peter Bently and illustrated by John Bond. Each collaborator is contracted separately – for most deals this will be an advance and royalty – and the royalty rate is usually split 50/50 between author and illustrator, although their advances are likely to vary as the illustrator has months of artwork to produce. The story may have started with the text, but it becomes a book when the illustrator comes on board – a true collaboration.

An illustrator's essentials

If you want to get started as an illustrator of picture books, it's vital to have a really strong, targeted, market-specific portfolio, even if you only intend to illustrate your own stories. What sort of things come up in picture books? Animals, toddlers, dragons, friendship … a varied mix. To give you some ideas for images, try going into a bookshop to take a look at the tables of new picture books, and making a list of their subjects, themes and settings.

Equally important is to find a stylistic voice of your own that also marries commercially with the market. Here again, research and inspiration are key. I think around 20 pages of work is about right for your portfolio, with a mixture of vignettes and spreads that allow you to show characterisation and how you would put a scene together. When your portfolio is ready, you can use this *Yearbook* to look up suitable agents to send it to (see the listings starting on page 210 and page 258). There are literary agents and also illustration agents; it's wise to think about which of those might be right for you. As a literary agent, I represent my illustrators for their book work only, whereas an illustration agent might cover many other areas. Make a list of agents and then look them up on their websites, social media and trade press – who do they represent? Are they doing plenty of deals? Does their reputation impress you? Follow each agent's submission guidelines and hopefully someone will connect with your work and want to progress a conversation. If things go well, this might lead to representation.

Advice for the picture book author

For authors of picture book, my first piece of advice is to be very creative and productive. Write, write and write some more. Have lots of texts and lots of ideas. This is important for several reasons.

Firstly, I assume you'd like to earn some money from your writing; advances for picture book texts are at the lower end of the scale, so selling and publishing multiple books each year is a way to increase your income.

Secondly, the picture book market moves quickly and is extremely focused on the new. You might have a text about a fussy-eating unicorn, but if your agent sends it to a publisher who has just bought a text about a fussy-eating dinosaur, or a unicorn with bad manners, then they're unlikely to have room for yours. It's not the fault of the text, but simply timing and elements that are out of your agent's control and yours. So, what do you do? Move on. Hopefully you've already got some other texts ready, and you try those.

The third reason to be prolific – which is also relevant to illustrators working on collaborative books – is that every new book, every new combination of text and illustration, is a new opportunity for a bestseller or an international success. The publishers use their market expertise to give the books the best possible chance, but sometimes it's simply down to inexplicable forces. For example, the magical combination of Rachel Bright's words with my client Jim Field's illustrations in their bestselling series of books beginning with *The Lion Inside* (Orchard Books 2015) has meant both UK commercial success and many international partner publishers. We might have hoped for that – but it's never a given.

I would always advise an aspiring picture book author looking for an agent to use the same strategy they will need when they're published: if you submit some stories to agents and they're not picked up – press on and write some more. Use feedback, read, research, and go again. The next one might be the one. And then you'll need another one.

If an agent connects with your work, be it texts or illustrations, it's vital you feel able to have an honest, open, productive relationship with them. Meet them, ask all the questions you have in mind; if you're offered representation, take some time to mull over your meeting before making your decision. We all hope an agent-client relationship is going to be long-term, so don't rush into it.

Dos and don'ts for authors and illustrators:

- If you're a picture book author, you **don't** need to find an illustrator yourself to be able to approach an agent. Have plenty of stories, make sure you're sending to agents representing picture book authors, and follow their guidelines – that's it.
- If you're an illustrator, you **don't** need to write a story. If you want to, and you've created a package that you feel could be a commercial picture book, that's great – but it's possible to have a very successful career as an illustrator who doesn't write.
- **Do** try to write your text with the book format in mind. It's good practice to write it out labelling the spreads 1–12. That way you can pace your story correctly and work with the page-turns to add jeopardy or humour.
- **Don't** provide extensive illustrative notes on your texts. If there's a visual joke that isn't spelt out in the text itself then, of course, mention it, but the reason a picture book royalty is split 50/50 is that the illustrator is equally as important as the author. I've seen projects completely transform when the illustrator takes the story to a different setting or casts it in a way the author just wouldn't have thought of. There will always be consultation; no one wants the author to be part of a book they don't recognise as their story any longer. More often than not, though, it's an extremely positive process.
- **Do** think about working outside the field of picture books. The skills used in writing and illustrating picture books can very often be transferred into other types of children's books – young fiction, chapter books, illustrated middle grade and young adult, non-fiction. It's thrilling to see creators branch out, with books like Rob Biddulph's *Peanut Jones* series (Macmillan Children's), or Jenny Løvlie illustrating both *The Boys* picture book (Caterpillar Books 2021) and the *Kitty* young fiction series (OUP 2019–). Once you've found an agent, you can talk about diversifying your writing or illustrating, or perhaps if you're struggling to find an agent with your picture book work, think about creating submissions for a different area of the market.
- **Don't** get carried away imagining the animated series and theme park of your picture book – even if you're lucky enough to have it published. It's natural, and desirable, to have ambitions, but expectation management is an undervalued and essential part of the publishing process and the life of an author and illustrator.

Submission rules

I want to assure you the 'slush' pile is a friend of the aspiring picture book creator. An agent can read the texts, or look through portfolio work, much more quickly than they can read a novel. So use that to your advantage by making your submission as easy to navigate as possible. For me this means a clear, short covering email, and separate attachments for each text or a single pdf portfolio I can scroll through. Submitting in the good old-fashioned way is your best chance of finding an agent – I've taken on countless clients this way. So don't imagine there's a shortcut. No good agent is ignoring their submissions – we want to find gold in there. I hope I might see some of your work in my own inbox soon.

Jodie Hodges is an agent with United Agents, representing children's illustrators and authors of picture books, middle grade, teenage and young adult, including Rob Biddulph, Jim Field, Smriti Halls, Sophie McKenzie, Jamie Smart and Harriet Muncaster. She began working with Rosemary Canter at Peters, Fraser & Dunlop in 2006, becoming an agent in 2010. For more information see www.unitedagents.co.uk/jhodgesunitedagentscouk. Follow her on X @jodiehodges31.

The many hats of a literary agent

In a role where no two days are the same, literary agents wear multiple 'hats'. Here, Christabel McKinley tells us more about her role, from deerstalker to fascinator by way of a beret.

I've long since wanted to build a career in children's books, and before I started my career at David Higham Associates seven years ago, I held jobs in translation rights, literary scouting and as an English language and literature teacher in Seoul. I've now worked with children's books from multiple vantage points, but from my first taste of agenting as an intern a decade ago, I knew it was the right fit for me. I still remember being told in my DHA interview that the role of the agent is to wear several hats, changing them back and forth in rapid succession. 'There are three main hats …,' they began. By the end of the interview, there were six hats. Well, sometimes we lose count! But if you'll bear with me, I'll walk you through the main aspects of my job – and the best hat to fit them all.

The deerstalker: reading submissions and sourcing clients

Finding new clients does sometimes make me feel like Sherlock Holmes – I have to get out my magnifying glass (I'll forego the pipe) and search through a wide world of talent to find the writing or artwork that really speaks to me. I have a very selective list, so every submission has to meet a few key criteria: once I start, do I feel compelled to keep reading? Does the concept feel saleable in the current market? Do I have a vision for it that means I'm adding to it in my own way, rather than simply taking it on?

As with all agents, I do keep a close eye on my submissions inbox, but I have disappointingly limited time in the working week to devote to it. I try to glance in there every couple of days, but this allows me only the briefest amount of time to review each submission – all the more reason why it's worth putting in the extra effort to really make your covering letter shine. When I'm writing my own submission letters, my objective is to make it as easy a process for the editor as possible – and I think this holds true for author subs, too. If you can help me by pitching your story and its merits in a succinct, well-formatted package, I'll be able to glean so much more from a quick perusal than I would otherwise.

These days, it's not only from submissions that I source clients; I've also scouted webcomic artists from Webtoon, self-published authors from Amazon, and debuts from writing competitions and in-house Open Days. So it's worth keeping an eye out for creative ways to get your book out there, to build up your network of contacts and get involved with any writing clubs, crit or feedback groups or other opportunities that may come your way.

The beret: editing manuscripts

I chose the beret for this because it's the most artistic hat I could think of, and editing is the most creative part of our jobs as agents. In fact, the editorial side of the job is one of the main things that attracted me to agenting, as I love looking at an excellent manuscript and thinking: 'right, how can we make this even better?'

I'll always read a manuscript through once without anything more than a few notes, just so that I can experience the story as a reader – to see how it unfolds from start to finish, where and when the important parts hit, and the general pacing. I usually do this very slowly, and then I'll do another read where I'll jot down notes ferociously to deliver later in a long Zoom call with my client. I prefer making this first round a conversation, as we can bounce ideas off each other and I can adjust my feedback accordingly. If I have the luxury of time, I'll also try and do this with authors I'm considering representing – it's a great way to see if we're a good match editorially.

After this, I could do any number of rounds of editing, depending on what the book needs – I'm a firm believer in sending out a submission only when it's the best we can possibly make it. My best advice at this stage: you're the creative piece of the puzzle, but your agent is the business bridge that is going to connect you to your potential readers. If they're advising something, it's with the book's best interests in mind, and something to consider with a professional eye rather than a personal one. One of my clients told me they need 24 hours to grumble about my notes to themselves before they suddenly snap into place – fair enough!

The cowboy hat: sales

Once the manuscript is ready to go, the author passes the baton to me and I send it forth into the world – the start of a great adventure! (I also do want to draw attention to this particular submission in an editor's inbox at this point, which I expect a cowboy hat would do if I were wearing one.)

I take a lot of pride in my submission letters, which have to stand out among all of the other submissions an editor is receiving and showcase the very best that the book has to offer in an immediate and eye-catching way. Aside from summarising the book's contents, I will spell out clearly who is the intended audience and why they're going to love it – sometimes with a picture or an attractive pitch deck full of details about the world and characters to further draw my reader in. In a recent offer call with a publisher, I explained that my dream would have been for the pitch deck to be like a TV trailer – to which the marketing and publicity staff responded, 'we'll make it one!'.

This gearing up and going out on submission is probably my favourite part of the job, even though it's one of the least frequent. It's a real moment of standing on the precipice and holding your breath, waiting for other people to love this story that your author wrote and that you believe in with your whole heart as much as you do. When the first offer comes in, it's such an electric moment and so exhilarating to tell your author 'you're going to be published!' Yee-haw!

The bowler hat: contracts and negotiations

I'll have to pick the most serious, business-minded type of hat for this one, because it is the most meticulous and detail-oriented part of the entire job. As fun as going out on submission is, there's a very careful science going on behind the scenes to ensure we move forward with the best terms possible when we finalise a deal. It's my job to make sure the publisher's offer is as good as it can possibly be, meeting both our established agency standards, as well as any other specific improvements.

Then it's on to the contract, the legally binding piece of paper that protects the rights of my client for this book – so it's vital to get it as good as it can be! I'm lucky enough to work at an agency with a Contracts Wizard (unofficial title, but she does deserve a Wizard's Hat) who ensures that all our contracts are in tip-top shape. Then, the process of going back and forth with a publisher on a draft can take anything from one to six months (although the latter is highly unusual!). This task is my highest priority, and one I am always careful to take the required time to get absolutely right.

Contracts is one of the key areas in which we earn our commission: by helping you make the most money and the overall best deal possible. It's not just about the size of the advance, but also about which rights are being signed away, the level of royalties, the high discount rates, the joint vs separate accounting, the bonuses, the audio rights, the fair reversion clause, and more. These terms will affect the author in both the short and long term so, if you don't have an agent, please do make use of other available resources, such as the Society of Authors.

The firefighter's helmet: project (and crisis) management

When people ask how my day was, I often respond that I've been 'putting out fires all day'. Luckily, these are only metaphorical! Agents look after a book from its early drafts right up to publication and beyond, a timeline that often spans several years. Inevitably, there will be speed bumps and hiccups along the way – and it's my job to keep an eye on things and make sure they're resolved quickly and effectively.

Time is really of the essence here, so this is the type of thing that shoots itself right to the top of my to-do list and elbows out everything else I was planning for my day. Some of these issues are fairly commonplace – a manuscript submitting late, a publication date being shifted – and, while not ideal, can usually be resolved quite easily. Others may be unexpected and require more delicate handling, and will need me to jump on calls with clients and editors to figure out how to procure an outcome everyone is happy with.

It's important to keep in mind that agenting isn't all the 'yee-haw's of selling a book, but also the 'uh oh's of dealing with tricky situations down the line. This is why it is important, when signing with an agent, to consider the process of working with them beyond just that initial sale. Are you looking for an established agent with a lot of experience, or a more junior agent with lots of time? Do you want them to follow your timelines, leave you to your own devices, or set their own deadlines – and is one of those better suited to you? Ideally, this will be a long-term partnership, so think about what aspects of the working relationship matter most to you.

The fascinator: networking

Not a hat I've ever worn, but to me this is a party hat, and socialising is a big part of the agenting job. I'm constantly in touch with people – whether it's discussing work or catching up with clients, asking and sharing advice with colleagues, checking in with editors or other industry professionals – but it's so important to get out there and keep an ear to the ground for news about the market.

Every Spring, I go to Bologna for the Children's Book Fair, where I spend three days wedged into a table meeting editors from around the world back to back. (Then in the evenings, I make my way through wedges of Parmesan – can't complain!) It's one of the crucial events throughout the year that brings publishing professionals together to take stock of the market and issue the new decrees: what sort of books are doing well? Which are not? How cautious are publishers right now? How are the book chains and the national literacy rates affecting what books are selling?

Aside from these industry doorstop events, I'm meeting editors throughout the year: in person over coffee, at industry events and launches. (Last year I had the added enjoyment of the WorldCon in Glasgow, where an editor and I had an unexpected meeting on the floor outside a conference room hoping to get in to see Holly Black. We were unsuccessful, but had a good discussion about fanfiction anyway!) I also sell into the USA, Australian and Canadian markets, so these meetings usually take place on Zoom (sometimes at bizarre hours) although there is some occasional international travel. Apart from being very enjoyable, these meetings help me target each of my submissions so that I make sure each submission is going to the exact right person. Win-win!

One of the best things about being an agent is that the work is always varied; no two days look the same. Several years into my career as a literary agent, I am still learning new things on a regular basis, and the ever-changing landscape of the publishing world is something that intrigues and excites me. It can become a bit all-consuming in terms of time spent on it (not listed above: the 10pm work Zooms, the evenings at work events and the weekends turning down plans to read manuscripts; the very real Hulk-like rage you feel on a personal level when someone disrespects your author's time or work). But, at the end of the day, it's a real privilege to be in a position to hear the words 'you've made my dream come true' when you've found the perfect home for your client's book. And that, in itself, is a bit of a dream come true.

Christabel McKinley is an agent at David Higham Associates (DHA), where she represents authors and illustrators across the whole range of children's publishing, from picture books to YA, including non-fiction and graphic novels. She also has a select list of adult sci-fi and fantasy writers. She was one of *The Bookseller's* Rising Stars in 2024.

Submitting your sci-fi/fantasy novel to an agent

Agent Molly Jamieson describes the magic of discovering well-written fantasy and science fiction for children, with absorbing narrative and world-building, and has advice for writers on the essential elements and qualities she looks for in a standout submission.

I didn't always know that I wanted to be an agent, but I started in publishing at Curtis Brown for an internship and then moved to United Agents in 2017 as part of a maternity cover ... and I've been here ever since. I have worked across both adult and children's lists, working on titles from board books (for children three years and under) right up to crime fiction, and I'm now building my own list with a particular focus on science fiction and fantasy titles for all ages.

Although I still work closely with Jodie Hodges, here at United Agents, on her list of children's authors and illustrators and review submissions for both of us, SFF (Science Fiction and Fantasy) is where my heart really lies. It is what I read in my spare time, what I gravitate towards naturally, and what I crave when I'm looking for comfort reading: something to really get lost in. When I was a kid, I went to see *The Lord of the Rings* in the cinema and I never looked back.

I love big stories with high stakes, both globally and personally, as well as quieter stories that focus on characters and the complexities of everyday relationships. I like traditional stories of good trumping evil, but I'm also drawn to stories with shades of grey, that subvert expectations. I'm always on the lookout for new talent in this space, both in writing for adults and children, so I'm delighted to have the opportunity to help you get your submission to the best possible place. So, let's start with the basics ...

Your submission package

For the most part, in a submission I look for the same things everyone else does. I hope that you'll get my name right (though it's not a deal breaker – I'd just prefer no 'Dear Sir's, if you can possibly help it) and I ask to see the synopsis and first three chapters.

While I know that agents' submission guidelines can feel restrictive, tricky, and often very tedious, we're not trying to trip you up with these; the traditional submission package is designed this way to make it as simple and straightforward as possible for us to review your work in its best light. You've got the opportunity to pitch it in the short form in your *cover letter*, to describe every major event in your *synopsis*, and to show me your most polished writing in the *first chapters* of your book – to draw me in. There are endless resources online, both free and paid for, to help you hone your pitch. Believe me, we know pitching isn't easy (if anyone understands that, it's us), but it's a skill that is worth investing your time in, even at this early stage. It will serve you well for the rest of your career.

- **The synopsis**: ideally this would be about one A4 page but, if that means cramming it onto the single side of A4 with the narrowest margins and the tiniest font, I'd rather it just eked out onto a second page. Aim for 350–500 words and I'll be happy. If you're struggling with your synopsis, I always recommend having a trusted reader go through your manuscript and then describe, from memory, the major events of the story. As a writer, it can

become so easy to get too close to your book – so much so that you can't necessarily see which information is vital for the synopsis. So fresh eyes are always a good idea.
- **First three chapters**: if your first three chapters are very short or your book isn't split into chapters, then feel free to send me the first 10,000 words. What I want to see is a good chunk of text that invites me into your story from the get-go. For me, it always comes down to the writing. A pitch might hook me, a synopsis might intrigue me, but when it comes to a final decision about taking a submission further, it's all about whether or not I love the writing. That is always going to be the deciding factor. So do make sure your draft is in the best shape possible. As with the synopsis, a fresh perspective on your manuscript is invaluable when you're struggling with edits or final touches so, ideally, I shouldn't be the first person to read it.
- **Cover letter**: there are common threads that run through my wish list for both the adult and children's SFF markets, and I don't necessarily look for the same thing in both places. In your cover letter for children's SFF, perhaps even more than in adult SFF, I want to see that you've got a good sense of the market as it is now. The easiest way to do this is to give me comparison titles for your book, which I know is not always the most straightforward process. I don't expect you to have read every book in your category, but I do think you should have a more contemporary comparison point for your book than *The Chronicles of Narnia* or *Harry Potter and the Philosopher's Stone* – there are so many great stories out there! Comparison titles are also useful, of course, because they help me to understand where you see your book on the shelf, and thus which publishers might be especially keen to see it.

Fantasy and fun

For the younger end of science fiction and fantasy, the scope of possible things to write about is huge – but my particular favourite space is probably fantasy middle grade. I really love middle-grade fiction that leans into whimsy in a big way, with soaring and surreal imaginative scenes that take the protagonist(s) on a wondrous journey; you can see this in the market with the success of series like Jessica Townsend's *Nevermoor* (Orion Children's 2018–), A.F. Steadman's *Skandar and the Unicorn Thief* (Simon & Schuster 2022–) and Rob Biddulph's *Peanut Jones* (Pan Macmillan 2021–). A strong narrative voice plays a big part in this, as well as a sense of humour throughout. You can definitely be serious in this space, too, but balance is very important and, if you're going to err on one side, let that be on the side of the funny.

World-building that works

One thing I do look for in both adult and children's SFF is thorough world-building, and magic systems that have consistent rules. That's not to say I want to be overloaded with information about these things – far from it – but I want to feel that you, the author, have a really grounded understanding of the world or 'magics' you have created. Essentially, as a reader, I want to feel safe in your hands. The best way to show me how your world works is to let me watch a character live in it, let me walk its streets and interact with its society. This can be a character who has lived in this world all their life, or a fish out of water emerging into a new world for the first time, but the thing that matters most is that I get to experience the world alongside that character. I won't remember lists of names, or extensive histories, but I'll remember the particular scents of a bustling market or an old, dusty library. I may not remember every new magical term or name that you tell me, but I'll have a better chance of understanding it if I see how it is used by your protagonist (or against them).

When it comes to magic systems in books for children, you can arguably get away with a little more whimsy and looseness than in adult books. But any inconsistencies or breaks with the rules of magic should not just be incidental; they need to be used for maximum impact. Again, as a reader, I must believe that *you* know how it works – I don't need to understand how all of the cogs fit together, as long as I *feel* sure that they do. Similarly, with sci-fi (a famously impenetrable genre for the uninitiated) I'm always keen on seeing authors find ways to make it feel more approachable, especially for younger readers. You can do this by keeping technical jargon to a minimum and establishing clear stakes for the characters, key pieces of tech, and some strong grounding principles to help ease the reader into the unknown.

Audience is key

Finally, it's important to remember, with any writing for children, that you need to take into account the age of your intended audience and know the limitations of formats for each age group. Anything for readers under the age of 13 is likely to be illustrated, so bear that in mind when considering your word count. Middle-grade fantasy is an overcrowded area of the market, and yet is still a sector where editors are actively acquiring and perhaps always will be. All areas of publishing run in cycles; a few years ago it seemed that YA was on the way out, but now it is having another resurgence, with a focus on that transitional 'New Adult/crossover' space. But there is also still an appetite for contemporary stories for teen readers. The main thing is to keep your audience in mind, always, and write what feels good rather than towards a particular trend.

There is so much fun to be had in writing science fiction and fantasy for children, and a delight in finding new stories. I can't wait to see what you write, and I wish you the best of luck with your journey to publication.

Molly Jamieson joined United Agents in 2017 as an assistant and is now an Associate Agent. She continues to work closely with Jodie Hodges and Emily Talbot on their lists of children's authors and illustrators as well as building her own list. For more information see www.unitedagents.co.uk/mjamiesonunitedagentscouk. Follow her on X @MollyJamieson.

See also...
- *Plotting and pace in your middle-grade adventure*, page 123
- *World-building in your fantasy fiction*, page 132
- *Writing magic into fiction*, page 148

Why teachers make great children's writers

Kate Scarborough shares her thoughts on how a teacher's experience and skills can empower and benefit them as a children's writer, as well as the essential advice, tools and tips she can offer new writers since setting up her own agency.

If you are thumbing through this book wondering whether your dreams of becoming a published writer can become a reality, my story and practical advice might be useful. By giving you a little background into how and why I set up my literary agency – Tyild's Agency – in 2021, I hope to help you on that journey. In the best teacherly tradition, I've highlighted in bold type the bits that are particularly pertinent to you, the aspiring writer.

Writers often talk about suffering from 'Imposter Syndrome' and, in this new post-pandemic publishing life I have created for myself, it's a condition I understand. As I dive deeper into the publishing world, I see fledgling writers revealing their unease through nervous tweets, published authors writing articles on how they can't believe they have been published, agents trying to find the next big thing, and publishers never being sure that a book they adore is going to fly on the open market. But amid all that self-doubt, I take comfort from accepting that **none of us really know for sure what makes a successful book and that the route to success is laced with huge amounts of luck.**

That said, it is easy to forget that **experience, planning, perseverance, persistence and craft account for a great deal**. I was an editor, writer and publisher in children's publishing for the first 14 years of my working life. I had a fabulous time, being creative, coming up with ideas, pitching them, putting them together and selling them, and ultimately being responsible for a team of people doing the same. Following a different dream, I then moved to teaching. Ironically – because I was always a bit of a rebel as a pupil, and *not* the teacher's favourite – I adored going back to the classroom, and loved planning ways to enthuse children about learning and especially about reading. The chance to use books in the classroom, find out what children particularly enjoy, and study how those books are written, was invaluable.

But upheavals, such as the pandemic, can have a dramatic effect on personal priorities. Like many, I found myself asking: What do I really want to do? What do I love doing? How do I make the most of my experience? I have always loved books and the creative process, and I know how to put them together. I love teaching and inspiring readers of all kinds. My wonderful colleague and friend for many years, Frances McKay (a successful illustrator's agent), gave me a nudge. Why not use these experiences to become an agent? There are many experienced, dynamic agents out there who have been digging out and nurturing writers for years. What could I bring to this market that would make my experience count? It had always struck me that **so many of our top children's authors previously worked in the classroom.** An agency that championed all those aspiring teacher writers might be exactly what I should do. And so Tyild's Agency was born.

Starting from scratch is daunting. I had to publicise my credentials and persuade authors to join the agency before I could begin to approach publishers with news that the agency was live. It is not easy to promote yourself – I had to work hard to remember that I was, in fact, qualified to do this job. However, this self-promotion is really important, and it is equally so for you, as authors. **In your covering letters to agents and publishers**, make sure you **mention all your training and your writing successes so far**. I had to spend a lot of time making connections through X (Twitter), LinkedIn, Facebook and Instagram. I could not have found my authors and developed the business without these tools. Teachers are one of the most communicative and vibrant communities online; they support and encourage one another across all these platforms and welcome newcomers with enthusiasm. And teacher writers are the best of these. I found that word spread quickly and, in no time, I had an inbox bulging with hopes and dreams.

Choosing authors to represent is extremely difficult, as there are so many talented writers out there. I have been fairly ambitious in my scope, in that I represent authors of picture books, chapter books and middle-grade titles. Most of the authors I have taken on, however, are keen to work across the age ranges, which is something I do look out for. Versatility and imagination are key, but it all starts with the initial email. And – forgive me – but if the email from a potential author is not addressed to me but has clearly been lumped in with a mailshot to lots of other agents, I tend not to prioritise it. **An agent will work very closely with an author and striking a good relationship right at the start is vital**. I check to see if an email shows that the sender has done their research and that they have followed my guidelines. The tone and style of the email also helps me to judge whether or not I should spend time reading the submission. When I started the agency, I had such high hopes of reading every word of each submission and of being able to give thoughtful feedback. I now know that this is absolutely impossible, given everything I need to do. And the same applies for all agents and publishers – so give yourself a head start, **do your research, follow the guidelines**, and **make it personal**.

Being a start-up, I am very conscious that the writers who have signed up with me are taking a gamble, and I speak to every potential writer to make sure that they understand this. It is a risk that is not for everyone and I understand that. The agency is in its infancy and each milestone – taking on new authors, meeting publishers, getting those first contracts signed – is fantastic, but (with a small child and a dog to support) I still have to earn in order to follow this dream. So, I am **not giving up the day job** … yet. I tutor children in English, which I love because it ties in so well with the agency work. It means I am reading, studying and critiquing books with the target market, which provides the perfect insight.

But why do I feel so strongly that teachers can be great writers for children? And what can we learn from their experience to help our own writing? Some of the biggest names in children's publishing started in teaching – J.R.R. Tolkien, C.S. Lewis, Philip Pullman, Eva Ibbotson, David Almond, Michael Morpurgo – even J.K. Rowling and Julia Donaldson dabbled. On a X exchange, **Philip Pullman** explained his journey by revealing that in class '… I told stories (not my own – myths, folk tales) because I thought it was a good thing to do. **I learned to tell [stories] by doing it'**. And **David Almond**, who said that teaching is central to his life as a writer, explained that in his lessons, he '… **wrote stories with the children**, inspired their own stories, dramatised stories with them. [This] helped me explore the varieties of form, and a connection to voice/movement'.

Why teachers make great children's writers 205

When writing for children, you need to **know your audience** in so many ways, from the practical (**what are they *able* to read**) to the inspirational (**what do they *want* to read**). A teacher works with children in the classroom, helping them to become readers. They can witness first-hand the impact stories have on young readers. The teacher will see which stories open eyes, widen horizons, encourage questions, unlock imagination and switch on light bulbs in their heads! Teachers also come to **know the book market** pretty well, especially those who take a professional interest in it. Most teacher writers will try out their own fledgling books on their class – who are always a willing audience. This can have a very direct effect, in that the teacher writer is able to edit on the fly and they quickly, even sometimes painfully (George, don't do that ...), **learn how to hold a reader's attention, how to build suspense, how to move them and how to make them laugh**.

It can seem that, as adults, we forget what it is like to be a child, but the teacher hopefully never forgets. Teachers are part of children's daily lives, and are there to share their joys, successes, struggles, battles and humour. This awareness of their audience that results from working with children means that teachers **never underestimate their reader**. Teaching children to write also lays bare the creative process for teachers. Every teacher writer that I work with writes with their pupils, and there is nothing more powerful than modelling writing for children, sharing what is good and exploring the difficulties. If children can see you struggle, change your mind, make mistakes and self-edit, then it is fine for them to do it. This **constant practice in editing helps hone a writer's craft**.

I spend a huge amount of my teaching time **exploring inference and empathy**. These are the skills you need to be a good reader (indeed, person), and which frankly give the child reader such a fantastic head start in life. As a writer, you need to know how to encourage inference and empathy in your reader, but you also must understand when your carefully crafted inference will go sailing right over the top of your reader's head. **Pitching it right for your reader** with enough to stretch children, and enough to help them begin to see it, is a delicate skill and the teacher writer has a distinct advantage with their insider knowledge. Good teachers **never stop learning**. There is so much help and support out there for writers, both of the teacher variety and others. My authors have writing groups, critical partners, go on courses for writing, attend conferences about the industry, join communities (see *Children's writing courses and conferences*, page 398 and *Societies, associations and organisations*, page 315). Using this book will help you to find those communities, as will the *Writers' & Artists'* website (www.writersandartists.co.uk).

Once your book is published you will need to do **school visits, festivals and presentations to children in order to market your work**. These are uplifting experiences, but can be extremely nerve-racking. Although – dare I say it – not to a teacher. Most teachers are more than happy to show off in front of children (any excuse) and know exactly how to manage that crowd so they don't lose them in the excitement. Not all great writers are teachers and not all teachers are great writers – but, if you talk to any writer who *has* taught, they will tell you the experience was invaluable. So, try to **get into a classroom and meet teachers**; they will be your strongest allies.

My own journey has really only just begun, and I hope the agency, which has been warmly welcomed by the publishing community, will flourish. I am and will go through the same highs and lows that everyone has in this industry. **It is not easy, but it is worth it**. It is worth it for so many different reasons: you get to meet wonderful people; you share your creative vision; and ultimately, if all goes well, you get to inspire the next generation. You will feel what all teachers feel – that sense of vocation.

[With thanks to these teacher writers who shared their thoughts on X Gaynor Andrews, Barbara Henderson, Mark Smith, Catherine Bruton, Lindsay Galvin, David Almond and Philip Pullman.]

Kate Scarborough is the founder of Tyild's Agency, a literary agency particularly for teachers who write for children. She has, over the last 30 years, been an editor, writer, publisher and teacher and now combines all this experience and enthusiasm into promoting teacher writers whose talent crosses over from the classroom to the page. For more information see www.tyildsagency.co.uk and follow on X @TyildS.

The life and works of a literary scout

Sophie Clarke explains just what a literary scout's role and life entails, with its varied and challenging workload and often all-consuming pace, the buzz of staying well-informed and well-connected, and the satisfaction that comes from matching the right book to the right client.

Entitling this article 'the life and works of a literary scout' seems unusually apt because, as with many jobs in publishing, trying to separate the personal from the professional in the career of a literary scout is almost impossible. It is a job that relies on forming, maintaining and nurturing connections, assessing the industry with a finely-honed eye to see which way the winds are blowing, and on reading accurately and critically at speed. Your role is to deliver professional judgement with a personal touch to your clients, who need guidance or advice to help them find the books which will work best for them. You are, in effect, a literary matchmaker. The clients of a literary scout are foreign publishers seeking to buy titles originally published in one language in order to translate them into their own, for publication and sale in their territory or market. Scouts can work across a range of languages, for example all literature from the Scandinavian countries, or in one language, such as just the UK or USA.

The information game

Literary scouts, unlike agents and editors, do not work directly with authors. They trade in information, gossip, industry buzz and foreign-market knowledge. A good scout has their finger on the pulse of the market they are scouting. They know which books are out on submission from agents to editors and, of those, which are making noise and going up for auction or being pre-empted. They are aware of which editors are moving between publishing houses, going on parental leave or sabbatical, or looking to acquire specific types of titles. They stay up-to-date on which new authors an agent might be representing; announcements on X (Twitter) are particularly helpful for this. Before titles go on submission (the process where agents send manuscripts to editors for them to sign-up or 'buy' for publication), scouts actively check in with agents about any titles which sound particularly interesting, or any which might be particularly suited to specific clients of theirs.

In order to gather this information, at least half of the scout's role is to talk – and to as many people as possible. Scouts are in contact day-to-day with primary agents (representing authors), rights agents (selling titles internationally) and publishing editors (acquiring titles and working with authors) via email and WhatsApp, as well as via video, phone and in-person meetings. These conversations allow scouts to build up a picture of what is currently going on in UK publishing. The wider and warmer a scout's network of contacts, the better the overall picture they can provide, and the better informed their clients will be – ideally ahead of competitors – and thus able to make decisions faster. A scout's network is more than a directory of contacts. Most become friends or – at the very least – valued acquaintances. It's almost impossible not to build up a close relationship; a scout may talk to a client once a day in peak season to check in on a title that's moving quickly and being acquired widely. Over the course of many meetings and emails, both parties get to know each other well. But of course, the core aspect of the relationship requires that, however kindly one might think of a contact personally, each has professional duties to the other.

Reading ... with a difference

The other half of a scout's role is to read, and to read quickly, professionally and widely in the area they scout in. Some scouts cover all genres; some specialise, for example in children's and young adult, like me. Reading and reporting on titles – providing a brief summary of the plot, information on the author and any notable facts or sales for the title – must be prioritised. Often, it must be done at speed. When titles are submitted for acquisition and begin to gather buzz domestically and/or internationally, translation sales begin to fall like dominoes in the right territories. A scout's reading does not always take place in the office or within office hours; with their clients in a variety of different time zones and territories, scouts must always be prepared to support and respond at any time of the day or night. As titles begin to move, auctions (multiple publishing houses bidding and offering on a title) and pre-empts (making an offer so convincing that the title is bought quickly and exclusively without the hassle of an auction) can happen overnight or even within a matter of hours from submission. This means that speed of reading, responding and reporting to clients is of the essence. You may be reading several manuscripts at one time, especially if you cover a broad range of titles. It's not uncommon for an individual scout to read between seven and ten titles a week – sometimes even more, around the busy book-fair seasons. You read with several different hats on, as there are many considerations: Will this title work in the UK market? Will it work in any of my client markets? Will any of the client's editors like it, even if it might not seem to be something for their market? Is it, objectively, any good? Do you, personally, like it – and would you be willing to recommend it, based on your own tastes, despite any other minor flaws to it? Addressing such questions, while reading to tight deadlines before reporting back to clients on a title, turns a seemingly simple task into one filled with nuance that requires a scout's expertise and professional knowledge.

Networking nous

Networking, as with the reading, isn't entirely limited within office hours either. Scouts are a regular fixture at parties, book launches and other publishing industry events – in fact anywhere where it's possible to hobnob and mix with the widest possible number of people and have the most wide-ranging conversations, gleaning titbits of gossip and information. Breakfasts, lunches, coffees, dinners and drinks meetings all feature regularly in scout life as well – meaning that we're extremely well-fed, as well as well-informed! As a scout, you quickly become very comfortable with walking into events where you might only know a few people, and leaving having befriended at least a few more. This skill comes in particularly useful at the international trade book fairs. These happen throughout the year, but the main ones are in Frankfurt in the autumn, London and Bologna in the spring. Bologna is specifically focused on children's and young adult titles. Editors, agents and rights agents from a multitude of countries gather to buy, sell and discuss titles. Scouts are at the heart of it – talking to their clients, meeting with editors and rights agents from outside their home territory and attending as many events as possible to meet the maximum number of people. Rights fairs are key for rights sales and for getting material, authors and passion in front of editors' noses. A scout's enthusiasm for a particular title, and their awareness of information ahead of it being public knowledge, can create excitement and help their publisher clients strike deals.

Author's friend

Indirectly, a scout is helping an author, even though they'll probably never meet and an author may be unaware of a scout's role across the publishing process. Across the course of many weeks, months or years, a scout may constantly re-flag an author's work or a specific title to their clients, demonstrating the momentum that a book or author is gathering both in their home territory and across other territories too. Sometimes, a book moves very quickly and there are swift acquisitions in the UK, the USA and a host of international territories – that's the dream scenario. But often books and authors take time to garner success and recognition and, as each building block of that process is achieved (e.g. sales figures, prize-shortlisting or -winning, accrued rights sales), a scout can be instrumental in reminding their clients of a title, seeing whose publishing list or taste might have changed enough to acquire it now, even if they passed over it previously.

To be a successful scout involves a high level of networking and reading, but of course there is far more to it than that. It also involves a huge volume of email traffic, lots of administration to stay on top of contacts – their changing roles and keeping up-to-date on correct territory contacts at each publisher and agency, organising meeting schedules for the book fairs, and reporting regularly to clients. All of this builds up to an ever-changing and shifting role – which is precisely what makes it one of the most exciting jobs in publishing. Scouts come from a variety of different backgrounds: some have started as interns at scouting agencies and worked their way up; others have previously worked at a publisher in rights or in editorial; others have come from a literary agency and are able to employ their already keen understanding of the industry. Most have some knowledge of a foreign language and culture, although almost all communication between scout and client is in English, and all reading is done in English too. Regardless of how they entered the industry, the key element a scout must have is a passion for, and deep knowledge of, the area of literature they are working in – no matter how broad or narrow that patch. Also helpful are the enthusiasm and energy to work more than occasional long hours, a curiosity about foreign markets, a desire to be well-informed about as much as possible, and the ability to read and network and manage emails beyond the office. And you need to be prepared – at peak book-fair season, when the pace becomes frenetic and the pressure to remain ahead of competitors becomes high – to be almost consumed by the job!

Reading back through this, I'm afraid I may have made scouting sound far too serious, when actually it's the most fun job I've ever had. There's a lot of stress, to be sure, but there also is a lot of laughter and camaraderie in the team as everyone works so closely together to deliver a great service to their clients. It's nigh on impossible to complain about drinks, events, book launches, parties and trips to the book fairs, even if they are outside office hours. You read books months and even years before the general public sees them. It's fair to say that scouting, in both little and big ways, shapes your life because it dictates the structure of your social and professional weeks, months and seasons; but it also shapes the lives of authors. For a scout, when a client acquires a title that you loved – one that has the potential to be successful for them and you also know the deal will be wonderful for the author – it really is the best feeling. Literary match ... made.

Sophie Clarke is senior scout for children's and young adult books, Sci-fi and Fantasy, and romance across the UK and US at Daniela Schlingmann Literary Scouting (https://schlingmann.co.uk). She has previously worked at the publisher Penguin Random House Children's and at the literary agencies Curtis Brown and Bell Lomax Moreton.

Children's literary agents
UK and Ireland

The *Children's Writers' & Artists' Yearbook*, along with the Association of Authors' Agents and the Society of Authors, do not recommend literary agents who ask potential clients for a fee prior to a manuscript being placed with a publisher. We advise you to treat any such request with caution and to let us know if that agent appears in the listings below. Agents may charge additional costs later in the process but these should only arise once a book has been accepted by a publisher and the author is earning an income. We recommend that you check agents' websites and familiarise yourself with submission guidelines, agent preferences and manuscript formatting.

Full-service agencies offer representation to writers across all territories, formats and business interests. They are likely to have a legal team and foreign/sub-right agents in-house or have established partnerships with specialist agencies who handle translation, film/TV or dramatisation rights.

NOTE: Where an agency is named after a specific agent, they are listed in alphabetical order by surname, i.e. Anne Clark Literary Agency can be found under C.

The country code for phoning UK offices from overseas is +44.
*Member of the Association of Authors' Agents
†Member of the Personal Managers' Association
sae = self-addressed envelope

The Agency (London)*
24 Pottery Lane, London W11 4LZ
tel 020-7727 1346
email childrensbooksubmissions@theagency.co.uk
website https://theagency.co.uk/childrens-books/childrens-home
X @TheAgencyBooks
Instagram @theagencybooks, @theagencyldn_
Head of Department Jessica Hare

Represents picture books, including novelty books, fiction for all ages including YA fiction and series fiction. Works in conjunction with overseas agents. Also represents screenwriters, directors, playwrights and composers. *Commission* Home 15%, overseas 20%. Submission guidelines on website. *Founded* 1995.

Darley Anderson Children's Book Agency*
Unit 19, Matrix Studios, 91 Peterborough Road, London SW6 3BU
tel 020-3940 9012
email childrens@darleyanderson.com
website www.darleyandersonchildrens.com
X @DA_Childrens
Instagram @da_childrens
Managing Director Clare Wallace, *Director* Lydia Silver, *Agent* Becca Langton, *Assocaite Agent* Chloe Davis, *Head of International Rights* Kristina Egan

Children's fiction and non-fiction for all ages from picture book to middle grade through to YA and crossover. For illustrators, refer to the Darley Anderson Illustration Agency (see page 258). *Commission* Home 15%, USA/translation 20%, film/TV/radio 20%. Send covering letter, short synopsis and first three chapters by email. No scripts or screenplays.

Clients include Mark Bradley, Sarah Bowie, Lindsay Galvin, Jamie Hammond, Polly Ho-Yen, Nathanael Lessore, Ayaan Mohamud, Rachel Morrisroe, Claire Powell, Christen Randall, Beth Reekles, J.P. Rose, Josh Silver, Rashmi Sirdeshpande, Deirdre Sullivan, S.F. Williamson. *Founded* 1988.

ASH Literary*
email info@ashliterary.com
website www.ashliterary.com
X @ashliterary
Instagram @ashliterary
Agents Alice Sutherland-Hawes, Saffron Dodd, Paula Weiman

Represents fiction authors and illustrators covering picture books through to YA titles, including graphic novels. Interested in all genres. *Commission* Home 15%, translation/dramatisation 20%. Send first three chapters and synopsis through QueryManager or by email to submissions@ashliterary.com. Does not handle adult fiction or non-fiction.

Clients include Alex Falasa-Koya, Jess McGeachin, Harry Woodgate, Amy Leow, Jennifer Iacopelli, Ravena Guron, Katie Cottle. *Founded* 2020.

Bath Literary Agency*
5 Gloucester Road, Bath BA1 7BH
email john.mclay@btinternet.com
website www.bathliteraryagency.com
X @BathLitAgency
Instagram @bathlitagency
Agent Gill McLay

Specialist in fiction for children and YA. Also accepts adult fiction, non-fiction and author-illustrator submissions. *Commission* UK 15%, overseas 20%, film/TV 20%. For full submission details, refer to the website.

Clients include Jake Biggin, Conor Busuttil, Mariesa Dulak, Philippa Forrester, Dr Jess French, Joe Haddow, Demelsa Haughton, Ben Hoare, Laura James, Gill Lewis, Pippa Pixley, Luke Scriven, Dr Shini Somara, Anna Terreros-Martin, Paul Westmoreland. *Founded* 2011.

Bell Lomax Moreton Agency*
Suite C, Victory House, 131 Queensway, Petts Wood, Kent BR5 1DG
tel 020-7930 4447
email agency@bell-lomax.co.uk
website www.belllomaxmoreton.co.uk
X @BLM_Agency
Executives Paul Moreton, Lauren Gardner, Jo Bell, Katie Fulford, Justine Smith, John Baker, Lorna Hemingway, Julie Gourinchas, Callen Martin, Rory Jeffers, Sarah McDonnell

Will consider most fiction, non-fiction and children's (including picture books, middle grade and YA) book proposals. Submission guidelines on website. Physical submissions should be accompanied by sae for return and an email address for correspondence. Does not represent poetry, short stories or novellas, education textbooks, film scripts or stage plays. *Founded* 2000.

The Bent Agency*
Greyhound House, 23/24 George Street, Richmond TW9 1HY
email info@thebentagency.com
website www.thebentagency.com
Agents Nicola Barr, Molly Ker Hawn, Zoë Plant

Full-service literary agency with offices in the UK and USA. Represents a diverse range of genres including literary, commercial and sci-fi and fantasy, including author-illustrators who write chapter books, middle-grade and YA fiction. Only accepts email queries. See website for detailed query and submission guidelines.

Clients include Faridah Abike-Iyimide, Sophie Anderson, Dhonielle Clayton, Stephanie Garber, Alwyn Hamilton, Frances Hardinge, Beth Linclon, Hilary McKay, Mo O'Hara, Sibeal Pounder, Jo Spain, Louie Stowell, Robin Stevens, Angie Thomas, Jessica Townsend. *Founded* 2009.

The Blair Partnership*
PO Box 7828, London W1A 4GE
tel 020-7504 2520
email info@theblairpartnership.com
website www.theblairpartnership.com
X @TBP_agency
Bluesky @tbpagency.bsky.social
Instagram @theblairpartnership_agency
Founding Partner & Agent Neil Blair, *Managing Director, Client Management* Rory Scarfe, *Lead Children's Agent* Rachel Petty

Represents a range of writers internationally from debut to established, with a strong focus on TV/film alongside literary publications. Considers fiction and non-fiction across YA and middle grade, graphic novels and picture books. Will consider unsolicited MSS. Fiction: email the specific agent with a covering letter, one-page synopsis and first three chapters. Non-fiction: email a proposal document and writing sample. Picture books: email your query and full project. Not currently accepting screenplays, short stories or poetry.

Clients include Bana Alabed, J.J. Arcanjo, Emma Farrarons, Sir Chris Hoy, Ramsey Hassan, Hazel Gardner, Frank Lampard, Kieran Larwood, Rose Lihou, J.K. Rowling, Emanuel Wallace. *Founded* 2011.

The Bright Agency*
103–105 St John's Hill, London SW11 1SY
tel 020-7326 9140
US Office 157 - A First Street, c/o Bright Group US Inc #339, Jersey City, NJ 07302
tel +1 646-525-9040
email mail@thebrightagency.com
website https://thebrightagency.com/uk
Global Managing Director James Burns, *Managing Agents* Nicky Lander, Alex Gehringer, Amy Fitzgerald, Anne Moore Armstrong, Susan Penny

Children's fiction and non-fiction, adult fiction and non-fiction, graphic novels and children's illustration. Other areas of representation include greeting and gift (cards, social stationery, giftwrap), design and advertising (editorial, branding, adult publishing, packaging, web and digital, typography), animation, and licensing (toys and games, digital gaming, fabric and apparel, and homewares). See website for illustration, writing and animation submissions guidelines. No submissions by post.

Clients include Aura Lewis, Benji Davies, Carys Bexington, David Litchfield, Galia Bernstein, Hannah Peck, Lucy Fleming, Mechal Roe, Meggie Johnson, Karl James Mountford, Subi Bosa, Yasmeen Ismail. *Founded* 2002.

Jenny Brown Associates*
42 The Causeway, Edinburgh EH15 3PZ
email childrens@jennybrownassociates.com
website https://jennybrownassociates.com
Contact Lucy Juckes

Writing and illustration for children and YA, fiction and non-fiction. Has a preference for working with writers or illustrators based in Scotland. *Commission* Home 15%, overseas/translation 20%. Submission by email with covering letter in body of the message. For picture books include three samples of completed stories as attachments. For illustrators include samples of work and link to website/portfolio.

Clients include Christopher Edge, Keith Gray, Helen Kellock, Emily MacKenzie, Jonathan Meres, Alison Murray. *Founded* 2002.

Felicity Bryan Associates*

2A North Parade, Banbury Road, Oxford OX2 6LX
tel (01865) 513216
email agency@felicitybryan.com
website www.felicitybryan.com
Managing Director Catherine Clarke, *Agents* Caroline Wood, Carrie Plitt, Angelique Tran Van Sang, James Gill, *Associate Agent* Sally Holloway

Translation rights handled by Andrew Nurnberg Associates; works in conjunction with US agents. Fiction for children aged 8–14 and YA, and adult fiction and general non-fiction. *Commission* Home 15%, overseas 20%. All submissions and queries through website. No high-concept sci-fi and fantasy (including romantasy), horror, graphic novels, picture books, scripts or poetry.

Children's authors include David Almond, Katya Balen, Matt Burton, Jenny Downham, Sally Gardner, Natasha Farrant, Clare Furniss, Liz Kessler, Annabel Pitcher, Meg Rosoff, Alom Shaha, Lauren St John, Chris Vick, Lisa Williamson. *Founded* 1988.

C&W Agency*

(previously Conville & Walsh)
Cunard House, 15 Regent Street, London SW1Y 4LR
tel 020-7393 4200
website www.cwagency.co.uk
X @CWAgencyUK
Instagram @cwagencyuk

A boutique and very select list of adult literary, commercial and genre fiction and non-fiction, and film/TV tie-ins. Handles some middle grade and teenage fiction. *Commission* Home 15%, overseas 20%. Part of the Curtis Brown Group of Companies; simultaneous submission accepted. Send cover letter, first three chapters and synopsis by email to the agent you would like to consider your work.

Children's authors include Katie Davies, Matt Haig, P.J. Lynch, Maxine Beneba Clarke, Paula Rawsthorne, Piers Torday, Steve Voake, the estates of John Burningham and Nicky Singer. *Founded* 2000.

Georgina Capel Associates*

29 Wardour Street, London W1D 6PS
tel 020-7734 2414
email [firstname]@georginacapel.com
website https://georginacapel.com
Directors Georgina Capel, Rachel Conway, Irene Baldoni, *Film/TV Agent* Simon Shaps, *Agency Assistant* Polly Halladay

Literary and commercial fiction including children's and YA; broad range of non-fiction including history, biography, science and nature. *Commission* Home/overseas 15%. Accepts submissions by email (preferred) and post. Include a covering letter, synopsis and first three chapters. See website for full submission guidelines. *Founded* 1999.

The Catchpole Agency

53 Cranham Street, Oxford OX2 6DD
tel 07789 588070
email james@thecatchpoleagency.co.uk
website www.thecatchpoleagency.co.uk
Instagram @thecatchpoles
Proprietor James Catchpole

Agents for authors and illustrators of children's books from picture books through to YA novels, with a specialism in story-editing work. Email submissions@thecatchpoleagency.co.uk with a covering letter which includes a one- or two-sentence elevator pitch, the intended readership and a writing sample pasted directly into the body of the email.

Authors include Polly Dunbar, S.F. Said, Michelle Robinson, Emer Stamp, Sean Taylor, Eoin McLaughlin. *Founded* 1996.

Children's Books North Agency*

email emma@childrensbooksnorthagency.co.uk
website www.childrensbooksnorthagency.co.uk
Bluesky @cbnagency.bsky.social
Instagram @childrensbooksnorthagency_
Threads @childrensbooksnorthagency_
Agent Emma Layfield

Represents authors, illustrators and author-illustrators who are based in the north of England (North West, North East and Yorkshire) and Scotland. Specialises in picture books, pre-school, illustrated non-fiction, young fiction and graphic novels. Email submissions only to submissions@childrensbooksnorthagency.co.uk. Authors: covering email with bio and location with synopsis and full manuscript (up to three for picture books) as attachments. Illustrators: covering email with links to social media channels and website, bio and location with pdf of your work attached. Author-illustrators: covering email with links to social media channels and website, bio and location with synopsis, full manuscript (or dummy book pdf) and pdf of illustration work as attachments. Solely focused on the children's market, no adult fiction or non-fiction.

Clients include Joely Badger, Bethan Clarke, Lucy Farfort, Catherine Fortey, Olivia Holden, Jess Mahy, Francis Martin, Rachel Plummer. *Founded* 2024.

Anne Clark Literary Agency*

email submissions@anneclarkliteraryagency.co.uk
website www.anneclarkliteraryagency.co.uk
Facebook www.facebook.com/anneclarkliterary

X @AnneClarkLit
Bluesky @anneclarklit.bsky.social
Contact Anne Clark

Specialist in fiction, non-fiction and picture books for children and young adults. *Commission* Home 15%, overseas 20%. Submissions by email only. See website for details.

Clients include Mike Barfield, Anne Booth, Max Boucherat, Moira Butterfield, Lou Carter, Emily-Jane Clark, Patricia Forde, Pippa Goodhart, Cath Howe, Ruth Lauren, Ben Lerwill, Leah Mohammed, Rebecca Patterson, Lucy Rowland. *Founded* 2012.

Colwill & Peddle*
email submissions@colwillandpeddle.com
website www.colwillandpeddle.com
Bluesky @colwillandpeddle.bsky.social
Instagram @colwillandpeddle
Agent Charlotte Colwill

Works with a number of foreign, film and TV co-agents to sell the rights to clients' work internationally, in all formats and mediums. Charlotte is looking for commercial children's fiction and non-fiction for all ages up to YA. *Commission* Home 15%, USA/overseas 20%. See website for detailed submission guidelines. Not interested in picture books or poetry.

Authors include Kat & Brian Keaney, Mark Illis, Andrew Lane, Clifford Samuel, Kate Walker. *Founded* 2022.

Gemma Cooper Literary*
email info@gemmacooperliterary.com
website www.gemmacooperliterary.com
X @gemma_cooper
Instagram @gemmacooperliterary
Founder & Literary Agent Gemma Cooper

Primary focus is children's and YA authors, and adult fiction in a few, select categories. Open to all genres in children's fiction. For adult fiction: cosy crime, smart contemporary crime with humour, and crime with a fantasy twist. Actively looking for something on the lighthearted side that is clever with an unusual or interesting hook. *Commission* Home 15%, overseas 20%, film/TV 20%. Submit by email to gemmaqueries@gemmacooperliterary.com. Include book title, short pitch, author bio and the first ten pages of the MS in the body of the email. For graphic novels or illustrated non-fiction: in addition to the above, include links to website or social media, if work is shared there, or attach up to five low-res images. Not seeking YA fantasy, but will consider light speculative with a twist. No contemporary adult fiction, adult non-fiction, literary novels, romance or poetry. Not interested in dark thriller, or crime that is gritty and includes gratuitous violence or child death.

Authors include B.B. Alston, Sophie Anderson, P.G. Bell, Abiola Bello, Claire Fayers, Beth Garrod, Siobhan McDermott, Katrina Charman, Sibéal Pounder, Sam Hay, Robin Stevens, Mo O'Hara, Jessica Townsend, Katy Watson, Freja Nicole Woolf. *Founded* 2024.

Creative Authors
11A Woodlawn Street, Whitstable, Kent CT5 1HQ
email write@creativeauthors.co.uk
website www.creativeauthors.co.uk
X @creativeauthors
Instagram @creativeauthors
Director Isabel Atherton

Children's fiction, picture books and illustrators. Also fiction and non-fiction for adults. *Commission* Home 15%, overseas 20%. Only accepts email submissions.

Authors and illustrators include Guojing, Ged Adamson, Graham Howie. *Founded* 2008.

Creative Roots Studio*
71–75 Shelton Street, Covent Garden, London WC2H 9JQ
website www.creativerootsstudio.com
X @Creative_Roots_
Instagram @creative.roots.studio
Agents Rachael Davis-Featherstone, Fiz Osborne

Boutique agency for children's book creatives including authors and illustrators. Offers consultancy, workshops and coaching. Open to traditionally published authors and illustrators. Use contact form on website. Occasionally welcomes non- or self-published writers, with submission windows announced through social media and newsletter. *Founded* 2024.

Rupert Crew*
Southgate, 7 Linden Avenue, Dorchester DT1 1EJ
tel (01305) 260335
email info@rupertcrew.co.uk
website www.rupertcrew.co.uk
Facebook www.facebook.com/RupertCrew
Bluesky @rupertcrewltd.bsky.social
Instagram @rupertcrew
Managing Director Caroline Montgomery

International representation, handling accessible literary and commercial fiction and non-fiction for adult and children's (8+) markets. *Commission* Home 15%, overseas 20%, film/TV/radio 20%. No unsolicited MSS: see website for current submission guidelines policy. No picture books, plays, screenplays, poetry, journalism, sci-fi and fantasy or short stories. *Founded* 1927.

Curtis Brown*†
Cunard House, 15 Regent Street, London SW1Y 4LR
tel 020-7393 4400
email cb@curtisbrown.co.uk
website https://curtisbrown.co.uk/section/books, www.curtisbrowncreative.co.uk
X @CBGBooks, @cbcreative

Children's Agents Davinia Andrew-Lynch, Isobel Gahan, Roxane Edouard (translation rights and French writers), Enrichetta Frezzato

Children's fiction ranges from picture books to YA novels across all genres. Represents prominent writers, from debut authors to established prize winners and bestsellers. Actively seeking talented new writers, particularly for books aimed at 8–12 years, adventure, fantasy, gothic stories and humour. Manages the international careers of authors with strong relationships in translation and US markets. *Commission* Home 15–20%. See website and individual agent web pages for submission guidelines. Founded 1899.

Dark House Literary & Screen Agency

19 Tottenhall Road, London N13 6HY
tel 07812 004546
email submission@darkhouse.uk
website www.darkhouse.uk
X @DarkHouseAgency
Managing Director Andreas Charalambous

Represents the works of authors and creatives working within the horror and dark fantasy genres, including adult fiction, non-fiction, graphic novels, children's (with subtle horror themes) and YA. Also interested in screenplays for film and TV. Email submissions only. Fiction: attach a Word document that includes a brief synopsis and the first three chapters of the MS. Non-fiction: include a proposal, short synopsis and up-to-date CV. Does not represent works of poetry, picture books, theatrical scripts and any other genres except horror and dark fantasy. Founded 2023.

DHH Literary Agency*

23–27 Cecil Court, London WC2N 4EZ
tel 020-3954 5999
email enquiries@dhhliteraryagency.com
website www.dhhliteraryagency.com
Facebook www.facebook.com/dhhliteraryagency
X @dhhlitagency
Bluesky @dhhlitagency.bsky.social
Instagram @dhhlitagency
Agents David H. Headley, Broo Doherty, Harry Illingworth, Emily Glenister, Abi Fellows, Diana Beaumont

Children's fiction and YA fiction. Also adult fiction, women's commercial fiction, crime, literary fiction, sci-fi and fantasy; and non-fiction including history, cookery and humour. *Commission* UK 15%, overseas 15% (where a sub-agent is used 20%). Send informative preliminary email with first three chapters and synopsis. Consult website for correct email address for each agent. New authors welcome. No picture books, plays or scripts, poetry or short stories.

Authors include James Goodhand, Lizzie Huxley Jones, Thomas Leeds, Clare Weze, Suzie Edge, Nicola Garrard. Founded 2008.

Diamond Kahn & Woods Literary Agency*

Office 378, Salisbury House, 29 Finsbury Circus, London EC2M 5QQ
tel 020-3514 6544
email info@dkwlitagency.co.uk
email submissions.ella@dkwlitagency.co.uk
email submissions.bryony@dkwlitagency.co.uk
website www.dkwlitagency.co.uk
Instagram @dkwliteraryagency
Agents Ella Diamond Kahn, Bryony Woods, Camille Burns

Children's, YA and crossover fiction; literary and commercial fiction (including all major genres) and non-fiction. Interested in new writers. *Commission* Home 15%, USA/translation 20%. Ella and Bryony accept email submissions only. Send three chapters and synopsis to one agent. For Camille, please submit via QueryManager at https://querytracker.net/query/camille.

Clients include Virginia Macgregor, Nicole Burstein, David Owen, Sharon Gosling, Sylvia Bishop, Katharine Orton, Dan Smith, Jamie Russell, Tom Huddleston, Caroline O'Donoghue, Daisy May Johnson, Sandra Lawrence, Rebecca Orwin, Calum McSwiggan, Laura Jane Williams. Founded 2012.

Eddison Pearson*

West Hill House, 6 Swains Lane, London N6 6QS
tel 020-7700 7763
email enquiries@eddisonpearson.com
website www.eddisonpearson.com,
https://eddisonpearson.blog
Contact Clare Pearson

Small, personally run agency. Children's and YA books, fiction, non-fiction and poetry. *Commission* Home 10–15%, overseas 15–20%. Enquiries and submissions by email only; email for up-to-date submission guidelines. May suggest revision.

Authors include Valerie Bloom, Sue Heap, Caroline Lawrence, Robert Muchamore, Mary Murphy, Megan Rix. Founded 1997.

Fraser Ross Associates

42 Hadfast Road, Cousland, Midlothian EH22 2NZ
email agentlmfraser@gmail.com
email kjross@tiscali.co.uk
website www.fraserross.co.uk
Facebook www.facebook.com/fraserrossassociates
Instagram @fraserrossassociates
Threads @fraserrossassociates
Partners Lindsey Fraser, Kathryn Ross

Writing and illustration for children and adults. See website for client list and submission information. Founded 2002.

Annette Green Authors' Agency

5 Henwoods Mount, Pembury, Tunbridge Wells TN2 4BH
tel (01892) 263252

email annette@annettegreenagency.co.uk
website www.annettegreenagency.co.uk
Partners Annette Green, David Smith

Fiction: literary, general, women's, historical, romance and fiction for older children. Non-fiction: popular culture, history and science. *Commission* Home 15%, overseas 20–25%. Preliminary email or letter, synopsis, sample chapter and sae essential. No picture books, dramatic scripts, poetry, sci-fi or fantasy. *Founded* 1998.

The Greenhouse Literary Agency
email info@greenhouseliterary.com
website www.greenhouseliterary.com
Director Chelsea Eberly, *Agent* Kristin Ostby

Children's fiction and non-fiction: illustrators who write picture books, middle grade, teen/YA and graphic novels. Some women's fiction. Submissions via QueryManager only; see website for submission guidelines. No poetry, short stories or film scripts.

Authors include Gavin Aung Than, Sarwat Chadda, Winifred Conkling, Andrea Contos, Alexandra Diaz, Bill Doyle, Theanne Griffith, Michelle Lam, Rebecca Mock, Kelis Rowe, Ali Standish, Emily Thiede, Ngozi Ukazu. *Founded* 2008.

Greyhound Literary*
6 Warwick Court, London WC1R 5DJ
email info@greyhoundliterary.co.uk
website www.greyhoundliterary.co.uk
Instagram @greyhoundliteraryagency
Founder Charlie Campbell, *Agents* Charlotte Atyeo, Salma Begum, Alexander Cochran, Sam Edenborough (Rights Director), Natalie Galustian, Dotti Irving, Philip Gwyn Jones, Julia Silk

Fiction and non-fiction for adults and children. Represents YA and some picture books for authors whose work is represented in other areas. *Commission* Home 15%, USA/film/TV 20%, translation 20%. Submissions via website. No plays, poetry or scripts.

Authors include Beach, Victoria Belim, S.J. Bennett, Edward Brooke-Hitching, Jen Campbell, Rebecca Front, Julian Gough, Saskia Gwinn, Ed Hawkins, Maisie Hill, Will Hill, Michael Holding, Jennifer Lane, Anthony McGowan, Lias Saoudi, the estates of Alan Rickman and Mal Peet. *Founded* 2022.

Marianne Gunn O'Connor Literary, Film/TV Agency
Morrison Chambers, 32 Nassau Street, Dublin 2, Republic of Ireland
tel +353 (01) 677 9100
email submissions@mariannegunnoconnor.com
website www.mariannegunnoconnor.com
Contact Marianne Gunn O'Connor

Represents children's books, middle grade, YA, New Adult and crossover fiction, as well as literary fiction, upmarket fiction and non-fiction for adults. No screenplays. *Founded* 1996.

Antony Harwood
103 Walton Street, Oxford OX2 6EB
email mail@antonyharwood.com
website www.antonyharwood.com
Contacts Antony Harwood, Jo Williamson

General and genre fiction; general non-fiction. *Commission* Home 15%, overseas 20%. Will suggest revision.

Children's authors include Andrea Shepherd, Tamsyn Murray, Jennifer Gray, Peter Bunzl. *Founded* 2000.

A.M. Heath & Co.*
6 Warwick Court, London WC1R 5DJ
tel 020-7242 2811
email enquiries@amheath.com
website www.amheath.com
Instagram @a.m.heath
Contact Julia Churchill

Children's fiction and non-fiction from picture books to YA. Also handles adult literary and commercial fiction and non-fiction. *Commission* Home 15%, USA/translation 20%, film/TV 20%. Digital submission via website. No screenplays, poetry or short stories except for collections.

Authors include Nicholas Allan, Abi Longstaff, Julie Sykes, Sarah Crossan, Pip Jones, Michelle Harrison, Az Dassu, Jenny McLachlan, Joanna Nadin, Amy Sparkes, Patricia Toht, Holly Webb, Harry Hill, the estates of Noel Streatfield and Joan Aiken *Founded* 1919.

Sophie Hicks Agency*
Providence Yard, Ezra Street, London E2 7RJ
email info@sophiehicksagency.com
website www.sophiehicksagency.com
X @SophieHicksAg
Agents Sophie Hicks, Sarah Williams

Fiction for 9+. Also handles adult fiction and non-fiction. *Commission* Home/USA 15%, translation 20%. Email submissions only, see website for guidelines. No poetry, scripts or illustrated books.

Authors include Anne Cassidy, Lucy Coats, Eoin Colfer, Andrew Donkin, Kathryn Evans, Emerald Fennell, Rohan Gavin, Padraig Kenny, Siobhan Parkinson, Kate Thompson, Sif Sigmarsdóttir, Kiah Thomas, the estate of Herbie Brennan. *Founded* 2014.

David Higham Associates*†
6th Floor, Waverley House, 7–12 Noel Street, London W1F 8GQ
tel 020-7434 5900
email dha@davidhigham.co.uk
website www.davidhigham.co.uk
Managing Director Lizzy Kremer, *Books* Veronique Baxter, Caroline Walsh, Christabel McKinley, *Children's Rights* Allison Cole, Mariam Quraishi, *Film/TV/Theatre* Nicky Lund, Clare Israel, Georgie Smith

Children's fiction and non-fiction. 35% of the agency's list is for the children's market. Represented in all foreign markets. Also represents illustrators for children's book publishing. Handles novelty books, picture books, fiction for 5–8 and 9–12 years, teen and YA fiction, series fiction, poetry, plays, film/TV tie-ins, non-fiction and audio. Also handles adult fiction, general non-fiction, plays, film and TV scripts. *Commission* Home 15%, USA/translation 20%, scripts 10%. See website for submissions policy.

Clients include Emma Chichester Clark, Cressida Cowell, Nicola Davies, Anna Kemp, Geraldine McCaughrean, Tom McLaughlin, Michael Morpurgo, Kate O'Hearn, Liz Pichon, Catherine Rayner, Nick Sharratt, Jonathan Stroud, Jenny Valentine, Jacqueline Wilson, the estate of Roald Dahl. *Founded* 1935.

Holroyde Cartey*
email claire@holroydecartey.com
email penny@holroydecartey.com
website www.holroydecartey.com
Contacts Claire Cartey, Penny Holroyde

A literary and artistic agency representing a list of award-winning and bestselling authors and illustrators for the children's market. Welcomes submissions from debut and established authors. *Commission* Home 15%. See website for submission guidelines. Does not handle proposals for the adult market. *Founded* 2015.

Oscar Janson Smith Agency
53 Turnham Green Terrace, Chiswick, London W4 1RP
email oscar@oscarjansonsmith.com
website www.oscarjansonsmith.com
Instagram @oscarjansonsmith
Founder Oscar Janson Smith

Fiction, non-fiction, cookery and children's. Email submissions. Consult website for interests.

Clients include Niall Kirkland, Georgia Harrison, Moses Swaibu, Abby Rawlinson, Ro Mitchell, Sarah Asuquo, Grant Brydon, Emmanuel Asuquo, Elly Smart, Jay McGuiness. *Founded* 2023.

Kane Literary Agency*
2 Dukes Avenue, London N10 2PT
tel 020-8351 9680
email submissionskaneliterary@gmail.com
website www.kaneliteraryagency.com
Director Yasmin Kane

Interested in discovering and launching the careers of debut writers. Children's fiction: middle grade to YA. Also handles literary and commercial fiction for adults. *Commission* Home 15%, overseas 20%. Send submissions by email only; no submissions by post. For fiction, send a covering letter with the first three chapters and a synopsis; for non-fiction, send a covering letter and full book proposal plus two sample chapters. See website for further information. Currently closed to submissions. No picture books.

Authors include Richard Butchins, Sarah Harris, Ruchita Misra, Min Day. *Founded* 2004.

LBA Books*
91 Great Russell Street, London WC1B 3PS
tel 020-7637 1234
email info@lbabooks.com
website www.lbabooks.com
X @LBA_Agency
Instagram @lba_litagency
Agents Luigi Bonomi, Amanda Preston, Louise Lamont, Hannah Schofield

Fiction and non-fiction. Keen to find new authors and help them develop their careers. Works with foreign agencies and has links with film and TV production companies. YA and children's fiction, as well as adult fiction and non-fiction. *Commission* Home 15%, overseas 20%. Send preliminary letter, synopsis and first three chapters. No postal submissions. No poetry, short stories or screenplays.

Authors include Anna Carey, Rebecca Cobb, Bea Fitzgerald, Helen Hancocks, Sarah Harrison, Anne Miller, Nazneen Ahmed Pathak, S.A. Patrick, Jess Popplewell, Lucy Strange, Eve Wersocki Morris, Tamsin Winter, Laura Wood, Katherine Woodfine, Emma Yarlett. *Founded* 2005.

Lindsay Literary Agency*
East Worldham House, Alton, Hants GU34 3AT
tel (01420) 831430
email info@lindsayliteraryagency.co.uk
website www.lindsayliteraryagency.co.uk
X @LindsayLit
Founder Becky Bagnell

Specialists in children's fiction and non-fiction, teen/YA, middle grade and picture books. *Commission* Home 15%, translation 20%. Send first three chapters, synopsis and covering letter by email, unless submitting a picture book which requires the submission of the full text. No submissions by post. Will suggest revision.

Authors include Pamela Butchart, Christina Collins, Donna David, James Davis, Louise Finch, Sam Gayton, Sital Gorasia Chapman, Ruth Hatfield, Larry Hayes, J.M. Joseph, Nicola Penfold, Beth O'Brien, Kate Peridot, Lui Sit, Daniel Tawse, Rachel Valentine, Sue Wallman, Joe Wilson. *Founded* 2008.

The Literary Office
71–75 Shelton Street, London WC2H 9JQ
tel 07910 267336
email jenny.todd@theliteraryoffice.com
website www.theliteraryoffice.com
Founder Jenny Todd

Represents literary and commercial fiction, non-fiction, YA, film and TV. Drawn to works of originality by inventive, relevant and multi-faceted writers and artists, and committed to developing long-term strategies for their careers. *Commission* Home 15%, overseas 20%. Submissions via website. Send covering letter, synopsis and three sample chapters. *Founded* 2021.

Luithlen Agency
88 Holmfield Road, Leicester LE2 1SB
tel 0116 273 8863
email penny@luithlenagency.com
website www.luithlenagency.com
Agent Penny Luithlen

Children's fiction, all ages up to YA. *Commission* Home 15%, overseas 20%, performance rights 15%. Currently no accepting submissions or new clients. *Founded* 1986.

Eunice McMullen
Low Ibbotsholme Cottage, Troutbeck Bridge, Windermere, Cumbria LA23 1HU
email eunice@eunicemcmullen.co.uk
website www.eunicemcmullen.co.uk
Director Eunice McMullen

Specialises exclusively in children's books, especially picture books and older fiction. Handles novelty books, picture books, fiction for all ages including teenage, series fiction and audio. *Commission* Home 15%, overseas 15%. No unsolicited MSS.

Authors include Alison Friend, Charles Fuge, Cally Johnson Isaacs, James Mayhew, Momoko Abe, Mark McKinley. *Founded* 1992.

Marjacq Scripts*
The Space, 235 High Holborn, London WC1V 7DN
tel 020-7935 9499
email [firstname]@marjacq.com
website www.marjacq.com
X @MarjacqScripts
Contact Catherine Pellegrino (children's and YA), Sandra Sawicka (YA only)

Full-service agency. Handles all rights. In-house legal, foreign rights, book-to-screen and interactive media support. Middle grade through to crossover fiction. *Commission* Home 15%, overseas 20%, film 20%. See website for submission guidelines. Does not represent picture book authors or illustrators.

Clients include Mel Darbon, Rose Edwards, Roopa Farooki, Gemma Fowler, Finbar Hawkins, Maria de Jong, Bryony Pearce, T.C. Shelley, Claire Waller, Harriet Whitehorn. *Founded* 1973.

May Literary Agency*
email carolyn@mayliteraryagency.com
website www.mayliteraryagency.com
Instagram @mayliteraryagency
Agent Carolyn May McGlone

Fiction and non-fiction for all ages, including picture books, middle grade and YA. Submissions currently closed. Does not represent sci-fi, horror, crime or cookery books. *Founded* 2024.

MBA Literary and Script Agents*†
62 Grafton Way, London W1T 5DW
tel 020-7387 2076
email submissions@mbalit.co.uk
website https://mbalit.co.uk
Instagram @mbaliteraryagents
Children's Book Agent Sophie Gorell Barnes, *Film & TV Agent* Diana Tyler

Fiction, non-fiction and children's books. Foreign rights handled by Louisa Pritchard Associates. *Commission* Home 15%, overseas 20%, TV/theatre/radio 10%, film 15%. Submission by email only. Include the first three chapters and a synopsis as attachments and a covering letter in the body of the email. All attachments must be in Word, pdfs or Final Draft format. Not currently accepting unsolicited film and television submissions.

Clients include Sufiya Ahmed, Christopher William Hill, Mark Wheeller. *Founded* 1971.

Madeleine Milburn Literary, TV & Film Agency*
The Factory, 1 Park Hill, Clapham, London SW4 9NS
tel 020-7499 7550
email childrens@madeleinemilburn.com
website www.madeleinemilburn.co.uk
Facebook www.facebook.com/MadeleineMilburnLiteraryAgency
X @MMLitAgency, @agentmilburn
Instagram @madeleinemilburn
*Director*s Madeleine Milburn, Giles Milburn, *Director of Children's & YA* Chloe Seager, *Literary Agent* Maddy Belton

Represents a range of children's and YA fiction and non-fiction. Also award-winning and popular fiction including fantasy, real life/contemporary, YA thrillers, mystery, action, historical, sci-fi, romance, coming of age and film/TV tie-ins. Handles all rights in the UK, US, Canada and foreign markets including film/TV/theatre/radio (for clients with book deal in place only) and digital. Areas include 6–8 years, 9–12 years, 12+, teen, YA, New Adult and books appealing to both children and adults. *Commission* Home 15%, USA/Canada/translation 20%, film/TV 20%. No submissions by post. See submission guidelines on website.

Authors include Holly Bourne, Katie Kirby, Jordan Lees, Lex Croucher, Laura Steven, Faridah Abike-Iyimide, Benjamin Dean, Maisie Chan, Kathryn Foxfield, Danielle Jawando, Heba Al-Wasity, Natasha Hastings, Kate Weston, Sarah Hagger-Holt, Ben Oliver, Rosie Talbot, Alexandra Christo. *Founded* 2012.

MMBcreative*
(Mulcahy Sweeney Associates Ltd)
165 Highlever Road, London W10 6PH
tel 020-3582 9379

email mulcahyadmin@mmbcreative.com
website https://mmbcreative.com/literary-agency/books
X @my_agent_secret
Instagram @myagentsecret
Contacts Ivan Mulcahy, Sallyanne Sweeney, Edwina de Charnacé, Sidney Jones

Children's fiction and YA. *Commission* Home 15%, Overseas/US 20%. See website for full list of submission email accounts and current guidelines.

Clients include Ha-Joon Chang, Juno Dawson, Ian Kelly, David Mitchell, Steven Lenton, Lisa McInerney, Sheena Demspey, Robert Webb, Dapo Adeola, Nathan Bryon, Brian Cox, Poppy Kuroki, James Roseman, Bridget Hourican, Africa Brooke. *Founded* 2016.

Morgan Green Creatives
157 Ribblesdale Road, London SW16 6SP
email kirsty@morgangreencreatives.com
website www.morgangreencreatives.com
Founder Kirsty McLachlan

Actively looking for fresh talent and to be challenged with new ideas, inspired and moved by great writing. Represents fiction, non-fiction and children's book writers. Submission by email which includes a covering letter within the body of the email, plus 30 pages of your work attached. Does not represent picture books for 0–5 year olds (other than for existing clients). *Founded* 2020.

Andrew Nurnberg Associates*
43 Great Russell Street, London WC1B 3PD
tel 020-3327 0400
email info@nurnberg.co.uk
website www.andrewnurnberg.com
X @nurnberg_agency
Instagram @andrewnurnbergassociates
Managing Directors Jenny Savill, Doug Wallace

Represents adult and children's authors, agent and publisher clients in the fields of literary and commercial fiction, and general non-fiction for the sale of rights throughout the world via offices in the UK and overseas. *Founded* 1977.

Originate Literary Agency*
71–75 Shelton Street, Covent Garden, London WC2H 9JQ
email info@originateliterary.co.uk
website www.originateliterary.co.uk
X @OriginateLit
Instagram @originateliterary
Founder & Literary Agent Natalie Jerome

Actively looking for new voices who push boundaries and want to create change on a global stage. Represents a broad range of genres including YA, commercial fiction and non-fiction. *Commission* Home 15%, overseas 20%. Send a covering note including a brief biography and the first three chapters (for illustrated titles send sample spreads with the proposal) by email to originatesubmissions@originateliterary.co.uk. Does not represent academic and educational texts.

Clients include Anchal Seda, Amir Khan, Sir Lenny Henry (children's publishing), Maya Jordan, Rene Germain. *Founded* 2023.

Paper Lion
13 Grayham Road, New Malden, Surrey KT3 5HR
tel 07748 786199, (01276) 61322
email katyloffman@paperlionltd.com
email lesleypollinger@paperlionltd.com
website www.paperlionltd.com
Agents Katy Loffman, Lesley Pollinger

A cross-media literary agency. The client list includes award-winning authors and literary estates. Has a strong focus on the exploration of digital opportunities, and expertise in solving complex copyright, dramatic rights and literary issues from the present and past.

Clients include Max Allen, Vince Cross, Catherine Fisher, Saviour Pirotta, the estates of authors including Gene Kemp, Bruce Hobson, Cordelia Feldman and Gwynedd Rae. *Founded* 2017.

Peters Fraser & Dunlop*
55 New Oxford Street, London WC1A 1BS
tel 020-7344 1000
email info@pfd.co.uk
website https://petersfraserdunlop.com
Facebook www.facebook.com/pfdagents
X @PFDAgents
Instagram @pfdAgents
Head of Children's Books Silvia Molteni, *Agent* Lucy Irvine

Represents authors of fiction and non-fiction, presenters and public speakers throughout the world. Email submissions addressed to individual agents. Include covering letter, synopsis or outline and first three chapters as well as author biographies. See website for submission guidelines. Does not represent scriptwriters.

Authors include Jeanette Winterson, Simon Schama, Bear Grylls, Sir Michael Caine, Onjali Q. Raúf, Jamie Bartlett, Lesley Pearse, Rose Tremain, Niall Williams, Jamie Susskind, Kenya Hunt, Ruby Wax, the estate of Edna O'Brien. *Founded* 1924.

RCW*
(formerly Rogers, Coleridge & White)
20 Powis Mews, London W11 1JN
tel 020-7221 3717
email info@rcwlitagency.com
website www.rcwlitagency.com
Instagram @rcwliteraryagency
Managing Director Peter Straus, *Deputy Managing Director* Georgia Garrett, *Directors* Nelka Bell, Sam Copeland, Stephen Edwards, Natasha Fairweather, Laurence Laluyaux, Zoë Waldie, Claire Wilson, Jon Wood, *Agents* Eleanor Birne, Cara Jones, Matthew Marland, Matthew Turner, Millie van Grutten

International representation for all genres of fiction, non-fiction, children's, YA and illustration. *Commission* Home 15%, USA 20%, translation 20%. See website for submissions information. Note that due to the volume of unsolicited queries, it is policy to respond (usually within six weeks) only if interested in the material.

Clients include David Baddiel, Frank Cottrell Boyce, Catherine Doyle, Lissa Evans, Hannah Gold, Anna James, Femi Fadugba, Tamzin Merchant, Alice Oseman, Katherine Rundell, A.F. Steadman, Holly Jackson, Katie and Kevin Tsang. *Founded* 1967 as Deborah Rogers Ltd, 1989 as RCW Ltd.

Redhammer Management
website https://redhammer.info
X @Litopia
Agent Peter Cox

A boutique literary agency providing in-depth management for a restricted number of clients. Specialises in works with international book, film and TV potential. Participates in Pop-Up Submissions every Sunday; submit a title, brief description and first 700 words of the work. No radio or theatre scripts.

Clients include Rt. Hon. Norman Baker, Michelle Paver. *Founded* 2006.

Seventh Agency
email info@seventhagency.co.uk
website www.seventhagency.co.uk
X @seventhagency_
Instagram @the_seventhagency
Agents Kemi Ogunsanwo, Joe Sedgewick, Lisa Goodrum, *Assistant* Lina Benosman

Specialises in fiction including literary, commercial, mystery/thriller, romance, historical, sci-fi and fantasy, New Adult and YA. Also represents children's middle-grade literature and select non-fiction. Fiction submissions welcome in the months of March and November. Non-fiction by invitation only. Consult website for specific details once the submission window is open. Not currently offering representation to scriptwriters.

Authors include Plestia Alaqad, Kenny Imafidon, Eric Collins, Mikaela Loach, Sharada Keats, Vasundra Tailor, Wenyan Lu, Yemi Dipeolu, Patrick Gallagher, Jeffrey Boadi, Verna Gao, Perri Drayton Shakes, Chidi-Ebere Onwuka. *Founded* 2024.

The Shaw Agency
website www.theshawagency.co.uk
X @KateJShaw
Instagram @agentkateshaw
Agent Kate Shaw

Interested in literary and commercial fiction, fact and fiction books for children (6+) and teens/YA, and narrative non-fiction. Submission by contact form on website. Include a cover letter of up to 300 words, the first six pages or approx. 3,000 words of the MS and a short synopsis of about 500 words (or in the case of non-fiction, a chapter plan and one sample chapter).

Clients include Lucy Adlington, Isabel Ashdown, Jasbinder Bilan, Lesley Lokko, Alan MacDonald, Mark Powers, Holly Smale, Isabel Thomas. *Founded* 2019.

Sheil Land Associates†
Room 9–25, LABS House, 15–19 Bloomsbury Way, London WC1A 2TH
tel 020-7405 9351
email info@sheilland.co.uk
website www.sheilland.co.uk
X @sheilland
Instagram @sheillandassociates
Agents UK & USA Sonia Land, Gaia Banks, Piers Blofeld, Ian Drury, Natalie Barracliffe, *Film/Theatre/TV* Lucy Fawcett, Rebecca Lyon, *Foreign Rights* Lauren Coleman

Literary and commercial fiction and non-fiction; adult and children's. Represents book club, commercial and literary fiction: thrillers, crime, romance, drama, sci-fi and fantasy and YA; and non-fiction: biography, politics, history, military history, gardening, travel, cookery and humour. *Commission* Home 15%, USA/translation 20%. Welcomes approaches from new clients to start or to develop their careers. Send cover letter, synopsis and first three chapters to submissions@sheilland.co.uk.

Clients include Peter Ackroyd, Pam Ayres, Steven Carroll, Nadine Dorries, Robert Fabbri, Janice Hallett, Graham Hancock, Susan Hill, Mark Lawrence, The Brothers McLeod, Gill Paul, Diane Setterfield, Julie Soto, the estate of Catherine Cookson. *Founded* 1962.

Caroline Sheldon Literary Agency – see RCW

Hannah Sheppard Literary Agency*
email enquiries@hs-la.com
website www.hs-la.com
Bluesky @hslanews.bsky.social
Instagram @hs_la_News
Founder & Literary Agent Hannah Sheppard, *Associate Agent* Louise Buckley

Actively seeking new authors, particularly from under-represented groups. Current wish lists can be found on the website. Represents children's fiction (primarily across middle grade, teen and YA), commercial adult fiction (with a focus on crime/thriller, women's fiction and upmarket/book-club fiction) and a very small amount of non-fiction. *Commission* Home 15%, overseas 20%, film/TV 20%. Submission via form on website between the 1st and 7th of each month. No poetry, short story collections, novellas or screenplays.

Clients include Dee Benson, Jim Beckett, Zoë Cookson, Abi Elphinstone, Keris Fox, Rosie Hopes,

Gabrielle Kent, Jon Lander, Philippa Leathley, Kate Mallinder, Morgan Owen, Yasmin Rahman, Felicity Yeoh. Founded 2023.

Show Me The Rabbit
Somerset House Exchange, New Wing, Somerset House, Strand, London WC2R 1LA
tel 07774 264826
email showmetherabbit2@gmail.com
website www.showmetherabbit.com
Instagram @showmetherabbit
Agents Philippa Perry, Claire Gill

Literary representation, management and PR support for our children's writers. Consult website for submission guidelines. Founded 2024.

Dorie Simmonds Agency*
email info@doriesimmonds.com
website https://doriesimmonds.com
Contact Dorie Simmonds

Children's fiction, general non-fiction and commercial fiction. Commission Home 15%, USA 15%, translation 20%. Email submissions only. Fiction: send the first chapter plus a full synopsis and a covering letter, with a brief CV. Non-fiction: send a detailed proposal, alongside the covering letter and CV. Full-length MS submission on request. Does not represent poetry or screenplays. Founded 1997.

Skylark Literary*
19 Parkway, Weybridge, Surrey KT13 9HD
tel 020-8144 7440
email info@skylark-literary.com
email submissions@skylark-literary.com
website www.skylark-literary.com
Facebook www.facebook.com/SkylarkLiteraryLtd
X @skylarklit
Directors Joanna Moult, Amber Caraveo

Specialists in children's and YA fiction. Keen to support new and established authors. Agents have editorial backgrounds and will work closely with clients on their manuscripts to increase chances of publication. All genres considered. Commission Home 15%, overseas 20%. Will consider unsolicited submissions by email only. Will suggest revision where appropriate. No adult fiction/non-fiction.
  Clients include Amy Wilson, Simon James Green, Alyssa Hollingsworth, Rachel Burge, Nizrana Farook, Lesley Parr, Em Lynas, Lily Dyu, Sarah Todd Taylor, Naomi Gibson, Lucy Hope, Lee Newbery, Aislinn O'Louglin, Clare Harlow, Eilish Fisher. Founded 2014.

The Soho Agency*†
16–17 Wardour Mews, 2nd Floor, London W1F 8AT
tel 020-7471 7900
email admin@thesohoagency.co.uk
website https://thesohoagency.co.uk
X @TheSohoAgencyUK
Instagram @thesohoagencyuk
Managing Director Rowan Lawton, Agent Philippa Milnes-Smith

Novelty books, picture books, fiction for 5–8 and 9–12 years including series, YA, film/TV and non-fiction. Special interests: projects with cross-media potential, diverse voices, visual storytelling and innovative non-fiction. Commission Home 15%, USA/translation 20%. Representation in all markets. Unsolicited and debut work considered. Submissions for children's, YA and artwork to be sent to sohoagencychildrenssubmissions@gmail.com. Include a covering letter, synopsis and first three chapter. Send the complete work if it is for young children and less than 1,000 words. No postal submissions.
  Clients include Lauren Child, Steve Cole, Linda Chapman, Gillian Cross, Emily Gravett, Chris Judge, Sophie Kinsella, Philip Reeve, Chris Riddell, Niamh Sharkey, Sarah Webb. Founded 2019.

Spring Literary
email submissions@springliterary.com
website www.springliterary.com
Instagram @springliterary
Agent Neil Dunnicliffe

Specialises in children's and YA writing and illustration. Searching for beautiful, entertaining, funny and thought-provoking books for children from picture books up to YA fiction. Send covering letter by email only. As attachments include: a one-page synopsis and sample chapters up to 10,000 words (fiction); a synopsis, short CV and three sample sections/chapters (non-fiction); one to three full book texts (picture book authors); or a portfolio of up to ten images (illustrators).
  Clients include Sarah Massini, Sam Usher, Ross Collins, Pam Smy, Mick Jackson, David Melling, Rose Blake, Matt Sewell, Maisie Paradise Shearring. Founded 2022.

Abner Stein*
Suite 137, China Works, 100 Black Prince Road, London SE1 7SJ
tel 020-7373 0456
email info@abnerstein.co.uk
website www.abnerstein.co.uk
Contacts Caspian Dennis, Sandy Violette

Fiction, general non-fiction and children's. Commission Home 15%, overseas 20%. Not taking on any new clients at present.

Rochelle Stevens & Co†
2 Terretts Place, Upper Street, London N1 1QZ
tel 020-7359 3900
email info@rochellestevens.com
website https://rochellestevens.com
Directors Rochelle Stevens, Frances Arnold

Scripts for TV, theatre and radio. *Commission* Home 10%. Recommendation from industry professional required. Email to introduce yourself and include your CV and the recommendation. Will request a writing sample if interested. Does not accept book submissions. *Founded* 1984.

StoryWise*
41 Jubilee Road, Swanage, Dorset BH19 2SE
email submissions@storywise.uk
website https://storywise.uk
Facebook www.facebook.com/storywiseagency
X @StoryWiseAgency
Instagram @storywiseagency
Owner & Agent Mandy Suhr

Boutique, specialist children's literary agency representing bestselling and award-winning authors and illustrators of preschool, novelty, picture books, young and middle-grade fiction and non-fiction. Deliberately small and therefore highly selective. Represent both debut and established authors and illustrators bringing something new to the children's market. Follow submission guidelines on website. Does not represent YA or poetry. *Founded* 2023

Sarah Such Literary Agency
38 Church Road, Barnes, London SW13 9HN
tel 020-8741 2107
email info@sarah-such.com
website https://sarahsuchliteraryagency.tumblr.com
X @sarahsuch
Bluesky @sarahsuch.bsky.social
Instagram @sarahsuch1
Director Sarah Such

High-quality literary and commercial non-fiction and fiction for adults and children. Always looking for original children's and YA writers and projects. Translation representation by The Buckman Agency. Film/TV representation by Lesley Thorne, Aitken Alexander Associates. Particular focus on debut YA novels, topical middle-grade non-fiction, children's fiction series, picture books and graphic novels. *Commission* Home 15%, overseas 20%, film/TV 20%. Will suggest revision. Submit synopsis and three sample chapters (as a Word attachment by email) and an author biography. No postal submissions unless requested. No unsolicited MSS or telephone enquiries. Film/TV scripts for established clients only. No radio or theatre scripts, poetry, fantasy, self-help or short stories (unless full collections).

Authors include Jeffrey Boakye, Kit Caless, Maxim Jakubowski, Antony Johnston, Amy Lankester-Owen, Louisa Leaman, Ruby Lewis, Vesna Maric, Sabrina Pace-Humphreys, Rachel Pashley, John Rowley, Caroline Sanderson, Nikhil Singh, Sara Starbuck, Hazell Ward. *Founded* 2007.

Nick Turner Management[†]
tel 020-3723 8833
email nick@nickturnermanagement.com
website https://nickturnermanagement.com
X @nickturnermgmt
Agents Nick Turner, Phil Adie, *Agency Assistant* Andrew Allen

Represents writers and directors for film, TV and radio worldwide. Specialises in TV drama, comedy, continuing drama and children's. *Commission* Home 10%, overseas 15–20%. *Founded* 2016.

Tyild's Agency
email submissionstotyildsagency@gmail.com
website www.tyildsagency.co.uk
X @tyilds
Agents Kate Scarborough, Frances McKay

Set up particularly for teachers who write for children. Represents authors of picture books, young readers and middle-grade fiction, as well as non-fiction. Actively looking for new voices – wonderful storytellers with an innate understanding of children. Actively seeking submissions from teachers and educators. *Commission* Home 15%, overseas 20%. Email submissions only. Consult the detailed guidelines on the website as criteria varies by age group and MS type.

Authors include Mark A. Smith, Jonny Daymond, Barbara Henders, Gaynor Andrews, Roy Peachey, Jane Dimond, Claire Lewis, Kathryn Williams, Simon Bell. *Founded* 2020.

United Agents*[†]
12–26 Lexington Street, London W1F 0LE
tel 020-3214 0800
email info@unitedagents.co.uk
website www.unitedagents.co.uk
X @UA_Books
Bluesky @unitedagents.bsky.social
Instagram @unitedagentsbooks
Agents Jodie Hodges, Emily Talbot, Molly Jamieson

Fiction and non-fiction. *Commission* Home 15%, USA/translation 20%. See website for submission details. *Founded* 2008.

Watson, Little*
Suite 315, ScreenWorks, 22 Highbury Grove, London N5 2ER
tel 020-7388 7529
email office@watsonlittle.com
website www.watsonlittle.com
X @watsonlittle
Managing Director James Wills, *Agents* Laetitia Rutherford, Megan Carroll, Hannah Weatherill, *Rights Manager* Gabrielle Demblon

Offers a full service to its clients across all aspects of media. Handles a wide range of fiction and non-fiction for adults and children and works directly and in conjunction with US agents. YA and middle-grade fiction, picture books and children's non-fiction in all genres. *Commission* Home 15%, USA/translation 20%. Email submissions@watsonlittle.com with an informative preliminary letter, synopsis and sample chapters. No poetry, TV, play or film scripts.

Authors include Adam B, Tom Clempson, Rebecca Elliott, T.K. Hall, Hayley Hoskins, Greg Jenner, Richard Joyce, Hiba Noor Khan, Lynne Reid Banks, Margaret Mahy. Founded 1970.

Whispering Buffalo Literary Agency
97 Chesson Road, London W14 9QS
tel 020-7385 4655
email info@whisperingbuffalo.com
website www.whisperingbuffalo.com
Director Mariam Keen

Commercial and literary fiction, non-fiction, children's and YA fiction. Special interest in book-to-screen adaptations; TV and film rights in novels and non-fiction handled in-house. Commission Home 15%, overseas 20%. See website for current submission guidelines; only accepts submissions by email. Founded 2008.

Eve White Literary Agency*
15 Alderney Street, London SW1V 4ES
tel 020-7630 1155
email [firstname]@evewhite.co.uk
website www.evewhite.co.uk
Bluesky @evewhiteagency.bsky.social
Instagram @evewhiteliteraryagency
Contacts Eve White, Ludo Cinelli, Steven Evans

Boutique agency representing young, middle grade, teenage and YA fiction, picture books and film/TV tie-ins. Also handles adult commercial and literary fiction and non-fiction; 35% of the list is for the children's market. Commission Home 15%, overseas 20%. Will suggest revision where appropriate. See website for up-to-date submission requirements. No submissions by post.

Clients include Andy Stanton, Iona Rangeley, Tia Fisher, Sarah Coyle, Tracey Corderoy, Elli Woollard, Sarah Naughton, Simon Fox, Alexia Mason, Mayo Agard-Olubo, Kate Francis, Ivan Brett. Founded 2003.

Alice Williams Literary*
tel 020-7385 2118
email submissions@alicewilliamsliterary.co.uk
website www.alicewilliamsliterary.co.uk
Instagram @agentalicewilliams
Contact Alice Williams

Specialist literary agency representing writers and illustrators of picture books, children's fiction, teen/YA fiction and children's non-fiction. Commission Home 15%, USA/translation 20%, film/TV 20%. Submission by email only; attach full manuscript and synopsis, two picture book texts or illustration portfolio. See website for further guidelines and whether the agency is currently open or closed to submissions.

Clients include Zeshan Akhter, Fiona Barker, Lauren Beard, Ruby Clyde, Rachel Delahaye, Meg McLaren, Natelle Quek, Matt Ralphs, Santiago, Suzy Senior, Ciara Smyth, Hannah Tolson, Cat Weldon, Clare Helen Welsh, Pete Williamson. Founded 2018.

WME*
(William Morris Endeavour, UK)
100 New Oxford Street, London WC1A 1HB
tel 020-8929 8400
email hogden.assistant@wmeagency.com
website www.wmebookdepartment.com
X @WMEBooksUK, @WMEBooks
Books Matilda Forbes Watson, Hellie Ogden, Fiona Baird, Lucy Balfour, Suzannah Ball, Karolina Kaim, Francesca Ali, Translation Rights James Munro, Florence Dodd, Cody Siler, Book to Film Sanjana Seelam

Worldwide talent and literary agency with offices in London, New York, Beverly Hills, Nashville, Washington and Sydney. Handles translation rights directly in most territories. US rights handled by one of the US-based WME offices. Represents bestselling authors, critically acclaimed literary writers, award-winning thought leaders and up-and-coming talent. Sponsors the Lucy Cavendish Fiction Prize. Picture books, middle-grade and YA including illustrated fiction and graphic novels. Commission UK 15%, USA/translation 20%, film/TV 10%. Submit via the website following the indivdual guidelines set out by each agent.

Clients include Kiran Millwood Hargrave, Ladbaby, Lev Grossman, Kat Dunn, Jessica Goodman, Sharna Jackson, Nat Luurtsema, Judy Blume, Jacqueline Woodson, Brad Montague. Founded 1898.

Susan Yearwood Agency*
2 Knebworth House, Londesborough Road, London N16 8RL
tel 020-7503 0954
email submissions@susanyearwoodagency.com
website https://susanyearwoodagency.com
Facebook www.facebook.com/susanyearwoodagency
X @sya_susan
Instagram @susanyearwoodagency
Contact Susan Yearwood

Children's fiction 9+ and teen/YA. Commission Home 15%, overseas 20%. Send submission with covering letter and brief synopsis via email. Submissions not accepted by hand or post. Tends not to read sci-fi and fantasy in adult fiction, short stories or poetry.

Authors include Fil Reid, Katie Brewer. Founded 2007.

YMU Literary*
180 Great Portland Street, London W1W 5QZ
tel 020-8742 4950
email ymuLiterarySubmissions@ymugroup.com
website www.ymugroup.com
X @YMULiterary
Instagram @ymuLiterary
Global Managing Director Briony Gowlett, UK Managing Director Anna Dixon, Literary Executive Elise Middleton

A bespoke literary agency within the UK's largest talent management agency, YMU Management, represents a broad range of writers of fiction and non-fiction across all genres. *Commission* Home 15%, USA 20%. Submissions should include an introductory email, detailed synopsis, and sample chapter. See website for further details.

Clients include Nathan Anthony (Bored of Lunch), Dr Whitney Bauman, Francis Bourgeois, Poppy Cooks, Fearne Cotton, Tom Daley, Jake Humphrey, Matt Lucas, Davina McCall, Ant McPartlin and Dec Donnelly, Rob Rinder, Stephen Mulhern, Dr Julie Smith, Stacey Solomon. *Founded* 2021.

Zeno Agency*

Primrose Hill Business Centre,
110 Gloucester Avenue, London NW1 8HX
tel 020-7096 0927
email info@zenoagency.com
website www.zenoagency.com
X @zenoagency
Bluesky @zenoagency.bsky.social
Instagram @zenoagency
Director John Berlyne, *Agent* Stevie Finegan, *Associate Agent* Bianca Gillam

Most adult fiction genres represented (commercial, crime/thriller, romance) with a specialism in sci-fi, fantasy and horror. Children's fiction from picture books through to YA. Non-fiction from specialists in their fields and authors with strong personal stories to tell (narrative, memoir, biography). Some illustrated non-fiction considered. *Commission* Home 15%, overseas 15% (via sub-agents 20%). Refer to the website for current submission guidelines. Does not consider poetry, plays or filmscripts.

Authors include Ben Aaronovitch, Aliette de Bodard, Travis Baldree, Jonathan Carroll, Charlaine Harris, Elizabeth Helen, Grady Hendrix, William Gibson, Emily Rath, Brandon Sanderson, Lavie Tidhar, M. A. Wardell, the estate of Roger Zelazny. *Founded* 2008.

Children's literary agents overseas

This list includes only a selection of agents across the English-speaking world. Before submitting material, writers are advised to visit agents' websites for detailed submission guidelines and to ascertain terms.

AUSTRALIA AND NEW ZEALAND

Alex Adsett Literary
PO Box 694, Tugun, QLD 4224
email agent@alexadsett.com.au
website https://alexadsett.com.au
Principal Alex Adsett, *Agents* Rochelle Fernandez, Abigail Nathan, Lisa Fuller

Full-service agency, representing works of fiction and non-fiction for children, teens and adults. Fiction: literary and commercial fiction, crime, mystery, romance, sci-fi and fantasy. Children's: chapter book, middle grade and YA fiction (chapter or genre). Non-fiction: narrative non-fiction with a hook. Submission by invitation only; no unsolicited submissions. *Founded* 2008.

ALM: Australian Literary Management
Suite 1, 2A Booth Street, Balmain, NSW 2041
tel +61 (0)2 9818 8557
email alphaalm8@gmail.com
website http://austlit.com
Proprietor Lyn Tranter

For full details of genres represented, see website. Unsolicited submissions welcome from Australian writers. Not currently accepting submissions. Does not consider TV or film scripts of any kind, poetry, self-help, sci-fi and fantasy or books for children by unpublished authors. Does not accept self-published work or previously published works, including ebooks. *Founded* 1980.

Annabel Barker Agency
email hello@annabelbarker.com
website https://annabelbarker.com
Instagram @annabelbarkeragency
Contact Annabel Barker

Specialises in books for children and young adults. The agency has a focus on international rights and looks for work that showcases the depth of the Australian experience by writers and illustrators. Submissions are open in December only. Outside this period, submission is by invitation or referral only. *Founded* 2020.

Margaret Connolly & Associates
PO Box 945, Wahroonga, NSW 2076
tel +61 (0)2 9449 6342
email contact@margaretconnolly.com
website https://margaretconnolly.com
Proprietor Margaret Connolly

Represenets novelists and non-fiction adult writers, children's writers and illustrators. Works closely with co-agents and sub-agents around the world. Consult website for submission information. *Founded* 1992.

Curtis Brown (Australia)
email submission@curtisbrown.com.au
website www.curtisbrown.com.au
X @curtisbrownaus
Managing Director Fiona Inglis, *Head of Agents* Pippa Masson, *Agents* Alexandra Christie, Tara Wynne, *Associate Agent* Caitlin Cooper-Trent

Australia's oldest and largest literary agency representing a diverse range of Australian and New Zealander authors. Submissions open in the months of March and August. Send cover email, synopsis and first three chapters. Not currently seeking stage/screenplays, poetry, self-help, children's picture books, early reader books, middle-grade fiction, comics, short stories, cookery books, educational, corporate, translated or comedy books.
Founded 1967.

Drummond Agency
PO Box 572, Woodend, VIC 3442
tel +61 (0)3 5427 3644
email info@drummondagency.com.au
website www.drummondagency.com.au/index.htm

Considers both fiction and non-fiction for adults and YA fiction. Query by telephone, email or letter. Do not send attachments unless requested. Represents Australian and New Zealander authors. Currently closed to submissions. No sci-fi or fantasy. Does not represent educational materials, poetry, plays, film scripts or children's picture books.
 Authors include Randa Abdel-Fattah, Vikki Wakefield, Claire Zorn, Deborah Burrows, Margareta Osborn, Yvette Walker. *Founded* 1997.

Golvan Arts Management
website www.golvanarts.com.au
Facebook www.facebook.com/Golvan-Arts-Management-153871021304383

Represents a wide range of writers including writers of both adult and children's fiction and non-fiction, poetry, screenwriters and writers of plays. Also represents visual artists and composers. See the General Information section on the website before making contact via online form. *Commission* Home 16.5%. Send a brief introductory letter about your work in first instance. Do not send any sample material unless requested.

Sarah McKenzie Literary Management
tel +61 (0)4 1603 5061
email submissions@smlm.com.au
website www.smlm.com.au
Contact Sarah McKenzie

Representation for Australian and New Zealander authors. Actively seeks established and emerging authors of commercial, literary and genre fiction, non-fiction and children's fiction (including picture books, middle grade, YA and graphic novels). Submissions via email only. For fiction and memoir, include a covering letter, one- to two-page synopsis and 20 consecutive pages of the MS. For non-fiction, include a covering letter, one-page summary, author bio, one or two sample chapters and a table of contents. Does not represent works that have been previously self-published in any form, academic or spirituality titles, sci-fi, novellas or poetry collections.

CANADA

CookeMcDermid
219 Dufferin Street, Unit 208B, Toronto, ON M6K 3J1
tel +1 647-788-4010
email admin@cookemcdermid.com
website https://cookemcdermid.com
Facebook www.facebook.com/CookeMcDermid
X @CookeMcDermid
Instagram @cookcmcdermid
Agents Martha Webb, Suzanne Brandreth, Ron Eckel, Paige Sisley, Cody Caetano, Hana El Niwairi, Amy Moore-Benson

Represents authors of literary, commercial, sci-fi and fantasy fiction; a broad range of narrative non-fiction; health and wellness resources; middle-grade and YA books. Sells Canadian and American rights directly. The in-house rights team sells UK and translation rights, in conjunction with a network of co-agents around the world. CMD also sells film and TV rights directly, in addition to working with associates in New York and LA. Submission via QueryManager.

Clients include John Irving, Geddy Lee, Alicia Elliot, Paul Sun-Hyung Lee, Billy-Ray Belcourt, Michael Crummey, Claudia Dey, Elamin Abdelmahmoud, Robyn Doolittle, Scaachi Koul, Jen Agg, Robert Munsch, Carol Off, Sonya Lalli, Rick Mofina *Founded* 2017.

Donaghy Literary Group
tel +1 647-527-3153
email [firstname]@donaghyliterary.com
website www.donaghyliterary.com
X @DonaghyLiterary
Agents Stacey Donaghy, Valerie Noble

Provides full-service literary representation to clients at all stages of their publishing career. Specialises in commercial fiction and seeking YA and adult novels. Genres represented include romance, psychological and domestic thriller, suspense, LGBTQ+, diverse stories, sci-fi, fantasy, historical fantasy and historical fiction. Visit agent pages on the website for information on each agent and what they are currently looking for. Only accepts submissions via QueryManager accessed via website through a link button on each agents' page. Do not query by phone or email. Welcomes both established and new writers.

Clients include K.A. Tucker, Jay Crownover, Jamie Shaw, Diana Gardin, Gustavo Florentin, Annika Sharma, Christopher Francis, Ara Grigorian, Kate L. Mary, Valerie Noble, Anita Kushwaha, Joe Bright, Desmond McLean, Shira Shiloah, Lisa Kusel.

P.S. Literary Agency
2nd Floor, 2010 Winston Park Drive, Oakville, ON L6H 5R7
email info@psliterary.com
website www.psliterary.com
Threads @psliteraryagency
President & Principal Agent Curtis Russell, *Senior Literary Agents* Carly Watters (Senior Advisor), Maria Vicente (Advisor), *Literary Agents* Eric Smith, Claire Harris, Cecilia Lyra, *Associate Agents* Rose Ferrao, Nour Sallam

Represents both fiction and non-fiction works to publishers in North America, Europe and throughout the world. Categories include commercial, upmarket, literary, women's fiction, mystery, thriller, romance, sci-fi, fantasy, historical, LGBTQ+, YA, middle grade, picture books, graphic novels, memoir, history, politics, current affairs, business, wellness, cookery books, sports, humour, popular science, popular psychology, popular culture, design and lifestyle. Send queries to query@psliterary.com. Do not send email attachments unless specifically requested. Does not accept submissions via mail or telephone. *Founded* 2005.

Transatlantic Agency
68 Claremont Street, Suite 100, Toronto, ON M6J 2M5
tel +1 416-488-9214
website www.transatlanticagency.com
Facebook www.facebook.com/TransLitAgency
Instagram @transatlantic_agency

Represents more than 800 American, Canadian and internationally bestselling and award-winning clients, with a team of 20 experienced agents based in cities across North America. Offers a full spectrum of career representation to authors (adult, children's and YA, and illustrators) and storytellers (speakers, industry leaders and influencers) across all genres and formats for book, content development, speaking, TV and film. *Founded* 1993.

Literary agents

Westwood Creative Artists
386 Huron Street, Toronto, ON M5S 2G6
tel +1 416-964-3302
email wca_office@wcaltd.com
website https://wcaltd.com
X @WCA_LitAgency
Instagram @westwoodcreativeartists
President Jackie Kaiser, *Executive Vice President* Hilary McMahon, *Agents* Chris Casuccio, Sara Harowitz, Bridgette Kam, John Pearce, Meg Wheeler, *Associate Agent* Briar Heckman

Represents Canadian authors. Interested in high-quality writing and illustration for children, literary and commercial YA fiction and select graphic novels and illustrated works for all age catergories. Email submissions to submissions@wcaltd.com. Send a covering letter and 10–20 pages of MS in body of email. See website for full submission guidelines. Does not represent screenwriters, playwrights or poets.

USA

*Agency includes agents who are members of the Association of American Literary Agents

Adams Literary*
7845 Colony Road, C4 Suite 215, Charlotte, NC 28226
tel +1 704-542-1440
email info@adamsliterary.com
website www.adamsliterary.com
X @adamsliterary
Instagram @adamsliterary
Agents Tracey Adams, Josh Adams

Selectively children's through to adult fiction. Submissions currently closed; check website for updates.

  Authors include John David Anderson, Hafsah Faizal, Margaret Peterson Haddix, Amie Kaufman, Jay Kristoff, Cynthia Lord, Vaunda Micheaux Nelson, C.S. Pacat, Wendy Shang, Tom Taylor. *Founded* 2004.

David Black Agency*
335 Adams Street, Suite 2707, Brooklyn, NY 11201
tel +1 718-852-5500
email dblack@dblackagency.com
website www.davidblackagency.com
X @dblackagency
Instagram @davidblackagency
Contacts David Black, Rica Allannic, Jennifer Herrera, Gary Morris, Susan Raihofer, Sarah Smith, Mark Tavani, Joy Tutela, Anna Zinchuk, Ellen Scott

Represents an extensive list of both prescriptive and narrative non-fiction including business, memoir, history, politics, fitness and sport. Also represents both commercial and literary fiction, middle grade and YA. Queries to be addressed to specific agent and by email, unless otherwise specified. For most up-to-date submission guidelines and agent preferences see website.

  Clients include Mitch Albom, Billie Jean King, Jonathan Eig, Julia Cameron, Bruce Feiler, Deborah Lipstadt, Lev Rosen, Emily Timberlake, Lindy West, Rodney Scott, Jessie Damuck, Devon Price, Joshua David Stein, Matt Laney, Maggie Smith. *Founded* 1989.

The Booker Albert Literary Agency
PO Box 20931, York, PA 17402
email bookeralbertinfo@gmail.com
website www.thebookeralbertagency.com
X @BookerAlbertLit
Co-Founders Jordy Albert, Brittany Booker, *Junior Agents* Rebecca Lawrence, A.J. Van Belle

Full-service agency representing adult, New Adult, YA and middle-grade fiction. Particularly interested in sci-fi, fantasy, horror and romance (including contemporary and paranormal). Non-fiction interests include science, popular science, self-help and health/wellness. Welcomes writers with expertise links with evolution, ecology, statistics, microbiology and biogeoscience. Submission via QueryManager only. See agents' individual profiles on website for specific guidelines and areas of interest. No picture books, memoirs or screenplays at this time.

  Clients include Charlotte Barnes, C.L. Bleek, Roberto Cofresí Hopgood, Jayne Denker, Lee A. Everett, Suzanne Feldman, Patrick Hurley, Zachary Long, Nicole Luiken, Ziah Miller, Rachel Reddick, Chris Scheina, Eva Siedler, Temma Thomas, Sheri Yutzy. *Founded* 2013.

Bradford Literary Agency*
5694 Mission Center Road, Suite 347, San Diego, CA 92108
email queries@bradfordlit.com
website www.bradfordlit.com
X @bradford_agents
Bluesky @bradfordagents.bsky.social
Instagram @bradfordlitagency

Currently looking for picture books, chapter books, middle grade and YA in both fiction and non-fiction categories. Queries accepted only via QueryManager. See website for detailed submission guidelines and for links to each agent's QueryManager form. Not currently looking for poetry, screenplays, short stories, Westerns, inspirational/spiritual, New Age, religion, inspirational, business, self-help, lifestyle, parenting, crafts or gift books. *Founded* 2001.

Andrea Brown Literary Agency*
website www.andreabrownlit.com
Facebook www.facebook.com/AndreaBrownAgency
Bluesky @andreabrownlit.bsky.social
President Andrea Brown, *Agents* Laura Rennert, Caryn Wiseman, Jennifer Laughran, Jennifer Rofé, Kelly Sonnack, Jamie Weiss Chilton, Jennifer

Mattson, Kathleen Rushall, Lara Perkins, Saritza Hernández, Jennifer March Soloway, Jemiscoe Chambers-Black, Paige Terlip, Sally Kim, Analía Cabello.

Exclusively all kinds of children's books. Represents both authors and illustrators. Email and form submissions only. See website for guidelines. Founded 1981.

Maria Carvainis Agency*
Rockefeller Center, 1270 Avenue of the Americas, Suite 2915, New York, NY 10020
tel +1 212-245-6365
email mca@mariacarvainisagency.com
website www.mariacarvainisagency.com
President & Literary Agent Maria Carvainis

YA fiction. Also handles adult fiction and non-fiction. Commission Home 15%, overseas 20%. Email and postal submissions are accepted. Send a query letter, a synopsis of the work, first five to ten pages and a note of any writing credentials. See website for full submission guidelines. Does not represent screenplays, children's picture books, sci-fi or poetry. Founded 1977.

Corvisiero Literary Agency
125 Park Avenue, 25th Floor, New York, NY 10017
119 Maple Avenue, Suite 204, Red Bank, NJ 07701
email info@corvisieroagency.com
website www.corvisieroagency.com
X @CorvisieroLit
Instagram @corvisierolit
Founder Marisa A. Corvisiero, Vice President Tessa Shaffer, Associate Agents Maggie Sadler, Kendyll Drilling, Catherine Ross, Alexandra Grana, Micah Brocker, Mira Landry, Lisa Gouldy, Gabrielle Harbowy, Ciara Smith, Film & TV Agent Ken Boxer

Offers international literary representation, management, and coaching services to fiction and non-fiction for all ages, in a wide spectrum of genres including screenplays. Only submit to one agent at a time via QueryManager. For fiction, send a query letter, one- to two-page synopsis and first five pages. For graphic novels, include 20 pages of the work along with illustration samples, query letter and synopsis. For non-fiction, include a full proposal and sample chapter. For screenplays, include a logline, genre, and upload the first 20 pages of the script. Not currently representing collections of short stories, novellas, essays or poetry. Founded 2012.

Curtis Brown*
228 East 45th Street, Suite 310, New York, NY 10017
tel +1 212-473-5400
email info@cbltd.com
website www.curtisbrown.com
X @CurtisBrownLtd
Instagram @curtisbrown.ltd
Ceo Timothy Knowlton, President Peter Ginsberg, Vice President Elizabeth Harding, Executive Vice President Ginger Knowlton, Contacts Kerry D'Agostino, Jonathan Lyons, Jazmia Young, Film & TV Rights Holly Frederick, Film & TV Rights Associate Alexandra Franklin, Translation Rights Karin Schulze

Fiction and non-fiction, juvenile, film and TV rights. Commission 15% Home, 20% overseas. No unsolicited MSS. See individual agents' entries on the Agents page of the website for specific query and submission information. No screenplays. Founded 1914.

Liza Dawson Associates*
121 West 27th Street, Suite 1201, New York, NY 10001
website www.lizadawsonassociates.com
X @LizaDawsonAssoc
Founder Liza Dawson, Agents Caitlin Blasdel, Hannah Bowman, Tom Miller, Rachel Beck, Lauren Bajek

A full-service agency which draws on expertise as former publishers. YA and middle grade: thrillers, mysteries, romance, historical fiction, contemporary, sci-fi and fantasy. See website for full details of genres represented by individual agents, submission guidelines and email contacts.

Clients include Annie Barrows, Bob Brier, Pierce Brown, Zen Cho, David Santos Donaldson, Britt Frank, Ross Gay, R.F. Kuang, Victoria Law, Julia Lee, Victoria Christopher Murray, Charles Stross, the estate of Eleanor Roosevelt. Founded 1996.

Sandra Dijkstra & Associates*
1155 Camino Del Mar, PMB 515, Del Mar, CA 92014
tel +1 858-755-3115
website www.dijkstraagency.com
Contacts Sandra Dijkstra, Elise Capron, Jill Marr, Thao Le, Andrea Cavallaro, Jessica Watterson, Jennifer Kim, Jake Lovell, Nick Van Orden

YA sci-fi, fantasy and contemporary; middle-grade fiction and non-fiction; picture books by author/ illustrators only. Works in conjunction with foreign and film agents. Commission Home 15%, overseas 20%. Email submissions only. See website for the most up-to-date guidelines.

Clients include Amy Tan, Maxine Hong Kingston, Lisa See, Chitra Divakaruni, Jasmin Darznik, Eric Foner, Ian Morris, Walter Johnson, Erika Lee, Mae Ngai, Lillian Faderman, Elena Armas, Jessie Sima, Ali Hazelwood. Founded 1981.

Dunham Literary*
email query@dunhamlit.com
website www.dunhamlit.com
Contact Jennie Dunham, Anjanette Barr

Children's books: handles picture books, fiction for 5–8 and 9–12 years and teenage fiction. Also handles adult literary fiction and non-fiction; 50% of list is for the children's market. Commission Home 15%, overseas 20%. Send query by email including a synopsis and first five pages in the body of the email. Founded 2000.

Dystel, Goderich & Bourret*
1 Union Square West, Suite 904, New York, NY 10003
tel +1 212-627-9100
website www.dystel.com
Facebook www.facebook.com/DGandB
Threads @dystelgoderichbourret
Contacts Michael Bourret, Jim McCarthy, Stacey Glick, John Rudolph, Lauren Abramo, Michaela Whatnall

Children's fiction: handles picture books (including author/illustrators), fiction for 5–8 and 9–12 years, teenage fiction and series fiction. Looking for quality YA fiction. Also handles adult fiction, non-fiction and graphic novels. *Commission* Home 15%, overseas 19%, film/TV/radio 15%. Electronic submission by either email or QueryManager. Include a query letter and 25 pages of MS or proposal sample chapters. Does not represent poetry, plays or screenplays. *Founded* 1994.

The Ethan Ellenberg Literary Agency*
548 Broadway, 5C, New York, NY 10012
tel +1 212-431-4554
email agent@ethanellenberg.com
website www.ethanellenberg.com
President & Agent Ethan Ellenberg, *Senior Agent* Evan Gregory, *Agents* Bibi Lewis, Ezra Ellenberg

Interested in all types of children's fiction: New Adult, YA, middle grade, chapter books and picture books. Will consider all genres: literary, mystery, romance, fantasy, sci-fi, humorous. Will consider other illustrated works. *Commission* Home 15%, overseas 20%. Accepts unsolicited MSS by email and seriously considers all submissions, including first-time writers. For fiction, submit query letter, one- or two-page synopsis and first 50 pages. For non-fiction, send a query letter and proposal (outline, sample material up to 50 pages, author CV). Illustrators should send four to five sample illustrations along with query letter. Unable to return any material from overseas. No poetry, short stories or screenplays. *Founded* 1984.

Fairbank Literary Representation*
21 Lyman Street, Waltham, MA 02452
tel +1 617-576-0030
email queries@fairbankliterary.com
website https://fairbankliterary.com
X @FairbankLit
Instagram @FairbankLit
Contacts Sorche Elizabeth Fairbank

Represents literary fiction than commercial. Seeking children's works (picture books and middle grade) by author-illustrators, as well as diverse illustrators of any type. Query by email preferred but accepted by mail as well. For full submission guidelines see website. No genre romance, sci-fi, fantasy, sports fiction, YA, screenplays or childrens unless by an author-illustrator. *Founded* 2002.

Flannery Literary
email jennifer@flanneryliterary.com
website https://flanneryliterary.com
Contact Jennifer Flannery

Specialises in children's and YA, juvenile fiction and non-fiction. *Commission* Home 15%, overseas 20%. Currently closed to submissions. *Founded* 1992.

Folio Literary Management*
The Film Center Building, 630 9th Avenue, Suite 1009, New York, NY 10036
tel +1 212-400-1494
website www.foliolit.com, www.foliojr.com
X @FolioLiterary, @FolioJr
Instagram @folioliterary, @foliojr
Agents Emily Van Beek, John Cusick, Erin Harris, Marcy Posner, Quressa Robinson, Melissa Sarver White, Lauren Spieller, Estelle Laure

Represents both first-time and established authors. Folio Jr is a division of Folio Literary Management devoted exclusively to representing children's book authors and artists. Represents fiction and non-fiction works from picture books through to YA. Consult individual agents' pages on the website for current wish lists and submission guidelines. Submission by email or QueryManager only. Does not represent poetry, plays or screenplays. *Founded* 2006.

Barry Goldblatt Literary
c/o Industrious – Brooklyn, 594 Dean Street, Brooklyn, NY 11238
tel +1 718-832-8787
website http://bgliterary.com
Contact Barry Goldblatt

Represents YA and middle-grade fiction, as well as adult sci-fi and fantasy. Has a preference for quirky, off-beat work. Submission via QueryManager only. No non-fiction. *Founded* 2000.

Irene Goodman Literary Agency*
27 West 24th Street, Suite 804, New York, NY 10010
email irene.queries@irenegoodman.com
website www.irenegoodman.com
Facebook www.facebook.com/IreneGoodmanAgency
X @IGLAbooks
Instagram @iglabooks
Agent Irene Goodman, *Foreign Rights Agents* Danny Baror, Heather Baror-Shapiro

Represents middle-grade and YA books, including fantasy. Also represents commercial fiction with an emphasis on women's voices, romantic novels, historical fiction, mystery, crime and suspense novels. Non-fiction areas of interest include health, business, anything French, Judaica, cookery books, and pop culture. Works in collaboration with the foreign rights agency Baror International who deal with foreign publishers directly. Query by email. For fiction, send query letter and first ten pages of a

Specialising in creating Children's Books
We offer the complete package! From initial ideas, layout design, unique illustrations, character design and logo design. Here at Happydesigner, we do it all!

www.happydesigner.co.uk

Members of:

Society of Children's Book Writers and Illustrators

AOI ASSOCIATION of ILLUSTRATORS

ARVON WRITING COURSES

You are a writer.

EXPERT TUITION TO BRING YOUR WORDS TO LIFE

Follow in the footsteps of Piers Torday, Mark Haddon, and Ciara Smyth and learn from the finest writers at work today

Online and residential courses available. Tutors include Anna Wilson, Ashley Hickson-Lovence, Emma Shevah, MG Leonard, and many more.

Book now arvon.org

---

ciep — Chartered Institute of Editing and Proofreading

Looking for an editor or proofreader?

Search our free online directory of editorial talent. Our members:
- are skilled and experienced
- cover all subjects and genres
- abide by our professional standards.

A reliable source of professional editorial help

@the_ciep | @EditProof | @the-ciep.bsky.social
Linkedin.com/company/the-ciep

ciep.uk

Web Services for Writers & Artists

Website Design
Every author needs a website for books, bio, events, and contact details.

Starting from £50 per month.

SEO
Boost your Google ranking and sell more books with Search Engine Optimisation.

Starting from £175 per month.

www.LoyalWebSolutions.co.uk

team@LoyalWebSolutions.co.uk

Writers & Artists
THE INSIDER GUIDE TO THE MEDIA

www.writersandartists.co.uk

Work through practical exercises and creative prompts to draft, craft and polish your ideas and writing. Transform a desire to write into a joyful writing practice.

> I found this book so valuable – it allowed me to step back and really think about my writing practice. **Louie Stowell**

> Empowering and bursting with kindness, *A Writer's Journal Workbook* is a must-have for writers. **Rashmi Sirdeshpande**

> It's a wonderful warm hug of a book, packed with practical help and inspiring goodness. Just the tonic to boost the moral of any writer. It might (might!) even help me finish this blasted draft! **Chris Callaghan**

The bestselling Writers & Artists brand provides up-to-date, impartial and practical advice on how to write and get published.

Writers & Artists
The essential toolkit on how to publish like a pro

- 2026 Writers' & Artists' Yearbook — RECOMMENDED BY WGGB – THE WRITERS' UNION
- 2026 Children's Writers' & Artists' Yearbook
- The Ultimate Guide to Editing your Novel — Sara Grant
- Poetry Writers' Handbook — Sophia Blackwell
- Guide to Writing for Children and YA (New Edition) — Linda Strachan
- Guide to How to Write — William Ryan
- Guide to How to Hook an Agent — James Rennoldson
- Guide to Getting Published — Alysoun Owen
- The Right Word: A Writer's Toolkit
- The Organised Writer — Antony Johnston

Available from your local bookshop or online at
https://www.writersandartists.co.uk/shop

www.writersandartists.co.uk

BLOOMSBURY PUBLISHING
LONDON · OXFORD · NEW YORK · NEW DELHI · SYDNEY

STORYMIX
THE INCLUSIVE FICTION STUDIO

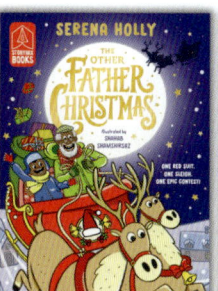 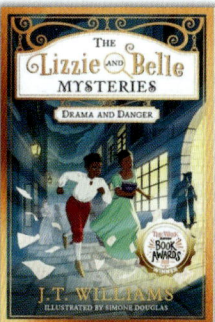  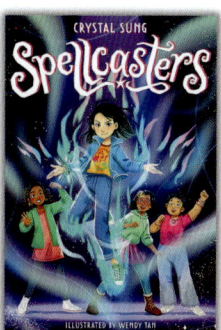

WITH YOUR HELP AND TALENT, STORYMIX CREATES INCLUSIVE CHILDREN'S FICTION FOR PUBLISHERS

WE'RE LOOKING FOR CREATIVES WHO:

- Are keen to write or illustrate for children;
- Can work collaboratively and to a brief;
- Are from a Black, Asian or Minority Ethnic background.

Fewer than 2% of published authors and illustrators in the UK are British people of colour.

Storymix imagines differently.

We work with agented and unagented, published, self-published and unpublished creatives to make heroes for all kids.

STORYMIX.CO.UK

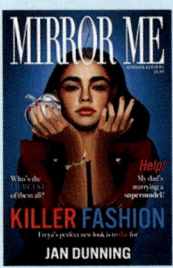 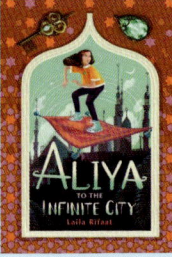 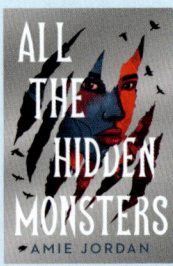 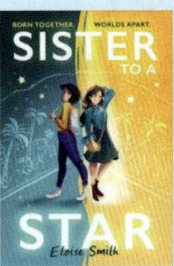 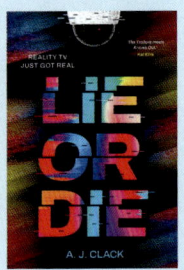

'I want to see everything Golden Egg recommends.'

Barry Cunningham, Publisher, The Chicken House
Discoverer of J K Rowling

Over 120 published and agented authors since 2014.

We are *the* trusted academy for writers of children's books.

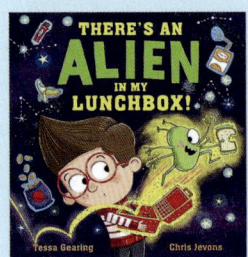 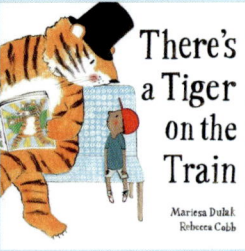 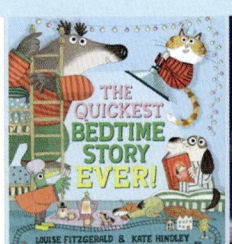 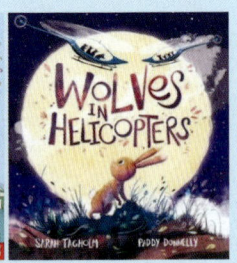

www.goldeneggacademy.co.uk

faber *academy*

Manuscript *Assessment*

Just finished a new draft? Getting ready to submit to agents? Or looking for an honest, professional steer on your work-in-progress? Our experienced readers provide constructive, comprehensive reports to help your manuscript stand out from the crowd.

ook now with the code **WAYB26** to receive a 10% discount

Visit faberacademy.com or call 0207 927 3827

ff

THE WRITING SCHOOL FROM THE
MAJOR LITERARY & TALENT AGENCY

Craft compelling stories for young readers

Raise your writing or illustrating game and get expert advice from top children's authors, literary agents and publishing professionals.

250+ former students with publishing deals

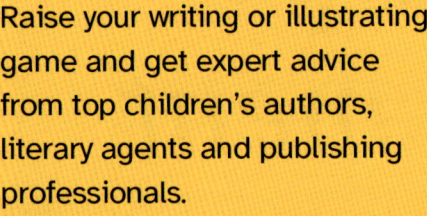

Writing courses
Unleash your imagination and fulfil your potential as a children's writer. Our online courses will help you develop brilliant YA, middle grade fiction or picture books.

Editorial services
Get detailed feedback on your manuscript from a professional editor. Receive tailored advice on how to get the best out of your story and learn what literary agents are looking for.

'The course gave m[e] drive and focus . . . came away confiden[t] and bursting with ideas.'

Clare Harlow
Waterstones Children[s] Book Prize shortliste[d] author of *Tidemagic*

Join our writing community today
www.curtisbrowncreative.co.uk

manuscript. For non-ficton, send a proposal that includes an overview, descriptions of each chapter and comparison titles. Does not represent picture books, poetry or screenplays. *Founded* 1989.

The Greenhouse Literary Agency*
website www.greenhouseliterary.com
Director Chelsea Eberly, *Agent* Kristin Ostby

Children's fiction from picture book authors/ illustrators through to teen/YA. Occasional non-fiction projects and women's fiction will also be considered. Submissions via QueryManager only; see website for submission guidelines. No picture book text unless author illustrates also, poetry, short stories or film scripts.

Authors include Gavin Aung Than, Sarwat Chadda, Winifred Conkling, Andrea Contos, Alexandra Diaz, Bill Doyle, Gabriela Epstein, Theanne Griffith, Michelle Lam, Rebecca Mock, Kelis Rowe, Ali Standish, Emily Thiede, Ngozi Ukazu. *Founded* 2008.

The Joy Harris Literary Agency*
1501 Broadway, Suite 2605, New York, NY 10036
tel +1 212-924-6269
email contact@joyharrisliterary.com
website www.joyharrisliterary.com
X @JoyHarrisAgency
Instagram @joyharrisliterary
Agents Joy Harris, Adam Reed

Represents literary and commercial fiction and non-fiction including narrative non-fiction, biography and memoir. Submissions should be emailed, comprising of a query letter and an outline or sample letter. See website for detailed submission guidelines. No unsolicited manuscripts at this time. Does not currently accept poetry, screenplays, genre fiction or self-help. *Founded* 1990.

John Hawkins & Associates*
80 Maiden Lane, Suite 1005, New York, NY 10038
tel +1 212-807-7040
email jha@jhalit.com
website www.jhalit.com
President Moses Cardona, *Agents* Warren Frazier, Anne Hawkins

Fiction and non-fiction; YA. *Founded* 1893.

HG Literary*
6 West 18th Street, Suite 7R, New York NY 10011
email [firstname]@hgliterary.com
website www.hgliterary.com
X @HGLiterary
Instagram @hgliterary
Partners Carrie Hannigan, Josh Getzler, *Agents* Victoria Wells-Arms, Soumeya Bendimerad Roberts, Wedni Gu, Julia Kardon, Bri Johnson, Jon Cobb, Ellen Goff, Alex Reubert

Represents children's picture books, middle-grade and YA fiction. Represents a variety of both commercial and literary fiction, including women's literature, crime and mystery novels, historical fiction and thrillers. Non-fiction areas of interest include memoir and narrative non-fiction relating to business, current affairs, popular psychology, science, food and select works of photography. Query one agent only by email or QueryManager. For full submission guidelines and agent preferences see website. Does not represent screenplays, romance or religious fiction. *Founded* 2011.

Janklow & Nesbit Associates
285 Madison, 21st Floor, New York, NY 10017
tel +1 212-421-1700
email info@janklow.com
website www.janklowandnesbit.com
Instagram @janklownesbit
President Luke Nesbit

Commercial and literary fiction, and non-fiction. Works in conjunction with Janklow & Nesbit (UK). Submissions: send an informative cover letter, synopsis/outline and the first ten pages. For picture book submissions, include a dummy and at least one full-colour sample. For graphic novels, send ten illustrated pages with text and a synopsis. Address submissions to an individual agent, including your email address to submissions@janklow.com. For postal submissions, a return envelope with sufficient postage for material must be included for your work to be returned. *Founded* 1989.

kt literary*
9249 South Broadway, 200–543, Highlands Ranch, CO 80129
tel +1 720-344-4728
email contact@ktliterary.com
website https://ktliterary.com
Instagram @ktliterary
Agents Kate Testerman, Adria Goetz, Renee Nyen, Kelly Van Sant, Kari Sutherland, Savannah Brooks, Tara Gilbert, Laurel Symonds, Arley Sorg, Maria Napolitano

Representing all ages and genres of fiction, from picture books through adult, and some select non-fiction. Queries are accepted via QueryManager. No postal submissions.

Clients include Maureen Johnson, Stephanie Perkins, Trish Doller, Amy Spalding, Christy Mandin, Saadia Faruqi, S.T. Gibson, Isabel Canas, Jamie Pacton. *Founded* 2008.

Levine Greenberg Rostan Literary Agency*
307 Seventh Avenue, Suite 2407, New York, NY 10001
tel +1 212-337-0934
email submit@lgrliterary.com
website https://lgrliterary.com
X @LGRLiterary
Instagram @lgrlit

Principals Jim Levine, Daniel Greenberg, Stephanie Rostan, *Agents* Sarah Bedingfield, Lindsay Edgecombe, Victoria Skurnick, Kerry Sparks, Danielle Svetcov, Monika Verma, Courtney Paganelli, *Associate Agent* Rebecca Rodd, *Agents-At-Large* Arielle Eckstut

Represents literary and commercial fiction, non-fiction and books for young readers across a diverse range of genres. Submissions via online form.

Gina Maccoby Literary Agency*
PO Box 60, Chappaqua, NY 10514
tel +1 914-238-5760
email query@maccobylit.com
website www.publishersmarketplace.com/members/GinaMaccoby
Contact Gina Maccoby

Looking for high-quality upmarket fiction and non-fiction for adults and children. An engaging narrative voice and strong premise are most important; across all forms the agency is looking for compelling stories and fresh perspectives. Children's: YA and middle grade. Picture books of writer/illustrators only. Non-fiction areas of interest include history, biography, popular science and narrative journalism. No unsolicited submissions. Query first via email. Due to the volume of submissions received, will only reply if interested. *Founded* 1986.

McIntosh & Otis*
235 Main Street, Suite 318, White Plains, NY 10601
tel +1 212-687-7400
email info@mcintoshandotis.com
website https://mcintoshandotis.com
X @McIntoshAndOtis
Head of Children's Department Christa Heschke

Board books, picture books (fiction and non-fiction), fiction for 5–8 and 9–12 years, teenage fiction, series fiction, poetry and non-fiction for children. For children and YA submissions, send a query letter, author bio, synopsis, the first three chapters and any relevant illustrations. Does not represent poetry, screenplays, and original theatrical or dramatic works of any kind. *Founded* 1928.

Jean V. Naggar Literary Agency*
216 East 75th Street, Suite 1E, New York, NY 10021
tel +1 212-794-1082
email jvnla@jvnla.com
website www.jvnla.com
X @JVNLA
Instagram @jvnlainc
President Jennifer Weltz, *Partners* Alice Tasman, Ariana Philips, *Junior Agent* Cole Hildebrand, *Senior Agent and Head of Culinary Division* Sally Ekus

Works in conjunction with foreign and film agents. Commercial and literary fiction, non-fiction (narrative, memoir, journalism, psychology, history, pop culture, humour and culinary), and young readers (picture, middle grade, YA) and illustrators. Submit queries via form on website. *Founded* 1978.

Olswanger Literary*
email anna@olswangerliterary.com
website www.olswanger.com
Instagram @annaolswanger
Contact Anna Olswanger

Specialises in representing author-illustrators of picture books and graphic novels. *Commission* 15% Home, 20% overseas.

Clients have won the Newbery Honor, Asian/Pacific American Honor Award for Literature, Flora Stieglitz Strauss Award for Non-fiction, Orbis Pictus Honor Award, PEN/Steven Kroll Award for Picture Book Writing, Parents' Choice Gold Award, Bank Street College of Education Best Children's Books, Sibert Award Honor, Ezra Jack Keats Award Honor, Sydney Taylor Silver Medal, Boston Globe-Horn Book Nonfiction Honor, International BolognaRagazzi Non-fiction Honor, CCBC Choices and have been Junior Library Guild Selections and on the *New York Times* Bestseller list.

Ayesha Pande Literary
tel +1 212-283-5825
email queries@pandeliterary.com
website www.pandeliterary.com
Facebook www.facebook.com/AyeshaPandeLiterary
X @pande_literary
Instagram @pandeliterary
Agents Ayesha Pande, Serene Hakim, Annie Hwang, Kayla Lightner, Paloma Hernando, *Affiliate Agents* Stephany Evans, Madison Smartt Bell, Luba Ostashevsky, Anne Edelstein

Represents writers and illustrators across fiction and non-fiction, children's and graphic novels. Interested in literary, upmarket and genre fiction. Non-fiction interests include narrative, popular science, health and history. Complete query form on website.

Clients include Danielle Evans, Patricia Engel, Ibram X. Kendi, Peter Rostovsky, Giaae Kwon, Tiffany Jewll, Lisa Ko, Shilip Somaya Gowda, Minda Honey, Russell Shorto. *Founded* 2007.

Alison Picard, Literary Agent
PO Box 2000, Cotuit, MA 02635
tel +1 508-477-7192
email ajpicard@aol.com

Adult fiction and non-fiction, children's and YA. *Commission* Home 15%. Send query via email (no attachments). No short stories, poetry, plays, screenplays or sci-fi and fantasy.

Clients include David Housewright, Caryl Rivers, Jessica Fisher, David Alan Johnson, Susan Froetschel. *Founded* 1985.

Pippin Properties
110 West 40th Street, Suite 1704, New York, NY 10018

tel +1 212-338-9310
email info@pippinproperties.com
website www.pippinproperties.com
Facebook www.facebook.com/pippinproperties
X @LovethePippins
Instagram @pippinproperties
Contacts Holly McGhee

Focuses on children's book authors and artists, including picture books, middle grade, graphic novels and YA novels, and adult trade books on occasion. *Commission* Home 15%, overseas 25%. Query specific agent by email. For authors, include the first chapter and short synopsis, or entire picture book. For illustrators, send a query letter detailing your background in illustration and links to website with a dummy or other examples of your work.
Clients includes Kate DiCamillo, Peter H. Reynolds, Jandy Nelson, Doreen Cronin, Jon Agee, LeUyen Pham, Edel Rodriguez. *Founded* 1998.

Rees Literary Agency
One Westinghouse Plaza, Suite A203, Boston, MA 02136-2075
tel +1 617-227-9014
email [firstname]@reesagency.com
website www.reesagency.com
Instagram @reesagency
Agents Ann Collette, Lorin Rees, Rebecca Podos

Represents literary and commercial fiction, memoirs, history, biography, business, YA and middle grade, self-help, psychology and science. *Commission* Home 15%. See the website for individual agents' submission guidelines. *Founded* 1983.

Rodeen Literary Management
email submissions@rodeenliterary.com
website www.rodeenliterary.com
Facebook www.facebook.com/RodeenLiterary
X @RodeenLiterary
Instagram @rodeenliterary
Contact Paul Rodeen

Open to submissions from writers and illustrators of all genres of children's literature including picture books, early readers, middle-grade fiction and non-fiction, graphic novels, YA fiction and non-fiction. Submit covering letter with synopsis in body of the email and attach the first 50 pages of a novel (authors), a portfolio (illustrators) or a picture book dummy. Not currently seeking authors who exclusively write picture books. *Founded* 2008.

Susan Schulman Literary Agency*
454 West 44th Street, New York, NY 10036
tel +1 212-713-1633
email susan@schulmanagency.com
website www.schulmanagency.com
X @SusanSchulman
Agents Susan Schulman, Emelie Burl, *Foreign Rights* Linda Migalti

Agents for negotiation in all markets (with co-agents) of fiction and general non-fiction; for picture books, middle-grade and YA markets; and associated subsidiary rights including plays, TV adaptation and film. *Commission* Home 15%, UK 7.5%, overseas 20%. Return postage required. Email enquiries to queries@schulmanagency.com.

Stimola Literary Studio*
tel +1 508-696-9351
website www.stimolaliterarystudio.com
President & Founder Rosemary B. Stimola, *Vice President* Peter K Ryan, *Senior Agent* Erica Rand Silverman, *Agents* Adriana Stimola, Allison Hellegers, Allison Remcheck, *Literary Assistant* Hillary Godwin

Children's fiction and non-fiction, from preschool to YA; adult fiction, non-fiction, cookery books, lifestyle and mind, body & spirit. *Commission* Home 15%, overseas 20%. Most clients come via referral. Please refer to website for agent interests and submission guidelines *Founded* 1997.

3 Seas Literary Agency*
PO Box 444, Sun Prairie, WI 53590
tel +1 608-332-3430
website www.threeseasagency.com
Facebook www.facebook.com/profile.php?id=100057827492698#
X @threeseaslit
Agents Michelle Grajkowski, Cori Deyoe, Stacey Graham, Kara Grajkowski, Wynter Graham (sub-rights)

A full-service literary agency representing authors who write romance, women's fiction, sci-fi and fantasy, thrillers, YA and middle-grade fiction, as well as select non-fiction titles and picture books. Submission through QueryManager only. See individual agent pages for preferences. Will only reply if interested in your work. *Founded* 2000.

Trident Media Group
355 Lexington Avenue, 12th Floor, New York, NY 10017
tel +1 212-333-1511
email info@tridentmediagroup.com
website www.tridentmediagroup.com
Facebook www.facebook.com/TridentMediaGroup
X @Trident_Media
Instagram @trident_media

Adult and children's fiction and non-fiction across a variety of genres. *Commission* Home 15%, overseas 20-25%, in conjunction with co-agents/theatre/films/TV 15%. Will suggest revision. Query one agent via online form. Writing sample on request. *Founded* 2000.

Upstart Crow Literary
594 Dean Street, Office 47, Brooklyn, NY 11238
website www.upstartcrowliterary.com
Instagram @upstartcrowliterary
Agents Danielle Chiotti, Kayla Cichello, Susan Hawk, Ted Malawer, Alexandra Penfold, Michael Stearns

Adult fiction, non-fiction and children's books (picture books, chapter books, middle grade and YA). Currently seeking adult upmarket commercial and literary fiction, and non-fiction which covers narrative, memoir, lifestyle, relationships, humour, current events, food, wine and cookery. For children's, all genres are welcome. Submissions vary by agent; consult website for details. *Founded* 2009.

Caroline Wakeman Literary Agency
31 Hudson Yards, 11th Floor, New York, NY 10001
email submissions@carolinewakeman.com
27 Old Gloucester Street, London WC1N 3AX
tel 020-7046 9416
website www.carolinewakeman.com
Instagram @carolinewakemanliterary
Ceo Caroline Wakeman, *Senior Sales Agent* Kate Johnson, *Sales Agents* Mike Cowley, Flora Rees-Arredondo, *Executive Assistant* Milly England

An international agency with a focus on picture, chapter and non-fiction books. Represents children's fiction and non-fiction from picture books to YA, and author-illustrators. Works closely with authors on their storylines to ensure they stand the best chance of being selected by a publisher. Also offers a range of editorial services from proof-reading to project managing. *Commission* Home/overseas 22%. Email in first instance to introduce yourself and your work. Tends to work with published authors, however opens submissions from non-published authors several times throughout the year, announced via social media. Picture books: send the full manuscript in a Word document without artwork. Chapter books: send a synopsis and the first three chapters in Word. No submissions by post. Does not accept previously self-published work. *Founded* 2019.

WME
11 Madison Avenue, 18th Floor, New York, NY 10010
tel +1 212-586-5100
website https://wmebookdepartment.com
X @wmebooks
Instagram @wmebooks

Worldwide talent and literary agency with offices in New York, Beverly Hills, Nashville, Washington, Sydney and London. Represents bestselling authors, critically acclaimed literary writers, award-winning thought leaders and up-and-coming talent. *Founded* 1898.

Writers House*
120 Broadway, 22nd floor, New York, NY 10271
tel +1 212-685-2400
7660 Fay Avenue, #338H, La Jolla, CA 92037
email info@writershouse.com
website www.writershouse.com
President Simon Lipskar

Fiction and non-fiction for adults and children, including illustrators and film/TV rights. Represents literary and commercial fiction, women's fiction, sci-fi and fantasy, narrative non-fiction, history, memoirs, biographies, psychology, science, parenting, cookery books, how-to, self-help, business, finance, YA and juvenile fiction/non-fiction and picture books. Send a query letter, a synopsis and ten pages of the MS addressed to one agent; email preferred. Does not represent original screenplays. *Founded* 1973.

Illustration
Pitching your work to an illustration agent

A good agent can be a true champion of your work and help you reach your creative potential. In this article, Anna Zieger explains the role of the illustration agency in that journey.

Introduction

I would like to think that I still remember leafing clumsily through my first children's anthology of *Grimms' Fairy Tales* when I was only a few years old. What I know for a fact is that it was a beautifully illustrated edition: still one of my most prized possessions, it is now to be found in its special place on my parents' bookshelf in rural Germany. I was too young to read the text on my own at the time – which may have been a blessing, as the original versions of our beloved fairy stories can be quite dark – but I didn't need to. The beautiful illustrations managed to bring these timeless tales to life on their own.

Jump to over a decade later, when I applied for an internship at the Bright Agency in London. For seven months, I was immersed in working for one of the most exciting businesses in publishing, learning from awe-inspiring professionals. After returning to Germany to finish my degree in Media and English, I returned to the UK seven years later during the COVID-19 pandemic and eventually found my way back to Bright, this time as an agent. After having worked on and guided my artists through numerous projects over the past few years in almost every division of children's publishing, I am now writing this article to help guide and demystify some of the processes behind illustration agencies and how we work.

The Bright Agency

Fuelled by the desire to create an inspiring space for artists to grow and create their best work, our Ceo and Creative Director, Vicki Willden-Lebrecht, founded The Bright Agency in 2003. Over the years, the company has grown internationally, championing some of the brightest talent in the industry.

I feel very lucky to be part of a team of incredibly passionate professionals who love what they do and are immensely proud of the work they help to create. There is nothing quite like walking into your local bookshop and seeing all of the wonderful books created by the talent of your hard-working artists. At Bright, we champion a variety of talent, managed by specialists in each of their respective fields, and although children's publishing has always been the core of the company, we have expanded over the years to categories such as licensing, design & advertising, greetings & gifts, and literary, just to name a few. Our offices are based in Clapham Junction and New Jersey, and we are proud to say that we work with artists and clients from all around the world.

What is an illustration agent, and what can they do for you?

Put simply, an agent is a champion of your work and your career. We help you navigate the (at times) turbulent waters of the publishing industry and guide you to where you want to go. Maybe you want to become a bestselling children's book illustrator/author or work on exciting advertising projects for large brands. As an agency, we also help develop your portfolio and connect you with the right publishers. We specialise in networking and take care to represent your work in the most professional and efficient way to clients.

We also support you with the more practical side of the commissioning process, which leads me to three very important additional services that an agency can provide. First, legal matters. Navigating an industry as large as publishing without a fundamental knowledge and experience of publishing contracts can be difficult. Specialists in the legal issues common in the publishing world, agencies help with contract negotiations and related matters. As an agency, we are also passionate about being at the forefront of (sometimes) controversial industry developments, making sure that our artist's work is protected. Agencies can also help with authors' financial concerns. This includes credit controlling and making sure payments are received regularly and on time. Lastly, our incredible team of in-house marketing and design specialists also create wonderful content, sharing and shouting about your work on the right channels. We also provide portfolio services, creating curated artwork selections for fairs and meetings.

Curating your portfolio
Something that we like to see in a portfolio is a consistent style. I'm not saying in any way that you should limit your work to one area of illustration/design only. However, if you are looking for work in picture books, we want to see that your artwork can match industry standards and have a consistent, commercially viable, unique style. Think of it this way: if a publisher is looking for the perfect artist for their picture book project, they will want reassurance that they will receive artwork in line with what they have commissioned. We need to see that you can work on an entire project in one style. Of course, you can diversify your portfolio, but keep each section market-specific. This is helpful to keep in mind when you are building an online presence. Curating your website is one way of making sure potential clients and agents are directed to the appropriate section of your portfolio for them. Also, take time to think about yourself and your brand. What is it that makes you special?

There are a few topics that will never go out of fashion – think animals, children, dragons, vehicles and fairy tales. When adding pieces to your portfolio, consider taking your characters further and creating scenes, showing interactions between characters, and most importantly, creating emotion! Also, consider producing beautiful work to complement non-fiction writing, which can be equally as rich in its storytelling as fiction work.

If you are feeling a little lost, look around your local bookshop. When doing so, keep the following questions in mind: What types of books would I like to be working on? What types of books do I enjoy reading and what makes them special? What are the current trends? How could my work fit alongside already established artists?

Submitting your work
Submissions can be a scary thing, but I hope that the following will make the process a little more accessible. First and foremost, do your research! Look at all the different agencies out there and what they have to offer. Every agency has different strengths and often a slightly different focus within the industry. Once you have chosen an agency to apply to, go to their website and find out as much as you can about them, including the types of artists they represent, the projects they work on, and more.

And then, most importantly, check their submission guidelines properly! A well-curated portfolio that is presented according to the individual agency's guidelines will take you one step closer to catching someone's eye. It helps to be patient, as it can take some time for a portfolio to be reviewed and for you to get a response. Agencies often receive a large number of submissions, but that doesn't mean that submissions get overlooked – on the contrary! Every agency is keen to find strong new talent, and submissions are one of the best ways to do so.

Only the beginning

Securing an agent doesn't mean you get to rest on your laurels: it's when the real work begins! It is very important to keep developing and honing your craft. With every illustration and every project that you work on, you will get better and expand your talent. As an agency, we value development very highly and pride ourselves on our continuous work with our artists, making sure to provide constructive feedback and ongoing evaluation of their work. Since we operate in the heart of the publishing industry, we are always informed about new trends and developments in that world and are at the forefront of any market developments.

Publishing is a beautiful thing, but it can be a very demanding industry. An agent can help guide you through its turbulent waters, but to succeed, you need to show dedication and a positive attitude towards your work. One of our principal goals to secure for our clients projects that will help them build relationships with key contacts in the publishing world. Showing up with a positive attitude and a strong work ethic can go a long way when it comes to strengthening those relationships. If a publisher knows they can count on you, they are more likely to want to work with you again – it can be as simple as that! As agents, we are always on your side and try to help you wherever possible, but ultimately it is you that needs to show up and create the work. Again, as wonderful as it is, publishing is still an industry.

The most important person

I touched on this earlier in the article, but I cannot stress enough how important it is for you to think about what you are looking to gain from your time in the publishing industry. Where do you want to go, what do you want to achieve, and how do you think an agent will be able to help you get to where you want to go? Working with an agent is a partnership based on mutual trust and respect. Communication is key and can start as early as telling your agent exactly what you are looking for from your career and your professional goals. A first conversation can be a great way for you to decide if an agent is the right fit for you!

I hope this article has demystified some of the mechanisms behind agency work and has highlighted the benefits of working with an agent. Building your portfolio is an exciting time, and there are wonderful opportunities out there! Get ready to make your mark on the industry; we can't wait to see your work.

Anna Zieger joined the children's illustration team at The Bright Agency in 2021, and works with a wide range of artists and projects. For more information, visit: https://thebrightagency.com/uk.

Picture books: the illustrator's story

Illustrated children's books are some the great joys of the publishing world. Creating them, though, involves a lot of hard graft, tenacity and resilience. In this article, Siân Roberts tells us her tale of illustration success.

A bit about me

I've been working as a children's book illustrator since 2019. My debut picture book published in 2021 and I have since had the opportunity to work with multiple wonderful authors and publishers on stories ranging from pirate princesses to sparkling unicorns, dancing dinosaurs to creepy crawlies. I have now worked on over 30 books including the *Don't Disturb* series with Rhiannon Findlay (Puffin Books), *Kindness Comes Back* with Sital Gorasia Chapman (Farshore Books) and the early reader *Bug Tales* (Usborne). Very excitingly, my debut picture book, *Never Mess with a Pirate Princess* (Little Tiger Press), written by Holly Ryan, was chosen to be read by Rachel Zegler on *Cbeebies Bedtime Story* in March 2025.

Starting out

My route to illustration started during a foundation course in Art and Design where I focused on visual communication. Seeing how my work naturally leant itself towards children's illustrations, I went on to study illustration at university, which meant I was able to dedicate a big chunk of time to working on my drawing abilities and developing my own style. It was also beneficial to study other artists and how they use colour, composition and characters to tell a story.

My final project was creating my own (somewhat rough) picture book, which I enjoyed enormously. Keen to get into the industry, after graduating I took on a part-time job as a teaching assistant, which allowed me the time to continue developing my illustration portfolio alongside getting some paid work. I also created an Etsy shop, setting up an account to sell different designs for Christmas cards and nursery pieces, doing my best to keep in mind what artwork could be used for both sales and my growing portfolio.

Finding an agent

I soon decided that having an illustration agent would be the best route to go for my career. An agent can allow you to dedicate more time to your work instead of spending your time sourcing and contacting potential clients or stressing over contract details and fees! They will also be industry experts, so full of helpful insights into the publishing world.

Do research the different agencies out there: things to consider could be how many artists they represent, what kind of work their artists get, the range of styles they represent and what commission they take per job.

I approached The Plum Agency in 2019 with my portfolio, which included a mix of university work alongside some newer pieces I had put together: in hindsight, these had been created far too quickly without much thought behind the characters and settings within them, and unsurprisingly my work wasn't ready yet. Luckily for me, though, they could see some potential, and as I didn't live too far from their offices, they invited me in for a chat where we discussed my work and I was told to keep in touch. I would recommend trying to get all the feedback you can when it comes to any agent or client rejections: it all helps to move you forward, so do your best not to feel too disheartened!

Portfolio reviews/Bologna Children's Book Fair

So off I went to work on some new portfolio pieces as well as organising to attend the Bologna Children's Book Fair that year. I wanted to fully dive into the world of children's publishing and get a feel for what it's all about. That said, once at the Fair it all felt hugely overwhelming, to the point where my friend and I had to sit down with a coffee and a pastry within the first five minutes to comprehend the size of it all. With no meetings booked (which was perhaps an oversight from us), we headed to the open portfolio reviews where we queued up for hours at a time alongside many other aspiring illustrators, to have what was a very quick review from whichever publishers would see us that day. Maybe it wasn't the greatest use of our time but we still managed to get some feedback on our work from the experts, which felt well worth it. For myself, perhaps more importantly, I popped my head round the Plum Agency's stand to show my face again where Mark, the agency director, kindly agreed to look at my portfolio for a second time. Unfortunately the work still wasn't quite ready for representation and I was sent away again but with some helpful pointers on where to improve – and some optimism!

Back in the UK and still trying to get my work up to industry standard, I tried a couple of new things. The AOI (The Association of Illustrators) is a great source of industry advice and also offers its members portfolio reviews. I got myself signed up for a review in London which I found really helpful; it opened my eyes to how I might have focused too much on getting an agent rather than looking into what clients were out there and who I wanted to work for. Focusing solely on book publishers meant I hadn't considered other aspects of print, such as children's magazines.

Online course

I also made the decision to enrol in the online course for illustrating children's books, Make Art That Sells (MATS). This was a big turning point for my portfolio work and I would highly recommend investing in the course if you can, or finding a similar one with a good structure to follow if you feel your portfolio needs a kick-start or update for picture-book work.

From that course I learnt that it's key to show your ability to draw the same character with multiple expressions and in a variety of different poses. For example, you have to able to show them being extremely happy, jumping for joy, as well as looking tired and cosily curled up in a ball. Taking the time to create character sheets full of all of these different sketches before rushing into a full spread is a great way to build your character and their world fully. It also mirrors how you would work on a picture book project in real life. You work on the characters first, thinking of their personality, what type of outfit would they wear, what items are poking out of their backpack, whether or not their shoes are brand new or worn and muddy, and so on. And you need to do all that before you start to look at the environment and scenes they'll be in.

Enjoying the artwork you create

This is something that was really pushed during the course and it's stayed with me ever since. It's so important to have fun creating your portfolio pieces and personal work as first of all, that's the style and area of work you will then get commissioned for, and second, if you enjoy creating the artwork, the audience will enjoy looking at it. I find my best spreads now are the ones that I've had the most fun with.

Internship
In an attempt to get as much feedback and insight into the world of children's books, I also applied for internships at different publishers, ending up with having a month's work at Walker Books. Unfortunately they didn't have anything to offer within the design department, but I took a role within the lovely PR team, spending my days sending out posters, books and marketing materials. It was great to get that experience working within the publishing world, surrounded by children's books, and even though I didn't work directly alongside any of the design team, they did take the time to meet with me and look through my work, letting me know of any areas I could improve on. I remember being reassured that the work you see in published books is always a big team effort, which will have had numerous rounds of feedback and revisions with inputs from designers to sales teams. When starting out your portfolio doesn't need to be perfect and completely match what you can see out there, you just need to show the art directors that you have the potential to get there.

It was then, with my newly updated portfolio, that I sent another email to Plum, who at this point after all the various meetings and messages, offered to represent me as one of their illustrators. I've been with them ever since!

Early professional work
My first professional projects were with clients such as children's magazines and educational publishers. These jobs were shorter in length, such as a few illustrations to run alongside poems or texts. These were a good step into the world of children's publishing and gave me experience of working with designers to briefs and deadlines. I then worked on a text within a compilation book of different animal stories, where each story had a different artist. Again this was a good step into the picture book world without the pressure of being the sole illustrator and on the cover. After that, I landed my first solo illustrator project, where I worked on *Never Mess with a Pirate Princess*, written by Holly Ryan and published by Little Tiger Books. My main work is now illustrating colourful and fun picture books whilst also working on board books, early reader books and I have just started work on a middle-grade title, too (for which I had to create new black-and-white portfolio work recently).

Picture book commissions
When being commissioned for picture books, you may be asked to work on a sample to begin with. It can be good to give a few variations if possible to show how you would take on the project or character in your style whilst following your brief.

Always remember your audience. Picture books are mostly aimed at three to six year-olds, so you want your work to be engaging for them and their adults who are reading the stories. As well as portraying the author's text, I love to think about the little details within a scene that might not be spotted the first time round. It's nice to think that the audience can enjoy spotting something new with each read and have fun spending time delving into each spread.

Composition
Creating a picture book has multiple stages. It starts with thumbnail artwork (small sketches of each spread to get an idea of how the composition could look), to the roughs (black-and-white sketches of each spread in more detail and to scale) to the final colour

artwork, with feedback and revisions given at each stage. From the start it's important to keep in mind where the text is going to fit on the page and how the illustration will sit around it. The text will most likely be black on the page so try to avoid dark colours or any details from sitting behind it. You may also want to consider leaving extra space around the text for potential foreign editions, where the story will be translated into a different language and therefore could take up more room on the page.

When making a book, the author will work with the editor on the text and the illustrator will work with the designer who provides the artwork briefs. Having a call with the design team is a great way to generate ideas together and to discuss feedback. Considering freelance illustration can be quite solitary, it's always nice to speak to another human wherever possible.

Once your new work has been published, it's a great idea to get that added into your portfolio straight away to keep it fresh and up to date, ready to be shared with more potential clients. You will also find that the more work you create, the more your style will naturally develop, so keeping your portfolio in line with your newest work is ideal. I'd also regularly clear out older work that you're less keen on or have moved away from. As mentioned earlier, whatever is in your portfolio is what you will be commissioned for, so make sure it's the work you want to create!

Hopefully my journey into the publishing world shows you that rejection is often part of the process. However, keeping optimistic, being keen to improve and unafraid to approach the same client or agency more than once could be what you need to kick-start your career in this creative industry.

My own process

When creating artwork for picture books, I will start off more traditionally with initial sketches on paper. I find this helpful with idea generation and a nice change from looking at a screen.

Next, I work from my iPad on the app Procreate before sending this work onto Photoshop, where I piece together the spreads and make adjustments to the colour, adding extra highlights and shadows and playing around with the composition before I'm happy to send it off to the designer for feedback. It's so much fun to bring an author's text to life and to see it come together with the designer's layouts. Seeing your work in print is a lovely, tangible element to the job that never gets old.

Siân Roberts is an illustrator based in the South-East of England. She has worked with some of the UK's leading children's publishers. She has most recently illustrated (all published in 2025): *Bug Tales and The Exceedingly Greedy Centipede* for Usborne, *My Best Friend is an Otter* and *My Best Friend is a Turtle* for Priddy Books, and *Do NOT Eat the Egg* for Scholastic. For more information go to https://sian-roberts.com and follow her on Instagram @sianrobertsillustration.

Picture books: the writer's story

Given they are the first books most of us come across, picture books play a vital role in children's publishing and readers' lives. In this article, Sital Gorasia Chapman explains how her writing journey started.

I fell in love with picture books when I started reading them to my then six-month-old daughter in 2014. I picked up a copy of *Giraffes Can't Dance* by Giles Andreae and Guy Parker-Rees at a children's centre. It was unlike anything I'd read before. The words flowed off the page and the pictures literally danced. I could totally identify with Gerald the Giraffe and his story warmed my heart. I immediately bought a copy when we got home and I read it over and over to my daughter. It was a joy to read out loud and even though my daughter was too young to understand the words, she could feel my joy and was excited by my excitement! It was the beginning of her love for books. This is what a good picture book can do. We soon filled up our bookshelf with lots of other amazing books (mostly rhyming) that had the same effect.

I had no idea at this point that I would one day write my own. It had never crossed my mind that I could be a writer. As a child, I read loads. I escaped into books. I wrote my own stories and poems and imagined all kinds of exciting adventures in my head. But as I grew up and became a responsible adult, that's where the stories stayed, locked somewhere in the back of my brain.

I got a sensible job, working in a bank, where I stayed for far too many years until I eventually left to become a yoga teacher and mum. I have three daughters and they were all terrible sleepers, nodding off only if they were in my arms. I spent many hours stuck on the sofa with a slumbering child. It was during one of these naps in 2019, when my youngest was a few months old, that some words bubbled out from my brain and I wrote them down in the Notes app on my phone with my one free hand. It was the first creative thing I had written as a grown-up. It came out in rhyme and I thought maybe it could make a good picture book. But I had no idea how to make that happen. I couldn't even draw.

Luckily after a bit of online research, I realised I didn't have to draw the pictures myself. Phew! I could just write the words. I also found the FAB Prize (see page 337) and the timing couldn't have been more perfect. The deadline was the following day. I entered my story, titled 'The Tantrum', and hoped for the best. If I'd had more time to think about it (and had been a little less sleep-deprived), I might have talked myself out of entering but I'm so glad I didn't.

I wrote more stories and enrolled in a picture book writing course at City Lit which I would highly recommend. I learnt so much, including how to structure a picture book manuscript (not the way I did for my entry to the FAB Prize! oh well …) and how to submit to agents. I joined SCBWI (Society for Children's Book Writers and Illustrators) and bought a copy of the *Children's Writers' & Artists' Yearbook*. I absorbed all the advice and made a list of the agents I'd like to submit to.

Then out of the blue, I received an email to say my entry to the FAB Prize had been commended. Although I didn't win, my story was shared with lots of agents and a few days later, two of them got in touch. I signed with my dream agent, Becky Bagnell (who was top of my agent list).

I realise how lucky I am to have bypassed the slush pile, but my story isn't that unusual. I saw a chance to get my work seen and I took it. And it changed my life. There are many competitions and opportunities to get your work in front of an agent or editor. Take every opportunity you can to get your work out there. You never know what will come of it.

Some tips to get started
Read, read, read
To write a good picture book, you have to really know (and love) picture books. I read hundreds before I ever attempted to write one of my own. I got to know what I liked and what I didn't.

Read the books you loved as a child. Are they still as good as you remember? Look at the most recently published books and see what's changed. Visit a bookshop and see what's on the shelves. Which books appeal to you? Join your local library and borrow books (it benefits the creators too). Examine the books closely. Pay attention to how the books are laid out over the pages and where the page turns are. How does the text work with the illustrations?

Picture books are meant to be read out loud, so try reading them that way. If you can, read with a child. It's really interesting to see how they react to a story. Often they notice things you don't.

The more books you read, the more you'll internalise what makes a story work.

Practise. A lot
Picture books are short, usually no more than 500 words, but that doesn't make them easy to write. They have to do a lot in those few words. Every word matters. I sometimes take all day to find that one perfect word that fits the story.

Like any skill, though, writing gets better with practice. The first story I wrote and submitted to the FAB Prize got attention because there was something in it, but it wasn't ready to be a picture book and it never became one. I wrote many more stories before I sold one. My writing improved with time and practice. So write lots and work on improving your craft.

But don't feel that you have to spend all of your writing time physically chained to a desk. I do a lot of 'writing' in my head as I go about my day, especially when I'm out walking. I find being outside and the rhythmic movement of my footsteps helps me to untangle my thoughts and solve story problems much more effectively than just staring at a screen. Find creative ways to add writing into your day.

Know who you're writing for
It's important to keep in mind the age you are writing for. Picture books are usually aimed at children aged three to five. Try to think like a child and see things through their eyes. What does the world look like when you're that little? Read books on child development. Watch kids' TV shows. And if you can, spend time with children. It's the best way to see how they interact with the world and with each other. Find out what fascinates them, what frightens them, what frustrates them. My kids are an endless source of story ideas. Every day is full of drama.

But picture books are not (usually) read by the child themselves. They are read to the child. So try to write a story that appeals to the child, but keep in mind the grownup that will be reading it (hopefully over and over!).

Leave space for the pictures

One of the great things about picture books is that the words don't have to do all the work. Half the story is in the illustrations. When you're writing the text, think about what the illustrations can add. Include some illustration notes with your manuscript. I don't put in too many, but I might give some ideas about how I imagine a scene to look, especially where it's different to the text.

You don't need to include long, detailed descriptions in the text itself when the pictures can do it for you. Leave space for the illustrator to work their magic.

I've been really lucky to work with some very talented illustrators who have brought my words to life with beautiful art. But what I didn't know before I started writing was that the author and the illustrator (whose names are right next to each other on the front cover) rarely ever meet. In fact, I've only met one of the illustrators who I've worked with, and that was after the book was published.

So how does it work? A picture book is a team effort. The author writes a story and works with an editor to make the words the best they can be. Then an art director works with the illustrator to create the pictures and lay out the finished book. There might be some back and forth, but the author and illustrator don't speak directly. The illustrator is free to put their own creative stamp on the book without too much interference from the author.

That doesn't mean the author has no input into the illustrations. I've always been asked for my opinion at each stage of the process. I've made very few comments, though, that haven't been something like 'I love it!' But when I have asked for a minor change, it has been taken on board.

Publishers don't choose the illustrator at random; they are selected carefully to suit the book. When I first saw the artwork for *The Bedtime Boat* (illustrated by Anastasia Suvorova), it had the exact dreamy feel that I had hoped for. Some of the scenes were different to how I had pictured them, but worked really well.

Sometimes illustrators might add little surprises that aren't in the text. In *Little Spruce*, Vicky Lommatzsch added a hidden mouse on each page with its own story – exactly the kind of detail that kids love.

Sometimes the illustrations might result in a change in the text. In *Kindness Comes Back* (illustrated by Siân Roberts), the lion's evening stroll became a morning stroll – a minor change that made the whole story flow better.

I love seeing see how the illustrator interprets the story and getting that first look of my words in pictures is like being given a very special gift.

Be patient

Publishing a picture book is a long process. On average it takes roughly two years from signing a contract to seeing the book on a bookshelf. And that's not including the time it takes to write the book in the first place, find an agent and sell it to a publisher. There is a lot of waiting and a lot of patience is required.

Sometimes I can write a story in a weekend, but usually it takes much longer. The idea for *Little Spruce* came to me years before I actually knew what the story would be. Sometimes an idea needs time to brew. Make a note of ideas as they come and if you get stuck on a story, put it away for a bit and work on something else.

Although I was lucky to find an agent quite quickly, getting the first publishing deal took a very long time. A lot of stories that I wrote (and my agent loved) were rejected by publishers. It can be disheartening, but don't give up. As soon I send something out for submission, I don't wait for a response; I begin working on something new. I'm always creating.

Get to know other writers

Children's writers and illustrators are the most supportive people and I've made some wonderful friends through SCBWI. It's great to hang out with people who love children's books as much as you do, who can celebrate with you when things go well and lift you up when things don't. And just keep you company while you're waiting!

Have fun

My most important tip of all is to enjoy yourself. Have fun with your writing and enjoy the process. I love playing with words and creating something new that didn't exist before.

Sital Gorasia Chapman is the author of 14 books for children including *The Bedtime Boat* (Farshore 2023), which was shortlisted for *The Week Junior* Book Awards 2024, *Celebrations and Festivals: Diwali* (Quarto 2024), which has been longlisted for the SLA Information Book Awards 2025, *Little Spruce* (Sweet Cherry 2024), which was featured on *CBeebies Bedtime Story*, *Kindness Comes Back* (Farshore 2024) and *The Maths Adventurers* series (DK 2023–25). For more information, see www.sitalgorasiachapman.com or follow her on Instagram @sital_gorasia_chapman.

How to become a book illustrator: Q&A with Dapo Adeola

Getting started in any industry is challenging, and publishing is harder than most. Here, award-winning illustrator Dapo Adeola explains how he set out on his path.

So, I'm gonna admit I was a bit surprised when I was asked to write this article. I've only been an illustrator for 5 years and I still feel like I've only just got started; there's still so much to learn. But I can share what I've learned on my journey so far, and hopefully that'll help anyone looking to get started on their own.

Starting out: when did you know you wanted to be a book illustrator? What training and experience do you have and do you think it is necessary to follow this career?

I've always known I wanted to be an illustrator; I just didn't actually know what an illustrator was. Growing up, I loved reading and would spend days and days lost in a book, especially Roald Dahl books containing Quentin Blake's artwork and the *Redwall* books by Brian Jacques. This was the first time I remember feeling like I was seeing something magical happen on the page. That, coupled with my love of Saturday-morning cartoons, comics and Nintendo and Sega video games, was enough to make it so that there was nothing else I wanted to do than draw all these characters every day.

This love for the visual media I was consuming was enough to carry me through early education up until A level, and then everything suddenly became very serious and I wasn't having fun anymore.

People are often surprised when I tell them I'm an academic failure on account of failing A level Art & Design, Graphic Design and later on my BA in Graphic Design and Advertising.

At the time I thought it was a 'me' problem, as admittedly I found it really hard to focus as a student, but I've since come to understand it's a problem with the way some creative courses are taught in academia.

It might have changed since, but the arts weren't taught in a way that was fun when I was a student. The need to keep and feed the love for your craft while working wasn't covered at all; instead we were told nightmare stories about how hard it is to thrive in the creative arts. Looking back, I think my lecturers were jaded, to be honest.

While I learned a lot in higher education, I learned infinitely more when I started working as a freelancer and cobbling together my own education in illustration. I made use of any free and affordable online or offline resources I could get my hands on and followed a ton of artists on social media for insights into their process and nuggets about the industry.

I also started building a library of picture books which became my most valuable resource for learning that particular field of illustration. I can't recommend that particular approach enough: there's no better teacher than the actual product you want to make, to show you how it's done well.

I studied books from my fave authors and illustrators and the works of those who were at the top of the industry, to learn about how they structured their stories and composed their illustrations. This is something I still do today, and probably will always do.

I was never trying to reinvent the wheel with my work, but wanted to learn how to do it at a really high standard. Any innovations that come from me are more of a result of this process than any intention of being innovative.

Routes to success: How did you get your portfolio under the noses of publishers and agents?

My route to success was an unorthodox one. I wasn't actually trying to get into the children's book industry when my agent found me. I didn't even have a website at the time. I had started putting my work out on social media, though, and built a small following over a few years as I documented my journey as an aspiring illustrator.

It was during this period that my friend Nathan Bryon approached me to design the character that would go on to pave the way for my success in the publishing world – Rocket.

Nathan took my work to his literary agent who, upon seeing my art, immediately asked for an introduction and proceeded to sign me up straightaway. She then took my artwork in pitch form to the Bologna Children's Book Fair, and everything went crazy from there.

So in a way, my first book proposal ended up being the portfolio that got me through the door. This is not how I'd advise anybody to do things, though: I was extremely fortunate. Most agents will want to see a portfolio of work that demonstrates your knowledge of the craft and ability to work to a high standard.

My tips for a good portfolio:
• Show your range across at least three of the different age groups that can be found in children's publishing. Examples of these are preschool titles, picture books, early readers chapter books, middle grade and YA.
• A well-rounded portfolio should have strong examples of character design, thumb-nailing and planning, as well as finished artwork and some book cover examples to round things off nicely. This'll show that you can execute a brief for a book from cover to cover.
• I'd also recommend using classic stories that are already well established as your source material if you don't have any stories of your own to get you started. This is really smart way of showing *your* unique take on something people are already familiar with. Try to show your range in these drawings too. You should have a mix of character designs and explorations as well as fully illustrated scenes and spot illustrations. This is your chance to show that you can do the full job.
• And my final tip is to put out the kind of work you want to come back to you. By this I mean make sure your portfolio contains examples of the kind of art and subject matter you want to actually work on for a living. There's no point in having a portfolio that's full of the kind of art you wouldn't be happy working long hours on.

Getting the call: how do you work with publishers and authors? Are you commissioned or do you send in unsolicited submissions?

Working with a publisher took a bit of getting used to.

I'd become so accustomed to working on my own that it took me a long time to get comfortable working with an editor and designer. Now, though, I feel the difference in the way I work when I don't have a team to bounce things off.

It's definitely possible to make children's books on your own, but working with a team really frees you up to focus on the more creative aspects of the work, as a good team will help you by staying on top of the bigger picture aspects of any project.

As a rule, I tend not to take unsolicited commisions that don't come through the proper or preferred channels, as more often than not they're badly organised and don't pay nearly enough for me to live on while I work. The commissions and book texts I get come to my agent via various publishers, before making their way onto my desk. A great tip I have for choosing a text is to be aware of whether the drawings are literally forming in your head while you read it: if this happens, then you're probably onto a winner.

I've been very fortunate to work with some amazing authors and illustrators so far in my career. Each of them has been awesome at leaving room for me to bring something of myself to the project in the form of my words or drawings. This is another important part of my process. Whether you're drawing or writing, when it comes to collaboration, no one person's contribution is more or less important than the others.

When you're doing two roles – writing and illustrating – what are the benefits and challenges?

There's definitely a massive benefit to being able to draw *and* write your own stories. Amongst other things, this means you don't have to wait on anyone before you can come up with and conceptualise your own ideas and stories. If you play your cards right, it also means you'll almost always have work.

The pros of writing and illustrating your own stories is the control you have over the decision-making in the narrative direction and visual style of the work. My advice would be to map things out and explore as much as possible before you take things to pitch, because it's much trickier to do all of that once the book has been sold to a publisher.

The drawbacks of writing and drawing your own stories is the amount of work involved and the responsibility for it all being solely on your shoulders. Working with another talent gives you someone to bounce ideas off as well as someone to share the workload. It does mean less control and more compromise, but it's worth it when the creative chemistry is just right.

Specialising or not: what are the positive points and your pet hates?

I'm definitely one for specialising, if only to learn everything you can about a specific field before moving on and growing in another direction. I honestly feel like it's a disservice to the craft of storytelling if you hop around willy-nilly from one side of it to another. By all means explore til you find what fits, but when you do find it, try and take some time to really get the hang of it as best as you can before moving on

What should those starting out as illustrators look out for? What are your top tips: what to do and what to avoid?

The most important thing to avoid is exploitation. Never work for free for anyone … EVER. You're much better off developing your own ideas and stories if that's the case. Learn as much as you can about the business side of things. Make sure you know about:
- What are the market rates for various jobs?
- What are the contractual obligations?
- How is your work going to be used?
- Do you own the work?
- Will you be paid a royalty?

Don't be afraid to talk about the money, and if you're met by anyone who is afraid to have those conversations, that's usually a bad sign. These days, it seems like the world is trying to exploit creativity, so try your best not to make it easy for anyone to do that to you.

Your next book: what are you working on now?

I'm currently learning about different writing forms and ways of telling stories in preparation for this next stage of my career. I want to write stories for myself and other artists to illustrate, that challenge me and allow me to express a range of different things. My next set of books will be a much longer form of storytelling and I can't wait to explore the new worlds and characters within them.

I'm going to close this off with what's probably the most important lesson I've learned so far. Your journey is yours and yours alone: it won't look like anybody else's. You owe it to yourself to prioritise being self aware when it comes to pursuing your craft. It takes a certain level of honesty with yourself to navigate the creative industry, especially with how things are changing these days when it comes to various areas of the visual arts.

Try to keep on top of what motivates you to create artwork, making sure you know this will always guide you in the right direction when it comes to choosing work.

Try to keep an open mind where possible, too. I say this as someone who never intended to make a career out of children's books, but kept an open mind when the opportunity presented itself. This is supposed to be a journey and if you're open to where the road leads, you'll be open to growing and learning about yourself through the work you do. Godspeed and good luck.

Dapo Adeola is a British-Nigerian illustrator. He is the co-creator (with Nathan Bryon) and illustrator of *Look Up!*, winner of the 2020 Waterstones Children's Book Prize. Follow him on Instagram @dapsdraws.

Do judge a book by its cover

Thomas Taylor explains how a good cover can tell you, at a glance, just how it feels to read the book. He describes the key, defining, attention-grabbing elements that, thanks to the skills of designer, publisher and marketing team, combine to sell your book to the reader.

Not its contents, of course – I would never suggest that the quality of someone's writing or their ability to tell a story can be fairly assessed by how the book appears; but do judge the book as an object – by how it looks on the shelf or feels in your hand – because a lot of effort went into making it that way.

When my middle-grade novel *Malamander* (Walker Books 2019) was being prepared for publication, I was eager to do the cover art myself. I am, after all, an illustrator, and my first published piece of illustration – straight out of art school – was the cover art for *Harry Potter and the Philosopher's Stone* (Bloomsbury 1997) by J.K. Rowling. Editor Barry Cunningham contacted me, after seeing some sample drawings I left at the offices of Bloomsbury, and invited me to make a painting for the cover of a debut book by an unknown author. The brief was simple: paint Harry beside the Hogwarts Express, on Platform Nine and Three Quarters, and then paint a wizard ('any wizard will do') for the back cover. After some to-ing and fro-ing with rough sketches, I produced the paintings, which were then whisked into book cover shape by a designer. At the time I had little inkling what this 'whisking' entailed.

Given this experience – and the years of working on picture books that followed – it seemed only natural that I would do the cover art for my own middle-grade novel too, and not just the incidental interior drawings and the map. Indeed, I'd doodled and sketched right through the process of writing *Malamander*, so I was ready to go. But that's not what happened.

One of the questions I get asked most by up-and-coming writers looking to break into traditional publishing and asking for guidance is: 'Do I need to find an illustrator before I submit to publishers?'. This comes up especially frequently with picture book writers, who correctly sense the importance images will have as a vehicle for their storytelling, but don't always know how to handle it if they're not doing the art themselves. Well, there's some good news. The answer to this is: you *never* need to find an illustrator. Not if you are following the traditional publishing route.

Selecting the right visual match for your writing and storytelling is a complex business, and one the publishers will definitely want to be in control of. Art directors bring enormous expertise to this process, as well as the contact details of some of the best cover artists and designers in the industry. Actually, be *glad* that they'll handle all this for you; querying an agent or prospective publisher as a double act will make you much harder to deal with anyway, and will throw up unnecessary complications that no editor wants to deal with.

When you have a publishing contract, you may get some say in the look of the book – probably further down the line, once the work has essentially been done. But this is likely to be a polite request for comment, rather than an invitation to send the designers back to the storyboard. Well-established writers may be able to exert more influence on the process, perhaps thanks to a clause they (or more likely their agent) were able to insert into the contract. Whether they *should* or not is a point for debate, though; an author may have strong feelings about how the book should look, but their preferences may not marry up with current trends or other marketing factors that could be crucial to a book's success in a highly competitive market.

Sometimes it can be hard when an author sees their cover for the first time and it is nothing like they imagined it would or should be. The publishing process can often appear mysterious and veiled, especially for new writers, who may feel that they are on the receiving end of arcane decisions made in secret conclave. But it's important to trust that the publishers know the market and how to position your book successfully in it, and to remember that they are on your side and have every interest in seeing your book succeed. This isn't to say you shouldn't use your chance to comment on the cover design, or that you should be shy of sharing your ideas. Just be aware that your voice is only one of many.

The first thing I noticed when the cover art for *Malamander* was being discussed was just how many people had input or a say in the process – from publishing and sales directors, through marketing and PR reps, to representatives of export sales, special sales, book club sales, and designers of course. That's before even factoring in key account (bookshop chains, for example) managers and buyers who have to actually sell the book, and who may well have strong views on what does or doesn't work on the shop floor. And yes, these views are sometimes strong enough to get a book cover design changed, in order to secure a substantial order.

This process has become more intense since my own experience of producing the cover art for *Harry Potter* back in 1996, due not only to ever-increasing competition in children's fiction but also to the rise of digital platforms. For example, the question of how a cover will display as a thumbnail is more important than ever, because that tiny postage-stamp-sized image that scrolls down an iPhone screen in a second may be the book's only chance to connect with potential readers. If the actual physical book benefits from a foil finish, or sprayed edges or embossed lettering, it still has to look good at just 107 pixels wide by 160 high (standard thumbnail dimensions), where all these flourishes will be invisible. Delicate typography might vanish altogether at that resolution, and subtle artwork become little more than a blob.

For similar reasons, the spine of a book – so often overlooked – might be the only side of your work a browsing reader sees as they scan the shelves. But a good designer can tell them the author's name, the title, the publisher and something of the flavour of the story – all in the narrow strip of paper that holds the book together. And in a way that catches the eye too.

Series recognition and author branding often rests entirely on how that author's books appear. Get this right from the beginning and you can create a graphic language that tells us, at a glance, that the new book by X is out. Often this is achieved simply by choosing (and sticking with) a distinctive font for the author's name and making this the dominating graphic element of the cover. Think Rankin, Ellroy and Le Carré, and now you know where the term 'Big Name author' comes from.

They say a good cover tells you how it will *feel* to read the book. So alongside the practical considerations of text hierarchy – the relative graphic importance of the title, author's name, and straplines and quotes – there are other, less literal design components at play. Photography, painted or decorative elements that conjure a sense of the story for the reader and entice them in, are complex considerations and easy to overdo. Clever font choice can straddle both of these fields, clearly communicating key information, whilst also hinting at the regional or temporal flavour of the story or summing up that elusive 'feel'.

There's only so much 'room' on a book cover. Doing a lot with font, for example, means you can't also add complex imagery without potentially overloading the design and creating a mess that the eye struggles to read at a glance. And when it comes to selling books by cover alone, a glance might be all you get.

What is or is not a good design is not entirely subjective. There are certain key elements that are usually combined to create a harmonious whole: what the book is called and who wrote it; how reading the story will make you feel; how the book can grab attention on displays; how the book cover fares when miniaturised to a thumbnail or glimpsed from across the street in a bookshop window. I now have a far greater appreciation for what designers do than I did when I painted those *Harry Potter* cover pictures way back at the start of my career.

I had my own lesson in the importance of the content of book cover art too, when the wizard I painted for the back cover of *Harry Potter* (the 'any wizard will do' wizard I mentioned at the start) became the subject of much fan speculation, and even consternation. With the rise of Pottermania, the identity of the wizard I originally painted there became the subject of debate – even some conspiracy theories. I was accused by some of having secret advance information about the then unwritten books, and of deliberately leaving clues and toying with readers. Nobody wanted to hear that the character I painted was just a generic wizard based on my own dad! Bloomsbury asked me, some years later, to paint a replacement picture – the image of Albus Dumbledore that most fans seemed to expect – and my father's brief career as an infamous magician came to an end.

In the ever-narrowing bricks-and-mortar retail space, and across the expanding and fiercely visual digital landscape, the appearance of your book has probably never been more important. So while it's still true that a good cover should tell you how it feels to read the book, these days it can't hurt if it also looks stunning on a coffee table, turns heads from across the street or launches a viral 'This was totally a cover buy, but …' Instagram wave.

I didn't do the cover art for *Malamander* in the end. I quickly became overwhelmed by how complex the process was, and how much editing and writing time it would take away. It was genuinely a relief to pass the task over to George Ermos, whose gorgeous art adorns the cover now – subtly suggesting the tone of the story within and how it will feel to read it, whilst also making a splash in a bookshop window. And yes, thanks to George, it also looks fabulous in an Instagram post.

Thomas Taylor is an author and illustrator. He has illustrated and contributed to dozens of books, and has also written and illustrated four of his own picture books, including *The Loudest Roar* (2003) and *The Biggest Splash* (2005), both published by OUP. His most recent books, in the *Legends of Eerie-on-Sea* series published by Walker Books for middle-grade readers, are *Malamander* (2019), *Gargantis* (2020), *Shadowghast* (2021), *Festergrimm* (2022) and the concluding title *Mermedusa* (2023). For more information see www.thomastaylor-author.com or follow him on X @ThomasHTaylor.

Creating successful comic books

Comics are very often a young reader's gateway to the book world. But if you want to create and eventually sell your own comics, how do you get started? Read on to find more about the path taken by Jamie Smart.

Before we start, I should perhaps say that I'm going to be using the word 'comics' instead of 'graphic novels'. The phrase 'graphic novels' has always felt a bit dry to me, as well as sounding like a derivative of some more noble artform. So, for me, it's all about comics. I make comics. Just the word itself sounds so fun, so vibrant, so much more alive. And while my particular interest is funny comics, particularly funny children's comics, comics as a medium can encompass so many different styles.

Comics can be huge, thrilling epics, or tiny, minimal gags; they can be dramatic, heartbreaking, autobiographical, life changing. Comics convey information in such a uniquely immediate way they can not only be educational and informative, but can also swing your opinion, make you laugh or just take you on a wonderfully bananas adventure.

If you want to tell a story – any kind of story, as far as I'm concerned – comics are one of the purest ways of doing it. If you're reading this, however, you probably already know that. Comics have been going through something of a resurgence in the UK, especially children's comics, kickstarted partly by the runaway success of *Dog Man* by Dav Pilkey and then carried along by a huge swell of homegrown talent. It wasn't always this way. I grew up in the 1980s, when I would go to the newsagents and scoop up every weekly comic from the shelves; *Buster*, *The Dandy*, *Monster Fun*, *Oink!*, to name but a few. But in the 90s and early 00s, children's comics faded out of the mainstream. A few stalwarts held strong – *The Beano* has remained on the shelves, week in and week out, since 1938, and for the last ten years *The Phoenix* has carved its own path into the world of weekly children's comics, which is quite some feat for any new title. Both of them have survived this long on the belief that comics deserve a more prominent place in society. And now, thankfully, they're being proved right. Right now, publishers are super keen to put out new comics and try new creators. And if you're looking to make comics professionally, whether as an artist, a writer, a letterer, a colourist, an editor, or all those things combined, it's a great time to be considering it.

On the long walks I took thinking about how best to write this article, however, I realised that I can't tell you how to make a success of comics. Like anything, there's no one way of doing it. And comics in particular can be hard graft, low pay and difficult to break through. We might as well be honest about that. But there's a huge, huge amount of joy to be found in creating comics, and that joy in your work will be what keeps you going. And publishers, just like any readers, really will notice that joy shining out from the comics you create.

So if I'm to offer any advice, it is that you need to be making comics for you, to fulfil yourself. This will give you your best chance at wherever you want comics to take you.

Beyond that, I thought it might be more helpful to explain how I, personally, built a career in comics. Some of it will be outdated (we used fax machines, can you imagine?), but I think there should be some perpetual truths in my story, and hopefully sharing it might help you on your own path.

As a kid, reading comics was very quickly followed by making comics, and I became obsessed. Comics were a speed-run way of telling stories. With childishly loose lines, I could draw panel after panel roughly, quickly, wrap the story up with a gag and then jump onto the next one. That's part of the reason children enjoy making their own comics so much: they don't need the right materials, an artistic style or even a big enough vocabulary; they just need heart. Anyway, by the time I was a teenager, I was already sending the comics I'd made out to publishers. I was raised in a family of artists and writers, and we shared our (very annotated) copies of the *Writers' & Artists' Yearbook* between us. The ritual of going to the library, photocopying my newest work, shuffling it into manila envelopes, and sending it out to a load of publishers became a real thrill for me. I was sending them examples of my slowly growing portfolio, sure, but I was also sending them excerpts from whatever new idea I was working on at the time. I'd send comic publishers pages from my new comic. I would send book publishers previews from an illustrated storybook I wanted to make. I would send greetings card companies a handful of designs for birthday cards. The point is, I was always working on something new, a project of my own, not catered to what any publisher might be looking or asking for, but something I wanted to make for myself.

Rejection quickly becomes the norm, and you just have to adapt to that. I got around the initial despondency by having a rapid turnover of ideas. By the time the rejections were coming in for one project, I'd already be working on (and sending out) the next. That's not to say I didn't love each project I was working on. I did, completely, and I longed to see each and every thing published. But they were branches on a tree rather than the tree itself, and I was too busy having fun to mind if I lost a few of them along the way.

I went to art college for a few years, drew a lot more cartoons, and by the time I left I was starting to get the occasional bite on my submissions. My first gig was drawing a six-panel funny comic for a cookery magazine, which also gave me my first experience of going into WHSmith and seeing my work on the shelves: it was such an incredible rush. After that I started picking up work on greetings cards, then comic strips in *The Dandy* and *The Funday Times*. In my early twenties, I did another big push of my work. This time I had some earnings behind me, so I invested those into getting A6 spiral-bound booklets of my work printed up, and sent copies out to a number of different agents. I made them fun, silly, hopefully enjoyable little books in themselves. Something memorable, at least. Alongside that I was making alternative 'goth' comics, and was lucky enough to find a US publisher for those. I spent weeks, months, making websites, not just to promote my work, but also to host little choose-your-own-adventure minisites, for which I'd hand-paint countless illustrations. In the 00s and 10s, webcomics started to become a thing, and that was a great way to get comics seen by large audiences. I drew whole books and posted them online, a page a week, never quite grasping how to make money out of it, but it worked for me in other ways.

It built me an audience. As did the alternative comics. As did the children's comics. Even a few people who found my greetings cards in Asda – why not? And although I'd been dipping my toes into several slightly different arenas, they were all connected: it was all still my work.

The reason I think this may be relevant to your journey is that I learnt the audiences you build often include the occasional publishers, agents, booksellers. They might see your work because you pitched it to them, but they might also be seeing it because its crossed their path in other ways. So try everything. Back when Twitter was a fun place to be (and filled with a community of friendly artists), I picked up a few great illustration gigs just by posting my work up and having it be shared across the screen of the right person at the right time. Artists posting comics online, whether on social media or dedicated websites, can and do grab book deals from them. Hey, it's rare, let's not be silly here, but it's not impossible.

Another great avenue for comic creators is self-publishing. Go to a dedicated comic show such as Thought Bubble (or there'll doubtless be others nearer to you) and you'll see table after table of comic creators all showing and selling their own work. Seriously, if you want to make comics but you haven't been to a convention yet, you should absolutely do it. See what other people are making, how they're making it, talk to them (comics people are the best people), read their work. It might help you see what's possible for your own work. You could even get some of your comics printed up and exhibit them, if you fancy it. If you don't, that's fine too. Earlier on I said there's no right way of making it in comics, and there really isn't. Take the road that works best for you.

One last thing. Agents. It's a question that gets asked a lot, whether it's better to send work to agents, or direct to publishers. When I was scouring the *Yearbook*, I never knew what the right answer was, so I just went for both. Now I'm nearly thirty years into making children's comics as a full-time job, I do have an agent, Jodie, and she's amazing. So this is what I'd advise. If you're busy making comics, posting them online and printing them yourself, you probably don't need an agent. If you want to send your work to publishers, by all means you can try by yourself, and you may have some luck, but it's worth considering that since now the more traditional publishers are publishing comics too, they'll likely expect to find new work via agents, just like they do with prose novels and non-fiction. So if you can get an agent, then it's a pretty good idea. Agents step in when there are deals to be made, whether that's with publishers, or once you're published, perhaps even with TV companies looking to adapt your work, and more. When you're at this stage, an agent is invaluable. They will defend you, fight for you, argue for you and make any contract as agreeable to you as possible. They will take the stress and the headaches out of the business side of things, so you can concentrate on what you love doing – making The Things. And, as long as you come out of it earning what's comfortable for you, then a good agent can be worth their weight in gold.

I hope this has helped in some way, somehow. As comics, especially children's comics, enjoy a renaissance, it's a double-edged sword for creators. On the one hand, publishers are really keen to look for new talent (even just ten years ago, it was incredibly difficult to get them to notice comics), and that's fantastic. On the flip side, maybe things are becoming more competitive now. There are a lot of great comic artists. And, like any corner of children's books, celebrities invariably muscle their way in, not to mention the ever looming threat of AI comics, if that transpires. If you're going to get noticed, or get published, you're going to need your voice to be authentic and true to you. You're going to need your comics to sing with your personality, and tell the stories you love to tell. You're going to need to be making comics because comics are how you connect with the world.

And if you're doing that, however you're doing that, then that's a success in itself.

Jamie Smart is a comic artist and author. His works include the bestselling comic series *Bunny Vs Monkey*, as well as *Looshkin*, *Max And Chaffy*, and *Flember*, his series of illustrated novels. Follow him on social media @jamiesmart.bsky.social.

How to create a graphic novel

Isabel Greenberg has valuable advice for the would-be graphic novelist, provides tried-and-tested practical rules and tips for visual storytellers, and shares her knowledge of this creative and engaging medium.

Contrary to how they are often presented, graphic novels (or comics) are not a genre – like science fiction or fantasy or crime or historical fiction, but a medium – like film, poetry, interpretative dance or prose novels. They are a way of telling stories. I can introduce you to some of the conventions or 'un-conventional' aspects of this medium and talk you through my own process, but to instruct you in how to create a graphic novel in one short article is as impossible a task as instructing someone on how to write a novel or make a film. That said, what I can do is tell you how I make *my* graphic novels. I'll present you with some tips, pointers and thoughts that I think might be useful for anyone embarking on this creative route … for it is a mammoth undertaking.

Definitions

Whether you choose to call it a graphic novel or a comic book, or just a story told in pictures, is entirely up to you. For me, if it's the length of a novel, I call it a graphic novel. This doesn't mean its content is necessarily more 'highbrow' than your average comic; for me it simply denotes the length of the book. A short episodic periodical or a zine, regardless of its content, I would refer to as a comic. But hot debate surrounds this issue, with many comic fans feeling that the term 'graphic novel' has been used to make the medium more palatable to audiences who might balk at reading 'comic books'. I tend to feel that whether this is true or not doesn't matter, so long as it means more readers are willing to access this wonderful medium.

Where to start?

With your story of course – and how you begin to find this is up to you. For some writers, a character might be their catalyst; for others it's a plot or premise. This is a visual medium, however, so that is something worth thinking about. Much as a film-maker might struggle to make an arresting film that takes place entirely in a pitch-black room, so you, as a visual storyteller, might also (that being said, you may be up for a challenge!).

As with standard novels, graphic novels encompass a vast array of genres. You can read a graphic novel adventure, a thriller, horror, biography or history. And yes, there are graphic novels that feature superheroes! Autobiography is extremely popular too; the most well-known examples of the medium are *Persepolis* by Marjane Satrapi (Jonathan Cape 2003) and *Maus* by Art Speigelman (Pantheon Books 1991), to name two of the most seminal.

Many graphic novelists write and draw their own books. I am one of these. But if you are an aspiring writer who would like to team up with an artist, that is also possible. Some publishers may be willing to help facilitate this but, with such a visual medium, it is hard to pitch the project on words alone, and you might want to consider approaching an artist to work on the pitch with you. A note here: do not ask an artist to illustrate your graphic novel pitch free of charge, unless you are equally invested artistic partners in the project.

If you need someone to facilitate your vision, you must pay for this service. Illustrating a graphic novel is an extremely complex and time-consuming task.

For me, everything starts with the story. I would not even begin to sketch or imagine characters or setting until I had the bare bones of a premise to work upon. Even my first book, which was set in an imaginary world called Early Earth, started with a creation story, rather than the building of the world itself. Many people like to start by building the world, but this aspect can be addictive, and your world can swiftly become too huge to handle. Remember that you are sculpting a narrative; the richer your world, the better. Of course, you can and should know all the back stories and places that go on off the page – but keep your focus on the story you want to tell in your book.

My most recent graphic novel, *Glass House* (Jonathan Cape 2020), began with research, as it is part biography, part fantastical interpretation of the Bronte siblings' childhood world-building. Many graphic novelists write their words like a film script. I do this to some extent, but I often play with writing as prose, and I'll frequently break off from the script to draw little moments or scenes so I can see how they might play out.

Rules to break or keep

I won't tell you how many panels should be on a page, or how many words should be in a speech bubble. Some of my favourite graphic novels are totally silent, such as *The Arrival* by Shaun Tan (Hachette Children's 2007) and *Bad Island* by Stanley Donwood (Hamish Hamilton 2020), and some have so many words it's almost a challenge to separate them from the images, so of course these rules and conventions are there to be broken. But there are a few important maxims I do try to stick to:

• One action per panel

You cannot direct a character to cross a room and open a window in a single panel (writers who have written for film are often the worst culprits in this area). You are working with still images. A character may be pictured mid-stride, crossing a room in the first panel, and opening a window in the next.

• Communication is paramount

Test your story out on a reader at every point. If they do not understand what is happening, if your images are too oblique or you have too much going on, then you will need to adapt. I particularly like to test my work out on readers who are not familiar with, or do not read a lot of, this medium. If a reader does not understand what you want them to, then you need to rethink how you are telling the story. Writers who work with artists can sometimes assume that the images can clear up confusing motives or explain things they do not want to say in words. Sometimes this is the case, but remember that – unlike with film – you cannot control how long your reader lingers on a moment or panel, or puzzles over the expression and emotion of a character. If there is something important you want them to know, you must endeavour to communicate it. Above all, remember that if your reader doesn't understand something, this is not their fault; the responsibility is on you, as the creator, to convey your own message adequately.

• If a moment is important, make them stay

I just said above that you cannot control how long a reader lingers on a panel. This is quite true, but you can certainly try. If a moment is important, emotionally or as a crux to your story, let your reader know this. You could signify it with a full bleed spread for example (this is a single image that runs the entire width and height of your double page). It can create impact if not used too frequently in your story. This might be a point of emotional significance, or perhaps a scene-setting moment – to introduce a character's arrival in a certain setting, or to show a moment of excitement or action.

- **The page-turn is powerful**

Don't show a big reveal as the last panel on a spread or page. Your reader will first see the page as one image before their eye adjusts and they read it as panels. This means you cannot stop spoilers if you show them on the same page. If you have a surprise, let the reader discover it as they turn the page.

- **If your picture is saying something, your words don't need to**

If your images are showing or saying something, then there is no need for you to say it in words too. If your image shows a character looking into a beautiful sunrise, you do not need to say '[XX] looked at the beautiful sunrise'. But you might use your words to say something your image cannot convey, or to add another layer to the narrative: '[XX] had not seen a sunrise for nearly a year'. Or you may choose to let the image breathe, and speak for itself, letting your reader decide what your character is feeling at this moment of sunrise contemplation.

I tend to use narration in my work, rather than leaving the story to be told purely through dialogue and action. But this is a stylistic choice, and many writers and artists will try to avoid narration; it can seem like unnecessary, or obvious, exposition. I do use such exposition to capitalise on the humour of having an omniscient narrative voice.

- **Consider keeping your text on a separate layer**

Whether you are hand lettering or using a font, this is worth considering. In all likelihood, your editor may come back to you with tweaks or spelling and grammatical corrections. I found early on that if I kept my text on a separate layer to my artwork, this made shuffling and changing much easier. Furthermore, it meant that when the works went into foreign translation, I was able to easily provide my font (which I made from my own handwriting) when appropriate, and when it needed to be re-lettered (for different alphabets) my text was easy to remove.

Pitching

Most publishers will require a full synopsis and plot breakdown, as well as at least six to ten example spreads, showing your words and artwork together. Some will require even more of a completed script. When choosing your example spreads, pick a variety that can show your range. Perhaps you want some quiet, some dialogue-heavy spreads, and some action or full-page images, if your story will call for these, so that they can see the full visual scope of the story.

You may choose to approach an agent to represent you before approaching a publisher. Choose who you approach prudently. Not all publishers or agents will be right for your work. Pick a selection of graphic novels by writers or artists whose work you feel has a parallel with your own stylistically, and see who publishes or represents them. Remember you have to appeal to a publisher both visually and in terms of your story; one is no good without the other. Consider both of these things when deciding who to approach. Look through a publishers' back catalogue and see if they have a house 'style'. Don't attempt to change your work to fit that style, but do bear it in mind if you get a rejection – they just may not be the right place for you. An agent can advise you on this, and will guide you through the process of pitching, should you choose to get one.

Making graphic novels your profession

Be aware that even the most generous advance from a publisher is unlikely to be enough for you to live on entirely whilst you make your book. The market is neither as large, nor as lucrative, as regular fiction, and the advances publishers offer will sadly reflect this. Most graphic novelists and comic artists will have several strings to their bow. Some may also do children's books, freelance writing, commercial illustration, hire themselves out to be the artist on another writers' work or have another day job completely.

And finally ...

Good luck! Graphic novels are a mammoth undertaking. But they are also a unique medium in that you have the power to do absolutely everything: you are in charge of set design, lighting, script, costume and location. You are the director of your own world, and it can be created without having to source a million-dollar budget and deal with a staff of hundreds. This is a wonderful thing, so enjoy it.

Illustrator and writer **Isabel Greenberg** studied Illustration at the University of Brighton and completed an MA at the Royal College of Art in experimental animation. Her bestselling graphic novels, all published by Jonathan Cape in the UK, are *The Encyclopaedia of Early Earth* (2013), winner of the Best Book category at the British Comic Awards, *The One Hundred Nights of Hero* (2016), a *New York Times* Graphic Books Bestseller and *Glass Town* (2020). Her work also includes comics and illustration, animation and children's books. For more information, see www.isabelgreenberg.co.uk. Follow her on X @isabelgreenberg and Instagram @isabel_greenberg.

Illustration agents

Before submitting work, artists are advised to make preliminary enquiries and to ascertain terms of work. Commission varies but averages 25–30%. The Association of Illustrators (see page 317) provides a valuable service for illustrators, agents and clients. The country code for phoning UK offices from overseas is +44.

*Member of the Society of Artists Agents
†Member of the Association of Illustrators
sae = self-addressed envelope

Advocate Art
27 Old Gloucester Street, London WC1N 3AX
tel 020-8390 6293
email mail@advocate-art.com
website www.advocate-art.com
Facebook www.facebook.com/advocateart
X @advocateart01
Instagram @advocateart01
Global Manager Amanda Hendon

Represents artists for children's, middle-grade and YA books, greeting cards and licensing. Also advertising. Has 12 agents representing over 300 artists globally. For illustrators' submission guidelines see the website. Also has offices in New York City, Los Angeles and Seville, with agents located internationally. The website is in German, Spanish, Italian and French. Founded 1992.

Allied Artists/Artistic License
tel 07971 111256
email gary@allied-artists.net
website www.alliedartists-illustration.co.uk
Contact Gary Mills

Represents leading international illustrators specialising in children's books and magazines from pre-school to YA for fiction, non-fiction, picture books, novelty, graphic novels and educational books with a range of styles covering realistic, stylised, cute, sci-fi and cartoon and comic. Founded 1983.

Darley Anderson Illustration Agency
Unit 19, Matrix Studios, 91 Peterborough Road, London SW6 3BU
tel 020-3940 9012
website www.darleyandersonillustration.com
Instagram @darleyanderson_illustration
Managing Director Clare Wallace, Agents Lydia Silver, Becca Langton, Chloe Davis, Head of International Rights Kristina Egan

Represents bestselling and award-winning illustrators. Works across all areas of publishing, from picture books to gift titles to graphic novels, across fiction and non-fiction, collaborating with both adult and children's publishers worldwide. Actively looking for new talent, especially illustrators from under-represented backgrounds. Commission: 20%. Submission guidelines: send an email with portfolio attached as a pdf or in the body of the email, along with information about yourself and links to social media channels used to display your work. Author-illustrators should send texts as pdf or Word attachments, along with a brief synopsis and illustration samples. Submissions should be made directly to the agent of choice. Founded 1988.

Arena Illustration*†
31 Eleanor Road, London E15 4AB
tel 020-8555 9827
website www.arenaillustration.com
Facebook www.facebook.com/arena.illustration
X @arenatweet
Instagram @arenaillustration
Contact Tamlyn Francis

Represents 29 artists. Average commission: 25%. Founded 1970.

The Art Agency
21 Morris Street, Sheringham, Norfolk NR26 8JY
tel (01263) 823424
email artagency@me.com
website www.the-art-agency.co.uk
Facebook www.facebook.com/illustrationagency
Director Peter Kavanagh

Provides non-fiction, reference and children's book illustration. Specialises in non-fiction illustrations across a wide variety of subjects and age groups. Submit up to six samples by email along with a link to your website. Founded 1990.

The Artworks*
4th Floor, 107 Charterhouse Street, London EC1M 6HW
email submissions@theartworksinc.com
website www.theartworksinc.com
Facebook www.facebook.com/artworksillustration
X @ArtworksIllos
Instagram @theartworks_inc
Contacts Stephanie Alexander-Jinks, Alex Hadlow, Lucy Scherer

Represents 35 illustrators for design and advertising work as well as for non-fiction children's books, book jackets, illustrated gift books and children's picture books. Commission: 30% design and advertising, 25% publishing advances, 15% royalties, 25% book jackets. Founded 1983.

Astound US
27 Old Gloucester Street, London WC1N 3AX
tel 020-7046 9410
email contact@astound.us
website https://astound.us/publishing/
Facebook www.facebook.com/astound.us
X @astound_us
Instagram @astoundusagency
Global Manager Christina Doffing, UK Manager Rosie Barlow

A new kind of artist representation business based in New York City and London. Offers contemporary children's book illustration, and both licensing and commercial art from around the world. Founded 2014.

Beehive Illustration
42A Cricklade Street, Cirencester, Glos. GL7 1JH
email enquiries@beehiveillustration.co.uk
website www.beehiveillustration.co.uk
X @beehive_illus
Instagram @beehive_illustration
Contact Paul Beebee

Represents 200 artists specialising in ELT, education and general children's publishing illustration. Commission: 25%. Founded 1989.

The Big Red Illustration Agency
29 Marlborough Ave, Cheadle Hulme, Cheadle SK8 7AP
tel 0808 120 0996
email enquiries@bigredillustrationagency.com
website www.bigredillustrationagency.com
Facebook www.facebook.com/thebigredillustrationagency
X @big_red_author
Director Adam Rushton

Represents a number of professional illustrators. Works with a variety of clients including children's book publishers, design agencies, greetings card companies and toy manufacturers. Founded 2012.

The Bright Agency*
103–105 St John's Hill, London SW11 1SY
tel 020-7326 9140
US Office 50 West Street, C12, New York, NY 10006
tel +1 646-604-0992
email mail@thebrightagency.com
website www.thebrightagency.com
X @bright_agency
Instagram @bright_agency
Global Managing Director James Burns

Areas of representation include: children's illustration, greeting and gift (cards, social stationery and giftwrap), design and advertising (editorial, branding, adult publishing, packaging, web, digital and typography), animation, literary (children's fiction and non-fiction, adult fiction and non-fiction, and graphic novels) and licensing (toys and games, digital gaming, fabric and apparel, and homewares). For illustration, writing and animation submissions guidelines see website. No submissions by post. Clients include: Benji Davies, David Litchfield, Yasmeen Ismail, Chris Chatterton, Diane Ewen, Laura Hughes, Galia Bernstein, Mechal Roe, Aura Lewis, Karl James Mountford, Jane Newland, Brenna Nation and Hannah Peck. Founded 2002.

Jenny Brown Associates – see page 211

The Catchpole Agency
53 Cranham Street, Oxford OX2 6DD
tel 07789 588070
email james@thecatchpoleagency.co.uk
email celia@thecatchpoleagency.co.uk
website www.thecatchpoleagency.co.uk
Instagram @thecatchpoles
Proprietors James Catchpole, Celia Catchpole

Agents for authors and illustrators of children's books from picture books through to YA novels, with a specialism in story-editing. See website for contact and submissions details. See also page 212. Founded 1996.

Creative Sparrow
12 Conqueror Court, Sittingbourne, Kent ME10 5BH
email contact@creativesparrow.co.uk
website https://creativesparrow.co.uk/
Instagram @creativesparrowart
Managing Director Hannah Curtis

An agency representing creatives across all industries. Working with clients and artists globally, facilitates collaborations for the art licensing, branding, advertising and publishing sectors. Founded 2021.

Good Illustration
40 Bowling Green Lane, London EC1R 0NE
tel 020-8123 0243 (UK), +1 347-627-0243 (US)
email draw@goodillustration.com
website www.goodillustration.com
Facebook www.facebook.com/goodillustration
X @gillustration
Instagram @goodillus
Directors Doreen Thorogood, Kate Webber, Tom Thorogood

Represents 50+ artists for advertising, design, publishing and animation. Send sae and samples. Commission: 25% publishing, 30% advertising. Founded 1977.

David Higham Associates – see page 215

IllustrationX*†
4th Floor, Silverstream House, 45 Fitzroy Street, London W1T 6EB

tel 020-7720 5202
email hello@illustrationx.com
website www.illustrationx.com/uk
Facebook www.facebook.com/weareillustrationx
X @illustrationx
Contact Juliette Lott

Welcomes submissions from illustrators and animators whose work is distinctive and innovative. Only accepts applications from artists through submissions page: www.illustrationx.com/applications. Founded 1929.

Inky Illustration

Kemp House, 152–160 City Road,
London EC1V 2NX
tel 0121 270 5828
email info@inkyillustration.com
website https://inkyillustration.com/
Facebook www.facebook.com/inkyillustration
X @inkyillo
Instagram @inkyillo

Illustrators have experience working with clients on international advertising campaigns, publications and editorials, as well as commissions for smaller companies. Always happy to receive new work. Fill out the application form on the website or email to: submissions@inkyillustration.com. Hard copies of work are accepted with an sae if the work is to be returned. Founded 2009.

B.L. Kearley Art & Antiques

Glebe House, Bakers Wood, Denham,
Bucks. UB9 4LG
tel (01895) 832145
email christine.kearley@kearley.co.uk
website www.kearley.co.uk
Agent C. R. Kearley

Represents 30+ artists. Mainly specialises in children's and educational illustration worldwide. Known for realistic figurative work. Also specialises in the sale of original book illustration artwork. Commission: 25%. Founded 1948.

Kids Corner

1 Mailing Street, West Street, Lewes BN7 2NZ
tel 020-7593 0506
email claire@meiklejohn.co.uk
website www.kidscornerillustration.co.uk
Facebook www.facebook.com/p/Kids-Corner-Illustration-100054277520017
X @KidsCornerIllos
Instagram @kidscornerillustration_
Managing Director Claire Meiklejohn

Represents illustrators, from award-winning to emerging artists for children's publishing. Styles include fun, cute, stylised, picture book, young fiction, reference, graphic, traditional, painterly and digital. Founded 2015.

Lemonade Illustration Agency

167–169 Great Portland Street, 5th Floor,
London W1W 5PF
tel 07891 390750
email studio@lemonadeillustration.com
US office 347 Fifth Ave, Suite 1402, New York, NY 10016, USA
website www.lemonadeillustration.com
Instagram @lemonadeillustrationagency

Represents 190+ illustrators working across all media from branding to children's picture books. Works with leading children's book publishers and educational publishers globally. Artists' submissions must contain a website link and a letter. Unfortunately unable to reply to all submissions. Serves clients in all global markets with offices in London, New York, Sydney and Wakefield. Founded 2001.

David Lewis Illustration Agency

3 Somali Road, London NW2 3RN
tel 020-7435 7762, 07931 824674
email info@davidlewisillustration.com
website https://davidlewisillustration.com/
Director David Lewis, *Associate* Lisa Britton

Representing approx. 25 illustrators, mostly for all areas of children's publishing, including educational, merchandising and toys. Also considers complete picture books with text. Send A4 colour or b&w copies of samples with sae. Commission: 30%. Founded 1974.

Frances McKay Illustration

17 Church Road, West Mersea, Essex CO5 8QH
tel 07703 344334
email frances@francesmckay.com
website www.francesmckay.com
Proprietor Frances McKay

Represents 10–15 artists for illustration and writing children's books. For information on submissions please look at the website. Submit email with low-res scans or colour copies of recent work; sae essential for return of all unsolicited samples sent by post. Commission: 25%. Founded 1999.

NB Illustration*

Home Farm, East Horrington, Somerset BA5 3EA
tel 07720 827328
email info@nbillustration.co.uk
website www.nbillustration.co.uk
Facebook www.facebook.com/nbillustrationltd
X @nb_illustration
Instagram @nb.illustration
Directors Joe Najman, Charlotte Dowson

Represents 50+ artists, 40% of whom produce children's material for picture books and educational publishing. For submission details see website. Commission: 30%. Founded 2000.

The Plum Agency
Chapel House, St Lawrences Way, Reigate, Surrey RH2 7AF
tel (01737) 244095
email letterbox@theplumagency.com
website https://theplumagency.com/
Instagram @plum_agency
Directors Mark Mills, Hannah Whitty

Represents 100+ artists and authors, producing texts and illustrations for children's publishing, advertising, editorial, greeting cards and packaging. See website for submission procedure. Commission: 30%. Founded 2006.

Sylvie Poggio Artists Agency
62 Ainsdale Road, London W5 1JX
tel 07775 894870
email sylvie-p@sylviepoggio.com
website www.sylviepoggio.com
Facebook www.facebook.com/Sylvie-Poggio-Artists-agency-700285410097943
X @sylviepoggioart
Directors Sylvie Poggio, Bruno Caurat

Represents 40 artists producing illustrations for publishing and advertising. Founded 1996.

RCW
20 Powis Mews, London W11 1JN
tel 020-7221 3717
email info@rcwlitagency.com
website www.rcwlitagency.com
Instagram @rcwliteraryagency
Contact Millie van Grutten

Represents leading illustrators of children's books, selling their work throughout the world in all media. Welcomes a broad range of styles across all genres of children's publishing including preschool, picture book, educational, gift, fiction, non-fiction, graphic novel and activity. Founded 1967.

The Soho Agency
16–17 Wardour Mews, 2nd Floor, London W1F 8AT
tel 020-7471 7900
email admin@thesohoagency.co.uk
website www.thesohoagency.co.uk
X @thesohoagencyuk
Instagram @thesohoagencyuk
Contact Philippa Milnes-Smith

Illustrators for children's publishing for children 0–16 years. See website for submission requirements. Special interests: authors/artists creating their own projects, projects with cross-media potential, illustrators from diverse backgrounds, original talent. Commission: UK 15%, US 20%. Clients include Lauren Child, Emily Gravett, Chris Judge, Steve McCarthy, Jane Porter, Chris Riddell and Niamh Sharkey. See also page 220. Founded 1996.

Studio Canal Kids & Family
3 Pancras Square, London N1C 4AG
tel 020-3880 0134
website www.studiocanal.co.uk
Facebook www.facebook.com/studiocanalUK
X @studiocanaluk
Instagram @studiocanaluk
Ceo UK Alex Hamilton

Full-service international brand licensing company offering strategic worldwide brand development, licensing and retail expertise. Focuses on the long-term development of IP and quality merchandise programmes. Properties include *Paddington Bear*, *Mush-Mush and the Mushables*, *Father Christmas*, *Fungus the Bogeyman*. Previously known as The Copyrights Group, acquired by global brand Studio Canal in 2016 and rebranded in 2024. Founded 1984.

Tallbean
tel (01728) 454921
email heather@tallbean.co.uk
website www.tallbean.co.uk
Founder Heather Richards

Provides specialist illustrators offering a range of styles. The team of well-established and creative illustrators is kept small to ensure a close working relationship. Founded 1996.

Vicki Thomas Associates
195 Tollgate Road, London E6 5JY
tel 020-7511 5767
email contact@vickithomasassociates.com
website www.vickithomasassociates.com
X @VickiThomasA
Instagram @vickithomasa
Consultant Vicki Thomas

Represents approx. 30 artists, 75% of whom produce children's material for all ages. Specialises in gift products and considers images for publishing, toys, stationery, clothing and decorative accessories. Email sample images, covering letter and CV. Commission: 30%. Founded 1985.

United Agents
12–26 Lexington Street, London W1F 0LE
tel 020-3214 0800
email info@unitedagents.co.uk
website www.unitedagents.co.uk
Agents Jodie Hodges, Emily Talbot

Illustrators of children's books for all ages. Commission: home 15%, USA/translation 20%. See website for submission details. Founded 2008.

Magazines and newspapers
Writing for teens

Chloe Rhodes describes the possibilities, challenges and rewards of writing for today's teenage magazine market, explains what writers need to bear in mind to find that crucial, supportive connection with young readers and provides essential tips on how to pitch your own ideas for features.

In a market that's often overly focused on looks, fashion and lifestyle, our magazine, *Teen Breathe*, gives attention to readers' inner lives. It exists to provide a safe, reassuring and uplifting space at a time when many young adults are facing a crisis of confidence and experiencing worries that affect their physical and mental wellbeing. Published every seven weeks in print along with a digital edition, it's aimed at 11–14 year-olds (though some readers are as young as eight); its message is that *all* feelings and ways of being are valid, all questions readers might be asking themselves are normal, and that there are all kinds of ways to slow the pace and make meaningful connections in the world. Based on the experience I've had connecting with our readers (all 30,000 of them) at *Teen Breathe*, here is my advice on how to write for this demanding but rewarding market.

Pick 'n' mix

Teen Breathe tries, in myriad ways, to suggest that thinking about who you are, why you feel as you do and how you experience the world can be enriching, especially during the formative teen years. That's not to say, however, that every feature has to offer profound insight or a therapeutic message. Creativity, humour and lightness are crucial ingredients too. Although they fall into the catch-all category of 'teens', our readers are as individual and unique as the rest of the population. Their family circumstances, cultural backgrounds, maturity levels, hobbies and interests vary wildly. As a result, we have no set list of subjects to constrain new contributors – just let the imagination flow! What the most powerful features we publish have in common are a) a curious approach, b) thorough, fact-backed research and c) the sense that there might be something interesting for readers to glean … something that sheds light on themselves or the world they're beginning to explore.

For would-be contributors, choosing a subject can be liberating and fun. The young reader's thirst for knowledge means that things adults might take for granted, like potted plants, book groups or their sense of smell, can be approached with fresh wonder. In every issue we aim for a mixture of topics, so pieces might range from bullying to baking, grief to gardening, perhaps alongside a recipe for boba pearl ice lollies and a DIY guide to building a wormery. But some areas are given a wide berth, including celebrity, romantic relationships and losing or gaining weight (anything to do with how to sculpt the so-called 'perfect body' is *not* for us). We also avoid using the term 'teenagers' (readers know that's what they are) and usually sidestep anything that's self-consciously cool or edgy. On the whole, we also try to steer clear of using online trends as a starting point for features. While it's important, of course, to acknowledge the role social media plays in readers' lives, its impact on young minds is complex. We're careful to present a balanced and nuanced picture.

Tips on tone
While gentle guidance and suggestion is great, most readers, whatever their age, will baulk slightly if they feel they're being lectured – so we try hard to ensure content doesn't sound formal, condescending or overtly educational. Instead, we try to channel the voice of a supportive older sibling – chatty, warm, conversational – giving comfort and empathy while acknowledging that we're in it together in not having all the answers. The aim is to convey a positive message that no one needs to be perfect and that most people sometimes experience uncertainty as well as happiness, self-doubt as well as confidence, loneliness as well as friendship. We remind them there's support available to help with sad or challenging issues, ways to learn from mistakes and manageable methods which help bring balance and contentment.

Wise words
From a practical perspective, language is important. Pieces need to be accessible to 12-year-olds, so it's best not to use overly complex vocabulary – but it's fine to include two or three tricky words per piece if they flow in the text and are explained by the surrounding sentences. Examples, quotes and points of reference also need to be suitable for this age group. Paragraphs are generally kept short (35–40 words) and features run to approximately 850 words.

Pitch perfect
Every magazine will have its own submissions guidelines. At *Teen Breathe* we have a dedicated form for writers to use to send in a pitch (see www.teenbreathe.co.uk/contact-us). We welcome new voices and fresh perspectives, so please do get in touch if you'd like to collaborate with us on a feature. Follow these tips to give your idea the best chance of success:

1. Have at least one clear, age-appropriate idea for a feature you'd like to write. We receive a lot of enquiries from would-be writers who tell us how much they'd like to contribute to the magazine but forget to include a specific piece they have in mind. Links to websites or articles published elsewhere are useful background reading if your idea sounds promising, but you need to outline a clear, **concise and concrete proposal** that we can consider.

2. Give a **clear summary** of the piece. Ideally think of a title and write a sentence or two that could be used as a 'standfirst' – a compelling subheading that fills the reader in on what they can expect.

3. Do some **research**. We wouldn't expect you to have read every back issue, but being able to refer to a past article that you've enjoyed, or one that includes thematic parallels to your proposal, is helpful in two ways. Firstly, it tells us you know what kind of features work for a teen readership. Secondly, it allows us to imagine your piece alongside others we've commissioned.

4. If your subject matter would benefit from the inclusion of expert insight, make suggestions for **who you might interview**. Just a couple of pithy quotes from a professional in the relevant field can be invaluable and ensure the magazine is offering the right kind of help.

5. Provide suggestions for **how the piece might be presented**. We try to break up blocky text with subheadings, bullet points and panels, so include ideas for these, alongside exercises, writing prompts or activities that might complement the main article.

6. Include a brief outline of **your writing background** (with one or two links to previously published work, if appropriate) and any other relevant experience or subject-related qualifications. We'd like to know why you're the best person to write the piece.

Handle with care

One of the joys of writing for teens is they're often open-minded, curious and compassionate. This makes exploring subjects like neurodiversity, self-acceptance or care for the natural world all the more rewarding. The feedback we receive from young adults, plus their guardians and teachers – via email and through social media – is that there's a willingness to see things from different perspectives and an interest in the experiences of others that is refreshing and inspiring.

The other side of this coin, though, is the challenge presented by writing for such an open-hearted audience; the sensitivities of some readers might not at first occur to older writers. This means thinking carefully about word choice, subtext and potential triggers. Some of the messages we receive from readers reveal the struggles and vulnerabilities they're facing and the important role the magazine plays in dealing delicately with raw emotions. It's important to consider every possible interpretation of what you're saying so that no one feels judged or hurt and to avoid making assumptions of any kind.

Write for everyone

Teen Breathe has subscribers of all genders from all over the world, from the USA and Australia to Sweden and South Korea, so any activities suggested should be accessible and varied. It's impossible to cover every base, of course, but international examples should be in the mix. For example, local-interest stories or features based on a project targeted only at girls in one part of the UK, could leave readers who don't fit into those categories feeling as though they're on the outside of things. It's important, too, that all our readers feel valued – which means seeing themselves on the page. We encourage all our writers to cast their net wide when sourcing case studies and professionals, and try to include as diverse, representative and authentic a set of voices as possible.

Consult your inner teen

There's one final point worth mentioning: writers sometimes think they need to have teenage children to write for the teen market. My own view is that – while that experience might equip you well to write parenting articles – the best preparation for writing for teens is simply to remember what it was like to *be* one. There's a gradual and natural loosening of the connection between the present version of yourself and the 'you' of your youth. But … if it's possible to re-inhabit that mindset for a little while, and even to let that teenage part of you pipe up with their ideas before you begin to write, you'll be better placed to get on readers' wavelength and connect with them more directly.

Chloe Rhodes is a commissioning editor at *Teen Breathe* (www.teenbreathe.co.uk). She is a former *Daily Telegraph* features commissioning editor and is also the author of several books on language and folklore published by Michael O'Mara and a series of reading books for children published by Oxford University Press. Her freelance work has been published in the *Guardian*, *The Sunday Times* and the *Independent*.

Magazines and newspapers for children

Listings of magazines about children's literature and education start on page 269.

Anorak
3rd Floor, 86–90 Paul Street, London EC2A 4NE
email anorakmagazine@gmail.com
website www.anorakmagazine.com
Instagram @anorakmag
Editor Cathy Olmedillas
4 p.a. £8.50

Aimed at children aged 6 years and above, and designed to encourage creativity. Founded 2006.

Aquila
Studio 2, 67A Willowfield Road, Eastbourne, East Sussex BN22 8AP
tel (01323) 431313
email submissions@aquila.co.uk
email illustrators@aquila.co.uk
website www.aquila.co.uk
Facebook www.facebook.com/AquilaChildrensMagazine
Instagram @aquila.magazine
Editorial Director Freya Hardy
Monthly £8

Dedicated to encouraging children aged 8–14 years to reason and create, and to develop a caring nature. Short stories and serials of up to three parts. Occasional features commissioned from writers with specialist knowledge. Approach in writing with ideas and sample of writing style, along with sae or via e-mail (fiction and non-fiction pitches should be sent to the first email address above). Length: 700–800 words (features), 1,000–1,100 words (stories or per episode of a serial). Payment: by arrangement. Founded 1993.

Beano
D.C. Thomson & Co Ltd, Courier Buildings, 2 Albert Square, Dundee DD1 1DD
email contactus@beano.com
website www.beano.com
Facebook www.facebook.com/BeanoOfficial
X @BeanoOfficial
Instagram @beano_official
Editor John Anderson
50 p.a. £3.25

Comic strips for children aged 6–12 years. Series, 8–20 pictures. Artwork and scripts. Payment: on acceptance.

Cocoa Boy
Studio 210, 134–146 Curtain Road, London EC2A 3AR
email admin@thecocoadream.com
website https://cocoaboy.com
Instagram @cocoaboymag
Publisher and Creative Director Serlina Boyd
4 p.a. £3.99

The first UK magazine aimed specifically at young Black boys. Includes empowering content aimed at teaching children about Black culture and celebrating role models. Actively encourages submissions from children aged 7–11 years via email. Founded 2020.

Cocoa Girl
Studio 210, 134–146 Curtain Road, London EC2A 3AR
email admin@thecocoadream.com
website www.cocoagirl.com/submissions
Instagram @cocoagirlmag
Publisher Serlina Boyd, *Editor* Faith Boyd
4 p.a. £3.99

The first UK magazine aimed specifically at young Black girls. Includes empowering content aimed at teaching children about Black culture and celebrating role models. Actively encourages submissions from children aged 7–11 years via email. Winner of Launch of the Year at the British Society of Magazine Editors' Awards 2020. Founded 2020.

Commando
DC Thomson & Co Ltd., 2 Albert Square, Dundee DD1 1DD
email generalenquiries@commandomag.com
website www.commandocomics.com/submissions
Facebook www.facebook.com/C0mmandoComics
X @CommandoComic
Instagram @commandocomics
8 per month (four new, four reprints) £2.99

Fictional stories set in time of war told in pictures. Scripts: about 135 pictures. Synopsis required as an opener. See website for submissions information. Payment: on acceptance. Founded 1961.

DOT
3rd Floor, 86–90 Paul Street, London EC2A 4NE
email anorakmagazine@gmail.com
website www.anorakmagazine.com/dot
Editor Cathy Olmedillas
4 p.a. £7.50

Ad-free magazine aimed at encouraging creativity and learning in the under-5s. Founded 2015.

Magazines and newspapers for children

Eco Kids Planet
86–90 Paul Street, London EC2A 4NF
tel 0800 639 1365
email hello@ecokidsplanet.co.uk
website www.ecokidsplanet.co.uk
Facebook www.facebook.com/ecokidsplanet
Instagram @ecokidsplanetmag
Editor Anya Dimelow
11 p.a. £4.90

Aimed at 7–11 year-old children. Each issue is dedicated to a different ecosystem and contains facts, photographs, puzzles and projects. The magazine uses fun, fictional characters in a story format to convey facts about nature and the environment. It also provides children with real-world examples of how they can make a difference on the planet. Length: 500–1,200 words (themed articles). Requirements: well-researched, up-to-date, informative articles, creative approach and interesting language. Specially commissions most material. Payment: by arrangement. Founded 2014.

FirstNews
7 Playhouse Court, 62 Southwark Bridge Road, London SE1 0AT
tel 020-3195 2000
email newsdesk@firstnews.co.uk
website www.firstnews.co.uk
X @First_News
Instagram @first_news
Editor-in-Chief Nicky Cox
Weekly Fri £2.85

Covers news and events in the UK and internationally for children aged 8–14 years. Founded 2006.

Girl Talk
Immediate Media Co. Ltd, Vineyard House, 44 Brook Green, London W6 7BT
tel 020-7150 5000
email hello@girltalkmagazine.com
Instagram @girltalkmag
Editor Clare Norman
Fortnightly £5.99

Magazine for children aged 7–12. Contains pop, TV and film celebrity features, personality features, quizzes, fashion, competitions and stories. Length: 500 words (fiction). Payment: by arrangement. All material is specially commissioned. Founded 1995.

Headliners
tel 0191 231 4394
email enquiries@headliners.org
website www.headliners.org
Facebook www.facebook.com/HeadlinersUK
Instagram @headlinersuk

Award-winning journalism and multi-media charity, offering young people aged 8–18 the opportunity to write on issues of importance to them, for newspapers, radio and TV. Founded 1995.

KiCK!
Kennedy Publishing, Greenway Farm, Bath Road, Wick, Bristol BS30 5RL
tel 0117 937 3003
email info@kennedypublishing.co.uk
X @KiCKmagazine
Editor Ash Rose
13 p.a. £5.99

Football magazine for readers aged 7–14 years. Reports on leading players and teams from a variety of divisions, including the Premier League; also includes puzzles, competitions and interviews.

Kids Alive! (The Young Soldier)
The Salvation Army, 1 Champion Park, London SE5 8FJ
tel 020-7367 4911
email kidsalive@salvationarmy.org.uk
website www.salvationarmy.org.uk/kidsalive
Editor Cara Mott, *Deputy Editor* Ibukun Baku
Weekly 60p

Children's magazine: scripts and artwork for cartoon strips, puzzles, etc; Christian-based articles with emphasis on education and lifestyle issues. Illustrations: half-tone, line and four-colour line, cartoons. Payment: by arrangement. Founded 1881.

Kurio
1–5 Vyner Street, London E2 9DG
email info@okido.com
Instagram @kuriomagazine
6 p.a. From £42.99

Science, cartoons, stories, puzzles and book reviews for readers aged 7 to 12. Monthly themed issues.

Match!
Kelsey Media, The Granary, Downs Court, Yalding Hill, Yalding, Kent ME18 6AL
email match.magazine@kelsey.co.uk
website www.matchfootball.co.uk
Facebook www.facebook.com/matchmagazine
Fortnightly £4.99

Aimed at teenage football fans. News, statistics and information on leading Premier League, Football League and Scottish Premier League teams.

National Geographic Kids
Unit 10, Tomas Seth Business Park, Argent Road, Queenborough, Kent ME11 5TS
email kids@ngkids.co.uk
website www.natgeokids.co.uk
Facebook www.facebook.com/natgeokids
Instagram @natgeokidsuk
Editor Tim Herbert
13 p.a. From £39 p.a.

Fun facts, photos and features about animals, science, geography, history, the environment and popular culture, aimed at children aged 7–12 years.

National Geographic Little Kids
Unit 10, Tomas Seth Business Park, Argent Road, Queenborough, Kent ME11 5TS
email georgia@ngkids.co.uk
website www.natgeokids.com/uk
Editor Georgia Harrison
13 p.a. £4.99

Fun facts, stickers and games focused on animals and the environment for children aged three to six.

Okido
1–5 Vyner Street, London E2 9DG
email info@okido.com
website www.okido.com
Facebook www.facebook.com/OKIDO.OFFICIAL
Instagram @okido.official
Monthly £60 p.a.

Award-winning, eco-friendly illustrated science and arts magazine for children aged 3–7 years. Created by scientists and educators to promote fun, immersive STEAM learning, with a new topic to explore every month. Each edition includes science experiments, activities, recipes, doodles and games. Founded 2007.

Oyla
128 City Road, London EC1V 2NX
email info@oyla.uk
website www.oyla.uk
Facebook www.facebook.com/oyla.uk
Instagram @oyla.uk
12 p.a. £60 p.a. (print)

Print and online science magazine for readers aged 12 and above. Part of a suite of international editions compiled by science journalists, educators and scientists.

The Phoenix
31 Beaumont Street, Oxford OX1 2NP
email theeditor@thephoenixcomic.co.uk
website www.thephoenixcomic.co.uk
Facebook www.facebook.com/phoenixcomic
Instagram @phoenixcomicuk
Editor Tom Fickling
Weekly From £1 (introductory offer; other options available)

32pp weekly anthology comic for boys and girls aged 7–14 years. Features serialised stories and one-off stories as well as non-fiction. Encourages reading for pleasure and children's critical thinking, creative writing and drawing skills. Contributors include Jamie Smart and Neill Cameron. Founded 2011.

PONY Magazine
DJ Murphy Publishers Ltd, Olive Studio, The Timber Yard, Grange Road, Tilford, Farnham, Surrey GU10 2DQ
tel (01428) 601020
email pony@djmurphy.co.uk
website www.ponymag.com
Instagram @ponymaguk
Editor-in-Chief Louise Kittle
13 p.a. from £4.25

Lively articles and short stories with a horsey theme aimed at readers aged 8–16 years. Technical accuracy and young, fresh writing essential. Length: up to 800 words. Payment: by arrangement. Illustrations: by arrangement. Founded 1949.

Storytime
61 Bridge Street, Kington HR5 3DJ
email hello@storytimemagazine.com
website www.storytimemagazine.com, www.storytimeforschools.com
Facebook www.facebook.com/StorytimeMag
X @StorytimeMag
Monthly From £4.99

Illustrated bedtime story magazine for children aged 3–8. Accepting submissions from illustrators: see website for full submission guidelines. Calls for submissions from short-story writers also occur periodically; check online for details of forthcoming opportunities.

Teen Breathe
GMC Publications, 86 High Street, Lewes BN7 1XN
tel (01273) 477374
email hello@breathemagazine.com
website www.teenbreathe.co.uk/submissions
Publisher Jonathan Grogan
Bi-monthly £5.99

Tips, exercises and ideas on how to make mindfulness part of teenagers' lives so that they can stay positive and improve their wellbeing. Submissions welcomed from experienced or new writers, and from illustrators; see website for specific requirements for each type of potential contributor. Founded 2017.

What on Earth!
The Black Barn, Wickhurst Farm, Leigh, Tonbridge, Kent TN11 8PS
tel (01732) 464621
email editor@whatonearth.co.uk
website https://www.britannicamagazine.com/contact
Facebook www.facebook.com/WhatonEarthMag
X @WhatonEarth_Mag
Instagram @whatonearth_mag
Editor-in-Chief Andrew Pettie
10 p.a. £5.99

Illustrated non-fiction magazine for children aged 7–14 years and featuring facts, quizzes, puzzles and real-life stories. Written in the UK; all content fact-checked by experts from Britannica. Founded 2021 as *Britannica Magazine*.

Magazines about children's literature and education

Listings of magazines and newspapers for children start on page 266.

Armadillo
32 Cannon Court Road, Maidenhead SL6 7QN
email armadilloeditor@gmail.com
website www.armadillomagazine.co.uk
Facebook www.facebook.com/Armadillomag
X @Armadillomag
Instagram @armadillomagazine
Editor Louise Ellis-Barrett
6 p.a. Free

Online children's book review magazine including reviews, interviews, features, competitions, profiles and downloadable activities. Free weekly newsletter for subscribers. Weekly blog; daily social media posts; issues posted February, April, June, August, October, December. New reviewers and writers always welcome. Founded 1999.

Books for Keeps
30 Winton Avenue, London N11 2AT
tel 07807 893369
email andrea@booksforkeeps.co.uk
website www.booksforkeeps.co.uk
X @BooksforKeeps
Bluesky @booksforkeeps.bsky.social
Instagram @booksforkeepsuk
Editor Andrea Reece
Bi-monthly Free

Children's book review journal including features, reviews and news on the genre. Readership is both professionals and parents. Founded 1980.

The Bookseller
The Stage Media Company Ltd,
47 Bermondsey Street, London SE1 3XT
tel 020-3403 1818
email tom.tivnan@thebookseller.com
website www.thebookseller.com
X @thebookseller
Editor Philip Jones, *Managing Editor* Tom Tivnan
Weekly £5.95

Journal of the UK publishing and bookselling trades. The *Children's Bookseller* supplement is published regularly and there is news on the children's book business in the main magazine. Produces the *Children's Buyer's Guide*, which previews children's books to be published in the following six months. The website features news on children's books, comment on the children's sector, author interviews and children's bestseller charts. Founded 1858.

Educate
National Education Union, Hamilton House, Mabledon Place, London WC1H 9BD
tel 020-7380 4708
email educate@neu.org.uk
website https://neu.org.uk/latest/union-journals/educate-magazine
Editor Max Watson
6 p.a. Free to NEU members

Articles, features and news of interest to all those involved in the education sector. Email outline in the first instance. Length: 500 words (single page), 1,000 (double page). Payment: NUJ rates to NUJ members. Founded 2019.

Inis – The Children's Books Ireland Magazine
Children's Books Ireland,
17 North Great George Street, Dublin D01 R2F1, Republic of Ireland
tel +353 (0)1 872 7475
email publications@childrensbooksireland.ie
website www.childrensbooksireland.ie
Instagram @kidsbooksirel
Publications Officer Ruth Concannon
3 p.a. €5

Solely devoted to children's books and the wider world of literature for young people. The three annual print issues each feature 44 reviews of current or upcoming titles; the features section includes five to six articles, ranging from artist interviews, project overviews or a broader focus on a topic or theme. Each issue is printed in Ireland, distributed to Children's Books Ireland members and is available for individual purchase. Back issues become available online one year after print publication. The archive of back issues is available from childrensbooksireland.ie/our-recommendations. Founded 1989.

Literacy
UK Literacy Association, Room 9 c/o VAL,
9 Newarke Street, Leicester LE1 5SN
tel 0116 254 4116
website https://onlinelibrary.wiley.com/journal/17414369
Editors Sam Duncan, Sinead Harmey, Rachael Levy, Lucy Taylor
3 p.a. Free to UKLA members or £106 p.a.

Official journal of the United Kingdom Literacy Association (see page 331), aimed at those interested in the study and development of literacy. Readership comprises practitioners, teachers, educators, researchers, undergraduate and graduate students. It offers educators a forum for debate through scrutinising research evidence, reflecting on analysed accounts of innovative practice and examining recent policy developments. Length: 2,000–6,000 words (articles). Illustrations: by arrangement. Formerly known as *Reading – Literacy and Language*. Founded 1966.

Nursery World

MA Education, St Jude's Church, Dulwich Road, London SE24 0PB
tel 020-8501 6693
email karen.faux@markallengroup.com
website www.nurseryworld.co.uk
Editor Karen Faux
Fortnightly From £11 per month

For all grades of primary school, nursery and childcare staff, nannies, foster parents and all those concerned with the care of expectant mothers, babies and young children. Authoritative and informative articles, 800 or 1,300 words, and photos on all aspects of child welfare and early education, from 0–8 years, in the UK. Practical ideas, policy news and career advice. No short stories. Illustrations: by arrangement. Payment: by arrangement.

Tes (The Times Educational Supplement)

70 Gray's Inn Road, London WC1X 8NH
tel 020-3194 3000
email newsdesk@tes.com
email features@tes.com
website www.tes.com
X @tes
Editor Jon Severs
Daily £3.50 (£19 per quarter, £40 per year for the first year, £59 per year thereafter)

Publishes daily online articles on educational subjects: the latest news, analysis and teaching and learning research for those who work in schools. Specialist knowledge required and ideas should be emailed to the relevant sector editor. Payment: by arrangement. Founded 1910.

Tess (The Times Educational Supplement Scotland)

70 Gray's Inn Road, London WC1X 8NH
email henry.hepburn@tes.com
website www.tes.com/magazine/hub/scotland
X @TesScotland
Scotland Editor Henry Hepburn
Daily See website for subscription options

Publishes online articles on education subjects. Looking for articles on education, preferably 600–800 words, written with special knowledge or experience. News items about Scottish educational affairs, especially those affecting schools. Payment: by arrangement. Founded 1965.

Stage, screen and audio
Adapting children's books for stage and screen

Emma Reeves offers her experience of the challenges and rewards of adapting other people's literary creations for the television or stage, giving practical advice on securing rights and successfully reimagining and reshaping a story you love in a way that works for the new medium.

If you are a working writer for stage, screen or radio, whether you're writing for children, adults or both, it's highly likely that adaptations will form a regular part of your work – and income. Audio drama, film, TV and theatre have a voracious appetite for valuable IP (intellectual property) and the rights to successful books are fought over ruthlessly. TV companies working in children's television are constantly reading and keeping up with the latest events in children's publishing.

CBBC's two biggest home-grown brands are probably *Horrible Histories* (based on the books by Terry Deary) and *The Dumping Ground*, evolved from *Tracy Beaker Returns* (created by Elly Brewer and Ben Ward), an original TV series which continued the story of Jacqueline Wilson's popular protagonist, Tracy Beaker, and introduced a whole new set of characters and problems. Tracy and her world have now been a vital part of the CBBC landscape for over 20 years – yet the CBBC development exec who initially championed Tracy's cause admits that it was an uphill struggle to get the powers that be to buy into the realistic story of a brutally neglected child who experiences bed-wetting, meltdowns, rages and attachment issues as an all-too-plausible result of a heartbreaking upbringing. In the end, Tracy's inimitable spirit (and 20 plus years of fierce audience loyalty) won the day; but it's worth keeping in mind that, when it comes to commissioning, nothing is ever really a 'no-brainer' – and if you truly believe in an idea, it's probably worth fighting for.

Book adaptations have a strong appeal for TV and theatre producers, who like to have a tangible idea of what they're getting before commissioning a new series or play. This can be frustrating for new writers who are desperate to get their own big new idea out there. It does mean, though, that producers are often looking for the 'right' writer to match with a project, which can be a shortcut to a paid commission. And artistically, it can give you the chance to experience the joy, fear and pain of taking control of a group of beloved characters in a rich, well-realised world.

Riding the highs and lows

The highs and lows of adaptation are dizzying. It's certainly not easier than original work. If you do happen to find it easier, I will sincerely try to be happy for you, but I enviously suspect that you're doing it wrong. In my personal experience, it doesn't hurt any less to fail as an adapter than as an originator – in fact, it's worse. You haven't just let yourself down, you've betrayed your original author, your guide, your travelling companion, maybe even your hero.

Of course, when things *do* work and people profess to love the resulting show, the Bad Voices in every writer's head lose no time in pointing out that *everything good is because* of the original author ... everything bad is your *fault*. And if those voices should ever abandon you (unlikely), there's always the internet ...

Which brings me to Rule One of adapting – no, Rule One of everything, ever: Never, *ever* search the internet. Just don't do it.

Rule Two: when you inevitably ignore my advice and search the internet – remember, they're just people, like you; maybe too much like you. As a child, I was an obsessive reader, and I still suffer from very strong 'fannish' tendencies. I know very well that there are certain books and authors of which no adaptation will ever satisfy me. The people who are hardest to please are the most devoted. If someone comes down hard on your adaptation, console yourself by imagining the review you'd give to any adaptation of *your* favourite book of all time.

The real high of adaptation is that you get to play inside someone else's incredible creation. And what could be better than that? As a stage adapter, I've been privileged to reimagine childhood favourites – *Little Women, Carrie's War, Anne of Green Gables, Sherlock Holmes, Cool Hand Luke, Doctor Jekyll and Mr Hyde* – and also to discover the work of a new generation of children's writers. I've written for *The Story of Tracy Beaker, Tracy Beaker Returns* and *The Dumping Ground* – all based on Jacqueline Wilson's work – and also worked on both the stage and TV versions of her *Hetty Feather*.

Every experience is different and brings its own challenges. Even within the same medium, there are different types of show. On TV, for example, at one end of the scale is the straight, closed-ended adaptation, where you are expected to more or less follow the story of the book. At the other end of the spectrum is the open-ended drama which may take nothing more from its source material than a few names and a situation, relying on the ingenuity of the script writers to come up with episodic plots. Most TV shows are somewhere in between – perhaps a novel may provide the protagonist's journey for series one, but then it's up to the writers to come up with new material.

Check out the rights

A lot of my adaptation work has come about through people approaching me. But what if you've fallen in love with an original work and you just have to adapt it or write a sequel? What should you do? Before you type your first words, make sure the rights are available and that you've got a realistic chance of getting them. The only exception is for out-of-copyright material (where the author has been dead for 70 years or more). Otherwise, anything you write without the blessing of the author or their estate is basically fan fiction; you may enjoy it, your friends may enjoy it, but you can never reach a mass audience, and certainly never make any money, unless you want a lawsuit on your hands. So, if you're serious about sharing your vision with the world, check out the rights before doing anything else.

If you have an agent, or an interested production company, they will be able to help you approach the rights-holders. If not, you can search online for the writer's agent or go through the publisher. Bear in mind that the latest hot properties and surprise hits will almost always be optioned already – but options lapse, so it's worth enquiring about the length of the option and trying again at the appropriate time. Read more obscure work in the hope of finding an un-optioned gem.

Despite all this, securing book rights is comparatively easy compared to getting the rights to adapt film or TV shows. This is particularly tricky for lone writers, as TV and film properties tend to have multiple owners and sorting out the various claims requires an army of showbiz lawyers. As a general rule, it's only worth pursuing if you have a major producing force on your side (both to give you credibility and to pay those lawyers' fees!), but there are always exceptions. If you're really passionate about a project and you think you can persuade the rights-holders, go for it. Our business is built on stories of those few lucky people whose tenacity and love for their project enabled them to break all the rules and succeed.

Reimagining the story

What happens next? A producer friend regularly chides me that he doesn't know why my scripts take so long, when all I have to do is copy down the book and cross out the description. Although I generally laugh bitterly at such comments, adaptation is a broad church and there are some gigs which are perhaps better described as abridging – such as when I worked out a three-hander version of *King Lear* and a four-hander version of *The Importance of Being Earnest* for a small touring company. Although you have to be a bit creative in situations like that, you're working within the intended medium and almost exclusively using the author's original text. At the other end of the scale of fidelity to the original work, I once worked on a children's TV show for two years before anyone informed me that it was actually based on a novel!

These two extremes aside, the job of the adapter is usually to reimagine the story in a way which works for the medium. For example, when I worked on the stage version of *Hetty Feather*, we started with Jacqueline's book and created the show in the rehearsal room with six actors. Using the wealth of material in the book, and even more which was generated by the actors, my job was to steer the story into a coherent structure which would fit into two hours' stage time, streamlining plot moments and making some tough calls about which brilliant bits to jettison. When I wrote episodes of the TV show, I had to come up with self-contained plots lasting half an hour. In the first case I had an overabundance of other people's material to deal with; in the second, it was up to me to tell new stories. People asked if I found it confusing but, to me, the worlds of *Hetty* the book, *Hetty* the stage show and *Hetty* the TV show were so different that I never struggled in that way. In some respects, the medium informs the writing experience possibly more than the original material does.

When you start to adapt a book, you are entering somebody else's world, and meeting their characters. In order to feel comfortable in that world, I always try to read as much of the writer's other work as I can. This may seem like obvious advice, but the benefits are so great that it's worth emphasising. If the author writes a lot about a specific time and place, that's useful for research and background colour. If they are preoccupied with certain ideas or social issues, you can get a greater understanding of where they were coming from when they wrote the book. I have actually transposed scenes from (out-of-copyright!) lesser-known works of authors, in order to illuminate important moments which I felt were glossed over somewhat in the work I was adapting. Cheeky perhaps, but it worked for me.

Creating the shape

So, you've got a handle on the world and the characters. Everything may be clearly set out for you, or you may need to fill the gaps – or change certain elements. You may discover what you need to change as you go along. At this stage, you take a step back from the source material (and its potentially seductive prose) and ask the normal questions of dramatic writing: Whose story is it? What do they want? Who is trying to stop them getting it?

A specific problem I have encountered is that many beloved books are episodic in nature: this happens, then that happens, then this happens … In drama, stories tend to need ongoing hooks: this happens, SO that happens, SO that happens … I find I need to work hard to create a sense of building drama and inevitability. Also, coincidence feels much harder to mask in drama than in novels. I find myself investigating plot conveniences – are they really just happenstance? Or did someone plan it? If you can decide that the events are the result of someone's plan, it immediately feels easier to dramatise plausibly.

You have to keep your characters active and keep your hooks dangling. Keep your protagonist pushing through to the end. When you're watching previews, or in the edit, try to resist the temptation to keep a 'good bit' in if your gut is screaming at you that it's slowing down the story and risks letting the audience's interest drop. Sometimes that comedy interlude just sits too awkwardly at a moment when the hero has to make a life-or-death choice and risk everything. Sometimes it's time to stop piling torture, misery and despair on a character and let the audience know that they're ready to fight back. As an adapter, you need to take responsibility for the work as a whole – the shape is now up to you. And you may have to keep a mediocre bit at the expense of a good bit if, after a lot of consideration (and discussion with the director, editor or whoever), you realise that that's what the shape of the story needs.

Interestingly, not a word of the paragraph above couldn't also be usefully applied to original drama scripts.

So in summary: enjoy the highs, the fun and the privilege; appreciate the work that other people have done so you don't have to; but if something's not working, don't shrug it off as the original author's problem – look at it from all angles until you find a way to make it work for you. It's the very least that the author deserves. After all, it's probably their name that got you the gig.

Emma Reeves is a three times BAFTA-nominated writer. Her credits include adapting numerous Jacqueline Wilson titles, including *My Mum Tracy Beaker, The Beaker Girls, The Dumping Ground* and *Hetty Feather* (all for the BBC). Other TV credits include *The Hardacres* for Channel 5 plus *Young Dracula* and a co-created original science fiction show, *Eve,* for CBBC. West End stage adaptations include *The Worst Witch, Carrie's War, Little Women, Hetty Feather* and *Cool Hand Luke*. *The Worst Witch* won the Olivier Award for Best Family Show, while *Hetty Feather* (the stage show) was nominated for an Olivier Award and won the first ever CAMEO award for best page-to-stage adaptation. She is currently Chair of the Writers' Guild of Great Britain. Follow her on X @emmajanereeves.

Children's literature on radio, podcast and audio

The technologies for transmitting the spoken word to children are developing rapidly. Neville Teller describes the fast-changing world of radio, podcasting and audio, and explores what a writer for the microphone needs to know to break into this market.

'Read me a story' – one of childhood's perennial cries. Until radio arrived, parents found little relief from it (palming it off on grandma or uncle was perhaps the best bet). But from its very beginning, radio included in its schedules stories read aloud for children. So, for part of the time at least, the loudspeaker was able to provide a fair substitute for mummy or daddy by providing literature, specially prepared for performance at the microphone, read by professional actors.

Very early on, actors learned that performing at the microphone was a new skill – the techniques were specialised and quite different from those required on the stage. Writers, too, had to acquire a whole range of new skills in preparing material for radio. Two things quickly became apparent. First, the time taken to read a complete book on the air would be far too long to be acceptable, and in consequence most books would need to be abridged. Second, literature simply read aloud from the printed page often failed to 'come across' to a listening audience, because material produced to be scanned by the eye is often basically unsuited to the requirements of the microphone.

Today there are two main outlets in this country for aspiring writers for children in the radio/podcasting sphere: online radio/audio/podcasts and audiobook publishers. How has this market reached its present position?

Radio/podcasts

Children's radio in the UK came into existence in December 1922, just a few weeks after the BBC itself was born, and for some 40 years the daily *Children's Hour* became an established and much-cherished feature of life. However, in the 1960s the imminent death of radio was a generally accepted prognostication. Starting in 1961, in the belief that television was their preferred medium, children's radio was slowly but surely strangled.

The demise of children's radio naturally evoked a massive groundswell of protest. In response the BBC of the day did grant some sort of reprieve. *Story Time* – a programme of abridged radio readings – started life in the old *Children's Hour* slot with a strong bias towards children's literature. It was not long, however, before more general literature began to be selected, and finally, in 1982, that programme too was dropped. For the next 20 years the only regular children's programme left on BBC radio was *Listen with Mother*, the 15-minute slot for the under-fives.

Early in the new millennium, the BBC – moved, doubtless, by mounting evidence of the undiminished popularity of radio – decided to reintroduce a regular programme for children. All they could offer at the time was a 30-minute programme each Sunday evening on Radio 4 called *Go4It*, a magazine-type show which included a ten-minute reading, and I found myself abridging books for it like *The Lion, the Witch and the Wardrobe* by

C.S. Lewis and *The Wolves of Willoughby Chase* by Joan Aiken. Unfortunately, this renaissance was typically short-lived. *Go4It* was axed on 24 May 2009.

But the door had been pushed ajar, and in the autumn of 2002, when the BBC launched its new digital radio channel, BBC7, its schedules included, as a basic ingredient, daily programmes for children incorporating readings from children's literature, both current and classic. I prepared a considerable number of books for these programmes, including not only classical children's literature like *Robinson Crusoe* and *The Prince and the Pauper*, but also more general classics like *20,000 Leagues Under the Sea* and *Oliver Twist*. The programme for older children also featured up-to-the-moment favourites such as Anthony Horowitz's series about his boy secret agent, Alex Rider, the *Artemis Fowl* novels by Eoin Colfer, Terry Pratchett's *A Hat Full of Sky* and *The Amazing Maurice* and Jackie French's *Callisto* series. For younger listeners, I abridged books like the *Whizziwig* series by Malorie Blackman, the *Lily Quench* books by Natalie Jane Prior and Kaye Umansky's *The Silver Spoon of Solomon Snow*.

All seemed set fair, but towards the end of 2006 came news of major changes. The programme for younger listeners was converted into a radio extension of CBeebies, the BBC's digital television channel for the youngest children, while the BBC7 schedule included readings drawn from the programme's extensive archive, including my own abridgements of, among many others, *Bootleg* by Alex Shearer, *Stop the Train* by Geraldine McCaughrean, *Huckleberry Finn* by Mark Twain, *Slaves of the Mastery* and *Firesong* by William Nicholson, *Stig of the Dump* by Clive King, *The BFG* by Roald Dahl, *The Little House on the Prairie* by Laura Ingalls Wilder, *Dream Master* by Theresa Breslin and *Point Blanc* by Anthony Horowitz.

Nothing lasts for ever, and 2011 saw BBC7 transformed into BBC Radio 4 Extra. With the transformation came a new shape to children's radio – almost a return to the *Children's Hour* concept of yesteryear, *The Four O'Clock Show* always including abridged readings of children's literature. Among the specially commissioned readings I abridged *Chitty Chitty Bang Bang Flies Again* by Frank Cottrell Boyce, *Wonder* by R.J. Palacio and *Maggot Moon* by Sally Gardner.

Sadly, *The Four O'Clock Show* too succumbed to the rapidly changing technological needs of its audience. 30 April 2015 saw its final transmission. The axing of this hour of dedicated children's radio meant that there is no longer any children's programming on Radio 4 Extra, and its service licence has been amended to remove its commitment to the content.

However, the BBC is now providing a wealth of children's programmes online. BBC Sounds has built up an impressive selection of radio programmes. Search its app or website for 'CBeebies' (for preschool children) or 'CBBC' (for older kids) to find loads of audio material suitable for youngsters of all ages.

Targeted at primary school pupils, BBC School Radio offers audio learning resources covering a variety of subjects. While traditional broadcasts have ceased, the content remains accessible online and via BBC Sounds.

In addition to the BBC, there is a national digital radio station dedicated entirely to children aged 6–12 years. Fun Kids is a nationwide station available on digital radio, mobiles, tablets, online and via smart speakers. Its podcasts and videos include stories, drama and educational material.

All these outlets require dedicated writers for children, prepared to adapt existing, or provide new, material in audio format specifically for young listeners.

Audiobooks

Audiobooks are literary works of all types, read by actors and available as CDs or as downloads from the internet. Industry data reveals that the audiobook market is expanding rapidly, but estimates of its actual size vary widely. One source suggests that total UK audiobook revenue has increased year-on-year and reached £257.5 million in 2024. Another claims that the figure topped £1 billion. Factors such as direct-to-consumer sales, subscription services, and content from international sources could account for the variation in the estimates. Exact figures for the children's share of the UK audiobook market are not available, but children's literature represents about 23% of total book sales in the UK, and that may serve as a broad-brush guide.

Audible dominates the audiobook market and its sales are booming, but it faces growing competition from newcomers such as audiobooks.com, Kobo and BookBeat, as well as Google and Apple.

Nowadays, it is common for major publishers to launch a fair number of their new books, including books for older children, in printed and audiobook form simultaneously. Publishers of books for younger children often adopt the 'twin pack' concept – packaging book and audiobook together – so that children can read and listen at the same time. Such products are zero-rated for VAT. However VAT at 20% is still being charged on audiobooks; the UK book industry has mounted a campaign ("Axe the Reading Tax") to have it removed. The subject was debated in the House of Commons in June 2023.

How children listen

The ways in which children listen to the readings intended especially for them are multiplying at what seems an ever-increasing rate. In addition to online radio heard via digital radio sets, children listen on laptops and PCs, smartphones, tablets and smart speaker voice assistants like Amazon's Alexa, Google's Assistant, and Apple's Siri. Primary school teachers download BBC School podcasts and play them back in class.

Downloads are a growing method for children to access audiobooks especially for them. There are a range of online outlets, including Audible and Apple iTunes through its audiobooks store. Taken together, these DTO (download to own) providers have available an enormous and expanding list of children's books, and stories are proving a popular second-best to music for many children. Subscribers pay either a monthly fee for the right to download a specific number of titles or pay for downloads book by book. However, these days a surprising number of websites are offering free downloads of children's stories. Just google "free children's audiobook downloads" for a list of sites.

For example, Amazon has some 30,000 children's audiobooks available to be purchased and downloaded. Users can start listening within seconds and can transfer the audiobook to another device or burn it to a CD. Other specialist providers of audiobooks for children include Children's Storybooks Online (www.magickeys.com/books) and the Story Home (www.thestoryhome.com). All commission new stories for children.

Young people are increasingly accessing not only their social networks via their smartphones, but also audiobooks. Google, Amazon and Audible are providing access to audiobooks via phones, and other providers are crowding into the marketplace.

Amazon's ebook readers, the Kindle and Kindle Fire (which offers a colour touchscreen), have been runaway successes. The Kindle can download a book in about 30 seconds, either to be read on its 6-inch wide screen or to be read aloud to you (albeit in a somewhat robot-like voice). Audiobooks can also be downloaded, though the process is easier on the later versions of Kindle.

Kindle's biggest rivals as a non-print reading device are Kobo, Onyx Boox, PocketBook and Nook, and its growing number of tablet competitors, all of which have loudspeaker and headphone facilities for audio transmission via Bluetooth. These include iPad, Samsung Galaxy, Remarkable 2 and Boox Tab series.

In-car MP3 playback, via the car radio, now widely available, is becoming increasingly popular as a means of keeping children happy on long journeys. Children's audiobooks are also now part of in-flight entertainment on long-haul flights.

A recent phenomenon is 'podiobooks', or podcast audiobook novels, released on the internet in instalments and for free. They are now often categorized as kids' fiction podcasts or serialized audio stories, and are featured on platforms like Audible, Pinna and Apple Podcasts, and on Spotify. The pioneer is Scott Sigler, whose website offers free audio fiction, together with videos, ebooks and blog posts via social media; see https://scottsigler.com. The whole concept is aimed particularly at teenagers and young people.

The message of all this for writers is that the radio/audio/podcast/'podiobook' market is mushrooming, and that burgeoning technological developments and innovations seem designed to appeal particularly to the internet-savvy younger generations. If you are keen to break into the rapidly changing world of children's literature on radio and audio, this seems as favourable and opportune a time to succeed as ever. For contact details for children's radio, see *Children's television and radio* (page 284) or search online for children's audiobook publishers, and offer your services. Do not be discouraged by initial rejection – that is often a writer's early experience. Persevere. As in all professional fields, the tyro is faced with the classic catch-22 situation: radio producers and audio publishers are reluctant to offer commissions to people without a track record, while it is of course impossible to gain a track record without having won a commission or two. The only advice is to keep plugging away, hoping for that elusive lucky break – and the only consolation on offer is that even the most experienced of today's professionals was once a complete novice.

Writing for the microphone

Unabridged readings are becoming increasing popular in the audiobook sphere, but there is still a need, especially in the children's sphere, to write and to convert the written word, in a way that can be performed by an actor with ease at the microphone, and bring real listening pleasure to the child at the other end.

Where the writer is called on to abridge specifically for download, the audiobook publishers will specify the length either in terms of time or of wordage. Remember, an actor can normally get through about 2,200 words in 15 minutes.

What makes a good abridgement? To reproduce the sense of an original in fewer words while, in addition and quite as important, to retain the character of the original writing. That demands the capacity to respond sympathetically to the feel of an author's style and to be able to preserve it, even when large chunks of the original are being cut away.

In crafting a radio/audio script, the needs of the listener must be one of the prime considerations. The needs of the actor who will read it at the microphone are another. The writer must keep in the forefront of their mind the fact that the script has to be performed. The words must, as Hamlet says, 'flow trippingly on the tongue'.

Neville Teller MBE has been contributing to BBC radio for over 50 years. He is credited with over 250 abridgements for radio readings, 50 radio dramatisations and 300 audiobook abridgements. His publications include *5-Minute Bedtime Stories*, based on classic children's tales he wrote for BBC radio. His radio dramatisations of *Aladdin* and the *Wonderful Lamp* (broadcast by the BBC), and *Ozma of Oz* by Frank Baum (broadcast across the USA), were included in his book *Audio Drama: 10 Plays for Radio and Podcast*. Included in his second book of radio plays, *Audio Drama 2*, is his dramatisation of the Zane Gray classic *Riders of the Purple Range*, also broadcast in the USA and Canada. His own radio play *Little Boy Lost* was broadcast in 2022. He is a past chairman of the Society of Authors' Broadcasting Committee and of the Audiobook Publishing Association's Contributors' Committee. He was made an MBE in 2006 for 'services to broadcasting and to drama'.

See also...
- *Children's audio publishers*, page 78
- *Children's television and radio*, page 284

Writing for visual broadcast media

Jayne Kirkham shares her experience of writing for the ever-changing world of children's broadcast media, confident that the writer's role remains essentially unchanged: the writer needs to tell a story with characters and concepts that their audience will remember and love all their lives.

'Writing for kids' telly? Easy! I mean … how hard can it be?'

So says someone who doesn't write for children. For a start, are kids actually watching a telly? If you watch much children's content (and, if you're interested in writing for children, you should) you'll know they are more likely to be watching YouTube on a phone. Depending on what it is, you may be even more inclined to think, 'No, seriously, how hard can it be?' But what looks so simple has been put through a furnace of development: even a 30-second TikTok, if money is involved somehow, will have been shaped, moulded, reshaped, possibly with a good deal of firing, before it is finally hammered into something that perfectly suits a broadcaster's or platform's particular audience. And that audience is very particular; children have all the myriad tastes and genre preferences of adults but with the different stages of a child's personal, social and physical development thrown in. Furthermore, the content has to be fun or, as kids in a 2019 report put it, 'amazing/cool/excellent' (*Social Media, Television and Children Report 2019* by University of Sheffield, BBC Children's and Dubit). Even the serious stuff must engage or children simply won't watch.

When I started writing for children's TV, it was a hugely competitive but fairly straightforward world to navigate, with only a handful of broadcasters and producers that commissioned shows. If you went to the Children's Media Conference (CMC; or Showcomotion, as it was called then), you could fit everyone you needed to meet into one room. Nowadays, if you go to the Children's Media Conference (and if you're interested in writing for children, you should), everyone you need to meet will still be there – that 'everyone' covers not just traditional TV but streaming services, online, games, books, apps and toys. Changes in children's media policy, and advances in technology, mean children and young people have never known anything but access to content (what used to be called 'programmes') whenever and wherever they like, and in all sorts of formats. They might watch something on a smart TV while accessing extra information about it on their tablet and simultaneously playing along on their phone; what's more, they are making and broadcasting their own content.

To write professionally, this looks like a much harder, more bewildering world to get into. But actually, whatever innovations arise and throw the industry into flux, for a writer the basics remain the same: know your audience and know how to tell a story, with characters and concepts that kids will remember and love all their lives. If you know your audience, you will know what they are watching and where. You will understand that they prefer to watch their content on YouTube rather than CBBC, and you will be aware of the growth of Sky Kids, TikTok, smart speakers and whatever new players are on the scene by the time you read this.

For a writer, things haven't changed as much as everyone would have us believe; children still enjoy drama, comedy, animation, game shows, documentaries and news made by professional media companies. Those companies need writers like you and me, but getting

Writing for visual broadcast media 281

in touch with them can take a bit of detective work – and a decent pause button, so that you can read a programme's credits properly. Another source of information is the programme's entry on www.imdb.com (International Movie Database). Once you know the name of the production company, you can do an online search for their website where you can generally find contact details for particular producers and/or development departments. Before you contact anyone about writing for them, however, find out as much as you can about the producers, production companies and their intellectual properties (IP). What have they made in the past? What are they developing now? What do they want to develop? Remember, the show that you have just watched and enjoyed will probably have been written two years before; what are they doing now?

The children's channels or platforms also have websites you can explore. By 'platforms', I'm referring to online providers such as Disney+, Netflix, Amazon, Apple TV, Azoomee and Hopster, as well as the public service broadcasters (BBC, ITV, Channel 4 and Five) and the commercial digital channels (Nickelodeon, Pop, Cartoon Network, Disney Channel, etc). To get beyond the shiny, public pages of games and fan chat, enter words like 'producer guidelines' or 'commissioning' into your search engine; you need to find the broadcasters' business pages which show what they are looking for. Remember, each channel/platform has its own brand identity, catering for a specific audience. Make sure you know the difference between a Nickelodeon and a Netflix show.

An easy way to compare and contrast the different platforms is to attend a trade event, such as the Children's Media Conference held in Sheffield every July. There are other conferences and festivals, but the CMC is the best for UK children's media professionals; all the significant platforms and broadcasters attend and hold commissioning sessions where they explain what they want to produce in the next few years. It's also a great opportunity to meet producers and other professionals you may want to collaborate with or work for, with lots of time in the conference schedule for networking. While attending in person is best, it is possible to attend online if money and time are limited. See www.thechildrensmediaconference.com for more details.

Having enjoyed a few years' respite from underfunding and lack of political support, thanks to the campaigning of organisations such as the Children's Media Foundation and the WGGB (Writers' Guild of Great Britain; see page 300), children's media is once more facing difficult times. Government funds have been cut, advertising restrictions and other threats to the public service broadcasters (BBC, ITV, C4 and C5) are making it increasingly difficult to finance content. If you've been watching the credits carefully (and if you're interested in writing for children, you should), you will have noticed that very few shows are the product of one producer and one broadcaster. With multinational streamers and international co-production as the norm, your writing has to appeal to an international audience. It can also mean that you are competing not just with British writers but writers from overseas. Rather than despair, let this open your eyes to other markets and territories. Countries like China, Brazil, India and many others have looked to the UK for writing talent in recent years. Annual international conferences, such as the Children's Media Conference mentioned above, MIPJUNIOR now held in London (www.mipjunior.com) and the Kidscreen Summit in the United States (http://kidscreen.com), are great places to meet international companies face to face. Attending these can be costly and time-consuming – it's easier and cheaper to subscribe to their regular newsletters for excellent insider information that you can follow up.

Working for an overseas company is one of the few reasons why a screenwriter might need an agent. I know a good number of non-agented writers working in the UK on existing shows; the contracts are generally straightforward and many follow WGGB guidelines. But when I have had overseas commissions, I've been grateful to have an agent used to dealing with other territories – not least getting the exchange rate and tax implications right.

It surely must be the dream of every screenwriter to get their own show produced. When the traditional broadcasters were the only players in town, new shows were generally commissioned from writers who had already proven themselves on other series. To get their ideas on screen, writers were dependent on the broadcaster's own producers or independent production companies and they often lost control. The internet has created more routes for entrepreneurial writers to reach their intended audience; for example, *Night Zookeeper* – available on Sky Kids – started as a web-based teaching aid to encourage children to start writing their own stories.

However, no matter how you intend to get your idea in front of your audience, it needs to go through the same rigorous development process: interrogating the concept and the characters to make sure that it is age-appropriate and will engage the audience utterly, not just in its main format but also in different 'transmedia' guises (as an app, books, in social media, videogames). Don't forget to consider toys and other merchandising, as appropriate. Different genres will, of course, have different opportunities and limitations. A drama like *The Dumping Ground* is unlikely to sell as many lunchboxes as, say, preschool animation *Paw Patrol*, but that doesn't mean it shouldn't get made. Just remember to allow the potential revenue returns to determine the budget. Rather confusingly, industry people tend to bandy the term 'genre' in their own special way, using it to describe animation, drama, preschool or comedy. If you watch enough kids' content, you will know that nearly all dramas have a lot of comedy, that animation covers everything from wacky shorts to sitcoms to intense re-enactments for documentaries, and that preschool covers everything but in a way that's appropriate for the under-sixes. As I've mentioned, the specific requirements for each broadcaster/platform brand should be available on their websites.

Once you have sufficiently developed your idea – and in that development I would include writing some sample scripts to fully prove whether your idea works or not – and have researched the market, it is time to get it out there. Does your intended recipient give guidelines on submitting your IP? They may ask you to use an online submission portal. If there are no guidelines, write a brief email introducing yourself and your project as succinctly as possible. Can you pitch it in one sentence? Can you explain the series on a single sheet of A4 paper? Do you have a decent sample script to show off your writing talents? Some producers are wary of unsolicited attachments, so you may want to start with just the email and then follow up when they have responded. Again, be led by their specific guidelines.

If you have the opportunity to pitch in person, practise. These are very busy people, so clarity and passion are essential for you and your idea to stand out. Show that you know your audience and any business or creative constraints: how easy would it be to animate your idea? Would young actors be able to deliver your stunts? The first time I pitched in person, I was a quivering jelly and just about as coherent. But – you know what? – I wasn't eaten, and the world didn't end. It sounds silly, but producers and commissioners are people and, in this industry, they're usually lovely people at that.

Being realistic, it is unlikely that your first project will get picked up. The thing to remember is that this is a business and your IP is a commodity and your skills are a service for hire so don't take rejection personally. There is a lot to learn, so learn it; take feedback when it is offered and get better. It can feel galling to take what feels like a barrage of criticism from a salaried executive, but they will know better than you do what works on their platform. They may well be in a position to offer you work on another show – it happens. There can be many reasons why an executive doesn't want your project, but that doesn't mean they don't like you or your style of writing. They may not get back to you. But then again, I was once called out of the blue by a producer who had rejected an idea of mine several years before; I ended up writing an animation series and a feature film (and, while the feature is in interminable 'pre-production', I still enjoy the residual fees from the international sales of the TV series).

The best advice I was ever given as a new writer was that you only fail when you give up. So, keep on writing; keep on submitting; keep on keeping on.

Jayne Kirkham is a screenwriter and a script and development consultant. With over 30 years' experience working with, and writing for children and young people, she has worked on a wide range of theatre, film, TV, radio and online scripts, ranging in size from small conservation films in Africa to international feature films. She taught at the Northern Film School for 14 years and is a member of the board of directors of the Children's Media Foundation. See her website https://jaynekirkham.com for more information.

Children's television and radio

The information in this section has been compiled as a general guide for writers, artists, agents and publishers to the major companies and key contacts operating within the children's broadcasting industry. As personnel, corporate structures and commissioning guidelines can change frequently, please check the relevant websites for the most up-to-date information.

REGULATION

Advertising Standards Authority
Castle House, 37–45 Paul Street, London EC2A 4LS
tel 020-7492 2222
website www.asa.org.uk
Facebook www.facebook.com/adauthority
X @ASA_UK
Chief Executive Guy Parker

The UK's independent regulator of advertising across all media. Its work includes acting on complaints and taking action against misleading, harmful or offensive advertisements.

Ofcom
Riverside House, 2A Southwark Bridge Road, London SE1 9HA
tel 020-7981 3000, 0300 123 3000
website www.ofcom.org.uk
Facebook www.facebook.com/ofcom
X @Ofcom
Instagram @ofcom.org.uk
Chief Executive Melanie Dawes

Accountable to parliament. Exists to further the interests of consumers by balancing choice and competition with the duty to encourage plurality, protect viewers and listeners, promote diversity in the media and ensure full and fair competition between communications providers.

TELEVISION

BabyTV
Baby Network Ltd, 3 Queen Caroline Street, Hammersmith, London W6 9PE
email info@babytvchannel.com
website www.babytv.com
Facebook www.facebook.com/BabyTVChannel
X @BabyTVChannel
Instagram @babytv

The world's leading baby and toddler network, for children under five years and their parents, airing 24 hours a day and completely ad-free. BabyTV features top-quality shows created by child development experts, designed for children and parents to enjoy together.

The BBC
BBC Broadcasting House, Portland Place, London W1A 1AA
website www.bbc.co.uk
Director, Children's & Education Patricia Hidalgo Reina, Head of Children's Content & Programming Strategy Anna Taganov

The world's largest broadcasting organisation, with a remit to provide programmes that inform, educate and entertain. Established by Royal Charter, the BBC is a public service broadcaster funded by a licence fee. The Children's Director is responsible for the overall direction and management of all of the BBC's services for children, including broadcasting, streaming, radio and websites.

Commissioning
CBeebies and CBBC are self-commissioning and self-scheduling, and proposals may be submitted at any time throughout the year. All submissions for TV and online should be made via PiCos. For further details and commissioning guidelines visit:
- www.bbc.co.uk/commissioning/childrens
- www.bbc.co.uk/commissioning/childrens/0-6
- www.bbc.co.uk/commissioning/childrens/7-12
- www.bbc.co.uk/commissioning/picos

CBeebies
website www.bbc.co.uk/cbeebies
Facebook www.facebook.com/cbeebies
X @CBeebiesHQ
Instagram @cbeebieshq
Head of Commissioning & Acquisitions (0–6 years) Kate Morton, Commissioning Editor (0–6 years) Beth Gardiner, Commissioning Executives (0–6 years) Joel Wilenius, Nick Hall, Mark Barton, David Mercer, Guy Phenix

CBeebies offers mixed genre output for TV, online and radio and is specifically produced for a young audience using a variety of formats including live action and animation. Content covers drama, comedy, entertainment and factual, and the target audience is children aged 0–6 years. CBeebies is on air daily from 6am–7pm.

CBBC
website www.bbc.co.uk/cbbc
Facebook www.facebook.com/cbbc
X @cbbc

Children's television and radio

Instagram @cbbc
Head of Commissioning & Acquisitions (7–12 years) Sarah Mueller, *Senior Commissioning Editor (7–12 years)* Melissa Hardinge, *Commissioning Editors (7–12 years)* Jo Allen, Amy Buscombe, *Commissioning Executives* Aubrey Clarke, Anita Burgess

CBBC content covers drama, factual, comedy, entertainment, animation and news. Prioritises stories that are relatable and fun, appeal to multiple generations and reflect the diversity of the UK and the wider world. The target audience is children aged 7–12 years. CBBC is on air daily from 7am to 7pm.

BBC Writers

website www.bbc.co.uk/writers
Facebook www.facebook.com/BBCWriters
X @bbcwritersroom
Instagram @bbcwriters

BBC Writers is a cross-genre department for scripted content, working with drama, comedy, CBeebies, CBBC, radio, online and others. It is the first port of call at the BBC for unsolicited scripts and new writers.

The BBC Writers blog provides a wealth of behind-the-scenes commentary from writers and producers who have worked on BBC TV and radio programmes: www.bbc.co.uk/writers/blogs.

See website and blog for opportunities, writing tips, success stories, interviews, competitions and events.

Channel 4

124–126 Horseferry Road, London SW1P 2TX
tel 0345 076 0191
website www.channel4.com
Facebook www.facebook.com/Channel4
X @Channel4
Instagram @channel4
Chief Executive Alex Mahon, *Chief Content Officer* Ian Katz

A publicly-owned television network freely available to all in the UK. Its commercially-funded, publicly-owned structure enables all profit generated to be directly reinvested back into its public service remit. As a publisher–broadcaster, Channel 4 commissions UK content from the independent production sector and currently works with over 300 creative companies across the UK every year. Provides a digital streaming service, All 4, and a network of six television channels, aiming to create change by representing unheard voices and reinventing entertainment.

Channel 4 does not produce content specifically for children but many of its programmes appeal to young people and address issues that are relevant to them.

4Skills supports people to build their careers in the media industry across a range of disciplines. Visit https://careers.channel4.com/4skills.

Commissioning

Information about commissioning and related processes and guidelines can be found at www.channel4.com/4producers. Email addresses for most individuals named below can be found on the relevant parts of the website.

Channel 5

17–29 Hawley Crescent, Camden Town, London NW1 8TT
tel 020-3580 3600
website www.channel5.com
Facebook www.facebook.com/channel5uk
X @channel5_tv
Instagram @channel5_tv
Director of Programming Ben Frow

Brands include Channel 5, 5Star, 5USA and 5Select, and an on-demand service, My5. Channel 5 broadcasts over 24 hours of children's programmes every week under the Milkshake! brand, which is aimed at children aged 2–5 years and airs daily from 6–9.15am (10am at weekends). Commissions, co-produces and acquires preschool programming through a wide range of deals and arrangements.

Commissioning

Children's Programming: Milkshake!

Senior Vice President Kids & Family Louise Bucknole

Disney+

website www.disneyplus.com/en-gb
Facebook www.facebook.com/DisneyPlusUK
X @DisneyPlusUK
Instagram @disneyplusuk
President Alisa Bowen

Programmes run by the Walt Disney Company specialising in programming for children from preschoolers to teens. There are three channels: Disney Channel (6–14 years), Disney Junior (2–7 years) and Disney XD (6–14 years). They are available through the Disney+ subscription streaming service.

ITVX Kids

White City, White City Place, 201 Wood Lane, London W12 7RU
website www.itv.com/watch/categories/children
Chief Executive Carolyn McCall

ITV is the UK's largest commercial TV network. The ITV network is responsible for the commissioning, scheduling and marketing of network programmes on its television channels and its digital channel portfolio.

ITVX Kids is online only and replaced ITV's children's channel, CITV. New content is acquired from UK distributors and released online monthly.

Content covers comedy, gameshows, live action, animation and sport. Children's content is also aired daily on ITV2 from 6–9am.

Nickelodeon UK
17–29 Hawley Crescent, London NW1 8TT
website www.nick.co.uk
Facebook www.facebook.com/NickelodeonUK
X @NickelodeonUK
Instagram @nickelodeonuk

Nickelodeon UK is comprised of three channels with a target audience spanning children aged approx. 2–12 years: Nickelodeon aimed at children aged 2–12 years; and NickJr (www.nickjr.co.uk) and NickJr Too aimed at children aged 2–5 years. Nickelodeon channels are available to watch on broadcast television and through the streaming service Paramount+.

POP
website https://player.pop.co.uk
Facebook www.facebook.com/POPUKTV
X @POPTV_UK
Instagram @poptv_uk

A free-to-air children's channel that broadcasts cartoons and live-action series for children aged 6–10 years. Has two sister channels: Tiny Pop broadcasts cartoons and live action series for children aged 3–7 years; Pop Max broadcasts cartoons, sci-fi, action and anime for children aged 7–15 years.

RTÉ
Donnybrook, Dublin 4, Republic of Ireland
tel +353 (0)1 208 3111
email info@rte.ie
website www.rte.ie
Facebook www.facebook.com/RTEjr
X @RTEjr
Instagram @rtejr
Head of Children's and Young People's Content Suzanne Kelly

RTÉ offers a comprehensive range of programmes for children and young people. RTÉjr broadcasts original and acquired live-action and animated content for children aged 2–7 years, airing each day from 7am–7pm. Additional content (podcasts, short films, activities) is available online as well as through RTÉjr radio. TRTÉ is aimed at children aged 7–15 years and airs on RTÉ2.

Commissioning
website https://about.rte.ie/commissioning/commissioning-briefs/rte-young-peoples

See website for information about commissioning and submitting proposals for children and young people.

S4C
Canolfan S4C Yr Egin, Carmarthen SA31 3EQ
tel 0370 600 4141
email gwifren@s4c.cymru
website www.s4c.cymru/en
Facebook www.facebook.com/S4C
X @S4C
Instagram @s4c
Chief Operating Officer Elin Morris, *Young Audiences Commissioner (16–24)* Guto Rhun

S4C is the world's only Welsh language TV channel, broadcasting programmes on sport, drama, music, factual, entertainment and culture. Cyw (https://cyw.cymru/en), a programming block for children aged 3–6 years, broadcasts every weekday from 6am–12pm, on Saturdays from 6–8am and on Sundays from 6–9 am. Awr, a programming block for primary school children, broadcasts every weekday from 4–5pm. Stwnsh (www.s4c.cymru/en/stwnsh), a programming block for children aged 7–13 years, broadcasts every weekday from 5–6pm and on Saturdays from 8–10am.

ORGANISATIONS CONNECTED TO TELEVISION BROADCASTING

BARB
4th Floor, 114 St Martin's Lane, London WC2N 4BE
email enquiries@barb.co.uk
website www.barb.co.uk
X @BarbAudiences
Chief Executive Justin Sampson

The Broadcasters Audience Research Board is the official source of viewing figures in the UK. Shares what people are watching and how, providing insights into trends and most viewed shows.

Ipsos MORI
3 Thomas More Square, London E1W 1YW
tel 020-3059 5000
website www.ipsos.com/en-uk
X @IpsosUK
Instagram @ipsos_uk
Ceo Ben Page

One of the UK's leading research companies; conducts surveys for a wide range of major organisations (such as BARB and RAJAR), as well as for other market research agencies.

Pact – see page 342

Public Media Alliance
Room 02.101, Lawrence Stenhouse Building, University of East Anglia, Norwich NR4 7TJ
tel (01603) 592335
email info@publicmediaalliance.org
website www.publicmediaalliance.org
Facebook www.facebook.com/publicmediaalliance

X @PublicMediaPMA
Ceo Kristian Porter

World's largest association of public broadcasters. Provides advocacy, support, knowledge exchange, research and training opportunities for public media worldwide.

Royal Television Society
3 Dorset Rise, London EC4Y 8EN
tel 020-7822 2810
email info@rts.org.uk
website www.rts.org.uk
X @RTS_media
Instagram @royaltelevisionsociety
Ceo Theresa Wise

An educational charity promoting the art and science of television and the leading forum for discussion and debate on all aspects of the TV community. Runs events, masterclasses and workshops, and provides training and bursaries.

RADIO

BBC School Radio
website www.bbc.co.uk/schoolradio

BBC School Radio provides audio resources for schools including podcasts, downloads, audio and video clips, learning resources and teachers' notes that are curriculum-linked to Early Years Foundation Stage (EYFS) and Key Stages 1, 2, 3 and 4.

CBeebies Radio
website www.bbc.co.uk/cbeebies/radio

CBeebies Radio is aimed at encouraging preschool children to develop their listening skills. In addition to radio output, the website contains games, songs, craft ideas and story-time activities.

Fun Kids
website www.funkidslive.com

A British children's digital radio station (not national) providing programming to entertain children aged 7–12 years, alongside podcasts, videos, articles, quizzes and competitions. Fun Kids Jnr provides content for children under seven years. Available to listen via the website or on DAB Digital Radio across Edinburgh, London and select English cities.

ORGANISATIONS CONNECTED TO RADIO BROADCASTING

Media.info
website https://media.info/uk

This website provides detailed listings of UK radio stations alongside information about TV, newspapers, magazines and media ownership in the UK.

The Radio Academy
Suite 303, The Pill Box, 115 Coventry Road, London E2 6GH
email info@radioacademy.org
website www.radioacademy.org
Facebook www.facebook.com/radioacademy
X @radioacademy
Instagram @radioacademy
Chair Helen Thomas

The Radio Academy is a registered charity with branches across the UK dedicated to the promotion of excellence in radio broadcasting and production. Runs the annual Audio and Radio Industry Awards (ARIAS), which celebrate content and creativity in the industry.

Radiocentre
15 Alfred Place, London WC1E 7EB
tel 020-7010 0600
website www.radiocentre.org
X @Radiocentre
Ceo Matt Payton

Radiocentre is the voice of UK commercial radio. Works with government, policy makers and regulators, and provides a forum for industry-wide debate and discussion.

RAJAR
15 Alfred Place, London WC1E 7EB
tel 020-7395 0630
website www.rajar.co.uk
X @RAJARLtd
Ceo Jerry Hill

Radio Joint Audience Research is the official body in charge of measuring radio audiences in the UK. It is jointly owned by the BBC and the Radiocentre on behalf of the commercial sector.

Theatre for children

London and regional theatres are listed below; listings of touring companies start on page 291.

LONDON

Chickenshed Theatre
290 Chase Side, Southgate, London N14 4PE
tel 020-8292 9222
email info@chickenshed.org.uk
website www.chickenshed.org.uk
Facebook www.facebook.com/Chickenshed_UK
X @CHICKENSHED_UK
Bluesky @chickenshed.bsky.social
Instagram @chickenshed_UK
Managing Director Louise Perry, *Executive Director of Education, Training and Outreach* Paul Morrall

Productions, performance training, education courses and outreach projects that aim to create change by sharing experiences. Founded 1974.

Polka Theatre
240 The Broadway, London SW19 1SB
tel 020-8543 4888
email helenm@polkatheatre.com
website www.polkatheatre.com
Facebook www.facebook.com/polkatheatre
Instagram @polkatheatre
Artistic Director and Joint Ceo Helen Matravers, *Executive Director and Joint Ceo Lynette* Shanbury

Theatre of new work for children up to the age of 12 years, with targeted commissions. Founded 1967.

The Questors Theatre
12 Mattock Lane, London W5 5BQ
email enquiries@questors.org.uk
website www.questors.org.uk
Facebook www.facebook.com/questorstheatre
X @questorstheatre
Instagram @questors_theatre
Executive Director Michael Eppy

Largest independent community theatre in Europe. Produces 15–20 shows a year, specialising in modern and classical world drama. Visiting productions hosted too. Also runs a youth theatre group, QYT, for young people aged between five and 18, as well as summer workshops. No unsolicited scripts. Founded 1929.

Theatre-Rites
Unit 3, Energy Centre, Bowling Green Walk, London N1 6AL
tel 020-7164 6196
email info@theatre-rites.co.uk
website www.theatre-rites.co.uk
Facebook www.facebook.com/TheatreRites
Instagram @theatrerites
Artistic Director Sue Buckmaster, *Executive Producer* Claire Templeton

Creates devised theatre for family audiences and young people using a mix of performance, installation, puppetry, dance and sound. Working within the UK and internationally, the company creates site-specific and touring productions. Founded 1995.

Unicorn Theatre
147 Tooley Street, London SE1 2HZ
tel 020-7645 0560
email hello@unicorntheatre.com
website www.unicorntheatre.com
Facebook www.facebook.com/unicorntheatre
X @unicorn_theatre
Instagram @unicorn_theatre
Artistic Director Rachel Bagshaw, *Executive Director* Rebekah Jones

Produces a year-round programme of theatre for children and young people under 21. In-house productions of full-length plays with professional casts are staged across two auditoria, alongside visiting companies and education work. Rarely commissions plays from writers who are new to it, but it is keen to hear from writers who are interested in working with the theatre in the future.

Do not send unsolicited MSS, but rather a short statement describing why you would like to write for Unicorn along with a CV or a summary of your relevant experience. Founded 1949 as Caryl Jenner Mobile Theatre.

REGIONAL

Yvonne Arnaud Theatre Management
Millbrook, Guildford, Surrey GU1 3UX
tel (01483) 440077
email yat@yvonne-arnaud.co.uk
website www.yvonne-arnaud.co.uk
X @YvonneArnaud
Director and Chief Executive Joanna Read

Presenting and producing theatre which also makes its own productions. Runs creative learning and community activities throughout the year. Founded 1965.

Bristol Old Vic Young Company
King Street, Bristol BS1 4ED
tel 0117 949 3993
email getinvolved@bristololdvic.org.uk
website https://bristololdvic.org.uk/interact/young-company

Facebook www.facebook.com/bristololdvic
Writer, Director and Dramaturg Krista Matthews

Large regional youth theatre hosting workshops, weekly sessions, masterclasses, community projects and performances for young people. Financial assistance is available for participants.

Chichester Festival Theatre
Oaklands Park, Chichester, West Sussex PO19 6AP
tel (01243) 784437
email leap.mailbox@cft.org.uk
email hello@cft.org.uk
website www.cft.org.uk
Instagram @chichesterft
Executive Director Kathy Bourne, *Artistic Director* Justin Audibert

Stages annual Summer Festival Season from April–October in the Festival and Minerva Theatres together with a year-round education programme, winter touring programme and youth theatre Christmas show. Does not accept unsolicited scripts. The Learning, Education and Participation (LEAP) department runs a programme of events for all ages, including workshops, performances, talks and tours. Founded 1962.

Contact Theatre Company
Oxford Road, Manchester M15 6JA
tel 0161 274 0600
website https://contactmcr.com
Instagram @contactmcr
Chief Executive Director Jack Dale-Dowd

Multidisciplinary arts organisation focused on working with and for young people aged 13 years and above. Offers a range of free projects, from writing to music and drama, including the Contact Young Company ensemble. Founded 1972.

Creation Theatre Company
tel (01865) 766266
email boxoffice@creationtheatre.co.uk
website www.creationtheatre.co.uk
Facebook www.facebook.com/CreationTheatre
X @creationtheatre
Instagram @creationtheatre
Ceo and Artistic Director Dr Helen Eastman

Award-winning producing theatre company, specialising in site-specific and digital theatre in extraordinary locations. Also runs drama classes during term-time for ages 5–19 and theatre & creativity workshops during the school holidays in Oxford. Does not accept unsolicited manuscripts.

Derby Theatre
15 Theatre Walk, St Peter's Quarter, Derby DE1 2NF
email creatives@derbyplayhouse.co.uk
website www.derbytheatre.co.uk
Facebook www.facebook.com/DerbyTheatre
X @DerbyTheatre
Artistic Director and Chief Executive Sarah Brigham,
Creative Learning Director Caroline Barth

Regional producing and receiving theatre. Offers opportunities for theatre-makers in the region. Founded 1975.

The Dukes
Moor Lane, Lancaster LA1 1QE
tel (01524) 598500
email ask@dukes-lancaster.org
website https://dukes-lancaster.org
Instagram @thedukeslancaster
Chief Executive Chris Lawson

Producing theatre and cultural centre. The Lancaster Writing Prize is open to young writers aged between 12 to 18. See website for information about the theatre's forthcoming productions and programming approach. Founded 1971.

The Edge Theatre and Arts Centre
Manchester Road, Chorlton, Manchester M21 9JG
tel 0161 282 9776
email info@edgetheatre.co.uk
website www.edgetheatre.co.uk
Instagram @edgemanchester
Artistic Director and Chief Executive Janine Waters,
Musical Director Simon Waters

Produces and presents theatre for all ages, including families and children. Musical and children's theatre specialities. 70-seat flexible theatre space and studio spaces. Also runs classes, courses and workshops in theatre, dance, music, writing and other creative genres, including the Edge Youth Theatre for ages 9–12 and Aspire for young people with learning challenges between 13–19 years. Founded 2011.

The Egg
Sawclose, Bath BA1 1ET
tel (01225) 823409 (reception and administration)
email egg.reception@theatreroyal.org.uk
website www.theatreroyal.org.uk/the-egg
X @theeggbath

Part of the Theatre Royal Bath. Purpose-built theatre for young people and their families. Hosts and produces shows for children and young people alongside a year-round participation and outreach programme for people aged 0–21 years. Founded 2005.

Everyman Theatre Cheltenham
7 Regent Street, Cheltenham, Glos. GL50 1HQ
tel (01242) 512515
email admin@everymantheatre.org.uk
website www.everymantheatre.org.uk
X @Everymanchelt
Creative Director Paul Milton

Regional presenting and producing theatre promoting a wide range of plays. Small-scale experimental, youth and educational work encouraged in The Studio Theatre. Contact the Creative Director before submitting material. Founded 1891.

Leeds Children's Theatre

c/o The Carriageworks Theatre, The Electric Press, 3 Millennium Square, Leeds LS2 3AD
email enquiry@leeds-childrens-theatre.co.uk
website www.leeds-childrens-theatre.co.uk
Facebook www.facebook.com/LeedsChildrensTheatre
X @LeedsCT

Oldest established Children's Theatre society in the UK. Its members (both adults and children) bring live theatre to young people, often for the very first time. Many of the plays produced are based on well-known children's literature. Stages two productions each year at the purpose-built Carriageworks Theatre, typically in spring (March/April) and late autumn (November). Welcomes school groups as well as families and friends. Founded 1935.

Leeds Playhouse

Playhouse Square, Quarry Hill, Leeds LS2 7UP
tel 0113 213 7700
website https://leedsplayhouse.org.uk
Instagram @leedsplayhouse
Chief Executive Shawab Iqbal, *Artistic Director* Tom Wright

Seeks out the best companies and artists to create theatre in the heart of Yorkshire. Its artistic development programme, Furnace, discovers and supports new voices, while developing work with established practitioners. It provides a creative space for writers, directors, companies and individual theatre-makers to refine their practice at all stages of their career. The Playhouse Connect team works with more than 12,000 people every year reaching out to refugee communities, young people, students, older people and people with learning challenges. Founded 1990.

Live Theatre

Broad Chare, Quayside, Newcastle upon Tyne NE1 3DQ
tel 0191 232 1232
email info@live.org.uk
website www.live.org.uk
website https://www.live.org.uk/children-young-people/schools-teachers
Instagram @livetheatrenewcastle
Executive Director & Joint Ceo Jacqui Kell, *Artistic Director & Joint Ceo* Jack McNamara

New writing theatre company and venue. Stages three to six productions per year of new writing, plus touring plays from other new writing companies. The Live Youth Theatre programme is free and open to young people between the ages of ten and 25. CPD and INSET support for teachers is also available. Founded 1986.

Norwich Puppet Theatre

St James, Whitefriars, Norwich NR3 1TN
tel (01603) 629921 (box office), (01603) 615564 (admin)
email info@puppettheatre.co.uk
website www.puppettheatre.co.uk
Facebook www.facebook.com/NorwichPuppetTheatre
Instagram @norwichpuppettheatre
Theatre Director Peter Beck

Home to a professional theatre company which creates family puppet shows. The company tours to schools and venues around the country and occasionally internationally. As a venue, the Theatre also presents a programme of puppetry performances and workshops for family and adult audiences. Norwich Puppet Theatre is also a charity and a creative engagement organisation with an extensive outreach programme.

Nottingham Playhouse

Nottingham Playhouse Trust Ltd, Wellington Circus, Nottingham NG1 5AF
tel 0115 941 9419
website https://nottinghamplayhouse.co.uk/get-involved/young-people
X @NottmPlayhouse
Artistic Director Adam Penford, *Chief Executive* Stephanie Sirr

Seeks to nurture new writers from the East Midlands primarily through its Artist Development programme, Amplify. Also offers a range of groups and youth theatres for young people aged two and above; see website for full details. Founded 1963.

Pegasus

Magdalen Road, Oxford OX4 1RE
tel (01865) 812150
email info@pegasustheatre.org.uk
website https://pegasustheatre.org.uk/spark-artists/
Instagram @pegasusoxford
Artistic Director and Joint Ceo Georgia Bradley, *Creative Learning Director and Joint Ceo* John McCraw

Theatre, dance and comedy for young people. Runs the two-year SPARK programme, which offers a range of support to artists, including development sessions, marketing and fundraising support, and rehearsal spaces. See website for details on future application windows.

Queen's Theatre, Hornchurch

Billet Lane, Hornchurch, Essex RM11 1QT
tel (01708) 443333
email info@queens-theatre.co.uk
website www.queens-theatre.co.uk, www.queens-theatre.co.uk/get-involved/youth-theatre
X @QueensTheatre

Regional theatre working in outer East London, Essex and beyond. Each annual programme includes homegrown theatre, visiting live entertainment and learning and participation projects.

The Queen's Youth Theatre Programme (QYouth) provides the opportunity for young people aged 6–18 years to develop creativity, confidence and teamwork, as well as offering valuable opportunities to perform on the Queen's Theatre stage and elsewhere. Younger members begin with the QSteps Programme before moving on to the Young Company Programme, which offers performance, technical and dance opportunities for those who wish to develop further a range of theatre skills. Founded 1953.

Royal Shakespeare Company

The Royal Shakespeare Theatre, Waterside, Stratford-upon-Avon, Warks. CV37 6BB
tel (01789) 296655
email newwork@rsc.org.uk
website www.rsc.org.uk/about-us/new-plays-and-writers
Facebook www.facebook.com/thersc
X @TheRSC
Instagram @thersc
Co-Artistic Directors Daniel Evans, Tamara Harvey

Produces new work by contemporary writers on all three of the company's permanent stages: the Royal Shakespeare Theatre, the Swan Theatre and The Other Place, in Stratford-Upon-Avon in Warwickshire. This programme of new plays, musicals, adaptations and translations sits alongside the work of Shakespeare and his contemporaries and contemporary revivals of modern classics. The company produces work regularly in London and tours nationally. The New Work department does not accept unsolicited scripts but rather seeks out writers for commission and monitors writers in production in the UK and internationally. Writers are welcome to invite the New Work Department to attend readings, showcases or productions by emailing the address above. Founded 1961.

Sherman Theatre

Senghennydd Road, Cardiff CF24 4YE
tel 029-2064 6900
email scripts@shermantheatre.co.uk
website www.shermantheatre.co.uk/theatre-makers
Instagram @shermantheatre
Chief Executive Julia Barry, *Artistic Director* Joe Murphy

Produces two Christmas productions (for ages 3–6 years in English and Welsh and an actor/musician-led production for ages 7+ years) and actively seeks high-quality work for children and young people as part of its programming. Participatory work with youth theatres. Founded 2007.

Taking Flight Theatre Company

Chapter Arts Centre, Market Road, Cardiff CF5 1QE
tel 029-2023 0020
email louise@takingflighttheatre.co.uk
website www.takingflighttheatre.org.uk
Facebook www.facebook.com/Takingflightco
X @takingflightco
Instagram @takingflighttheatre
Artistic Director Elise Davison, *Executive Director* Louise Ralph

Boundary-pushing productions featuring Deaf, disabled and non-disabled performers.

Theatr Clwyd

Raikes Lane, Mold, Flintshire CH7 1YA
tel (01352) 344101
email writers@theatrclwyd.com
website www.theatrclwyd.com
Instagram @theatrclwyd
Executive Director Liam Evans-Ford, *Artistic Director* Kate Wasserberg

Largest producing theatre in Wales, creating up to 14 productions each year in English, Welsh and bilingually. Productions are a mix of classic plays, contemporary revivals, musicals and new writing. Will consider plays by writers, particularly Welsh, Wales-based or with Welsh themes, and usually offers six writing residencies each year. No literary department, so authors should expect to wait for a response to unsolicited scripts.

Visible Fictions

Suite 325/327, 4th Floor, 11 Bothwell Street, Glasgow G2 6LY
email laura@visiblefictions.co.uk
website https://visiblefictions.co.uk
X @visiblefictions
Artistic Director Dougie Irvine, *Producer* Laura Penny

Specialises in professional productions for young audiences and their families across a range of artforms, from theatre to film, puppetry to immersive experiences. Also works in creative learning settings – community, educational, institutional, and professional – to make bespoke projects to accompany and enhance artistic experiences of young audiences. Founded 1991.

TOURING COMPANIES

Arad Goch

Stryd y Baddon, Aberystwyth, Ceredigion SY23 2NN
tel (01970) 617998
email post@aradgoch.org
website www.aradgoch.cymru
Instagram @aradgoch
Artistic Director Ffion Wyn Bowen, *Business Director* Nia Wyn Evans

Performs in Welsh and English and tours nationally throughout Wales, and occasionally abroad. The company is particularly interested in enabling children and young people to recognise and appreciate their own unique cultural identity through theatre. Some of the company's work is based on traditional material and children's literature, but it also commissions new work from experienced dramatists and new writers. Arad Goch performs in theatres and other locations, including schools, and also offers seminars/workshops for students and teachers. The company has its own production house in Aberystwyth which is used by other arts and community organisations and where it programmes a variety of participatory activities for young people. It organises the biennial 'Agor Drysau–Opening Doors' Wales International Festival of Performing Arts for Young Audiences (www.agordrysau.cymru). Founded 1989.

Booster Cushion Theatre
75 How Wood, Park Street, St Albans,
Herts. AL2 2RW
tel (01727) 873874
email admin@booster-cushion.co.uk
website www.boostercushiontheatreforchildren.com
Facebook www.facebook.com/boostercushiontheatre
X @BoosterCushion
Director Philip Sherman

Comic theatre company formed especially to re-tell traditional tales to primary-school pupils and their families using surprising Big Books. BCT has performed to over 500,000 people in schools, libraries, museums and theatres across the UK using pop-up books up to 3m tall and concertina books over 5m wide.

All productions are solo performing shows using mime, voice and some sign language. They involve a high level of audience participation. Each show is completely portable and can be performed inside or outside; technical requirements are minimal. Founded 1989.

Boundless Theatre
12 South Norwood Hill, London SE25 6AB
tel 020-7072 0140
email hello@boundlesstheatre.org.uk
website www.boundlesstheatre.org.uk
website https://boundlessdrama.club/welcome
Instagram @boundlessabound

Creates new plays with and for audiences aged 15–25 years. Tours the UK and internationally. Resources, exclusive deals, workshops and more are available to members of the Boundless Drama Club, a community of young creatives.

Cahoots NI
Cityside Retail Park, 100–150 York Street,
Belfast BT15 1WA
tel 07434 661671
email info@cahootsni.com
website www.cahootsni.com
Facebook www.facebook.com/Cahoots NI
X @CahootsNI
Instagram @cahoots_ni
Artistic Director Paul Bosco Mc Eneaney, *Creative Engagement Manager* Hannah Fullerton

Professional children's touring company which concentrates on the visual potential of theatre and the age-old popularity of magic and illusion as an essential ingredient in the art of entertaining. The company tours in Ireland, the UK, the US and Asia in theatres, schools and healthcare settings. Founded 2001.

Catherine Wheels Theatre Company
22B High Street, East Linton, East Lothian EH40 3AB
tel 07500 847473
email admin@catherinewheels.co.uk
website www.catherinewheels.co.uk
Facebook www.facebook.com/CatherineWheelsCompany
X @cwheelstheatre
Artistic Director Gill Robertson

Producing company that tours the UK and internationally, performing for children and young people. One of the founders of the Theatre in Schools Scotland initiative.

Fevered Sleep
15A Old Ford Road, London E2 9PJ
tel 07349 962243
email admin@feveredsleep.co.uk
website www.feveredsleep.co.uk
Facebook www.facebook.com/feveredsleeponline
X @feveredsleep
Instagram @feveredsleep
Co-Artistic Director and Ceo David Harradine, *Co-Artistic Director* Sam Butler

Creates performances, installations and digital art for children and adults. Founded 1996.

Half Moon Theatre
43 White Horse Road, London E1 0ND
tel 020-7709 8900
email admin@halfmoon.org.uk
website www.halfmoon.org.uk
Facebook www.facebook.com/halfmoontheatre
X @HalfMoonTheatre
Instagram @halfmoon_theatre
Artistic Director and Joint Ceo Bradley Travis, *Executive Director and Joint Ceo* Louise Allen

Stages professional plays for young people and family audiences; also tours work around the UK. Youth theatre groups offer opportunities for participants aged 5–18 years (or 25 for young people with disabilities).

Hopscotch Theatre Company
2nd Floor, 7 Water Row, Govan G51 3UW
tel 0141 440 2025
email info@hopscotchtheatre.com
website https://hopscotchtheatre.com
Facebook www.facebook.com/hopscotchtheatre

Instagram @hopscotch_theatre
Producer and General Managers Thomas McCulloch, Stephanie Black-Daniels

Producer of touring theatre for young people aged 4–12 years and families, including an annual pantomime tour. An artist-support programme for new writers and theatre-makers enables artists to make accessible work for young audiences. Founded 1988.

Kazzum Arts
Oxford House, Derbyshire Street, London E2 6HG
tel 020-7749 1123
email hello@kazzum.org
website www.kazzum.org
Facebook www.facebook.com/Kazzum
Instagram @kazzumarts
Artistic Director Alex Evans, *Executive Director* Lauren Irving

Uses creativity to enable children and young people who have been impacted by trauma and adversity to feel seen, heard and valued. Provides opportunities to explore creative expression and agency through multidisciplinary arts activities. Founded 1989.

Konflux Theatre in Education
4100 Park Approach, Thorpe Park, Leeds LS15 8GB
tel (01937) 832740
email info@konfluxtheatre.com
website www.konfluxtheatre.com
Facebook www.facebook.com/KonfluxTheatre
X @KonfluxTheatre

Theatre in Education company and Arts Award Supporter. Works with approx. 700 schools each year, building close working relationships with teachers and other education professionals and ensuring its programmes and their delivery are tailored to the needs of each organisation. Konflux offers over 70 curriculum-based Play in a Day workshops designed to build confidence and promote team work. They give pupils the opportunity to learn through drama, increase their acting skills and present a performance back to peers and parents. Founded 1998.

Little Angel Theatre
14 Dagmar Passage, London N1 2DN
tel 020-7226 1787
email info@littleangeltheatre.com
website www.littleangeltheatre.com
X @LittleATheatre
Artistic Director Samantha Lane, *Executive Director* Peta Swindell

Committed to working with children and families through schools, the local community and the wider community through its extensive touring programme. Develops innovative projects, implements improved access to their creative work, increases opportunities for participation and provides stimulating learning and creativity for all using puppetry. Productions last approx. one hour. Termly activities are run for children, families and schools, including INSET training for teachers. Regular introductory and professional development courses are held throughout the year for teenagers and adults.

The London Bubble
(Bubble Theatre Company)
5 Elephant Lane, London SE16 4JD
tel 020-7237 4434
email admin@londonbubble.org.uk
website www.londonbubble.org.uk
Instagram @bubbletheatre
Co-Ceos Lucy Bradshaw, Marie Vickers

Aims to provide the artistic direction, skills, environment and resources to create inspirational, inclusive and involving theatre for the local community and beyond. Also runs a number of groups for children and young people as well as an adult drama group.

M6 Theatre Company
Studio Theatre, Hamer C.P. School,
Albert Royds Street, Rochdale, Lancs. OL16 2SU
tel (01706) 355898
email admin@m6theatre.co.uk
website https://m6theatre.co.uk
Facebook www.facebook.com/M6Theatre
Instagram @m6theatre
Artistic Director Gilly Baskeyfield

Touring theatre company specialising in creating and delivering innovative theatre for young audiences. Founded 1977.

Oily Cart
Smallwood School Annexe, Smallwood Road,
London SW17 0TW
tel 020-8102 0112
email oilies@oilycart.org.uk
website www.oilycart.org.uk
Instagram @oilycart
Artistic Director and Co-Ceo Ellie Griffiths, *Executive Director and Co-Ceo* Zoë Lally

Touring company staging interactive, sensory shows across the UK and internationally. Reimagines theatre for young audiences to make it more inclusive, and all productions are created for and with children and young people, regardless of age or perceived ability. Considers scripts from new writers, but at present all work is generated from within the company. Founded 1981.

The Pied Piper Theatre Company
1 Lilian Place, Coxcombe Lane, Chiddingfold,
Surrey GU8 4QA
tel 07748 983940

email info@piedpipertheatre.co.uk
website www.piedpipertheatre.co.uk
X @PiedPiperLive
Artistic Director Tina Williams

Specialises in bringing new writing for children to the stage. Typically tours one show a year in the UK, sometimes two, and occasionally tours in Europe and Asia. Founded 1984.

Prime Theatre
(formerly Sixth Sense Theatre for Young People)
c/o The Wyvern Theatre, Theatre Square, Swindon SN1 1QN
tel (01793) 614864
email info@primetheatre.co.uk
website www.primetheatre.co.uk
Facebook www.facebook.com/primetheatre
Instagram @primetheatre
Artistic Director Mark Powell

Professional theatre company prioritising work with young people. Produces both issue-based and creative theatre productions and performs in schools, theatres and arts centres in the South-West region and beyond. These productions are supported by additional young people-led work, workshops, training sessions and other projects.

Proteus Theatre Company
Proteus Creation Space, Council Road, Basingstoke, Hants RG21 3DH
tel (01256) 354541
email info@proteustheatre.com
website www.proteustheatre.com
Instagram @proteustheatre
Artistic Director and Chief Executive Mary Swan

Small-scale touring company particularly committed to new writing and new work, education and community collaborations. Produces up to three touring shows per year plus community projects. Founded 1981.

Replay Theatre Company
East Belfast Network Centre,
55 Templemore Avenue, Belfast BT5 4FP
tel 028-9045 4562
email info@replaytheatre.co.uk
website www.replaytheatre.co.uk
Facebook www.facebook.com/ReplayTheatreCo
X @ReplayTheatreCo
Instagram @replaytheatreco
Chief Executive Officer Brian Mullan, *Artistic Director* Janice Kernoghan-Reid, *Finance and Operations Manager* Hayley McBride, *Director of Inclusive Theatre* Andrew Stanford, *Company Stage Manager* Jordan Nelson

Innovative, high-quality work for audiences under the age of 19, including school groups, children and young people with disabilities, and families. Each show is shaped through creative consultation with its intended audience, and those who live and work with them. Tours locally, nationally and internationally. Founded 1988.

Rhubarb Theatre
7 Queensway, Leadenham, Lincoln LN5 0PF
tel (01400) 275133
email info@rhubarbtheatre.co.uk
website www.rhubarbtheatre.co.uk
Facebook www.facebook.com/rhubarbtheatre
Bluesky @rhubarbtheatre.bsky.social
Instagram @rhubarbtheatre
Artistic Directors Kirsty Baker, Philip Mead

Professional indoor theatre and street theatre predominantly aimed at family audiences (age 5+). Productions are newly created stories that include original music and lots of theatrical devices, i.e. masks, puppetry, dance, song, movement and mime. Most of Rhubarb's street shows are wordless and suitable for booking overseas. Tours nationally and performs in a host of different small- to middle-scale venues, including theatres, arts centres, village halls, rural touring schemes and schools, undertaking approx. 200 performances a year. Other activities include walkabout, interactive storytelling, workshops and teaching. Founded 2004.

Spectacle Theatre
c/o The Factory, Jenkin Street, Porth CF39 9PP
tel 07900 493691
email steve.davis@spectacletheatre.co.uk
website www.spectacletheatre.co.uk
Facebook www.facebook.com/Theatr-Spectacle-Theatre
X @SpectacleTheat1
Manager/Creative Director Steve Davis

Community theatre company. New writing. Unsolicited scripts accepted. Bilingual performance, health and wellbeing workshops, training and volunteering opportunities.

Tell Tale Hearts
c/o 4 Oxspring Road, Penistone, Sheffield S36 8AB
email info@telltalehearts.co.uk
website www.telltalehearts.co.uk
Facebook www.facebook.com/TellTaleHeartsTheatreCo
Instagram @telltaleheartstheatre
Artistic Director Natasha Holmes

Produces participatory theatre for primary-school pupils and younger years in a range of settings, from theatres to schools and community venues. Also runs workshops, INSET training and offers other consultancy services. Rarely produces theatre from written work but actively seeks out collaborations with contributing artists. Occasionally works with a writer as part of its collaborative team, but this is to produce new work. Contact the Artistic Director before sending any work in order to gauge interest. Founded 2003.

Theatr Iolo

c/o Chapter, Market Road, Canton, Cardiff CF5 1QE
tel 029-2061 3782
email hello@theatriolo.com
website www.theatriolo.com
Artistic Director Lee Lyford, *Executive Director* Michelle Perez, *Communications and Engagement Manager* Sarah Gilbert

Works with artists, writers and creatives to create memorable live theatre, workshops and activities in both English and Welsh. Its productions for babies, young children and teenagers is toured across Wales, the UK and internationally.

Theatre Centre

1 Town Barn Road, Crawley RH11 7XG
tel (01293) 304377
email admin@theatre-centre.co.uk
website www.theatre-centre.co.uk
Facebook www.facebook.com/TheatreCentreUK
X @TClive
Instagram @theatrecentre
Artistic Director Eleanor Manners, *Executive Director and Ceo* Emma Rees

Young people's theatre company producing plays and workshops which tour nationally across the UK. Productions are staged in primary and secondary schools, arts centres and other venues. Keen to nurture new and established talent, encouraging all writers to consider writing for young audiences. Also runs creative projects and manages writing awards: see website for details. Founded 1953.

Theatre Hullabaloo

The Hullabaloo, Borough Road, Darlington DL1 1SG
tel (01325) 405681
email info@theatrehullabaloo.org.uk
website www.theatrehullabaloo.org.uk
Facebook www.facebook.com/TheatreHullabaloo
Instagram @theatrehullabaloo
Artistic Producer Miranda Thain

Specialist theatre company that creates, promotes and tours work for young audiences, with a particular emphasis on early years. Encourages greater awareness of the value of theatre to children and young people by working with academic researchers, teachers and others through courses, events and publications. Tours professional theatre productions to schools and venues across the North East and nationally. Dedicated children's theatre and family venue, The Hullabaloo, offers theatre for children, creative play installations and more.

Travelling Light Theatre Company

Barton Hill Settlement, 43 Ducie Road, Lawrence Hill, Bristol BS5 0AX
tel 07305 085081
email info@travellinglighttheatre.org.uk
website www.travellinglighttheatre.org.uk
Facebook www.facebook.com/travellinglighttheatre
X @tl_theatre
Instagram @tl_theatre
Ceo Dienka Hines, *Artistic Director* Lizzy Stephens

Professional theatre company producing work for young audiences. Collaborates with many different arts organisations to create original, cross-artform productions that inspire and engage young people. Tours to theatres and festivals throughout the UK and abroad as well as to local schools. Also runs an extensive participation programme engaging with 0–25 year-olds through youth theatre groups, holiday and school projects, work experience, placements and mentoring. Founded 1984.

Tutti Frutti Productions

Hope House, 65 Mabgate, Leeds LS9 7DR
tel 07763 468556
email hello@tutti-frutti.org.uk
website www.tutti-frutti.org.uk
X @tuttifruttiprod
Artistic Director Wendy Harris, *Executive Director* Emma Killick

Professional theatre for family audiences (age 3+ and families/carers). Productions are adaptations of well-known stories or specially commissioned new shows with a focus on diversity, and have a very physical movement-based style with original music. Tours nationally to variety of different small- and middle-scale venues in isolated or deprived areas, including theatres, arts centres, village halls, rural touring schemes and schools, undertaking approx. 250 performances a year. Tours internationally to USA. Also creates local arts engagement projects for children in less affluent areas. Founded 1991.

Societies, prizes and festivals

Society of Authors

The Society of Authors (SoA) is the UK trade union for all types of writers, illustrators and literary translators at every stage of their careers.

Founded in 1884, the Society of Authors now has over 12,000 members. Members receive unlimited free advice on all aspects of the profession, including confidential clause-by-clause contract vetting, access to professional and geographic author communities and a wide range of exclusive offers. It campaigns and lobbies on the issues that affect authors and holds hundreds of events online and across the UK each year, offering opportunities for authors to network and learn from each other. It manages more than 58 literary estates, the income from which helps to fund the organisation's work.

Members

SoA members include household names, such as Malorie Blackman, Stephen Fry, Lemn Sissay and Kate Mosse, but they also include authors right at the start of their careers. Amongst the SoA membership are academic writers, biographers, broadcasters, children's writers, crime writers, dramatists, educational writers, ELT writers, health writers, ghostwriters, graphic novelists, historians, illustrators, journalists, medical writers, non-fiction writers, novelists, poets, playwrights, radio writers, scriptwriters, short story writers, translators, spoken word artists, YA writers and more.

The benefits available to all SoA members include the following:
- assistance with contracts, from negotiation and assessment of terms to clause-by-clause, confidential vetting;
- unlimited advice on queries, covering any aspect of the business of authorship;
- taking up complaints on behalf of members on any issue concerned with the business of authorship;

Membership

The Society of Authors
24 Bedford Row, London WC1R 4EH
tel 020-3880 2230
email info@societyofauthors.org
website https://societyofauthors.org
Chief Executive Anna Ganley

There are two membership options: Regular and Plus membership.

Regular membership is available to all types of writers, illustrators and literary translators at every stage of their careers. From journalists to webcomic artists, scriptwriters to bloggers, novelists to games writers, and translators to performance poets. This includes students and writers at the very start of their careers.

Plus membership brings you all the benefits of a Regular member, with the addition of public liability insurance for an additional £10 p.a.

Membership is subject to election and payment of subscription fees. The subscription fee (tax deductible) starts at £32.50 per quarter, or £22.75 for those aged 35 or under. A concessionary rate for over 65s or those on state benefits is available on request. Joint membership also available from £48.75.

- pursuing legal actions for breach of contract, copyright infringement and the non-payment of royalties and fees, when the risk and cost preclude individual action by a member and issues of general concern to the profession are at stake;
- conferences, seminars, meetings and other opportunities to network and learn from other authors;
- regular communications and a comprehensive range of publications, including the SoA's quarterly journal, *The Author*;
- discounts on books, exclusive rates on specialist insurance, special offers on products and services and free membership of the Authors' Licensing and Collecting Society (ALCS; see page 413).

> 'It does no harm to repeat, as often as you can, "Without me the literary industry would not exist: the publishers, the agents, the sub-agents, the accountants, the libel lawyers, the departments of literature, the professors, the theses, the books of criticism, the reviewers, the book pages – all this vast and proliferating edifice is because of this small, patronised, put-down and underpaid person."' – *Doris Lessing*

Networks and groups for members include:
- Authors with Disabilities and Chronic Illnesses – a peer support network for authors living and working with health challenges;
- Comics Creators Network – a professional support network for all types of comics creators;
- Children's Writers and Illustrators Group – a professional community of writers and illustrators who create content for the children's publishing market;
- Educational Writers Group – protecting the interests of educational authors in professional matters, especially contracts, rates of pay, digitalisation and copyright;
- Poetry and Spoken Word Group – a new, increasingly active group to which all new member poets are subscribed on joining SoA;
- Scriptwriters Group – representing members working in radio, TV, film and games development;
- Carers Network – a new group designed to help keep writers writing when they take on caring responsibilities for someone with an illness or disability;
- The SoA also coordinates a growing network of over 49 local author communities across the UK.

Campaigning and lobbying

The SoA is a voice for authors and works at a national and international level to improve terms and treatment of authors, negotiating with all parties including publishers, broadcasters, agents and governments. Current areas of campaigning include contract terms, copyright, freedom of expression, tax and benefits arrangements and Public Lending Right (PLR; see page 381) – which the SoA played a key role in establishing.

In the UK the SoA lobbies parliament, ministers and departments and makes submissions on relevant issues, working closely with the Department for Culture, Media and Sport and the All Party Parliamentary Writers Group. The SoA is a member of the British Copyright Council and was instrumental in setting up ALCS. They chair the Creators for Rights Alliance (CRA), a partnership of unions and member organisations from across the creative industries, working together on common interests such as copyright, payment and credit, and in 2022 launched the cross-industry 'Pay the Creator' campaign. It is recognised by the BBC in the negotiation of rates for authors' contributions to radio drama, as well as for the broadcasting of published material.

The SoA is a member of the European Writers' Council and applies pressure globally, working with sister organisations as part of the International Authors' Foundation.

The SoA also works closely with other professional bodies, including the Association of Authors' Agents, the Booksellers Association, the Publishers Association, the Independent Publishers Guild, the British Council, the National Union of Journalists and the Writers' Guild of Great Britain.

Awards and grants

The SoA supports authors through a wide range of awards and grants. Over £900,000 in awards and grant are given annually. The following prizes and awards are administered:
- the annual SoA Awards – ten prizes for poetry, fiction and non-fiction, and illustration, awarding authors at the beginning of their careers as well as those well established;
- two audio drama prizes: the Imison Award for a writer new to radio drama and the Tinniswood Award for best original audio drama;
- awards for translations from Arabic, Dutch/Flemish, French, German, Hebrew, Italian, Japanese, Spanish and Swedish into English;
- *The Sunday Times* Charlotte Aitken Young Writer of the Year Award;
- the ALCS Educational Writers' Awards;
- the Ilse Schwepcke Prize for Women's Travel Writing;
- the Authors' Foundation and K. Blundell Trust, which give grants to assist authors working on their next book;
- the Authors' Contingency Fund, which offers hardship grants to authors in financial difficulty;
- the SoA Access Fund;
- Strachey Trust Grant.

Writers' Guild of Great Britain (WGGB)

The WGGB is the TUC-affiliated trade union for writers.

WGGB represents writers working in film, television, audio, theatre, books, poetry, animation, comedy and videogames. Formed in 1959 as the Screenwriters' Guild, the union gradually extended into all areas of freelance writing activity and copyright protection. It comprises professional writers in all media, united in common concern for one another and regulating the conditions under which they work.

Apart from necessary dealings with government and policies on legislative matters affecting writers, the WGGB is, by constitution, non-political, has no involvement with any political party and members pay no political levy.

WGGB employs a permanent general secretary and other permanent staff and is administered by an Executive Council of around 20 members.

Membership

Writers' Guild of Great Britain
1st Floor, 134 Tooley Street, London SE1 2TU
tel 020-7833 0777
email admin@writersguild.org.uk
website https://writersguild.org.uk
Facebook www.facebook.com/thewritersguild
X @The WritersGuild
General Secretary Ellie Peers

WGGB has a range of membership options, and welcomes writers at all stages of their careers – whether they are professional writers with credits and an agent, or just starting out. There is also a membership level for students and for those who work professionally with writers, for example agents. Find out about eligibility criteria, subscription amounts and join online via the WGGB website: https://writersguild.org.uk/join-renew

Members receive a weekly email newsletter. The WGGB website contains full details of collective agreements and WGGB activities, plus a 'Find a Writer' service and a dedicated members' area; information is also made available on X, Facebook, Instagram and other social media channels. Other benefits include legal advice and contract vetting; free training; member events, discounts and special offers (subject to membership tier).

WGGB agreements

WGGB's core function is to negotiate minimum terms in areas in which its members work. Agreements form the basis of the individual contracts signed by members. It also gives individual advice to its members on contracts and other matters and maintains a welfare fund to help writers in financial trouble. Details of negotiations outlined below represent just some of the union's work in this area.

Television

WGGB TV agreements regulate minimum fees, residuals and royalties, copyright, credits and general conditions for television plays, series and serials, dramatisations and adaptations, soaps, sitcoms and sketch shows. One of the WGGB's most important achievements has been the establishment of pension rights for members. The BBC, ITV and independent producers pay a pension contribution on top of the standard writer's fee on the understanding that the WGGB member also pays a contribution.

The switch to digital television, subscription-video-on-demand and download-to-own services, mobile phone technology and the expansion of the BBC's commercial arm have seen WGGB in constant negotiation over the past two decades. WGGB now has agreements for all of the BBC's digital channels and for its joint venture channels. In May 2012 it signed new agreements with the BBC extending minimum terms over online services such as iPlayer. From April 2015 the first payments under the Writers Digital Payments scheme (a not-for-profit company) were paid out to writers whose work had been broadcast on BBC iPlayer and ITV Player. In 2016 WGGB negotiated a 75% fee increase for writers working under its 2003 Pact agreement, and also started work on rewriting the agreement. In 2017 it negotiated a new script agreement for television and online with the BBC, which was renegotiated in 2024 to provide additional compensation for writers' work across a number of new platforms.

Film

In 1985 an agreement was signed with two producer organisations: the British Film and Television Producers' Association and the Independent Programme Producers' Association (now known as Pact). Since then there has been an industrial agreement covering UK film productions and pension fund contributions have been negotiated for WGGB members. The agreement was renegotiated in February 1992 and consultations on an updated arrangement are in progress.

Audio

WGGB has a standard agreement for Radio Drama with the BBC, establishing a fee structure that is reviewed annually. It was comprehensively renegotiated in 2005 resulting in an agreement covering digital radio. In 1985 the BBC agreed to extend the pension scheme already established for television writers to include radio writers. WGGB has special agreements for Radio 4's *The Archers* and for BBC iPlayer. A separate agreement covers the reuse of old comedy and drama material on digital BBC Radio 4 Extra. It has also negotiated rates for podcasts.

Books

WGGB fought for the loans-based Public Lending Right (PLR, see page 381) to reimburse authors for books lent in libraries. The scheme is now administered by the British Library; WGGB is represented on its advisory committee. WGGB has a Books Committee, which works on behalf of book writers and poets. Issues affecting members include authors' earnings, self-publishing, print-on-demand services and ebooks, and in 2022 the union launched the *Is It A Steal?* (see page 378) joint campaign with the Society of Authors to tackle bad practice in the hybrid/paid-for publishing sector.

Theatre

In 1979 WGGB, together with the Theatre Writers' Union, negotiated the first industrial agreement for theatre writers. The Theatres National Committee Agreement (TNC) covers the Royal Shakespeare Company, the Royal National Theatre Company and the English Stage Company at the Royal Court. When their agreement was renegotiated in 2007, WGGB achieved a long-standing ambition of a minimum fee of £10,000 for a new play; for current minimum rates see the WGGB website.

In June 1986, a new agreement was signed with the Theatrical Management Association (now UK Theatre), which covers 95 provincial theatres. In 1993, this agreement was comprehensively revised and included a provision for a year-on-year increase in fees in line with the Retail Price Index. The agreement was renegotiated in 2015, and in 2024 (following a deal struck by WGGB and the Scottish Society of Playwrights), playwrights working under the agreement received landmark new terms for the digital exploitation of their work).

After many years of negotiation, an agreement was concluded in 1991 between WGGB and the Independent Theatre Council (ITC), which represents 200 of the smaller and fringe theatres as well as educational and touring companies. This agreement was revised in 2002 and the minimum fees are reviewed annually. WGGB is currently talking to the ITC about updating the agreement. The WGGB Theatre Committee runs the Olwen Wymark Theatre Encouragement Award scheme. In 2022 the union launched a landmark New Play Commission Scheme to address the severe impact Covid-19 had on playwrights and new writing in the theatre sector, resulting in commissions for 18 new plays, which have now started to be performed at theatres across the UK.

Videogames

WGGB counts games writers amongst its members and holds regular networking events for them. The union publishes guidelines for games writers and those who work with them, outlining best practice in this growing area.

Other activities

WGGB is in touch with government and national institutions wherever and whenever the interests of writers are in question or are being discussed, for example submitting evidence to a Parliamentary inquiries and responding to consultations, for example on copyright and AI. It holds cross-party Parliamentary lobbies with Equity and the Musicians' Union to ensure that the various artforms they represent are properly cared for and writers' voices are heard during, for instance, the Brexit transition and the Covid-19 pandemic. In the run up to the 2024 General Election the union launched a manifesto, 'Putting writers at the heart of the story', calling for the next government to take urgent action around fair pay, fair treatment, a sustainable sector and copyright and AI. Working with the Federation of Entertainment Unions, WGGB makes its views known to bodies, such as Arts Council England and Ofcom on a broader basis.

WGGB is an active affiliate of the British Copyright Council, Creators' Rights Alliance and other organisations whose activities are relevant to professional writers. Internationally, it plays a leading role in the International Affiliation of Writers Guilds, which includes the American Guilds East and West, the Canadian Guilds (French and English) and the Irish, Mexican, French, Israeli, South African and New Zealand Guilds. When it is possible to make common cause, the guilds act accordingly. WGGB takes a leading role in the Fédération des Scénaristes d'Europe.

On a day-to-day basis, WGGB gives advice on contracts and takes up issues that affect the lives of its members as professional writers. Other benefits include access to free and discounted training, exclusive events and discounts and a dedicated online members' area. Full members are entitled to submit a profile for inclusion in the WGGB online *Find A Writer* directory; pay no joining fee for membership to Writers Guild of America East or West (if they meet joining criteria); and are eligible for Cannes accreditation. Regular committee meetings are held by specialist WGGB Craft Committees, and its active branches across the UK organise panel discussions, talks and social events. WGGB also has an Equality & Diversity Committee where activists have been involved in many initiatives, including an access rider to reduce access barriers for freelance writers and a new series of member networks for under-represented writing groups.

Campaigns include Save Audio Drama at the BBC and sustained campaigning and lobbying around Artificial Intelligence and threats to writers' copyright and remuneration. In 2018 the union's Equality Writers campaign was launched following Equality Writes, following an independent report commissioned by WGGB which revealed the lack of gender equality in the UK screen industries. The union has also campaigned against the privatisation of Channel 4. It has spoken out on arts funding cuts and the impact of the cost-of-living crisis.

Alliance of Independent Authors

ALLi is the professional association for self-publishing writers and advisors.

The Alliance of Independent Authors (ALLi) is a global non-profit membership organisation focused on ethics and excellence in self-publishing.

Since its foundation in 2012 by Orna Ross, ALLi has offered its members and the wider author community a wide range of publishing, marketing and business guidance through its Self-Publishing Advice Centre blog, podcast, annual online conference and series of guidebooks. It issues a directory of publishing services vetted for quality, value and ethical behaviour and maintains an active Watchdog desk which rates self-publishing providers and provides community alerts.

ALLi commissions original research as well as compiling facts and figures across the industry, making it the best source of data on self-publishing in the world: www.allianceindependentauthors.org/facts.

It also advocates for the interests of independent authors within and outside the literary, publishing and bookselling sectors through its outreach campaigns relating to ethics, diversity, opening up literary opportunities and raising the average income for authors through encouraging excellence in creative business practice.

Membership

The Alliance of Independent Authors
7 Bell Yard, City of Westminster, London WC2A 2JR
email info@allianceindependentauthors.org
website www.allianceindependentauthors.org, https://selfpublishingadvice.org
X @IndieAuthorALLi

ALLi offers three grades of membership for authors:

Associate membership (£69 p.a.) is open to writing/publishing students with an interest in self-publishing and non-published writers (or translators) preparing a book for self-publication.

Author membership (£89 p.a.) is open to writers or translators of books for adults who have self-published a full-length title (55,000+ words) or series of shorter books; writers of children's/young adult books who have self-published one or more titles.

Authorpreneur membership (£119 p.a.) is open to full-time self-publishing authors who earn their living from their author business and can show evidence of 50,000 book sales in the last two years; applications are assessed.

Benefits include self-publishing advice, guidance and community; vetted services, service ratings and watchdog desk; legal and contract appraisal; discounts and deals; professional and business development; campaigns and advocacy.

ALLi also has two partner memberships: for self-publishing services; and for other authors' associations that align with ALLi's ethos.

Society of Children's Book Writers & Illustrators

The Society of Children's Book Writers & Illustrators (SCBWI) is the only international professional organisation for authors, illustrators or translators of books for children and young adults. It is a global community of writers, illustrators, translators, publishers, librarians, advocates and other industry professionals working to establish a more imaginative and inclusive world through the power of children's literature. Its mission is to support the creation of quality children's books, so that young people everywhere have the books they need and deserve. There can never be too many good children's books, and this simple belief guides everything they do. SCBWI are committed to breaking down barriers and opening doors for everyone with a story to tell.

Whether you are a professional children's writer, illustrator, translator or a newcomer to the field, SCBWI has plenty to offer, from local, national to international events, from advice on getting your first deal to help in navigating your career. Established in 1971, it has over 26,000 members in 70 regional chapters worldwide, serving as a consolidated voice for members within the publishing industry. Membership benefits include professional development and networking opportunities, marketing information, events, publications, online profiles, grants and awards. Through awards, events and publications SCBWI provides established writers, illustrators and translators tools and resources to manage and develop their careers, and educates those just starting out.

What does SCBWI British Isles do?

It is a dynamic and friendly chapter of over 1,000 members, which supports aspiring and published writers and illustrators and provides opportunities for them to network, market their work, hone their craft, make industry connections and develop their careers. Volunteer-run events include an annual two-day conference, a fiction and picture book retreat, an annual Agents' Party, the Industry Insiders series (six talks a year in London aimed at professional development), the illustrators' masterclasses (Saturday workshops with a hands-on craft element), sketch-and-scrawl crawls. (See also the next paragraph.) A network of volunteers run local critique groups, workshops and social events across the British Isles. SCBWI British Isles is committed to offering free and subsidised places to attend and participate in all of its events and initiatives for authors and illustrators traditionally under-represented in publishing.

Further information

Society of Children's Book Writers & Illustrators
website www.scbwi.org,
www.scbwi.org/regions/british-isles
Co-Regional Advisors (Co-chairs) Natascha Biebow and Alison Gardiner
email britishisles-ra@scbwi.org
Membership Coordinator Anita Loughrey
email membership@britishscbwi.org
Membership £80 p.a.; £20 p.a. for students

What SCBWI does for its members
• A professional guild speaking as a consolidated global voice for professional children's writers and illustrators. In recent years, SCBWI has successfully lobbied for such issues as new copyright legislation, equitable treatment of authors and artists, and fair contract terms.
• Provides a showcase of authors' and illustrators' work through Featured Illustrator Showcase and Member Awards.
• Keeps members up to date with industry developments through the SCBWI PULSE series of events, with opportunities to learn more about the 'business' of writing and illustrating, including marketing and publicity, school and festival visits, and exclusive networking events with librarians and booksellers.
• Offers members invaluable exposure to editors, art directors and agents through one-to-one manuscript or portfolio reviews at the annual conference and retreats, the members-only Agents' Party, the Slush Pile Challenge and biennial SCBWI Undiscovered Voices (www.undiscoveredvoices.com) competitions.
• Supports professional development for members to hone their craft through the Masterclass series, conference workshops and critique groups.
• Gives members increased visibility online with a free profile on its website, which is a port of call for agents, art directors and editors.
• Provides support and a network of like-minded people, helping to answer members' queries through a variety of online resources including a popular social networking site.
• Facilitates networking opportunities with professionals worldwide.
• Publishes *Insight* and *PRO-Insider* e-newsletters; bi-weekly *Words & Pictures* newsletter blog (www.wordsandpics.org) and annual publications: *The Book: The Essential Guide to Children's Publishing* and *The Essential Guide to Self-Publishing Books for Children*.
• Has website resources, including book launch parties, members' bookshop, discussion boards, illustrator gallery, Find a Speaker Directory, webinars and podcasts.

Awards and grants
The SCBWI administers a number of awards and grants.

British Isles Regional Grants
• There are six Conference Scholarships to attend the annual SCBWI-BI conference.
• A number of scholarship places are awarded at all British Isles region events for under-represented groups in children's publishing, including SCBWI British Isles members who have financial need; SCBWI British Isles members and non-members who identify as a person of colour, LGBTQ+, disabled or working class.
• SCBWI British Isles also offers scholarship memberships to the All Stories Mentorship programme and Undiscovered Voices competition for participants who have been traditionally under-represented in children's publishing.

For SCBWI Members
• Several Work-in-Progress Grants are available each year to assist children's book writers. illustrators and translators in the completion of a specific project currently not under contract, in the categories of Picture Book Text, Chapter Books/Early Readers, Middle Grade, Young Adult Fiction, Non-fiction, and Multicultural Fiction or Non-Fiction.

Society of Children's Book Writers & Illustrators

• The Stephen Fraser Encouragement Fund offers three no-strings attached yearly grants of $2,000 each to three children's book authors, artists or translators who have traditionally published at least one book.

For Writers
• A. Orr Fantasy Grant: For young adult and middle-grade writers working in the fantasy or science fiction genre.
• Ann Whitford Paul and Writer's Digest Most Promising Picture Book Manuscript Award: For the Most Promising Picture Book manuscript. There will be two awards given, one for a work of fiction and one for a work of non-fiction and each winner will receive a $1500 cash prize.
• BIPOC Scholarship: For an all-expense paid trip to the Winter or Summer Conference for a writer who identify as Black, Indigenous, and/or a Person of colour.
• The Emerging Voices Award: For fostering the emergence of diverse voices in children's books.
• Karen Cushman Late Bloomer Award: For a work-in-progress from an unpublished author over 50 years old.
• Out from the Margins Award: For early career under-represented creators of children's literature.
• Volemos – The Meg Medina Grant: For authors of Hispanic/Latinx/Ibero-American heritage who are in the early stages of their career (between 1 and 3 traditionally published books) or not yet traditionally published.
• The Russell Freedman Award for Non-Fiction for a Better World: For a work of non-fiction that contributes to our understanding of how to make our world and society better. The winner will receive a prize of $2500 plus $500 to purchase copies of the winning book for distribution to schools and libraries.

For Illustrators
• Bologna Illustrators Scholarship: For two illustrators to receive a ticket to the Bologna Book Fair, travel fare, and a stipend for accommodations.
• Don Freeman Work-in-Progress Grant: For assisting illustrators in the completion of a book dummy or portfolio.
• Ezra Jack Keats Showcase Prize: For a promising BIPOC illustrator.
• Narrative Art Award: For an illustrator of promise based on a given prompt.
• Out from the Margins Award: For early career under-represented creators of children's literature.
• The Portfolio Awards: For the best art portfolios on view at the Juried Portfolio Display at the Summer or Winter Conference. Gold Award: Free tuition to the Summer or Winter Conference of the following year; appointments with two art directors for a portfolio/style/illustration critique. Silver and Bronze Awards: Zoom conversation with an art director for a portfolio/style/illustration critique.
• Student Illustrator Scholarships: For Summer or Winter Conference tuition for full-time university students studying illustration.

For PAL Published Members
• The Crystal Kite Awards: For the most outstanding books published by SCBWI members each year, voted for by SCBWI peers.

308 Societies, prizes and festivals

• The Golden Kite Awards: the Golden Kite Awards recognize outstanding achievement in seven categories: Young Reader and Middle Grade Fiction, Young Adult Fiction, Nonfiction for Younger Readers, Nonfiction for Older Readers, Picture Book Text, Picture Book Illustration, and Illustration for Older Readers. Each category winner receives $2,500, while honor recipients are awarded $500.
• The Charlotte and Wilbur Award for Compassion For Animals awards one winning book (prize of $2,500) and one honour book (prize of $1,000) for their dedication to promoting compassion and respect for animals in their readers. If the winning or honour book is a picture book, the prize will be split between the author and illustrator.

For Translators
• The SCBWI Pitch-Perfect Translation Grant assists children's book translators in the development of a specific translation project into English, which is not currently under contract. Up to two winners will be selected annually and will receive $500 and the opportunity to craft a longer sample of up to 4000 words, which will be made available on a secure webpage and presented to a hand-selected group of editors, along with the pitch.

For Independently Published Members
• Independently Published Pre-publication Grant provides $2,500 to help offset the price of self-publishing.
• The annual Spark Award recognises excellence in a children's book published through a non-traditional publishing route.

Community Grants
• Amber Brown Grant commemorates the author and beloved school speaker Paula Danziger. One school is awarded each year with an author or illustrator visit and new books to continue Paula's love of connecting children with creative influences.
• The SCBWI Disability Fund gives grants to disabled members for anything that would help them create children's literature. For non-members with disabilities, the funds may support memberships and/or registration to events.
• The SCBWI Emergency Fund gives a grant of up to $1,500 to a member for anything that would help them create children's literature. For non-members with disabilities, the funds may support memberships and/or registration to events.

See also...
- *Seven Stories – The National Centre for Children's Books*, page 309
- *Federation of Children's Book Groups*, page 311
- *Opportunities for under-represented writers*, page 350

Seven Stories – The National Centre for Children's Books

At Seven Stories the rich heritage of British children's books is collected, explored and celebrated.

seven stories
National Centre for Children's Books

Once upon a time an idea was born on the banks of the Tyne to create a national home for children's literature – a place where the original work of authors and illustrators could be collected, treasured and celebrated. After ten years of pioneering work by founding directors Elizabeth Hammill and Mary Briggs, that dream became a reality. In August 2005 Seven Stories, the Centre for Children's Books, opened in an award-winning converted seven-storey Victorian granary in the Ouseburn Valley, a stone's throw from Newcastle's vibrant quayside. Seven Stories is now officially known as The National Centre for Children's Books, following approval by Arts Council England in 2012. It is the only accredited museum in the UK that specialises in children's books.

The collection

At the heart of Seven Stories is a unique and growing collection of manuscripts, artwork and other pre-publication materials. These treasures record the creative process involved in making a children's book and provide illuminating insights into the working lives of modern authors and illustrators. The collection focuses on work created in modern Britain. It already contains thousands of items by authors such as Judith Kerr, Peter Dickinson, Michael Morpurgo, Enid Blyton, Berlie Doherty, Jan Mark, Philip Pullman, Michael Rosen, Robert Westall and Ursula Moray Williams; illustrators like Edward Ardizzone, Faith Jaques, Harold Jones, Anthony Maitland, Pat Hutchins, Helen Cooper, Jan Ormerod and Jane Ray; and editors and other practitioners such as Kaye Webb. Many more bodies of work are pledged. A catalogue of the collection is available via the Seven Stories website. In 2022, Seven Stories launched a new platform designed to attract and encourage new audiences to explore the stories behind the stories and widen access to a digitised archive of children's literature through https://sevenstories.online.

Exhibitions

A celebration of creativity underpins the Seven Stories project: its collection documents the creative act, and its exhibitions and programmes interpret this original material in unconventional but meaningful ways. The aim is to cultivate an appreciation of books and their making, and inspire creativity in its audience.

Seven Stories has been mounting exhibitions since 1998 – first in borrowed venues and now in its own home. Here it provides the only exhibition space in the UK wholly dedicated to showcasing the incomparable legacy of British writing and illustrating for children. With exhibitions changing every year, Seven Stories have showcased the impressive work of children's authors such as Judith Kerr, Michael Morpurgo and David McKee, as well as working alongside communities to showcase their collection in ways that reflect a modern and ever-changing landscape.

Throughout its seven storeys – from the galleries, Story Station, independent bookshop, coffee shop to the Attic – visitors of all ages are invited to engage in a unique, interactive exploration of creativity, literature and art. In this ever-changing literary playground and landscape for the imagination, they can become writers, artists, explorers, designers, storytellers, readers or collectors, in the company of storytellers, authors, illustrators and Seven Stories' own facilitators and learning team.

Seven Stories aims to place children, young people and their books at the heart of the UK's national literary culture. An independent educational charity, it is committed to access for all and it has initiated several innovative participation projects. For example working with its regional universities to develop their collection, while utilising the archive of over one million items from the making of children's literature, to broaden access and improve inclusivity.

Seven Stories is dedicated to the celebration of children's literature. It is supported by Arts Council England and Community Foundation Newcastle Culture Investment Fund.

Further information

Seven Stories – The National Centre for Children's Books
30 Lime Street, Ouseburn,
Newcastle upon Tyne NE1 2PQ
tel 0300 330 1095
email info@sevenstories.org.uk
website https://sevenstories.org.uk
X @7stories

Public opening hours Open every day except Wednesdays, 10am–5pm. Open daily during school holidays.

Admission charges General admission free. Events, story time, and workshops tickets start at £2.

Please check the website for the most up-to-date opening and booking information.

See also...
- *Society of Children's Book Writers & Illustrators*, page 305
- *Federation of Children's Book Groups*, page 311

Federation of Children's Book Groups

The aim of the Federation of Children's Book Groups is simple: to bring children and books together, promote children's books and inspire a love of reading through its national and local events. If you are a parent, carer, author, illustrator or professional with a passion for encouraging children to read, the Federation will be of interest to you.

Federation history

The Federation of Children's Book Groups was formed in 1968 by Anne Wood to coordinate the work of the many different children's book groups already in existence across the country, and in 2018 it celebrated 50 years of bringing children and books together.

Celebrating its 40th anniversary in 2020, the Children's Book Award is the only national award voted for entirely by children. Throughout the year Federation Testing Groups read and vote on new fiction supplied by publishers. Each year 90,000 votes are cast involving nearly 250 schools and families across the UK. A shortlist (Top Ten) is drawn up with four picture books in the Younger Children category, three shorter novels for Younger Readers and three novels for Older Readers, with children from all over the UK voting in their groups or online. You do not have to be a member to vote in the Top Ten. The Award has a track record of identifying future bestsellers: the first Overall Winner was *Mr Magnolia* by Quentin Blake; other winners include *The Hunger Games*, *Noughts and Crosses* and the *Harry Potter* books.

In 1976 National Tell-A-Story-Week was established and it has now grown into National Share-A-Story-Month (NSSM), which takes place each May. It enables groups to focus on the power of stories and to hold events which celebrate all forms of storytelling. The theme in 2025 is 'Saving the World One Book at a Time'. The website hosts the NSSM pack, full of ideas and activities, which is sent to each book group and can also be downloaded by non-members.

In 1977, the first Federation anthology was published, and since then they have compiled booklists covering the whole age range from picture books to the latest teen and young adult novels (downloadable from the website). In 2010 the Federation created National Non-Fiction Day to celebrate the quality and variety of information books available for children. It has expanded to be National Non-Fiction November; further details can be found on the website, along with downloadable free resources. The theme for 2024 was 'Why Don't You' encouraging children to take up new hobbies and activities.

Each year the Federation holds a conference: three days of author and illustrator events, panel discussions and seminars enable group and individual members, publishers, authors, illustrators, teachers, librarians and booksellers to meet and exchange ideas. Delegates are inspired by meeting others who share their passion. The 2025 Conference, 'Weaving Magic with Words', was held in April at Haberdashers' Monmouth School in Wales. See http://fcbg.org.uk/conference for more details about future events.

The Children's Book Groups

Federation Book Groups exist throughout the UK: from Plymouth to Dundee, from Ipswich to Somerset and from Harrogate to Lewes. Their activities are as varied and diverse as the groups themselves, serving their own community's needs, including author and illustrator visits, bonfire parties, museum and library events, book swaps and parties. But, above all, FCBG are passionate about children's books, bringing together ordinary book-loving families, empowering parents, grandparents, carers and children to become enthusiastic and excited about all kinds of good books. Some book groups are based around schools run by enthusiastic librarians and teachers. You can still be a member of the Federation if there is no book group near you. Individual, schools and professional membership enables everyone to participate in sharing their passion for children's books.

Further information

Federation of Children's Book Groups
Wakananai Firs Road, Mardy, Abergavenny, Wales NP7 6NA
tel 07591 380434
email info@fcbg.org.uk
website http://fcbg.org.uk

See also...
- *Society of Children's Book Writers & Illustrators*, page 305
- *Seven Stories – The National Centre for Children's Books*, page 309

National Literacy Trust

Authors and artists can spark a lifelong love of reading – it just takes one book. Jonathan Douglas explains how the National Literacy Trust is raising literacy levels across the UK.

Writers and artists are essential to the National Literacy Trust's mission to raise literacy levels in the UK. We work to improve reading, writing, speaking and listening abilities in the most disadvantaged communities. Creators are not just our natural allies, they are key partners in our campaign to make a difference. It goes without saying that a literacy charity cannot exist without books.

> **Further information**
>
> **National Literacy Trust**
> 68 South Lambeth Road, London SW8 1RL
> *tel* 020-7587 1842
> *email* contact@literacytrust.org.uk
> *website* https://literacytrust.org.uk
> *Facebook* www.facebook.com/nationalliteracytrust
> *X* @Literacy_Trust
> *Instagram* @literacy_trust

The literacy challenge in the UK is significant: last year, around a third of children left primary school without the expected reading and writing skills to thrive, with children from disadvantaged backgrounds falling even further behind. With 4.3 million children already living in poverty (2022/23 figures) and the cost-of-living crisis continuing to grow, the literacy levels of the most vulnerable children are at risk.

Authors have the power to transform the way a child engages with books and in doing so unlock a lifetime of benefits. Our research shows that author visits to schools have a tangible impact on literacy skills: twice as many children and young people who had a writer visit their school read above the expected level for their age compared with their peers who didn't have such a visit. What's more, children who have had an author visit their school have higher levels of confidence in their reading and enjoy reading and writing more. We are grateful when writers ask how they can collaborate with us, and are always looking for support with our campaigning. As a charitable organisation, we are thankful to the people who help us spread the word about our initiatives. Every new like, comment or share is vitally important in helping us reach the people who need our assistance.

One of the National Literacy Trust's priorities is increasing access to books by transforming and equipping primary school libraries. 1 in 7 state primary schools do not have a designated library space and 1 in 10 children (rising to 1 in 8 children from disadvantaged backgrounds) in the UK do not own, or have access to, books at home. To combat this, the Libraries for Primaries campaign, formerly the Primary School Library Alliance, was founded in November 2021 by the National Literacy Trust and Penguin Random House UK. The campaign works with its flagship partners to address the chronic lack of investment in primary school libraries and bring together relevant parties to help solve this urgent issue. The aim is to ensure that every primary school in the UK has a library or dedicated library space. To date, the campaign has transformed over 1,000 school reading spaces in underserved communities in the UK, including donating 732,200 books. We believe bringing together expertise and resources from partners across a number of sectors can more effectively support children's educational outcomes, ensuring the wider emotional and economic benefits of reading for pleasure can be felt by all children.

The unequal impact of school closures during the Covid-19 pandemic, coupled with the pressures of the cost-of-living crisis, highlights the need to help children, young people, families, teachers and communities. Our Arts Council England-funded project 'Connecting Stories' is an excellent example of our work to deepen connections with communities where engagement with reading for pleasure is traditionally low. Publishers are donating books and writers' time to encourage children in 14 areas with low literacy levels to read for pleasure, enjoy their local libraries, and boost their wellbeing. Since its launch, Connecting Stories has reached more than 200,000 individuals. It has been supported by 43 publishers and 95 authors and creatives, including celebrated children's writers Cressida Cowell, Matt Haig and Joseph Coelho.

We are working hard to make sure more children will have greater access to books and their brilliant benefits. Our five-year campaign, Early Words Matter, has a mission to to support 250,000 children in areas most impacted by poverty. We will continue our work developing programmes, resources, activities and materials to give children across the country the best chance to develop literacy skills that will help them throughout their lives.

Jonathan Douglas CBE is the Chief Executive of the National Literacy Trust.

See also...
- *Opportunities for under-represented writers*, page 350

Societies, associations and organisations

The societies and associations listed here include appreciation societies devoted to specific authors, professional bodies and national institutions. Some also offer prizes and awards (see page 333).

Action for Children's Arts
c/o Mousetrap Theatre Projects,
33 Shaftesbury Avenue, London W1D 7EH
email admin@childrensarts.org.uk
website www.childrensarts.org.uk
Facebook www.facebook.com/ActionChildrensArts
X @childrensarts
Membership £18 p.a. student and school; £30 p.a. individual; from £50 p.a. organisation

A membership charity organisation that values children, childhood and the arts. It embraces the UN Convention on the Rights of the Child by campaigning for the right of all children in the UK to experience high-quality arts as an integral part of their childhood; by connecting people within and across the cultural and education sectors, across art forms and across the regions and nations of the UK; and by celebrating achievement, dedication and best practice in artistic activity for and with children.

Alliance of Independent Authors
7 Bell Yard, City of Westminster, London WC2A 2JR
email info@allianceindependentauthors.org
website www.allianceindependentauthors.org, https://selfpublishingadvice.org
X @IndieAuthorALLi
Instagram @indieauthoralli
Membership £69 p.a. Associate; £89 p.a. Author; £119 p.a. Authorpreneur

A global collaborative collective of self-publishing writers. Founded in 2012 at the London Book Fair by former author and former literary agent, Orna Ross, in response to her personal experience of self-publishing. Supports and advocates for the interests of independent, self-publishing authors everywhere and promotes the interests of indie authors within the literary and publishing industries; engages with booksellers, festivals, prize-giving committees, libraries, book clubs and the media.

It issues a directory of publishing services vetted for quality, value and ethical behaviour and maintains an active Watchdog desk which rates self-publishing providers and provides community alerts.

ALLi commissions original research as well as compiling facts and figures across the industry, making it the best source of data on self-publishing in the world: www.allianceindependentauthors.org/facts. Benefits for members include self-publishing advice, guidance and community; vetted services, service ratings and watchdog desk; legal and contract appraisal; discounts and deals; professional and business development; campaigns and advocacy.

American Booksellers Association
tel +1 800-637-0037
email info@bookweb.org
website www.bookweb.org
Facebook www.facebook.com/americanbooksellers
Instagram @americanbooksellers

A national non-profit trade organisation that works with booksellers and industry partners to ensure the success and profitability of independently owned book retailers and to assist in expanding the book community. Provides education and information dissemination, offers business products and services, creates relevant awareness programmes and engages in public policy. Founded 1900.

American Society of Composers, Authors and Publishers
250 West 57th Street, New York, NY 10107, USA
tel +1 212-621-6000
website www.ascap.com
Facebook www.facebook.com/ascap
X @ASCAP
Instagram @ascap
Threads @ascap

An organisation founded and governed by its members, it is the leading performance rights organisation representing more than one million songwriters, composers and music publishers.

Arts Council/An Chomhairle Ealaíon
70 Merrion Square, Dublin D02 NY52, Republic of Ireland
tel +353 (0)1 618 0200
website www.artscouncil.ie/home
Facebook www.facebook.com/artscouncilireland
X @artscouncil_ie
Instagram @artscouncilireland

The national development agency for the arts in Ireland. Promotes the arts through funding, research, information sharing, setting standards and encouraging appreciation. Founded 1951.

Arts Council England
tel 0161 934 4317
website www.artscouncil.org.uk
Facebook www.facebook.com/artscouncilofengland

X @ace_national
Instagram @aceagrams

The national development agency for arts and culture in England, distributing public money from the government and the National Lottery. Organisations, artists, events and initiatives can receive funding to help achieve the Council's mission of providing art and culture for everyone. There are five area councils: London, Midlands, North, South East and South West. Visit the website for information on funding support and advice, an online funding finder and funding FAQs. Founded 1946.

Arts Council of Northern Ireland

The MAC, 10 Exchange Street West, Belfast BT1 2NB
tel 028-9262 3555
email info@artscouncil-ni.org
website www.artscouncil-ni.org
Chief Executive Roisín McDonough

Promotes and encourages the arts throughout Northern Ireland. Artists in drama, dance, music and jazz, literature, visual arts, traditional arts and community arts can apply for support for specific schemes and projects. The value of the grant will be set according to the aims of the programme. Artists of all disciplines and in all types of working practice, who have made a contribution to artistic activities in Northern Ireland for a minimum period of one year within the last five years, are eligible.

Arts Council of Wales

Bute Place, Cardiff CF10 5AL
tel 0330 124 2733
website https://arts.wales
Facebook www.facebook.com/celfyddyau
X @Arts_Wales_
Instagram @celfcymruarts

The official body that funds and develops the arts in Wales. The funding it distributes comes from both the Welsh government and the National Lottery; most funding goes to artists and arts organisations carrying out programmes of work across Wales. Founded 1994.

North Wales Regional Office
Princes Park II, Princes Drive, Colwyn Bay LL29 8PL

Mid and West Wales Regional Office
Yr Egin, College Road, Carmarthen SA31 3EQ

Association for Library Service to Children

American Library Association,
225 North Michigan Avenue, Suite 1300, Chicago, IL 60601, USA
tel +1 800-545-2433
email alsc@ala.org
website www.ala.org/alsc
Facebook www.facebook.com/Associationforlibraryservicetochildren
X @wearealsc

Develops and supports the profession of children's librarianship by enabling and encouraging its practitioners to provide the best library service to US children.

Association for Scottish Literature

c/o Department of Scottish Literature,
University of Glasgow, 7 University Gardens, Glasgow G12 8QH
tel 0141 330 5309
email office@asls.org.uk
website www.asls.org.uk
Facebook www.facebook.com/groups/scotlit
Bluesky @asls.org.uk.bsky.social
Instagram @associationforscotlit
President David Goldie, *Secretary* Moira Hansen, *Director* Duncan Jones
Membership £70 p.a. individuals; £20 p.a. UK students; £100 p.a. corporate

Promotes the study, teaching and writing of Scottish literature and furthers the study of Scottish languages. Publishes annually an anthology of new Scottish writing, *New Writing Scotland*; an edited text of Scottish literature; a series of academic journals; and the eZine *The Bottle Imp*. Also publishes *Scotnotes* (comprehensive study guides for major Scottish writers), literary texts and commentaries designed to assist the classroom teacher, and a series of occasional papers. Organises two conferences a year. Founded 1970.

Association of American Literary Agents

302A West 12th Street, Suite 122, New York, NY 10014, USA
email info@aalitagents.org
website https://aalitagents.org

A professional organisation of over 500 agents who work with authors and illustrators. Founded 1991.

Association of American Publishers

1730 Pennsylvania Avenue NW, Washington, DC 20006, USA
tel +1 202-347-3375
email info@publishers.org
website https://publishers.org
X @AmericanPublish

AAP is the trade association for US books, journals and education publishers, providing advocacy and communications on behalf of the industry and its priorities nationally and worldwide. Founded 1970.

The Association of Authors' Agents

The Society of Authors, 24 Bedford Row, London WC1R 4EH
tel 020-3880 2230
website www.agentsassoc.co.uk
President Claire Wilson, *Secretary* John Baker

Exists to provide a forum that allows member agencies to discuss issues arising in the profession; a collective voice for UK literary agencies in public affairs and the media; and a code of conduct to which all members commit themselves. Please note that the AAA is not able to offer advice on finding representation by an agent or getting published. Founded 1974.

Association of Canadian Publishers
401 Richmond Street West, Studio 258, Toronto, ON M5V 3A8, Canada
tel +1 416-487-6116
email admin@canbook.org
website https://publishers.ca
Executive Director Jack Illingworth

Represents approx. 115 Canadian-owned and controlled book publishers from across the country. Activities include government and public relations, marketing initiatives, research and communications, and professional development. Founded 1976.

Association of Freelance Editors, Proofreaders and Indexers of Ireland
email info@afepi-ireland.com
website www.afepi-ireland.com
Facebook www.facebook.com/AFEPI.Ireland
X @AFEPI_Ireland
Membership €100 p.a. full; €55 p.a. associate

AFEPI Ireland is an organisation for publishing and editorial freelancers in Ireland. Fosters high standards in editing, proofreading and indexing; protects the interests of its members; and helps to match authors, indie writers, publishers, businesses, public bodies and charitable organisations with suitable editorial freelancers. Membership is available to experienced professional editors, proofreaders and indexers. For services for publishers and authors, see the online directory of freelance professional editors, proofreaders and indexers based in Ireland and Northern Ireland. Founded 1985.

Association of Illustrators
Somerset House, Strand, London WC2R 1LA
tel 020-7759 1010
email info@theaoi.com
website www.theaoi.com
Facebook www.facebook.com/theaoi
X @theaoi
Instagram @theaoi

Trade association that supports illustrators throughout their careers with business, licensing and contract advice, promotes illustration and encourages professional standards in the industry. Presents an annual programme of events and holds an annual competition, the World Illustration Awards, in partnership with the *Directory of Illustration*. Founded 1973.

Australian Copyright Council
PO Box 1986, Strawberry Hills, NSW 2012, Australia
tel +61 (0)2 9101 2377
email info@copyright.org.au
website www.copyright.org.au
Facebook www.facebook.com/AusCopyrightCouncil
X @AusCopyright
Instagram @auscopyrightcouncil
Ceo Eileen Camilleri

Provides easily accessible and affordable practical information, legal advice, education and forums on Australian copyright law for content creators and consumers. Represents the peak bodies for professional artists and content creators working in Australia's creative industries and Australia's major copyright collecting societies, including the Australian Society of Authors, the Australian Writers' Guild and the Australian Publishers Association.

Advocates for the contribution of creators to Australia's culture and economy and the importance of copyright for the common good. Works to promote understanding of copyright law and its application, supports appropriate law reform and fosters collaboration between content creators and consumers. Founded 1968.

Australian Publishers Association
60/89 Jones Street, Ultimo, NSW 2007, Australia
tel +61 (0)2 9281 9788
website www.publishers.asn.au
X @AusPublish
President Julie Burland

The APA is the national representative body for the Australian publishing industry. Founded 1948.

Australian Writers' Guild
Level 4, 70 Pitt Street, Sydney, NSW 2000, Australia
tel +61 (0)2 9319 0339
email admin@awg.com.au
website www.awg.com.au

The professional association representing writers for stage, screen, radio and online. Protects and promotes creative and professional interests. Founded 1962.

Authors Aloud UK
72 Castle Road, St Albans, Herts. AL1 5DG
tel (01727) 893992
email info@authorsalouduk.co.uk
website www.authorsalouduk.co.uk
Facebook www.facebook.com/Authors-Aloud-UK-497942623573822
X @AuthorsAloudUK
Instagram @authorsalouduk
Directors Naomi Cooper, Annie Everall

An author booking agency that brings together authors, illustrators, poets, storytellers and trainers with schools, libraries and festivals, in the UK and internationally, to promote enthusiasm for reading.

Works with children's authors who wish to visit schools and libraries, in person and virtually, and who are published by mainstream children's publishers. Also arranges author tours and book-related events for publishers and other organisations.

Authors' Licensing and Collecting Society Ltd – see page 413

Bardd Plant Cymru (Welsh-Language Children's Poet Laureate)
Books Council of Wales, Castell Brychan, Aberystwyth, Ceredigion SY23 2JB
tel (01970) 624151
email castellbrychan@books.wales
website https://llyfrau.cymru/en

Raises the profile of poetry amongst children and encourages them to compose and enjoy poetry. During their term of office the bard visits schools and conducts online workshops. The scheme's partner organisations are: S4C, the Welsh Government, the Books Council of Wales, Urdd Gobaith Cymru and Literature Wales.

Quentin Blake Centre for Illustration
1 Myddelton Passage, London EC1R 1XJ
email info@qbcentre.org.uk
website www.qbcentre.org.uk
Instagram @qbcentre

Will open in Clerkenwell, London in 2026. The Centre will be a home for Quentin Blake's archive, host events and workshops, and feature a cafe, shop and public gardens. The Centre also tours nationwide exhibitions and schools projects.

Book Marketing Society
email admin@bookmarketingsociety.co.uk
website www.bookmarketingsociety.co.uk
X @BMSoc
Membership £84 p.a. standard; £120 p.a. freelancer

Launched with the objective of becoming the representative body of marketing within the book industry. Provides a forum for sharing best practice, inspiration and creativity through regular awards and a lively programme of member meetings, development workshops, masterclasses and social events. Anyone who works for a book publisher, book retailer or book wholesaler is eligible for membership, including those working in associated areas.

Books Council of Wales/Cyngor Llyfrau Cymru
Castell Brychan, Aberystwyth, Ceredigion SY23 2JB
tel (01970) 624151
email castellbrychan@books.wales
website https://llyfrau.cymru/en, www.gwales.com
Ceo Helgard Krause

Supports and develops the publishing industry in Wales. Promotes literacy and reading for pleasure through a range of public campaigns, activities and events across Wales, often working in partnership with schools, libraries and other literary organisations. Works with publishers to nurture new talent and content in Welsh and English, and offers specialist editing, design, marketing and distribution services. Administers grants to publishers and independent booksellers. Partly funded by the Welsh Government through Creative Wales and from the commercial operations of its wholesale book distribution centre. Founded 1961.

The Booksellers Association
6 Bell Yard, London WC2A 2JR
tel 020-7421 4640
email mail@booksellers.org.uk
website www.booksellers.org.uk
Facebook www.facebook.com/thebooksellersassociation
X @BAbooksellers
President Fleur Sinclair

A membership organisation for all booksellers in the UK and Ireland, representing over 95% of bookshops. Key services include National Book Tokens, Batch Payment Services and BatchLine. Founded 1895.

BookTrust
BookTrust HQ: 1 Aire Street, Leeds LS1 4PR
London Office: BookTrust, 29 Clerkenwell Road, Farringdon, London EC1M 5RN
tel 020-7801 8826
email query@booktrust.org.uk
website www.booktrust.org.uk
Facebook www.facebook.com/booktrust
X @Booktrust
Instagram @booktrust
Ceo Diana Gerald, Chair of Trustees John Coughlan

The UK's largest children's reading charity, dedicated to getting children reading. Supports parents and carers to share stories and books with children from a young age, with especial focus on disadvantaged children who need reading the most.

BookTrust reviews at least one children's book each day and runs the Waterstones Children's Laureate, BookTrust Storytime Prize and BookTrust Represents.

BookTrust Represents
BookTrust HQ 1 Aire Street, Leeds LS1 4PR
London Office 29 Clerkenwell Road, Farringdon, London EC1M 5RN
tel 020-7801 8826
email booktrust.represents@booktrust.org.uk
website www.booktrust.org.uk/booktrustrepresents
X @Booktrust

A project to support and promote authors and illustrators of colour and to reach more readers

Societies, associations and organisations 319

through school visits, special events and festivals. Also supports aspiring and new authors and illustrators of colour with training, mentoring, events and an online community. Find out more about the project and the associated research on the website. Founded 2019.

The British Council
Bridgewater House, 58 Whitworth Street,
Manchester M1 6BB
tel 0161 884 0291
website www.britishcouncil.org
Facebook www.facebook.com/britishcouncil
X @BritishCouncil
Instagram @britishcouncil
Chief Executive Scott McDonald, *Director of Cultural Engagement* Mark Stephens

The UK's international organisation for cultural relations and educational opportunities. Builds connections, understanding and trust between people in the UK and other countries through arts and culture, education and the English language. Working in close collaboration with book trade associations, the Literature team participates in major international book fairs.

Collaborates with offices overseas to broker relationships and create activities that link artists and cultural institutions around the world. Works with writers, publishers, producers, translators and other sector professionals across literature, publishing and education. The Visual Arts team connects professionals internationally through collaborative exhibition programmes, digital networking, training and development, and delegations. Manages and develops the British Council Collection and the British Pavilion at the Venice Biennale.

Canadian Authors Association
Aurora, ON L4G 2R6, Canada
tel +1 877-905-1921 (ext. 800)
email office@canadianauthors.org
website www.canadianauthors.org
Facebook www.facebook.com/canadianauthorsassociation
X @canauthors
Administrative Director Brandi Tanner

A membership-based organisation for writers in all areas of the profession. Has chapters across Canada that provide writers with a wide variety of programmes, services and resources to help them develop skills in the craft and business of writing. Founded 1921.

The Canadian Children's Book Centre
1 Centre Street, Unit 102, Scarborough,
ON M1J 3B4, Canada
tel +1 416-975-0010
email info@bookcentre.ca
website https://bookcentre.ca
Facebook www.facebook.com/kidsbookcentre
X @kidsbookcentre
Bluesky @kidsbookcentre.bsky.social
Instagram @kidsbookcentre

The CCBC is a national, not-for-profit organisation that is dedicated to encouraging, promoting and supporting the reading, writing, illustrating and publishing of Canadian books for young readers. Programmes, publications and resources help teachers, librarians, booksellers, parents and caregivers select the very best for young readers. Founded 1976.

Canadian Publishers' Council
Suite 6060, 3080 Yonge Street, Toronto,
ON M4N 3N1, Canada
tel +1 647-255-8880
email dswail@pubcouncil.ca
website https://pubcouncil.ca
Facebook www.facebook.com/people/Canadian-Publishers-Council/100089305355472
X @pubcouncil_ca
Instagram @pubcouncil_ca
President David Swail

Represents the interests of Canadian publishing companies that publish books and other media for schools, colleges and universities, professional and reference markets, and the retail and library sectors. Founded 1910.

Canadian Society of Children's Authors, Illustrators & Performers
720 Bathurst Street, Suite 412, Toronto,
ON M5S 2R4, Canada
tel +1 416-515-1559
email office@canscaip.org
website www.canscaip.org
X @CANSCAIP
Administrative Director Helena Aalto
Membership $90 p.a. member; $50 p.a. friend

CANSCAIP is a membership-based non-profit organisation that supports the professional development of Canada's community of authors, illustrators and performers for children and teens. Founded 1977.

The Center for Children's Books
School of Information Sciences,
501 East Daniel Street, Champaign, IL 61820, USA
tel +1 217-244-9331
email ccb-asst@illinois.edu
website https://ccb.ischool.illinois.edu
Facebook www.facebook.com/CenterforChildrensBooks
X @iSchoolCCB
Instagram @ischoolccb

CCB houses a non-circulating collection of recent and historically significant trade books for children, plus review copies of nearly all trade books published in the USA in the current year.

Includes professional and reference books on the history and criticism of literature for youth, literature-based library and classroom programming, and storytelling. The collection is available for examination by scholars, teachers, librarians, students and other educators.

Centre for Literacy in Primary Education
Webber Street, London SE1 8QW
tel 020-7401 3382/3
email info@clpe.org.uk
website https://clpe.org.uk
Facebook www.facebook.com/CentreforLiteracyinPrimaryEducation
X @clpe1
Instagram @clpe.org.uk
Ceo Rebecca Eaves

The CLPE is a small independent charity working with all those involved in teaching literacy in primary schools. Raises the achievement of children by helping schools to teach literacy more effectively and by showing teachers how quality children's literature can be placed at the heart of all learning.

CIEP (Chartered Institute of Editing and Proofreading)
Studio 651, Milton Keynes Business Centre, Foxhunter Drive, Linford Wood, Milton Keynes, Bucks. MK14 6GD
tel 020-8785 6155
email office@ciep.uk
website www.ciep.uk
Facebook www.facebook.com/EditProof
X @The_CIEP

A membership organisation promoting excellence in English language editing, setting and demonstrating editorial standards, and providing a community, training hub and support network for editorial professionals. Runs online courses and workshops in copy-editing, proofreading and related skills, for people starting an editorial career and those wishing to broaden their competence, and maintains an online directory of experienced editorial professionals. Also publishes factsheets and guides on various aspects of editing and business skills for the self-employed. Previously the Society for Editors and Proofreaders before being awarded its Royal Charter in 2019.

The Children's Book Council and Every Child A Reader
54 West 39th Street, New York, NY 10018, USA
email cbc.info@cbcbooks.org
website www.cbcbooks.org
website www.everychildareader.net

The CBC is the non-profit trade association of North American publishers for children and young adults. Runs Every Child a Reader, its charitable component that sponsors Children's Book Week; Get Caught Reading; and the National Ambassador of Young People's Literature, in conjunction with the Library of Congress.

Offers children's publishers the opportunity for educational programming, diversity advocacy, and national literacy campaigns. The CBC connects member publishers to librarians, teachers, booksellers and caregivers across the country, providing reading lists, student resources and community outreach in coordination with prominent national organisations.

The Children's Book Council of Australia
Level 2, State Library of Queensland, Stanley Place, South Brisbane, QLD 4101, Australia
email admin@cbca.org.au
website www.cbca.org.au
Facebook www.facebook.com/cbca.national
X @TheCBCA
Instagram @cbcaustralia

Fosters children's enjoyment of books through managing the Book of the Year Awards; providing information on and encouragement to authors and illustrators; organising exhibitions and activities during Children's Book Week; supporting children's library services; promoting high standards in book reviewing; and promoting greater equity of access to reading through community projects.

The Children's Book Guild of Washington DC
email membership.cbg@gmail.com
website www.childrensbookguild.org
Facebook www.facebook.com/bookguilddc
X @BOOKGUILDDC
Instagram @bookguilddc

A regional association of writers, artists, librarians and other specialists dedicated to the field of children's literature. Its aims are to uphold and stimulate high standards of writing and illustrating for children; to increase knowledge and use of better books for children in the community; and to cooperate with other groups having similar purposes. Founded 1945.

Children's Books Ireland
17 North Great George's Street, Dublin D01 R2F1, Republic of Ireland
tel +353 (0)1 872 7475
email info@childrensbooksireland.com
website www.childrensbooksireland.ie
Ceo Elaina Ryan, *Deputy Ceo* Jenny Murray, *Programme & Events Manager* Aoife Murray

Champions every child's right to develop a love of reading. Engages young people in reading, fosters a greater understanding of books for young people and acts as a core resource for those with an interest in books for children in Ireland. Celebrates the importance of authors and illustrators and works in partnership with the people and organisations who enhance children's lives through books. Core projects include: the Children's Books Ireland International Annual Conference; the KPMG Children's Books Ireland Awards and its Junior Juries' programme for school groups and book clubs; the annual Children's Books Ireland Reading Guide; nationwide Book Clinics; various book gifting initiatives including Every Child A Reader; and *Inis* magazine in print and online – a forum for discussion, debate and critique of Irish and international books. Also administers the Laureate na nÓg project on behalf of the Arts Council and runs live literature events throughout the year. Founded 1996.

Children's Books North Network

email info@childrensbooksnorth.co.uk
website www.childrensbooksnorth.co.uk
X @books_north
Bluesky @cbnnetwork.bsky.social
Instagram @childrens_books_north
Co-leaders Emma Layfield, Rebecca Mortimer

A voluntary network group that connects published children's authors, illustrators and publishing professionals living in the North West, North East, Yorkshire and Scotland. The network seeks to promote their members' work, new books and events, and highlights the importance of regional diversity in children's books and the publishing industry. Founded 2020.

Children's Literature Association

140B Purcellville Gateway Drive, Suite 120, Purcellville, VA 20132, USA
tel +1 504-203-9055
email info@childlitassn.org
website https://chla.memberclicks.net
Facebook www.facebook.com/ChildLitAssn
X @chlatweets
Membership From $40 p.a. (dependent on income)

An organisation encouraging high standards of criticism, scholarship, research and teaching in children's literature. Hosts events, admissions, awards and grants, and organises committees. Founded in 1966.

Children's Writers and Illustrators for Stories and Literacy

email enquiries@cwisl.org.uk
website https://cwisl.org.uk
X @CWISL

CWISL (pronounced quizzle) is a voluntary group of children's authors and illustrators who run festivals and workshops that inspire a love of reading, writing, drawing and storytelling in children aged 2–16 years. Events take place in schools and libraries throughout England and online.

The Comics Cultural Impact Collective (CCIC)

email helloccic@gmail.com
website www.thecomicsculturalimpactcollective.org
Instagram @comicsculturalimpact

Established to raise the profile of comics and help establish viable careers in the industry. CCIC collaborates with institutions, organisations and individuals who work in and with comics to campaign for increased funding and support, and for greater awareness of the cultural, educational, artistic and economic value of the medium.

Contact An Author

2 Burns Close, Carshalton SM5 4PY
tel 020-8642 0884
email info@contactanauthor.com
website https://contactanauthor.co.uk
Facebook www.facebook.com/contactanauthor
X @contactanauthor
Instagram @contactanauthor

An author-booking agency that connects children with compassionate and creative people to enhance education. Helps schools, libraries, festivals and organisations all over the world to book authors for their events. Its mission is to celebrate books and help to arrange as many author visits as possible. Founded 2006.

Coram Beanstalk

Coram Campus, 41 Brunswick Square, London WC1N 1AZ
tel 020-7729 4087
email admin@corambeanstalk.org.uk
website www.beanstalkcharity.org.uk
Facebook www.facebook.com/Beanstalkreads
X @beanstalkreads
Instagram @beanstalkreads

Recruits and trains volunteers to provide individually tailored, one-to-one reading support to children aged 3–11 years in primary schools. Focuses on reading for pleasure to give children the support they need to improve their reading ability and confidence. Also provides training courses for students in secondary schools, offering them the opportunity to become Reading Leaders and mentor younger students.

Creative Australia

PO Box 576, Pyrmont, NSW 2009, Australia
tel +61 (0)2 9215 9000
email enquiries@creative.gov.au
website www.creative.gov.au
Facebook www.facebook.com/creative.gov.au
X @creative_gov_au
Instagram @creative.australia
Ceo Adrian Collette

Provides a broad range of support for the arts, embracing music, theatre, literature, visual arts and crafts, dance, First Nations arts, and community and experimental arts.

Creative Rights in AI Coalition
website www.creativerightsinai.co.uk

An umbrella group advocating for the protection of the rights of content creators in response to AI. Members include a diverse range of businesses and organisations from the creative industries. The three pillars of their policy are allowing intellectual property owners control over their own work, transparency in how AI developers are using content and how they are held responsible for infringing copyright, and support for growth and innovation in the creative industries. Founded 2024.

Creative UK
Tomorrow Building, 130 Broadway, 2nd Floor, Suite 7, MediaCityUK, Salford M50 2UW
tel 0333 023 5240
email info@wearecreative.uk
website www.wearecreative.uk
Facebook www.facebook.com/WeAreCreativeUK
Instagram @wearecreativeuk

The national network for the creative industries. Champions the social and economic value of the creative industries by connecting and supporting talent, businesses and organisations; providing development opportunities at a local and national level through a network of partners; and offering tailor-made resources and financial expertise.

The Roald Dahl Museum and Story Centre
81–83 High Street, Great Missenden, Bucks. HP16 0AL
tel (01494) 892192
email hello@roalddahlmuseum.org
website www.roalddahlmuseum.org
Facebook www.facebook.com/roalddahlmuseum
X @roalddahlmuseum
Instagram @roalddahlmuseum

Based in the village of Great Missenden, where Roald Dahl lived and wrote for 36 years. The museum's immersive spaces feature interactive audio and video, activities and crafts, alongside original material from the Roald Dahl archive. Hosts school visits and creative workshops for young people year round.

Discover Children's Story Centre
383–387 High Street, Stratford, London E15 4QZ
tel 020-8536 5555
email bookings@discover.org.uk
website https://discover.org.uk
Facebook www.facebook.com/DiscoverChildrensStoryCentre
X @Discover_Story
Instagram @discover_story

The UK's first hands-on creative literacy centre for children aged 0–11 years and their families, carers and teachers. Sparks children's and adults' imagination, curiosity and creativity in a stimulating environment through creative play. Offers a variety of creative family events led by children's writers and illustrators.

Editors' and Proofreaders' Alliance of Northern Ireland
email info@epani.org.uk
website www.epani.org.uk
Bluesky @epani.bsky.social
Coordinator Averill Buchanan

Establishes and maintains high professional standards in editorial skills in Northern Ireland. For services for authors, see the directory of freelance professional editors, proofreaders and indexers.

Empathy Lab
email info@empathylab.uk
website https://www.empathylab.uk
Facebook www.facebook.com/EmpathyLabUK
X @EmpathyLabUK
Instagram @empathylabuk

A non-profit with a mission to raise an empathy-educated generation. EmpathyLab builds children's empathy, literacy and social activism through high-quality literature. Their strategy is built on scientific evidence showing that empathy is learnable and that reading is a crucial tool to build this skill. EmpathyLab provides training, free resources, an in-depth schools programme and an annual Read for Empathy Book Collection. Empathy Day Festival, a free ten-day nationwide festival that features authors and illustrators and takes place every June, teaches children about empathy and inspires them to develop and put into action key empathy skills. Empathy Action Month, during which themed booklists and learning resources are shared, takes place in November. Founded 2014.

English Association
Senate House, Malet Street, London WC1E 7HU
email hello@englishassociation.ac.uk
website www.englishassociation.ac.uk
X @englishassoc
Ceo Dr Rebecca Fisher
Membership From £55 p.a.

A membership association and a learned society for people passionate about English language, literature and creative writing. Brings together individuals and organisations from all sectors of education and English studies, and has a long history of engagement with national and international bodies. The elective Fellowship recognises outstanding achievement in English studies, and Officers and Committee members are leaders in their field. Through a portfolio of publications, an events programme, networking and campaigning, the association has shaped the discipline and continues to connect English teachers in schools, colleges and universities. Founded 1906.

Federation of Children's Book Groups – see page 311

Federation of European Publishers
Chaussee d'Ixelles, 29/35 Box 4, 1050 Brussels, Belgium
tel +32 2770 1110
email info@fep-fee.eu
website www.fep-fee.eu
X @FEP_EU
Director Anne Bergman-Tahon

Represents the interests of European publishers on EU affairs and informs members on the development of EU policies that could affect the publishing industry. Founded 1967.

Forward Arts Foundation
Somerset House Exchange, The Strand, London WC2R 1LA
tel 020-8187 9861
email info@forwardartsfoundation.org
website www.forwardartsfoundation.org

Promotes appreciation and engagement with poetry through programmes and initiatives that run throughout the year. As well as advocating for the positive social impact of poetry and growing poetry audiences, the foundation supports and celebrates poets, works closely with schools and libraries, organises National Poetry Day each year and runs the Forward Prizes for Poetry.

Free Books Campaign
8A Gloucester Circus, Greenwich SE10 8RX
website https://freebookscampaign.co.uk
X @bookscampaign
Founder Sofia Akel, *Head of Community* Princess Adenrele, *Head of Book Curation* Fatima Saleh

A social enterprise dedicated to ensuring that books are accessible to everyone, regardless of financial barriers. The Campaign's mission is to increase book ownership among under-represented communities; to foster literacy, inspire creativity and provide a sense of escapism, particularly for those affected by austerity; and to amplify the voices of authors of colour.

The Gaelic Books Council/Comhairle nan Leabhraichean
32 Mansfield Street, Glasgow G11 5QP
tel 0141 337 6211
email alison@gaelicbooks.org
website www.gaelicbooks.org
Director Alison Lang

Stimulates Scottish Gaelic publishing by awarding publication grants for commissioning new works from established and emerging authors and providing editorial advice and guidance to Gaelic writers and publishers. Has a bookshop in Glasgow that stocks all Gaelic and Gaelic-related books in print. All stock is listed on the website. Founded 1968.

GLL Literary Foundation
Greenwich Leisure Limited, Middlegate House, The Royal Arsenal, London SE18 6SX
tel 0330 123 1500
email literaryfoundation@gll.org
website www.better.org.uk/library/gll-literary-foundation
Facebook www.facebook.com/GLLLiteraryFoundation
Instagram @gll_literaryfoundation
Ceo Peter Bundey, *Head of Libraries* Rebecca Gediking, *Children's Librarian* Jenny Hawke, *Patron* Joseph Coelho

Established by Greenwich Leisure Limited, the largest public library operator in the UK, the GLL Literary Foundation supports local authors, encourages reading and champions public libraries. Provides authors with the skills and knowledge necessary to self-promote and host author events, recognising that these are essential to a successful career as a children's author, and supports publishers to promote their authors. Connects authors and publishers to their community libraries, allowing young people to meet local authors, and promote diverse and inclusive texts, celebrating the impact that both can have on young people's literacy.

Greeting Card Association
PO Box, Teddington TW11 1EL
tel 020-7619 9266
email hello@gca.cards
website www.gca.cards
Facebook www.facebook.com/GreetingCardAssociation
X @GCAUK
Instagram @gca_uk
Chief Executive Amanda Fergusson

The GCA is an independent, not-for-profit trade organisation operating for the benefit of members, who include greeting card publishers, retailers and suppliers, and individuals working in the card industry. Supports members by providing a forum to promote their businesses, sharing specialist information, and organising events and networking opportunities. Founded 1919.

IBBY (International Board on Books for Young People)
Nonnenweg 12, CH–4055 Basel, Switzerland
tel +41 (0)61 272 2917
email ibby@ibby.org
website www.ibby.org
Facebook www.facebook.com/ibby.international
X @IBBYINT
Instagram @ibby.international

A non-profit organisation that represents an international network of people from all over the world who are committed to bringing books and children together. Promotes international understanding through children's books; gives children everywhere the opportunity to have access to books with high literary and artistic standards; encourages the publication and distribution of quality children's books, especially in developing countries; provides support and training for those involved with children and children's literature; and stimulates research and scholarly works in the field of children's literature.

Is composed of National Sections all over the world and represents countries with well-developed book publishing and literacy programmes, and other countries with only a few dedicated professionals who are doing pioneer work in children's book publishing and promotion. Founded 1953.

IBBY UK (International Board on Books for Young People)
119 Victoria Road, London N22 7XG
website www.ibby.org.uk
Facebook www.facebook.com/IBBYUK
X @IBBYUK

A unique international alliance of people interested in children's literature including academics, librarians, publishers, booksellers, writers, illustrators, teachers, literacy workers, parents and others. Committed to increasing children's access to books and promoting the power of books to transform lives.

Imaginate
30B Grindlay Street, Edinburgh EH3 9AX
tel 0131 225 8050
email info@imaginate.org.uk
website www.imaginate.org.uk
Facebook www.facebook.com/EdChildrensFest
Bluesky @edchildrensfest.bsky.social
Instagram @edchildrensfest
Chair Lynne Halfpenny

The national organisation in Scotland that develops, celebrates and presents theatre and dance for children and young people. Works to enable more children in Scotland to experience work that is deeply engaging, innovative and inspiring, and believes that all children deserve the opportunity to develop their creativity and emotional intelligence and reach their true potential. Runs the Edinburgh International Children's Festival, delivers a year-round programme for schools, and provides a year-round Creative Development Programme for artists who make theatre and dance for children, including projects to develop artistic practice and support productions, networking events, mentoring and a Go and See Fund.

Imaginative Book Illustration Society
email ibissec@martinsteenson.co.uk
website www.bookillustration.org
Membership Secretary Martin Steenson

Established to encourage research into, and to facilitate, the exchange of information on book and periodical illustrations, the artists and their publishers. The Society has a worldwide membership including artists, collectors, bibliographers, writers and general enthusiasts. Whilst IBIS embraces all aspects of illustrative art, the main emphasis is on the illustration of texts in English since the 1830s. Founded 1995.

Inclusive Books for Children
Suite 332, 56 Gloucester Road, London SW7 4UB
email contact@inclusivebooksforchildren.org
website www.inclusivebooksforchildren.org
Facebook www.facebook.com/InclusiveBooksforChildrenplatform
X @IBCplatform
Bluesky @ibc-reads.bsky.social
Instagram @ibcplatform
Threads @ibc_reads
Co-founders Sarah Satha, Marcus Satha

Spotlights authors and illustrators of inclusive children's books on their website and social media, and through other creative media and bookseller collaborations. Offers expert reviews, advice and research to help families source inclusive books for babies and older children. Showcases stories that represent all types of families and identities, feature a variety of ethnicities and identities, include positive depictions of neurodivergence and disabilities, and do not draw on gender stereotypes or other negative tropes. Also celebrates own-voice authors and illustrators. Administers the annual IBC Awards, which recognise the best new inclusive children's books published in the UK. Runs a bookgifting initiative for schools and libraries, and provides funding to other not-for-profit organisations working to improve inclusivity in children's books. Founded 2022.

Independent Publishers Guild
PO Box 12, Llain, Login SA34 0WU
tel (01437) 563335
email info@independentpublishersguild.com
website www.independentpublishersguild.com
Facebook www.facebook.com/independentpublishersguild
Bluesky @ipghq.bsky.social
Chief Executive Bridget Shine

The IPG is the UK's largest network of publishers, open to independent publishers from all sectors and of all sizes, plus suppliers and providers. Their events, resources and services are intended to help independent publishers and their teams. Events include the Spring and Autumn Conferences and the Independent Publishing Awards. Learning and development support is delivered via the online Skills Hub, mentoring schemes and training in AI tailored to the needs of publishers. Other benefits include weekly ebulletins, discounts on products and services, collective stands at book fairs, industry briefings and reports, and special interest groups focused on DEI, sustainability and various publishing sectors. Founded 1962.

Independent Theatre Council
The Albany, Douglas Way, London SE8 4AG
tel 020-7403 1727
email admin@itc-arts.org
website www.itc-arts.org
Facebook www.facebook.com/independenttheatrecouncil
X @itc_arts
Membership £200 p.a.

Enables the creation of high-quality professional performing arts by supporting, representing and developing the people who manage and produce it. Has over 450 members from a wide range of companies, venues and individuals in the fields of drama, dance, opera, musical theatre, puppetry, mixed media, mime, physical theatre and circus. Founded 1974.

International Authors Forum
6th Floor, International House,
1 St Katherine's Way, London E1W 1UN
tel 020-7264 5707
email luke.alcott@internationalauthors.org
website www.internationalauthors.org
X @IntAuthors
Instagram @internationalauthorsforum
Executive Administrator Luke Alcott

Represents over 700,000 authors around the world and has a membership made up of authors' organisations from every continent. Campaigns for authors' rights at national and international levels. Organises events, publications and opportunities to promote the importance of creative work financially, socially and culturally, and keeps members up to date with international developments in copyright law.

International Publishers Association
23 Avenue de France, 1202 Geneva, Switzerland
tel +41 (0)22 704 1820
email info@internationalpublishers.org
website www.internationalpublishers.org
Facebook www.facebook.com/InternationalPublishersAssociation
X @IntPublishers
Instagram @intpublishers
President Gvantsa Jobava, Secretary-General José Borghino

The IPA is a federation of national, regional and international publishers' associations. Promotes and protects publishing worldwide with a focus on copyright and freedom to publish. Membership comprises 105 organisations from 84 countries worldwide. Founded 1896.

Irish Writers Centre
19 Parnell Square, Dublin D01 E102,
Republic of Ireland
tel +353 (0)1 872 1302
email info@irishwriterscentre.ie
website https://irishwriterscentre.ie
Facebook www.facebook.com/irishwritersctr
X @IrishWritersCtr
Instagram @irishwriterscentre
Ceo Mags McLoughlin

Leading resource and development organisation for writers in Ireland. Year-round programme (online and in person) provides creative writing courses, resources, mentoring opportunities and literary events. Each September the centre welcomes submissions to its international Novel Fair competition for aspiring novelists. Also supports the careers of writers through a series of free development programmes for writers resident on the island of Ireland. Founded 1991.

Laureate na nÓg/Ireland's Children's Laureate
Children's Books Ireland,
17 North Great George's Street, Dublin 1 D01 R2F1,
Republic of Ireland
tel +353 (0)1 872 7475
email info@childrenslaureate.ie
website www.childrenslaureate.ie
Project Manager Ruth Ní Eidhin

Recognises the role and importance of literature for children in Ireland. Established to engage young people with high-quality literature and to underline the importance of children's literature in Ireland's cultural and imaginative life. The Laureate participates in selected events and activities around Ireland and internationally during their three-year term.
 The Laureate is chosen in recognition of their high-quality children's writing or illustration and the positive impact they have had on readers as well as other writers and illustrators. The current Laureate is Patricia Forde (2023–26). Founded 2010.

Literature Alliance Scotland
email admin@literaturealliancescotland.co.uk
website https://literaturealliancescotland.co.uk/membership/
X @LitScotland

Scotland's largest literary network, LAS is a collective voice dedicated to advancing the interests of Scotland's literature and languages locally, nationally and internationally. Brings together a network of writers, publishers, educators, librarians, literature organisations and national cultural bodies.

Literature Wales
Tŷ Newydd Writing Centre, Llanystumdwy,
Criccieth, Gwynedd LL52 0LW
tel 029-2047 2266, (01766) 522811
email post@literaturewales.org
website www.literaturewales.org
Facebook www.facebook.com/LlenCymruLitWales

X @LitWales
Instagram @llencymru_litwales
Executive Director Claire Furlong, *Artistic Director* Leusa Llewelyn

The national company for the development of literature in Wales. Works to inspire communities, develop writers and celebrate Wales' literary culture. Activities include the Wales Book of the Year Award; the Children's Laureate Wales and Bardd Plant Cymru schemes; creative writing courses at Tŷ Newydd Writing Centre; the professional development scheme Representing Wales; and the National Poet of Wales initiative. A member of the Arts Council of Wales' Arts Portfolio Wales.

Little Theatre Guild of Great Britain
tel 07971 474721
email secretary@littletheatreguild.org
website www.littletheatreguild.org
National Secretary Anne Gilmour

Promotes closer cooperation amongst the 122 amateur theatres that constitute its membership (all based in the UK), acts as a coordinating and representative body on behalf of its members, and maintains and advances the highest standards in the art of theatre.

LoveReading4Kids
157 Shooters Hill, London SE18 3HP
tel 020-3004 7204
website www.lovereading4kids.co.uk
Facebook www.facebook.com/lovereading4kids
X @lovereading4kids

A book recommendation site and online bookstore for children's books ranging from board books to YA. Supports parents, teachers and school librarians in helping children find books that they will love and engendering a lifelong love of reading. Offers a variety of free services alongside the ability to read and write reviews. The website features Kids' Zone, an area designed specifically for children, with competitions, quizzes and book-related material. The LoveReading4Schools portal offers educational resources, recommended reading lists for all ages, topics and curriculum, and funding benefits.

National Association for the Teaching of English
Marshall House, 2 Park Avenue, Sale, Manchester M33 6HE
email membership@nate.org.uk
website www.nate.org.uk
Facebook www.facebook.com/nationalassociationfortheteachingofenglish
X @NATEfeed

NATE is a not-for-profit educational charity that provides publications and training for English teachers at all key stages. Works to promote standards of excellence in the teaching of English, make teacher's voices heard on issues that affect their practice and provide a platform for teachers to share their expertise. Activities include campaigning, research and partnerships. Founded 1963.

National Association of Writers and Groups
Old Vicarage, Scammonden, Huddersfield HD3 3FT
email chairman@nawg.co.uk
website www.nawg.co.uk
Facebook www.facebook.com/NAWGNews
Chairman Chris Huck
Membership £50 p.a. group, £25 p.a. individual (UK); £56 p.a. group, £32 p.a. individual (EU); £62 p.a. group, £39 p.a. individual (R.O.W)

Advances the education of the general public throughout the UK, including the Channel Islands, by promoting the study and art of writing in all its aspects. Publishes *LINK*, a bi-monthly magazine; holds annual festivals and events; and runs competitions with cash prizes (some open to all). Founded 1995.

National Association of Writers in Education
Tower House, Mill Lane, off Askham Fields Lane, Askham Bryan, York YO23 3FS
email admin@nawe.co.uk
website www.nawe.co.uk
X @NaweWriters
Membership £75 p.a. professional; £37.50 professional graduate; £30 p.a. student/associate/overseas

National membership organisation that furthers knowledge, understanding and enjoyment of creative writing and supports good practice in its teaching and learning at all levels. NAWE promotes creative writing as both a distinct discipline and an essential element in education generally. Its membership includes those working in higher education, the many freelance writers working in schools and community contexts, and the teachers and other professionals who work with them. Runs a national database of writers, produces a fortnightly opportunities bulletin, publishes a journal, *Writing in Education*, and holds a national conference (takes place 7–8 November, online for 2025). Professional Membership includes public liability insurance cover.

National Centre for Research in Children's Literature
website https://ncrcl.wordpress.com
X @NCRCL

NCRCL members work on a range of projects related to children's literature and the culture of childhood, publishing in such diverse areas as: ethics and metaphysics; YA fiction; the Robinsonade; Romantic childhood; print culture; graphic novels; posthumanism; and ecocriticism and environmental humanities. News of regular conferences and events hosted by the NCRCL can be found on the NCRCL Blog. Founded 1995.

National Centre for Writing
Dragon Hall, 115–123 King Street,
Norwich NR1 1QE
email info@nationalcentreforwriting.org.uk
website https://nationalcentreforwriting.org.uk
Facebook www.facebook.com/NationalCentreforWriting
X @WritersCentre
Bluesky @WritersCentre.bsky.social
Instagram @writerscentre

Celebrates and explores the artistic and social power of creative writing and literary translation. An ongoing programme of innovative collaborations engages writers, literary translators and readers in projects that support new voices and stories and respond to the rapidly changing world of writing. Workshops and mentoring available for writers at all levels, both face-to-face and online. Projects range from the Emerging Translator Mentorships to festivals such as the City of Literature strand of Norfolk & Norwich Festival. Founded 2018.

National Literacy Trust – see page 313

National Society for Education in Art and Design
3 Masons Wharf, Potley Lane, Corsham,
Wilts. SN13 9FY
tel (01225) 810134
email info@nsead.org
website www.nsead.org
Facebook www.facebook.com/NationalSocietyforEducationinArtandDesign
Instagram @nsead1
General Secretary Michele Gregson

The leading national authority concerned with art, craft and design across all phases of education in the UK. Offers the benefits of membership of a professional association, a learned society and a trade union. Has representatives on national and regional committees concerned with art and design education. Publishes *International Journal of Art and Design Education* online and *AD* magazine for teachers. Founded 1888.

New Writing North
New Writing North, 120 Squires Building,
Northumbria University, Sandyford Road,
Newcastle upon Tyne NE1 8ST
tel 0191 204 8850
email office@newwritingnorth.com
website https://newwritingnorth.com
Facebook www.facebook.com/newwritingnorth
X @NewWritingNorth
Instagram @nwnnewwritingnorth

Supports writing and reading in the North of England. Commissions new work, creates development opportunities and nurtures talent. Founded 1996.

The Office for Standards in Education, Children's Services and Skills
Piccadilly Gate, Store Street, Manchester M1 2WD
tel 0300 123 1231
email enquiries@ofsted.gov.uk
website www.gov.uk/ofsted

Ofsted is a non-ministerial government department. Ensures excellence in the care of children and young people, and in education and skills for learners of all ages. Regulates and inspects childcare and children's social care, and inspects the Children and Family Court Advisory and Support Service (Cafcass), schools, colleges, initial teacher training, further education and skills, adult and community learning, and education and training in prisons and other secure establishments. It assesses council children's services, and inspects services for looked after children, safeguarding and child protection.

Pen to Print
tel 020-8227 2267
email pentoprint@lbbd.gov.uk
website https://pentoprint.org
Facebook www.facebook.com/OfficialPentoPrint
X @Pen_to_Print
Instagram @officialpentoprint

An Arts Council funded library organisation providing a safe, collaborative environment to develop storytellers' authentic voices. Aspiring writers, especially those from backgrounds that are under-represented in publishing, are encouraged to reach communities with their stories and inspire potential in others. Runs writing classes and workshops; competitions including The Book Challenge; author talks; and ReadFest literary festival. Publishes *Write On!* magazine (print), *Write On! Extra* magazine (online) and *Write On! Audio* podcast.

PICSEL (Picture Industry Collecting Society for Effective Licensing)
112 Western Road, Brighton, East Sussex BN1 2AB
tel 07377 535095
email info@picsel.org.uk
website www.picsel.org.uk

A not-for-profit collecting society. Ensures that all visual artists, creators and representative rights holders of images receive fair payment for various secondary uses of their works following the initial publication, such as copying pages from books and magazines for use in schools and universities. Works to ensure all licence fees collected are distributed equitably, efficiently and in a transparent manner. Founded 2016.

Societies, prizes and festivals

The Poetry Book Society – see page 179

The Poetry Society – see page 179

Poetry Society Education – see page 183

Publishers Association (PA)
1st Floor, 50 Southwark Street, London SE1 1UN
email mail@publishers.org.uk
website www.publishers.org.uk
X @PublishersAssoc
Instagram @publishersassoc
President Mandy Hill, *Ceo* Dan Conway

A member organisation for UK publishing, representing companies of all sizes and specialisms – including children's books. Their members produce digital and print books, research journals and educational resources across genres and subjects. Exists to champion publishing to the wider world and has helped change laws, improve business conditions and inspire people to become publishers. Founded 1896.

Publishers Association of New Zealand (Te Rau o Tākupu)
Level 6, 19–21 Como Street, Takapuna, Auckland 0622, New Zealand
tel +64 (0)9 242 3820
email admin@publishers.org.nz
website www.publishers.org.nz
X @Publishers_NZ

PANZ represents book, educational and digital publishers in New Zealand. Members include the largest international publishers and companies in the independent publishing community.

Publishing Ireland/Foilsiú Éireann
63 Patrick Street, Dun Laoghaire, Dublin A96 WF25, Republic of Ireland
email info@publishingireland.com
website www.publishingireland.com
Facebook www.facebook.com/PublishingIreland
X @PublishingIRL
Instagram @publishing_ireland
General Manager Orla McLoughlin

Enables publishers to share expertise and resources in order to benefit from opportunities and solve problems that are of common concern to all. Comprises most of the major publishing houses in Ireland, including trade, general and academic. Founded 1970.

Publishing Scotland
Scott House, 10 South St Andrew Street, Edinburgh EH2 2AZ
tel 0131 228 6866
email enquiries@publishingscotland.org
website www.publishingscotland.org
Facebook www.facebook.com/publishingscotland
X @PublishScotland
Bluesky @publishingscotland.bsky.social

A network for trade, training and development in the Scottish publishing industry. Runs events throughout the year, including workshops and courses, spotlights opportunities and supports the Scottish publishing industry. Founded 1974.

The Queen's Reading Room
email info@thequeensreadingroom.co.uk
website https://thequeensreadingsroom.co.uk
Facebook www.facebook.com/TheQueensReadingRoom
Instagram @thequeensreadingroom

Champions reading and its wellbeing benefits to individuals and communities. Through neuroscientific research the charity proves the benefits of reading to brain health, mental health and social connection; and through partnering with other organisations, sharing educational content and organising events and festivals makes reading more accessible. Founded 2023.

Read for Good
26 Nailsworth Mills, Nailsworth, Glos. GL6 0BS
tel (01453) 839005
email reading@readforgood.org
website www.readforgood.org
Facebook www.facebook.com/readforgood
X @ReadforGoodUK
Bluesky @readforgood.bsky.social
Instagram @readforgood

A charity that wants all children and young people in the UK to be able to develop a lifelong love of reading, positively shaping their futures and creating a more equal society. Runs Readathon, Track My Read and Read for Good in Hospitals. Founded 1984.

The Reading Agency
24 Bedford Row, London WC1R 4EH
tel 07933 181889
email info@readingagency.org.uk
website www.readingagency.org.uk
Facebook www.facebook.com/readingagency
X @readingagency
Instagram @readingagency
Ceo Karen Napier

A charity whose mission is to tackle life's big challenges through the proven power of reading. Works closely with public libraries, publishers, health partners and volunteers to bring reading programmes to children across the UK. Funded by Arts Council England, The Reading Agency supports a wide range of reading initiatives for children including the Summer Reading Challenge, run in partnership with libraries, which helps get around three-quarters of a million children into libraries each year; and Chatterbooks reading clubs, which help children build a lifelong reading habit.

Societies, associations and organisations 329

RNIB Reading Services
RNIB, Northminster House, Northminster, Peterborough PE1 1YN
tel 0303 123 9999
website www.rniblibrary.com
website https://readingservices.rnib.org.uk
website www.rnibbookshare.org

The largest specialist library for readers with sight loss in the UK, run by the Royal National Institute of Blind People. Offers a comprehensive range of books and accessible information for children and adults in braille and Talking Books. Books are also available for download in audio and braille from the RNIB Reading Service. RNIB Bookshare opens up the world of reading in education for learners with a print-disability, including those with dyslexia or who are blind or partially sighted.

Scattered Authors' Society
email scatteredauthorssociety@gmail.com
website www.scatteredauthors.org

Provides a forum for informal discussion, contact and support for professional writers in children's fiction. Founded 1998.

School Library Association
1 Pine Court, Kembrey Park, Swindon SN2 8AD
tel (01793) 530166
email info@sla.org.uk
website www.sla.org.uk
Facebook www.facebook.com/schoollibraryassociation
X @uksla
Instagram @uksla

The SLA is a UK-focused charity that supports everyone involved in school libraries. It believes that every pupil is entitled to effective school library provision and the educational, emotional and developmental benefits that come with it. Provides training, networking and an information service, and publishes guidelines for school library and resource centres, book lists and a quarterly journal that includes current book and digital resources for all school-age children.

Scottish Book Trust
Sandeman House, Trunk's Close, 55 High Street, Edinburgh EH1 1SR
tel 0131 524 0160
email info@scottishbooktrust.com
website www.scottishbooktrust.com
Facebook www.facebook.com/scottishbktrust
X @ScottishBkTrust
Instagram @scottishbooktrust

Scotland's national agency for the promotion of reading, writing and literature. Offers mentoring and professional development for emerging and established writers. Programmes include Bookbug, a free universal book-gifting programme that encourages families to read with their children from birth; an ambitious schools programme including national tours; Authors Live, the virtual events programme; the Live Literature funding programme, a national initiative enabling Scottish citizens to engage with authors, playwrights, poets, storytellers and illustrators; and Book Week Scotland, held during the last week in November. Founded 1998.

Scottish Storytelling Forum
Scottish Storytelling Centre, 43–45 High Street, Edinburgh EH1 1SR
tel 0131 652 3273
email storytelling@tracscotland.org
website www.scottishstorytellingcentre.com
website www.storytellingforum.co.uk
Facebook www.facebook.com/ScotStoryForum
X @ScotStoryCentre, @scotstoryforum

Scotland's national charity for oral storytelling, established to encourage and support the telling and sharing of stories across all ages and sectors of society, in particular those who, for reasons of poverty or disability, are sometimes excluded from artistic experiences. The Scottish Storytelling Centre is the Forum's resource and training centre that presents a year-round programme of storytelling and traditional arts events, workshops and the Scottish International Storytelling Festival in autumn. The Storytelling Network has over 150 professional storytellers across Scotland. Founded 1992.

Seven Stories – The National Centre for Children's Books – see page 309

Society for Storytelling
Lytchett House, 13 Freeland Park, Wareham Road, Poole BH16 6FA
tel 07942 344259
email membership@sfs.org.uk
website www.sfs.org.uk
Facebook www.facebook.com/societyforstorytelling
Instagram @sfsintheuk

SfS is a registered charity and community organisation for both professional and non-professional oral storytellers. It provides a directory of registered storytellers across the UK and listings of events, clubs and free online resources. Its volunteers have specialist knowledge of storytelling in education, health, therapy and business settings. To increase public awareness and support storytellers they created National Storytelling Week and organise an annual 'gathering' that includes workshops and talks. The SfS provides a network for anyone interested in the art of oral storytelling whether they are full-time storytellers, use storytelling in their work, tell stories for the love of it or just want to listen. Founded 1993.

Society of Artists Agents
website https://saahub.com
X @SaaAgents

Formed to promote professionalism in the illustration industry and to forge closer links between clients and artists through proper terms and conditions that protect the interests of both. Actively campaigns to protect copyright and intellectual property. Founded 1992.

Society of Authors
– see page 297

SCBWI (Society of Children's Book Writers and Illustrators) – see page 305

Society of Editors
Stationers Hall, Ave Maria Lane, London EC4M 7DD
tel 07599 954636
email office@societyofeditors.org
website www.societyofeditors.org
President Sarah Whitehead

Formed from the merger of the Guild of Editors and the Association of British Editors, it has members in national, regional and local newspapers, magazines, broadcasting and digital media, journalism, education and media law. Campaigns for media freedom, self-regulation, the public's right to know and the maintenance of standards in journalism.

Society of Young Publishers
The Publishers Association, 1st Floor, 50 Southwark Street, London SE1 1UN
email sypchair@thesyp.org.uk
website www.thesyp.org.uk
X @SYP_UK, @SYPIreland, @SYP_LDN, @SYPNorth, @SYP_Oxford, @SYPScotland, @SYP_SouthWest, @SYP_Wales
Instagram @syp_uk, @syp_london, @syp.north, @oxford_syp, @sypscotland, @syp_southwest, @syp_wales
Membership £30 p.a. employed standard; £24 p.a. student/unemployed; £18 p.a. digital membership

Supports those of any age looking to get into publishing, or those within the first ten years of a career who are looking to get ahead. It is made up of seven regional committees (Ireland, Scotland, Wales, North, South West, London and Oxford), and a UK team responsible for the organisation's oversight. Runs a mentorship scheme for current and aspiring publishers based in the UK and Ireland. Two conferences are held each year, as well as numerous in-person and digital events; also shares a range of digital content and a quarterly magazine for members. Hosts the First Chapter Award alongside *The Publishing Post*. Founded 1949.

Speaking of Books
tel 07931 929325
email ellie@speakingofbooks.co.uk
website www.speakingofbooks.co.uk
X @SpeakingofBks

Arranges school visits from writers, illustrators, poets and storytellers, plus other high-quality speakers and workshop facilitators. Also provides speakers for festivals and events relating to literacy and the arts.

Spread the Word
The Albany, Douglas Way, London SE8 4AG
email hello@spreadtheword.org.uk
website www.spreadtheword.org.uk
Facebook www.facebook.com/spreadthewordwriters
X @STWevents
Bluesky @spread-the-word.bsky.social
Instagram @spreadthewordwriters

London's literature development agency, a charity and a National Portfolio client of Arts Council England. Develops the careers and creative talents of London's under-represented writers. Initiates change-making research and developmental programmes that prioritise equity and access. Partners with people and organisations to diversify storytelling and enrich the UK's literature ecology. Founded by Bernardine Evaristo and Ruth Borthwick.

The Story Museum
42 Pembroke Street, Oxford OX1 1BP
tel (01865) 790050
email hello@storymuseum.org.uk
website www.storymuseum.org.uk
Facebook www.facebook.com/TheStoryMuseum
X @TheStoryMuseum
Bluesky @thestorymuseum.bsky.social
Instagram @thestorymusuem

Celebrates the power of stories to teach and entertain. Its 100-seat theatre, gallery and activity spaces encourage visitors of all ages to lose themselves in their imagination. Highlights include a Whispering Wood; an Enchanted Library; Small Worlds, a dedicated space for younger children; the Magic Common Room, a learning studio inspired by Hogwarts; and the Treasure Chamber, a temporary exhibition space. Offers a full programme of events including family storytelling shows, clubs, courses, workshops and school sessions, as well as funded community and school participation projects.

Story Therapy
1 Sugworth Lane, Radley, Abingdon-on-Thames, Oxon OX14 2HZ
email admin@storytherapyresources.co.uk
website www.storytherapyresources.co.uk
Facebook www.facebook.com/storytherapy
X @StoryTherapy
Contact Hilary Hawkes

A non-profit social enterprise creating stories and resources, especially story-themed resources, that support children's emotional health and mental wellbeing. Founded 2016.

The Swedish Institute for Children's Books
email info@barnboksinstitutet.se
website www.barnboksinstitutet.se

Svenska barnboksinstitutet is a research and information centre for children's and YA literature with a special library open to the public. Founded 1965.

United Kingdom Literacy Association
Room 9, 9 Newarke Street, Leicester LE1 5SN
tel 0116 254 4116
website www.ukla.org
X @the_ukla
Bluesky @uklitassociation.bsky.social
Instagram @ukliteraryassociation
Membership £65 p.a. individuals; £30 p.a. concessionary

UKLA is a registered charity, which has as its sole object the advancement of literacy in education. It conducts research into literacy education and encourages teachers and librarians to take an active role in finding and sharing a wider range of books that children will love. Members receive access to a community focused on improving literacy, resources and guides, literacy journals, *English 4-11* magazine and conference discounts. Founded 1963.

Voice of the Listener & Viewer
The Old Rectory Business Centre, Springhead Road, Northfleet DA11 8HN
tel (01474) 338716
email info@vlv.org.uk
website www.vlv.org.uk
Facebook www.facebook.com/VLVUK
X @vlvuk
Administrator Sarah Stapylton-Smith
Membership From £30 p.a.; academic, corporate and student rates available

VLV campaigns for accountability, diversity and excellence in UK broadcasting, seeking to sustain and strengthen public service broadcasting to the benefit of civil society and democracy in the UK. It holds regular conferences and seminars and publishes a bulletin and an e-newsletter. Founded 1983.

Waterstones Children's Laureate
BookTrust, 1 Aire Street, Leeds LS1 4PR
tel 020-7801 8800
email childrenslaureate@booktrust.org.uk
website www.childrenslaureate.org.uk
X @UKLaureate

The idea for the Children's Laureate originated from a conversation between (the then) Poet Laureate Ted Hughes and children's writer Michael Morpurgo. The post was established to celebrate exceptional children's authors and illustrators and to acknowledge their importance in creating the readers of tomorrow. Managed by BookTrust and sponsored by Waterstones, the current Children's Laureate is Frank Cottrell-Boyce (2024–26). Founded 1999.

World Book Day
email wbd@education.co.uk
website www.worldbookday.com
Facebook www.facebook.com/worldbookdayuk
X @WorldBookDayUK
Ceo Cassie Chadderton

The charity's purpose is to champion the fun of reading, recognising the impact that it has on children's lives. Encourages children, particularly those from disadvantaged backgrounds, to form a life long habit of reading for pleasure and benefit from the improved life chances this brings them. World Book Day takes place on the first Thursday in March. Events include distributing £1 book tokens to children and providing activity packs and resources to schools, libraries and community groups. Founded 1988.

WriteMentor
email florianne@write-mentor.com
website https://write-mentor.com
Facebook www.facebook.com/WriteMentor1
X @writementor
Instagram @writementor
Brand Manager Florianne Humphrey

Promotes the craft and careers of a community of storytellers, with support from a network of authors, agents, editors and other publishing professionals. Open internationally, both online and in person. Provides courses, mentoring, conferences, awards and an online membership platform. Welcomes writers in any genre and at any stage of their career across children's, YA and adult fiction.

Writers Advice Centre for Children's Books
17A Electric Lane, Brixton, London SW9 8LA
tel 07938 819510
email info@writersadvice.co.uk
website www.writersadvice.co.uk
Facebook www.facebook.com/writersadvice
Instagram @writersadvice1
Managing Editor Louise Jordan

Dedicated to helping new and published children's writers. Offers both editorial advice and tips on how to get published. The Centre also runs workshops and an online children's writing correspondence course, and publishes a small list of its own under the name Wacky Bee Books. Founded 1994.

WGGB (Writers' Guild of Great Britain) – see page 300

Writing East Midlands
The Garage Studios, Unit 4, 41-43 St Mary's Gate, Notts. NG1 1PU
tel (01157) 934110

332 Societies, prizes and festivals

email info@writingeastmidlands.co.uk
website https://writingeastmidlands.co.uk
Facebook www.facebook.com/WritingEM
Bluesky @writingeastmidlands.com.bsky.social
Instagram @writingeastmidlands
Threads @writingeastmidlands

Supports writers of all ages, from all communities, at all stages in their careers. Services include writing masterclasses, workshops, mentorship programmes and internship schemes. Facilitates writing projects with communities that face barriers to the publishing industry, including Beyond the Spectrum for Autistic writers. Also runs The Writers' Conference, the Aurora Prize for Writing and *Pulse* magazine for writers.

Young at Art
Cotton Court, 30–42 Waring Street, Belfast BT1 2ED
tel 028-9023 0660
website www.youngatart.co.uk
Facebook www.facebook.com/young.a.art.3
X @Young_at_Art

Northern Ireland's leading arts provider for children and young people. Coordinates the annual Belfast Children's Festival as well as a wide variety of projects that encourage children and young people to enjoy the arts, develop an awareness of its impact on their lives, and have a say in what their arts provision should be. These include engagement programmes, workshop programmes, commissions, seminars, training, research and online resources.
Founded 2000.

Young V&A
Cambridge Heath Road, Bethnal Green,
London E2 9PA
tel 020-7942 2000
website www.vam.ac.uk/young
Facebook www.facebook.com/youngvam
X @young_vam
Instagram @young.vam

A world-leading museum of design and creativity for children and young adults. Inspires young people to be active citizens and creative change-makers in their communities; empowers educators to drive forward creative education in art, design and performance from early years to secondary school; connects young people with the creative ingenuity of designers, entrepreneurs, innovators, inventors and each other; and influences the sector through child-centred museum practice.

Youth Libraries Group
CILIP, Room 150, British Library, 96 Euston Road, London NW1 2DB
email secretary.YLG@cilip.org.uk
website www.cilip.org.uk
X @youthlibraries
Secretary Alison Cassels

YLG is open to all members of the Chartered Institute for Library and Information Professionals (CILIP) who are interested in children's work. At a national level its aims are to influence the provision of library services for children and the provision of quality literature; to inspire and support all librarians working with children and young people; and to liaise with other national professional organisations in pursuit of such aims.

At a local level, the YLG organises regular training courses, supports professional development and provides opportunities to meet colleagues. It holds an annual conference and judges the Carnegie Awards.

Children's book and illustration prizes and awards

This list provides details of prizes, competitions and awards relevant to children's writers and artists. The awards featured here cover a variety of different forms of writing, including books, poetry, TV and film; and genres, from picture books to YA novels, and fairytales to non-fiction. There are also prizes celebrating illustrations, cover artwork and graphic novels.

Many of these prizes seek entries from specific writers or artists based, for example, on country or region of residence, stage of career or cultural identity. A selection of these prizes are free to enter, and many more offer free or subsidised entries for writers on low income. Check individual websites for entry guidelines and deadlines.

Academy of British Cover Design: Annual Cover Design Competition
Underbelly, 11 Hoxton Square, London N1 6NU
website https://abcoverd.co.uk
X @ABCoverD

Awards covers produced for any book published between 1 January and 31 December each year, by any designer in the UK, for a UK or overseas publisher. Designers may enter their own work or the work of other designers. There are three children's categories: Children's (0–5) and (6–12), and YA. Voting takes place during the awards ceremony. Founded 2014.

ALCS Educational Writers' Award
The Society of Authors, 24 Bedford Row, London WC1R 4EH
tel 020-3880 2230
email prizes@societyofauthors.org
website https://societyofauthors.org/prizes/other-prizes/alcs-educational-writers-award
Facebook www.facebook.com/TheSocietyofAuthors
X @Soc_of_Authors
Instagram @thesocietyofauthors
Grants & Prizes Manager Aine Pullan, *Grants & Prizes Design Manager* Natalie Thorpe, *Head of Fundraising, Grants & Prizes* Robyn Law

A collaboration between the Society of Authors and the Author's Licensing and Collecting Society. Alternates each year between books for ages 5–11 years and 11–18 years. Given to an outstanding example of traditionally published non-fiction (with or without illustrations) that stimulates and enhances learning. The work must have been first published in the UK, in the English language, within the previous two calendar years. Prize fund: £2,000. Founded 2008.

The Alligator's Mouth Award for Illustrated Early Fiction
2A Church Court, Richmond, Surrey TW9 1JL
tel 020-8948 6775
email award@thealligatorsmouth.co.uk
website www.thealligatorsmouth.co.uk/award
X @alligatorsmouth
Instagram @alligatorsmouth, @the_bright_agency

Celebrates highly illustrated early fiction. The children's book prize, launched by The Alligator's Mouth and the Bright Agency, celebrates the best books for 6–8-year-olds and champions authors and illustrators. Open to books first published in the UK in English from the last year which have illustrations on the majority of the internal spreads. Entry form, submissions criteria and entry rules can be downloaded from the website. The winner of the prize receives a trophy. Founded 2018.

The Hans Christian Andersen Awards
International Board on Books for Young People, Nonnenweg 12, 4055, Basel, Switzerland
tel +41 (0)61 272 2917
email ibby@ibby.org
website www.ibby.org
Facebook www.facebook.com/ibby.international
Instagram @ibby.international

Given every other year by IBBY, they recognise lifelong achievement and are presented to an author and an illustrator whose complete works have made an important, lasting contribution to children's literature. The selection criteria include the aesthetic and literary qualities of writing and illustrating, as well as the ability to see things from the child's point of view and stretch the child's curiosity and imagination. The complete works of the author and of the illustrator are taken into consideration. Nominations are presented to IBBY by its Member Sections, which can put forward one candidate in each category. The Sections also recommend judges, ten of whom are picked by the Jury President to form the Jury that decides the winners. The Author's Award has been given since 1956 and the Illustrator's Award since 1966.

334 Societies, prizes and festivals

Association for Library Service to Children Awards
American Library Association,
225 North Michigan Avenue, Suite 1300, Chicago, IL 60601, USA
tel +1 800-545-2433
email alsc@ala.org
website www.ala.org/alsc/awardsgrants/bookmedia
Facebook www.facebook.com/Associationforlibraryservicetochildren
X @wearealsc

The following awards are administered by ALSC:
- The Caldecott Medal (named in honour of the 19th-century English illustrator Randolph Caldecott) awarded annually to the artist of the most distinguished US picture book for children;
- The Newbery Medal (named after the 18th-century British bookseller John Newbery) awarded annually to the author of the most distinguished contribution to US literature for children;
- The Geisel Medal (named after the world-renowned children's author a.k.a. Dr Seuss) given annually to the author(s) and illustrator(s) of the most distinguished beginning reader books published in the USA during the preceding year;
- The Robert F. Sibert Informational Book Medal given annually to the author of the most distinguished informational book published in English during the preceding year;
- The Children's Literature Legacy Award honouring authors and illustrators published in the US whose books have made a substantial and lasting contribution to literature for children;
- The Excellence in Early Learning Digital Media Award given to a digital media producer that has created distinguished digital media for an early learning audience;
- The Batchelder Award awarded annually to an outstanding children's book translated from a language other than English and originally published in a country other than the United States;
- The Belpré Awards presented annually to a Latino/Latina writer and illustrator whose work best portrays, affirms and celebrates the Latino cultural experience;
- The Odyssey Award given for the best audio book produced for children and/or young adults.

BAFTA Rocliffe New Writing Competition
email office@rocliffe.com
website www.rocliffe.com
Facebook www.facebook.com/BAFTARocliffe
X @rocliffeforum
Instagram @rocliffeproductions

Established to champion emerging writing and directing talent and develop diverse stories with an international outlook. Run in partnership with BAFTA, there are three categories, of which only one is open each year: Children & Young Adult Media and TV Drama for 2025; Comedy for 2026; Film for 2027. All categories are judged by readers, a script selection panel and an industry jury, selected for their proven expertise in that medium. Three winners receive access to an industry showcase with professional actors and directors, industry introductions, bespoke masterclasses and a tailored career planning and profile building session to provide support navigating the industry. Bursaries are available for applicants who cannot afford the admission fee. Founded 2000.

The Bath Children's Novel Award
PO Box 5223, Bath BA1 0UR
email info@bathnovelaward.co.uk
website www.bathnovelaward.co.uk
Facebook www.facebook.com/bathnovelaward
X @bathnovelaward
Bluesky @bathnovelaward.bsky.social
Instagram @bathnovelaward

This annual international prize is for unagented, emerging children's authors. Submissions: first 5,000 words plus one-page synopsis or up to three picture book texts. Entries open March until November. Entry fee: £29.99 per novel with sponsored places available for low-income writers. Prize: £5,000.

Bibliobuzz Children's Award
Alexandra Palace, Alexandra Palace Way, London N22 7AY
email learning@alexandrapalace.com
website www.alexandrapalace.com/creative-event/biblio-buzz/
X @APChBookAward

An award scheme aimed at encouraging readers aged 9–12 years. Participants are asked to read six shortlisted books and vote for their favourite. The winner is announced at a ceremony at Alexandra Palace where children get to meet the shortlisted authors, get their books signed and take part in workshops.

BolognaRagazzi Award
Viale della Fiera, 20 40128, Bologna, Italy
tel +39 051-282-111
email bolognaragazziaward@bolognafiere.it
website www.bolognachildrensbookfair.com/premi/bolognaragazzi-award/8382.html
Facebook www.facebook.com/BolognaChildrensBookFair
X @BoChildrensBook
Instagram @bolognachildrensbookfair

One of the world's most highly regarded international prizes in the sector of children's publishing. Celebrates the finest illustrated children's books and honours the best productions in terms of their graphic and editorial qualities, providing an international launch pad for authors and illustrators. There are five main award categories: Fiction, Non-fiction, First Feature, Comics and Toddlers. Special categories are introduced each year and a special New Horizons award can be made to a particularly innovative book at the judges' discretion. Founded 1966.

Book Edit Writers' Prize
email writersprize@thebookedit.co.uk
website www.thebookedit.co.uk/writers-prize
X @EmilyJPedder
Instagram @bookeditors
Founder Emily Pedder

Supports British- and UK-based unpublished novelists who are from backgrounds and communities currently under-represented in publishing. Eight winners are invited to read their work at a showcase in front of key literary agents; an anthology of the readings is published online. All entrants receive career advice. Entrants should submit the first 1,000 words of an adult or YA novel, a synopsis of the novel and details of their writing experience to date. Free to enter. Founded 2021.

Books Are My Bag Readers Awards
website www.nationalbooktokens.com/vote
Facebook www.facebook.com/nationalbooktokens
X @book_tokens
Bluesky @nationalbooktokens.bsky.social
Instagram @book_tokens
Threads @book_tokens

Curated by bookshops and chosen by readers across seven categories: Fiction, Non-Fiction, Poetry, Young Adult Fiction, Children's Fiction, Breakthrough Author and Readers' Choice, which is nominated exclusively by readers.

BookTrust Storytime Prize
BookTrust, 29 Clerkenwell Road, Farringdon, London EC1M 5RN
tel 020-7801 8800
email queries@booktrust.org.uk
website www.booktrust.org.uk/what-we-do/awards-and-prizes/current-prizes/booktrust-storytime-prize/

Celebrates the best books for sharing with young children between 0–5 years, with a particular focus on books that have a wide appeal to parents and carers and stories that can be read and enjoyed over and over again. The Prize is run in collaboration with public libraries who receive copies of the shortlisted books and are invited to vote on the shortlist alongside children and families. 1st prize: £5,000.

The Branford Boase Award
30 Winton Avenue, London N11 2AT
tel 020-8889 1292
email branford.boase@gmail.com
website www.branfordboaseaward.org.uk
Facebook www.facebook.com/branfordboaseaward
X @BranfordBoase

An annual award of £1,000 is made to a first-time writer of a full-length children's novel (seven years and older) published in the preceding year; the editor is also recognised. Encourages new writers for children and highlights the role of perceptive editors in developing new talent. The award was set up in memory of the outstanding children's writer Henrietta Branford and the gifted editor and publisher Wendy Boase who both died in 1999. Closing date for nominations: end of December. Founded 2000.

The British Book Awards
The Bookseller, The Stage Media Company Ltd., 47 Bermondsey Street, London SE1 3XT
email awards@thebookseller.com
website www.thebookseller.com/awards

Also known as The Nibbies, showcase and honour the books that have had the biggest impact on readers, and the publishers and booksellers who supported them. There are 12 categories recognising authors, illustrators, fiction, non-fiction, children's fiction, children's non-fiction and audiobooks. In 2024 a new category was introduced in association with The Reading Agency: Library of the Year. Founded 1990.

British Book Design and Production Awards
email heena.bulsara@bpif.org.uk
website www.britishbookawards.org/
X @BPIF
Instagram @bpifofficial

Recognises beautiful books across 18 categories: Best British Book, Best Student Book, Fine Binding & Limited Edition, Brand/Series Identity, Self-Published Books, Exhibition Catalogues, Photographic Books, Art & Architecture Monographs, Trade Illustrated, Lifestyle Illustrated, Literature, Educational Books, Scholarly, Academic & Reference Books, Children's Trade, Best Jacket/Cover Design, Graphic Novels, Sustainable Books and Book of the Year. Winners are announced at a ceremony each year.

Caledonia Novel Award
email caledoniaaward@gmail.com
website https://thecaledonianovelaward.com
Facebook www.facebook.com/caledoniaaward
X @caledoniaaward
Instagram @caledonianovelaward

International competition for unpublished and self-published novelists. Novels can be of any genre for adults or young adults. The award is open to writers of any nationality, aged 18 years and older. Entrants should submit the first 20 pages of a completed novel and a 200-word synopsis. 1st prize: £1,500; highly commended prize: £500; the author of the best novel from the UK and Ireland wins a free place on a writing course at Moniack Mhor Creative Writing

Centre. Entry fee: £28. The award provides a number of sponsored places to low-income writers who are unable to afford the fee.

The Carnegies
Room 150 British Library, 96 Euston Road, London NW1 2DB
email carnegies@cilip.org.uk
website https://carnegies.co.uk
Facebook www.facebook.com/CarnegieMedals
X @CarnegieMedals
Bluesky @carnegiemedals.bsky.social
Instagram @carnegiemedals
Threads @carnegiemedals

Nominations for the following two awards are invited from members of CILIP (the library and information association), who are asked to submit one title per Medal, accompanied by an explanation of how the book they have selected meets the medal criteria. Submissions must have been first published in the UK during the preceding year or co-published elsewhere within a three-month time lapse. The awards are selected by librarian judges from the Youth Libraries Group of CILIP. Prizes are given from the Colin Mears Award fund.

As part of the Medals scheme, children read, review and vote on the shortlists; their favourite books receive the Shadowers' Choice Awards.

Carnegie Medal for Writing
Awarded annually for an outstanding book for children (fiction or non-fiction) written in English. 1st prize: £5,000.

Carnegie Medal for Illustration
Awarded annually for an outstanding illustrated book for children. Books intended for older as well as younger children are eligible. 1st prize: £5,000.

The Caterpillar Poetry Prize
Ardan Grange, Milltown, Belturbet, Co. Cavan H14 K768, Republic of Ireland
tel +353 (0)87 265 7251
email enquiries@thecaterpillarmagazine.com
website www.thecaterpillarmagazine.com
Facebook www.facebook.com/thecaterpillarmagazine
X @thecaterpilla20

For unpublished poems written by adults for children. The winners are chosen by a different judge each year; previous judges have included Michael Morpurgo and Michael Rosen. 1st prize: €1,000 and a week at Circle of Misse in France; 2nd prize: €500; 3rd prize: €250. Winning poems appear in the *Irish Times* online. The prize is open to anyone over the age of 16. The entry fee is €16 per poem and writers can submit as many poems as they like. Closing date 31 March. Founded 2015.

CBCA Book of the Year Awards
Level 2, State Library of Queensland, Stanley Place, South Brisbane, QLD 4101, Australia
email admin@cbca.org.au
website https://cbca.org.au/entry-information/
Facebook www.facebook.com/theCBCA
X @TheCBCA

Established to support children's writers, illustrators and publishers, prizes are given in six categories: three Book of The Year Awards for Older Readers, Younger Readers and Early Childhood; Picture Book of the Year; the Eva Pownall Award (non-fiction); and the Award for New Illustrator. All entrants must be citizens or permanent residents of Australia; all entries must have been pubished in the preceding year. Submissions are only accepted from publishers. Winners in each category receive cash prizes and medallions. Entry deadline: November. Founded 1946.

Cheltenham Illustration Awards
email pittvillepress@gmail.com
website www.cheltenham-illustration-awards.com

The awards are divided into two sections: Student (aged 18 and over), and Emerging and Established Illustrators. Entries must relate to that year's theme. The selected work is showcased in an exhibition and published in the *Cheltenham Illustration Awards Annual*, which is distributed to education institutions and publishers.

The Cheshire Novel Prize
website https://cheshirenovelprize.com
Facebook www.facebook.com/cheshirenovelprize
X @prize_novel
Instagram @cheshirenovelprize

Only accepts entries from unagented writers; self-published writers may apply. Every unsuccessful entrant receives at least one paragraph of feedback explaining why they were not longlisted. Submit a one-page synopsis and the first 5,000 words of a novel for adults or young adults (not children). 1st prize: £1,500; 2nd prize: £500. Entry fee £29; sponsored entries are available for writers who are under-represented in publishing. Founded 2021.

The Children's Book Award
email childrensbookaward@fcbg.org.uk
website https://fcbg.org.uk/cba-home
Facebook www.facebook.com/fcbgnews
X @FCBGNews
Instagram @fcbg_news
Administrator Sarah Stuffins

Awarded annually to authors and illustrators of children's fiction published in the UK. The only national award voted for solely by children. Awards are made in the following categories: Books for Younger Children, Books for Younger Readers and Books for Older Readers. The overall winner receives a silver acorn and holds the Oak Tree trophy for a year. Contact the administrator by email for submission criteria. Founded 1980.

CLiPPA (Centre for Literacy in Primary Poetry Award)
CLPE, Webber Street, London SE1 8QW
tel 020-7401 3382/3
email info@clpe.org.uk
website https://clpe.org.uk/poetry/CLiPPA
Facebook www.facebook.com/CentreforLiteracyinPrimaryEducation
X @clpe1
Instagram @clpe.org.uk

Organised by the Centre for Literacy in Primary Education (CLPE). Presented annually for a book of poetry for children published in the preceding year. The book can be a single-poet collection or an anthology. Submissions window is open from November to January; shortlist announced in Spring and winner announced in Summer. A Shadowing Scheme for Primary schools runs alongside the Award. Founded 2003.

The Alice Corrie Award
email orangebeakstudio@gmail.com
website www.orangebeakstudio.com/
Instagram @orangebeakstudio

Offers picture book authors the chance to have their writing assessed by, and receive advice from, an industry professional. Open to unpublished authors and those who have not been published or contracted in the last five years. Entrants should submit one picture book text only, 1,000 words or less. The top two entries receive £200 each and the opportunity to meet with an industry professional. Entry fee: £10. Entry deadline: March.

The Diverse Book Awards
email hello@thediversebookawards.co.uk
website www.thediversebookawards.co.uk

Administered by author Abiola Bello and publicist Helen Lewis to celebrate diversity in book publishing in the UK and Ireland. There are four fiction award categories: Adult, YA, Children's and Picture Books. Entries can be traditionally or self-published but must have been published in the preceding year. 1st prize: £500. Entry deadline: March. Founded 2020.

Edinburgh Young Adult Novel Award
email info@scottishartstrust.org
website www.scottishartstrust.org
Facebook www.facebook.com/edinburghwritingawards
Instagram @edinburghwritingawards

Open to writers and illustrators working in traditional novel or graphic novel formats. The Award is seeking the most engaging novels and graphic novels on any topic, suitable for readers age 12 and older. Writers should initially submit a short extract of a novel or graphic novel suitable for adults (5,000 words or 6–8 pages with finished art and text) plus a 300 word synopsis. Longlisted and shortlisted authors will be asked for more material but at no stage are writers asked to submit a completed novel. 1st prize: £1,500; all shortlisted entries are reviewed by a literary agency. Entry fee: £15; free entries are available for writers in need of support. Entries open 1 November; free entry applications close 31 December; paid entries close 28 February.

English Association English 4–11 Children's Picture Book Awards
The English Association, Senate House, Malet Street, London WC1E 7HU
email awards@englishassociation.ac.uk
website https://englishassociation.ac.uk/english-4-11-picture-book-awards

Presented by the English Association to the best children's picture books of the year, both fiction and non-fiction, in the age ranges 4–7 years and 7–11 years. The winning books are chosen by the editorial board of *English 4–11*, the magazine for primary teachers, from a shortlist selected by a panel of teachers and primary specialists. Each year, one of the books submitted is selected as the recipient of the Margaret Mallett Prize for Children's Non-Fiction. Founded 1995.

FAB Prize for Undiscovered Talent
email prize@fabfaber.co.uk
website www.fabprize.org
Facebook www.facebook.com/faberchildrensbooks
X @FaberChildrens
Instagram @faberchildrens

An annual competition for unagented and unpublished writers and illustrators from Black, Asian and/or non-white minority ethnic backgrounds. The Prize provides a unique opportunity to kickstart a writing or illustrating career. There are two categories: Text and Illustration. Entries must be text or artwork for children aged 1–18 years; writers should submit no more that 5,000 words of text (or the entirety of a picture book text); illustrators should submit a portfolio of their work. 1st prize in each category: £1,500 and access to mentoring and development opportunities. Founded 2017.

The Klaus Flugge Prize
email klausfluggeprize@gmail.com
website www.klausfluggeprize.co.uk
X @KlausFluggePr
Instagram @klausfluggeprize
Administrator Andrea Reece

Awarded to the most promising and exciting newcomer to children's picture book illustration. Honours the work of publisher Klaus Flugge in the field of illustration and children's picture books. The winning debut illustrator receives £5,000. Founded 2016.

Foyle Young Poets of the Year Award – see page 183

GLL Literary Foundation Author Placements

Greenwich Leisure Limited, Middlegate House, The Royal Arsenal, London SE18 6SX
tel 0330 123 1500
email library.foundation@gll.org
website www.better.org.uk/library/gll-literary-foundation
Facebook www.facebook.com/GLLLiteraryFoundation
Instagram @gll_literaryfoundation
Ceo Peter Bundey, *Head of Libraries* Rebecca Gediking, *Children's Librarian* Jenny Hawke, *Patron* Joseph Coelho

The GLL Literary Foundation offers children's authors placements to improve their promotional skills and ability to deliver events, recognising the importance of these skills to an author's career. Authors must write for children in any of the following genres: picture books, early readers, chapter books, YA, poetry, non-fiction, novels, graphic and verse novels; must reside in an area where Greenwich Leisure Limited (GLL) manage public libraries (see website for a list); and must have published between one and three books in the previous five years. The one-year in-person placements include bursaries, access to business courses, opportunities to attend networking events with publishers and authors, and support and training to deliver literary events. Authors must be nominated by their publishing house; self-published authors are not eligible. Applications open in November and close in January; successful recipients are announced in February. Founded 2024.

The Goldfinch Novel Award

24 High Street, Alton GU34 1BN
tel 07810 122426
email gary@goldfinch-books.com
website www.goldfinch-books.com
Facebook www.facebook.com/goldfinchbooks
X @GoldfinchBooks_
Instagram @goldfinchbooks
Director Gary Clark

Administered by Goldfinch Books in association with the Alton Arts Festival. The prize is for emerging authors (aged 16 years and older) who have completed a YA or adult novel that is at least 50,000 words in length. Entrants should submit the first 3,000 words of a novel and a one-page synopsis. The winning novel is chosen by a literary agent. 1st prize: £500 and a place on a creative writing course. Entry fee: £10. Entry deadline: May. Founded 2022.

The Shirley Hughes Sketchbook Award

email shaward@orangebeakstudio.com
website www.orangebeakstudio.com/shirley-hughes-sketchbook-award
Instagram @orangebeakstudio

Celebrates the work of children's illustrator Shirley Hughes. Entrants should submit up to ten sketchbook pages of observational drawings of real life as a pdf. 1st prize: £1,000; 2nd prize: £250; the top three entries also receive access to an online tutorial with Orange Beak Studio designed to support children's authors and illustrators. Submission deadline: June. Founded 2024.

I AM Writing Competitions

Kingfisher House, Rownhams Lane, North Baddesley, Southampton SO52 9LP
email competitions@iaminprint.co.uk
website www.iaminprint.co.uk
Facebook www.facebook.com/iaminprint
X @IAminPrint
Instagram @iaminprint

Awards are given in the following genres: Action/Adventure, Cosy Crime, Crime/Thriller, Historical, Horror, Literary, Romance, Sci-Fi/Fantasy, Chapter Books, Middle Grade/YA and Picture Books. Prizes include cash, feedback from literary agents and online meetings with publishing professionals.

Inclusive Books for Children Awards

Suite 332, 56 Gloucester Road, London SW7 4UB
email contact@inclusivebooksforchildren.org
website www.inclusivebooksforchildren.org
Facebook www.facebook.com/InclusiveBooksforChildrenplatform
X @IBCplatform
Bluesky @ibc-reads.bsky.social
Instagram @ibcplatform
Threads @ibc_reads
Co-founders Sarah Satha, Marcus Satha

Recognise the authors and illustrators of the best inclusive children's books across three categories: Books for Babies and Toddlers (1–3 years), Picture Books (3–7 years) and Children's Fiction (5–9 years). Eligible books must include at least one of the following forms of representation at main-character level: ethnic minority, disability, neurodivergence, LGBTQ+. The judges will also take into consideration an own-voice perspective, a challenge to gender stereotypes, representation of diverse family structures and a diverse cast of characters beyond the main character. Books must have been traditionally published in the UK in the preceding year (November to November). 1st prize: £10,000 in each category, shared between the author(s) and illustrator(s), plus promotional opportunities at Hay Festival. Submissions via publishers only. Entry deadline: September. Free to enter. Founded 2023.

Indie Book Awards

6 Bell Yard, London WC2A 2JR
tel 020-7421 4694
email katie.connor@booksellers.org.uk
website www.booksaremybag.com/IndieBookAwards/About

Facebook www.facebook.com/booksaremybag
X @booksaremybag
Instagram @booksaremybag

The only awards given to an author or illustrator on behalf of independent bookshops and booksellers. Showcase the best paperback reads for the summer. Awards are given in four categories: Fiction, Non-Fiction, Children's Fiction and Picture Book.

Indie Champions Awards
website https://uk.bookshop.org/lists/annual-indie-champions-awards
Facebook www.facebook.com/BookshopOrgUK
X @bookshop_org_uk
Instagram @bookshop_org_uk

Celebrate writers, industry professionals, publishers and organisations who have taken concrete steps to financially support independent bookshops through Bookshop.org sales, alongside using the platform in innovative ways. Founded 2022.

International Award for Illustration Bologna Children's Book Fair/Fundación SM
Viale della Fiera, 20 40128, Bologna, Italy
tel +39 051 282 111
email bookfair@bolognafiere.it
website www.bolognachildrensbookfair.com
Facebook www.facebook.com/BolognaChildrensBookFair
X @BoChildrensBook
Instagram @bolognachildrensbookfair

Supports the illustration work of artists under the age of 35 years, the special quality of whose work has yet to be acknowledged. This annual award is granted to one of the illustrators selected each year from the Bologna Children's Book Fair Illustrators Exhibition. The winner receives €15,000 as well as publication and exhibition opportunities. Founded 2009.

Jhalak Children's & YA Prize
email info@jhalakprize.com
website www.jhalakprize.com/childrens-ya
X @jhalakprize
Instagram @jhalakprize

Seeks out the best books by British or British resident BAME writers. Entries can be for fiction, non-fiction, short stories, graphic novels, picture books and all other genres intended for children and young adult readers. For submission guidelines and details of key dates see the website. 1st prize: £1,000, and a unique work of art created by artists of colour for the annual Jhalak Art Residency. Submissions open in September and close in December. Founded 2020.

Jhalak Poetry Prize
email info@jhalakprize.com
website www.jhalakprize.com
X @jhalakprize
Instagram @jhalakprize

Administered by the Jhalak Foundation, the Prize celebrates poetry by writers of colour in the UK and Ireland. Accepts entries of poetry aimed at adults as well as children and young adults, and both traditionally published and self-published entries. 1st prize: £1000 and a unique work of art created by artists of colour as part of the annual Jhalak Art Residency. Submissions open in September and close in December.

The Kelpies Prizes for Writing and Illustration
Floris Books, Canal Court, 40 Craiglockhart Avenue, Edinburgh EH14 1LT
email kelpiesprize@florisbooks.co.uk
website https://discoverkelpies.co.uk/kelpies-prizes
Facebook www.facebook.com/discoverkelpies
X @DiscoverKelpies
Instagram @discoverkelpies

Annual awards for emerging writers and illustrators who are committed to developing their skills and creating quality books for children. The Kelpies Prizes are open to anyone who lives in Scotland. Entrants should submit a writing or illustration sample online. 1st prize: £500 cash, nine months of mentoring with an experienced editorial or design team, and consideration for a publishing contract with Floris Books. Free to enter. Entry deadline: end of February. Founded 2004.

The KPMG Children's Books Ireland Awards
17 North Great George's Street, Dublin 1 D01 R2F1, Republic of Ireland
tel +353 (0)1 872 7475
email info@childrensbooksireland.ie
website www.childrensbooksireland.ie

Leading annual children's book awards in Ireland. The awards are: Book of the Year, Eilís Dillon Award (for a first children's book), Honour Award for Fiction, Honour Award for Illustration, Judges' Special Award and Junior Juries Award. Schools and reading groups nationwide take part in the Junior Juries programme: participating groups make their own selection of suitable titles from the books shortlisted for the awards in March, using a specially devised activity pack to guide them in their reading; each group then votes for their favourite book. Entries close in November; shortlist announced in February; winners announced in May. Founded 1990.

Lancashire Book of the Year Award
tel 0300 123 6703
email culturaldevelopment@lancashire.gov.uk
website www.lancashire.gov.uk/libraries-and-archives/libraries/lancashires-book-of-the-year

Awarded to the best work of fiction for children in the 12–14 year group, published in the UK. It is the longest-running regional book award in the country and the award is voted for by Year 9 students in high schools around the county of Lancashire. Entries must be submitted by publishers. Winner announced in July. Founded 1987.

Laureate na nÓg/Ireland's Children's Laureate

Children's Books Ireland,
17 North Great George's Street, Dublin 1 D01 R2F1, Republic of Ireland
tel +353 (0)1 872 7475
email info@childrenslaureate.ie
website www.childrenslaureate.ie
Project Manager Ruth Ní Eidhin

Recognises the role and importance of literature for children in Ireland. Established to engage young people with high-quality literature and to underline the importance of children's literature in Ireland's cultural and imaginative life. The Laureate participates in selected events and activities around Ireland and internationally during their three-year term.

The Laureate is chosen in recognition of their high-quality children's writing or illustration and the positive impact they have had on readers as well as other writers and illustrators. The current Laureate is Patricia Forde (2023–26). Founded 2010.

Leapfrog Global Fiction Prize

Can of Worms Press, 7 Peacock Yard, Iliffe Street, London SE17 3LH
email prize@leapfrogpress.com
website www.leapfrogprize.org, www.canofworms.net/prize
Facebook www.facebook.com/Leapfrogpress
X @LeapfrogPress1
Instagram @leapfrogpress

Aimed at writers of literary and commercial fiction in two categories: the Adult Fiction category includes novels, novellas and short story collections; the YA and Middle-Grade Fiction category includes novels only. For both categories the minimum word count is 22,000 and work must be unpublished (individual stories in a collection may have already been published and self-published work that sold less than 200 copies is considered unpublished). 1st prize: publication with Leapfrog Press in the USA and Can of Worms Press outside the USA. Finalists receive $150 and a manuscript critique from one or more of the judges. Founded 2009.

The Astrid Lindgren Memorial Award

Borgvagen 1–5, Stockholm, Sweden
tel +46 851-926-400
email literatureaward@alma.se
website https://alma.se/en
Facebook www.facebook.com/AstridLindgrenMemorialAward
Instagram @astridlindgrenmemorialaward
Head of Office Åsa Bergman, *Senior Advisor* David Nygård, *Communications Officer* André Vifot Haas

Honours the memory of Astrid Lindgren, Sweden's favourite author, and promotes children's and youth literature around the world. The award is five million Swedish kronas, the world's largest for children's and youth literature, and the second-largest literature prize in the world. It is awarded annually to one or more recipients, regardless of language or nationality.

Authors, illustrators, storytellers and promoters of reading are eligible. The award is for life-long work or artistry rather than for individual pieces. The prize can only be awarded to living people. The winner is selected by a jury based on nominations for outstanding achievement from selected nominating bodies around the world. Administered by the Swedish Arts Council. Founded 2002.

Little Rebels Children's Book Award

email info@letterboxlibrary.com
website https://littlerebels.org
X @littlerebsprize
Instagram @littlerebelsaward

Recognises children's fiction for readers aged 0–12 years that promotes social justice or social equality, challenges stereotypes or is informed by anti-discriminatory concerns. The award is given by the Alliance of Radical Booksellers. 1st prize: £2,000. Founded 2010.

The London Writers Awards

The Albany Centre, Douglas Way, London SE8 4AG
email bobby@spreadtheword.org.uk
website www.spreadtheword.org.uk/projects/london-writers-awards

Set up by Spread the Word for London-based prose writers who identify as being from a background currently under-represented in publishing. The awards are given across three genres: literary fiction (including short stories), commercial fiction and children's (including middle-grade and YA fiction, excluding picture books). Recipients of the award receive a place on a programme that includes feedback, masterclasses and professional development. Founded 2018.

The Macmillan Prize for Illustration

Macmillan Children's Books, 6 Briset Street, London EC1M 5NR
email macmillanprize@macmillan.co.uk
website www.panmacmillan.com/mac-prize-entry-page

Seeks picture books from non-professional illustrators in the UK over the age of 18. Submitted books should be between 24–32 pages, the text can be fiction or non-fiction and the artwork must meet the specifications given on the website. 1st prize: £1,000; 2nd prize: £500; 3rd prize: £250. Founded 1985.

Mslexia Competitions: Novel (Children's & YA)
PO Box 656, Newcastle upon Tyne NE99 1PZ
tel 0191 204 8860
email postbag@mslexia.co.uk
website https://mslexia.co.uk/competitions/childrens-and-ya-novel/
Facebook www.facebook.com/Mslexia/
X @mslexia
Instagram @mslexia

A biennial prize for writers of novels for children and young adults who identify as women. Novels should be at least 20,000 words long; entrants should not have traditionally published a novel before; self-published novels are eligible if they sold less than 500 copies. Entrants should submit the first 3,000 words of a novel online or by post. 1st prize: £5,000; the winner and three finalists also receive manuscript feedback from the Literary Consultancy, and pitch training and introductions to agents and editors from New Writing North. Entry fee: £26. Submission deadline: September.

The Mythopoeic Fantasy Award for Children's Literature
email awards@mythsoc.org
website www.mythsoc.org

Honours books for younger readers (ages 12 years and under) in the tradition of *The Hobbit* or *The Chronicles of Narnia*. The Mythopoeic Awards are chosen from books nominated by individual members of the Mythopoeic Society and selected by a committee of society members. Authors, publishers and their representatives may not nominate their own books for any of the awards, nor are books published by the Mythopoeic Press eligible for the awards. The Mythopoeic Society does not accept or review unsolicited MSS.

The Mythopoeic Fantasy Award for Young Adult Literature
Honours YA books (for readers aged 13–18 years) that follow in the fantasy tradition of the Inklings.

Nero Book Awards
c/o The Booksellers Association, 6 Bell Yard, London WC2A 2JR
email info@nerobookawards.com
website https://nerobookawards.com
Facebook www.facebook.com/NeroBookAwards
X @nerobookawards
Instagram @nerobookawards

Administered by the Booksellers Association and in partnership with Brunel University London and Right to Dream. Recognises books that the judges most want to recommend across four categories: Fiction, Debut Fiction, Non-Fiction and Children's Books. Judging panel includes publishing professionals, authors, booksellers and influencers. Shortlist announced in December, category winners in January and overall winner in March. 1st prize: £5,000 in each category; one overall winner receives the Nero Gold Prize and £30,000. Submissions accepted from publishers only. Founded 2023.

New Writers Award
Scottish Book Trust, Sandeman House, Trunk's Close, 55 High Street, Edinburgh EH1 1SR
tel 0131 524 0160
email info@scottishbooktrust.com
website www.scottishbooktrust.com/writing-and-authors/new-writers-awards/
Facebook www.facebook.com/scottishbktrust/
X @scottishbktrust

An annual awards programme supporting individuals committed to developing their writing. There are five categories: Fiction, Narrative Non-Fiction, Poetry, Children's and YA. In association with Gaelic Books Council the Gaelic New Writing Awards are given to two writers working in Gaelic; The Callan Gordon Award is an additional award given every two years for a writer of poetry or short stories by a writer aged 18–35; The Next Chapter Award is given to a writer over the age of 40. Applicants should supply a personal statement, details of their writing experience, a description of the project they plan to work on and a sample of their writing. Award winners receive a tailored package of support, including £2,500; mentoring from writers and industry professionals; PR, performance and presentation training; the opportunity to showcase work to publishers and agents; and a week-long writing retreat. Applications close July.

New Zealand Book Awards for Children and Young Adults
72 Te Wharepōuri Street, Wellington 6023, New Zealand
tel +64 (0)2 7773 9855
email childrensawards@nzbookawards.org.nz
website www.nzbookawards.nz/new-zealand-book-awards-for-children-and-young-adults
Facebook www.facebook.com/NewZealandCYABookAwards
X @nzcya
Instagram @nzcya_awards
Trust Manager Belinda Cooke, *Awards Administrator* Joy Sellen

Celebrates excellence in, and provides recognition for, the best children's books published in New Zealand. Awards are presented in six categories: Picture Book, Junior Fiction (the Wright Family Foundation Esther Glen Award), Young Adult Fiction, Non-Fiction (the Elsie Locke Award), Illustration (the Russell Clark Award) and te reo Māori (the Wright Family Foundation Te Kura Pounamu Award). Each of these awards carries prize money of $8,500. The overall prize, the Margaret

Mahy Book of the Year award, carries a further prize of $8,500. A $2,500 prize (The NZSA Best First Book Award) is awarded to a previously unpublished author or illustrator. Eligible books must have been published in New Zealand between April and March in the period preceding the awards' August ceremony date. Governed by the New Zealand Book Awards Trust Te Ohu Tiaki i Te Rau Hiringa. Founded 1945.

The Next Big Story
25 Eccleston Place, London SW1W 9NF
tel 07700 153560
email hello@thenovelry.com
website www.thenovelry.com/prize
Facebook www.facebook.com/thenovelry
X @thenovelry
Instagram @thenovelry

Seeks works of fiction that showcase a gripping story and a unique voice. Entrants should submit the first three pages (maximum 1,500 words) of a novel for children or adults. Entries will be judged on the following five criteria: person, problem, place, plot and prose. The winner will be decided by a panel of judges and a public vote. 1st prize: £75,000; eight shortlisted entrants will receice a place on The Finished Novel Course. Entry deadline: 31 July 2025. Entry fee: £15. Founded 2025.

North East Book Award
Cramlington Learning Village, Cramlington, Northumberland NE23 6BN
tel (01670) 712311
email earmstrong@cramlingtonlv.co.uk
website www.nebookawards.org.uk
Contact Eileen Armstrong

Awarded to a book written by an author resident in the UK or Ireland and first published in paperback the previous year. The shortlist is selected by school librarians, teachers and the previous year's student judges. The final winner is decided entirely by the student judges (Year 7/8) and is announced in June.

North East Teen Book Award
Cramlington Learning Village, Cramlington, Northumberland NE23 6BN
tel (01670) 712311
email earmstrong@cramlingtonlv.co.uk
website https://www.nebookawards.org.uk
Contact Eileen Armstrong

Awarded to a book written by an author resident in the UK or Ireland and first published in paperback during the previous year. The shortlist is selected by school librarians, teachers and the previous year's student judges. The final winner is decided entirely by the student judges (Year 9+) and is announced in April.

Nottingham Children's Book Awards
Nottingham Library Service,
Nottingham Central Library, Carrington Street,
Nottingham NG1 7FH
email charlotte.blount@nottinghamcity.gov.uk
website www.nottinghamcitylibraries.co.uk/ncba
Facebook www.facebook.com/NottmLibraries
X @readingnottm
Contact Charlotte Blount

Nottingham children aged 2–4 years choose their favourite picture books from books published the previous year. The shortlist of titles is drawn up with the help of local schools and nurseries. Then library staff visit settings to read the three shortlisted books to preschool children, asking them to vote for their favourite. Families can also vote in libraries and via the website. Founded 1999.

Oscar's Book Prize
email info@oscarsbookprize.co.uk
website www.oscarsbookprize.co.uk
Facebook www.facebook.com/oscarsbookprize
X @OscarsBookPrize
Instagram @oscarsbookprize

This £10,000 prize, supported by Amazon and in partnership with the *Evening Standard*, is awarded to the best preschool book published in the UK in the previous year. Publishers may enter up to five books per imprint. Collections and anthologies are not eligible. Previously published, self-published books and ebooks are not eligible. Founded 2013.

Pact (Producers Alliance for Cinema and Television)
3rd Floor, Fitzrovia House,
153–157 Cleveland Street, London W1T 6QW
tel 020-7380 8230
website www.pact.co.uk
X @PactUK
Chief Executive John McVay

The UK trade association that represents and promotes the commercial interests of independent feature film, television, animation and interactive media companies. Headquartered in London, it has regional representation throughout the UK in order to support its members, including an office in Leeds. An effective lobbying organisation, it has regular dialogues with government, regulators, public agencies and opinion-formers on all issues affecting its members, and contributes to key public policy debates on the media industry. It negotiates terms of trade with all public service broadcasters in the UK and supports members in their business dealings with cable and satellite channels and streaming services. It also lobbies for a properly structured and funded UK film industry and maintains close contact with other relevant film organisations and government departments.

The People's Book Prize
website www.peoplesbookprize.com
Facebook www.facebook.com/pages/The-Peoples-Book-Prize/200637717319384
X @PeoplesBkPrize

Founder & Prize Administrator Tatiana Wilson, *Director* Julie Hyde Mew, *Patron Emeritus* Frederick Forsyth CBE, *Founding Patron* Dame Beryl Bainbridge DBE

Awards are given in six categories. Publishers are invited to submit up to three titles for each of the first three categories: the Frederick Forsyth Fiction Award, Non-Fiction and Children's. The winners of the next three categories are chosen from the same pool of submissions: the Beryl Bainbridge First-Time Author Award, Best Publisher and Best Achievement.

Peters Children's Book of the Year Award

Peters, 120 Bromsgrove Street, Birmingham B5 6RJ
tel 0121 666 6646
email hello@peters.co.uk
website https://peters.co.uk/pboty2025
Facebook www.facebook.com/Petersbooksbirmingham
X @Petersbooks
Instagram @petersbooks

Administered by Peter's Bookshop, the Award celebrates the best children's fiction and non-fiction published in the preceeding in the UK. There are four categories: Picture Books, Junior Fiction, Teen Fiction and Non-Fiction. The award's shortlists are chosen by Peters' in-house team of librarians and children's book specialists, who between them read and review more than 10,000 newly published UK children's books every year. Winners are selected by public vote, open to all UK teachers, school librarians and public libraries. Shortlists are announced in November/December each year, with winning titles confirmed in March. Winners in each category and an overall winner each receive a trophy and are promoted across social media and online to schools and librarians. Peters also create book packs for schools featuring these titles to encourage sales.

Phoenix Award

140B Purcellville Gateway Drive, Suite 120, Purcellville, VA 20132, USA
email info@childlitassn.org
website www.childlitassn.org/phoenix-award, www.childlitassn.org/phoenix-picture-book-award

Presented by the Children's Literature Association (ChLA) for the most outstanding book for children originally published in the English language 20 years earlier, which did not receive a major award at the time of publication.

A second award, the Phoenix Picture Book Award, follows the same rubric but awards picture books. Books can be text and pictures or pictures only. Both authors and illustrators are recognised.

Polari Book Prize

email paulburston@btinternet.com
website www.polarisalon.com
Facebook www.facebook.com/groups/36989183143
X @polarisalon

Established by Paul Burston, the Prize recognises emerging and establised LGBTQ+ literary talent. Any book for children or young adults published in the preceding year is eligible. The winner receives £1,000. Full eligibility and submission guidelines can be found on the website. Founded 2011.

The Queen's Knickers Award

The Society of Authors, 24 Bedford Row, London WC1R 4EH
tel 020-3880 2230
email prizes@societyofauthors.org
website https://societyofauthors.org/prizes/the-soa-awards/queens-knickers-awards
Facebook www.facebook.com/TheSocietyofAuthors
X @Soc_of_Authors
Instagram @thesocietyofauthors
Grants & Prizes Manager Aine Pullan, *Grants & Prizes Design Manager* Natalie Thorpe, *Head of Fundraising, Grants & Prizes* Robyn Law

Funded by Nicholas Allan, author of *The Queen's Knickers*, for a quirky children's illustrated book for children aged 0–7 years. Submissions must be made by the print publisher. The winner receives £5,000 as well as a golden Queen's Knickers badge, and the runner-up receives £1,000 and a silver badge. The prize is shared between the author and illustrator (if applicable). Founded 2019.

The Queen's Reading Room Medal

email info@thequeensreadingroom.co.uk
website https://thequeensreadingroom.co.uk
Facebook www.facebook.com/TheQueensReadingRoom
Instagram @thequeensreadingroom

Celebrates individuals who promote reading and its benefits in their communities. Nominees may have championed reading in a variety of ways, including increasing access to books, encouraging non-readers to pick up books, creating literary events and volunteering for reading organisations. The winner receives a specially designed medal. Nomination deadline: December. Founded 2025.

RatedWriters.com Book Awards

tel 07948 392634
email info@ratedwriters.com
website www.ratedwriters.com

Developed with Arts Council funding, the review site is free to join and offers writers an opportunity to share extracts of their work for others to review. This allows writers to develop their craft and view which audiences enjoy their work. Writers can also submit their extracts to the annual competition. Two winning extracts receive £500 and a full book or script critique; runners-up also receive full critiques. Entry fee: £12. Founded 2024.

Reading for Pleasure Awards

Collins Education, HarperCollins Publishers, Westerhill Road, Bishopbriggs, Glasgow G64 2QT
email collinspressenquiries@harpercollins.co.uk
website https://collins.co.uk/pages/reading-for-pleasure-awards

Recognise teachers, librarians and reading champions who instill a love of reading in children. Entrants should submit a research-informed case study (1,000–1,500 words) on the strategy that they have used to encourage children to read for pleasure, including information on research, aims and objectives, and impact. Winners receive books for their classroom or setting. Entry deadline: June.

Ruth Rendell Award

68 South Lambeth Road, London SW8 1RL
tel 020-7587 1842
email contact@literacytrust.org.uk
website https://literacytrust.org.uk/about-us/ruth-rendell-award/
Facebook www.facebook.com/nationalliteracytrust/
X @Literacy_Trust
Instagram @literacy_trust

Named after the author Ruth Rendell who championed literacy throughout her life. Recognises authors who exert special effort to promote literacy development. Authors can be traditionally or self-published but must have demonstrated a commitment to furthering literacy through working with charities, schools, adult education settings, or communities; using their platform to highlight literacy issues; and participating in events, workshops, awards, festivals and initiatives dedicated to reading and writing. Nominations can be made by publishers, libraries, booksellers, schools, charities and individuals through the website. Founded 2016.

Deborah Rogers Foundation Writers Award

email admin@deborahrogersfoundation.org
website www.deborahrogersfoundation.org
X @DRFWritersAward
Instagram @deborah_rogers_org/
Administrator Alison Menzies

Set up in memory of Deborah Rogers, a literary agent, who died in 2014. A biennial award that gives £10,000 to an unpublished author to enable them to complete a first book. Entrants should submit between 15,000 and 20,000 words of a work of fiction, non-fiction or short stories, for adults, young adults or children. Two shortlisted authors also receive £1,000 each. Submissions open in January 2027 and the winner is announced in November.

The Royal Society Young People's Book Prize

The Royal Society, 6–9 Carlton House Terrace, London SW1Y 5AG
tel 020-7451 2500
email sciencebooks@royalsociety.org
website https://royalsociety.org/medals-and-prizes/young-peoples-book-prize/
Facebook www.facebook.com/theroyalsociety
X @royalsociety
Bluesky @royalsociety.org.bsky.social
Instagram @theroyalsociety
Threads @theroyalsociety

Open to books for children aged 14 years and younger that have science as a substantial part of their content, narrative or theme. An expert adult panel chooses the shortlist, but the winner is chosen by groups of young people in judging panels across the UK. Pure reference works including encyclopedias, educational textbooks and descriptive books are not eligible. The winning entry receives £10,000 and shortlisted entries receive £2,500. Entries open in February each year. Founded 1988.

Rubery Book Award

2 Weights Drive, Worcestershire B97 6DZ
email enquiries@ruberybookaward.com
website www.ruberybookaward.com
Facebook www.facebook.com/ruberybookaward
X @RuberyBookAward
Instagram @ruberybookaward

Celebrates books on any subject in the following categories: Fiction, Non-Fiction, Short Fiction, Poetry, and Children and YA. Category winners receive £200 each and one overall Book of the Year receives £2,000. Books published by independent presses and self-published books are eligible. Founded 2010.

The Scholastic Graphic Novel Award

Scholastic Limited, 1 London Bridge, London SE1 9BG
tel 020-7756 7756
email graphicnovelprize@scholastic.co.uk
website https://shop.scholastic.co.uk/graphic-novel-prize
Facebook www.facebook.com/ScholasticUK
X @scholasticuk
Instagram @scholastic_uk

Created in recognition of the growth of the graphic novel market and graphic novels' ability to improve literacy skills and spark a love of reading. Awarded across three categories: 6–8-year-olds, 9–12-year-olds and Teens. Submissions accepted from publishers only and close in February. Founded 2023.

Scholastic Laugh Out Loud Book Awards

Scholastic Limited, 1 London Bridge, London SE1 9BG
tel 020-7756 7756
email laughoutloud@scholastic.co.uk
website https://shop.scholastic.co.uk/lollies
Facebook www.facebook.com/ScholasticUK
X @lolbookawards
Instagram @scholastic_uk

Known as The Lollies. Awarded to books in seven categories: Illustrator of the Year, Best Picture Book, 6–8-year-olds, 9–12-year-olds, Teens, Non-Fiction and Poetry. A judging panel selects four books to make up a shortlist for each category, but winners are decided entirely by children's votes, with voting taking place via the website and promoted through Scholastic Book Clubs and Book Fairs. See website for full entry and submission guidelines.

Scottish BPOC Writers Network (SBWN)
email scottishbpocwriters@gmail.com
website https://scottishbpocwritersnetwork.org/
Facebook www.facebook.com/groups/ScottishBPOCWriters/
Bluesky @scotbpocwriters.bsky.social
Instagram @scotbpocwriters
Threads @scotbpocwriters

SBWN is an advocacy and profession development group for Black and POC writers and literary professionals who are Scottish, based in Scotland or with strong connections to Scotland. Inclusive programming includes workshops, masterclasses, seminars and industry panels; curatorial roles; feedback and mentoring; and partnerships with literary and arts organisations.

The Selfies Book Awards
email selfies@bookbrunch.co.uk
website https://theselfies.co.uk/

Established to discover and recognise self-published authors, the Awards are judged on the following criteria: an entertaining story, a well-produced book, an engaging cover and blurb, and a creative marketing and publicity plan. Entries must have been self-published in the preceding year. There are three categories: Adult Fiction, Children's Fiction (including YA) and General Non-Fiction. 1st prize in each category: £750 and a package of support including a profile in BookBrunch, advertising and PR. Shortlisted authors receive free entry to the London Book Fair and the Author HQ. Entry deadline: January. Entry fee: £34.50. Founded 2018.

Sheffield Children's Book Award
Schools Library Service, Stadia Technology Park, 60 Shirland Lane, Sheffield S9 3SP
tel 0114 250 6840
email sheffieldchildrensbookaward@sheffield.gov.uk
website www.sheffield.gov.uk/home/libraries-archives/book-awards
Facebook www.facebook.com/shefflibraries
Instagram @shefflibraries

Presented annually in November to the book chosen as the most enjoyable by the children of Sheffield. Categories include: Baby Books, Toddler Books, Picture Books, Emerging Reads, Shorter Novel, Longer Novel and Young Adult.

Wilbur Smith Adventure Writing Prize
The Wilbur & Niso Smith Foundation, Unit 9, 5–7 Wells Terrace, London N4 3JU
email submissions@wilbur-niso-smithfoundation.org
website www.wilbur-niso-smithfoundation.org/
Facebook www.facebook.com/WNSmithFoundation
X @Wilbur_Niso_Fdn
Instagram @adventurewritingprize

Supports and celebrates today's best adventure writing. Open to writers of any nationality, writing in English. The Best Published Novel (1st prize: £10,000) is for full-length novels for adults or young adults. The New Voices Award (1st prize: one year of editorial support and one-to-one mentoring for five aspiring writers) is for a novel-in-progress, intended for adult readers. Entrants should submit the first three chapters (no more than 10,000 words) and a plot outline of no more than 1,000 words.

The Author of Tomorrow award seeks the adventure writers of the future and is open to young people across the world who have completed a short piece of adventure writing in English. There are three categories: 11 years and under, 12–15 years and 16–21 years.

SCBWI Awards and Grants – see Society of Children's Book Writers & Illustrators

The Edward Stanford Travel Writing Awards
Stanfords, 7 Mercer Walk, Covent Garden, London WC2H 9FA
tel 020-7836 1321
email press@stanfords.co.uk
website www.stanfords.co.uk
Facebook www.facebook.com/stanfordstravel
X @StanfordsTravel
Instagram @standfordstravel

Administered by Stanfords and sponsored by Viking. Recognise exceptional travel writing published in the previous year. The categories include: Travel Book of the Year, Children's Travel Book of the Year, Bradt New Travel Writer of the Year, and The Viking Award for Fiction with a Sense of Place. The winner in each category receives a personalised handmade globe trophy.

Bram Stoker Awards
PO Box 14387, Columbus, OH 43214, USA
email stokerchair@horror.org
website www.thebramstokerawards.com

Administered by the Horror Writers Association, they recognise superior achievement in horror writing. There are 13 categories: Novel, First Novel, Short Fiction, Long Fiction, Middle Grade, YA, Fiction Collection, Poetry Collection, Anthology, Screenplay, Graphic Novel, Non-Fiction and Short Non-Fiction. Longlisted works are nominated by society members and the jury; authors can submit their own work to the jury. Submission deadline: 30 November. Awards are presented each year as part of an association banquet. Founded 1988.

Thriller Awards
PO Box 1402, Medina, OH 44258, USA
email AwardsVP@thrillerwriters.org
website https://thrillerwriters.org
Facebook www.facebook.com/ThrillerWritersOrganization
X @thrillerwriters
Instagram @internationalthrillerwriters

Recognises the best thrillers of the year in seven categories: Standalone Thriller, Standalone Mystery, Series Novel, First Novel, YA Novel, Short Story and Audiobook. Submissions must have been written in English and published in the preceding year.

TikTok Book Awards
6th Floor, One London Wall, London EC2Y 5EB
website www.tiktok.com
Facebook www.facebook.com/tiktok
X @tiktok_uk
Instagram @tiktok_uk

Celebrates the best books and authors discussed on TikTok and the most popular creators who post videos about them. Judged by a panel of authors and publishing professionals, TikTok users vote on a shortlist and winners are announced in summer. Founded 2023.

The Times/Chicken House Children's Fiction Competition
Chicken House, 2 Palmer Street, Frome, Somerset BA11 1DS
tel (01373) 454488
email competitions@chickenhousebooks.com
website www.chickenhousebooks.com
Facebook www.facebook.com/chickenhousebooks
X @timeschprize
Instagram @timeschprize
Contact Jazz Bartlett Love

Open to unpublished writers of a full-length children's novel (7–18 years). Entrants must be over 18 and novels must be between 30,000 and 80,000 words in length. 1st prize: a worldwide publishing contract with Chicken House with a royalty advance of £10,000. The winner is selected by a panel of judges that includes children's authors, journalists, publishers, librarians and other key figures from the world of children's literature.

A second prize, The Lime Pictures New Storyteller Prize, runs alongside the main prize and seeks completed fiction manuscripts for TV and film for children aged seven years and older or young adults. 1st prize: £7,000, representation and consideration for TV or film development.

Entrants to both prizes should submit the full MSS, a one-page cover letter and a one-page synopsis. Entry deadline: June. Entry fee: £20.

Tir na n-Og Awards
Books Council of Wales, Castell Brychan, Aberystwyth, Ceredigion SY23 2JB
tel (01970) 624151
email wbc.children@books.wales
website https://llyfrau.cymru/en/gwobrau/tir-na-nog
Facebook www.facebook.com/LlyfrDaFabBooks
X @LlyfrDaFabBooks

Established to promote and raise the standard of children's and young people's books in Wales. Three awards (prize: £1,000 each) are presented annually by the Books Council of Wales and are sponsored by the Chartered Institute of Library and Information Professionals Cymru/Wales. Awards the best English-language book of the year with an authentic Welsh background (fiction and factual books originally in English are eligible, translations from Welsh or any other language are not eligible); the best original Welsh-language book aimed at the primary school sector; and the best original Welsh-language book aimed at the secondary school sector. Founded 1976.

Tower Poetry Competition – see page 184

UKLA Book Awards
Room 9, 9 Newarke Street, Leicester LE1 5SN
tel 07933 724030
website www.ukla.org/awards/ukla-book-award
X @the_ukla
Bluesky @uklitassociation.bsky.social
Instagram @ukliteraryassociation

The only UK children's book awards voted for by teachers. Encourage teachers and school librarians to increase their knowledge of recently published children's books and to share them with their students. The selection committee is looking for books that can be read aloud, studied and discussed and inspire creative classroom activities. Teachers are looking for books that evocatively express ideas and offer layered meanings through the use of language, imaginative expression and rich illustration/graphics.

The V&A Illustration Awards
Victoria & Albert Museum, London SW7 2RL
email villa@vam.ac.uk
website www.vam.ac.uk/info/va-illustration-awards

Biennial awards open to illustrators living or publishing in the UK and students who have attended a course in the UK over the last two years. Categories: Adult Fiction, Adult Non-Fiction, Advertising and Commercial, Illustration for Children and Unpublished Emerging Illustrator. One winner in each category receives £3,000 and a runner-up in each category receives £750. One overall winner is named the Moira Gemmill Illustrator of the Year; they receive an additional £5,000 and their artwork becomes part of the V&A's collection.

Children's book and illustration prizes and awards

The Wainwright Prize
email danielle@agile-ideas.com
website https://wainwrightprize.com/
Facebook www.facebook.com/WainwrightPrize
X @wainwrightprize
Instagram @wainwrightprize

Awarded annually to the books that most successfully encourage their readers to explore the outdoors and nurture a respect for the natural world. The Prize celebrates nature and our environment and informs readers of the threats the earth currently faces. There are three categories: Nature Writing, Writing on Conservation and Children's Writing on Nature and Conservation. A prize fund of £7,500 is shared between three winners. Founded 2014.

The Warwick Prize for Women in Translation
email womenintranslation@warwick.ac.uk
website https://warwick.ac.uk/fac/cross_fac/womenintranslation
Coordinator Holly Langstaff

Addresses the gender imbalance in translated literature and increases the number of international women's voices accessible to a British and Irish readership. Awarded annually to the best eligible work of fiction, poetry, literary non-fiction, work of fiction for children or young adults, graphic novel or play text; entries must be written by a woman, translated into English by a translator (or translators) of any gender, and published by a UK or Irish publisher. The £1,000 prize is divided between writer and translator. Entry deadline: May. Founded 2017.

Waterstones Children's Book Prize
Waterstones, 203–206 Piccadilly, London W1J 9HD
website www.waterstones.com

Rewards and champions new and emerging children's writers, voted for by booksellers. There are three categories: Illustrated Books, Books for Younger Readers and Books for Older Readers. There is also an overall winner. Each category winner receives £2,000; the overall winner receives a further £3,000; all winners are publicised in Waterstones shops and online.

The Week Junior Book Awards
Future 121–141 Westbourne Terrace, Paddington, London W2 6JR
website www.theweekjuniorbookawards.co.uk
Facebook www.facebook.com/Theweekjunior
X @theweekjunior
Instagram @theweekjunior

Celebrates authors, illustrators and publishers who inspire children to read for pleasure and recognise original ideas, captivating illustration and intelligent storytelling. Books can be nominated by fellow authors, illustrators and publishers across 14 categories: Fiction (Younger and Older), Graphic Novel, Poetry Book, Factual, Animals and Nature, Wellbeing, Hobbies and Interests, STEM Book, Illustrated Book, Audiobook, Cover, Children's Choice and Breakthrough. Winners receive coverage in The Week Junior and The Bookseller and are part of the marketing campaign that supports the awards. Entry deadline: March.

Wildlife Photographer of the Year
The Natural History Museum, Cromwell Road, London SW7 5BD
website www.nhm.ac.uk/visit/wpy/competition.html

Open to photographers of all experience levels, aged 18 and over. There are 16 categories, ranging from Animal Portraits to Photojournalism and Urban Wildlife to Underwater Photography. The Grand Title award (£10,000) is given to the photographer whose individual image is judged to be the most striking and memorable. Prizes range in value depending on the category. The Young Wildlife Photographer of the Year recognises photographers aged 17 and under.

World Illustration Awards
Association of Illustrators, Somerset House, Strand, London WC2R 1LA
tel 020-7759 1010
email awards@theaoi.com
website https://worldillustrationawards.com
Facebook www.facebook.com/theaoi
X @theaoi
Instagram @worldillustrationawards

Presented by the Association of Illustrators in partnership with the Directory of Illustration, the awards programme celebrates contemporary illustration across the globe. A panel of international judges create a 500–strong longlist and shortlists 200 projects across 10 categories, which are celebrated in an online showcase with an industry events programme. For submission guidelines, categories and prizes, see the website.

WriteMentor Novel and Picture Book Award
email florianne@write-mentor.com
website https://write-mentor.com
Facebook www.facebook.com/WriteMentor1
X @writementor
Instagram @writementor
Brand Manager Florianne Humphrey

Recognises authors across three categories: Picture Books, Children's (Chapter Book, Middle Grade, Young Adult) and Adult Fiction. Entrants should submit a finished picture book MSS or the first 3,000 words of a completed novel, and a one-page synopsis.

1st prize in each category: £500 and a one-year membership to WriteMentor. Entry fee: £12. Submission deadline: 1 April.

YA Book Prize
email caroline.carpenter@thebookseller.com
website www.yabookprize.com
Facebook www.facebook.com/YABookPrize
X @yabookprize
Instagram @yabookprize

First prize to specifically focus on fiction for young adults. Organised by *The Bookseller*, in partnership with the Edinburgh International Book Festival. Open to titles published between 1 January and 31 December of the previous year. The author must have been living in the UK or Ireland for at least six months prior to publication. Publishers must submit on behalf of an author. 1st prize: £2,000. Founded 2014.

Sheikh Zayed Book Award
Department of Culture & Tourism, PO Box 7050, Abu Dhabi, UAE
email info@zayedaward.ae
website www.zayedaward.ae/en
Facebook www.facebook.com/ZayedBookAward
X @ZayedBookAward
Instagram @zayedbookaward

Celebrates writers and publishers whose work contributes to Arab literature and culture. Awards are divided into nine categories including Literature, Children's Literature, Literary and Art Criticism and Young Author. Entries must be in Arabic unless being submitted to the Arab Culture in Other Languages, Editing of Arabic Manuscripts or Translation categories, which accept work in any language. Winners in each category receive a gold medal and 750,000 UAE dirhams. See website for specific entry requirements for each category. Founded 2006.

Prize winners

This is a selection of high-profile literary prize winners from the last year presented chronologically. Entries for many of these prizes are included in the *Yearbook*, starting on page 333.

May 2024

KPMG Book of the Year Award
Catfish Rolling by Clara Kumagai

Jhalak Children's & YA Prize
Safiyyah's War by Hiba Noor Khan

Tir na n-Og Awards
Jac a'r Angel by Daf James, illustrated by Bethan Mai (Primary); *Astronot yn yr Atig* by Megan Angharad Hunter (Secondary); *Where the River Takes Us* by Lesley Parr (English Language)

The Macmillan Prize for Children's Picture Book Illustration
It's Swing Time by Abi Bi

June

The Carnegie Medal
The Tree and the River by Aaron Becker (Medal for Illustration); *The Boy Lost in the Maze* by Joseph Coelho (Medal for Writing)

UKLA Book Awards
The Hare-Shaped Hole by John Dougherty, illustrated by Thomas Docherty (3–6+ years); *Wildsmith: Into the Dark Forest* by Liz Flanagan, illustrated by Joe Todd-Stanton (7–10+ years); *Crossing the Line* by Tia Fisher (11–14+ years); *The Boy Who Didn't Want to Die* by Peter Lantos (Information Book 3–14+ years)

July

Lancashire Book of the Year Award
The Midnight Game by Cynthia Murphy

CLiPPA (Centre for Literacy in Primary Poetry Award)
The Final Year by Matt Goodfellow, illustrated by Joe Todd-Stanton

Branford Boase Award
Steady for This by Nathanael Lessore (and his editors Ella Whiddett and Ruth Bennett)

August

YA Book Prize
Gwen & Art Are Not in Love by Lex Croucher

Mythopoeic Fantasy Award for Children's Literature (USA)
The Moth Keeper by K. O'Neill

December

Scholastic Laugh Out Loud Book Awards
I Did See a Mammoth! by Alex Willmore (Picture book); *Bunny vs Monkey: Machine Mayhem!* by Jamie Smart (Book for 6–8 year-olds); *How to Survive Time Travel* by Larry Hayes (Book for 9–12 year-olds); *You're Not the Boss of Me!* by Catherine Wilkins (Book for Teens); *The Gecko and the Echo* by Rachel Bright and Jim Field (Poetry Book); *Cats: Understanding Your Whiskered Friend* by Dr John Bradshaw and Clare Elsom (Non-Fiction Book); Jamie Smart (Illustrator of the Year)

March 2025

Waterstones Children's Book Prize
The Cafe at the Edge of the Woods by Mikey Please (Best Illustrated Book and Overall Winner); *Rune: The Tale of a Thousand Faces* by Carlos Sánchez (Best Book for Younger Readers); *King of Nothing* by Nathanael Lessore (Best Book for Older Readers)

April

BolognaRagazzi Award
House of Wisdom by Bodour Al Qasimi (Fiction); *For a Thousand Blouses a Day* by Serena Ballista (Non-Fiction); The Multilingual Cockerel by Marie Darme-Rizzo (Toddler), *Through the Window* by Laura Cattabianchi (New Horizons); *If You Want to Eat a Red Apple* by Jin Joo (Opera Prima)

Opportunities for under-represented writers

There has been an acknowledgement across the publishing industry that many voices have not been heard, supported or promoted. Many publishers, agents and literary organisations now actively encourage and nurture a more diverse range of writers, through open submissions, prizes, bursaries and other schemes. Under-represented groups include writers of colour, LGBTQ+ writers, disabled writers, d/Deaf writers, neurodivergent writers and working-class writers. This list is not exclusive; the opportunities below will have their own definition of 'under-represented' in the submission guidelines on their websites.

PRIZE AND AWARDS

The Times/Chicken House Children's Fiction Competition – see page 346

The Diverse Book Awards – see page 337

Golden Egg Award – see page 398

Jhalak Children's & YA Prize – see page 339

SCBWI Diversity Awards and Grants – see page 305

EVENTS, BURSARIES AND OTHER SCHEMES

All Stories
email info@allstories.org.uk
website www.allstories.org.uk
Facebook www.facebook.com/AllStoriesWrite
X @AllStoriesWrite
Instagram @allstorieswrite
Founder & Director Catherine Coe

An initiative offering free opportunities for children's book writers from under-represented groups to develop their work, especially those who would not otherwise be able to pay for writing support. Opportunities available include mentorships with experienced editors, writing workshops from award-winning authors and writing support groups. All Stories is funded by the ALCS, Arts Council England and Inclusive Books for Children, with support from SCBWI.

The Malorie Blackman Scholarships for Unheard Voices
email writing@citylit.ac.uk
website www.citylit.ac.uk/malorie-blackman-scholarships

Offers three annual awards, worth up to £1,000 each, to fund one year's study within the Creative Writing department at City Lit. The awards especially welcome entries from 'Unheard Voices'. Open for submissions from December to the end of January. Founded 2020.

BookTrust Represents – see page 318

Creative Access
ITV, Westworks, 195 Wood Lane, London W12 7FQ
email info@creativeaccess.org.uk
website www.creativeaccess.org.uk
Facebook www.facebook.com/CreativeAccessUK
X @_CreativeAccess
Instagram @_creativeaccess

One of the UK's leading diversity, equity and inclusion organisations providing career support and development for those from under-represented communities. Works with hundreds of creative organisations across the UK to create inclusive workspaces, providing services such as recruitment, mentoring, research-driven consultancy and training. Founded 2012.

Curtis Brown Creative – see page 398

Design. Publishing. Inclusivity.
email contact@dpi.org.uk
website www.dpi.org.uk
X @dpi_org
Instagram @dpi_org

The mentorship scheme runs annually and offers ten applicants an opportunity to develop skills to pursue a career in book design. No prior education or experience is required; existing designers are eligible to apply. Each successful applicant is matched with a mentor for a period of six months. Applicants must be from a group that is under-represented in publishing. Founded 2022.

Emerging Writers Programme
tel 020-7766 4765
email emergingwriters@londonlibrary.co.uk
website www.londonlibrary.co.uk/about-us/ll-emerging-writers

Open to all writers above the age of 16, the programme offers writers, in all genres, one year's free membership to The London Library, writing development masterclasses and peer support. The programme runs from July to June each year and sessions take place in the evening. The Emerging Writers Programme Access Bursary assists writers who require financial assistance to take part in the scheme. The Virago Participation Bursary is awarded to Black women and Black non-binary writers to assist with any financial issues that might prevent them from accessing the full programme. Applicants should be working on a project that is intended for publication and must submit a personal statement and a sample of their writing. Founded 2019.

Megaphone Writer Development Scheme
email megaphone.write@gmail.com
website https://megaphonewrite.com
X @MegaphoneWrite

An Arts Council England funded project that offers a year of one-to-one mentoring and masterclasses for writers of colour based in England who are writing a novel for children or teenagers. Bursaries are available for writers who cannot afford the fees.

Pathways Into Children's Publishing
Pop Up Projects, Seesaw Space, 86 Princess Street, Manchester M1 6NG
email pathways@pop-up.org.uk
website https://pop-up.org.uk/pathways-into-childrens-publishing/

Two-year programme for writers, editors, illustrators and designers from under-represented backgrounds offering development opportunities. The programme is designed and organised by Pop Up Projects, with support from over 25 publishers and leading universities. The next programme will run from autumn 2025 to autumn 2027.

Storymix – see page 79

TLC ACE Free Reads Scheme
East Side, Platform 1, King's Cross Station, London N1C 4AX
tel 020-3751 0757 (ext. 800)
email info@literaryconsultancy.co.uk
website www.literaryconsultancy.co.uk/editorial/ace-free-reads-scheme
Director Aki Schilz

TLC receives funding from Arts Council England to enable the provision of bursaried MSS assessments for writers from low-income households. The scheme is known as the Free Reads Scheme and offers access to TLC's core services to writers who might not be able to afford them. Free Reads are selected by a range of literature development bodies from across the UK. For detailed submission guidelines and eligibility information, see the website.
Founded 2001.

Writers & Artists: Accessible to All
Bloomsbury Publishing, 50 Bedford Square, London WC1B 3DP
tel 020-7631 5985
email AccessWA@bloomsbury.com
website www.writersandartists.co.uk/accessible-to-all

Financial assistance to a combined value of £4,000 has been made available to help ensure that everything W&A offers – events, writing courses and editing services – is accessible to all. See the website for more details and eligibility.

Children's literature festivals and trade fairs

Some of the literature festivals in this section are specifically related to children's books and others are general arts festivals that include literature events for children.

Accessible Book & Story Festival
12 Clearburn Crescent, Edinburgh EH16 5ER
tel 0131 662 9834
email ailie@mykindofbook.org.uk
website https://mykindofbook.org.uk/festival
Facebook www.facebook.com/people/My-Kind-of-Book/100043995404469
Instagram @mykindofbook
Director Ailie Finlay
Takes place October

Showcases some of the ways that books and stories are being made accessible for children with additional needs, in response to research showing a lack of fun and engaging picture books for children with additional or complex needs. Provides a unique opportunity for parents, teachers, authors, artists, publishers, booksellers and performers to share knowledge and learn new skills. Alongside the main festival in Edinburgh, outreach work takes place across Scotland. Founded 2024.

AIM Literary Festival
tel (01494) 265002
email events@authorinme.com
website https://aimliteraryfestival.com
Facebook www.facebook.com/authorinmepublishing
X @AuthorInMeUK
Instagram @authorinme_publishing
Takes place October

Developed by Author In Me Publishing. A week-long celebration of the power of storytelling and cultural diversity to connect and inspire. Brings together readers, authors and publishers for a range of events including panel discussions, workshops and book launches. Founded 2019.

Alton Arts Festival
email info@altonartsfestival.com
website www.altonartsfestival.com
Facebook www.facebook.com/people/Alton-Arts-Festival/61550842865597
Instagram @altonartsfestival
Chair Annie Lancaster
Takes place 3–12 July 2026

A not-for-profit festival featuring a programme of literary, music, theatre and visual arts events. Run entirely by volunteers for the benefit of the local community. Founded 2024.

Aspects Irish Literature Festival
City Hall, The Castle, Bangor BT20 4BT
website www.aspectsfestival.com
Facebook www.facebook.com/CultureArdsandNorthDown
X @aspectsfestival
Instagram @cultureardsandnorthdown
Takes place September–October

An annual celebration of contemporary Irish writing, based in Bangor, featuring novelists, poets and playwrights. Includes readings, children's events and exhibitions.

Barnes Children's Literature Festival
website www.barneskidslitfest.org
Facebook www.facebook.com/BarnesKidsLitFest
X @kidslitfest
Instagram @barneskidslitfest
Takes place June

Dedicated children's literature festival with more than 100 family-friendly author and illustrator events, performances and workshops. Barnes is also the home of the largest free literature festival primary schools programme in England.

Barnsley Book Festival
Barnsley Libraries, The Glassworks, Barnsley S70 1GW
tel (01226) 770770
email barnsleylibraryenquiries@barnsley.gov.uk
website https://visitbarnsley.co.uk/barnsleybookfestival
Facebook www.facebook.com/barnsleylibraries
X @BarnsleyLibs
Instagram @barnsleylibs
Takes place February

Featuring a diverse line-up of authors, poets, artists and performers, events include book launches, performances, workshops and talks for all ages. Founded 2024.

Bath Children's Literature Festival
tel (01225) 614180
email info@bathfestivals.org.uk
website https://bathfestivals.org.uk/childrens-literature
Facebook www.facebook.com/BathKidsLitFest
X @BathKidsLitFest
Instagram @bathkidslitfest
Takes place 26 September–5 October

An annual dedicated children's literature festival with events for families featuring writers and illustrators. Builds children's confidence and communication skills through year-round activities and opportunities.

Black British Book Festival

Moseley Exchange, 149–153 Alcester Road, Birmingham B13 8JP
email info@blackbritishbookfestival.com
website https://blackbritishbookfestival.com
X @BBBookFestival
Instagram @bbbookfestival
Founder & Ceo Selina Brown
Takes place October

Europe's largest Black Literature Festival, dedicated to highlighting Black writers across genres and career levels, improving the accessibility of the publishing process for Black writers and generating valuable opportunities for them. Also promotes literacy, nurturing a passion for reading in both children and adults through year-round projects within local communities and national campaigns and collaborations. Founded 2021.

Bologna Children's Book Fair

Viale della Fiera 20, 40128 Bologna, Italy
tel +39 051-282-111
email bookfair@bolognafiere.it
website www.bolognachildrensbookfair.com
Facebook www.facebook.com/BolognaChildrensBookFair
X @BoChildrensBook
Instagram @bolognachildrensbookfair
Takes place Spring

A leading children's publishing event. Publishers, authors and illustrators, literary agents, app developers, e-publishing professionals, licensors and licensees, and many other members of the children's content community meet in Bologna. Attendees buy and sell copyrights, establish new contacts and strengthen their professional relationships, discover new illustrators, develop new business opportunities, learn about the latest trends and developments, and explore children's educational materials, including new media products. Entry is restricted to professionals in children's content.

Borders Book Festival

Harmony House, St Mary's Road, Melrose TD6 9LJ
email info@bordersbookfestival.org
website www.bordersbookfestival.org
Facebook www.facebook.com/bordersbookfestival
X @BordersBookFest
Instagram @bordersbookfest
Takes place June

An annual festival with a programme of events featuring high-profile and bestselling writers, including a Family Festival programme. The winner of the Walter Scott Prize for Historical Fiction is announced during the festival. Founded 2004.

Boswell Book Festival

website www.boswellbookfestival.co.uk
Facebook www.facebook.com/boswellbookfestival
X @bozzyfest
Instagram @boswellbookfest
Takes place May

The world's only festival of biography and memoir, named after Ayrshire biographer James Boswell. Programmed around stories taken from the inspirational lives of people past and present, shared through writing, drama, art and music. Features children's authors, illustrators and performers, and runs a school's programme that encourages primary and secondary students to engage in storytelling.

Bournemouth Writing Festival

6 Wilfred Road, Bournemouth BH5 1NB
email info@bournemouthwritingfestival.co.uk
website www.bournemouthwritingfestival.co.uk
Facebook www.facebook.com/BournemouthWritingFestival
Instagram @bournemouthwritingfestival
Festival Director Dominic Wong
Takes place April

A variety of self-published, published and writing professionals impart their knowledge and advice to writers of all ages, backgrounds, abilities and genres, regardless of where they are on their writing journey. Free and ticketed events include workshops, talks, walks, writing competitions and networking opportunities. Founded 2023.

Bradford Literature Festival

Horton Building, University of Bradford, Richmond Road, Bradford BD7 1DP
tel (01274) 044140
email info@bradfordlitfest.co.uk
website www.bradfordlitfest.co.uk
Facebook www.facebook.com/bradfordlitfest
X @BradfordLitFest
Instagram @bradfordlitfest
Ceo & Artistic Director Syima Aslam
Takes place June–July

An annual arts event, and year-round cultural outreach programme, that hosts a diverse range of authors, poets, speakers, musicians and artists from Bradford, the UK and around the world. Taking place over ten days, the programme includes over 400 events with a mix of topic-led events, author talks, poetry line-ups, live music, film, theatre and more. Operates an extensive ethical ticketing policy, offering free or discounted tickets to those who might otherwise be unable to attend the festival. Founded 2014.

Budleigh Salterton Literary Festival

10 Fairfield Close, Exmouth EX8 2BN
tel (01395) 262635
email festival@budlitfest.org.uk
website https://budlitfest.org.uk
Facebook www.facebook.com/BudleighSaltertonLiteraryFestival

Instagram @budlitfest
Chair Sue Briggs
Takes place 17–21 September 2025

Held beside the sea on the Jurassic Coast, the festival features leading writers and celebrities, events for families and workshops for writers. Includes an outreach programme in schools. Founded 2009.

Cambridge Literary Festival
Unit 7, Hope Street Yard, Hope Street, Cambridge CB1 3NA
tel (01223) 515335
email hello@cambridgeliteraryfestival.com
website https://cambridgeliteraryfestival.com
Facebook www.facebook.com/CamLitFest
X @camlitfest
Takes place April and November

Brings together an eclectic mix of writers, thinkers and speakers, covering poetry, politics, fiction, finance, history, hip-hop, comedy and current affairs. Founded 2003.

Cardiff Children's Lit Fest
County Hall, Atlantic Wharf, Cardiff CF10 4UW
tel 029-0287 3394
email events@cardiff.gov.uk
website www.cardiffkidslitfest.com
Facebook www.facebook.com/CDFKidsLitFest
X @CDFKidsLitFest
Takes place March/April

Inspires a love of reading in young people aged 3–12 years. The festival includes events with local and national authors and illustrators and comprises a number of educational sessions for schools. Founded 2013.

China Shanghai International Children's Book Fair
email ccbf@bfchina.net
website www.ccbookfair.com/en
Facebook www.facebook.com/ccbookfair
X @ccbookfair
Instagram @ccbookfair
Takes place 14–16 November 2025

A leading fair entirely dedicated to books and specific content for children aged 0–16 years in Asia Pacific. Offers unique opportunities for face-to-face interaction with publishers, popular authors, translators and illustrators from the region. Located on the ground floor of the Shanghai World Expo Exhibition and Convention Centre. Founded 2013.

Chiswick Book Festival
email admin@chiswickbookfestival.net
website www.chiswickbookfestival.net
Facebook www.facebook.com/chiswickbookfestival
X @W4BookFest
Instagram @chiswickbookfest
Takes place 10–15 September 2025

Brings writers and readers together to support reading-related charities. Since its inception it has raised over £140,000. Hosts a range of literary events, covering history, poetry, biography, fiction, thrillers, gardening, food, wine, politics, creative writing and self-help. Children's book events are also central to the festival, encouraging a love of both reading and writing. Founded 2009.

Cuckfield Book Festival
email info@cuckfieldbookfest.co.uk
website https://cuckfieldbookfest.co.uk
Facebook www.facebook.com/cuckfieldbookfest
X @CuckfieldBF
Instagram @cuckfieldbookfest
Takes place 3–5 October 2025

Includes talks and workshops featuring authors from a wide range of genres across fiction, non-fiction and poetry. Also runs a programme of events for young people. Founded 2016.

Deptford Literature Festival
email festival@spreadtheword.org.uk
website https://deptfordlitfest.com
Producer Tom MacAndrew
Takes place March

Celebrates the diversity and creativity of Deptford and Lewisham through words, stories and performance. Features writers, artists and arts organisations based in the area, and hosts creative writing workshops and a programme of events for children and families. Events are free to attend.

Derby Book Festival
13 Lavender Row, Darley Abbey, Derby DE22 1DF
website www.derbybookfestival.co.uk
Facebook www.facebook.com/DerbyBookFestival
X @DerbyBookFest
Instagram @derby_book_festival
Takes place May/June

Celebrates the joy of books and reading for all ages and interests, with a programme featuring writers, poets, historians, politicians, illustrators, storytellers and musicians. Each year the festival welcomes internationally celebrated bestselling authors as well as a broad range of local writing talent. In addition, runs a small Autumn festival and a year-round community and schools programme. Founded 2015.

DESIblitz
Spaces Crossway, 156 Great Oxford Charles St, Queensway, Birmingham B3 3HN
tel 0121 285 5288
email arts@desiblitz.com
website www.desiblitz.com/literaturefestival/
Facebook www.facebook.com/desiblitz
X @desiblitz
Instagram @desiblitz
Managing Director Indi Deol
Takes place October

Children's literature festivals and trade fairs

Dedicated to celebrating British South Asian writing and storytelling, supporting, inspiring and amplifying diverse voices, and providing a platform for emerging and established authors to connect with readers and the wider literary community. Features a programme of book launches, panel discussions, author interviews, creative writing and publishing workshops, and live performances. Also provides opportunities for unpublished writers to share their work, engage with publishers and gain valuable insights from experienced authors. 90% of events are free to attend, making literature available to all.

Ealing Book Festival
email info@ealingbookfestival.com
website https://ealingbookfestival.com
X @EalingBkFest
Instagram @ealingbookfestival
Takes place April

Spotlights writers from the London borough of Ealing and beyond. Events include panel discussions, book signings and activities that aim to connect the writing community and literary scene within Ealing with readers of all ages. Founded 2024.

Edinburgh Comic Art Fair
website https://ecaf.uk
Takes place November

ECAF is a gathering of artists, comic authors, fans and readers that expands the reach and creativity of the genre and offers unique events, from writing poetry graphic novels to illustrating folk tales to publishing zines. Comic creators take part in panels, talks, workshops and portfolio reviews.

Edinburgh International Book Festival
121 George Street, Edinburgh EH2 4YN
tel 0131 718 5666
email admin@edbookfest.co.uk
website www.edbookfest.co.uk
Facebook www.facebook.com/edbookfest/
X @edbookfest
Instagram @edbookfest
Takes place 9–24 August 2025 / 8–23 August 2026

A key event in Edinburgh's annual August festival season and one of the largest public celebrations of words and ideas in the world. Around 600 UK and international writers appear in over 500 events for adults, children and schools. Programme details available in June. Founded 1983.

Edinburgh International Children's Festival
30B Grindlay Street, Edinburgh EH3 9AX
tel 0131 225 8050
email info@imaginate.org.uk
website www.imaginate.org.uk
Takes place May/June

Presents theatre and dance for young audiences aged 0–15 years, with performances that are deeply engaging, innovative and inspiring. With an emphasis on striking visual productions, the international programme goes beyond expectations of children's and young people's work. The shows include a mix of theatre and dance and attract an audience of over 17,000 children, families and schools every year. The festival regularly attracts over 300 industry delegates from around the world.

Fleet Street Quarter Festival of Words
Unit 411, 160 Fleet Street, London EC4A 2DQ
email info@fleetstreetquarter.co.uk
website www.fleetstreetquarter.co.uk/news/festival-of-words
X @fleetstquarter
Instagram @fleetstquarter
Takes place May

Recognises the power of words to change the world. Features authors of fiction, non-fiction and poetry, broadcasters, journalists, screenwriters and spoken word artists. Events are diverse in nature and topic and include a programme for children. Founded 2024.

Free Books Festival
8A Greenwich Circus, Greenwich SE10 8RX
website https://freebookscampaign.co.uk/
X @bookscampaign
Founder Sofia Akel, *Head of Community* Princess Adenrele, *Head of Book Curation* Fatima Saleh
Takes place July

Established by The Free Books Campaign, the annual Festival is a celebration of diverse literature that brings together authors, readers and communities. By centring authors of colour, the Festival challenges the lack of representation in publishing and ensures that everyone sees themselves reflected in the stories they read. Events include panel discussions, author readings, workshops and interactive activities designed to ignite a passion for reading.

Hastings Book Festival
99 Cambridge Road, Hastings, East Sussex TN34 1EP
email info@hastingsbookfest.org
website www.hastingsbookfest.org
Facebook www.facebook.com/HastingsBookFest/
Instagram @hastingsbookfestival
Directors Helen Drake, Tola Dabiri, Julie Allen, Chris Connelly
Takes place Over two weekends in September

Annual book festival featuring author events, writing workshops, a book fair, an open mic poetry evening, competitions for short story and poetry, and writing workshops in various genres. Also includes events for children. Founded 2018.

Hay Festival
The Drill Hall, 25 Lion Street,
Hay-on-Wye HR3 5AD

tel (01497) 822620
email submissions@hayfestival.org
website www.hayfestival.com
Facebook www.facebook.com/hayfestival
X @hayfestival
Instagram @hayfestival
Takes place Late May–early June; Hay Festival Winter Weekend takes place late November

Brings together writers, comedians, musicians, filmmakers, historians, politicians, environmentalists and scientists from around the world to communicate challenging ideas. Hundreds of events take place over 11 days. Within the annual festival is a festival for families and children, HAYDAYS, which introduces young people, from toddlers to teenagers, to their favourite authors. Programme published April. Founded 1987.

Ilkley Literature Festival

Word Up North, 2nd Floor, Fairfax House, 38 The Grove Promenade, Ilkley LS29 9LW
tel (01943) 601210
email info@ilkleylitfest.org.uk
website www.ilkleyliteraturefestival.org.uk
Facebook www.facebook.com/ilkleylitfest
X @ilkleylitfest
Instagram @ilkleylitfest
Director Erica Morris, Programme Manager Becky Wholley
Takes place October

One of the UK's longest-running and widest-ranging literature festivals, delivered by arts charity Word Up North. Features author discussions, workshops, readings, literary walks and children's events. Founded 1973.

Imagine: Writers and Writing for Children

Southbank Centre, London SE1 8XX
tel 020-7960 4200
website www.southbankcentre.co.uk/events/imagine/imagine-festival/
X @southbankcentre
Takes place February

An annual festival celebrating writing for children. Features a selection of poets, storytellers and illustrators.

Independent Bookshop Week

6 Bell Yard, London WC2A 2JR
tel 020-7421 4656
email emma.bradshaw@booksellers.org.uk
website www.booksaremybag.com/IndependentBookshopWeek
Facebook www.facebook.com/booksaremybag
X @booksaremybag
Instagram @booksaremybag
Takes place June

An annual celebration of independent bookshops. Part of the Books Are My Bag campaign to promote high-street bookshops and shopping locally and sustainably. Founded 2006.

Jewish Book Week

email info@jewishliteraryfoundation.co.uk
website https://jewishliteraryfoundation.co.uk/
X @jlfbookweek
Instagram @jewishliteraryfoundation, @jewishbookweek
Festival Director Claudia Rubenstein
Takes place February–March

A festival of writing, arts and culture, with sessions at King's Place, London and online. Explores Jewish themes and writers, and is open to everyone. Includes events for children and teenagers. Founded 1952.

London Literature Festival

email literatureandspokenword@southbankcentre.co.uk
website www.southbankcentre.co.uk/whats-on/festivals-series/london-literature-festival
Facebook www.facebook.com/southbankcentre
X @southbankcentre
Takes place 21 October–2 November 2025

Combines year-round literature events with an engaging festival programme, encompassing free public programming, thematically focused talks and debates, newly commissioned performances and a family offer to coincide with the half-term school holiday. Founded 1967.

Lyra Bristol Poetry Festival

website www.lyrafest.com
Facebook www.facebook.com/lyrabristol/
Bluesky @lyrafest.com.bsky.social
Instagram @lyrafest

Annual festival in Bristol celebrating all forms of poetry. Events include readings, slam competitions, film screenings, walking tours, panels and lectures. Prioritises diversity, accessibility and bringing together communities. Also runs the Bristol City Poet and Young City Poet initiatives, both of which appoint a poet to speak on behalf of the Bristol community and the issues that matter most to them.

Margate Bookie Festival

email info@margatebookie.com
website www.margatebookie.com
Facebook www.facebook.com/MargateBookie
X @MargateBookie
Instagram @margatebookie
Takes place October

Brings together well-known writers and local authors across a weekend of events for both adults and children. Celebrates literature, comedy and music with over 4,000 visitors every year. Also runs a year-round programme of creative writing workshops and courses. Founded 2015.

Marlborough Literature Festival
email general@marlboroughlitfest.org
website www.marlboroughlitfest.org
Facebook www.facebook.com/MarlboroughLitFest
X @MarlbLitFest
Instagram @marlboroughlitfest
Festival Patron Sir Simon Russell Beale
Takes place 25–28 September 2025

An annual literary festival in the market town of Marlborough, the Festival offers varied events for all ages. Includes a children's programme featuring children's authors and an outreach programme offering free schools events to local primary and secondary school pupils. Also provides free storytelling sessions and drama performances during the festival weekend. Founded 2010.

Milton Keynes Literary Festival
Milton Keynes Central Library,
555 Silbury Boulevard MK9 3HL
email mklitfest@gmail.com
website www.mklitfest.org
Facebook www.facebook.com/MKLitFest
X @MKlitfest
Instagram @mklitfest
Threads @mklitfest
Takes place April

An annual Spring festival for writers and readers, including author events and writing workshops. Runs a year-round programme of online and in-person events and a writing competition. Founded 2017.

Monty Lit Fest
Montgomery Town Hall, Broad Street, Montgomery, Powys SY15 6PH
email enquiries@montylitfest.com
website https://montylitfest.com
Facebook www.facebook.com/montylitfest
X @montylitfest
Instagram @montylitfest
Takes place June

A diverse programme of events brings together a wide range of audiences to celebrate writers who live in or write about Wales. Founded 2016.

National Poetry Day
Forward Arts Foundation,
Somerset House Exchange, The Strand,
London WC2R 1LA
tel 020-8187 9861
email info@forwardartsfoundation.org
website https://nationalpoetryday.co.uk
Facebook www.facebook.com/PoetryDayUK
X @PoetryDayUK
Instagram @nationalpoetryday
Takes place 2 October 2025

Organised by the Forward Arts Foundation to encourage poetry reading and writing. Combines poetry recommendations and teaching resources with nationwide events to highlight the artistic and social value of poetry. Each year it takes place on the first Thursday in October and explores a different theme. Founded 1999.

Ness Book Fest
email nbfinverness@gmail.com
website https://nessbookfest.com
Facebook www.facebook.com/NessBookFest
Takes place October

Organised and run by the community, for the community. Events are free to attend and held in accessible, central locations throughout the city; recordings are shared online. Aims to encourage regular book festival demographics to attend, as well as those who have never visited a book festival before. Guest authors write in a wide range of genres, from crime and thriller to poetry, and events include author talks, panel discussions, workshops and a full children's programme brought to local schools.

New Delhi World Book Fair
National Book Trust, Ministry of Education, Government of India, Nehru Bhawan,
5 Institutional Area, Phase-II, Vasant Kunj,
New Delhi-110070, India
email ndwbf.nbt@gmail.com
website www.nbtindia.gov.in
Facebook www.facebook.com/nationalbooktrustindia
X @nbt_india
Instagram @nbt_india
Takes place February

Organised by India's National Book Trust. Facilitates the sale of rights and cultural exchanges, and features book launches, panel discussions, mentorship opportunities for emerging writers, a designated Children's pavilion and a themed pavilion (the theme for 2025 was the 75th anniversary of India as a Republic). Founded 1972.

Off the Shelf Festival of Words Sheffield
tel 0114 222 3895
email offtheshelf@sheffield.ac.uk
website www.offtheshelf.org.uk
Facebook www.facebook.com/OffTheShelf/
X @otsfestival
Instagram @offtheshelffestival
Takes place 10–26 October 2025

A diverse festival featuring children's authors and illustrators with activities and events for children, young people and families.

Oundle Festival of Literature
tel (01832) 270312
website www.oundlelitfest.org.uk
Facebook www.facebook.com/OundleFestivalofLit/
Bluesky @oundlefestoflit.bsky.social
Instagram @oundlefestivaloflit

Threads @oundlefestivaloflit
Festival Secretary Sue Pearson
Takes place March

Kid Lit Week includes author events and a writing competition for infant and junior school children. Also runs a programme of year-round events aimed at exciting, informing, entertaining and educating through talks, discussions and workshops by award-winning and local authors and poets.

Oxford Literary Festival

c/o Gravita, 40–41 Park End Street, Oxford OX1 1JD
tel 07931 560223
email info@oxfordliteraryfestival.org
website https://oxfordliteraryfestival.org
Takes place March/April

An annual festival held in venues across the city and university, in partnership with the *Telegraph*. Presents topical debates and discussion panels, and a programme of children's events. Topics range from contemporary fiction to discussions on politics, history, science, gardening, food, poetry, philosophy and art. Founded 1998.

Paisley Book Fest

email bookfest@renfrewshire.gov.uk
website https://paisleybookfestival.com
Facebook www.facebook.com/BookPaisley
Instagram @paisleybookfest
Takes place April

Celebrates Scottish arts and culture. Events include author talks, writing workshops and publishing advice, covering a range of genres, from flash fiction to memoir. Also runs a schools programme and facilitates the Janet Coats Memorial Prize.

SAIL Fest UK

29 Fortis Green Rd, Muswell Hill, London N10 3HP
email sailfestuk@gmail.com
website www.sailfest.org.uk
X @SailFestUK
Instagram @sailfest_uk
Co-founders Chitra Soundar, Sinead Gosai, Sanchita Basu de Sarkar
Takes place September

A celebration of the best in South Asian children's illustration and literature, dedicated to connecting and empowering South Asian authors, poets and illustrators creating books for younger readers aged 0-17 years. The Festival also features publishers, editors, agents, designers, sales and marketing specialists, book influencers, librarians, teachers and booksellers. Founded 2024.

Scottish International Storytelling Festival

43–45 High Street, Edinburgh EH1 1SR
tel 0131 556 9579
email reception@scottishstorytellingcentre.com
website www.sisf.org.uk
Facebook www.facebook.com/scotstoryfest
Instagram @scotstoryfest
Festival Director Donald Smith
Takes place October

A celebration of Scottish storytelling set in its international context, complemented by music, ballad and song. Takes place at the Scottish Storytelling Centre and partner venues across Edinburgh and Scotland.

The Self-Publishing Conference

Troubador Publishing Ltd, Unit E2,
Airfield Business Park,
Market Harborough LE16 7UL
tel 0116 279 2299
email conference@troubador.co.uk
website www.conference.troubador.co.uk
Facebook www.facebook.com/troubadorpublishing
X @matadorbooks
Instagram @troubador_publishing

Designed to educate, inform and inspire authors who are self-publishing or considering it as a publication route. Offers insight into diverse publishing options, opportunities to learn from and engage with industry experts, and the chance to network with experienced self-publishers. Fiction, non-fiction, business and children's writing are all represented. Tickets include access to workshops, keynote speakers, lunch, refreshments and an evening drinks reception.

Sevenoaks Literary Festival

email info@sevlitfest.com
website https://sevlitfest.com/
Facebook www.facebook.com/SevenoaksLitFest
X @Sevenoakslit
Instagram @sevenoaks_literary_festival
Takes place September

An eclectic festival featuring novelists, biographers, historians, poets and musicians talking about and performing their work. Also features a school's day for local children. Founded 2001.

South Ken Kid's Festival

Institut français, 17 Queensberry Place,
London SW7 2DT
tel 020-7871 3515
website https://southkenkidsfestival.co.uk
Takes place November

Hosted by the French Institute, this bilingual festival celebrates children's literature and illustration, from comic books and graphic novels to films and music. Events include storytelling, live drawing, workshops, talks, screenings, concerts and book signings.

St Austell Festival of Children's Literature

Workshop 2, East Stables, Foundary Lane,
Hayle TR27 4BW

email info@staustellfestivalofchildrensliterature.com
website https://staustellfestivalofliterature.com
Facebook www.facebook.com/p/St-Austell-Festival-of-Childrens-Literature-100090003774954/?_rdr
X @StLiterature
Instagram @st.alitfest
Threads @st.alitfest
Takes place June

Celebrates the positive impact of reading on life outcomes and encourages families and communities to read for pleasure. Features a range of events to cater to different learning styles and interests, including opportunities to listen to and meet authors and creative workshops. Events are aimed at toddlers to pre-teens. Founded 2023.

StAnza: Scotland's International Poetry Festival
tel (01334) 475000 (box office)
email stanza@stanzapoetry.org
website www.stanzapoetry.org
Facebook www.facebook.com/stanzapoetry
X @StAnzaPoetry
Instagram @stanzapoetry
Executive Producer Suzie Kirk Dumitru
Takes place March

Dedicated to programming a wide diversity of poetries and poets, alongside other art forms such as music and visual art. International in focus and has a hybrid format, including both live and digital events. Founded 1998.

Stepping Into Stories Kid's Lit Fest
email steppingintostories@gmail.com
website www.steppingintostories.org
Facebook www.facebook.com/stationhallhernehill
X @stories_fest
Instagram @stories_fest
Takes place February

Organised by a team of three children's authors and one children's theatre director. Brings together children's poets, authors and illustrators in venues and schools across South East London. Celebrates storytelling through a programme of readings, performances, workshops and activities. Also runs school sessions, after school and holiday workshops, and a writing competition for children. Founded 2019.

Stratford-upon-Avon Literary Festival
email info@stratfordliteraryfestival.co.uk
website www.stratlitfest.co.uk
Facebook www.facebook.com/stratfordlitfest
X @StratLitFest
Instagram @stratfordlitfest
Festival Director Annie Ashworth
Takes place May and October

A feast of workshops, panel discussions, celebrity and author events. Also runs a year-round programme of events and projects for families and regional schools aimed at entertaining and inspiring children and encouraging literacy, as well as events in the community and writing workshops in prisons. Founded 2008.

The Times and Sunday Times Cheltenham Literature Festival
53–57 Rodney Road, Cheltenham GL50 1HX
email literature@cheltenhamfestivals.com
website www.cheltenhamfestivals.com/literature
Facebook www.facebook.com/cheltenhamfestivals
X @cheltfestivals
Takes place 10–19 October 2025

An annual festival and one of the oldest literary events in the world. Features adult, family and schools programmes. Events for families and schools include presentations from authors and illustrators alongside workshops, shows, storytellers, story trails, discussions and free drop-in craft activities. Founded 1949.

Tottenham Literature Festival
website www.berniegrantcentre.co.uk/whats-on/tottenham-literature-festival-2025
Facebook www.facebook.com/BGArtsCentre
X @BGArtsCentre
Instagram @bgartscentre
Takes place November

Brings together Black writers, poets, journalists and artists across a series of events including performances, panel discussions, workshops and film screenings. Also runs a family programme that aims to inspire and engage children and celebrate the diversity of children's publishing. Founded 2019.

Tring Book Festival
Our Bookshop, 87 High Street, Tring, Herts. HP23 4AB
tel (01442) 827653
website www.tringbookfestival.co.uk
Facebook www.facebook.com/tringbookfest
X @tringbookfest
Takes place November

Features interviews, debates and workshops across a wide range of genres, as well as events for children. Also runs year-round events, a schools programme and an independent bookshop in Tring. Founded 2023.

Wigtown Book Festival
11 North Main Street, Wigtown, Dumfries and Galloway DG8 9HN
tel (01988) 402306
email mail@wigtownbookfestival.com
website https://wigtownbookfestival.com
Facebook www.facebook.com/WigtownBookFestival

X @WigtownBookFest
Instagram @wigtownbookfest
Takes place 26 September–5 October 2025

Annual festival in Scotland's National Book Town, bringing readers, aspiring writers and published authors together across 200 events. Big Wig (for children) and Wigtwon YA (for young people) runs alongside the main festival; Big DoG Book Festival runs in March and includes a schools tour around the region. Events foster a love of reading and incorporate art, drama and music. Founded 1999.

Wimbledon Book Fest

35 Wimbledon Hill Road, London SW19 7NB
email boxoffice@wimbledonbookfest.org
website www.wimbledonbookfest.org
Facebook www.facebook.com/Wimbledonbookfest/
Instagram @wimbookfest
Takes place 16–26 October 2025

Fosters a space for art and culture within the community. Guest speakers include writers from all genres, with a focus on inspiring stories, diversity and inclusion. Runs educational workshops and projects for young people during the festival and throughout the year. Founded 2006.

Winchester Books Festival

Avebury House, 6 St Peter Street, Winchester SO23 8BN
email info@winchesterbooksfestival.com
website https://winchesterbooksfestival.com
Instagram @winchester_books_festival
Co-founders Sophie Liardet, Sian Searles
Takes place April

Hosts a well-rounded programme of talks, panel discussions and workshops covering fiction and non-fiction, aimed at both children and adults. Celebrates regional authors and local history and culture. Founded 2023.

WOWCON

email florianne@write-mentor.com
website https://write-mentor.com
Facebook www.facebook.com/WriteMentor1
X @writementor
Instagram @writementor
Brand Manager Florianne Humphrey
Takes place September

A virtual conference hosted by WriteMentor that brings together children's writers and industry professionals for a weekend of keynote speeches from leading authors, panel discussions, interactive workshops and a live pitching event with literary agents. Also includes a Saturday night party.

YALC (Young Adult Literature Convention)

email yalc@showmastersevents.com
website https://londoncomicconwinter.com/YALC
Facebook www.facebook.com/ukYALC
X @yalc_uk
Instagram @yalc_uk
Takes place 15–16 November 2025

A celebration of the best YA books and authors. An interactive event where YA fiction fans can meet their favourite authors, listen to panel discussions and take part in workshops. Founded 2014.

Resources for writers
How BookTok can help you engage with your readers

Author Beth Reekles reveals the huge potential and reach of BookTok, a community within TikTok built on a 'shared joy over all things bookish'; an almost limitless and varied audience for authors to tap into. She offers advice on using BookTok to engage with and grow your readership in your own individual way, and describes its power to boost confidence and creativity, as well as sales.

We've all seen those articles doing the rounds in recent years. You know the ones: someone gained a certain amount of viral fame and now they're signing an impressive book deal and living out their dreams – *your* dreams – of being a published author. There's a sensationalism about it that can go one of two ways. Either you want to burst with excitement (the book sounds great and, if it can happen to anybody, why not you?) or scream into a pillow and cry (because … why *wasn't* it you?).

I was one of those authors back in 2012. I'd written a YA romance (*The Kissing Booth*) that I shared on story-sharing platform Wattpad when I was 15 and then, after it gained over 19 million hits, I was offered a publishing deal at age 17. That was practically unheard of at the time; X (Twitter) was still relatively new, and I was just getting my first iPhone. The press dubbed me simultaneously 'The Dickens of the iPad Generation' and 'Fifty Shades of Youth' (apparently, I had the range). Nowadays, of course, the real powerhouse you hear about is TikTok – or, more specifically, BookTok. You'll see plenty of articles about book deals signed after the author gained some kind of notoriety on the app, and probably you'll have seen the stands in WHSmith or stickers on book covers in The Works declaring: 'As seen on BookTok!', rather than simply trying to showcase them as 'new' or 'bestselling'.

For those who are unfamiliar with BookTok, let's break it down. Simply put, BookTok is the name given to the bookish side of TikTok, encompassing everything from reader reviews, pretty aesthetics of bookshelves or unboxings of a Waterstones haul, authors discussing their writing process or promoting new books, character cosplays, mood boards of fictional worlds, reactions to snippets of an audiobook… It's niche, yes, but it is by no means small. At the time of writing, #BookTok has over 239 billion views and 49.6 million videos posted under the hashtag – and that's not counting all the denominations like #romancetok, #fantasytok, #authorsoftiktok, #booktoker, etc. BookTok is often cosy, but it's also vibrant and friendly and excited. It's a place where people can connect with a community and feel at home in this shared joy over all things bookish. This sense of community is what drives sales in such huge numbers, carves out new genres, and helps to lift up new writers and to help them secure book deals.

Bea Fitzgerald, known on TikTok as @chaosonolympus, may be best recognised for applying viral soundbites from pop culture to classic Greek myths, but she also posts videos sharing her publishing journey with her debut YA romance *Girl, Goddess, Queen* (Penguin 2023). Meanwhile, Hannah Nicole Maehrer shared episodic, minute-long scenes about being the 'morally grey fantasy villain's personal assistant', building overarching storylines, a vibrant cast of characters, and a romance over a series of 271 videos. Now, her novel adapted from this series, *Assistant to the Villain* (Transworld 2023), is a #1 *New York Times* bestseller, with a movie deal and third novel in the series on the way.

Even established authors can find BookTok success with their backlist, thanks to the bookish community on TikTok: Colleen Hoover's *It Ends With Us* was published in 2016, only to become a staple recommendation for BookTok and becoming a bestselling novel in 2021 with a movie adaptation following in 2024.

One particularly notable novel that gained massive traction on BookTok is Travis Baldree's cosy fantasy *Legends & Lattes* (Tor 2022). I first heard about this book in videos that started 'If you like playing Dungeons and Dragons, you'll like these novels …' but before long, I was seeing it everywhere. It featured in videos that racked up hundreds of thousands of views, gaining such massive reach from 'word of mouth' alone, to the point where 'cosy fantasy' has now become its own established subgenre – and a corner of BookTok where the term alone has amassed millions of views and around 40,000 videos using the hashtag. When a book finds its audience on TikTok, it well and truly finds its audience and, most importantly, often *continues* to gain traction after that initial wave of views and engagement.

The rise in BookTok also speaks to the shift in social media, both for readers and writers/publishers. There's often an expectation for authors and illustrators to leverage their social media presence to help sell their book (easier said than done), but these days that focus is less on X and Facebook or even Instagram, and more about tapping into that massive reach that BookTok has. *Publishers Weekly* reported that BookTok helped authors sell 47 million books in 2022 alone. And while romance is consistently a high-selling but under-recognised genre in certain traditional print media, BookTokers are loud and proud about their love for it. Huge romance hits like Ali Hazelwood's *The Love Hypothesis* (Sphere 2021) or Hannah Grace's *Icebreaker* (Simon & Schuster 2023) will be touted under headings like 'TikTok made me buy it', and this isn't down to things like in-app ads but word of mouth – people shouting about a book they loved, and sharing it with others.

Part of what allows BookTok to have such a chokehold on the market is the 'For You Page' (FYP), a key feature of TikTok that's been quickly adopted by other social media platforms in the last few years. The FYP is less concerned with showing you content from accounts you follow, but cares more about what you interact with (which videos you spend time watching, sharing, liking, commenting on) in order to show you more of that. Pushing content it thinks you want to see, rather than only videos from the people you've chosen to follow, makes it a great tool for offering readers new book recommendations. If you are sharing a lot of fanart videos of Sarah J. Maas's *A Court Of Thorns And Roses* (Bloomsbury 2020) with your friends, for instance, the app will realise you enjoy fantasy romance ('romantasy') novels and start pushing BookTokers showcasing other books in this subgenre you might like. Recommendations are usually driven by how a reader felt, what the vibes of the book were and its key tropes, rather than a critical deconstruction and analysis of the storytelling.

The FYP is obviously a fantastic tool if you're a reader (I know my TBR pile has grown exponentially since downloading TikTok) but it also works its magic for authors. Previously, you would have needed a large following on social media to get your content seen by as many eyes as possible – but that's not the case here. The majority of views on any given video will come from the FYP, not necessarily directly from existing followers, so the potential audience for anything you upload is practically limitless. The appeal of having social media profiles as an author is very simple and straightforward: it's a free way to promote your books, but also a chance to interact directly with readers. For a career that can be, in large part, sitting alone behind a computer screen indulging your imagination, being able to hear directly from a reader that they are excited about your new book or loved your characters is a wonderful feeling.

It's not essential to have a big online following to sign an agent or get a publishing deal; there are obviously cases when it might help new writers prove that there is interest in their story, but that won't always be the case. And it's not essential to have any online presence in order to get published, but it can help – and it's never too early to start. Sure, you could be one of the lucky few who build such a dedicated audience that it ultimately lays the path to getting you that book deal. Or maybe you'll just share an idea you're working on and find that two or three comments saying 'I love this! I'd read that!' is all the encouragement you need to finish your manuscript and gather the courage to submit it to an agent. These are both equally valuable outcomes – don't lose sight of that. Writing can be a lonely profession, so it's important to find community where you can.

Utilising your social media presence to build your readership can be tricky and, for a lot of people, it's a daunting experience to put yourself out there as a 'brand' rather than simply sharing photos and memes with your close friends. Many people find just the thought of being on camera uncomfortable enough but, the good news is, there are ways around this. The beauty (ironically) of BookTok (and its Instagram equivalent, Bookstagram) is that you can show as much or as little of yourself as you want. Your content might feature you chatting directly to the camera, or maybe just filming your morning coffee-making routine and then showing off your desk set-up while you do a voiceover – or even just add some text and lo-fi music so that your video doesn't have either your face or voice in it. BookTok loves everything from quiet bookshelf videos to clever, choppy transitions between different paperbacks, to chatty reviews, to *The Office's* Michael Scott holding up a speaker to blast music next to some text summarising the plot of a book in one line. Its content is as varied as its audience, which is a further part of its appeal on both sides of the screen.

One struggle that creators face with TikTok is the complexity of its seemingly ineffable algorithm. Compared to the more straightforward algorithms of previous X/Instagram/Facebook iterations which made for an easy rinse-repeat success model, TikTok's is both unnervingly specific and wildly inaccurate – all in the same five-minute scroll. This can be frustrating for creators, as you're never totally sure which of your videos will take off, even if you follow 'the formula' (for instance, by using a trending CapCut (www.capcut.com) template and sound, posting two hours before most of your followers are active – usually around 6pm, using the appropriate keywords in both your caption and as a text overlay in the video *and* vocally as the 'hook' in the first few seconds of your video, and avoiding pushing traffic to external websites/sources).

Ironically, TikTok loves consistency. Posting regularly is key to building an audience and boosting your views – three videos a day, at the same sort of times each day, is the typical recommendation for those building their channel. My recommendation? Save viral sounds and trends to recreate, set aside a few hours to film, and then edit afterwards. You'll soon have plenty of videos in your TikTok drafts to post later. After a couple of years posting on the app regularly, I'm now at a point where I easily have a month's worth of content in my drafts, even if I recorded nothing new and posted multiple times a day. It will build up quicker than you realise – and this 'backlog' is especially handy to have if you're stuck for ideas or simply too busy to film new content.

And for some concrete examples: last year I began a 'day in the life' series on TikTok to document my writing journey as I completed a first draft of a new book in a month. Loaded with SEO and posted at the same time each day, these videos got far higher engagement rates (comments/shares/likes) than most of my other content. But, in terms of views, they typically only did a tenth as well as a six-second lip-sync where I joked about the use of 'all right' versus 'alright' when copy-editing one of my books. Like I said, the algorithm can be unpredictable.

The complexity of the algorithm shouldn't be disheartening or intimidating, though. Let me put it this way: there's no telling exactly *which* of your videos will be the one to gain traction, and there's something very freeing about that. It allows you – encourages you – to try new things ... to be a bit silly, a bit serious, to have fun with it. To experiment with filters and filming techniques, photo carousels or trending lip syncs. One thing that's clear about TikTok is that it rewards people who engage and try new things. When you see someone else's video in your niche going viral, it's easy to wonder – why not yours? Just as when you see articles about someone else's book getting a publishing deal, that same jealousy can rear its head. But things like BookTok are a great reminder that – it *can* be yours. It can always be. If not this video, maybe the next. If not this exact moment or stage in your career, maybe the next. Any one of your videos could hit the algorithm at just the right time, finding just the right people, and take you from hundreds of views to hundreds of thousands. Even if your book only finds one or two new readers each time you post a video – well, those readers can add up pretty quickly.

BookTok is a behemoth. Its boundless potential in allowing you to access new readers directly means that it's worth a try, whether you're an established writer with published books under your belt or are only just beginning that journey.

Beth Reekles is the author of the bestselling young adult series *The Kissing Booth* (now a Netflix film trilogy) and several other rom-com novels. Aged 17 she was offered a three-book publishing deal with Penguin Random House before completing her degree in Physics at Exeter University. Beth's first book *The Kissing Booth* (Corgi Children's) was published in 2013; the series also includes *The Beach House* (2019), *Going the Distance* (2020) and *One Last Time* (2021). Her debut adult novel *Love, Locked Down* was published by Sphere in 2022, and her most recent books are *Do You Ship It* (Penguin 2025) and *The Layover* (Sphere 2025). Beth lives in South Wales. See www.authorbethreekles.com for more information. Follow her on Instagram @authorbethreekles and on TikTok @bethreekles.

ISBNs: what you need to know

The BookData ISBN Agency for UK & Ireland receives a large number of enquiries about the ISBN system; the most frequently asked questions are answered here.

What is an ISBN?
An ISBN is an International Standard Book Number and is 13 digits long.

What is the purpose of an ISBN?
An ISBN is a product number, used by publishers, booksellers and libraries for ordering, listing and stock control purposes. It enables them to identify a particular publisher and allows the publisher to identify a specific edition of a specific title in a specific format within their output.

Contact details

BookData ISBN Agency for UK and Ireland
3rd Floor, Station Place, Argyle Way,
Stevenage SG1 2AD
tel (01483) 712215
email isbn.agency@nielseniq.com
website www.nielsenisbnstore.com

Does an ISBN protect copyright?
A widely held misconception is that an ISBN protects copyright. The copyright belongs to the author and in the UK authors are protected by the Berne Convention, more information available here: *Berne Convention for the Protection of Literary and Artistic Works* (www.wipo.int/treaties/en/ip/berne). In general, publishers don't tend to buy copyrights for books. They license the copyrights, which the author retains.

What is a publisher?
The publisher is generally the person or organisation taking the financial and other risks in making a product available. For example, if a product goes on sale and sells no copies at all, the publisher loses money. If you get paid anyway, you are likely to be a designer, printer, author or consultant of some kind.

What is the format of an ISBN?
The ISBN is 13 digits long and is divided into five parts separated by spaces or hyphens.
- Prefix element: for the foreseeable future this will be 978 or 979.
- Registration group element: identifies a geographic or national grouping. It shows where the publisher is based.
- Registrant element: identifies a specific publisher or imprint.
- Publication element: identifies a specific edition of a specific title in a specific format.
- Check digit: the final digit which mathematically validates the rest of the number.

The four parts following the prefix element can be of varying length. Prior to 1 January 2007, ISBNs were ten digits long; any existing ten-digit ISBNs must be converted by prefixing them with '978' and the check digit must be recalculated using a Modulus 10 system with alternate weights of 1 and 3. The ISBN Agency can help you with this.

Do I *have* to have an ISBN?
There is no legal requirement in the UK and Ireland for an ISBN and it conveys no form of legal or copyright protection. It is simply a product identification number.

Why should I use an ISBN?

If you wish to sell your publication through major bookselling chains, independent bookshops or internet retailers, they will require you to have an ISBN to assist their internal processing and ordering systems.

The ISBN also provides access to bibliographic databases, such as the Nielsen BookData Database, which use ISBNs as references. These databases help booksellers and libraries to provide information for customers. Nielsen BookData has a range of bibliographic metadata and retail sales monitoring services which use ISBNs and are vital for the dissemination, trading and monitoring of books in the supply chain. The ISBN therefore provides access to additional marketing opportunities which could help sales of your product.

Where can I get an ISBN?

ISBNs are assigned to publishers in the country where the publisher's main office is based. This is irrespective of the language of the publication or the intended market for the book. ISBNs are geo-specific and must be acquired from the ISBN Agency in the country where you are based and publishing from. Each country has a National ISBN Agency that supplies ISBNs only to publishers within their territories.

The BookData ISBN Agency is the national agency for the UK, Republic of Ireland, and British Overseas Territories. If you are based in the UK and Ireland, you can purchase ISBNs online from the BookData ISBN Store: www.nielsenisbnstore.com.

A publisher based elsewhere will not be able to get ISBNs from the UK Agency (even if you are a British Citizen) but you can contact the International ISBN Agency for further information via their website www.isbn-international.org/agencies. Having a non-UK ISBN does not preclude you from registering your book for the UK trade with BookData or to sell your book through UK bookshops.

How long does it take to get an ISBN?

If you purchase your ISBNs online from the BookData ISBN Store you will receive your ISBN allocation within minutes. If you are purchasing ISBNs direct from the ISBN Agency via an off-line application, it can take up to five days. The processing period begins when a correctly completed application is received in the ISBN Agency and payment is received.

How much does it cost to get an ISBN?

ISBNs can be bought individually or in blocks of ten or more. Refer to www.nielsenisbnstore.com or email the ISBN Agency: isbn.agency@nielseniq.com.

Who is eligible for ISBNs?

Any individual or organisation who is publishing a qualifying product for general sale or distribution to the market. By publishing we mean making a work available to the public.

Which products do NOT qualify for ISBNs?

Any publication that is without a defined end should not be assigned an ISBN. For example, publications that are regularly updated and intended to continue indefinitely are not eligible for an ISBN.

> Some examples of products that do not qualify for an ISBN are:
> - Journals, periodicals, serials, newspapers in their entirety (single issues or articles, where these are made available separately, may qualify for ISBN);
> - Abstract entities and other abstract creations of intellectual or artistic content;
> - Ephemeral printed materials such as advertising matter and the like;

- Customised print-on-demand publications (Publications that are available only on a limited basis, such as customised print-on-demand publications with content specifically tailored to a user's request shall not be assigned an ISBN. If a customised publication is being made available for wider sale, e.g. as a college course pack available through a college book store, then an ISBN may be assigned);
- Printed music;
- Art prints and art folders without title page and text;
- Personal documents (such as a curriculum vitae or personal profile);
- Greetings cards;
- Music sound recordings;
- Software that is intended for any purpose other than educational or instructional;
- Electronic bulletin boards;
- Emails and other digital correspondence;
- Updating websites.

Following a review of the UK market, it is now permissible for ISBNs to be assigned to calendars and diaries, provided that they are not intended for purely time-management purposes and that a substantial proportion of their content is textual or graphic.

What is an ISSN?

An International Standard Serial Number. This is the numbering system for journals, magazines, periodicals, newspapers and newsletters. It is administered by the British Library, contact *tel* (01937) 546959 or *email* issn-uk@bl.uk.

Where do I put the ISBN?

The ISBN should appear on the reverse of the title page, sometimes called the copyright page or the imprint page, and on the outside back cover of the book. If the book has a dust jacket, the ISBN should also appear on the back of this. If the publication is not a book, the ISBN should appear on the product, and on the packaging or inlay card. If the publication is a map, the ISBN should be visible when the map is folded and should also appear near the publisher statement if this is elsewhere.

I am reprinting a book with no changes – do I need a new ISBN?

No.

I am reprinting a book but adding a new chapter – do I need a new ISBN?

Yes. You are adding a significant amount of additional material and altering the content of the book.

I am reprinting a book with a new cover design – should I change the ISBN?

No. A change of cover design with no changes to the title, author name, or content of the book does not need to have a new ISBN.

I am changing the binding from hardback to paperback. Do I need a new ISBN?

Yes. Changes in binding always require new ISBNs even if there are no changes to the content of the book.

I am changing the price – do I need a new ISBN?

No. Price changes with no other changes do not require new ISBNs and in fact must not change the ISBN.

Who's who in publishing

agent
See **literary agent**.

aggregator
A company or website that gathers together related content from a range of other sources and provides various different services and resources, such as formatting and distribution, to ebook authors.

art editor
A person in charge of the layout and design of a magazine, who commissions the photographs and illustrations and is responsible for its overall appearance and style.

audio editor
A person who edits the raw audio from the recording into the final, retail-ready audiobook.

audio producer
A person who supervises the entire production process of the audiobook.

author
A person who has written a book, article, or other piece of original writing.

book packager
See **packager**.

columnist
A person who regularly writes an article for publication in a newspaper or magazine.

commissioning editor
A person who asks authors to write books for the part of the publisher's list for which he or she is responsible or who takes on an author who approaches them direct or via an agent with a proposal. Also called **acquisitions editor** or **acquiring editor** (more commonly in the USA). A person who signs up writers (commissions them) to write an article for a magazine or newspaper.

contributor
A person who writes an article that is included in a magazine or paper, or who writes a chapter or section that is included in a book.

copy-editor
A person whose job is to check material ready for publication for accuracy, clarity of message, writing style and consistency of spelling, punctuation and grammar.

desk editor
Manages a list of titles, seeing them through the editorial and production processes, and works closely with authors.

distributor
Acts as a link between the publisher and retailer. The distributor can receive orders from retailers, ship books, invoice, collect revenue and deal with returns. Distributors often handle books from several publishers. **Digital distributors** handle ebook distribution.

editor
A person in charge of publishing a newspaper or magazine who makes the final decisions about the content and format. A person in book publishing who has responsibility for the content of a book and can be variously a senior person (**editor-in-chief**) or day-to-day contact for authors (**copy-editor**, **development editor**, **commissioning editor**, etc).

editorial assistant
A person who assists senior editorial staff at a publishing company, newspaper, or similar business with various administrative duties, as well as editorial tasks in preparing copy for publication.

illustrator
A person who designs and draws a visual rendering of the source material, such as characters or settings, in a 2D media. Using traditional or digital methods, an illustrator creates artwork manually rather than photographically.

journalist
A person who prepares and writes material for a newspaper or magazine, news website, television or radio programme, or any similar medium.

literary agent
Somebody whose job is to negotiate publishing contracts, involving royalties, advances and rights sales on behalf of an author and who earns commission on the proceeds of the sales they negotiate.

literary scout
A person who looks for unpublished manuscripts to recommend to clients for publication as books, or adaptation into film scripts, etc.

Who's who in publishing

marketing department
The department that originates the sales material – catalogues, order forms, blads, samplers, posters, book proofs and advertisements – to promote published titles.

narrator
A person who reads a text aloud into a recording device to create an audiobook. This may be the author of the text or a professional voice artist.

packager
A company that creates a finished book for a publisher.

picture researcher
A person who looks for pictures relevant to a particular topic, so that they can be used as illustrations in, for example, a book, newspaper or TV programme.

printer
A person or company whose job is to produce printed books, magazines, newspapers or similar material. The many stages in this process include establishing the product specifications, preparing the pages for print, operating the printing presses, and binding and finishing the final product.

production controller
A person in the production department of a publishing company who deals with printers and paper suppliers.

production department
The department responsible for the technical aspects of planning and producing material for publication to a schedule and as specified by the client. Their work involves liaising with editors, designers, typesetters, printers and binders.

proofreader
A person whose job is to check typeset pages and text for layout, design, spelling and grammatical errors missed at copy-editing, prior to publication.

publicity department
The department that works with the author and the media on 'free' publicity when a book is published – e.g. reviews, features, author interviews, bookshop readings and signings, festival appearances, book tours, and radio and TV interviews.

publisher
A person or company that publishes books, magazines or newspapers.

rights manager
A person who negotiates and coordinates rights sales (e.g. for subsidiary, translation or foreign rights). Often travels to book fairs to negotiate rights sales.

sales department
The department responsible for selling and marketing the publications produced by a publishing company, to bring about maximum sales and profit. Its tasks include identifying physical and digital outlets, ensuring orders and supplies of stock.

self-publishing services provider
Company that provides (for a fee) the complete range of activities to support a self-publishing author get their book into print or ebook. These include editorial, design, production, marketing and selling (i.e. all tasks carried out by a traditional publisher for their authors).

sensitivity reader
A person who assesses a manuscript with a particular issue of representation in mind, usually one that they have personal experience of.

sub-editor
A person who corrects and checks articles in a newspaper before they are printed.

translator
A person who translates copy, such as a manuscript, from one language into another.

typesetter
A person or company that 'sets' text and prepares the final layout of the page for printing. It can also now involve XML tagging for ebook creation.

vanity publisher
A publisher who charges an author a fee in order to publish his or her work for them and is not responsible for selling the product.

web content manager
A person who controls the type and quality of material shown on a website or blog and is responsible for how it is produced, organised, presented and updated.

wholesaler
A person or company that buys large quantities of books, magazines, etc from publishers, transports and stores them, and then sells them in smaller quantities to a range of retailers.

Glossary of publishing terms

advance
Money paid by a publisher to an author before a book is published which will be covered by future royalties. A publishing contract often allows an author an advance payment against future royalties; the author will not receive any further royalties until the amount paid in advance has been earned by sales of the book.

AI (advance information sheet)
A document that is put together by a publishing company to provide sales and marketing information about a book before publication and can be sent several months before publication to sales representatives. It typically includes details of the format and contents of the book, key selling points and information about intended readership, as well as information about promotions and reviews.

auction
An auction, usually arranged by a literary agent, takes place when multiple publishing houses are interested in acquiring a manuscript and bid against one another to secure the domestic or territorial rights.

B format
See **trade paperback**.

backlist
The range of books already published by a publisher, or indie author, that are still in print.

backmatter
See **endmatter**.

beta reader
A person who reads a book before it is published in order to mark errors and suggest improvements, typically without receiving payment.

BIC
A group of categories and subcategories that can be applied to a book to accurately describe it and to help place it in the market.

BISAC
Subject heading codes that categorise a book into topics and subtopics. Used by sellers to place your book in the correct section of their store or online listings.

blad (book layout and design)
A pre-publication sales and marketing tool. It is often a printed booklet that contains sample pages, images and front and back covers, which acts as a preview for promotional use or for sales and rights teams to show to potential retailers, customers or reviewers.

blurb
A short piece of writing or a paragraph that praises and promotes a book, which usually appears on the back or inside cover and may be used in sales and marketing material.

book club edition
An edition of a book specially printed and bound for a book club for sale to its members.

book proof
A bound set of uncorrected reading proofs. Traditionally publisher sales teams send pre-publication copies to reviewers.

brief
A set of instructions given to a designer about a project, such as a cover or internal design.

C format
A term most often used to describe a paperback edition published simultaneously with, and in the same format as, the hardback original.

co-edition
The publication of a book by two publishing companies in different countries, where the first company has originated the work and then sells sheets to the second publisher (or licenses the second publisher to reprint the book locally).

copy-editing
The editorial stage where an editor looks for spelling mistakes, grammatical errors and factual errors. They may rework sentences or paragraphs to add clarity to the work.

copyright
The legal right, which the creator of an original work has, to only allow copying of the work with permission and sometimes on payment of royalties or a copyright fee. An amendment to the Copyright, Designs and Patents Act (1988) states that in the UK most works are protected for 70 years from the creator's death. The copyright page (or imprint page)

Glossary of publishing terms

at the start of a book asserts copyright ownership and author identification.

crowdfunding
A publishing model that requires a book to surpass a financial goal before it can go into production. This money comes from pledges made by readers who back the project. In return, each backer usually receives a different level of acknowledgement (based on the amount pledged) from the author within the published book.

developmental edit
See **structural edit**.

double-page spread (DPS)
Two facing pages of an illustrated book.

edition
A quantity of books printed without changes to the content. A 'new edition' is a reprint of an existing title that incorporates substantial textual alterations. Originally one edition meant a single print run, though today an edition may consist of several separate printings, or impressions.

endmatter
Material at the end of the main body of a book which may be useful to the reader, including references, appendices, indexes and bibliography. Also called back matter.

ePub files
Digital book format compatible with all electronic devices and e-readers.

extent
The number of pages in a book.

first edition
The first print run of a book. It can occasionally gain secondhand value if either the book or its author become collectable.

folio
A large sheet of paper folded twice across the middle and trimmed to make four pages of a book. Also a page number.

frontlist
New books just published (generally in their first year of publication) or about to be published by a publisher. Promotion of the frontlist is heavy, and the frontlist carries most of a publisher's investment. On the other hand, a **backlist** which continues to sell is usually the most profitable part of a publisher's list.

frontmatter
The pages before the main chapters of a book with information about the publication and contents. This may include a copyright page, reviews, table of contents, etc.

HTML markup
Instructing the text that will appear on a webpage to look a certain way, such as bold (<b></b>) or italic (<i></i>). These markup indicators are often called tags.

imagery
The use of pictures, photographs, illustrations and other type of images within a book.

impression
A single print run of a book; all books in an impression are manufactured at the same time and are identical. A 'second impression' would be the second batch of copies to be printed and bound. The impression number is usually marked on the copyright/imprint page. There can be several impressions in an edition, all sharing the same **ISBN**.

imprint
The publisher's or printer's name which appears on the title page of a book or in the bibliographical details; a brand name under which a book is published within a larger publishing company, usually representing a specialised subject area.

inspection copy
A copy of a publication sent or given with time allowed for a decision to purchase or return it. In academic publishing, lecturers can request inspection copies to decide whether to make a book/textbook recommended reading or adopt it as a core textbook for their course.

internal(s)
Refers to the actual page design and layout of the pages that make up a book.

ISBN
International Standard Book Number. The ISBN is formed of 13 digits and is unique to a published title.

ISSN
International Standard Serial Number. An international system used on periodicals, magazines, learned journals, etc. The ISSN is formed of eight digits, which refer to the country in which the magazine is published and the title of the publication.

kill fee
A fee paid to a freelance writer for material written on assignment but not used, typically a percentage of the total payment.

manuscript
The pre-published version of an author's work, now usually submitted in electronic form.

metadata
Data that describes the content of a book to aid online discoverability – typically title, author, ISBN, key terms, description and other bibliographic information.

moral right
The right of people such as editors or illustrators to have some say in the publication of a work to which they have contributed, even if they do not own the copyright.

MS (*pl* MSS)
The abbreviation commonly used for 'manuscript'.

nom de plume
A pseudonym or 'pen-name' under which a writer may choose to publish their work instead of their real name.

out of print or o.p.
Relating to a book of which the publisher has no copies left and which is not going to be reprinted. Print-on-demand technology, however, means that a book can be kept 'in print' indefinitely.

page proofs
A set of designed and typeset pages in a book used to check the accuracy of typesetting and page layout before publication, and also as an advance promotional tool. These are provided in electronic form, such as a pdf.

paper engineering
The mechanics of creating novelty books and pop-ups.

pdf
Portable Document Format. A data file generated from PostScript that is platform-independent, application-independent and font-independent. Acrobat is Adobe's suite of software used to generate, edit and view pdf files.

point of sale (POS)
Merchandising display material provided by publishers to bookshops in order to promote particular titles.

prelims
The initial pages of a book, including the title page and table of contents, which precede the main text. Also called front matter.

pre-press
Before going to press, to be printed.

print on demand (POD)
The facility to print and bind a small number of books at short notice, without the need for a large print run, using digital technology. When an order comes through, a digital file of the book can be printed individually and automatically.

print run
The quantity of a book printed at one time in an **impression**.

public lending right
An author's right to receive from the public purse a payment for the loan of works from public libraries in the UK.

publisher's agreement
A contract between a publisher and the copyright holder, author, agent or another publisher which lays down the terms under which the publisher will publish the book for the copyright holder.

publishing contract
An agreement between a publisher and an author by which the author grants the publisher the right to publish the work against payment of a fee, usually in the form of a royalty.

query letter
A letter from an author to an agent pitching their book. Also known as a covering letter.

reading fee
Money paid to an editor for reading a manuscript and commenting on it. Reputable literary agents should never charge such a fee.

recto
Relating to the right-hand page of a book, usually given an odd number.

reprint
Copies of a book made from the original, but with a note in the publication details of the date of reprinting and possibly a new title page and cover design.

review copy
An advance copy of a book sent to magazines, newspapers or other media outlets (such as social media channels) for the purposes of review. A 'book proof' may be sent out before the final book is printed or published.

revises

If any corrections are made to your typeset proofs by the proofreader, a new round of proofs will be produced which are known as revises or revised proofs.

rights

The legal right to publish something such as a book, picture or extract from a text.

royalty

Money paid to a writer for the right to use their property, usually a percentage of sales or an agreed amount per sale.

royalty split

The way in which a royalty is divided between several authors or between author and illustrator.

royalty statement

A printed statement from a publisher showing how much royalty is due to an author.

sale or return

An arrangement between a retailer and publisher where any unwanted or unsold books can be returned to the publisher and the purchase costs reimbursed to the retailer. If no arrangement is in place, retailers cannot return unwanted or unsold stock to the publisher.

sans serif

A style of printing letters with all lines of equal thickness and no **serifs**. Sans faces are less easy to read in print than seriffed faces and they are rarely used for continuous text, although some magazines use them for text matter.

SEO (Search Engine Optimisation)

The process of using keywords in your content so that it can be found through search engines such as Google. Keyword can be used in metadata, titles or website URLs.

serialisation

Publication of a book in parts in a magazine or newspaper.

serif

A small decorative line added to letters in some fonts; a font that uses serifs, such as Times. The addition of serifs (1) keeps the letters apart while at the same time making it possible to link one letter to the next, and (2) makes the letters distinct, in particular the top parts which the reader recognises when reading.

slush pile

Unsolicited manuscripts which are sent to publishers or agents.

STM

The accepted abbreviation for the scientific, technical and medical publishing sector.

structural editing

Also known as **developmental edit**. This type of editing looks at the overall structure and content of your book. It should address story structure alongside plot, characters, and themes.

style sheet

A guide listing all the rules of house style for a publishing company which has to be followed by authors and editors.

submission guidelines

Instructions given by agents or publishers on how they wish to receive submissions from authors.

subscription sale or 'sub'

Sales of a title to booksellers in advance of publication, and orders taken from wholesalers and retailers to be supplied by the publisher shortly before the publication date.

subsidiary rights

Rights other than the right to publish a book in its first form, e.g. paperback rights; rights to adapt the book; rights to serialise it in a magazine; film and TV rights; audio, ebook, foreign and translation rights.

sub-title

A secondary or subordinate title of a published work providing additional information about its content. More commonly found in works of non-fiction.

synopsis

A concise plot summary of a manuscript (usually one side of A4) that covers the major plot points, narrative arcs and characters.

territory

Areas of the world where the publisher has the rights to publish or can make foreign rights deals.

Thema

A globally applicable subject classification system for books to aid the merchandising and discoverability of the title. This type of classification can be used alongside **BIC**.

trade discount
A reduction in price given to a customer in the same trade, as by a publisher to another publisher or to a bookseller.

trade paperback (B format)
A paperback edition of a book that is superior in production quality to, and larger than, a mass-market paperback edition.

trim size or trimmed size
The measurements of a page of a book after it has been cut, or of a sheet of paper after it has been cut to size.

type specification (spec)
A brief created by the design department of a publishing house for how a book should be typeset.

typeface
A set of characters that share a distinctive and consistent design. Typefaces come in families of different weights, e.g. Helvetica Roman, Helvetica Italic, Bold, Bold Italic, etc. Hundreds of typefaces exist and new ones are still being designed. Today, 'font' is often used synonymously with 'typeface' though originally font meant the characters were all the same size, e.g. Helvetica Italic 11 point.

typescript
The final draft of a book. This unedited text is usually an electronic Word file. The term 'typescript' (abbreviated TS or ts) is synonymous with 'manuscript' (abbreviated MS or ms; plural is MSS or mss).

See also...
- *Who's who in publishing*, page 368

typographic error (typo)
A mistake made when keying text or typesetting.

typography
The art and technique of arranging type.

unsolicited manuscript
An unpublished manuscript sent to a publisher without having been commissioned or requested.

USP
Unique selling point. A distinctive quality or feature of a book that distinguishes it within the market.

verso
The left-hand page of a book, usually given an even number.

voice casting
The process of finding a suitable voice artist to narrate audiobooks.

volume rights
The right to publish the work in hardback, paperback or ebook.

XML tagging
Inserting tags into the text that can allow it to be converted for ebooks or for use in electronic formats.

YA
A term used within children's publishing to refer to books written to appeal to an audience of teenagers or young adults.

Self-publishing children's books

Publishing is an inherently innovative industry, and the rise of self-publishing over the past decade in particular has helped many authors make their dream a reality. There are, of course, challenges to navigate along the way. Here, Jeremy Thompson and Alex Thompson of Troubador Publishing explain how self-publishing your children's book might work.

Publishing a children's book is often seen as an easier option by many aspiring authors, but in truth, it can be a minefield. While children have less experience with language, it doesn't mean writing for them will be easier; in fact, it is often far harder to get the language level right. Children develop their linguistic abilities from a very early age through to adulthood (and beyond), so pitching your words correctly is essential. Add to that, the complexities of publishing illustrated books for younger children, and it becomes clear that self-publishing a children's book is not as simple as it might at first appear.

There are three main avenues to self-publishing.

- **The DIY approach**: you, as the author, do everything, from editing to page layout, cover design, print and distribution. While the author retains full creative and financial control, it does demand an amount of expertise (design, market knowledge, linguistic ability, technical knowledge and significant time). Such expertise is generally found among industry professionals. Going it alone is fine, but the more savvy self-publisher will understand their own limitations, recognise when they need assistance and pay for relevant advice and support. Sadly, many DIY self-published books *look* too DIY, reflecting the author's lack of industry experience.
- **Authorpreneurs**: as the author, you commission freelancers to undertake all the publishing activities required. This route is better for those with some experience in publishing, as you need to be able to identify what aspects of the publishing processes you need assistance with and how to go about accessing them. Try Reedsy, Indie-Go.co.uk, the listings in this *Yearbook* (which start on page 395) or the CIEP to source individual production services. This approach offers flexibility, but it can be very time-consuming and costly.
- **All-in-one service suppliers** (see below).

Defining key terms

- **Self-publishing**: the process of publishing a book without the involvement of a traditional publishing company. The author retains full control over all aspects of the process, from editing through design, print and distribution.
- **Partnership publishing** involves a collaboration between the author and the publishing company, where each makes a financial contribution to the publication of a book. The author brings the book, and the publisher the publishing expertise. Care should be taken with this model, however, as some less reputable companies purport to be offering a partnership when in fact the author is bearing all the cost and taking all the risk. Check what is on offer, what you are being expected to pay, and what you will get in return; also find out what any company's authors say about their experience (Trustpilot and Google reviews are good places to start).
- **All-in-one self-publishing services companies**: many authors prefer the convenience of working with a service provider (such as Troubador Publishing) that offers end-to-end publishing solutions. This streamlines the process as everything is handled under one roof, but authors need to ensure that they choose the right company to achieve their aims – many self-publishing companies offer only print 'on demand' (where a book exists only on a website until someone orders it, at which point it is printed), giving far less market exposure than books printed in advance and made available through bookshops. As above, when choosing any self-publishing supplier, check the quality of books published by each company, exactly what you are getting for your money, and online reviews of your prospective publishing partner.

Self-publishing books for YA readers (10–16 years)

So here's a good starting point: what *you* wanted to read at the age of 15 is not what a 15-year-old today wants to read. Tastes, attitudes and expectations change all the time. If you are writing for a specific age range – and you really need to for a children's book, then make sure you understand your audience from the start. Take the authors of this article, for example. When Jeremy was a lad (okay, we're going back a bit here), Enid Blyton's *Famous Five* series was all the rage. For Alex, it was Anthony Horowitz's *Alex Rider* ... and today? Well, we've lost touch, so if we were to write for this age range, we'd need to do our research before starting.

Getting the content right is vital. You are writing for today's younger audience, not for yourself, so you need to ensure that your audience will identify with not only your story but with the characters that inhabit your story, the world they live in and the challenges they face. Harking back to 'things were better in my day' will not cut the proverbial mustard with your readers! With this age range more than any other, it is easy to pitch things at the wrong level, in terms of both content and language, so take the time to fully appreciate what your readers are interested in, and read widely within the genre yourself so that you fully understand it.

Self-publishing picture books

In the colourful world of young children's literature, self-publishing a picture book is a dream for many aspiring authors and illustrators. However, amidst the whimsy and wonder lie a myriad of challenges that can turn this dream into a daunting reality. From balancing the artistic vision with financial constraints to navigating the complex landscape of distribution, self-publishers face a unique set of obstacles with picture books – almost a perfect negative storm.

As with YA books, age-appropriate text that resonates with the target reader while maintaining literary quality is a delicate balance. Children's books require simple yet engaging language that stimulates the imagination and fosters language development. Self-publishers must ensure that the vocabulary, sentence structure and themes are suitable for the intended audience, whether it's preschool, early or middle-grade readers. Children's books are very specifically categorised into appropriate reading age ranges, so you must be certain that your language is pitched at the right level.

The words are only half the story, though. With picture books, illustrations are more than just accompaniments to the text – they are integral to storytelling. Visual elements play a crucial role in capturing a child's attention, conveying emotions and enhancing comprehension. As the publisher, you must collaborate closely with your illustrator to ensure the artwork complements and enriches the narrative, creating a cohesive and immersive reading experience. And quality counts with illustrations – don't be tempted to 'have a go' at illustrations yourself unless you are a very competent artist. That usually means you'll need to commission someone to create illustrations for you, and herein lie two more potential problems:

• Illustrated children's books rely heavily on captivating artwork to engage young readers. Yet commissioning quality illustrations is a skill: how do you convey your vision to an illustrator? What specific illustrations do you want? What do your characters look like? What style of illustration do you envisage? And it's also likely to be a significant financial investment – illustrators usually charge per illustration, and for a picture book consisting

of 24 or 32 pages, the costs can quickly escalate. Getting your illustrator's brief right is essential, as errors at the start of the process can have extensive knock-on effects.
• Knowing how and what to commission demands some skill, and it can be a daunting prospect when costs are likely to be high. Services like Reedsy.com can connect you with freelance illustrators, or you can use a one-stop shop like our illustration service (www.troubador.co.uk/illustrations), which coordinates the whole process between author and illustrator, backed by extensive experience in the field, to ensure the author's vision is fulfilled as cost-effectively as possible.

Illustrated picture books present challenges other than just the content. Unlike text-only books, children's picture books often require full-colour printing to showcase the vibrant illustrations. Yet colour printing is significantly more expensive than black and white, and while you might think that you can just hike the cover price to cover that extra cost, think again! The competitive nature of the children's book market, coupled with the expectation of affordable pricing, means that parents and caregivers are reluctant to purchase picture books with higher price tags, especially considering the relatively short reading duration. Look at the cover prices on picture books in any bookshop and you will see the price point you have to aim at. Any more, and readers and retailers just won't be interested. Self-publishers must find a balance between maintaining profitability and setting a cover price that remains competitive in the market which is no easy task.

Once you have your beautifully illustrated, carefully written, high-quality picture book in hand, how are you going to sell it? Securing distribution channels and getting books onto retailers' shelves can be difficult for self-publishers. Traditional bookstores have limited shelf space and will prioritise established publishers over indie authors, usually buying on a 'sale or return' basis (i.e. at no risk to them, as they can return unsold stock within a set timeframe). On top of that, bookshops rarely source print 'on demand' titles because of the additional timescales needed and the costs involved. Large commercial distributors are unlikely to take a self-publisher on unless they have numerous titles, and few one-stop self-publishing service providers offer a distribution service to retailers. You must think carefully about how you will get your book to market before you decide on a route to self-publishing.

In conclusion, while self-publishing a children's book offers creative freedom and entrepreneurial opportunities, it also comes with its fair share of challenges, particularly in the realm of picture books. Overcoming these hurdles requires careful planning, resourcefulness and a deep understanding of both the creative and the business aspects of book publishing. Despite the obstacles, however, the rewards of seeing a captivating story come to life – whether in words alone or a picture book – and touching the hearts of young readers will hopefully make the self-publishing journey both enjoyable and worthwhile.

Jeremy Thompson is the former Managing Director of Troubador Publishing Ltd, and **Alex Thompson** the company's current Managing Director. Troubador has offered a range of self-publishing services for more than 30 years. To find out more, visit www.troubador.co.uk.

See also ...
- *The next chapter ... being a successful self-publisher author,* page 25
- *Debut dilemma: your publishing options,* page 29

Paid-for publishing services: *Is it a steal?*

The UK writers' unions, the Society of Authors (SoA) and the Writers' Guild of Great Britain (WGGB), investigated the practices of companies that charge writers to publish their work while taking rights. The findings were published in their 2022 report *Is it a steal?* Their investigation into 'hybrid'/paid-for publishing services raises awareness and work for change in what is a growing section of the writer services sector. Authors are advised to read the report and heed its advice.

Below are key extracts from this report. The full version can be found at: https://writersguild.org.uk/wp-content/uploads/2022/05/REPORT-Is-it-a-steal.pdf

As part of an investigation into practices in the sector, the SoA and the WGGB carried out a survey of authors who had used 'hybrid'/paid-for publishing services. 240 writers responded to the survey which ran online between 28 February and 25 April 2021.

The findings of that survey have informed our in-depth assessment of the relationship between writers and companies who often refer to themselves as 'hybrid', 'partnership' or 'contributory' publishers (among other terms) but which have much in common with what have historically been described as 'vanity' publishers.

Summary findings:
- 94% of respondents lost money, typically in the thousands.
- The average loss was £1,861 with some writers reporting losses as high as £9,900.
- The median cost of publication was £2,000.
- A median of only 67 books were sold per deal, resulting in royalties of only £68.
- 59% of writers said their book was not available to buy in retail outlets.

We received reports of aggressive marketing tactics by 'hybrid'/paid-for publishers in their approaches to writers, their manipulative sales approaches, unclear contracts, obscure publishing processes and services that fell far short of expectations and value.

Recommendations

1. We have identified an urgent need to educate writers about all models of publishing and to support them through any publishing process they choose. We have made five recommendations for writers to follow.
2. We strongly urge all publishers to commit to 15 key publishing principles, including offering clarity about their business models, production and book-marketing capacity, as well as notifying people who enter into 'hybrid'/paid-for agreements about their Consumer Rights.
3. We are working with third parties – including the Publishers Association, the Independent Publishers Guild, and various advertising platforms – who in various ways give these 'hybrid'/paid-for companies credibility, to ensure that they are not helping to promote or validate companies whose operations are based on poor practice and the exploitation of writers.

What is 'hybrid'/paid-for publishing?

In a traditional or conventional trade publishing contract, a publisher provides everything from editing and printing to marketing, publicity and distribution. It takes a licence of rights and pays writers a fee or an advance, and royalties. It does not ask for payments from a writer. It funds its operation by sales of books and is therefore investing cash and resources, and taking a risk on the book's success.

'Hybrid'/paid-for publishing deals should also not be confused with self-publishing. Writers can self-publish at very little cost to themselves, but even if they pay a **self-publishing service provider** to edit, design, produce and market their book, the rights will remain with the writer. The writer receives all profits after the sales platform or distributor takes its cut and can extract themselves from the agreement at any time. Such service providers are funded by payments agreed, and preferably negotiated, with the author.

Defining 'hybrid'/paid-for publishing services

If a writer pays money for publication and grants the company a licence of rights or if the company takes a share of any profits, the writer is dealing with a 'hybrid'/paid-for publishing service.

The companies in question sometimes describe themselves as 'contributory', 'subsidy' or 'partnership' publishers, but they have much in common with what used to be called 'vanity' publishers. In their marketing approaches to writers, they often suggest that they operate as traditional publishing houses. In fact, some are run as imprints of major publishers, gaining legitimacy from their parent brands.

At first glance, 'hybrid'/paid-for publishing deals can look much like traditional publishing agreements, but they are very different. There is rarely any sign of expenditure by the 'hybrid'/paid-for publisher except what is funded by the author. As such, terms like 'hybrid', 'contributory' and 'partnership' can appear deliberately misleading. Writers pay the publisher. They are offered no advance, and there is usually no undertaking or intention by the 'hybrid'/paid-for publisher to publish the work other than as an ebook and/or as Print on demand ('POD'), or in an ultra-short print run. The writer does not own any of the books produced except for limited initial copies.

Anyone can set themselves up as such a publisher, regardless of their financial stability, publishing knowledge and experience, or commercial expertise. Start-up and overhead costs are minimal, and expenses are funded by writers, not by income from book sales.

At the point of submitting a work for publication, writers are vulnerable. They have invested a great deal of time, work, energy and creativity in their manuscript. Now they want to be read, and for their work to be legitimised.

'Hybrid'/paid-for publishing services often exploit this desire, sending excessive praise about manuscripts and telling writers what they want to hear. They might claim their approach is better than traditional publishing or self-publishing, without ever explaining what that means. They will stress how excited they are to be working with the writer. Of course, at the point of hearing a 'publisher' express interest in their work like this, it can be difficult for a writer to step back and see it for what it is: a sales approach, designed to take advantage of writers' hopes, their passion for their work and their desire for validation – not to mention their lack of knowledge about the complexities of the publishing industry.

In our view, of all the publishing approaches available, a 'hybrid'/paid-for deal is the worst option a writer can take. In our direct experience of working with SoA and WGGB members, and as our research bears out, 'hybrid'/paid-for publishing deals do not result in enough sales or exposure to justify the payment by the author. For many years, even before researching for this report, we have seen how such services fall short of expectations, with writers unnecessarily handing over rights and control over their manuscripts, along with large sums of money. We have seen the impact this has on writers' careers and confidence in their work, and on their finances. We have seen too many cases where the 'hybrid'/paid-for model amounts to a counterfeit approach to publishing. We invariably advise writers against it.

If you are a writer considering a 'hybrid'/paid-for deal, we recommend taking the following five steps before you commit:

1. Educate yourself.
The publishing industry is complex. Do your research to get a broad understanding of how it works and the options available before you commit to any publishing deal. For starters, download the free SoA guide *What type of deal is that?* for a no-nonsense introduction to the pros, cons and gotchas of five publishing approaches.

2. Consider carefully what you want from publication and whether a 'hybrid'/paid-for deal is the best way to achieve it.
Is a 'hybrid'/paid-for publishing deal a better option than self-publishing, with its substantial investment from you as well as surrendering rights in your work? To commission self-publishing services will probably cost you less and you will retain all rights in your work.

3. Look closely at the detail of the deal.
How much will you have to pay? What is covered for that payment? Are there guarantees on the number of books to be printed? And will you own any of them, or will you have to pay more to get hold of copies yourself ('author copies')? What rights are you giving away? Will you have to make further payments later? Can you terminate the deal, when and how?

4. Research the company offering the deal.
Ask the SoA and WGGB what we know about them. Ask others who have used the company. Look for online reviews (though be mindful of paid-for positive reviews) and check their history at Companies House. Check the Watchdog Advisory Ratings on the Alliance of Independent Authors' (ALLi) website. In short, don't sign with a company unless you are confident about what you can expect if you work with them.

5. Have your contract vetted.
Remember that all contracts are negotiable. If you are an SoA or WGGB member, get your contract vetted as part of your membership. We recommend that you always do this regardless of the type of deal or contract you are being offered.

Is it a steal? is supported by the Authors' Licensing and Collecting Society (ALCS). © The Society of Authors and Writers' Guild of Great Britain – April 2022.

See also...
- *Society of Authors*, page 297
- *Writers' Guild of Great Britain (WGGB)*, page 300

Public Lending Right

Under the PLR system, payment is made from public funds to authors and other contributors (writers, illustrators/photographers, translators, adapters/retellers, ghostwriters, editors/compilers/abridgers/revisers, narrators and producers) whose books (print, audiobook and ebook) are lent from public libraries. Payment is annual; the amount authors receive is proportionate to the number of times that their books were borrowed during the previous year (July to June).

How the system works

From the applications received, the PLR office compiles a database of authors and books (the PLR Register). A representative sample of book issues is recorded, consisting of all loans from selected public libraries. This is then multiplied in proportion to total library lending to produce, for each book, an estimate of its total annual loans throughout the country. The estimated loans are matched against the database of registered authors and titles to discover how many loans are credited to each registered book for the calculation of PLR payments, using the ISBN printed in the book (see below).

Parliament allocates a sum each year (£6.6 million for 2023/24) for PLR. This fund pays the administrative costs of PLR and reimburses local authorities for recording loans in the sample libraries (see below). The remaining money is divided by the total estimated national loan figure for all registered books in order to work out how much can be paid for each estimated loan of every registered ISBN.

Limits on payments

If all the registered interests in an author's books score so few loans that they would earn less than £1 in a year, no payment is due. However, if the books of one registered author score so high that the author's PLR earnings for the year would exceed £6,600, then only £6,600 is paid. (No author can earn more than £6,600 in PLR in any one year.) Money that is not paid out because of these limits belongs to the fund and increases the amounts paid that year to other authors.

The sample

Currently a statistical sampling method is employed to collect loans data. The sample represents only public lending libraries – academic, school, private and commercial libraries are not included. Only books which are loaned from public libraries can earn PLR; consultations of books on library premises are excluded.

The sample consists of the entire loans records for a year from libraries in more than 72 public library authorities spread through England, Scotland and Wales, and whole data

Further information

Public Lending Right – British Library
Boston Spa, Wetherby, West Yorkshire LS23 7BQ
tel (01937) 546030
website www.bl.uk/plr, www.plrinternational.com
Contact Head of PLR Operations

The UK PLR scheme is administered by the British Library from its offices in Boston Spa. The UK PLR office also provides registration for the Irish PLR scheme on behalf of the Irish Public Lending Remuneration office.

Application forms, information and publications are all obtainable from the PLR Office. See website for further information on eligibility for PLR, loans statistics and forthcoming developments.

British Library Advisory Committee for Public Lending Right
Advises the British Library Board, the PLR Head of Policy and Engagement and Head of PLR Operations on the operation and future development of the PLR scheme.

is collected from Northern Ireland. In 2023/24, sample loans represent around 37% of the national total. All the computerised sampling points in an authority contribute loans data ('multi-site' sampling). An amendment to PLR legislation came into force in October 2023, allowing a gradual increase in the number of public libraries in the sample, with an aim to transition to full loans data collection over the next few years. Therefore the need to replace seven libraries every year, the removal of a library after four years is no longer required. Loans are totalled every 12 months for the period 1 July–30 June.

An author's entitlement to PLR depends on the loans accrued by his or her books in the sample. This figure is averaged up to produce first regional and then finally national estimated loans.

ISBNs

The PLR system uses ISBNs (International Standard Book Numbers) to identify books lent and correlate loans with entries on the PLR Register so that payments can be made. ISBNs are required for all registrations. Different editions (e.g. 1st, 2nd, hardback, paperback, large print) of the same book have different ISBNs. See *ISBNs: what you need to know* on page 365.

Authorship

In the PLR system the author of a printed book or ebook is any contributor such as the writer, illustrator, translator, compiler, editor or reviser. Authors must be named on the book's title page, or be able to prove authorship by some other means (e.g. receipt of royalties). The ownership of copyright has no bearing on PLR eligibility. Narrators, producers and abridgers are also eligible to apply for PLR shares in audiobooks and e-audiobooks.

Co-authorship/illustrators. In the PLR system the authors of a book are those writers, translators, editors, compilers and illustrators as defined above. Authors must apply for registration before their books can earn PLR and this can be done via the PLR website.

Summary of the 42nd year's results

Registration: authors. When registration closed for the 42nd year (30 June 2024) there were 63,583 authors and assignees.

Eligible loans. The loans from UK libraries credited to registered books – approximately 33% of all library borrowings – qualify for payment. The remaining loans relate to books that are ineligible for various reasons, to books written by dead or foreign authors, and to books that have simply not been applied for.

Money and payments. PLR's administrative costs are deducted from the fund allocated to the British Library Board annually by Parliament. Total government funding for 2023/24 was £6.6 million. The amount distributed to authors was just over £6.4 million. The Rate per Loan for 2023/24 was 11.76 pence.

The numbers of authors in various payment categories are as follows:

*298	payments at	£5,000–6,600
375	payments between	£2,500–4,999.99
911	payments between	£1,000–2,499.99
939	payments between	£500–999.99
3,369	payments between	£100–499.99
18,383	payments between	£1–99.99
24,275	TOTAL	

* Includes 206 authors whose book loans reached the maximum threshold

There is no restriction on the number of authors who can register shares in any one book as long as they satisfy the eligibility criteria.

Writers and/or illustrators. At least one contributor must be eligible and they must jointly agree what share of PLR each will take based on contribution. This agreement is necessary even if one or two are ineligible or do not wish to register for PLR. The eligible authors will receive the share(s) specified in the application.

Translators. Translators may apply for a 30% fixed share (to be shared equally between joint translators).

Editors and compilers. An editor or compiler may apply to register a 20% share if they have written at least 10% of the book's content or more than ten pages of text in addition to normal editorial work and are named on the title page. Alternatively, editors may register 20% if they have a royalty agreement with the publisher. In the case of joint editors/compilers, the total editor's share should be divided equally.

Audiobooks. PLR shares in audiobooks are fixed by the UK scheme and may not be varied. *Writers* may register a fixed 60% share in an audiobook, providing that it has not been abridged or translated. In cases where the writer has made an additional contribution (e.g. as narrator), she/he may claim both shares. *Narrators* may register a fixed 20% PLR share in an audiobook. *Producers* may register a fixed 20% share in an audiobook. *Abridgers* (in cases where the writer's original text has been abridged prior to recording as an audiobook) qualify for 12% (20% of the writer's share). *Translators* (in cases where the writer's original text has been translated from another language) qualify for 18% (30% of the writer's share). If there is more than one writer, narrator, etc the appropriate shares should be divided equally.

Dead or missing co-authors. Where it is impossible to agree shares with a co-author because that person is dead or untraceable, then the surviving co-author or co-authors may submit an application to register a share which reflects their individual contribution to the book.

Transferring PLR after death. First applications may not be made by the estate of a deceased author. However, if an author registers during their lifetime the PLR in their books can be transferred to a new owner and continues for up to 70 years after the date of their death. The new owner can apply to register new titles if first published one year before, or up to ten years after, the date of the author's death. New editions of existing registered titles can also be registered posthumously.

Residential qualifications. To register for the UK PLR scheme, at the time of application authors must have their only home or principal home in the UK or in any of the other countries within the European Economic Area (i.e. EC member states plus Iceland, Norway and Liechtenstein).

Eligible books

In the PLR system each edition of a book is registered and treated as a separate book. A book is eligible for PLR registration provided that:
- it has an eligible author (or co-author);
- it is printed and bound (paperbacks count as bound);
- it has already been published;
- copies of it have been put on sale, i.e. it is not a free handout;

- the authorship is personal, i.e. not a company or association, and the book is not crown copyright;
- it has an ISBN;
- it is not wholly or mainly a musical score;
- it is not a newspaper, magazine, journal or periodical.

Audiobooks. An audiobook is defined as an 'authored text' or 'a work recorded as a sound recording and consisting mainly of spoken words'. Applications can therefore only be accepted to register audiobooks which meet these requirements and are the equivalent of a printed book. Music, dramatisations and live recordings do not qualify for registration. To qualify for UK PLR in an audiobook contributors should be named on the case in which the audiobook is held; or be able to refer to a contract with the publisher; or be named within the audiobook recording.

Ebooks. Previously only ebooks downloaded to fixed terminals in library premises and then taken away on loan on portable devices to be read elsewhere qualified for PLR payment. Information provided by libraries suggested that the vast majority of ebook and digital audio lending was carried out 'remotely' to home PCs and mobile devices, which meant the loan did not qualify for PLR.

On 27 April 2017 the Digital Economy Bill, which included provision to extend the UK PLR legislation to include remote loans of ebooks from public libraries, received Royal Assent. The new arrangements took effect officially from 1 July 2018, and remote ebook loans data is now collected, and the first payments arising from the newly eligible loans were made in February 2020. The PLR website provides updated information on this legislation.

Statements and payment

Authors who have registered their email address may view their statement online. Only registered authors with an offline account and no registered email address receive a statement posted to their address, if a payment is due.

Sampling arrangements

To help minimise the unfairness that arises inevitably from a sampling system, the scheme specifies the eight regions within which authorities and sampling points have to be designated and includes libraries of varying size. Prior to an amendment to legislation that came into force October 2024, part of the sample drops out by rotation each year to allow fresh libraries to be included. Since the amendment, once included in the sample a library will stay in the sample. The aim is to slowly transition to full public library loans data collection over the next few years. The following library authorities were designated for the year 1 July 2024–30 June 2025 (all are multi-site authorities). This list is based on the nine government regions for England plus Northern Ireland, Scotland and Wales. The composition of the PLR library authority sample changes annually and not all regions have to be represented each year.

- East – Bedford, Cambridgeshire, Central Bedfordshire, Lincolnshire, Norfolk, Peterborough, Suffolk, Southend-on-Sea
- East Midlands – Derbyshire, Leicester City, Leicestershire, North Northamptonshire, Nottinghamshire, West Northamptonshire

- London – Bexley, Brent, Bromley, Camden, City of London, Croydon, Ealing, Enfield, Hammersmith and Fulham, Haringey, Harrow, Havering, Hillingdon, Hounslow, Islington, The Royal Borough of Kensington and Chelsea (RBKC), Lambeth, Merton, Newham, Redbridge, Richmond Upon Thames, Southwark, Sutton, Tower Hamlets, Waltham Forest, Wandsworth, Westminster
- North East – Darlington, Durham, Gateshead, Hartlepool, Middlesborough, Newcastle, North Tyneside, South Tyneside, Stockton-on-Tees
- North West and Merseyside – Blackburn-with-Darwen, Blackpool, Bolton, Cheshire West, Chester, Cumberland, Halton, Knowsley, Liverpool, Manchester, Oldham, Rochdale, Sefton, St Helens, Stockport, Tameside, Warrington, Westmoreland and Furness, Wigan, Wirral
- South East – Brighton and Hove, Buckinghamshire, East Sussex, Kent, Luton, Medway, Oxfordshire, Portsmouth, Southampton, Surrey, West Berkshire, Windsor and Maidenhead
- South West – Cornwall, Devon, Gloucestershire, Hampshire, Isle of Wight, Plymouth, Swindon, Torbay, Wiltshire, Worcestershire
- West Midlands – Coventry, Sandwell, Shropshire, Solihull, Staffordshire, Stoke-on-Trent, Warwickshire, Wolverhampton
- Yorkshire and The Humber – Barnsley, Bradford, Doncaster, Kingston Upon Hull, Kirklees, Leeds, North Lincolnshire, North Yorkshire, Rotherham, Sheffield, Wakefield
- Northern Ireland – The Northern Ireland Library Authority
- Scotland – Aberdeen, Angus, Clackmannanshire, Dumfries and Galloway, Dundee, East Ayrshire, East Dumbartonshire, East Lothian, East Renfrewshire, Glasgow, Highland, Inverclyde, Moray, North Ayrshire, North Lanarkshire, Orkney, Perth and Kinross, Shetland, South Ayrshire, South Lanarkshire, Stirling, West Dumbartonshire, West Lothian
- Wales – Bridgend, Caerphilly, Cardiff, Carmarthenshire, Ceredigion, Conwy, Denbighshire, Gwynedd, Methyr Tydfil, Monmouthshire, Neath Port Talbot, Pembrokeshire, Powys, Rhondda Cynon Taf, Swansea, Torfaen, Wrexham

Participating local authorities are reimbursed on an actual cost basis for additional expenditure incurred in providing loans data to the PLR Office. The extra PLR work mostly consists of modifications to computer programs to accumulate loans data in the local authority computer and to transmit the data to the PLR Office.

Reciprocal arrangements

Reciprocal PLR arrangements now exist with the German, Dutch, Austrian and other European PLR schemes. Authors can apply for overseas PLR for most of these countries through the ALCS (Authors' Licensing and Collecting Society; see page 413). The exception to this rule is Ireland. Authors should now register for Irish PLR through the UK PLR Office. Further information on PLR schemes internationally and recent developments within the EC towards wider recognition of PLR is available from the PLR Office or on the international PLR website.

Libraries

Libraries are not just repositories for books and a source of reference, they provide an increasing range of different services, using a multitude of media to reach more diverse audiences. Countless writers attest to the importance of libraries in shaping and helping develop their creative ambitions. Local libraries are a good source of information about the writing process and how to get published. They often hold author events, reading groups and creative writing classes.

Note that the code needed for phoning UK libraries from overseas is +44.

TYPES OF LIBRARIES

- **Public libraries** are accessible to the general population and are usually funded by a local or district council. They typically offer a mix of lending and reference facilities. Public libraries are distinct from research libraries, subscription libraries and other specialist libraries in terms of their funding and access, but may offer some of the same facilities to visitors. Public library services are facing financial challenges and cuts to funding, so many library authorities are looking for new approaches to working with communities in order to build sustainable library services for the future.
- Most **community libraries** are part of the local public library network and many are considered part of the statutory library provision. Most authorities have found ways to ensure that community libraries can remain part of their network, often including the library management system. A list of community libraries in the UK can be found at www.publiclibrariesnews.com. Consult this website to find your nearest and local UK public and community libraries: www.gov.uk/local-library-services.
- An **academic library** is usually affiliated to an educational institution and primarily serves the students and faculty of that institution. Many are accessible to the public.
- A **subscription library** is one that is funded via membership or endowments. Access is often restricted to members but membership is sometimes extended to groups who are non-members, such as students.
- Many libraries belong to the Association of Independent Libraries and a list of members can be found on the Association's website (see below).

SOME OF THE BEST

Britain has such a wealth of comprehensive and historic libraries that a full list of them is not possible in this publication. Here is just a small selection of public libraries with outstanding collections in the UK.

Barbican Library
Barbican Centre, Silk Street, London EC2Y 8DS
tel 020-7638 0569
email barbicanlib@cityoflondon.gov.uk
website www.barbican.org.uk/your-visit/during-your-visit/library
Facebook www.facebook.com/Barbicanlibrary
X @barbicanlib

The largest of London's lending libraries with a strong arts and music section, a children's library, a London collection, literature events programme and reading groups.

Belfast Central Library
Royal Avenue, Belfast BT1 1EA
tel 028-9050 9150
email belfast.central@librariesni.org.uk
website www.librariesni.org.uk/libraries/greater-belfast/belfast-central-library
Facebook www.facebook.com/BelfastCentralLibrary
X @BelfastCentLib

The library holds the greatest number of titles in Northern Ireland. The library houses a number of special collections including a digital film archive and the Northern Ireland Music Archive.

Library of Birmingham
Centenary Square, Broad Street, Birmingham B1 2ND
tel 0121 242 4242
email enquiries@libraryofbirmingham.com
website www.birmingham.gov.uk/info/50132/visiting_the_library_of_birmingham
Facebook www.facebook.com/libraryofbirmingham
X @LibraryofBham
Instagram @the_library_of_birmingham

The largest public library in the UK and the largest regional library in Europe. Houses locally relevant collections of archives, photography and rare books. Facilities include an art gallery space. It is also home to the BFI Mediatheque, providing free access to the National Film Archive.

Bristol Central Library
Deanery Road, City Centre, Bristol BS1 5TL
tel 0117 903 7250
email bristol.library.service@bristol.gov.uk
website www.bristol.gov.uk/libraries-archives/central-library
Instagram @thelibrarybrisol

Includes collections related to Bristol's slave trade, 19th-century travel and art. An appointment must be made by email or phone five working days in advance to view rare items.

Canterbury Library
18 High Street, Canterbury, Kent CT1 2RA
tel 03000 413131
email canterburylibrary@kent.gov.uk
website www.kent.gov.uk/libs
Facebook www.facebook.com/KentLibrariesArchives
Instagram @canterburylibrary

The main library for the city of Canterbury. Canterbury Library was the first publicly funded library in Great Britain, through innovative interpretation of the Museums Act 1845 for provision of a museum of arts and science. It is now part of a large network of public libraries managed by Kent County Council. For services see website.

Cardiff Central Library
The Hayes, Cardiff CF10 1FL
tel 029-2038 2116
email centrallibrary@cardiff.gov.uk
website https://cardiffhubs.co.uk/hub/central-library-hub/
Facebook www.facebook.com/cardifflibraryservice
X @cdflibraries
Instagram @central_library_hub

The largest public library in Wales, opened in 2009, houses 90,000 books, 10,000 of which are in Welsh.

Leeds Library
18 Commercial Street, Leeds LS1 6AL
tel 0113 245 3071
email enquiries@theleedslibrary.org.uk
website www.theleedslibrary.org.uk
Facebook www.facebook.com/leedslibrary
X @theleedslibrary
Instagram @theleedslibrary

Founded in 1768 as a proprietary subscription library, it is now the oldest surviving example of this sort of library in the UK. It includes specialist collections in travel, topography, biography, history and literature. There are long runs of periodicals, popular novels, children's books, and Civil War pamphlets and Reformation Tracts. About 1,500 new books and audio/visual items are added every year.

Liverpool Central Library
William Brown Street, Liverpool L3 8EW
tel 0151 233 3069
email refbt.central.library@liverpool.gov.uk
website https://liverpool.gov.uk/libraries/explore-central-library/central-library/

The collection includes 15,000 rare books, some of which date back to the 13th century.

London Library
14 St James's Square, London SW1Y 4LG
tel 020-7766 4700
email reception@londonlibrary.co.uk
website www.londonlibrary.co.uk
Facebook www.facebook.com/thelondonlibrary
X @thelondonlib
Bluesky @thelondonlibrary.bsky.social
Instagram @thelondonlibrary

A subscription lending library containing over one million books and periodicals in over 50 languages, the collection includes works from 1700 to the latest publications in print and electronic form. Over 6,000 new books are added each year. Membership is open to all. The library's emerging writers' programme offers writers, in all genres, one year's free membership of The London Library and includes writing development masterclasses, literary networking opportunities, peer support and guidance in use of the Library's resources. For details: www.londonlibrary.co.uk/about-us/ll-emerging-writers.

Manchester Central Library
St Peter's Square, Manchester M2 5PD
tel 0161 234 1983
email libraries@manchester.gov.uk
website www.manchester.gov.uk/centrallibrary
Instagram @manchestercentrallibrary

Manchester's main library, the second biggest public lending library in the UK, houses a number of specialist collections such as Elizabeth Gaskell, Bellot Chinese and Thomas Penson De Quincey collections.

Mitchell Library
North Street, Glasgow G3 7DN
tel 0141 287 2999
email libraries@glasgowlife.org.uk
website www.glasgowlife.org.uk/libraries/venues/the-mitchell-library
Facebook www.facebook.com/GlasgowLibraries
X @GlasgowLib

One of the largest public reference library in Europe housing over one million items. Holds an unrivalled collection of material relating to the city of Glasgow. To contact the special collections team, email specialcollections@glasgowlife.org.uk or phone 0141 287 2988.

Newcastle City Library
Charles Avison Building, 33 Newbridge Street West, Newcastle upon Tyne NE1 8AX
tel 0191 277 4100
email information@newcastle.gov.uk
website https://new.newcastle.gov.uk/libraries/find-library/city-library
Facebook www.facebook.com/NewcastleLibraries
X @ToonLibraries

Newcastle's main public library includes a café, exhibition spaces, a rare books and watercolours collection, a viewing deck and six floors of books.

Westminster Reference Library

35 St Martin's Street, London WC2H 7HP
tel 020-7641 6200 (press 2)
email referencelibrarywc2@westminster.gov.uk
website www.westminster.gov.uk/library-opening-times-and-contact-details/westminster-reference-library
X @WCClibraries

Specialist public reference library with collections in performing arts and art and design. Hosts regular and varied events, includes an exhibition space and a Business Information Point. Also has a range of business resources including market research, company and legal databases. Includes collection from Westminster Music Library.

LIBRARIES OF LEGAL DEPOSIT IN THE UK AND IRELAND

A library of legal deposit is a library that has the power to request (at no charge) a copy of anything published in the UK. There are six legal deposit libraries in the UK and Ireland. To obtain a copy of a book, five out of the six legal deposit libraries must make a request in writing to a publisher within one year of publication of a book, newspaper or journal. This request comes via the Agency for the Legal Deposit Libraries and they distribute the five books to the individual locations. Different rules apply to the British Library in that all UK libraries and Republic of Ireland publishers have a legal responsibility to send a copy of each of their publications to the library, without a written request being made (although they may receive an electronic notification). The British Library is the only legal deposit library with its own Legal Deposit Office. Since April 2013, legal deposit also covers material published digitally and online, so that the legal deposit libraries can provide a national archive of the UK's non-print published material, such as websites, blogs, e-journals and CDs.

The Agency for the Legal Deposit Libraries (ALDL)

21 Marnin Way, Edinburgh EH12 9GD
tel 0131 334 2833
email publisher.enquiries@legaldeposit.org.uk
website www.legaldeposit.org.uk

The ALDL requests and receives copies of publications for distribution to five major libraries (not the British Library). It is maintained by five legal deposit libraries and ensures that they receive legal deposit copies of British and Irish publications. The agency must request copies on behalf of the libraries within 12 months of the date of publication. On receiving such a request, a publisher must supply a copy for each of the requesting libraries under the terms of the Legal Deposit Libraries Act 2003 (UK) and the Copyright and Related Rights Act 2000 (Ireland).

Bodleian Libraries of the University of Oxford

Broad Street, Oxford OX1 3BG
tel (01865) 277162
email reader.services@bodleian.ox.ac.uk
website www.bodleian.ox.ac.uk
Facebook www.facebook.com/bodleianlibraries
X @bodleianlibs
Instagram @bodleianlibrary

With over 13 million items, the Bodleian Libraries together form the second-largest library in the UK after the British Library, and is the main reference library of Oxford University. It is one of the oldest libraries in Europe. It holds special collections in classics and ancient history, English, history, history of science, local history, philosophy, reference, theology and patristics.

The British Library

St Pancras Building, 96 Euston Road,
London NW1 2DB
Legal Deposit Office: The British Library, Boston Spa, Wetherby, West Yorkshire LS23 7BQ
email legal-deposit-books@bl.uk
website www.bl.uk
Facebook www.facebook.com/britishlibrary
X @BritishLibrary
Instagram @britishlibrary

Cambridge University Library

West Road, Cambridge CB3 9DR
tel (01223) 333000
email library@lib.cam.ac.uk
website www.lib.cam.ac.uk
Instagram @cambridgeuniversitylibrary

Cambridge University Library houses its own collection and also comprises four other libraries within the university. The library dates back to the 15th century and now has a collection of over ten million items in electronic and physical formats. It is the only legal deposit library that keeps a large percentage of its books on Open Access. To visit the rare books collection email: rarebooks@lib.cam.ac.uk.

National Library of Scotland

Edinburgh (main location): George IV Bridge, Edinburgh EH1 1EW
tel 0131 623 3700
email enquiries@nls.uk
Glasgow (Kelvin Hall): 1445 Argyle Street, Glasgow G3 8AW
tel 0141 880 2329

website www.nls.uk
Facebook www.facebook.com/NationalLibraryOfScotland
X @natlibscot
Instagram @natlibscot

The National Library of Scotland holds over 34 million items. It is the world's central source for research relating to Scotland and the Scots. The library also holds a copy of the Gutenberg Bible, a First Folio of Shakespeare and the last letter written by Mary Queen of Scots. It contains important items relating to Jane Austen, Lord Byron and Sir Arthur Conan Doyle. The library is based in both Edinburgh and Glasgow. The George IV Bridge site in Edinburgh houses the main reading rooms, events centre and registration. The map rooms are at the Causewayside site (33 Salisbury Place, Edinburgh, EH9 1SL). The moving image archive can be found at the Kelvin Hall, Glasgow site.

National Library of Wales
Aberystwyth, Ceredigion SY23 3BU
tel (01970) 632800
email gofyn@llgc.org.uk
website www.library.wales
Facebook www.facebook.com/llgcymranlwales
X @nlwales

The National Library of Wales was established in 1907 and holds over 6 million books and newspapers, including many important works such as the first book printed in Welsh and the first Welsh translation of the Bible.

Trinity College Library Dublin
College Green, Dublin 2, Republic of Ireland
tel +353 (0)1 896 1127
email library@tcd.ie
website www.tcd.ie/library
Facebook www.facebook.com/tcdlibrary
X @tcdlibrary
Instagram @tcdlibrary

Trinity College Library is the largest library in Ireland and is home to the *Book of Kells* – two of the four volumes are on permanent public display. The library houses sound recordings, maps, databases, and a digital collection. Currently it has over seven million printed volumes with extensive collections of journals, manuscripts, maps and music reflecting over 400 years of academic development.

DESIGNATED OUTSTANDING COLLECTIONS

The Designated Outstanding Collections scheme was established in 1997 by the Museums and Galleries Commission to identify collections of national and international importance in non-national museums and galleries. In 2005 the scheme was extended to include libraries and archives. The scheme is now administered by Arts Council England and there are currently 163 Designated Outstanding Collections in England. To find out if there is a Designated Outstanding Collection library near you: www.artscouncil.org.uk/designated-collections.

SPECIALIST LIBRARIES IN THE UK

Writers often need access to specialised information sources in order to research their work. The following are a sample of specialist libraries in the UK. In addition to the libraries listed below, many university libraries hold special collections which are accessible to the public, usually by appointment. Check individual university library websites for details.

ORGANISATIONS THAT SUPPORT LIBRARIES

There are many organisations which are affiliated to, and champion the use of libraries in the UK. These include:

APPG for Libraries Information & Knowledge in Parliament
tel 020-4513 2831
website www.cilip.org.uk/page/APPGLInK
Facebook www.facebook.com/CILIPinfo/wall
X @CILIPinfo
Instagram @clip_uk

The goal is to provide information and opportunities for debate about the important role libraries play in society and their future; to highlight the contribution that a wide variety of library and information services make, including those in public, school, government, health sector, colleges, private companies and university libraries; and to promote and discuss themes in the wider information and knowledge sector including the impact of technology, skills and training, professional standards and broader issues. There are separate divisions for Cymru Wales, Ireland and Scotland so please see website for divisional contact details.

Arts Council England
tel 0161 934 4317
website www.artscouncil.org.uk
X @ace_national
Instagram @aceagrams

The developmental agency for libraries in England and has responsibility for supporting and developing libraries. See also page 180.

Association of Independent Libraries
Church Lane, Doncaster DN5 7AU
email info@independentlibraries.co.uk
website http://independentlibraries.co.uk/
Facebook www.facebook.com/IndependentLibraries
X @indielibraries

Develops the conservation, restoration and public awareness of independent libraries in the UK. Together, its members possess over two million books and have many listed buildings in their care.

Association of Senior and Children's Education Librarians (ASCEL)
Wolverhampton Central Library, Snow Hill, Wolverhampton WV1 3AX
email info@ascel.org.uk
website www.ascel.org.uk
X @ASCELUK

A national membership network of Senior Children's and Education Librarians. It aims to stimulate innovation and share initiatives relating to children and young people using public libraries and educational services.

BookTrust
No. 1 Aire Street, Leeds LS1 4PR
email queries@booktrust.org.uk
website www.booktrust.org.uk
Facebook www.facebook.com/booktrust
X @Booktrust
Instagram @booktrust

Charitable organisation that aims to give everyone access to books from an early age and the chance to benefit from reading. The focus is on children from birth to the first years of primary school, particularly children from low-income or vulnerable backgrounds. As well as the Leeds office, there are offices in London, Cardiff and Belfast. See also page 318.

Chartered Institute of Library and Information Professionals (CILIP)
7 Ridgmount Street, London WC1E 7AE
tel 020-7255 0500
email info@cilip.org.uk
website www.cilip.org.uk
Facebook www.facebook.com/CILIPinfo
X @CILIPinfo
Instagram @cilip_uk

The leading professional body for librarians, information specialists and knowledge managers. Aims for a fair and economically prosperous society underpinned by literacy, access to information and the transfer of knowledge. A registered charity. Offices in London, Wales, Scotland and Northern Ireland.

Friends of Libraries
Many libraries in the UK have Friends of Libraries organisations affiliated to them that support library use through charitable means. Sometimes Friends groups are set up to campaign against a potential council closure or reduction in budget. They have been known to set up their own community libraries.

Friends of National Libraries
email info@fnlmail.org.uk
website www.fnl.org.uk
X @FNL313
Bluesky @thefnl.bsky.social

Has awarded thousands of grants to regional, specialist and national libraries that have acquired rare books, manuscripts archives and fine bindings which are now accessible to all.

Internet Library for Librarians
email info@itcompany.com
website www.itcompany.com/inforetriever/index.htm

One of the most popular information resource sites for librarians since 1994, an information portal specifically designed for librarians to locate internet resources related to their profession.

Libraries Connected
email info@librariesconnected.org.uk
website www.librariesconnected.org.uk
X @libsconnected
Bluesky @librariesconnected.bsky.social
Instagram @librariesconnected

A charity, previously known as the Society of Chief Librarians (SCL). Partly funded by Arts Council England as the Sector Support Organisation for libraries. This funding provides increased capacity with a new team of staff and trustees to work alongside members. Remains a membership organisation, made up of every library service in England, Wales and Northern Ireland.

Libraries Week
website www.librariesweek.org.uk

The first Libraries Day took place in February 2012 and is now a week-long annual event in the UK dedicated to the celebration of libraries and librarians. Green Libraries Week, which took place in October 2024 led by CILIP, was the first national celebration of libraries, across all sectors, from public libraries on the high street to national, health and academic libraries, where the focus was on the climate and sustainability. Each year, author talks and competitions are arranged by local authorities, universities, library services and local community groups.

The Library Campaign
email thelibrarycampaign@gmail.com
website www.librarycampaign.com

Aims to advance the lifelong education of the public by the promotion, support, assistance and improvement of libraries through the activities of Friends of Library groups and user groups.

Library Planet
website https://libraryplanet.net/
Instagram @library_planet

Libraries

A crowdsourced travel guide for the libraries of the world. The intention is to inspire library travellers. To contribute to Library Planet, please send an email to: booksofkells@live.com.au. See website for details on how to contribute and what to write.

National Literacy Trust
tel 020-7587 1842
email contact@literarytrust.org.uk
website www.literacytrust.org.uk
Facebook www.facebook.com/nationalliteracytrust
X @literacy_trust
Instagram @literacy_trust

Aims to improve reading, writing, speaking and listening skills in disadvantaged communities, in part through access to libraries. See also page 313.

Private Libraries Association
email info@plabooks.org
website www.plabooks.org
X @PLAbooks
Instagram @pla_books

An international society of book collectors and lovers of books. Publications include *The Private Library* (quarterly), annual *Private Press Books*, and other books on book collecting.

Public Library News
website www.publiclibrariesnews.com

Promotes knowledge about libraries in the UK.

The Reading Agency
website https://readingagency.org.uk/
Facebook www.facebook.com/readingagency
X @readingagency
Instagram @readingagency

Aims to give everyone an equal chance in life by helping people become confident and enthusiastic readers, and that includes supporting library use.

School Library Association (SLA)
1 Pine Court, Kembrey Park, Swindon SN2 8AD
tel (01793) 530166
email info@sla.org.uk
website www.sla.org.uk
Facebook www.facebook.com/schoollibraryassociation
X @uksla
Instagram @uksla

The main goal is to support people involved with school libraries, promoting high-quality reading and learning opportunities for all. Founded 1937.

Software for writers

This is a selection of software programmes and applications designed to enhance your writing experience and aid productivity. Each product has its own selection of features; we recommend you check the cost carefully, as many involve a fixed-term subscription or licence fee but do also offer free trials.

WRITING SOFTWARE

Aeon Timeline
website https://timeline.app
£47.99 one-off fee

Includes tools and features to help you understand characters, avoid plot holes and inconsistencies, and visualise your story in new ways.

Atticus
website www.atticus.io
$147 one-off fee (exc. tax)

Allows authors to use the same platform for writing and formatting; writing can also be imported. A word counter and goal tracker allow you to monitor your progress.

Bear
website https://bear.app
Free; pro $2.29 monthly; $29.99 p.a.

A note-taking tool that allows you to link notes to create an outline and apply hashtags to organise notes, and provides a focus feature to aid concentration.

Bibisco
website https://bibisco.com
Community edition: free; supporters edition: pay what you want

Designed to allow a writer to focus on their characters and develop rounded and complex narratives, with particular emphasis on the manuscript's geographical, temporal and social context.

Dabble
website www.dabblewriter.com
From $9 monthly

Gives writers the freedom to plot, write and edit on a desktop, in a browser or offline, and automatically syncs all versions across your devices. Features include plot grids, progress tracking and goal setting.

Evernote
website https://evernote.com
Free; tiered from £6.66 monthly

Note-taking tool which allows you to sync notes across devices, identify tasks and assign schedules, mark-up webpages and add them to your notes along with documents, images, videos and audio files.

FocusWriter
website https://gottcode.org/focuswriter
Free

Provides a simple and distraction-free writing environment with a hide-away interface, so you can focus solely on your writing.

MasterWriter
website https://masterwriter.com/creative_writers
$9.95 monthly; $99.95 p.a.

An extensive catalogue of words and phrases that can help improve and enrich the vocabulary in your writing. The search function will return synonyms, words used in similar contexts, common phrases, rhymes and figures of speech.

Novel Factory
website www.novel-software.com
From $75 p.a.

Plan your book with confidence by using the Roadmap feature which provides tools and structures to suit your needs. Includes detailed character overviews including biographies and images, as well as scene tabs and writing statistics about your work.

Novel Suite
website www.novelsuite.com

Freely downloadable Novel Planner and Checklist guide, incorporating '16 steps' to help you structure your book. Novel Writing software available for a fee.

Novelize
website www.getnovelize.com
$9 monthly; $65 p.a.

Developed for fiction writers, this web-based writing app means you can work on your book anywhere on any device. Keep your research in one place in the notebook displayed on the writing screen and track your progress.

NovelPad
website https://novelpad.co
$15 monthly; $120 p.a.

A writing and editing application that provides plot boards, scene cards and a consistency checker which filters your writing for specific characters and plot lines.

Obsidian
website https://obsidian.md
Free

A mapping structure which helps writers to make new connections and identify relationships between ideas and key terms in order to create a coherent narrative.

Plottr
website https://plottr.com
$25 p.a.; $99 one-off fee

Created to aid book planning and story mapping. Tracks characters and plots for easy reference, provides templates for plot outlining and visualisation, and creates an automated outline of your writing.

Scrivener
website www.literatureandlatte.com/scrivener/overview
From £55 one-off fee

Tailored for long writing projects with everything you need housed in one place; it is a typewriter, ring binder and scrapbook, allowing you to optimise your digital workspace.

SmartEdit Writer
website www.smart-edit.com/Writer
Free

Organically build your book one scene or one chapter at a time, then drag and drop to arrange these on your document tree. Store your research images, URLs and notes alongside work for easy access, then export your manuscript into a single Word document when ready.

Ulysses
website https://ulysses.app
$5.99 monthly; $39.99 p.a.

Document management for all writing projects, with flexible export options including pdf, Word, ebook and HTML which are appropriately formatted and styled.

WriteItNow
website www.ravensheadservices.com
From $59.95 one-off fee

Includes sophisticated world-building features to create detailed and complex settings and characters. Recommends suitable names for your characters based on the historical period and geographical setting of your story.

EDITING SOFTWARE

After the Deadline
website www.afterthedeadline.com
Free

A context-driven grammar and spelling checker, it underlines potential issues and gives a suggestion with an explanation of how you can rectify the error.

AutoCrit
website www.autocrit.com
Free; pro from $30 monthly

Analyses your entire manuscript and suggests insightful improvements in the form of an individual summary report, showing where your strengths and weaknesses lie.

Ginger
website www.gingersoftware.com
From $4.99 monthly; $60 p.a

Combines a grammar checker with tools to improve your writing, including a synonym suggester and text rephrasing.

Grammarly
website www.grammarly.com
Free; premium from £10 monthly

Provides accurate and context-specific suggestions when the application detects grammar, spelling, punctuation, word choice and style mistakes in your writing.

Hemingway Editor
website https:/hemingwayapp.com
$19.99 one-off fee

Helps you write with clarity and confidence. This application is like a spellchecker but for style. It will highlight any areas that need tightening up by identifying adverbs, passive voice, and uninspiring or over-complicated words.

iA Writer
website https://ia.net/writer
From $29.99 one-off fee

Provides tools to help you improve your writing: syntax colour-coding identifies repetitive and extraneous text, text blocking allowing moving whole sections of text, and a style checker highlights cliches and weak phrases.

Linguix
website https://linguix.com
Free; pro $60 p.a.; $85 one-off fee

Combines a range of editing tools: checks your grammar, suggests ways to paraphrase your writing to make it more succinct and aids with style and flow for non-native English writers.

PerfectIt
website https://intelligentediting.com
From £7 monthly

Proofreading software which checks consistency, for example by applying style rules and highlighting undefined abbreviations.

ProWritingAid
website https://prowritingaid.com
Free; pro from £30 monthly; £120 p.a.; £399 one-off fee

For use via the web, or as an add-on to word processing software, it analyses your work for a multitude of potential issues such as passive voice, clichés, missing dialogue tags and pace, and suggests how you can rectify any errors or make style improvements.

SmartEdit
website www.smart-edit.com
Free

Software add-on Microsoft Word and runs 25 individual checks whilst you work, flagging areas that need attention, including highlighting repeated words, listing adverbs and foreign phrases used and identifying possible misused words.

Vellum
website https://vellum.pub
£159.99 (ebook only); £199.99 (ebook and print)

Print and ebook formatting package that provides templates for front and endmatter, styles pages and generates versions for different platforms. Allows the user to update ebooks after they have been published. Only available for Mac.

WordRake
website www.wordrake.com
From $149 p.a.

Automated in-line editing software to tighten and tone your work with one click.

Wordtune
website www.wordtune.com
Free; premium from $9.99 monthly

An extension which can be added to browsers, email providers, social media and Microsoft Word. Provides a rephrasing and rewriting tool and suggests ways to shorten sentences, expand your ideas and alter your tone.

Publishing services for independent authors

This is a selection of the expanding list of companies that offer editorial, production, marketing and distribution support predominantly (but not exclusively) for authors who want to publish independently. As with all the organisations mentioned in the *Yearbook*, we recommend that you check carefully what companies offer and their fees; also be aware of any minimum commitment requirements.

A longer list of companies and individuals who provide similar services is included in our subscription service: www.writersandartists.co.uk/shop/subscriptions.

POD = print on demand

BookPrinting UK
Remus House, Coltsfoot Drive, Woodston, Peterborough PE2 9BF
tel (01733) 898102
email info@bookprintinguk.com
website www.bookprintinguk.com
X @BookPrintingUK

Colour and b&w printing and POD books in a range of bindings. Can provide custom illustration and interior layout options, as well as typesetting. Supplies templates for formatting manuscript files before sending. Can also distribute print books direct to customers. Prints bookmarks, posters and flyers.

eBookPartnership.com
7 Bell Yard, London WC2A 2JR
email helpdesk@ebookpartnership.com
website www.ebookpartnership.com
X @ebookpartners

Ebook conversion service, producing digital files for authors, publishers and content owners worldwide. Also POD and worldwide distribution for clients, who can access daily reports and submit changes 24/7. Network includes retailers, subscription services and e-libraries. Founded 2010.

Fuzzy Flamingo
23 Haddonian Way, Market Harborough LE16 9GD
tel 07588 966425
email contact@fuzzyflamingo.co.uk
website https://fuzzyflamingo.co.uk/
Facebook www.facebook.com/FuzzyFlamingoDesign
X @FlamingoFuzzy
Editor Jen Parker

Design and editing services as well as self-publishing packages for children's and YA authors and multi-author collaborations.

Grosvenor House Publishing
Link House, 140 The Broadway, Tolworth, Surrey KT6 7HT
tel 020-8339 6060
website www.grosvenorhousepublishing.co.uk
Facebook www.facebook.com/GrosvenorHousePublishing
Founder Kim Cross

Publishes across a range of genres including children's and non-fiction in colour, b&w, POD, paperback, hardback and ebook formats. Offers a £795 publishing package which includes typesetting and five free print copies as well as an ISBN, and print and ebook distribution via online retailers. Marketing services include producing posters and postcards, and website set-up from template with two years' hosting. Ebook publishing costs £195 if the print edition of the book has been produced by the company and £495 otherwise. Print costs and royalties depend on book specification. A proofreading service is offered at a rate of £5 per 1,000 words. See website for full list of costs.

Jelly Bean Self-Publishing
Candy Jar Ltd, Mackintosh House, 136 Newport Road, Cardiff CF24 1DJ
tel 029-211 5702
email submissions@jellybeanselfpublishing.co.uk
website www.jellybeanselfpublishing.co.uk
Director Shaun Russell

Self-publishing imprint of Candy Jar Books. Bespoke services including editing, typesetting, illustration, cover design, audiobook production and marketing support. Can accommodate authors of various genres, budgets and timetables. Welsh Self-Publisher of the Year 2020. Founded 2012.

The JQ Ghostwriting Agency
17 Carlton House Terrace, London SW1Y 5AH
tel 07396 344505
email joey@jq-agency.co.uk
website www.jq-agency.co.uk
Editor Joey Quince

Specialist ghostwriter of memoir, sports memoir and historical fiction, taking authors from seed concept to final draft.

Kindle Direct Publishing
website https://kdp.amazon.com
Facebook www.facebook.com/KindleDirectPublishing
X @AmazonKDP

Ebook self-publishing and distribution platform for Kindle and Kindle Apps. Its business model offers up to a 70% royalty (on certain retail prices between $2.99–$9.99) in many countries and availability in Amazon stores worldwide. POD options are also available. Books are made exclusive to Amazon (which means they cannot be sold through an author's personal website, for example), but authors can share in the KDP every time the book is borrowed from the Kindle Owners' Lending Library.

Kobo Writing Life
email writinglife@kobo.com
website www.kobo.com/p/writinglife
Facebook www.facebook.com/KoboWritingLife
X @kobowritinglife
Instagram @kobo.writing.life

Ebook self-publishing platform where authors can upload manuscripts and cover images. These files are then converted into ebooks before being distributed through the Kobo Store. Authors are able to set pricing and DRM territories, as well as track sales. Royalty rates vary depending on price or territory; enquire directly. Free to join. Owned by Rakuten.

Little Steps
Vicarage House, 58–60 Kensington Church Street, London W8 4DB
email info@littlestepspublishing.co.uk
website www.littlestepspublishing.co.uk
Instagram @littlestepspublishinguk

Provides a complete service for the aspiring children's author, including printing, design, marketing, editing, proofreading, public relations, production and distribution. Authors invest financially in their own books, entitling them to receive majority royalties. Founded in the UK 2019; has been operating for over 10 years in Australia.

PublishNation
Suite 544, Kemp House, 152 City Road, London EC1V 2NX
email david@publishnation.co.uk
website www.publishnation.co.uk
Publisher David Morrison

Offers POD paperback and Kindle format ebooks, available through Amazon. Publication in both print and digital formats costs £495 or £215 for Kindle format. Images may be included from £3.95 each. A range of book sizes is available, as are free template book covers. Enhanced cover design costs £40. Marketing services include creation of a press release, social media accounts and author website. Standard proofreading is £8 per 1,000 words, while an 'express' option from £125 focuses on the beginning of the manuscript. Editorial critique reports range in price from £99 for manuscripts of up to 15,000 words to £219 for manuscripts of up to 120,000 words.

SilverWood Books
14 Small Street, Bristol BS1 1DE
tel 0117 910 5829
email enquiries@silverwoodbooks.co.uk
website www.silverwoodbooks.co.uk
X @SilverWoodBooks
Publishing Director Helen Hart

Complete self-publishing service for adult and children's books (including picture books), from manuscript feedback to editing and proofreading, professional cover and page design, typesetting, ebook hand-formatting and conversion, b&w and colour POD, short-run and lithographic printing, one-to-one support and coaching. Distributes to bookshops via wholesalers and to online retailers including Amazon. See website for price information.

Socciones Literary Consultancy
tel (01792) 687867
email info@socciones.co.uk
website www.socciones.co.uk/contact

Offers design, editing, and publishing services centred around the Amazon publishing ecosystem, with packages for fiction, non-fiction and children's books.

The Stardust Experience
email alex@thestardustexperience.com
website www.thestardustexperience.com
Facebook www.facebook.com/thestardustexperience
Instagram @the.stardust.experience
Creative Director Zoe Peart-Johnson

Works with both traditionally published writers and independent authors around the world, providing a range of ghostwriting services for children's books, including idea creation, outlining, developmental editing, writing picture books and writing chapter books. Editorial support also available. Prices for writing start from £195: see website for cost estimates, depending on requirements.

Tim Saunders Publications
49 Church Close, Locks Heath, Southampton, Hampshire SO31 6LR
tel (01489) 808621
email tsaunderspubs@gmail.com
website https://tsaunderspubs.weebly.com/

Offers a range of publishing services, including editorial and marketing support for adult and children's titles. Also monthly flash fiction, poetry and short story writing challenges: Four Words, Idea,

Proverbs, Title and Writing Prompt (accepted submissions published on website and in anthologies). Ongoing opportunities to contribute poetry and short stories to anthologies on various subjects.

Troubador
Troubador Publishing Ltd, Unit E2,
Airfield Business Park, Market Harborough,
LE16 7UL
tel 0116 279 2299
email books@troubador.co.uk
website www.troubador.co.uk
Facebook www.facebook.com/matadorbooks
X @matadorbooks
Instagram @troubador_publishing
Managing Director Alex Thompson, *Operations Director* Chloe May

Publishing services for independent authors. Offers support with editorial, marketing and sales and distribution activities. See website for pricing examples. Founded 1999.

Children's writing courses and conferences

Contact your local library, college or university for further information about the courses that might be most suited to you and the stage you are at with your writing. While many courses are now going ahead in person once more, some may have an online component.

Curtis Brown Creative
Cunard House, 15 Regent Street, London SW1Y 4LR
tel 020-7393 4266
email help@curtisbrowncreative.co.uk
website www.curtisbrowncreative.co.uk
Facebook www.facebook.com/CurtisBrownCreative
X @cbcreative
Bluesky @cbcreative.bsky.social
Instagram @curtisbrowncreative

The only creative writing school run by a major literary and talent agency (The Curtis Brown Group). Offers courses in London and online. Over 250 students to date have subsequently signed publishing deals; alumni include Bonnie Garmus, Julia Armfield, Lucy Rose and Sean Lusk. Subjects covered include fiction, short stories, children's fiction (YA, middle grade and picture books), memoir and screenwriting. Curtis Brown Creative also runs the Breakthrough Writers' Programme, which offers free courses, mentoring and scholarships for under-represented writer

The Federation of Children's Book Groups Conference
email conference@fcbg.org.uk
website www.fcbg.org.uk/conference
Facebook www.facebook.com/fcbgnews
X @FCBGnews
Takes place April

Held annually, guest speakers include well-known children's authors as well as experts and publishers in the field of children's books. Publishers also exhibit their newest books and resources.

The Golden Egg Academy
The Wool House, 6 Cork Street, Frome, Somerset BA11 1BL
email info@goldeneggacademy.co.uk
website www.goldeneggacademy.co.uk
Facebook www.facebook.com/GoldenEggAcademy
Instagram @thegeacademy
Founder and Managing Director Imogen Cooper

Runs writing courses for authors who want to develop their writing to publication standard. All courses are run online and include: Write Your Successful Children's Novel; Writing for Children and Young Adults; Work on Your Novel; How to be a Picture Book Writer; and Writing Picture Books for Young Children. Selective courses comprise virtual workshops, one-to-one editorial surgeries and regular online group seminars.

Students also have the opportunity to meet industry professionals and benefit from presentations by some of the best writers in their field. Middle grade and YA fiction writers enjoy an exclusive non-binding 'First Look' deal with Chicken House; Lower Middle Grade with Scholastic/Chicken House and Young Series Fiction with Nosy Crow; picture book writers with Andersen Press. Also runs the Golden Egg Award for BAME, LGBTQ+, disabled and financially disadvantaged groups.

IBBY Congress
Nonnenweg 12, CH-4055 Basel, Switzerland
tel +41 (0)61 272 2917
email info@ibbycongress2024.org
website www.ibbycongress2024.org/
Instagram @ibby.international

IBBY's biennial international congresses bring together IBBY (the International Board on Books for Young People) members and other people involved in children's books and reading development from all over the world. The congresses are excellent occasions to make contacts, exchange ideas and open horizons. Every two years a different National Section hosts the Congress. Several hundred people attend the lectures, panel discussions, seminar sessions and workshops on current congress themes. An IBBY International Congress also serves as a framework not only for the General Assembly and other meetings, but also for the presentation of different exhibitions and celebrations such as the Hans Christian Andersen Awards and the IBBY Honour List.

Jericho Writers
Box 321, 266 Banbury Road, Oxford OX2 7DL
tel 0345 459 9560, +1 646-974-9060 (US)
email info@jerichowriters.com
website https://jerichowriters.com
Instagram @jerichowriters
Founder Harry Bingham

Inclusive online writing organisation offering editorial services and events for all genres, including writing for children, and tutored courses. Also available: guidance for self-publishers, masterclasses,

Children's writing courses and conferences

agent one-to-ones, a free community for writers to connect, and expert guides to writing and publishing. See website for information on Festival of Writing.

The London School of Journalism
tel 020-7432 8140
email enquiries@lsj.org
website www.lsj.org/courses/distance-learning/writing-for-children

Part of the School's distance learning programme, the year-long Writing for Children course guides the writer as they work in their chosen genre, including picture books, story books, early readers, teenage fiction, activity books, non-fiction and books for the education market. Students will learn how to construct a story that children will enjoy reading, including how to create believable characters and realistic dialogue.

Oxford University Short Courses
Department for Continuing Education, 1 Wellington Square, Oxford OX1 2JA
tel (01865) 270360
email enquiries@conted.ox.ac.uk
website www.conted.ox.ac.uk
Instagram @oxfordconted

Online and in-person creative writing courses including Creative Writing and Writing Fiction for Young Adults. Courses range from day schools to weekly learning programmes.

SCBWI-BI Annual Conference and Masterclass Series
email scbwi@scbwi.org
website https://britishisles.scbwi.org/conference
website www.scbwi.org
Instagram @scbwi
Executive Director Sarah Baker

Annual series of author masterclasses, fiction and picture book retreats and conference, offering a mix of craft-based seminars, industry professional one-to-ones, inspiration and networking opportunities for writers and author/illustrators, both published and unpublished. Check website for information on future events.

SCBWI-BI Writers' Events
email araevents@britishscbwi.org
website www.scbwi.org/regions/british-isles
Instagram @scbwi_british_isles

Online listings of retreats and other writing and literary events across the UK organised by the Society of Children's Book Writers and Illustrators.

Tŷ Newydd Writing Centre
Tŷ Newydd, Llanystumdwy, Criciech, Gwynedd LL52 0LW
tel (01766) 522811
email tynewydd@literaturewales.org
website www.tynewydd.wales
Instagram @canolfantynewydd

Residential creative writing courses for writers of all abilities over the age of 16. Course topics range from poetry and popular fiction to writing for the theatre and developing a novel for young adults. No qualifications are necessary; staff can advise on the suitability of courses. Also offers courses for schools, corporate courses and awaydays for companies. Tŷ Newydd is home to Nant, the writers' retreat cottage located on site. Run by Literature Wales, the national organisation for the development of literature in Wales.

Writers & Artists
Bloomsbury Publishing plc, 50 Bedford Square, London WC1B 3DP
tel 020-7631 5985
email writersandartists@bloomsbury.com
website www.writersandartists.co.uk
Facebook www.facebook.com/WritersArtistsYearbook
X @Writers_Artists
Instagram @writers_artists_
Contacts James Rennoldson, Clare Povey, Amelia Brown

Hosts online and offline masterclasses, conferences and writing courses throughout the year. Masterclasses and conferences are run independently or in collaboration with literary festivals, universities and charities such as Book Aid International, Literature Works and the Open University. A series of events dedicated to writing and illustrating books for children and young adults is held in March each year. Online writing courses – which cover a variety of genres – take place on weekday evenings.

Also offers a range of editing services, and works regularly with literary agents to provide guidance on the submission process. The W&A platform is free to join, contains hundreds of writing and publishing advice articles, and offers a lively community area and personalisation features. Financial assistance on selected events and services made available each year.

The Writers' Summer School at Swanwick, Derbyshire
c/o Old Farmhouse, Station Road, Ulceby, N. Lincs DN39 6TT
tel 07827 671735
email secretary@swanwickwritersschool.org.uk
website www.swanwickwritersschool.org.uk
Facebook www.facebook.com/SwanwickWriters
X @swanwickwriters

Extensive choice of courses, talks and workshops. Offers several highly subsidised places for writers aged between 18 and 30, and assistance for writers unable to afford the full course fee. Full details of the programme and information on how to apply for the TopWrite Programme and Assisted Places Scheme are available on the website.

UNIVERSITY COURSES

Bath Spa University
Newton Park, Newton St Loe, Bath BA2 9BN
tel (01225) 876180
email admissions@bathspa.ac.uk
website www.bathspa.ac.uk/courses/course-index-a-z/

Offers a variety of postgraduate courses on subjects including Creative Writing, Writing for Young People, Travel and Nature Writing, Scriptwriting, and Children's Publishing.

University of Central Lancashire
School of Arts and Media,
University of Central Lancashire, Preston PR1 2HE
tel (01772) 893364
email mstuart1@uclan.ac.uk
website www.uclan.ac.uk/postgraduate/courses/childrens-book-illustration-ma

Offers MA Children's Book Illustration, a taught master's course which explores the practice of illustration for children's picture and story books, including graphic novels and other formats for children's publishing. The course is designed to encourage the pursuit of a unique and personal line of research into an artist's chosen area of children's book illustration. Many graduates have gone on to careers as published illustrators. The course runs both full and part time.

University of Chichester
Bishop Otter Campus, College Lane, Chichester,
West Sussex PO19 6PE
tel (01243) 816000
email h.frey@chi.ac.uk
email h.dunkerley@chi.ac.uk
website www.chi.ac.uk
Contacts Professor Hugo Frey (Head of Department), Professor Hugh Dunkerley (MA Creative Writing Programme Coordinator)

Offers BA, MA and PhD Creative Writing. Students work with practising writers. Specialisms include: novels, short stories, creative non-fiction, YA fiction, writing for children, fantasy and poetry.

Hosts regular visits by high-profile writers, editors and agents. Many students go on to publish and win prizes. Second in the country for Creative Writing Courses (*Guardian* University Guide 2023). Part-time or full-time study. MA begins 29 September 2025.

University of London, Goldsmiths
Goldsmiths, University of London,
London SE14 6NW
tel 020-7919 7171
website www.gold.ac.uk
Facebook www.facebook.com/GoldsmithsUoL
Instagram @goldsmithsuol

Postgraduate courses include Artists' Film and Moving Image, Art Psychotherapy, Art and Ecology, Arts and Learning, Black British Literature, Children's Literature, Children's Book Illustration, Computational Arts, Computer Games Art and Design, Creative and Life Writing, Creative Writing and Education, Curating, Digital Media, Dramaturgy and Writing for Performance, Film and Screen Studies, Filmmaking, Fine Art, Journalism, Performance Making, Audio, Radio and Podcasting, Script Writing and Translation.

The Manchester Writing School at Manchester Metropolitan University
Grosvenor East Building, Cavendish Street,
Manchester M15 6BG
tel 0161 247 2000
email writingschool@mmu.ac.uk
website www.mmu.ac.uk/writingschool
X @McrWritingSchl
Creative Director Professor Carol Ann Duffy, *Contact and Senior Lecturer (admission and general enquiries)* James Draper

Courses offered include Master of Fine Arts (MFA) and Master of Arts (MA) in Creative Writing with specialist routes in Novel, Poetry, Writing for Children & Young Adults, Scriptwriting and Creative Non-Fiction. Campus-based and international online distance learning, available to study full-time (MA: one year, MFA: two years) or part-time (MA: two years; MFA: three years). September and January enrolment. Scholarships available (including Joyce Nield Fund for non-UK Commonwealth students). Evening taught, with strong industry links. MFA students complete a full-length book/script. MA in Publishing presented in collaboration with industry partners. PhD in Creative Writing, including PhD by practice, and BA programmes also available.

Nottingham Trent University
School of Social Sciences, Clarendon Street,
Nottingham NG1 4FQ
tel 0115 848 4200
email rory.waterman@ntu.ac.uk
email hum.enquiries@ntu.ac.uk
website www.ntu.ac.uk/course/english-linguistics-creative-writing
X @ntuhum
Programme Leader Dr Rory Waterman

Offers a long-established and practice-based MA Creative Writing. Close links to the writing industry, an annual anthology, a programme of guest talks and workshops and many successful graduate writers. Diverse module options include: Fiction, Poetry, Writing for Stage, Radio and Screen, all taught by leading practitioners.

Plymouth Marjon University
Derriford Road, Plymouth, PL6 8BH
tel (01752) 636890

email admissions@marjon.ac.uk
website www.marjon.ac.uk/courses/ma-literature-for-children/
Course Leader Dr Leah Phillips

Offers MA Literature for Children and Young Adults, which includes creative writing modules.

University of Roehampton

Grove House, Roehampton Lane, London SW15 5PJ
tel 020-8392 3000
website www.roehampton.ac.uk/postgraduate-courses/childrens-literature-distance-learning
Facebook www.facebook.com/roehamptonuni
X @RoehamptonUni
Instagram @uni_roehampton

Postgraduate courses include Children's Literature.

University of Southampton

Avenue Campus, Highfield Road, Southampton, Hampshire SO17 1BF
tel 023-8059 5000
email enquiries@southampton.ac.uk
website www.southampton.ac.uk/courses/creative-writing-masters-ma
Course Leader Toby Litt

Offers MA Creative Writing, which includes modules on Writing for Young People, Scriptwriting, Fiction, Poetry and Narrative Non-Fiction. Lecturers include writers Rebecca Smith, Sarah Hayden, Carole Burns and Philip Hoare.

University of Suffolk

Waterfront Building, 19 Neptune Quay, Ipswich IP4 1QJ
tel (01473) 338833
email Lindsey.Scott@uos.ac.uk
website www.uos.ac.uk/courses/pg/ma-creative-and-critical-writing
X @UOSEnglish
Instagram @uosenglish
Course Leader Dr Lindsey Scott

The MA Creative and Critical Writing offers specialist modules and workshops focused on writing middle grade and YA fiction. Students are guided through the process of writing their opening chapters, an agent cover letter and a plot synopsis. Further MG/YA writing may be undertaken on the Dissertation Project module, enabling students to continue developing their novel-in-progress. A programme of events with industry professionals runs throughout the academic year, including the annual Suffolk Children's Literature Festival. This in-person event, held in May at the university's Waterfront campus provides agent talks, pitching sessions and author workshops for picture book, middle grade and young adult writers and illustrators.

Copyright and contracts
Copyright 101: top tips

Sarah Burton of the Society of Authors provides answers and advice for writers, illustrators and translators on copyright, with valuable tips on how to protect your work and avoid any pitfalls.

1. What is copyright, and what does 'in the public domain' mean?

Copyright is what allows you – whether you're an author, an illustrator or a translator – to control and make money from the exploitation of your work. A copyright owner has the exclusive right to copy the work, issue copies of the work to the public, rent or lend the work to the public, perform, show or play the work in public, communicate the work to the public, edit or adapt the work (including translation or dramatisation), sell or licence the copyright for use by others. Generally speaking, copyright in the UK lasts until 70 years after the end of the year of the creator's death. However, there are variations when it comes to unpublished or posthumously published works by older authors.

Copyright also gives you **moral rights**. You should check that your publishing contract upholds, rather than asks you to waive, your moral rights. These include:
- The right to be named as the author, translator or illustrator of your work. This right needs to be asserted in writing.
- The right to object to derogatory treatment, which means no one can distort or mutilate your work. In essence, significant changes cannot be made without your consent.
- The right of false attribution. This protects you from being named as the author of a work you did not create.
- There is also the moral right of privacy if someone is easily identifiable in a photograph or still from a film, taken for private purposes.

In the context of copyright, a work that is **in the public domain** is out of copyright and therefore can be freely used by anyone. Be careful when it comes to older works, though; for example, an old work that is out of copyright in the UK might still be protected in the USA.

2. Can I use quotations or images from other writers in my book?

You may wish to include quotations or images from in-copyright sources in your work. Be aware that you need to seek permission if you are using a 'substantial' amount of material from works that are in copyright. 'Substantial' is not defined in the Copyright Designs and Patents Act 1988 – but is a matter of fact and degree. It has often been said that the test is much more about quality than quantity. A short extract may be a vital part of a work. A few sentences taken from a long novel or biography are unlikely to constitute a 'substantial part', but a few lines of poetry may be. It can be helpful to imagine you are the rights holder – how would you feel about the proposed use?

There are some very specific circumstances, known as **copyright exceptions**, in which you can reproduce limited extracts from in-copyright works without consent, even if it's a substantial part.

You can quote without needing permission *if all of the following apply*:
- The use is 'fair dealing' (is the amount of the original being used reasonable and appropriate, and might it affect the market for the original work).
- The work you are quoting from has been previously published.
- You quote no more than is required by the specific purpose for which it is used.
- The use is genuinely for the purpose of quotation – for example in the context of criticism or review.
- You include proper acknowledgement (generally the title and author).

For a fuller explanation of fair dealing and copyright exceptions, the Society of Authors (SoA; see page 297) has a *Guide to Copyright Permissions* or you can find details on the Intellectual Property Office website (www.gov.uk/topic/intellectual-property/copyright).

If you are quoting from song lyrics or from films, some rights holders are notoriously rigorous about charging even for very short extracts, taking the view that any quotation, however short, is de facto 'substantial'. They often have deep pockets, can be litigious, and the fees they charge can be high. Even if they are overreaching, they are often large companies and you may wish to avoid a legal battle.

The use of an in-copyright work as an epigram will be regarded as substantial because its use is decorative, rather than forming an integral part of the text, and it would not be considered fair dealing.

3. I'm a self-published author and want to use a famous painting on the cover for my book. Is that okay?

If you wish to reproduce an in-copyright painting on the cover of your book, you will need permission. If you find an image online of the painting you want to use, do not assume it's copyright-free. You should also be aware that if you find a photograph of a painting, that photograph will have its own separate copyright for which permission is required. However, copyright in the photograph of an out-of-copyright work can be asserted only where the photographer has made free and creative choices, not if the photo is effectively a scan of an out-of-copyright work.

Whether or not a work of art is still in copyright, its owner (be they an individual, museum, picture library) may deny access or charge for their services of supplying or sourcing images. Such fees are separate from and in addition to any consent needed from a copyright owner.

If you're considering using a photograph of an identifiable living individual, you should be aware that people have a legal right not to have their privacy unreasonably invaded and you should not reproduce the photo without their consent.

4. How do I protect my story from plagiarism? Can I trust an agent or publisher I submit to?

Your work is automatically protected by copyright as soon as it is written or recorded, but it makes sense to keep drafts and notes should you ever need to prove ownership. Standard advice used to be for authors to post a copy to themselves and keep it unopened; now that most authors will have date-stamped digital files, that is rarely necessary. However, if you're uneasy, using the old-fashioned method will do no harm!

It's good practice to always mark your work with your name, the copyright symbol and the date when you submit. It's also sensible to make it clear you are submitting your work in strictest confidence (this means the recipient cannot share your work without your consent and gives you protection under the law of confidentiality) and send it to a named person, not e.g. 'the Editor'. Remember: there is no copyright in an idea or facts per se, but only in the unique arrangement of words you use to express those ideas or facts. You should therefore be particularly mindful of confidentiality when submitting ideas that are not fully developed.

Do your homework on any agent or publisher you wish to submit work to, and be wary of any unsolicited approach. It can be difficult to distinguish between legitimate offers and scams. The SoA is always happy to advise authors on any offer they receive.

5. When do I need to clear permissions for quotations and images in my book? Who does this – the author or the publisher?

Many contracts make the author responsible both for clearing and paying for permissions, and whether that is fair and/or negotiable depends on the work in question. It may be possible to negotiate with a publisher for them to cover the cost, share the cost, or pay upfront and deduct a corresponding sum from your royalties. If it's your responsibility, allow as much time as possible, particularly as your contract may say you need to deliver clearances at the same time as your book. Some publishers' permissions departments operate on a 12–16 week turnaround.

6. What can I do if I have written to seek permission but there has been no response from the rights holder?

If you're seeking permission for use of published material, it is best to write first to the publisher of the original edition of the book. Most publishers' websites tell you how to contact the Permissions Department. If the original publisher does not control the rights, it should let you know who does. The website for Writers, Artists and Their Copyright Holders (https://norman.hrc.utexas.edu/watch) is a very helpful resource. And if you still cannot discover or get a response from the rights holder, see the Intellectual Property Office's online guidance on **diligent search** (www.gov.uk/government/publications/orphan-works-diligent-search-guidance-for-applicants).

7. How do I earn money from a translation of my book or if a TV programme is made based on my story?

Anyone wishing to translate and publish your book in another language, or to create a TV, film or stage adaptation of your work, will need an agreement with you to do so and we would expect the terms of that agreement to include payment.

If you have granted translation rights and dramatisation rights to your publisher, they will handle any such deal on your behalf and split the income with you in the proportions agreed in your publishing contract. If you have retained the rights, either you or your agent (if you have one) will negotiate the deal directly. Members are welcome to consult the SoA on any proposed agreement.

8. My stories for 8–10 year-olds are retellings of fairy stories – do I need permission from anywhere to 'use' these original tales?

Very old tales, such as those first collected and published by Charles Perrault in the 17th century and the Brothers Grimm in the 19th century, are now out of copyright. But, as the nature of a fairy tale is to evolve each time someone writes it down, be careful you are not relying on an in-copyright version. An individual author's unique expression of a fairy tale will be protected, and permission is needed if you wish to reproduce a substantial amount of the text. Be mindful, too, of translations – even if the original work is out of copyright, a translation holds its own separate copyright and may still be protected.

9. If I forget to get permission to use a picture or quotation in my novel, will I be prosecuted?

You could be sued by a third party if you use a substantial amount of their in-copyright work without consent and therefore infringe their copyright. However, before taking legal action, any claimant must first take steps to settle the matter out of court. Anyone making a successful claim against you is entitled to claim the damage they have suffered by the infringement. Damages can be difficult to calculate, but typically they amount to the licence fee the claimant would have charged for authorised use; they could also include other sums, such as compensation for the loss of another contract due to the unauthorised use, or damage arising from the possibility of loss of reputation through a failure to credit the author.

Be aware in particular that rights holders of images often use detection agencies with software which searches the internet for unauthorised uses and, if any infringement is found, they pursue the matter aggressively.

10. I'm a YouTuber and use BookTok to advocate for children's books and reading. Do I need permission to read a(nother) writer's work online?

Yes, the usual rules apply: if you are reading a substantial amount of another author's work, you will need their permission to do so (or their publisher's, depending on who holds the relevant rights) unless you are confident that a copyright exception applies (see question 2 above).

This article is inevitably a brief summary of a very complex topic. Authors should also be aware of other potential danger areas, notably privacy, libel, trademarks and 'passing off'. The SoA's advisory team is always pleased to offer members confidential guidance on all business aspects of the writing profession.

Sarah Burton is Deputy Chief Executive at the Society of Authors (www.societyofauthors.org). She also leads the advisory team and advises members on all business aspects of the writing profession. As a coordinator of the Children's Writers and Illustrators Group, a special interest group within the SoA, she has a particular interest in industry issues affecting creators of children's books.

See also...
- Society of Authors, page 297
- Copyright Licensing Agency Ltd, page 411
- DACS (Design and Artists Copyright Society), page 415

Author–Publisher contracts

Publishing contracts can be lengthy; it's helpful to know what types of clauses they are likely to include and why they are there.

If you have an agent, they will negotiate your publishing contract on your behalf. Organisations such as the Society of Authors (see page 297) and WGGB (see page 300) offer contract review services. A contract is a legal agreement between two parties and exists to protect both author and publisher. It includes clauses on rights and obligations to avoid ambiguity as to the responsibilities of both parties. The clauses in your publishing contract are likely to include those listed below.

Definitions used throughout the contract will often be included at the beginning or in an appendix, and might include terms such as 'Net Receipts', 'Hybrid Product', 'First Serial', 'Territory' and 'Electronic Book'.

Legal operation and enforcement of the contract is covered by a few standard clauses, such as those relating to 'Interpretation', 'Arbitration', 'Confidentiality', 'Notices' and 'Entire Agreement'.

Free to publish

The author confirms that they are able to enter into the agreement and that the book they are writing is a unique, new property, their own work and will not contain any legally compromising material. Note that the first example below indicates the style of legalese in which your contract is likely to be couched:

Exclusivity 'The Author hereby grants to the Publishers during the legal term of copyright the sole and exclusive licence to publish the said work in volume form.'

Warranty and indemnity are confirmed, meaning the author states that they are freely able to enter into the agreement, is the sole author, owns the rights in the 'work' and that it is unique, i.e. has not been published elsewhere previously. It also confirms the work does not contain any libellous or defamatory material or content that isn't the author's to include, i.e. that is someone else's copyright and that the author has cleared permissions with the copyright holder for any part of somebody else's work being reproduced in the book. The author agrees to cover any legal costs, other fees or losses if they are in any way in breach of the warranty.

Territory

This is the geographical area where the book can be sold, for example UK and Europe, or North American, or World territories.

Rights

Legal Term is the period that the contract covers, from date of signature of the contract by both parties or until rights are reverted to the author.

Granting and Reversion is when an author agrees that the publisher is allowed to publish their Work during the legal term. Rights might revert (back to the author) automatically when sales dip below a minimum annual level, of say, 50 copies. An author may negotiate to have rights in their book reverted and will be able to purchase any remaining stock. At that stage the contract is also formally terminated.

Termination might also occur if either party breaches any of the terms of the contract, for example if the author fails to deliver a manuscript of the quality expected on time and if it is found to be plagiarised. Late delivery alone would not usually be grounds for termination, but an author should always inform the agent or publisher if a contracted delivery date cannot be fulfilled.

Copyright Notice and Infringement This covers how the author's name will appear in the book, i.e. © [name of author], 202X. These clauses confirm that copyright in the Work is the property of the author. They will also make it clear that, if the publisher decides to protect the copyright of a book insofar as it threatens the value of the rights sold to a publisher, the author will assist the publisher (at the publisher's expense).

Subsidiary rights include:
- Anthology and quotation rights
- Broadcast reading and audiobook rights
- Digital and electronic rights
- Dramatisation, film, documentary, television sound broadcasting video or other mechanical reproduction rights
- English language rights (royalty exclusive)
- First serial rights (e.g. in a magazine where an extract from an original Work is serialised or published)
- Large print, educational, reprint or paperback rights licensed to a book club or to another publisher
- Micrography reprography, merchandising and manufacturing rights
- Second serial rights (rights sold subsequent to the first serial rights, see above)
- Single-extract or digest or book condensation rights
- Translation rights (royalty exclusive)
- US rights (royalty exclusive)

Each set of rights will be subject to a royalty percentage, payable to the author when these rights have been exercised. Some rights are held back or retained by an agent or author, so they might be exploited at another time and be subject to negotiation with a third party after publication. These tend to be the potentially more lucrative rights if exploited, such as dramatisation and film, translation or audio. Some 'hybrid' authors will license print rights to a publisher but retain digital book rights to allow them to self-publish in that format; a contract would make clear in which territories each edition might be sold.

Practicalities

Delivery includes a realistic delivery date and the specifications as to what will be delivered in what format (e.g. complete digital manuscript), to what extent (70,000 words including any endmatter) and accompanied by any material (extracts, quotations) for which copyright might need to be cleared.

Payments

Advances are an example of financial goodwill, a pact that author and editor have cemented through the contract to agree to work together and to make money from the activity. It is usually paid in two or three equal tranches, payable on signature of the contract, on delivery and approval of the final manuscript, and on first publication. The advance against royalties means a payment made before any actual revenue from sales of a book have been received.

Author–Publisher contracts

Royalties are the fees paid to an author on the sale of copies of their book and are subject to sliding scales, so that as a book becomes more successful an author benefits more. As more and more copies are sold the investment the publisher made in producing the first print run will be recouped; subsequent runs might become very profitable for the publisher and rightly an agent will argue for an author to profit from this success too. Such rising royalty rates for a published price contract might look something like this:

- **on home sales**: 7.5% of the published price on the first ten thousand (10,000) copies sold; 10% of the published price up to twenty thousand (20,000) copies sold and 12.5% of the published price on all copies sold thereafter, such royalty not to be deemed a precedent between the publishers and author or agent;
- **on home sales where the discount is 52.5% or more**: four-fifths (4/5ths) of the prevailing royalty; on home sales where the discount is 60% or more: three-fifths (3/5ths) of the prevailing rate.

Free and presentation copies will be provided to the author (anywhere between six and 15 free copies) on publication and to potential reviewers as part of a promotional campaign; royalty payments are not made against these gratis copies. Authors may purchase copies of their own book at discount.

Payment process, accounting periods and other details about how and when the publisher will remunerate the author (or their agent on the author's behalf) will be included.

Publishing process

Author corrections and their proofreading responsibilities might be clearly laid out, covering what checking tasks an author will be expected to undertake and when and which might be carried out and paid for by the publisher, such as having an index prepared or clearing permissions for images or quotations. It might also include a clause in which the publisher 'reserves the right to charge the Author' for the cost of author corrections to page proofs if these are over and above the usual level of alterations. Such costs might be debited against the author's royalty account.

Promotion clauses advise that a publisher shall advertise, promote and market the Work as they deem appropriate 'in their sole discretion'. If an author feels strongly that they wish to be consulted about any aspect of promotion or cover design they could ask for such clauses to be modified. The most an author is likely to get is an amendment that agrees they will be 'consulted' and asked to 'agree' to the publisher's plan and that their agreement 'will not be unreasonably withheld'.

Publication date might not be firmly set when the contract is signed but the publisher's commissioning editor should have a clear idea of what quarter they would like the book to appear in. An agreement would usually stipulate that the book should be published within twelve months of date of delivery and acceptance 'unless prevented by circumstances over which they have no control or unless mutually agreed'.

New and updated editions for non-fiction titles might be referred to, defining what would constitute a 'new' rather than a 'revised' edition and how much new content it might include, say at least 10% new material. The author would be offered first refusal on preparing a new edition, but the publisher would want to include a clause to allow them to ask another writer to complete such a project if they perceived there was a market for it, but the original author was unable or unwilling to take on the commission.

Copyright and contracts

The contract should not daunt an author. It is supposed to be a joint declaration and not biased in favour of one party or the other.

By **Alysoun Owen**, Editor of the *Writers' & Artists' Yearbook* and author of the *Writers' & Artists' Guide to Getting Published* (Bloomsbury 2019).

Copyright Licensing Agency

The Copyright Licensing Agency (CLA) is a not-for-profit company, recognised by the UK government as the collective management organisation for published material (www.gov.uk/copyright-licensing-agency-licence). CLA provides content users with access to millions of titles worldwide, and in return ensures that creators, artists, photographers and writers, along with publishers, are paid royalties for the copying, sharing and re-use of limited extracts of their published work.

CLA was established in 1983 as a joint venture between Publishers' Licensing Services (PLS) and Authors' Licensing and Collecting Society (ALCS) (see page 413). It was placed in an unique position of representing authors and publishers by licensing the copying of their work and promoting the role and value of copyright. CLA later expanded its licensing agreement to include the Design and Artists Copyright Society (DACS) (page 415) and the Picture Industry Collective Society for Effective Licensing (PICSEL), meaning that visual artists and photographers could receive licence fee distributions, and licensees were covered to copy images and artistic works found in content being copied. The allocation of fees is based on subscriptions, library holdings and detailed surveys of copying activity (see link.cla.co.uk/about-us and read the 'Distribution Model Report').

> **Further information**
>
> **Copyright Licensing Agency**
> 3rd Floor, 6 Hays Lane, London SE1 2HB
> *tel* 020-7400 3100
> *email* cla@cla.co.uk
> *website* www.cla.co.uk

Helping organisations copy, right

CLA provides lawful access to over eight million print and online publications, and for over 40 years, has helped organisations to research, create and collaborate with a range of simple licensing solutions whilst ensuring creators' rights are respected.

With over 20 licences covering the UK's education, public and commercial sectors, CLA facilitates the efficient reuse of content by 12.7 million students and over 9.5 million employees in over 40,000 schools, universities, and organisations across the UK. These licences are tailored to each sector, taking into account the specific needs of those who rely on copying and reusing content as part of their day-to-day work.

Further to this, with 42 reciprocal agreements with countries around the world, CLA's licences allow content users to copy from publications published in more than 39 international territories. Visit link.cla.co.uk/copyright for further information.

Looking forward

CLA has demonstrated over the last forty years that copyright licensing is able to adapt to technological change, support innovation and play a vital role in connecting content users to content creators in an efficient and fair way. CLA has developed digital tools such as Check Permissions, Digital Content Store, and Education Platform to keep their licences and services relevant in a fast-changing environment while ensuring fair returns for copyright owners.

In 2023, the CLA set out to develop licensing solutions to help ensure this is the case for both Generative AI and Text and Data Mining (TDM). They published a research report looking into the dynamic relationship between UK creatives and generative AI. The aim was to spark further discussion and develop tools that protect and value human creative endeavour (https://cla.co.uk/ai-research). From 1 May 2025, CLA will be updating and extending their licences to cover Workplace Generative AI use - for corporate and public sector organisations. The launch of a groundbreaking new Generative AI Training Licence is set to launch in Q3 2025. This will provide a collective licensing solution that gives the rightsholder the opportunity to receive remuneration for the use of their works in generative AI models, whilst ensuring copyright and content protection. This initiative is a significant step forward and is the first of its kind to be developed in the UK. More information can be found at https://cla.co.uk/ai-and-copyright.

Authors' Licensing and Collecting Society

ALCS is the rights management society for UK writers.

ALCS is the largest writers' organisation in the UK with a membership of over 125,000. In 2024, ALCS paid their eligible members over £44 million. Once you've paid your £36 lifetime membership fee (which is simply deducted from the first payment you receive), whatever you've earned in secondary royalties is paid into your bank account during twice yearly distributions.

If you are a published writer, you can be part of this organisation committed to ensuring that writers' intellectual and moral rights are fully respected and fairly rewarded. ALCS represents all types of writer and includes educational, research and academic authors drawn from the professions, scriptwriters, adapters, playwrights, poets, novelists, editors and freelance journalists.

Established in 1977, ALCS is a non-profit that was set up in the wake of the campaign to establish a Public Lending Right (see page 381) to help writers protect and exploit their collective rights. The organisation now represents the interests of all UK writers and aims to ensure that they are fairly compensated for any works that are copied, broadcast or recorded.

Internationally recognised as a leading authority on copyright matters and authors' interests, ALCS is committed to campaigning on behalf of writers to ensure their intellectual property rights are respected and that they are fairly compensated for their invaluable work. It closely monitors all matters affecting copyright, both in the UK and internationally, and makes regular representations to the UK government and the European Union.

ALCS collects fees that are difficult, time-consuming or legally impossible for writers and their representatives to claim on an individual basis, money that is nonetheless due to them. To date, it has distributed over £700 million in secondary royalties to writers. Over the years, ALCS has developed highly specialised knowledge and sophisticated systems that can track writers and their works against any secondary use for which they are due payment. A network of international contacts and reciprocal agreements with foreign collecting societies also ensures that UK writers are compensated for any similar use overseas.

The primary sources of fees due to writers are secondary royalties from the following:

Photocopying, scanning and the digital reuse of electronic and online publications

This income is from licences issued by the Copyright Licensing Agency (CLA; see page 411), originally set up by ALCS and the Publishers' Licensing Services (PLS) to license

Membership

Authors' Licensing and Collecting Society
6th Floor, International House, 1 St Katharine's Way, London E1W 1UN
tel 020-7264 5700
email alcs@alcs.co.uk
website www.alcs.co.uk
X @ALCS_UK
Chief Executive Barbara Hayes

Membership is open to all writers and successors to their estates at a one-off fee of £36 deducted from your first payment. Members of the Society of Authors, the Writers' Guild of Great Britain, National Union of Journalists, Chartered Institute of Journalists and British Association of Journalists can join for free. ALCS charges a 10% commission rate on all payments to fund its operations.

reproduction rights on behalf of its member organisations. The CLA offers a number of licensing options for businesses, educational institutions and government agencies to ensure writers are paid fairly when their works are copied or scanned.

Overseas Public Lending Right (PLR)

PLR schemes are typically set up to pay authors when libraries lend their books (to compensate them for the lack of sales). Whilst UK PLR is administered by the British Library (see page 381), ALCS collects money due to UK writers from international PLR systems.

Retransmission of all types of scripted works broadcast on TV and radio

This is the simultaneous showing of one country's broadcasting in another country through a cable network. ALCS receives fees for the cable transmission of British programmes, and then distribute that money to the relevant writers.

Educational recording

The Copyright, Designs and Patents Act 1988 gave schools, colleges and other educational establishments the right to record any radio or TV broadcast for educational purposes without infringing copyright. The Educational Recording Agency (ERA), which was established in 1989, licenses this activity and collects fees to compensate the authors and other owners of rights in the broadcast works. ALCS pays writers their share of these fees.

Tracing authors

ALCS is dedicated to protecting and promoting authors' rights and enabling writers to maximise their income. It is committed to ensuring that royalties due to writers are efficiently collected and speedily distributed to them. One of its greatest challenges is finding those writers for whom it holds funds and ensuring that they claim the money that is owed to them. Any published writer could have funds held by ALCS for them. The amount may be nominal, or it could run into several thousand pounds. Either call or visit the ALCS website – see the **Membership** box for contact details.

DACS (Design and Artists Copyright Society)

A non-for-profit organisation, DACS is the UK's leading visual artists' rights management organisation.

Established by artists for artists in 1984, DACS is the flagship rights management organisation for visual artists in the UK. Passionate about transforming the financial landscape for visual artists, DACS acts as a trusted broker for 102,500 artists worldwide.

Contact details

DACS
33 Old Bethnal Green Road, London E2 6AA
tel 020-7336 8811
email info@dacs.org.uk
website www.dacs.org.uk
Membership Free to join

DACS is a leading voice in campaigning for artists' rights, championing their sustained and vital contribution to the creative economy. Through its services, DACS collects and distributes royalties to visual artists and their estates through Payback, Artist's Resale Right, Copyright Licensing and Artimage.

Payback
Every year, DACS pays artists for the use of artworks that are published in UK books, magazines and shown on TV. If their artwork has been published or broadcast on television, artists could be entitled to a share of millions in royalties. DACS' 2024 distribution saw the annual Payback scheme pay thousands of artists and their representatives a share of over £5.6 million.

Artist's Resale Right
The Artist's Resale Right is a royalty that is due when a work is resold by an art market professional for over £1,000 or the equivalent in pounds sterling. DACS collect resale royalties and provide a quick, efficient payment service trusted by thousands of UK artists and estates. Artists can sign up as a member and DACS will monitor sales of artwork by auction houses, galleries and dealers and collect royalties on their behalf.

Copyright Licensing and Artimage
DACS has 40 years of experience helping artists generate income through the licensed use of their work. Its dedicated team collaborate with artists and leading brands to facilitate partnerships that both parties can be proud of, while making sure artists' rights are always protected.

Artimage (www.artimage.org.uk) is DACS' curated image platform, which makes available over 30,000 hi-res, artist or estate-approved images to a wide range of clients. Through Artimage DACS offers a wraparound service: putting licences in place, collecting royalty fees, and releasing quality image files.

Additional Benefits for Members
DACS' Artist's Resale Right, Copyright licensing and Artimage members can all access DACS' Copyright Advice Service free of charge. This service includes advice and guidance about copyright matters and reviews of relevant sections in agreements. DACS also have a copyright enforcement service for licensing members, which aims to protect artists' rights and artistic integrity by pursuing action when work is misused.

Money, tax and benefits
Managing your finances: a guide for writers

Chartered accountants Jonathan and Louise Ford of Writers Tax Limited set out a clear view of the various financial issues that a writer needs to understand and consider at each stage of their writing career, with helpful links and valuable advice.

In some ways the financial issues of being a writer are no different to pursuing any other occupation. You earn money for your skill, you deduct the costs you have incurred earning your money, and you pay tax on what's left. However, there are several factors that, in combination, make the situation of a writer unique; many writers have income from multiple sources, as well as overseas tax issues and matters concerning copyright.

We'll look at the different stages of a writer's career and the financial aspects you may need to consider as your career develops: 1) getting started – unpaid writing done for love not money; 2) paid writing often running alongside traditional employed income; 3) paid writing as main source of income; and 4) lifelong considerations.

Stage 1: getting started
When you're at an early stage of your writing career and not earning any money from it, there is little you need to do to stay compliant. However, there are still some important things you can consider.

Setting up a dormant limited company
If you are planning to write a book and you would like the royalty income of that book to be held in a limited company, then consider setting up a company even before you start writing. This will allow you to write the book on behalf of your company. If you wait to set the company up until the book is complete, and publishers are interested, then you would have to transfer the copyright of the book to the company at market value; this could cause issues in terms of valuing the copyright and can create a tax problem that

> **Do I need an accountant?**
>
> If your financial situation is straightforward, there may be no need for you to appoint an accountant. If you are employed, then PAYE usually does a reasonable job of collecting the right amount of tax. Your writing income may be quite modest so it should be straightforward to deal with and – if the numbers are not very big – it may not cause too many issues if you get things a little wrong. To help you as your career develops, a good accountant can do the following:
>
> - Deal with HMRC on your behalf;
> - Submit your tax returns on time, so you don't get penalties for being late;
> - Make sure you are claiming for the things you can claim for (and not claiming for things you shouldn't);
> - Advise you on ways of saving tax legitimately;
> - Help you to keep your records accurately;
> - Help you to avoid nasty surprises and unexpected tax bills;
> - Be on hand for all your tax-related questions.
>
> Anybody can call themselves an accountant, even if they have no qualifications or experience. Try to choose someone who is a member of a professional accountancy body, such as ICAEW, ICAS, AAT, ACCA or CIOT. It is also worth getting recommendations from other writers. Social media groups can be a useful source when looking for accountants who act for lots of writers and understand their needs.

could have been avoided. To decide whether this is right for you, you need to weigh up the cost and hassle of having a dormant limited company against the possible future advantages.

Creative averaging

There are a number of conditions you need to satisfy to be eligible for creative averaging; more details are available on HMRC Helpsheet HS234. One such condition is that you cannot use your first year of trading as part of any creative averaging calculation. Using the example given in the box, Theo would need to be submitting information to HMRC about his writing business from the 2021/22 tax year to be able to claim creative averaging in 2023/24.

Loss relief against other income

It is possible for a sole trader to make a loss and to set that loss against other income. This can be beneficial for tax reasons. For example, if an author makes a loss of £5,000 and they also have *employed income* of £30,000, they could offset the £5,000 loss against their employed income so that they only have to pay tax on £25,000. To be able to offset losses against other income, you need to be able to show HMRC that the loss has been incurred on a commercial basis with a view to making a profit. A vague idea that one day you might write a book on Greece would not be sufficient evidence to get a tax deduction on the costs of your holiday.

> ### Creative averaging example
>
> Theo earns nothing in the tax year 2023/24 while he is writing his novel.
>
> In 2024/25 his book is published and he makes a profit of £30,000. Without creative averaging his tax bill in 2023/24 would be nothing, but in 2024/25 he would owe £3,486 in income tax and £1,045.80 in National Insurance – a total of £4,531.80.
>
> If he elects to use creative averaging, his £30,000 profit would be split across both tax years, giving him a total tax bill of £704.70 in 2023/24 and of £631.80 in 2024/25. By choosing to use creative averaging, Theo would have saved £3195.30 over the two tax years.

Pre-trading expenses

If you haven't been reporting expenditure to HMRC as losses, then it is still possible to get tax relief for 'pre-trading expenditure'. The relief allows you to claim for expenditure incurred within seven years of starting to trade and, in effect, gives tax relief as if it was incurred on the first day of trading. The 'wholly and exclusive' rule will still apply, so it is important to be able to link the expenditure you are claiming to the income you are receiving. The stronger the link, the more likely HMRC are to accept it. In order to maximise any possible pre-trading expenditure claim, it is important to try and keep records and receipts *just in case* you might need them in the future.

Stage 2: paid writing as additional income

Most writers at this stage will still be running their writing business as a sole trader (or freelancer – there is no difference in terms of tax). Legally you don't need to do anything to set up as a sole trader. As soon as you start writing with a view to making a profit, you've become a sole trader. The tax system is very flexible. You can have a part-time employed job, be a partner in a bookshop and be a published author, all at the same time. Important things to consider at this stage are:

Managing your finances: a guide for writers 419

Registering with HMRC

If you earn more than £1,000 from self-employment you need to register as a sole trader with HMRC. You can do this at www.gov.uk/register-for-self-assessment. You need to register by 5 October in your second tax year (tax years run from 6 April to 5 April).

For example, if you started on 20 November 2024 (tax year 2024/25) then you would need to register with HMRC by 5 October 2025 (tax year 2025/26). You would then get sent a tax return to complete by 31 January 2026 if filing online or 31 October 2025 if filing by paper.

Two or more writers working together may also need to consider if they are in partnership with each other. A partnership has to be registered in its own right with HMRC and submit a tax return each year.

Submitting a tax return

The tax system is called Self Assessment and this means that it is necessary for you to assess what rules and regulations apply to your tax position. There are a range of penalties that HMRC levy and, although it is possible in certain circumstances to appeal the penalties, it is well worth doing all you can to avoid them in the first place.

Keeping records

A self-employed person needs to keep records for at least five years from 31 January following the tax year they relate to. For example, if you have transactions in the tax year to 5 April 2025, you need to keep your records until 31 January 2031. You can keep records digitally or on paper. You should keep copies of bank statements, contracts, receipts for expenditure you are claiming for and any invoices you have raised. It is also worth keeping a note of any unusual non-business transactions. If you win £1,000 at the races or get a generous gift from Aunt Ethel, you want to be able to prove this wasn't undeclared income from writing.

> **Making Tax Digital for Income Tax**
>
> From 6 April 2026 there is a new system for reporting income to HMRC called Making Tax Digital for Income Tax (MTD for IT). This will affect landlords and sole traders. Those with qualifying income of £50,000 or more will have to join from April 2026 and those with qualifying income of more than £30,000 will join from April 2027. It is sales or turnover that matters rather than profit. Under the new system taxpayers will have to do the following:
> - keep their records digitally
> - provide a quarterly return to HMRC through compatible software
> - provide an annual tax return
>
> If you think you will be affected and you aren't currently keeping your records on cloud bookkeeping software then it would be worth exploring this further.
>
> There is more information available at www.gov.uk/guidance/check-if-youre-eligible-for-making-tax-digital-for-income-tax.

It is usually a good idea to have a separate business bank account that you use just for your writing income. This will help to keep things organised and could give you a little more privacy, as your accountant – and possibly HMRC – don't have to look through all your private outgoings.

Claiming expenses

A writer pays tax on their profit. Profit is income less allowable costs, often referred to as 'expenses'. Sometimes people talk about things being 'tax deductible', which means they can be deducted from your profit before calculating the tax bill, rather than being deducted from your tax bill. For example, if a higher-rate tax payer spends £100 on stationery, this is tax deductible and so it will reduce her profits by £100 and save income tax at 40%, i.e. £40.

Trading allowance

You can claim a £1,000 trading allowance against your self-employed income instead of claiming for expenses you have incurred. You cannot claim the trading allowance and expenses at the same time. Claiming the trading allowance would be suitable when the trading allowance is more than the expenses incurred. However, you can't use the trading allowance to turn your profit into a loss. There are also restrictions to prevent you from using the trading allowance if the income is received from a business controlled by you, or by someone connected to you.

What can you claim for?

The rule is that an expense must be 'wholly and exclusively' for the purpose of your business. Typical costs are:
- Accountancy
- Advertising
- Agent commission
- Bank charges
- Computing and IT
- Printing, postage and stationery
- Professional subscriptions
- Internet and telephone
- Software subscriptions
- Research
- Travel

Some costs may have an element of private use. In this case, HMRC will allow the cost to be apportioned provided you can justify the calculation. For example:
- Motor expenses – may be apportioned according to business use.
- Home as office – apportioned according to rooms and time spent in use.

Alternatively, you may be able to use HMRC Simplified Expenses. You can find more details at www.gov.uk/simpler-income-tax-simplified-expenses.

HMRC Self Assessment penalties

Late filing

Up to 3 months late £100, plus

after 3 months £10 per day for 90 days (max £900), plus

after 6 months penalties accrue at regular intervals based on 5% of the tax due or £300 – whichever is the greater.

You can estimate your penalty at www.gov.uk/estimate-self-assessment-penalties.

Late payment of tax

5% of tax due if not paid within 30 days with further 5% penalties every 6 months.

Interest is also charged (at the bank base rate plus 2.5%).

Incorrect returns

Penalties are charged for tax returns that HMRC consider to be incorrect. There is an appeals process. The penalties are all behaviour based and are as follows:
- Careless errors – 0% to 30% of the additional tax due.
- Deliberate errors – 20% to 70% of the additional tax due.
- Deliberate and concealed errors – 30% to 100% of the additional tax due.

Prizes and bursaries

There are many prizes and awards open to authors and other creatives, and entering competitions or seeking awards is a normal part of these professions and a good way for them to obtain extra income from their work. Such prizes are usually taxable. However, there are exceptions. When a prize is unsolicited, and awarded as a mark of honour, distinction or public esteem in recognition of outstanding achievement in a particular field, it won't be taxable. For example, if your publisher or agent enters you for a competition without your knowledge or consent, any prize money received should not be taxable.

> **Cloud bookkeeping**
>
> Recent years have seen the development of relatively cheap, simple bookkeeping packages like Xero and Quickbooks. These allow you to link up your business bank account to your accounting records, so you can quickly and accurately keep track of your income and expenditure. They have the advantage of being regularly backed up, less prone to error, and easy to use. You can also store your receipts and paperwork digitally.

Payments on account

For self-employed people the tax system can require payments on account of tax to be made every six months. Each payment on account is half of the previous year's tax bill.

For example: Jo's first year of trading is the tax year 2024/25; she owes tax of £4,000 for the 2024/25 tax year which is due for payment by 31 January 2026. Also, on 31 January 2026 she'll need to pay a payment on account of £2,000 towards her 2026/27 tax bill. She'll have to make a further payment of £2,000 in July 2026. Her actual tax bill for 2025/26 is £5,000. In January 2027 her payments will be:

	£
Tax due for tax year 2025/26	5,000
Less:	
Payment on account - paid 31 January 2026	2,000
Payment on account - paid 31 July 2026	2,000
Balance for 2025/26	1,000
Add:	
Payment on account for 2026/27 (50% of £5,000)	2,500
Total due 31 January 2027	3,500

When income is rising, payments on account can catch out the unwary, as each January there is both a shortfall of tax and a new, higher payment on account to pay. A sensible approach is to save for your tax throughout the year and to complete your tax return early in the tax year, so you have plenty of notice if the bill is higher than expected.

When income is falling (or ceasing) then it is possible to make a claim to HMRC to reduce payments on account so that you don't pay tax in advance that is more than necessary. If the payments on account you make are more than your tax bill, these will be offset against your next payments on account or refunded to you.

Setting up a limited company as a 'money box'

If you already have a paid job, then it's possible that your additional income from writing may take your total income into a higher tax band. If you don't need the money now, setting up a limited company could mean that the company pays corporation tax at a lower rate.

For example, Jamie earns £60,000 through his employment; he also receives £2,212 in Child Benefit in respect of his two children. He earns a further £20,000 in profit as a writer. He doesn't need to access the additional money now and is happy to leave it in his company. His tax liability as a sole trader can be compared with that of the limited company as follows:

Sole trader	£
Income tax on £20,000 @ 40%	8,000
High Income Child Benefit Tax Charge	2,212
Total due	10,212

Limited company	£
Corporation tax on £20,000 @ 19%	3,800
Total due	3,800

Although this is an extreme example, it shows that through using a limited company Jamie has saved £6,412 of tax on £20,000 of income. Once Jamie wants to take the money out of the company, it will be taxable on him personally, but he can control the amount paid so that it might be covered by his personal allowance entirely or subject to a lower rate of tax than he is paying now. If Jamie's plans are to build up a savings buffer, so that one day he can take the plunge and become a full-time writer, then this could be of real benefit.

Corporation tax is payable on the profit earned by a company. The first £50,000 of profit is taxed at 19%. Profits between £50,000 and £250,000 are taxed at a marginal rate of 26.5% and profits over £250,000 at 25%. There are also special rules that reduce the tax bands where more than one company is controlled by the same people.

Stage 3: writing as main source of income

Typically, a writer at this stage will either be self-employed or trade through a limited company. A limited company has to be 'incorporated' at Companies House and, once it is set up, it exists as a legal entity. It can enter into contracts, have a bank account, and exist without you. It is possible to trade both as a sole trader and through a limited company. It may even be the case that an author has some of their books taxed as a sole trader and other titles taxed within a limited company.

Issues on incorporation

If you do trade through a limited company, it is important to ensure that the underlying paperwork is correct. Here are some issues to bear in mind:
• For a company to receive copyright income, it must be legally entitled to the income. This can be achieved by ensuring the company exists before the book has been written and a service contract is in place between the director (i.e. the author) and the company.
• It isn't sufficient to simply 'bank' any proceeds into your company. All contracts need to be properly drawn up in the company's name.
• If you simply give your copyright to your company, it can create a tax issue; HMRC will expect you to pay income tax on the market value of the gift and will also expect the company to pay tax on the income it receives. In effect, the same income could be taxed twice.

- It is possible to sell the copyright to the company. This results in a better tax position, as the company would be able to get some tax relief for the cost of the copyright, but it will require a valuation of the copyright which brings with it costs and some uncertainty.
- Once your company owns the copyright, royalty income is 'locked' into being paid to the company. If you wished to own the copyright personally, it would need to be transferred out of the company at a fair value. You may find you have a company for a much longer time than you first anticipate, because it may not be practical to close it down until the copyright has a negligible value.

VAT

VAT (Value Added Tax) is a tax that businesses are required to charge their customers for goods or services. A writer is no different from any other business and therefore must charge VAT when supplying writing services. The standard UK rate of VAT is currently 20%. VAT is a complicated subject and much of it is beyond the scope of this book. However, there are some key things a writer should be aware of.

A VAT-registered business usually submits a quarterly VAT return within one month and seven days of the end of the VAT quarter. Any VAT due is then paid by the same deadline. Being VAT-registered is not entirely bad news; a VAT-registered business has to charge VAT on their relevant services, but they can also claim back VAT on things they buy for their business. For example, in the VAT quarter ending 31 December 2024 a writer gets a publishing deal for £10,000 plus £2,000 of VAT. Their agent charges them £1,500 plus £300 VAT, and they buy a computer for writing for £500 plus £100 VAT. They would submit a VAT return to HMRC by 7 February 2025 and pay over £1,600, as follows:

	£
VAT charged	2,000
Less:	
VAT on agent's fees	300
VAT on computer	100
Paid to HMRC	1,600

Although this may make you feel worse off, especially when you are paying £1,600 to HMRC, you are in fact better off by £400 – this being the difference between the VAT you have been paid and the VAT you have paid out.

IR35

IR35 was introduced in April 2000 to stop the practice of employees setting up a limited company (a 'personal service company') and invoicing their employer for their work rather than being paid as an employee. This practice led to a large tax saving for both the employer and the employee.

IR35 only applies to limited companies, so a writer who is trading as a sole trader can ignore it. From April 2021 both public entities and larger private companies have to look at the status of people working through personal service companies and, if necessary, deduct tax and National Insurance.

For most writers operating through a personal service company, it will be clear that they are not working for anyone as disguised employment. For other writers the situation may be more uncertain. For example, a copywriter with their own company providing weekly content for a client who describes them as their 'Content Manager', pays them a regular salary, expects them to attend meetings on site and doesn't allow a substitute, may be caught by the IR35 rules.

The IR35 rules are complex and, if caught by the rules, your limited company has to pay out most of the money it receives as a salary to the employee – together with Employers National Insurance.

Specialist help should be sought if you think your company may be affected by IR35.

Sole trader or limited company – the key differences

Sole trader	Limited company
Starting up	
Nothing legal required	Must be incorporated at Companies House
Closing down	
Nothing legal required	Must be formally struck off at Companies House
Legal protection	
None – you and the business are one and the same	Limited liability (but watch out for contracts that pass on liabilities to directors)
If you are sued, then all your assets are at stake	If the company is sued, then only the assets of the company are at stake
Tax on profits	
Income tax paid depending on total earnings from all sources in the year; rates may be 0%, 20%, 40% or 45% depending on income	Corporation tax paid; rates are between 19% and 26.5%
Tax on profits extracted	
Not applicable – you pay tax on profit whether extracted or not	Dividend tax due at rates of 0%, 8.75%, 33.75% or 39.35% depending on income
National Insurance	
Pay Class 4 National Insurance	Only pay National Insurance on salaries paid to employees if they earn over the limit
Reporting	
Must tell HMRC you are trading and must complete an individual Self Assessment tax return each year (and comply with MTD for IT form 6 April 2026)	Must file accounts each year with Companies House
	Must submit a Confirmation Statement each year to Companies House
	Must file a corporation tax return each year with HMRC
	May have to run a payroll and report to HMRC
	Likely that director/shareholder will have to complete an individual Self Assessment tax return each year
Separate business bank account	
Advisable	Essential
VAT	
Can be VAT registered; it is a person that is VAT registered, not a business, which may have unintended consequences	Can be VAT registered
Creative averaging	
Can be used	Cannot be used
Why choose this one?	
Simple; cheap; you want to take all the money out of business when it's earned, not concerned about legal liability	Possible to save tax if you don't require all the money or are able to take advantage of splitting income; provides legal liability protection

VAT registration threshold

A business needs to register for VAT when the level of sales exceeds the VAT threshold. The VAT threshold is currently £90,000 and it applies to the last 12 months. To know whether you need to register or not, you have to look back at your cumulative sales over the last 12 months and, if these exceed the VAT threshold, you must register. You are also required to register if you believe your sales in the next 30 days alone will be more than the VAT threshold – for example if you bag a big publishing deal.

Some writers will make an early 'protective' VAT registration, so that they know they are registered and don't have to worry about tripping over the VAT threshold. It is important to remember that the turnover figure is not necessarily the amount you receive. For example, a writer gets an advance of £10,000; their agent deducts 15% plus their VAT and so the writer only receives £8,200. The figure that counts towards the VAT threshold is £10,000.

You do not need to include employment income in your turnover calculation or non-UK income (such as royalties from Amazon).

Finally, you need to include services you buy that are subject to the 'reverse charge' rules in your turnover calculation. For example, a writer who uses Facebook and Amazon advertising and spends, on average, more than £7,500 per month on this type of service would be required to register for VAT even if they are not making any sales themselves that are subject to VAT.

Voluntary registration

You can voluntarily register for VAT even if your sales are under the VAT registration threshold. The reason you may want to do this is to recover the VAT you are being charged – typically by your agent. For example, a writer gets a publishing deal for £25,000; their agent charges 15% commission plus VAT. If they are not VAT-registered, they'll lose the agent VAT of £750 but, if they are VAT-registered, they'd be able to recover this.

Being in the 'VAT club' will allow you to recover VAT on all your other business expenditure, such as computer costs and accountancy fees. Whether it is a good idea to register early depends on your circumstances. If you're not incurring much VAT, then it may not be worth the hassle.

What to include in your sales for VAT

You need to include all your UK sales and any foreign sales collected by your UK publisher. You can exclude any direct foreign sales (such as Amazon self-publishing or sales you or your agent have agreed with a foreign publisher). If you're a sole trader, you can exclude any employed income. But, if you are self-employed as something else too (e.g. you're both a plumber and a writer), you need to aggregate both sets of income. The VAT registration belongs to the *person*, not the *business*.

Claiming back VAT

When you first register for VAT, you can reclaim VAT on goods purchased up to four years prior to registration provided those goods are still held when registration takes place. VAT on services supplied in the six months prior to registration may also be reclaimed. To claim VAT you'll need a valid VAT receipt; a credit card receipt isn't enough, and a VAT inspector will disallow any expenditure that you can't produce a valid VAT receipt for – even if it's obvious that you would have paid VAT.

Not all expenditure has VAT charged on it:

Usually has VAT	Usually has no VAT
Agent commission	Trains, planes and taxis
Accountancy fees	Software subscriptions from overseas
Stationery	Postage
Computers and UK software	Entertainment
Internet and mobile phone	Insurance

Withholding tax and double taxation relief

Writers will often receive some or, in the case of an author selling via Amazon Kindle Direct Publishing (KDP), most of their income from an overseas source. Many foreign countries will charge a 'withholding tax' on such royalty payments, for example 30% in the case of the USA. Once withholding tax is paid, it is often not cost effective to try to recover it from the country in question, as doing so may require local professional advice and tax returns to be submitted to the country in question.

It is often possible to avoid any withholding tax being deducted in the first instance by completing the information required by the overseas publisher, so they don't have to apply withholding tax. Amazon KDP has an online tax interview to make it as easy as possible for you to comply. Other publishers in other countries will have to follow their own rules and will often ask for a Certificate of Residence to prove you are a UK tax payer. There are more details on applying for a Certificate of Residence at www.gov.uk/guidance/get-a-certificate-of-residence.

If you do suffer withholding tax, then it may be possible to use the foreign tax you have paid to offset against your tax liability on the same income when you complete your tax return. A word of warning though: you may not get back the full amount of foreign tax paid and relief is restricted to the amount of UK tax you would have to pay on the same income or the amount of foreign tax you would have paid had you complied with the requirements to avoid withholding tax.

Stage 4: Lifelong considerations

As a writer's career becomes more established, there are other financial considerations.

Pensions

State Pension

To qualify for the new State Pension, you need a minimum of ten qualifying years and at least 35 qualifying years to receive the maximum payments. You can check your pension entitlement online at www.gov.uk/check-state-pension. If you have gaps in your pension contribution history, then you can consider making voluntary contributions.

> **Writers' Guild Pension Scheme**
>
> For their members writing for TV, radio and film, WGGB (Writers' Guild of Great Britain) have negotiated agreements with the BBC, ITV and PACT so that pension contributions are made to the Writers' Guild Pension Scheme. In return for the writer making a contribution to the scheme, the production company will also make a contribution, in addition to the writer's fee. More details are available from WGGB (see page 300 for contact details).

Private pensions

If you have been employed, you may have an occupational pension from your employment in place. Most writers who have been self-employed will depend upon their own pension arrangements using 'defined contribution' schemes. Contributions to a private pension by an individual are made net of basic rate income tax. This means that a contribution of £80 actually means the amount invested is £100, with £20 being claimed by the pension company from the government. A higher-rate tax payer would save another £20 in income tax, making the cost of putting £100 into a pension just £60. There are rules regarding how much you can invest each year and many people will need professional advice as to what scheme they invest in.

Insurances

Being a self-employed writer does mean that you don't have the same safety net that many employees may have. It is sensible to think about how you and your family would manage if you died or, through injury or illness, were unable to continue to earn a living. There are insurance policies that are available to help.

- **Life insurance** can provide a lump sum or a monthly income for a period of time if you die.
- **Critical illness insurance** can provide a lump sum or a monthly income for a period of time if you are diagnosed with a critical illness.
- **Income protection insurance** can provide a monthly income if you are unable to work due to ill health.

Wills

Making a will is important for a number of reasons. Amongst other things, you can specify who inherits your assets, make tax efficient choices and provide instructions as to who looks after your minor children. A writer also needs to consider what happens with any copyright they hold as part of their estate. Copyright can last up to 70 years after death, so it may represent a valuable asset. You may also have particular instructions as to what happens to your personal papers and unpublished works. It is also worth thinking about what happens with digital assets such as blogs, social media accounts, online videos, and access to cloud storage services like Dropbox. A bit of forward planning may save a lot of trouble for the people dealing with your estate.

Further advice: useful websites

HMRC
www.gov.uk/government/organisations/hm-revenue-customs

Institute of Chartered Accountants in England and Wales
www.icaew.com

Institute of Chartered Accountants of Scotland
www.icas.com

These author associations offer support and advice on financial matters to their members:

National Union of Journalists
www.nuj.org.uk

Society of Authors
https://societyofauthors.org (see page 297)

WGGB (Writers' Guild of Great Britain)
https://writersguild.org.uk (see page 300)

Accountancy and business software tools include:

Sage
www.sage.com/en-gb/sage-business-cloud/accounting

Quickbooks
https://quickbooks.intuit.com/uk

Xero
www.xero.com/uk

Jonathan Ford BSC FCA and **Louise Ford** BA FCA are the directors of Writers Tax Ltd, a firm of chartered accountants that specialises in helping authors, scriptwriters and other professional writers with their tax and accountancy needs, which they established in 2020. They both qualified as chartered accountants with Price Waterhouse in Liverpool. Jonathan worked at Grant Thornton and later as Financial Controller at Mersey TV before setting up his own company. See their website https://writers.tax for more information.

National Insurance contributions

Sarah Bradford sets out the facts about National Insurance, explaining the contributory principle that underlies it, the various classes of contribution payable by workers (both employed and self-employed), the related benefit entitlements and information on current rates and earnings thresholds.

Nature of National Insurance contributions

The payment of primary Class 1 and Class 4 National Insurance contributions secures access to the state pension and to contributory benefits. This is the contributory principle of National Insurance. National Insurance contributions are payable by employed earners and their employers and also by self-employed earners. People who do not have any earnings or whose earnings are not sufficient to trigger a liability to pay National Insurance contributions and who do not receive National Insurance credits can choose to pay Class 3 or Class 2 National Insurance contributions voluntarily to maintain their contribution record.

If sufficient National Insurance contributions of the right type are paid or credited for a tax year, the year will be a qualifying year for National Insurance purposes. A person needs 35 qualifying years in order to receive the full state pension when they reach state pension age. Where a person has at least ten qualifying years, they will receive a reduced state pension.

Classes of National Insurance

There are various different classes of National Insurance contribution. The class (or classes) that you pay will depend on whether you are an employed earner, a self-employed earner, an employer or a voluntary contributor. Contributions may be earnings-related, payable on profits or payable at a flat rate, depending on the class.

The different classes of contribution are shown in the box below. Class 1 and 4 contributions are only payable once earnings exceed certain thresholds and limits. The rates and thresholds applying to 2025/26 are set out in the box on page 434.

Classes of National Insurance

Nature of contribution	Payable by
Class 1 Earnings-related	Employed earners (primary Class 1 contributions)
	Employer (secondary Class 1 contributions)
Class 1A Earnings-related	Employer on taxable benefits in kind and taxable termination payments and sporting testimonials
Class 1B Earnings-related	Employer on items included within a PAYE Settlement Agreement and on the tax due under that agreement
Class 2 Flat rate	Voluntary contributions payable by self-employed earners with low profits
Class 3 Flat rate	Voluntary contributions
Class 3A Variable amount	Payable between 12 October 2015 and 5 April 2017 voluntarily by those who reached state pension age before 6 April 2016 to boost their state pension
Class 4 Profit-related	Self-employed earners

Contributions payable by writers and artists

As for other earners, the class of National Insurance payable by writers and artists depends on whether they are a self-employed earner or an employed earner. This is not something that they can choose – it will depend on the facts of the engagement. It is important that the employment status of the writer or artist is categorised correctly as this will affect not only what class (and therefore how) they pay, but also what benefits they are entitled to.

Categorisation – employed earner v self-employed earner

To ensure that writers and artists pay the right class of National Insurance contributions, it is important they are correctly categorised. Employed earners with sufficient earnings will pay Class 1 National Insurance contributions, whereas self-employed earners with sufficient profits will pay Class 4 contributions. Employed earners with low earnings and self-employed earners with low profits will receive a National Insurance credit if their earnings/profits exceed a minimum level. Self-employed earners whose profits are too low to benefit from the National Insurance credit can choose to pay Class 2 contributions voluntarily.

A worker's categorisation depends on the characteristics of the engagement. In many cases, it will be clear whether a worker is an employed earner or a self-employed earner. For example, a writer who is employed by a publishing firm and has a contract of employment will be an employed earner and will pay Class 1 National Insurance contributions on their earnings, whereas a freelance writer who undertakes commissions for a variety of people and is paid a fee for each commission will be a self-employed earner and will pay Class 4 contributions if their profits exceed the Class 4 lower profits limit.

Characteristics of employment

The following characteristics apply to an engagement where the worker is an employed earner:

- they are required to work regularly unless they are unwell or on leave;
- they are expected to work a minimum number of hours a week and expect to be paid for the time that they work;
- a manager or supervisor is responsible for their workload and will say when a job should be finished or how it should be done;
- they must do the work themselves – they can't send someone else to do it instead;
- the business deducts tax and National Insurance from their pay;
- they are entitled to paid holiday;
- they are entitled to statutory payments;
- they can join the business's pensions scheme;
- they are subject to grievance and disciplinary procedures;
- the contract sets out the procedure applying in the event of redundancy;
- they work at the business premises or at a location specified by the business;
- they work for only that business or, if they have another job, it is completely separate;
- the offer letter and contract refer to the 'employee' and the 'employer'.

For example, a staff writer who is paid a salary and contracted to work 35 hours a week would be an employed earner.

Characteristics of self-employment

The following characteristics indicate that the writer or artist is a self-employed earner:
- they are in business for themselves and are responsible for the success or failure of the business and can make a profit or a loss;
- they decide what work they take on and where and how they do it;
- they can hire someone else to do the work;
- they are responsible for fixing unsatisfactory work in their own time;
- they agree a fixed price for a job – the fee is the same regardless of how long it takes them to do the work;
- they use their own money to buy any equipment needed and to cover the running costs of the business;
- they work for more than one client.

For example, a writer who is commissioned to write specific articles for different publications and who works for a number of publishers, being paid a fee for each article, would be a self-employed earner.

Marginal cases

It will not always be clear whether a writer or artist is an employed earner or a self-employed earner. In this situation, it is necessary to look at the overall picture and see whether, on balance, the writer or artist is employed or self-employed. It should be noted that there is not one single definitive test, rather a question of seeing what characteristics of employment and what characteristics of self-employment are present.

In reaching a decision, the following factors need to be considered:
- The nature of the contract and the written terms – a contract for *services* indicates employment and a contract of *service* indicates self-employment.
- The nature of the engager's business and the nature of the job.
- Right of substitution – a right to send a substitute indicates self-employment.
- Mutuality of obligation – for a contract for services there must be minimum mutual obligations; the employer is obliged to offer work and the employee is obliged to do that work.
- Right of control – a high degree of control (on the part of the employer) over how and where the worker performs the work suggests employment.
- Provision of equipment – the provision by the worker of their own equipment suggests self-employment.
- Financial risk – a person who is self-employed bears a higher degree of financial risk than an employee.
- Opportunity to profit – a person who is self-employed has the opportunity to profit if they do the job quicker or under-budget.
- Length of engagement – while this is not a decisive factor, an open-ended contract is more likely to indicate employment.
- Part and parcel of the organisation – a worker who is seen as 'part and parcel' of the organisation is likely to be an employee.
- Entitlement to benefits – a worker who is entitled to employee-type benefits, such as a pension, is more likely to be an employee.
- Personal factors – a highly skilled worker may not need supervising but may still be an employee.

• Intention – while intention alone cannot determine status, it can be useful in forming an opinion on whether the worker is employed or self-employed.

Check Employment Status for Tax (CEST) tool

HMRC have produced a tool – the Check Employment Status for Tax (CEST) tool – which can be used to reach a decision on whether a writer or artist is employed or self-employed. The tool asks a series of questions on the engagement, which must be answered honestly, in order to reach a decision. As long as the information provided is accurate and represents the reality of the engagement, HMRC will stand by the decision that is reached. The CEST tool is available on the government website at www.gov.uk/guidance/check-employment-status-for-tax.

Workers providing their services through a personal service company

Anti-avoidance rules apply where services are provided through a personal limited company or another intermediary to an end client. There are two sets of rules to consider – the off-payroll working rules and the IR35 rules. The rules that apply depend on the nature of the end client.

• **Off-payroll working rules**

The off-payroll working rules were introduced from 6 April 2017. They applied from the date when services were provided through an intermediary to a private sector body. The rules were extended from 6 April 2021, and from that date they also apply when the end client is a medium or large private sector organisation.

The end client must carry out a status determination to ascertain whether the worker would be an employee of the end client if they provided their services to them directly. Where this is the case, the end client must deduct tax and National Insurance from payments made to the worker's personal company (after adjusting the bill for VAT and the cost of any materials), and report this to HMRC. The worker receives credit for the tax and National Insurance on payment made to them by their personal limited company. They do not need to consider the IR35 rules because the off-payroll working rules apply instead.

• **IR35**

From 6 April 2021 onwards, the IR35 rules only apply where a worker provides their services to a small private sector organisation through an intermediary, such as a personal service company. The worker's personal service company must determine whether the worker would be an employee of the small private sector organisation if they provided their services directly. If the answer is 'yes' the IR35 rules apply. The intermediary must calculate the deemed employment payment at the end of the tax year, and account for tax and National Insurance on that payment to HMRC.

Employed earners – Class 1 National Insurance

Class 1 National Insurance is payable on the earnings of an employed earner. The employed earner pays primary contributions and the secondary contributor (which is generally the employer) pays secondary contributions. The payment of primary Class 1 National Insurance contributions by the employed earner is the mechanism by which the employed earner earns the right to the state pension and contributory benefits. Secondary Class 1 contributions, payable by the employer, do not earn benefit entitlement – they are akin to a tax on the employee's earnings.

Contributions are calculated by reference to earnings for the earnings period on a non-cumulative basis; no account is taken of earnings previously in the tax year, only those for the earnings period. The earnings period will normally correspond to the pay interval. However, directors have an annual earnings period, regardless of their actual pay frequency. The employer must deduct primary contributions from the employee's pay and pay them over to HMRC together with tax deducted under PAYE and the employer's secondary contributions.

- **Primary Class 1 National Insurance**

Primary Class 1 National Insurance contributions are payable by employees aged 16 and over until they reach state pension age (which depends on their date of birth). No contributions are payable until earnings reach the *lower earnings limit* (set at £125 per week, £542 per month, £6,500 per year for 2025/26). They are then payable at a notional zero rate until earnings reach the *primary threshold*. This is important as it secures the year as a qualifying year for National Insurance purposes (as long as earnings are paid above the lower earnings limit for each earnings period in the tax year). Where earnings are below the lower earnings limit, the year is not a qualifying year (although may become one if the worker receives National Insurance credits or pays voluntary contributions).

Contributions are payable on earnings above the *primary threshold* at the main primary rate of 8% (2025/26 rate) until earnings reach the upper earnings limit and at the additional primary rate of 2% (2025/26) on earnings in excess of the *upper earnings limit* and at the additional primary rate of 2% (2025/26) on earnings in excess of the *upper earnings limit*

The *primary threshold is* set at £242 per week (£1,048 per month, £12,570 per year) for 2025/26 and is aligned with the personal allowance applying for tax purposes. The *upper earnings* limit is set at £967 per week, £4,189 per month and £50,270 per year for 2025/26.

- **Secondary Class 1 contributions**

Secondary contributions are payable by the secondary contributor, which in most cases is the employed earner's employer. They are payable on the earnings of an employee aged 16 and above; unlike primary contributions, the secondary liability does not stop when the employed earner reaches state pension age.

Contributions are payable at the secondary rate of 15% on earnings in excess of the *secondary threshold* (set at £96 per week, £417 per month, £5,000 per year for 2025/26).

A higher secondary threshold applies to the earnings of employees under the age of 21 (the upper secondary threshold for under 21s), to those of apprentices under the age of 25 (the apprentice upper secondary threshold) and to armed forces veterans in the first year of their first civilian employment since leaving the armed forces. Each of these thresholds are aligned with the upper earnings limit for primary Class 1 purposes (set at £967 per week, £4,189 per month and £50,270 per year for 2025/26).

A separate secondary threshold applies to the earnings of a new employee in the first 36 months of their employment with an employer with physical premises in a special tax site, such as a Freeport or an investment zone. For 2025/26, this threshold is set at £481 per week, £2,083 per month and £25,000 per year.

These upper thresholds only apply for secondary Class 1 purposes; the employee or apprentice pays the primary contributions at the usual rates.

Eligible employers can claim the Employment Allowance which is offset against their secondary Class 1 National Insurance liability. The Employment Allowance is set at £10,500 for 2025/26 (capped at the employer's secondary Class 1 liability where this is lower).

For 2025/26, employers whose secondary Class 1 liability exceeded £100,000 in 2024/25 are able to benefit from the Employment Allowance as the previous condition restricting the allowance to employers whose secondary Class 1 liability for the previous year was less than £100,000 has been lifted. Companies where the sole employee is also a director do not qualify for the allowance.

The Employment Allowance is not given automatically and must be claimed. This can be done through the employer's payroll software.

- **Earnings for Class 1 purposes**

Class 1 contributions are calculated on the earnings for the earnings period. The definition of 'earnings' includes any remuneration or profits derived from the employment. This will include payments of wages and salary, but will also include other items such as statutory sick pay, statutory payments, and certain share-based remuneration. Comprehensive guidance on what to include in earnings for National Insurance purposes can be found in the HMRC guidance CWG2 *Employer further guide to PAYE and National Insurance contributions*. The 2025/26 edition is available at www.gov.uk/government/publications/cwg2-further-guide-to-paye-and-national-insurance-contributions.

- **Class 1A National Insurance contributions**

Class 1A National Insurance contributions are employer-only contributions payable on taxable benefits in kind and also on taxable termination payments in excess of the £30,000 tax-free threshold and taxable sporting testimonials in excess of the £100,000 tax-free threshold. They are payable at the Class 1A rate, which for 2025/26 is set at 15%. The Class 1A rate is aligned with the secondary rate of Class 1 contributions.

- **Class 1B National Insurance**

Class 1B National Insurance contributions are employer-only contributions payable in place of the Class 1 or Class 1A liability that would otherwise arise on items included within a PAYE Settlement Agreement (PSA), and also on the tax due under the PSA. The Class 1B rate is aligned with the secondary Class 1 rate and is set at 15% for 2025/26.

Self-employed earners – Class 4 National Insurance contributions

Where a writer or artist is a self-employed earner, if their profits are high enough, they will pay Class 4 contributions on their profits. These are payable via the Self Assessment system and must be paid by 31 January after the end of the tax year to which they relate (i.e. by 31 January 2027 for 2025/26 contributions).

Self-employed earners whose profits are too low to pay Class 4 National Insurance contributions or receive a Class 4 National Insurance credit can choose to pay voluntary Class 2 contributions.

Class 4 National Insurance contributions are payable by self-employed earners on their profits if these are high enough. No contributions are payable on profits below the lower

National Insurance rates and thresholds 2025/26

National Insurance class	Rate or threshold
Class 1	
Lower earnings limit	£125 per week
	£542 per month
	£6,500 per year
Primary threshold	£242 per week
	£1,048 per week
	£12,570 per year
Secondary threshold	£96 per week
	£417 per month
	£5,000 per year
Upper earnings limit	£967 per week
	£4,189 per month
	£50,270 per year
Upper secondary threshold for under 21s	£967 per week
	£4,189 per month
	£50,270 per year
Apprentice upper secondary threshold	£967 per week
	£4,189 per month
	£50,270 per year
Veterans upper secondary threshold	£967 per week
	£4,189 per month
	£50,270 per year
Upper secondary threshold for special tax sites	£481 per week
	£2,083 per month
	£25,000 per year
Primary (employee) contributions	
On earnings between the primary threshold and the upper earnings limit	8%
On earnings above the upper earnings limit	2%
Secondary (employer) contributions	
On earnings above the relevant secondary threshold	15%
Class 1A and Class 1B	
Contribution rate (employer only)	15%
Class 2 (voluntary: self employed)	
Flat rate contribution	£3.50 per week
Small profits threshold	£6,845 a year
Class 3 (voluntary)	
Flat rate contribution	£17.75 per week
Class 4	
Lower profits limit	£12,570 a year
Upper profits limit	£50,270 a year
Main rate on earnings between the lower profits limit and the upper profits limit	6%
Additional rate on profits in excess of the upper profits limit	2%

National Insurance contributions

profits limit, set at £12,570 for 2025/26. Class 4 contributions are payable at the main rate, set at 6% for 2025/26, on profits between the lower profits limit and the upper profits limit, set at £50,270 for 2025/26, and on profits in excess of the upper profits limit, at the additional Class 4 rate, set at 2% for 2025/26.

A self-employed earner whose profits are between the small profits threshold (set at £6,845 for 2025/26) and the lower profits limit (set at £12,570 for 2025/26) is awarded a National Insurance credit. This provides them with a qualifying year for state pension purposes for zero contribution cost. Self-employed earnings whose profits are below the lower profits threshold do not receive a National Insurance credit.

- **Voluntary Class 2 National Insurance contributions**
Self-employed earners whose earnings are below the small profits threshold (set at £6,845 for 2025/26), and who so not have sufficiently high profits to receive a National Insurance credit, can opt to pay voluntary Class 2 contributions to secure a qualifying year for state pension purposes. For 2025/26, voluntary Class 2 contributions are payable at £3.50 per week. Contributions for 2025/26 must be paid by 31 January 2027. Paying voluntary Class 2 contributions is a much cheaper option that paying voluntary Class 3 contributions.

Voluntary contributions – Class 3

A person can pay voluntary Class 3 contributions to plug gaps in their contributions record. Class 3 contributions are payable at the rate of £17.75 per week for 2025/26. Where a person has profits from self-employment below the *small profits threshold* (set at £6,845 for 2025/26), they can instead pay voluntary Class 2 contributions; at £3.50 per week for 2025/26 this is a much cheaper option.

Maximum contributions

Where a person has more than one job, or is both employed and self-employed, there is a cap on the contributions that are payable for the year. The calculations are complex.

National Insurance credits

National Insurance credits are available in certain circumstances where people are unable to work or because they are ill. There are two types of credit. Class 1 credits count towards state pension and contributory benefits, while Class 3 credits only count towards the state pension. Further detail on National Insurance credits can be found on the government website at www.gov.uk/national-insurance-credits.

Benefit entitlement

Class of contributions	Benefit entitlement
Primary Class 1 (employed earner)	State Pension, contribution-based Jobseeker's Allowance, contribution-based Employment and Support Allowance, Maternity Allowance and Bereavement Payment, Bereavement Allowance, Bereavement Support Payment.
Class 2 (voluntary: self-employed earners)	State Pension, contribution-based Employment and Support Allowance, Maternity Allowance and Bereavement Allowance.
Class 3 (voluntary contributions)	State Pension and Bereavement Payment, Bereavement Allowance, Widowed Parent's Allowance.

Benefit entitlement

The payment of National Insurance contributions (and the award of National Insurance credits) earns entitlement to the state pension and certain contributory benefits. The payment of primary Class 1, Class 2, Class 3 and Class 4 contributions confers benefit entitlement. Benefit entitlement depends on the class of contribution paid.

Sarah Bradford BA (Hons), FCA CTA (Fellow) is the director of WriteTax Ltd and the author of *National Insurance Contributions 2025/26* (and earlier editions) published by Bloomsbury Professional. She writes widely on tax and National Insurance contributions.

Index

Index 439

This index includes all the 'listings' entries in this *Yearbook*: the companies, societies and organisations that you might wish to consult when looking for where and how you can share your work. They are listed alphabetically by surname, e.g. Yvonne Arnaud Theatre Management is under 'A'. This index also includes some general topics that are covered in the articles.

A

A. Orr Fantasy Grant   307
Abingdon Press   66
Harry N. Abrams   66
abridged books   275, 278
abridging   273
Academy of British Cover Design: Annual Cover Design Competition   333
Acair   37
Accessible Book & Story Festival   352
accountant   417
ACER Press   57
achieving goals   93
Action for Children's Arts   315
activism   161
Adams Literary   226
adapting books for stage and screen   271
Alex Adsett Literary   224
advances   193, 408
adventure stories   123, 154
Advertising Standards Authority   284
Advocate Art   258
Affirm Press   57
age-appropriate text   376
Agency for the Legal Deposit Libraries (ALDL), The   388
Agency (London), The   210
agents, attitude to poetry   175
agents, role of for comics   253
AIM Literary Festival   352
Aladdin Paperbacks *see* Simon & Schuster Children's Publishing Division
Alanna Max   37
ALCS Educational Writers' Award   333
All About Kids Publishing   67
All Stories   350
Allen & Unwin   57
Alliance of Independent Authors   304, 315, 380
Alliance of Literary Societies (ALS)   180
Allied Artists/Artistic License   258
Alligator's Mouth, The   81, 333
ALM: Australian Literary Management   224
Alton Arts Festival   352
Amazon   277, 426
Amber Brown Grant   308
American Booksellers Association   315
American Society of Composers, Authors and Publishers   315
Amgueddfa Cymru – Museum Wales   37
Grupo Anaya   66
Hans Christian Andersen Awards, The   333
Andersen Press   37
Darley Anderson Children's Book Agency   210
Darley Anderson Illustration Agency   258

Ann Whitford Paul - Writer's Digest Manuscript Award   307
Annick Press   59
Anorak   266
APPG for Libraries Information & Knowledge in Parliament   389
Aquila   266
Arad Goch   291
Arcturus Publishing   37
Arena Illustration   258
Armadillo   269
Yvonne Arnaud Theatre Management   288
Art Agency, The   258
artificial intelligence (AI)   302
Arts Council/An Chomhairle Ealaíon   315
Arts Council England   180, 314–15, 389
Arts Council of Northern Ireland   316
Arts Council of Wales   180, 316
artwork   376
Artworks, The   258
Arvon   182
ASH Literary   210
Aspects Irish Literature Festival   352
Association for Library Service to Children   316
Association for Library Service to Children Awards   334
Association for Scottish Literature   316
Association of American Literary Agents   316
Association of American Publishers   316
Association of Authors' Agents, The   316
Association of Canadian Publishers   317
Association of Freelance Editors, Proofreaders and Indexers of Ireland   317
Association of Illustrators   317
Association of Independent Libraries   389
Association of Senior and Children's Education Librarians (ASCEL)   390
associations   315
Astound US   259
Astra Publishing House   67
Atheneum Books for Young Readers *see* Simon & Schuster Children's Publishing Division
Audible   78, 277
audience, building and connecting with   31
audience, engaging with   238
audience, picture books   241
audio, children's literature   275
audiobook publishers   278
audiobooks   275, 277
Audiobooks.com   78
Aurora Metro   38
Australian Copyright Council   317
Australian Publishers Association   317
Australian Writers' Guild   317
authenticity   9

Author, The   298
author contracts   189
author visits   313
author website   120
author–agent contract, importance of   189
author–reader relationship   119
author-illustrator   192, 254
author/illustrator relationship, picture books   242
Authors Aloud UK   317
Authors' Licensing and Collecting Society (ALCS)   298, 385, 413
authors, tracing   414
authorship   382
Award Publications   38
awards   333

B

b small publishing   38
BabyTV   284
Badger Learning   38
BAFTA Rocliffe New Writing Competition   334
Bags-of-Books   81
BARB   286
Barbican Library   386
Bardd Plant Cymru (Welsh-Language Children's Poet Laureate)   318
Barefoot Books   67
Annabel Barker Agency   224
Barnes Children's Literature Festival   352
Barnsley Book Festival   352
Barrington Stoke   38
Bath Children's Literature Festival   352
Bath Children's Novel Award, The   334
Bath Literary Agency   211
Bath Spa University   400
BBC, The   284
BBC School Radio   287
Beano   266
becoming a children's author   103
becoming a writer   93, 99, 113
Beehive Illustration   259
Belfast Central Library   386
Bell Lomax Moreton Agency   211
benefits   428
Bent Agency, The   211
Bert's Books   81
Bibliobuzz Children's Award   334
Big Picture Press   38
Big Red Illustration Agency, The   259
Library of Birmingham   386
Black British Book Festival   353
David Black Agency   226
Malorie Blackman Scholarships for Unheard Voices, The   350
Blackwell's Bookshop, Children's Dept   81
Blackwell's Rare Books   86
Blair Partnership, The   211
Quentin Blake Centre for Illustration   318
Bloomsbury Publishing   38, 57
Bloomsbury Publishing USA   67
Blue House Bookshop, The   81

Bodleian Libraries of the University of Oxford   388
Bog Eyed Books   39
Bologna Children's Book Fair   353
Bologna Illustrators Scholarship   307
BolognaRagazzi Award   334
Bonnier Books UK   39
book adaptations   271
book auctions   208
Book Burrow @ Aardvark Books & Café, The   81
Book Corner   81
book covers   248
Book Edit Writers' Prize   335
book fairs   208
Book Guild, The   39
Book House, The   82
Book Marketing Society   318
Book Nook, The   82
book promotion   362
Booka Bookshop and Café   82
BookBeat   78
Bookbugs and Dragon Tales   82
Booker Albert Literary Agency, The   226
Bookmark Children's and Illustrated Books   87
BookPrinting UK   395
Books Are My Bag Readers Awards   335
Books Council of Wales/Cyngor Llyfrau Cymru   318
Books for Keeps   269
Books on the Hill Press   39
Bookseller, The   269
booksellers   121
Booksellers Association, The   318
BookTok   29, 361, 406
BookTrust   318, 390
BookTrust Represents   318
BookTrust Storytime Prize   335
Booster Cushion Theatre   292
Borders Book Festival   353
Boswell Book Festival   353
Boundless Theatre   292
Bournemouth Writing Festival   353
Bradford Literary Agency   226
Bradford Literature Festival   353
Branford Boase Award, The   335
Breakwater Books   59
Bright Agency, The   211, 259
Bright Red Publishing   39
Bristol Central Library   386
Bristol Old Vic Young Company   288
British Book Awards, The   335
British Book Design and Production Awards   335
British Council, The   182, 319
British Library, The   388
British Museum Press, The   39
broadcast media   280
broadcasting, children's   284
Broadway Bookshop, The   82
Brolly Books   57
Jenny Brown Associates   211
Brown Bear Books   79

Index 441

Andrea Brown Literary Agency   226
Browns Books For Students   82
Felicity Bryan Associates   212
Budleigh Salterton Literary Festival   353
bursaries   421
Buster Books   39

C

Cahoots NI   292
Caledonia Novel Award   335
Calkins Creek Books *see* Astra Publishing House
Cambridge Literary Festival   354
Cambridge University Library   388
Cambridge University Press & Assessment, Africa   65
Cambridge University Press & Assessment   39
Cambridge University Press & Assessment Education Australia   57
Campbell *see* Pan Macmillan
Canadian Authors Association   319
Canadian Children's Book Centre, The   319
Canadian Publishers' Council   319
Canadian Society of Children's Authors, Illustrators & Performers   319
Candlewick Press   67
C&W Agency   212
Candy Jar Books   40
Canterbury Library   387
Georgina Capel Associates   212
Cardiff Central Library   387
Cardiff Children's Lit Fest   354
Carlsen Verlag   62
Carnegies, The   336
Maria Carvainis Agency   227
Cassava Republic Press   40
Catchpole Agency, The   212   259
Caterpillar Poetry Prize, The   336
Catherine Wheels Theatre Company   292
Catnip Publishing   40
CBCA Book of the Year Awards   336
CBeebies Radio   287
Cengage Learning Australia   57
Center for Children's Books, The   319
University of Central Lancashire   400
Centre for Literacy in Primary Education   320
CGP   40
Channel 4   285
Channel 5   285
character development   126
character diversity, YA   167
character tagging   159
characterisation   126, 129–30
Charlesbridge Publishing   67
CIEP (Chartered Institute of Editing and Proofreading)   320
Chartered Institute of Library and Information Professionals (CILIP)   390
ChatGPT   135
Cheltenham Illustration Awards   336
Cheshire Novel Prize, The   336
Chicago Review Press   67

Chichester Festival Theatre   289
University of Chichester   400
Chicken & Frog   82
Chicken House   40
Chickenshed Theatre   288
children, writing about love and loss for   169
Children's Book Award, The   336
Children's Book Council and Every Child A Reader, The   320
Children's Book Council of Australia, The   320
Children's Book Guild of Washington DC, The   320
children's books, illustrated   236
Children's Books Ireland   320
Children's Books North Agency   212
Children's Books North Network   321
Children's Bookshop – Hay-on-Wye, The   87
Children's Bookshop (Huddersfield)   82
Children's Bookshop (Muswell Hill)   82
Children's Hour   275
Children's Literature Association   321
Children's Poetry Archive   174, 181
children's publishers   12
children's television   271
children's television, writing for   280
Children's Writers and Illustrators for Stories and Literacy   321
Child's Play (International)   40
China Shanghai International Children's Book Fair   354
Chiswick Book Festival   354
choosing an agent   21
Christian Education   40
Chronicle Books   68
Cicada Books   41
City Lit   182
Anne Clark Literary Agency   212
clauses   407
climate change   161
CLiPPA (Centre for Literacy in Primary Poetry Award)   337
co-authors, dead or untraceable   383
Cocoa Boy   266
Cocoa Girl   266
collaboration   192
Colourpoint Creative   41
Colwill & Peddle   213
comic books   254
comics, creating and selling   251
Comics Cultural Impact Collective (CCIC), The   321
Commando   266
commissioning   271
commissioning editor   23
commissions, picture books   238
Common Deer Press   59
Companies House   422
comparision titles   201
competitions   333
conferences   398
confidence to try   98

Index

connecting with readers   119, 130, 163, 205
Margaret Connolly & Associates   224
Contact An Author   321
Contact Theatre Company   289
contract negotiations, agent's role in   197
contract termination   408
contracts   407, 419
CookeMcDermid   225
Gemma Cooper Literary   213
copying   414
copyright   272, 300, 382, 403, 407, 411, 417
Copyright Licensing Agency   411
Coram Beanstalk   321
Alice Corrie Award, The   337
Corvisiero Literary Agency   227
cover design   248
covering letter   186, 200
Cranthorpe Millner Publishers   41
Creation Theatre Company   289
Creative Access   350
Creative Australia   321
Creative Authors   213
creative averaging   418
Creative Rights in AI Coalition   322
Creative Roots Studio   213
Creative Sparrow   259
Creative UK   322
Rupert Crew   213
Crown House Publishing   41
Editorial Cruilla   66
Crystal Kite Awards, The   307
Cuba Press, The   64
Cuckfield Book Festival   354
Curtis Brown   213, 227
Curtis Brown (Australia)   224
Curtis Brown Creative   398

D

DACS   415
Roald Dahl Museum and Story Centre, The   322
Dark House Literary & Screen Agency   214
Dawn Publications   68
Liza Dawson Associates   227
De Agostini Editore   63
debut author   18, 20
deciding what to publish   13
defamation   407
Deptford Literature Festival   354
Derby Book Festival   354
Derby Theatre   289
DESIBlitz   354
Design. Publishing. Inclusivity.   350
designers   248
Destino Infantil & Juvenil   66
DHH Literary Agency   214
Dial Books *see* Penguin Young Readers
Diamond Kahn & Woods Literary Agency   214
difficult topics   265
Sandra Dijkstra & Associates   227
Dinosaur Books   41
disappointment   109

Discover Children's Story Centre   322
Disney+   285
Diverse Book Awards, The   337
diversity   8, 265
DK   41
Donaghy Literary Group   225
DOT   266
Doubleday *see* Penguin Random House
Dover Publications   68
DRAKE The Bookshop   83
dramatisation rights   405
Dref Wen   41
Drummond Agency   224
dtv Verlagsgesellschaft mbH & Co. KG   63
Dukes, The   289
Dundurn Press   59
Dunham Literary   227
Dystel, Goderich & Bourret   228

E

Ealing Book Festival   355
ebb & flo bookshop   83
ebook readers   278
eBookPartnership.com   395
Eco Kids Planet   267
l'école des loisirs   62
EDCON Publishing Group   68
Eddison Pearson   214
Edge Theatre and Arts Centre, The   289
Edify   64
Edinburgh Bookshop, The   83
Edinburgh Comic Art Fair   355
Edinburgh International Book Festival   355
Edinburgh International Children's Festival   355
Edinburgh Young Adult Novel Award   337
editing   185, 205
editing, importance of in poetry   174
Editors' and Proofreaders' Alliance of Northern Ireland   322
Edizioni Arka srl   63
Edizioni El/Einaudi Ragazzi/Emme Edizioni   63
Educate   269
Educational Company of Ireland, The   42, 78
Eerdmans Publishing Company   68
Egg, The   289
ego   109
EK Books   57
ELK Publishing   58
Ethan Ellenberg Literary Agency, The   228
Elsewhen Press   42
Emerging Voices Award, The   307
Emerging Writers Programme   350
empathy   158
Empathy Lab   322
Enchanted Lion Press   68
Encyclopaedia Britannica   68
English Association   322
English Association English 4–11 Children's Picture Book Awards   337
Enslow Publishers   69
Evan-Moor Educational Publishers   69

Index

Everyman Theatre Cheltenham 289
Everything with Words 42
exclusivity 407
expenses, tax 419
Express Publishing 42
Ezra Jack Keats Showcase Prize 307

F

FAB Prize for Undiscovered Talent 337
Faber & Faber 42
fabulism 148
Fairbank Literary Representation 228
fairy tales 151
CJ Fallon 42
fantasy 132, 134, 148, 163, 200
Far from the Madding Crowd 83
Farrar, Straus Giroux Books for Young Readers 69
Farshore Books *see* HarperCollins Publishers
Federation of Children's Book Groups Conference, The 398
Federation of Children's Book Groups 311
Federation of European Publishers 323
feedback 194
Feminist Press, The 69
festivals 352
Fevered Sleep 292
David Fickling Books 42
fiction, YA 165
finance 417
Fincham Press 42
finding a literary agent 177, 185
finding a publisher 18
finding new clients, agents 196
Firefly Press 43
first drafts 34, 129, 149
FirstNews 267
Fitzhenry & Whiteside 60
Five Quills 43
Flammarion 62
Flannery Literary 228
Fleet Street Quarter Festival of Words 355
Floris Books 43
Klaus Flugge Prize, The 337
Flux 69
Flying Eye Books 43
Foggie Toddle Books 83
Folio Literary Management 228
football 34
Forward Arts Foundation 323
foundation course, art 236
Fox Eye Publishing 43
Foyle Young Poets of the Year Award 183
Fraser Ross Associates 214
Free Books Campaign 323
Free Books Festival 355
Free Spirit Publishing 69
freelance 418
Don Freeman Work-in-Progress Grant 307
Friends of Libraries 390
Friends of National Libraries 390
From You To Me 43

Fulcrum Publishing 69
Fun Kids 287
Fuzzy Flamingo 395

G

Gaelic Books Council/Comhairle nan Leabhraichean, The 323
Gale, part of Cengage Group 69
Gallimard Jeunesse 62
Galore Park Publishing 43
Gecko Press 69
Gemini Books Group 43
genre fiction 123
getting published 9, 103, 105, 113
ghostwriter, working with 135
Gibbs Smith 70
Ginger and Pickles Children's Bookshop 83
Girl Talk 267
Giunti Editore 63
GLL Literary Foundation 323
GLL Literary Foundation Author Placements 338
Global Blended Learning 79
glossary, publishing roles 368
Barry Goldblatt Literary 228
Golden Egg Academy, The 398
Golden Hare Books 83
Golden Kite Awards, The 308
Goldfinch Novel Award, The 338
Golvan Arts Management 224
Good Illustration 259
Irene Goodman Literary Agency 228
Graffeg 43
W.F. Graham 44
granting and reversion 407
graphic novels 5, 254
Annette Green Authors' Agency 214
Greenhouse Literary Agency, The 215, 229
Greeting Card Association 323
Greyhound Literary 215
Grosvenor House Publishing 395
Gryphon House 70
Guernica Editions 60
Marianne Gunn O'Connor Literary, Film/TV Agency 215
Guppy Publishing 44

H

Hachai Publishing 70
Hachette Australia 58
Hachette Book Group 70
Hachette Children's Trade 44
Hachette Learning 44
Hachette Livre/Gautier-Languereau 62
Hachette UK 44
Half Moon Theatre 292
Handprint Books 70
Carl Hanser Verlag 63
Happy Yak 44
Harbour Bookshop 83
Hardie Grant Children's Publishing 58
HarperCollins Publishers 44, 70

Index

HarperCollins Publishers (Australia)   58
HarperCollins Publishers (Canada)   60
HarperCollins Publishers (New Zealand)   64
Joy Harris Literary Agency, The   229
Antony Harwood   215
Hastings Book Festival   355
Hawcock Books   79
John Hawkins & Associates   229
Hawthorn Press   45
Hay Festival   355
Head of Zeus - Zephyr *see* Bloomsbury Publishing
Headliners   267
A.M. Heath & Co.   215
Heath Educational Books   83
Henningham Family Press   45
HG Literary   229
Sophie Hicks Agency   215
David Higham Associates   215
History Compass   71
Histria Books   71
HMRC   418, 431
Hogs Back Books   45
Holiday House   71
Holler   45
Holroyde Cartey   216
Hopscotch   45
Hopscotch Theatre Company   292
Hot Key Books   45
Houghton Mifflin Harcourt   71
House of Anansi Press and Groundwood Books   60
W. F. Howes   78
Shirley Hughes Sketchbook Award, The   338
Huia Publishing   64
Human & Rousseau *see* NB Publishers
Hungry Tomato   45
hybrid publishing   378

I

I Am a Bookworm   46, 79
I AM Writing Competitions   338
IBBY (International Board on Books for Young People)   323
IBBY Congress   398
IBBY UK (International Board on Books for Young People)   324
Igloo Books   46
Ilkley Literature Festival   356
Illuminate Publishing   46
IllustrationX   259
illustrated books   113, 375
illustrated non-fiction   192
illustration   248
illustration agency   233
illustration agent, finding   236
illustration portfolio, starting and developing   236
illustrations, space for in picture books   242
illustrator, children's books   236
illustrators   12, 192, 244, 305
Imaginate   324
Imaginative Book Illustration Society   324

Imagine: Writers and Writing for Children   182, 356
Impact Publishers   71
inclusion   8
Inclusive Books for Children   324
Inclusive Books for Children Awards   338
Independent Bookshop Week   356
independent publishers   14, 19
Independent Publishers Guild   324, 378
Independent Theatre Council   325
Independently Published Pre-publication Grant   308
Indie Book Awards   338
Indie Champions Awards   339
Inis – The Children's Books Ireland Magazine   269
Inky Illustration   260
insurance   427
intellectual property   271, 281
International Authors Forum   325
International Award for Illustration Bologna Children's Book Fair/Fundación SM   339
International Publishers Association   325
Internet Library for Librarians   390
internships   200, 238
Ipsos MORI   286
Irish Writers Centre   325
ISBNs   382, 384
   FAQs about   365
ISSNs   367
ITVX Kids   285
Ivy Kids   46
IWM (Imperial War Museums) Publishing   46

J

Jacqson Diego Story Emporium   84
Janklow & Nesbit Associates   229
Oscar Janson Smith Agency   216
Jelly Bean Self-Publishing   395
Jericho Writers   398
Jewish Book Week   356
Jhalak Children's & YA Prize   339
Jhalak Poetry Prize   339
Jolly Fish Press   71
Jolly Learning   46
JQ Ghostwriting Agency, The   395
Just Us Books, Inc.   71

K

Kaeden Books   72
Kane Literary Agency   216
Kane Press *see* Astra Publishing House
Karen Cushman Late Bloomer Award   307
Kazzum Arts   293
B.L. Kearley Art & Antiques   260
Miles Kelly Publishing   46
Kelpies *see* Floris Books
Kelpies Prizes for Writing and Illustration, The   339
KiCK!   267
Kids Alive! (The Young Soldier)   267
Kids Can Press   60
Kids Corner   260
Kindle Direct Publishing (KDP)   396, 426

Index 445

Knights Of 46
Alfred A. Knopf *see* Penguin Random House
Kobo 78
Kobo Writing Life 396
Konflux Theatre in Education 293
KPMG Children's Books Ireland Awards, The 339
kt literary 229
Kube Publishing 46
Kurio 267

L

Ladybird Books 46
Lancashire Book of the Year Award 339
language 131
language and style 264
Lantana Publishing 47
Laureate na nÓg/Ireland's Children's Laureate 325, 340
LBA Books 216
Leapfrog Global Fiction Prize 340
Leckie 47
Ledbury Poetry Festival 182
Lee & Low Books 72
Leeds Children's Theatre 290
Leeds Library 387
Leeds Playhouse 290
legacy books 7
Lemniscaat BV 63
Lemonade Illustration Agency 260
Lerner Publishing Group 72
Letterbox Library 84
Levine Greenberg Rostan Literary Agency 229
David Lewis Illustration Agency 260
libraries 120, 386
Libraries Connected 390
Libraries for Primaries project 4
Libraries Week 390
Library Campaign, The 390
Library Planet 390
Libros del Zorro Rojo 66
Editorial Libsa 66
Lightbox Learning Books 72
Frances Lincoln Children's Books 47
Astrid Lindgren Memorial Award, The 340
Madeleine Lindley 84
Lindsay Literary Agency 216
Literacy 269
literacy levels 313
literary agents 18, 20, 185, 192, 200, 203, 207, 272, 405
literary agents, main aspects of job 196
literary estates 272
Literary Office, The 216
literary prize winners 349
literary scout 207
Literature Alliance Scotland 325
literature festivals 352
Literature Wales 179, 325
Little Angel Theatre 293
Little Book Press 58
Little Bookshop, The 84

Little, Brown and Company Books for Young Readers 47, 72
Little Door Books 47
Little Island Books 47
Little People Books 79
Little Rebels Children's Book Award 340
Little Steps 396
Little Theatre Guild of Great Britain 326
Little Tiger Press 47
Live Theatre 290
lived experience 126
Liverpool Central Library 387
LOM ART 48
London Bubble, The 293
University of London, Goldsmiths 400
London Library 387
London Literature Festival 356
London School of Journalism, The 399
London Writers Awards, The 340
love and loss, children and teenagers 169
LoveReading4Kids 181, 326
luck 98
Luithlen Agency 217
Lyra Bristol Poetry Festival 356
lyrics 404

M

M6 Theatre Company 293
Mabecron Books 48
Gina Maccoby Literary Agency 230
Margaret K. McElderry Books *see* Simon & Schuster Children's Publishing Division
McGraw-Hill Canada 60
McGraw-Hill Education 48, 58
McGraw-Hill Professional 73
McIntosh & Otis 230
Frances McKay Illustration 260
Macmillan Education South Africa 65
Macmillan Prize for Illustration, The 340
Macmillan Publishers 73
Eunice McMullen 217
magazines 263
Magic Cat Publishing 48
magic in fiction 148, 202
magical realism 148
Mainstreet Trading Company, The 84
Mama Makes Books 48
managing your finances 417
Manchester Central Library 387
Manchester Poetry Library 180
Manchester Writing School at Manchester Metropolitan University, The 400
Mantra Lingua 48
manuscript edits, agent's role in 196
manuscript input from other readers, importance of 26
maps 115, 149
Margate Bookie Festival 356
Marjacq Scripts 217
marketing 249
marketing budgets, importance of 27

markets 207
  foreign markets 209
Marlborough Literature Festival 357
Maskew Miller Learning 65
Massey University Press 64
Match! 267
Maverick Arts Publishing 48
May Literary Agency 217
Kevin Mayhew 48
MBA Literary and Script Agents 217
Sarah McKenzie Literary Management 225
Media.info 287
Megaphone Writer Development Scheme 351
mentoring 177
Mercier Press, The 48
middle-grade fiction 5, 16, 123–4
Madeleine Milburn Literary, TV & Film Agency 217
Milton Keynes Literary Festival 357
Mitchell Lane Publishers 73
Mitchell Library 387
MMBcreative 217
models of publishing 378
Arnoldo Mondadori Editore (Mondadori) 63
Monty Lit Fest 357
Moon Lane Ink CIC 84
Moonlight Publishing 49
moral rights 403
Morgan Green Creatives 218
Mslexia Competitions: Novel (Children's & YA) 341
My Kind of Book 49
mystery stories 154
Mythopoeic Fantasy Award for Children's Literature, The 341

N

Jean V. Naggar Literary Agency 230
Narrative Art Award 307
National Association for the Teaching of English 326
National Association of Writers and Groups 326
National Association of Writers' Groups 180
National Association of Writers in Education 326
National Association of Writers in Education (NAWE) 183
National Centre for Research in Children's Literature 326
National Centre for Writing 327
National Geographic Kids 267
National Geographic Little Kids 268
National Insurance 428
  classes of contribution 428
National Library of Scotland 388
National Library of Wales 389
National Literacy Trust 327, 391
National Poetry Day 357
National Poetry Library (Children's Collection) 180
National Society for Education in Art and Design 327
Naxos AudioBooks 78

NB Illustration 260
NB Publishers 65
Neem Tree Press 49
Nelson Education 60
Thomas Nelson Publisher 73
Nero Book Awards 341
Ness Book Fest 357
networking 208
networking, importance of for agents 198
neurodivergence 126
New Africa Books 65
New Delhi World Book Fair 357
New Frontier Publishing 58
New Writers Award 341
New Writing North 327
New Zealand Book Awards for Children and Young Adults 341
New Zealand Council for Educational Research 64
Newcastle City Library 387
Next Big Story, The 342
Nickel Books 84
Nickelodeon UK 286
Nimbus Publishing 60
non-fiction 141
Norfolk Children's Book Centre 84
North East Book Award 342
North East Teen Book Award 342
North Parade Publishing 49
North Star Editions 73
Northern Poetry Library 181
NorthSouth Books 73
Norwich Puppet Theatre 290
Nosy Crow 49
Nottingham Children's Book Awards 342
Nottingham Playhouse 290
Nottingham Trent University 400
Andrew Nurnberg Associates 218
Nursery World 270

O

Oberon Press 60
O'Brien Press, The 49
Octavia's Bookshop 85
Ofcom 284
Off the Shelf Festival of Words Sheffield 357
offer of representation 194
Office for Standards in Education, Children's Services and Skills, The 327
Oily Cart 293
Okido 268
Old Barn Books 49
old stories for new readers 151
Olswanger Literary 230
Michael O'Mara Books 49
open submissions 16
Orca Book Publishers 61
Originate Literary Agency 218
Orpheus Books 79
Oscar's Book Prize 342
Otter-Barry Books 50
Oundle Bookshop, The 85

Oundle Festival of Literature 357
Out from the Margins Award 307
Overlook Press, The *see* Abrams Books for Young Readers
overnight success 109
Richard C. Owen Publishers 73
Owl and Pyramid 85
Owlet Press 50
Oxford Literary Festival 358
Oxford University Press 50
Oxford University Press Southern Africa 65
Oxford University Short Courses 399
Oyla 268

P

pace 123
Pact (Producers Alliance for Cinema and Television) 342
paid-for publishing 378
Paisley Book Fest 358
Pajama Press 61
Palazzo Editions 50
Pan Macmillan 50
Pan Macmillan Australia 58
Ayesha Pande Literary 230
Paper Lion 218
partnership publishing 379
partnerships 33
Pathways Into Children's Publishing 351
Pearson Canada 61
Pearson Education 73
Pearson UK 50
Pegasus 290
Pelican Publishing 74
Pen to Print 327
Penguin Random House 74
Penguin Random House Australia 58
Penguin Random House Canada 61
Penguin Random House Children's UK 50
Penguin Random House Grupo Editorial 66
Penguin Random House New Zealand 64
Penguin Random House UK 51
Penguin Random House UK Audio (Children's) 78
Penguin Young Readers 74
pensions 426
People's Book Prize, The 342
performance poetry 177
permissions 405
persistence 98
Peters Children's Book of the Year Award 343
Peters Fraser & Dunlop 218
Peters 85
PG Online 51
Phaidon Press 51
Phoenix, The 268
Phoenix Award 343
photocopying and scanning 414
Alison Picard, Literary Agent 230
Piccadilly Press 51
Pickled Pepper Books 85
PICSEL (Picture Industry Collecting Society for Effective Licensing) 327

picture book, composition stages 238
picture books 142, 192, 248, 376
picture books, writing 240
Pied Piper Theatre Company, The 293
Pikku Publishing 51
Pippin Properties 230
pitch 264
plagiarism 404
planning 129
plot 123–5, 130
plot structure 123–4
Plum Agency, The 261
Plymouth Marjon University 400
podcasting 275
'podiobooks' 278
poems, sharing on social media 175
Poetry Book Society, The 179
Poetry Business, The 179
Poetry Ireland 179
Poetry Kit, The 181
poetry organisations 179
Poetry School, The 182
Poetry Society, The 179
Poetry Society Education 183
Poetry Space 181
poetry, writing for children 173
Sylvie Poggio Artists Agency 261
point of view 126
Polari Book Prize 343
Polka Theatre 288
PONY Magazine 268
Poolbeg Press 51
POP 286
portfolio 193, 234, 245
Portfolio Awards, The 307
Post Wave Publishing 51
Priddy Books 51
Prim-Ed Publishing 51
Prime Theatre 294
Private Libraries Association 391
prize winners, literary 349
prizes 333, 421
promotion 204
proposal writing 142
Proteus Theatre Company 294
P.S. Literary Agency 225
public domain 403
public lending right (PLR) 381, 383, 414
Public Library News 391
Public Media Alliance 286
publishers, and ISBNs 366
Publishers Association (PA) 328, 378
Publishers Association of New Zealand (Te Rau o Tākupu) 328
publishers, what they are looking 12
publishing contracts 403, 407
publishing deal 33
Publishing Ireland/Foilsiú Éireann 328
publishing process 23
publishing roles glossary 368
Publishing Scotland 328

PublishNation 396
Puffin *see* Penguin Young Readers
Pure Indigo 52
Pushkin Press 52
Puzzle House, The 79

Q

Quarto Group Publishing UK 52
Quarto Publishing Group – Walter Foster Publishing 74
Queen's Knickers Award, The 343
Queen's Reading Room, The 328
Queen's Reading Room Medal, The 343
Queen's Theatre, Hornchurch 290
University of Queensland Press 59
querying 98
quest narrative 149
Questors Theatre, The 288

R

Rabbit Hole, The 85
radio, children's 271, 275, 284
Radio Academy, The 287
radio and audio for children 275
radio, children's literature 275
Radiocentre 287
RAJAR 287
Random House Children's Books 74
Ransom Publishing 52
RatedWriters.com Book Awards 343
Razorbill *see* Penguin Young Readers
RCW 218, 261
Read for Good 328
Reading Agency, The 328, 391
reading crisis 3
reading for pleasure 3
Reading for Pleasure Awards 344
real YA 4
Really Decent Books 52
reciprocal arrangements, PLR 385
Red Bird Publishing 79
Red Deer Press 61
Redhammer Management 219
Rees Literary Agency 231
reinventing fairy tales 151
rejection 21, 101, 109, 113, 194
Ruth Rendell Award 344
Replay Theatre Company 294
representation 20
research 9, 34, 161–2, 177, 193, 203, 263
Rhiza Edge 59
Rhubarb Theatre 294
R.I.C. Publications 59
rights 271, 407
   authors' 414
rights fairs 208
Rily Publications 52
RNIB Reading Services 329
Roaring Brook Press 74
Rocketship Bookshop, The 85
Rockpool Children's Books 52
Rodeen Literary Management 231

University of Roehampton 401
Deborah Rogers Foundation Writers Award 344
Ronsdale Press 61
Round Table Books 85
Royal Shakespeare Company 291
Royal Society Young People's Book Prize, The 344
Royal Television Society 287
royalties 408–9, 417
RTÉ 286
Rubery Book Award 344
Rubinstein Publishing 64
Ruby Tuesday Books 52
Running Press Group 74
Russell Freedman Award for Non-Fiction for a Better World, The 307

S

S4C 286
SAGE Publishing 53
SAIL Fest UK 358
Adriano Salani Editore 63
sampling arrangements, PLR 384
Editions Sarbacane 62
Sasquatch Books 75
Scallywag Press 53
Scattered Authors' Society 329
SCBWI 305
SCBWI Disability Fund, The 308
SCBWI Emergency Fund, The 308
SCBWI Pitch-Perfect Translation Grant, The 308
SCBWI PULSE 306
SCBWI-BI Annual Conference and Masterclass Series 399
SCBWI-BI Writers' Events 399
Schofield & Sims 53
Scholastic 53, 75
Scholastic Australia 59
Scholastic Canada 61
Scholastic Graphic Novel Award, The 344
Scholastic Laugh Out Loud Book Awards 344
School Library Association (SLA) 329, 391
school visits 121, 205
Susan Schulman Literary Agency 231
science 162
science fiction 163, 200
Scottish Book Trust 329
Scottish BPOC Writers Network (SBWN) 345
Scottish International Storytelling Festival 358
Scottish Poetry Library 181
Scottish Storytelling Forum 329
screenwriting 271
Scripture Union 53
Second Story Press 61
secondary characters 130
Secret Bookshelf, The 85
self assessment 419
self-eployment 419
self-publishing 25, 29, 119, 304, 375, 404
Self-Publishing Conference, The 358
self-publishing for comic creators 253
self-publishing service providers 378

Index 449

self-publishing vs traditional publishing 30
Selfies Book Awards, The 345
sensitivity readers 9
setting up a limited company 417
Seven Stories – The National Centre for Children's Books 181, 309
Seven Stories Bookshop 86
Sevenoaks Literary Festival 358
Seventh Agency 219
Shaw Agency, The 219
Sheffield Children's Book Award 345
Sheil Land Associates 219
Caroline Sheldon Literary Agency *see* RCW
Shepheard-Walwyn (Publishers) 53
Hannah Sheppard Literary Agency 219
Sherman Theatre 291
short stories 145
Show Me The Rabbit 220
Shuter and Shooter Publishers 65
SilverWood Books 396
Dorie Simmonds Agency 220
Simon & Schuster Children's Publishing Division 75
Simon & Schuster UK 53
Simply Books 86
Skylark Literary 220
slush pile 194
Wilbur Smith Adventure Writing Prize 345
Socciones Literary Consultancy 396
social media 120, 204, 207, 245, 362
social media, writing about 263
societies 315
Society for Storytelling 329
Society of Artists Agents 329
Society of Authors 297, 330, 378, 403, 407
SCBWI Awards and Grants *see* Society of Children's Book Writers & Illustrators
Society of Children's Book Writers and Illustrators (SCBWI) 305, 330
Society of Editors 330
Society of Young Publishers 330
Soho Agency, The 220, 261
sole author 407
sole trader 418
Le Sorbier 62
Henry Sotheran 87
Sourcebooks 76
South Ken Kid's Festival 358
Spark Award 308
Speaking of Books 330
Spectacle Theatre 294
Spread the Word 330
Spring Literary 220
SRL Publishing 54
St Austell Festival of Children's Literature 358
standard commission, author's 190
Edward Stanford Travel Writing Awards, The 345
StAnza: Scotland's International Poetry Festival 359
Stardust Experience, The 396
Abner Stein 220

Stella & Rose's Books 87
Stephen Fraser Encouragement Fund, The 307
Stepping Into Stories Kid's Lit Fest 359
stereotypes in children's fiction 10
Rochelle Stevens & Co 220
Stimola Literary Studio 231
Bram Stoker Awards 345
story arc 129
Story Museum, The 330
story structure 124
Story Therapy 330
storyboarding 149
Storymix 79
Storytellers, Inc. 86
Storytime 268
StoryWise 221
Stratford-upon-Avon Literary Festival 359
Studio Press 54
Studio Canal Kids & Family 261
submission letter, agent to publisher 197
submission process 113
submissions 15, 101, 109, 150, 185, 200, 264
submissions guidelines 235
submissions inbox, agents 196
submissions package 186, 200
submitting to agents 193–4, 200, 204
submitting to children's publishers 12
submitting work to an agent 150, 185
subsidiary rights 408
Sarah Such Literary Agency 221
Swedish Institute for Children's Books, The 331
Sweet Cherry Publishing 54
synopsis 186, 200

T

Tachyon Publications 76
Ta-Ha Publishers 54
Taking Flight Theatre Company 291
Tale Publishing 59
Tales On Moon Lane 86
Tallbean 261
Tarquin Publications 54
tax 417
  VAT 423
tax return 419, 421
Taylor & Francis Group 54
Teacher Created Resources 76
teachers 203
Teachit: English Teaching Resources 182
Teen Breathe 268
teenage author 97
teenagers, writing about love and loss for 169
television, children's 284
television, film and radio 300
television, writing for 280
Tell Tale Hearts 294
Templar Books 54
territory 407
Tes (The Times Educational Supplement) 270
Tess (The Times Educational Supplement Scotland) 270

450 Index

Theatr Clwyd 291
Theatr Iolo 295
Theatre Centre 295
Theatre Hullabaloo 295
Theatre-Rites 288
themes, treatment in YA 165
Vicki Thomas Associates 261
3 Seas Literary Agency 231
Thriller Awards 346
ThunderPoint Publishing 54
TikTok 29, 361
TikTok Book Awards 346
Tim Saunders Publications 396
Times and Sunday Times Cheltenham Literature Festival, The 359
Times/Chicken House Children's Fiction Competition, The 346
Tiny Owl Publishing 55
Tippermuir Books 55
Tir na n-Og Awards 346
TLC ACE Free Reads Scheme 351
tone 264
Tor Publishing Group 76
University of Toronto Press 62
Tottenham Literature Festival 359
Toucan Books 80
Tower Poetry 180
Christopher Tower Poetry Competition 184
trading allowance 420
traditional publishing 378
Transatlantic Agency 225
translation rights 405
translators 305
Travelling Light Theatre Company 295
Trident Media Group 231
'triggering' 265
Tring Book Festival 359
Trinity College Library Dublin 389
Troika 55
Trotman Indigo Publishing 55
Troubador 397
Tundra Books 62
Nick Turner Management 221
Tutti Frutti Productions 295
Two Windmills 55
Tŷ Newydd Writing Centre 399 182
Tyild's Agency 221

U

UCLan Publishing 55
UKLA Book Awards 346
under-represented writers 18, 350
Unicorn Theatre 288
Union Square & Co. 76
United Agents 221, 261
United Kingdom Literacy Association 331
University of Southampton 401
University of Suffolk 401
Upstart Crow Literary 231
Usborne Publishing 55

V

Van Goor/Van Holkema & Warendorf 64
V&A Illustration Awards, The 346
vanity publishers 378
Via Afrika 65
Vicens Vives SA 66
Viking *see* Penguin Young Readers
Visible Fictions 291
visual broadcast media 280
visual storytelling 254
Voice of the Listener & Viewer 331
Volemos: The Meg Medina Grant 307

W

Wacky Bee Books 55
Wainwright Prize, The 347
Caroline Wakeman Literary Agency 232
Walker Books 55
warranty and indemnity 407
Warwick Prize for Women in Translation, The 347
Waterstones Children's Book Prize 347
Waterstones Children's Laureate 331
Watson, Little 221
Wee Book Company, The 56
Week Junior Book Awards, The 347
wellbeing 263
David West Children's Books 80
West End Lane Books 86
Westminster Reference Library 388
Westwood Creative Artists 226
what are publishers looking for? 12
What On Earth! 56, 268
Whispering Buffalo Literary Agency 222
Eve White Literary Agency 222
white space, importance of in poetry 173
Albert Whitman & Company 76
Wide Eyed Editions 56
Wigtown Book Festival 359
Wildlife Photographer of the Year 347
Wildthought Books 56
Alice Williams Literary 222
Wimbledon Book Fest 360
Winchester Books Festival 360
Winstone's Hunting Raven Books 86
WME 222, 232
Wombat Books 59
Wonderland Bookshop 86
word count 264
WordSong *see* Astra Publishing House
working in collaboration 113, 192
Working Partners 80
Workman Publishing Company 77
World Book 77
World Book Day 331
World Illustration Awards 347
world-building 132–4, 200
WorthyKids 77
WOWCON 360
WriteMentor 331

WriteMentor Novel and Picture Book Award 347
Writers Advice Centre for Children's Books 331
Writers & Artists 399
Writers & Artists: Accessible to All 351
writers groups 205
Writers' Guild of Great Britain 300, 331, 378, 407
Writers House 232
Writers' Summer School at Swanwick, Derbyshire, The 399
writing a graphic novel 254
writing about disabilities 126
writing adventure stories 123, 154
writing characters 126
writing courses 205, 398
Writing East Midlands 331
writing for magazines 263
writing for teenagers 263
writing magic into fiction 148
writing mystery and adventure stories 154
writing non-fiction for children 141
writing picture books 193
writing poetry 177
writing poetry, benefits of 176
writing practice, importance of 241
writing short stories for children 145

Y

YA 169, 376
YA and adult fiction, differences between 165
YA Book Prize 348
YA fantasy 29
YA fiction 161
YALC (Young Adult Literature Convention) 360
Susan Yearwood Agency 222
Yen Press 77
YMU Literary 222
young adult novels 16, 19
young adult readers 263
young adults 151, 169, 263
young adults, dealing with difficult issues 23
young adults, writing for 151, 263
Young at Art 332
Young Poets Network 183
Young V&A 332
Youth Libraries Group 332
YouTube 406

Z

Sheikh Zayed Book Award 348
Zeno Agency 223
ZigZag Education 56
ZunTold 56

Writers & Artists

A FREE WRITING PLATFORM TO CALL YOUR OWN

- Exclusive discounts
- Regular writing competitions
- Free writing advice articles
- Publishing guidance
- Save margin notes
- Share your writings
- Bursary opportunities

REGISTER NOW
WWW.WRITERSANDARTISTS.CO.UK